"LET US
BEGIN
ANEW"

Other Books by Gerald S. Strober

"LET US BEGIN ANEW"

An Oral History of the Kennedy Presidency

GERALD S. AND
DEBORAH H. STROBER

HarperPerennial
A Division of HarperCollinsPublishers

A hardcover edition of this book was published in 1993 by HarperCollins Publishers.

"LET US BEGIN ANEW": AN ORAL HISTORY OF THE KENNEDY PRESIDENCY. Copyright © 1993 by Gerald S. and Deborah H. Strober. All rights reserved. Printed in the United States of America. No part of this book may be used or reproduced in any manner whatsoever without written permission except in the case of brief quotations embodied in critical articles and reviews. For information address HarperCollins Publishers, Inc., 10 East 53rd Street, New York, NY 10022.

HarperCollins books may be purchased for educational, business, or sales promotional use. For information please write: Special Markets Department, HarperCollins Publishers, Inc., 10 East 53rd Street, New York, NY 10022.

First HarperPerennial edition published 1994.

Designed by C. Linda Dingler

The Library of Congress has catalogued the hardcover edition as follows:

"Let us begin anew": an oral history of the Kennedy presidency/by Gerald S. Strober and Deborah H. Strober—1st ed.
   p. cm.
  Includes index.
  ISBN 0-06-016720-3 (cloth)
  1. Kennedy, John F. (John Fitzgerald), 1917–1963. 2. United States—Politics and government—1961–1963. 3. Presidents—United States—Election—1960. 4. Oral history. I. Strober, Gerald S. II. Strober, Deborah H., 1940– .
E842.L45 1993
973.922'092—dc20   92-53348

ISBN 0-06-092238-9 (pbk.)

94 95 96 97 98 ❖/CW 10 9 8 7 6 5 4 3 2 1

To our children,
Jeremy Benjamin, and Jonathan, Lori, and Robin Strober,
whose lively interest in the issues of today
inspired us to look back in time
to the issues of our young adulthood

Of those to whom much is given, much is required. And when at some future date the high court of history sits in judgment on each one of us—recording whether in our brief span of service we fulfilled our responsibilities to the state—our success or failure, in whatever office we may hold, will be measured by the answers to four questions: First, were we truly men of courage ... secondly, were we truly men of judgment ... third, were we truly men of integrity ... finally, were we truly men of dedication? Courage, judgment, integrity, dedication ... these are the qualities which, with God's help, this son of Massachusetts hopes will characterize our Government's conduct in the four stormy years that lie ahead. Humbly, I ask His help in this undertaking. But aware that on earth His will is worked by man, I ask for your help and your prayers, as I embark on this new and solemn journey.

—President-elect John F. Kennedy
in a farewell address to the Massachusetts legislature,
January 9, 1961

Contents

Preface   xi

Acknowledgments   xv

1. The 1960 Campaign   1
2. The Kennedy Appeal   50
3. Kennedy's Political Philosophy   64
4. The Kennedy Family and the Presidency   70
5. Was There a Dynasty in the Making?   102
6. Cabinet Appointments   110
7. Sub-Cabinet-Level Appointments   127
8. President Kennedy's Administrative Style   139
9. Lyndon Johnson   188
10. Foreign Affairs   201
11. Kennedy's Knowledge of, and Policy on, Various Issues   242
12. J. Edgar Hoover and the Kennedys   264
13. Civil Rights   271
14. The Bay of Pigs   323

15. The Vienna Summit   355
16. The Berlin Crisis   360
17. The Cuban Missile Crisis   373
18. Vietnam   402
19. The Assassination   435
20. Camelot   465
21. If Kennedy Had Lived   473
22. The Kennedy Legacy   482
   Appendix A   Schedule of Interviews   503
   Appendix B   The Interviewees: Where Are They Today?   511
   Index   525

Preface

In 1993, thirty years after the assassination of John Fitzgerald Kennedy, the first U.S. president to be born in the twentieth century remains a subject of intense fascination to people throughout the world who were alive during that era and engenders keen interest among many of those born in subsequent years.

At the time of Kennedy's election as president, we were young adults and thus very much aware of the impact on the world of his three immediate predecessors: Franklin D. Roosevelt, Harry S. Truman, and Dwight D. Eisenhower. Yet these three men, despite their unique personal characteristics and achievements, do not evoke either the memories or the emotions associated with John Fitzgerald Kennedy.

In 1989, attempting to better comprehend the Kennedy phenomenon, we embarked on this project. Bearing in mind the need for a new perspective, we decided to proceed through the medium of an oral history of the Kennedy presidency, which would provide the most comprehensive view of a significant era of political and social history.

In order to achieve our goal of documenting the Kennedy presidency—not, we emphasize, as historians but rather as reporters seeking to develop a far-reaching, broad portrait of that era—we assembled an original list of two hundred potential interviewees, including cabinet, subcabinet, and administration officials, congressional colleagues, personalities on the international scene, and others.

We then wrote to these individuals, apprising them of our project and requesting interviews. Approximately 140 of those on the list agreed to be interviewed, while others declined or were unable to comply with our request. During the course of our queries, four of those who had agreed to be interviewed died.

While we were aware of the vast resource of interviews contained in the Kennedy Library—a body of information compiled largely in the months and years immediately following President Kennedy's death— we believed that it was incumbent on us to seek interviews from the perspective of almost thirty years after the assassination. Hence we relied solely on material obtained through our own interviews, which were conducted from the autumn of 1989 through the summer of 1992.

Uppermost in our thoughts as we began our exploration of the Kennedy presidency was whether there was more myth than substance to the man: Were his actions as chief executive genuine accomplishments, or were they exaggerated as such in the aftermath of November 22, 1963?

Here the Cuban missile crisis and the issue of civil rights come to mind. Regarding the latter, did the Kennedys empathize with and encourage the aspirations of the black community? Could more have been achieved in the first term? Were the Kennedys holding back for fear of losing the 1964 presidential election?

What of President Kennedy's worldview: Was he a cold warrior or a dove? And what role did the Bay of Pigs debacle play in shaping his response to Nikita Khrushchev's placing of missiles in Cuba?

And what of Kennedy's role as a decision maker? Did he rely on his brother Robert, or was he his own master? Or was his father pulling the strings as the president grappled with major issues?

In seeking answers to our questions, we had to come to terms at the beginning of our endeavor with the way in which we would deal with the president's personal life, specifically his much-chronicled extramarital sexual activity.

As our goal was to reveal the presidency and the man through discussion of the major domestic and foreign issues of the day, we felt that it would be inappropriate for us to initiate questions regarding Kennedy's personal life. We did realize, however, that mention of the president's private behavior by his associates and contemporaries in the context of discussion of the issues could be relevant to the understanding of his performance as president. Thus, when such observations were offered in what we determined to be a relevant context, we included them.

We also realized that in organizing our material, we had—as far as was possible—to do so in an objective manner, and as we collected material and began to glean from the thousands of pages of verbatim transcripts the portions that would eventually be included in the text, we hit upon what we believed to be a fair way to arrange quotations of the various interviewees: namely, to place them in relation to one another as they related to the specific areas of our consideration.

The material contained in the following chapters consists of significant portions of more than 120 interviews, conducted on three continents.

Acknowledgments

We are deeply indebted to all our interviewees for their courtesy, frankness, and, most important, their willingness to participate in our project, which reinforced our view that a reconsideration of the Kennedy presidency at this time was warranted.

As we pursued our project, we were encouraged at many steps along the way by our friends, colleagues, and family. We are especially appreciative of the interest and support of Beate and Serge Klarsfeld, Carol Shookhoff (into whose word processor went endless pages, revisions, and drafts, and at all hours of the day and night!), our editor at Harper-Collins, Buz Wyeth, whose faxed messages pointed us many times along the right path, and our agent, Mitchell Rose, who responded to a telephone call from us in the summer of 1990, and from our initial meeting shortly thereafter, offered us invaluable advice regarding this text, above and beyond the call of professional duty.

Authors invariably bubble over with praise for and gratitude to their families, and we are no exception. To our siblings and their spouses, their offspring, and our cousins, many of whom have read excerpts of this text, we say: Thank you for your love and expressions of faith in our project.

"LET US BEGIN ANEW"

1

The 1960 Campaign

On January 2, 1960, John Fitzgerald Kennedy, who had lost the 1956 vice-presidential nomination to Tennessee senator Estes Kefauver, announced his candidacy for the presidency before an enthusiastic audience gathered in the Senate Caucus Room. Striking the predominant theme of his congressional years, he stated: "I have developed an image of America as fulfilling a noble and historic role as defender of freedom in a time of peril, and of the American people as confident, courageous and persevering. It is with this image that I begin my campaigning."

In his quest for the Democratic presidential nomination and later in the general campaign, Kennedy had to confront criticisms concerning his capacity to lead the nation. These involved his health (the possibility of Addison's disease as well as chronic back problems), his youth (he would be over forty-three in January 1961), his lack of experience (during his fourteen years in Congress he had held no major committee chairmanships nor had he authored any major legislation), and his religion (in 1960 the election of a Roman Catholic to the presidency seemed a dubious proposition).

The Prelude

Abraham Ribicoff, secretary of health, education and welfare; U.S. senator (D., Conn.) As soon as the 1956 election was over, John Bailey [chairman, Connecticut State Democratic Committee] and I and Kennedy started to plan for 1960. We spent a lot of time together. No one except me publicly came out for Jack. No one took him seriously. No one thought he could make it. Finally, he said, "Look, Abe, the only one who can make any statement about my intentions is you. We know each other so well that whatever you feel like saying, say it."

Now it got so embarrassing because nobody, nobody came out for Jack Kennedy. Finally, John Bailey and Jack met with Governor Mike DiSalle of Ohio at an airport motel in Pittsburgh. They told Mike that he had to come out for Kennedy or they were going to go into Ohio and run a primary race against him. So Mike DiSalle became the second person to come out for Kennedy.

I am a little ashamed of myself, because when I talked to governors, I inferred that Kennedy was considering them for vice president. But it was hard to get their commitment because nobody gave Jack a chance. In fact, everybody wanted to run. All the Catholics, Muskie [Edmund S. Muskie, U.S. senator (D., Maine)], Brown [Edmund G. ("Pat") Brown, Sr., governor of California], McCarthy [Eugene J. McCarthy, U.S. senator (D., Minn.)], they weren't going to go for Kennedy; they thought, If it's going to be a Catholic, why not me? They all felt they were smarter than Kennedy, had a better personality, were better known. So it was very, very hard to get the Catholics to come out for Jack.

Maurine Neuberger, U.S. senator (D., Oreg.)   I met Kennedy when my husband was in the Senate. We were neighbors in Georgetown and saw them a lot. One night he had Gene McCarthy and my husband and me over to dinner to talk about whether he should run for the presidency. It was germinating at that time. He probably had similar dinners for a lot of other people. He wanted to see what the mood was and how we all felt about it.

Frank Moss, U.S. senator (D., Utah)   I first actually met him on the floor of the Senate, when he came in and congratulated me and the other members who had just been sworn in. I didn't really think he was going to run until 1959. He and Jackie [Jacqueline Lee Bouvier Kennedy, wife of President John F. Kennedy] invited me and my wife and Ed Muskie and his wife over to have dinner with them one night. It was just a little social event, and I thought he was just being friendly with us—as he was with all the other senators—but as I look back on it, I could see he was already beginning to touch base with us. He was a very engaging conversationalist, and Jackie was quiet, but very pleasant.

THE PRIMARIES

Kennedy's drive for the nomination received its first major boost when he won the New Hampshire primary—then the first such contest of the presidential election process. This success was followed by key victories in Wisconsin and in West Virginia, where, on May 10, Kennedy ended Minnesota senator Hubert Humphrey's candidacy with a decisive win in the largely Protestant state.

Joseph L. Rauh, Jr., vice-chairman, Americans for Democratic Action; general counsel, Leadership Conference on Civil Rights
I'd been for Humphrey [U.S. senator (D., Minn.)] all the time. Humphrey and I started in the ADA back in 1947. I guess Humphrey was my closest friend in politics, and he could do no wrong, and here we are in 1960 and he'd done something wrong: He supported the Communist Control Act of 1954, which is a pretty terrible thing, but he was still my hero and it was a heartbreaker. What happened was in Wisconsin we lost, and we had a big fight whether we should go on or not, but we'd agreed we'd go on. And then we had a primary here in Washington, D.C., and we won. We didn't beat Kennedy because he didn't run. He was smart enough not to run against us, so we won the primary here against Stevenson [Adlai E. Stevenson, Democratic candidate for president, 1952 and 1956] and Wayne Morse [U.S. senator (D., Oreg.)] and the next week, to West Virginia, and we were—oh, we were crushed, absolutely crushed. I was standing beside Hubert, looking at the blackboard in our headquarters. We went in there after an hour or so of the returns. And it was incredible, we were losing sixty-forty almost everywhere. We thought we had a chance—we thought, well, it's a pretty Protestant state—that we were going to make it, it's a pretty liberal state, and it was just crushing. We had a banjo player traveling with Hubert, and he was crying and Hubert went up and comforted him. But the minute we stood side by side watching that blackboard was one of the most excruciating, painful moments of my life, because it was over. Then the question arose, What do we do? And I had no hesitation. I was for Kennedy.

Hubert went back to his hotel suite. Everybody was there. There was liquor, and so we all tried to dissolve some of our pain, and we went into the bedroom, and I can't remember exactly who was in the bedroom. I persuaded Hubert to issue a statement. Hubert said, "Okay, okay, Joe," so I read it to Bobby Kennedy [Robert F. Kennedy, brother of President John F. Kennedy, future U.S. attorney general] at his hotel. Then I went out in the living room where we all were watching television, and the phone rang. I happened to be closest to the phone, and the operator down below said, "Mr. Kennedy is on his way up." And I said, "Oh my God," because I was looking at Jack Kennedy live on television, so he wasn't on the way up. Bobby was on the way up. But if there was one person in this world that the Humphrey crowd didn't like—I didn't share this, but the dominant feeling was that a very bad thing had happened, and this was the perpetrator. Well, I knew it was Bobby, but I didn't say that. I just turned to everybody and said, "The operator says Mr. Kennedy is on the way up."

So somebody has the door open and says, "It's Bobby." Sort of a low-key gasp. And then it was like the Red Sea opening for Moses, with people sort of separated, with Hubert and Muriel [wife of Hubert Humphrey] standing at the far end of the suite and Bobby walking through that group saying thanks, but he was especially nice to me because I'd read the statement to him. Then he gets to Muriel and Hubert, and I knew Muriel hated his guts, so I wondered what was going to happen. And he leaned in and kissed her. I don't know—it was kinda quiet after that. Then Bobby took several of us over to Jack's headquarters. Hubert went and Muriel didn't go. But when we got over there, Hubert was wonderful with Jack. They were just wonderful together. Being nice to each other. Jack was obviously very happy. Hubert was moving to talk to some other people, and Jack said to me, "Joe, when are you coming out for me?" I was kinda taken aback. He said, "Do you remember our talk?" I said, "Yes, I remember." I said, "As soon as somebody asks me. I'm not going to pontificate, I'm not important enough to issue a statement." Well, he didn't answer that. I said, "If somebody asks me, I'll answer it."

THE CONVENTION

On July 13, 1960, following Kennedy's victories in the Wisconsin and West Virginia primaries, the Democratic National Convention, meeting at Los Angeles, nominated Kennedy on the first ballot. He received 806 votes, while his closest rival, Senator Lyndon Johnson of Texas, garnered 409.

The Prelude

Walt W. Rostow, deputy special assistant to the president for national security affairs; chairman, State Department Policy Planning Council   In August of 1958, I was about to go on a sabbatical, but I was in Washington writing Eisenhower's Lebanon-Jordan speech with C. D. Jackson [White House aide, speechwriter to President Dwight D. Eisenhower]. Kennedy asked me to have breakfast. It was one of those summer days in Washington where it was cool in the morning but you knew by the middle of the day it would be just awful. He picked me up in his convertible. The top was down, and the following conversation took place: He said, "People tell me I should get rid of this convertible because I have enough trouble running, because I am so young. But I like it, and I am going to keep it and take my chances." Then he said, "Isn't it ridiculous to say that you are going to run for the presidency? The task is so much bigger than any mortal person. But some mortal person is going to be president." Then he went through the candidates. He said, "Adlai has had two shots at it, and we don't really owe him a third shot. But I'll tell you something; I don't think Adlai would be very happy as president. The president, every day, has to make one choice after another between very unpleasant alternatives. Adlai thinks if you talk long enough you'll get a soft option, and there are very few soft options as president. I like Hubert [Humphrey], but honestly, I don't think he would make a better president than I would. Stu Symington [Stuart W. Symington, U.S. senator (D., Mo.)] is very intelligent and experienced, but he is lazy and it is not really a job for a lazy man. The man we owe the nomination to is Lyndon; he wants the same things for the country that I do. But it is too close to Appomattox for him to get the nomination."*

I never knew where Kennedy got that phrase about Appomattox from until when President Johnson was here, writing his memoirs, and he had a letter he had written to Joe Kennedy [Joseph P. Kennedy, businessman; former U.S. ambassador to the Court of St. James's; father of President John F. Kennedy] in 1956, saying he couldn't be elected president because it was too close to Appomattox.

*On April 9, 1865, at Appomattox Court House, Virginia, General Robert E. Lee surrendered his Army of Northern Virginia to Union General Ulysses S. Grant, thus effectively ending the Civil War. Kennedy meant that the war was too "recent" for a Southerner to be nominated.

I told my wife after that conversation that Kennedy would choose Johnson as his running mate.

Bernard Boutin, campaign aide; deputy administrator, General Services Administration; administrator, General Services Administration   We were in Los Angeles considerably in advance of the start of the convention. The coordinators were told to meet Bobby at our headquarters at eight o'clock in the morning. He stood on a stool so he could look down at everybody and said, "It has come to my attention that some of you think Disneyland is more important than nominating the next president of the United States. Those that do can just resign." Of course, we were all there as volunteers so there was nothing to resign from. But it was a sober crowd, and there was no more going to Disneyland.

Ralph Dungan, special assistant to the president   When we got to Los Angeles, I didn't think we had the nomination; I think we had it potentially, if you looked at the cards we carefully kept of all the delegates—and looked at them optimistically and counted all those who had in some way committed themselves to us. But I don't think that—going into the convention—the cards were reliable at all.

The Stevenson Nomination

In the spring of 1960 associates of Senator Kennedy traveled to Adlai E. Stevenson's home in Libertyville, Illinois, to offer him a deal: If the governor would nominate Senator Kennedy at the Los Angeles Convention, he would probably be selected as secretary of state.

Adam Yarmolinsky, member, transition team; special assistant to the secretary of defense   They were rivals for the presidential nomination. I don't know how hard Stevenson tried in '60, but I guess Kennedy saw him as a rival, and they never hit it off. I'm not sure why. They could have. They were not that different: They both had a detached view of the world. Stevenson was more of an intellectual, more overtly an intellectual, than Kennedy. But Kennedy had an intellectual view—he was interested in ideas as well as people. But Stevenson was not one of us, in the view of the people around Kennedy. He didn't come from Massachusetts.

Abraham Ribicoff   I was a floor manager at the convention, and I worked very closely with Bobby. We knew Jack was going to get the nomination. I think the only one he feared was Adlai Stevenson; he was the one person we were worried about.

In early 1960 Adlai came to Yale to give the Chubb Lectures. I called Jack and said, "Adlai is coming to Yale and as governor of the state, I will go down to New Haven and have dinner with him. Is there anything you would like me to say to him?" He said, "Yes, you tell Adlai Stevenson this. I would like his support. If he does not make a play for the presidency, I will make a commitment to him that if I can't get the nomination, I will publicly come out and say I would only run for vice president if Stevenson is the nominee. That would assure him the nomination. And if I am elected president and he has come out for me, I would make him secretary of state."

I met with Adlai and gave him that message. His tragedy was that he could never make up his mind. He hesitated, then turned Kennedy's offer down. So at the convention there was a big play for him. The galleries were full of his supporters. They thought they could swing the nomination to Stevenson. Of course, Jack knew he had it, and at that stage Stevenson wasn't going to get anything.

Adlai Stevenson III, former U.S. senator (D., Ill.)   The participants in that exchange were Kennedy supporters, or at least closet Kennedy supporters, urging my father to support Kennedy. He had no strategy, no camp, and no designs on the presidency—which is not to say that if a miracle happened, and the Convention deadlocked and turned to him, he wouldn't have gone the final campaign. But he felt very strongly that he'd had his opportunities. He was not a candidate, and as titular leader of the party, he had a duty to be neutral. In those days *titular leader* meant something; whatever it was, it meant more than it means today. There's no such thing now. He took that responsibility of titular leader very strongly. He campaigned strenuously, all over the country, for congressional candidates, but not à la Nixon [Richard M. Nixon, Republican candidate for president, 1960], as part of the strategy to win friends and, ultimately, the nomination. He did it because it was his duty as the party leader. He put together think tanks; he published publications and raised money; he had a brain trust in New York which helped to develop policy in the interim for the party. I never heard any suggestion from anyone around him that those efforts were part of the campaign to win the nomination in 1960. On the contrary.

Bernard Boutin   I was coordinator for the New England states and New Jersey. I was also cochairman, with Hy Raskin [campaign aide, 1960 presidential election], of the Kennedy headquarters at the Biltmore Hotel. We thought we had done a very good organizational job, and then we found that the Stevenson people had tapped into our communications system, which then made the whole system suspect.

I found out about it through a friend of mine who had worked with me in New Hampshire, who, from there, had gone to New York and was very high on Stevenson. He told me in confidence and we checked it out, and it was true. It was an early indication that Stevenson was going to make a major play.

I think Stevenson wasn't interested in having his name put forth until about a week before the convention. I refuse to believe that what I saw at the convention was spontaneous. Going into the convention, it looked initially that Johnson was the main opposition. Then the next thing that happened was that Gene McCarthy, who had agreed to give one of the seconding speeches for Kennedy, had changed his mind and was going to nominate Stevenson. Of course, they also found a way to pack the gallery with supporters, so between McCarthy and Eleanor Roosevelt [widow of Franklin D. Roosevelt, thirty-second president of the United States] and the young people up in the galleries, they scared the life right out of some people.

I was angry as this was building. Stevenson had indicated to Kennedy that he was not going to make a big play for the nomination. Adlai was a great man to vacillate anyway, as he did with the vice presidential nomination in 1956 and the presidential nomination in 1960. When it was obvious that, despite all the noise and a hell of a fine speech by McCarthy, he wasn't going to get the nomination, he went home.

Arthur M. Schlesinger, Jr., special assistant to the president
Stevenson consented to have his name brought forth. Bill Blair [William McCormick Blair, ambassador to Denmark] and Newton Minow [chair-

man, Federal Communications Commission] stayed with Stevenson, but they had no illusions as to what was going to happen. I think that—almost through passivity—Stevenson found himself in the situation. There were a lot of people who distrusted Kennedy and felt passionately for Stevenson, and he didn't want to let them down.

George Ball, undersecretary of state for economic affairs; undersecretary of state   It was not so much what happened at the convention as it was Stevenson's refusal to make the nomination address. Stevenson called me after Kennedy people went to see him at his house in Libertyville. He was absolutely furious. Stevenson was a fellow who was instinctively a gentlemanly type, and they had called him every name in the book. They had simply said, We are sorry, we are going to have to shit all over you. As far as he was concerned, this was outrageous. What did those young Irish types think they were doing to him? I think if he had agreed to nominate Kennedy that he could very well have been secretary of state, which was the job he was interested in. Whether he would have been a good secretary of state is arguable.

Arthur Schlesinger, Jr.   I came to know Kennedy quite well. He had been representative from the district in which I lived, and he became a senator from the state. I had been a classmate of his older brother, Joe. I was very much taken with Jack Kennedy. A group of us—Arthur Goldberg [secretary of labor], Henry Steele Commager [professor of history, Harvard University], Ken Galbraith [U.S. ambassador to India], and one or two others—in the spring of 1960 decided that we would issue a statement as liberals. At that time there was great mistrust of Kennedy among liberals, so we thought a statement on our part, supporting Kennedy, might help ease his way with that community. The only thing I regret about all of this was that the statement was leaked just after Stevenson had spent a weekend with us, and I felt badly that I hadn't warned him that the statement was coming out.

Had Stevenson declared his candidacy, I suppose I would have stayed with him, though I was among those who hoped he would not declare his candidacy. He had already run twice, and I felt that by 1960, he had had his time and that Kennedy, in some ways, might be a more effective president. A number of people were in this quandary, people close to Stevenson, like William Blair and Newton Minow, both of whom did their best to persuade him to say he wasn't a candidate. Stevenson never declared his candidacy but never effectively declared his noncandidacy either. There existed a realm of ambiguity about it. He was clearly draftable, but he did not declare himself as a candidate.

Harlan Cleveland, assistant secretary of state for international organization affairs   I was a delegate to the convention from New York, and I don't know if the Kennedys ever realized that Stevenson wasn't running. I saw him the evening of the demonstration, and he reiterated that he wasn't running and didn't know what all the shouting was about, which I thought was a bit disingenuous of him. Mrs. Roosevelt and others were trying to create a firestorm in his favor, but he kept saying he wasn't running.

Bobby Baker, secretary to the Senate majority   Gene McCarthy was for Lyndon Johnson; he hated Kennedy and he was for Lyndon Johnson; he was committed to me. I was going to some meeting at the Statler Hotel, and Gene was at the top of the escalator. He said, "Mrs. Roosevelt wanted me to second Adlai's nomination, and I'm committed to you; it's up to you what I do." I said, "We cannot win on the first ballot. I've got the California delegation screwed up, because Pat Brown is wishy-washy. You make the speech," and he made the best speech he ever made in his life.

Adlai Stevenson III   Eugene McCarthy made an eloquent nominating speech for my father; Eleanor Roosevelt made an appearance for him. For a time, I imagine, the Kennedys were a little apprehensive about what was going on. It was a great moment in American politics—totally unrealistic, actually. But I would guess that there were some resentments over that. It shouldn't have been allowed to happen. He should have supported Kennedy early; he should never have permitted the situation to get out of control in Los Angeles. But when it was over, my father supported him very faithfully and strenuously all across the country.

The Stevenson Demonstration

Adlai Stevenson III   I don't think there's any evidence at all to indicate it was just a "mark of respect." Of course, he and Kennedy didn't hit it off too well, but they weren't going to take unnecessary political risks in a total act of futility. There were other ways for that convention to show their respect. I don't believe that he wanted it put in nomination, but when others said, "There's this great groundswell of respect; you owe it to the country," his resistance broke down, and that was such an emotional, dramatic moment. It was hard for anybody—perhaps including the Kennedys—not to think there was a chance. They probably did think that there was a chance that maybe the convention could be just swept off its feet. It wasn't realistic, but I think that's what they were thinking, "they" being Gene McCarthy and Hubert Humphrey and, of course, Eleanor Roosevelt. I can't remember who the others were now.

Ralph Dungan   I personally thought that the demonstration was Stevenson's last hurrah. Bobby, of course, was irate; he was worried that it could turn things around, but he worried if anything was going different from the way he thought it would turn out.

Edward A. McDermott, campaign aide; director, Office of Emergency Planning; member, National Security Council   I felt rather badly for him on that occasion, because I think that his name was placed in nomination, and he was pushed into that contest, literally, by those who were more interested in their own personal welfare and fortunes than they were in him. I remember his entry into the hall in Los Angeles, where there were, literally, people behind him with their hands on his back, pushing him forward, and I thought that was rather pathetic.

Ben Bradlee, Washington correspondent, *Newsweek*   I was in the Stevenson demonstration at the 1960 convention, and it scared the bejesus out of me. I'd never covered a convention before in my life. I'd lived in Europe for seven years, and I'm back, and it's the first one I ever saw. I thought when Mrs. Roosevelt came in—with the spotlight on her, we knew she hated Kennedy—I didn't know anything about how you could make those demonstrations erupt. I had thought that this was a precise science; that you could count the delegates. I'd spent months talking to delegates and counting delegations, and I was astounded by that demonstration. The guy I was sitting next to was Ken Crawford, who was the bureau chief of *Newsweek*, and who was really one of the noble, nice guys in this world. He said to me: "Look at the delegates; who's cheering on the delegation floor?" And there wasn't anybody; he didn't have any delegates. It was all in the gallery; of course they packed the gallery.

Adlai Stevenson III   I wasn't with him at that minute. We were waiting in the galleries. I'm speculating again: I just don't see how he could have failed to be affected by this extraordinary outpouring of respect, support, and affection, inside and outside that convention, and he undoubtedly felt that he was the better qualified of the two, that the support which was welling up had been earned due to a very principled campaign, and he had certainly, by then, very strong ideas about how to lead the country, where to take it, and he probably looked upon Kennedy as very young, and inexperienced, and felt his time would come. But I certainly don't have any recollection of his ever being a party to any effort to draft him—to nominate him. It was totally reactive. There was that senator—the names keep slipping me—there were a number of senators, and other leaders, and then these grass-roots people, who'd come from all over the country, and they were just going at him, telling him he owed it to the country and the party needed him, and he could win.

Pierre Salinger, White House press secretary   I think Stevenson felt he had a chance. He appeared at the convention, walked around, and saw the delegates—maybe thinking he could change things around, but it didn't go anywhere. I'm sure he was thinking that he could beat the Republican candidate; I'm sure he was thinking about that potential. The Stevenson demonstration didn't bother me a bit: I had in front of me the names of all the delegates who were for us; I thought they were unturnable.

Ralph Yarborough, U.S. senator (D., Tex.)   As it turned out, I think Kennedy was the strongest candidate. A lot of people thought he was too young and untried. That drum was beating, just drumming, drumming. Back at the hotel I saw Bobby Kennedy and Ted Kennedy [Edward M. Kennedy, President John F. Kennedy's youngest brother and future U.S. senator (D., Mass.)], walking toward the New York delegation, to ask them to hold steady. I said, "I'll try to talk to them." So they said, "Mrs. Roosevelt overdid it when she came back and stayed there too long. Our delegation was just about to break, and she came back; she just overdid it and we just kind of resent it." It was dramatic—those last two or three days. I've never seen a convention since—compared to that one.

Harlan Cleveland   If he had asked me, I would have told him that the best thing he could have done at the end of the demonstration was to go to the podium and say, "Thank you, from the bottom of my heart, but I've run twice and it is somebody else's turn." I think that would have gotten him off to a better start with Kennedy. It might even have gotten him somewhere closer to the job he wanted, namely, secretary of state. But he didn't play it that way; he let it happen around him.

Selection of a Running Mate

In a move that both surprised and infuriated many Democratic politicians and party supporters, Kennedy chose Senator Johnson as the vice presidential candidate.

Joseph Rauh, Jr.   I said, "Who's going to be the vice president?" This was a conversation I had with him on June 9, 1960. "Is it going to be Johnson? Is it going to be Humphrey? Or is it going to be somebody else?" He said, "Joe, it will either be Hubert Humphrey or another Midwestern liberal." Well, that satisfied me.

I think Jack Kennedy was a great man. But great men tell whoppers too. I guess when he told me that it would be Humphrey or another Midwestern liberal, he thought that was his position that minute, but I don't think he ever thought he was bound by anything he said.

Bobby Baker   Old man Joe Kennedy was the guy who saw the wisdom of putting Johnson on the ticket.

Terry Sanford, governor of North Carolina   Kennedy selected him because it gave him balance and it gave him votes; it wasn't just Texas, it was the South. The fact that Johnson was on the ticket made it easier for us to do what we did in North Carolina. I went to Los Angeles saying that should be the ticket.

Joseph Dolan, campaign aide; assistant attorney general Right after the Wyoming vote that put Kennedy over the top, the phone rang in the Michigan delegation, where I was stationed. It was Hy Raskin, who was running the telephone operation from the trailer outside. He told me they were having trouble contacting the Pennsylvania delegation and that I should go get Governor Lawrence [David Lawrence, governor of Pennsylvania] and Congressman Green [William Green, U.S. congressman (D., Pa.)] and take them to the cottage. Senator Kennedy was coming out to the convention, and he wanted to see them. So I went over and got Lawrence. The first person Kennedy met when he came out to the convention was Lawrence, and Lawrence wanted Johnson. The next morning, O'Donnell [Kenneth P. O'Donnell, special assistant to the president] and O'Brien [Lawrence O'Brien, special assistant to the president for congressional relations and personnel] dictated a memorandum at eight o'clock, showing in what states Johnson could help the ticket.

Frank Moss I was invited to his suite after the presidential vote to talk about the vice presidential nomination; there was a lot of speculation about what was going on. Johnson was not there, but they were in communication with him. There must have been ten people there—mostly all senators. There was a great division of opinion as to who Kennedy should designate for the nomination. There was a particular area of opposition to Lyndon Johnson. The word was—as we discussed it—that Johnson wouldn't even consider it; he would be more powerful as majority leader than as vice president. The names ran all the way from Stuart Symington to even Adlai Stevenson and Hubert Humphrey. Senator Kennedy was in and out. He would be there and talking a bit, and then he would go into an adjoining room and be on a telephone; he had people stationed in different places, who were reporting in by phone. The word finally came in from one of those calls that Lyndon Johnson would accept. There was a bit of a flurry by some, who thought that that was a mistake. I don't think Sam Rayburn [Samuel T. Rayburn, Speaker of the House (D., Tex.)] was in the meeting, but the word was that Rayburn was strongly opposed to Johnson's accepting the nomination. There was some concern that Rayburn would be so strong in his opposition that Johnson would not accept. That dissipated because Johnson just plain said yes. When that word got out, the wave started and there was no stopping it.

John Seigenthaler, administrative assistant to the attorney general   There is no doubt in my mind they didn't think Johnson would take it. There is no doubt in my mind that the president wanted him to take it. Bob had talked to Symington two days before, and I had written in my newspaper that it was going to be Symington and that my source was Robert Kennedy. I had been outside the meeting where Bob and Symington talked, and when it was over, Bob said to me, "If I were you, I'd predict that tomorrow."

The morning after Jack got the nomination, Bobby invited me and two friends from Tennessee up to his hotel for coffee. It was clear that the place was in chaos, but you couldn't tell what was going on. We were in a bedroom, and Kenny O'Donnell was shuttling people through the room we were in, to the room where the Kennedys were. At some point Bob comes in and says, "This thing about the vice president has gotten all tangled up." And then Jack comes in and says, "Bobby, come back here with me." Then Bob comes out again and asks, "How would you fellows feel if it were Lyndon Johnson?" Both of my friends were elated. They immediately said, "We can carry Tennessee." All of these conversations had taken place before he goes down for the historic visit to Johnson's room. He asked us to keep this in confidence; it might change. We leave, and my two friends are ecstatic. Later Bob finds out Lyndon is going to take it. He goes down, in effect, to try to talk him out of it. But it is apparent that there is no way they can get out of it.

When the president says to Johnson, "Bobby is not up to date," what he is really saying is, "He came down to talk you out of it and he's not up to date on the fact that I realize I can't talk you out of it." Therefore, there is this feeling on Johnson's part, and on the part of the people around him, that the two brothers were divided on the subject. I don't think they were ever in disagreement about it, except they thought Bob might go down and tell him how difficult it would be, and how the convention might reject him, and how there would be a big floor fight. And he went down to tell him that, because Jack sent him down to tell him that.

In the meantime they discover that Lyndon is going to do it, so there are a couple of conversations and certainly one on the telephone in which the acceptance is clear: I'm going to take your offer. And Jack, in those circumstances, is talking back and forth with people in the suite, and he says, "You know, I am going to go with it." And Lyndon says,

"Bobby is down here." And Jack says, "Don't pay any attention to that; he doesn't know what he is saying; he's not up on that."

I think Bobby was trying to talk him out of it and was hoping that he would succeed. The bad blood that existed—and it got worse after the president was assassinated—that was bad throughout, started right there.

Orville Freeman, secretary of agriculture I don't remember exactly why he had called me to his suite to ask me about the vice presidency. He was sitting on a window sill. He told me that he had selected Lyndon Johnson. If you had hit me over the head with a telephone pole, I couldn't have been more surprised. I couldn't imagine Lyndon Johnson taking the job. He was miserable on the job the whole time, anyway, and why would he take it when he was the strongest, most powerful man in Washington? Then Bobby stuck his head in and said, "The son of a bitch is already talking, and if you want to make this announcement, you'd better make it right away." He got up and left the room to make the announcement.

Years later I was up at Camp David one time with LBJ—it was the two of us up by the swimming pool. All of a sudden, he grabbed me and rolled over and said, "If I hadn't taken the vice presidential thing, who do you think would have been named?" And I said, "I don't know." He said, "You would have. I asked him, and that's what he said." It almost happened.

Pierre Salinger We had been very tough with Johnson because he was a potentially tough candidate against us. Suddenly one morning, about twenty-four hours before the nomination, I get a call from Phil Graham [publisher of the *Washington Post*], saying: "Stop attacking Johnson." I said, "What do you mean?" He replied, "He's going to be the vice presidential candidate." That was the first time I had heard of that possibility. Graham had good relations with John Kennedy, so he may have known something behind the scenes that I hadn't heard about. I went to see Kennedy and told him that Phil Graham had told me not to attack Johnson anymore. He said, "That's not a bad idea."

Joseph Dolan I was up in the room where they were meeting. Pierre Salinger came out kind of all shook up. He says, "Circus Bar. Right away." That is where the press met.

Three times between 1956 and 1957, John Kennedy said to me, "After me, Lyndon is the best qualified." I was for Symington; Colorado was for Symington. He was popular there. When we tried to sell the Colorado delegation on Johnson after the announcement, we damn near got lynched.

Ben Bradlee   My wife went out to the convention in Los Angeles with Kennedy—sitting next to him on the plane, great with child—and I was out in Los Angeles a week earlier, and I had said to Toni: "Here are eight questions; ask them of Kennedy." Kennedy had a throat problem as he went out; he was not speaking. So she said to him: "Here's a list Ben gave me last night," and he wrote his answers. The first question was "What about LBJ for vice president?" He wrote: "He'll never take it." I assume he wasn't dissembling in that. The election was closer than it seemed. They [the Kennedy people] assumed they'd win on the first ballot, but they weren't all that sure, and they were directing all their attention to that. And Jack had promised everybody the vice presidency. Certainly Stu Symington; certainly Scoop Jackson [Henry M. Jackson, U.S. senator, (D., Wash.)]; Stu Symington even had a speech he was practicing. So I don't think he had settled it at all, and if he had had his druthers, I think it probably would have been okay with him if Lyndon had said no.

Pierre Salinger   Kenny O'Donnell and I went up to see Bobby at six-thirty A.M. the morning after Kennedy had won the presidential nomination, to start discussing the vice presidential nomination, and Bobby was taking a bath. He shouts from the bathroom: "How many electoral votes will we get if we take the South and the Northeast? Can we win the election with those regions?" O'Donnell said, "You're not thinking of nominating Lyndon Johnson, are you?" And Bobby said, "Yes." Then we got into a big fight with him; neither Kenny nor I were for Lyndon Johnson; I was pretty much for Symington, and I think Kenny was for Scoop Jackson. Bobby said, "No. It looks like it's going to be Johnson."

Bobby Baker   I was a delegate to the convention from South Carolina. I occupied rooms three doors north of Johnson's suite at the Biltmore Hotel. On the morning that presidential nominee Kennedy had called Lyndon Johnson at about six forty-five in the morning asking to come see him, Bill Moyers [aide to Lyndon Johnson]—who was at that time basically a telephone page—was sent by Johnson to my room to urge me to come down to the suite immediately, and I was angry with Johnson because he had been very rude the night after he had been defeated by Senator Kennedy—we had held a party at the Biltmore for all our people who had supported Johnson for the presidency, and he had done very well in view of his reticence to run. He had refused to run in the primaries and he'd been very difficult as the presidential candidate, but we had a lot of fine people, like Governor [Buford] Ellington of Tennessee and Connally [John B. Connally, Jr., later governor of Texas]—I guess we had three or four hundred people there. We had fought the good fight, and I think we were almost unanimous that because of the extreme ADA-liberal viewpoint of that convention, that Nixon would be elected. I had consumed too much whiskey—I had a terrible hangover.

I told Bill to tell him I wasn't coming down there. About five minutes later Bill came back and said that it was a crisis—that I had to come. So I took a cold shower and shaved and went down. Just he and Lady Bird [Claudia T. Johnson, wife of Lyndon Johnson] were in the room. Lyndon said, "Your friend, Kennedy"—Kennedy and I were closer in age than he was—"your friend, Kennedy, called me. What do you think he wants?" I said, "He's smart. He knows he doesn't have a chance in hell to be elected president unless you're on the ticket. So, if Kennedy offers you the nomination, you just tell him you'll take it." I'd been there with Johnson about ten minutes when he summoned Mr. Rayburn, who wouldn't come. But John Connally came. After about five minutes, Senator Kennedy came in and Senator Kennedy offered him to be his running mate.

Adlai Stevenson III There was some talk of the possibility of my father's being offered the vice presidency. It was mentioned, without any real conviction or enthusiasm, by the people around him, because they knew he wouldn't consider it for one second. That would have been very difficult for him—he never sought—his grandfather had been vice president. Besides, he wanted to be secretary of state.

George Smathers, U.S. senator (D., Fla.) I said, "Jack, take Stuart Symington." He said, "Stuart Symington can't get me votes. I can carry Missouri. I don't need Stuart Symington to take Missouri; I need somebody who's going to win some votes in the South for me. That's what I need." I said, "I'm a believer that you ought to mix it up a little bit," but I didn't believe Johnson would ever go for that. . . . You know, Johnson didn't like Kennedy; Kennedy didn't like Johnson.

So then, when he called me later in the afternoon—I was just two floors below him—to come on up, it was all pretty well decided. Bobby walked in and said, "It's all set."

Gaylord Nelson, governor of Wisconsin; U.S. senator (D., Wis.) At the convention Kennedy sent for me. He wanted me to talk to Senator Proxmire [William E. Proxmire, U.S. senator (D., Wis.)] because, although Johnson had not been selected, Kennedy had decided on him, and he didn't want a liberal senator denouncing the choice. He was clever. He said to me, "I am going to select Lyndon Johnson. Will Proxmire attack that?" He then said, "I have no choice. Sam Rayburn was in, pushing for Johnson. Can you imagine what kind of a success my presidency would be if Lyndon Johnson was still in the Senate and I don't select him, and he is the majority leader, and Sam Rayburn is running the House? How can I get anything through there?" I am not sure that Sam went and said that. I am sure Sam lobbied for Johnson. Kennedy was making a case and saying, "For heaven's sake, don't pick on me. I had no choice."

Terry Sanford   I said to Bobby, "I think Johnson should be the man." I was asked to come over to the Kennedy suite the morning after Jack was nominated. Soapy Williams [G. Mennen Williams, assistant secretary of state for African affairs] and Fritz Hollings [Ernest F. Hollings, governor of South Carolina], and a few other people were there. I believe it was Larry O'Brien who said to me, "Well, you're for Johnson, aren't you?" I said, "Oh yes, you know that." He said, "Speak up to him; urge him to take Johnson." I don't think I was urging him to take Johnson, I think I was cutting Soapy off before he objected too much to Johnson. I think they had already made the deal that morning; I thought we were going through a charade. My feeling was: This decision has been made; now I want to get people to support it. Soapy told Fritz, "You will understand I have to be against Johnson on the floor. It's going to work out all right." So when he spoke up and raised Cain, I told three or four people I was watching this with, "Don't you worry about that."

Abraham Ribicoff   I knew it was going to be Johnson pretty early. Jack was very smart, very calculating. There was only one person who wanted it, who could help him, and that was Lyndon Johnson. The Democrats never carried Texas; if Texas did not go for the Democrats, they could not win the presidency. Johnson was the only one who could bring him something. The Catholic thing was going to come up, and the only one who could do it was Johnson. Sam Rayburn didn't want Johnson to take it; feelings were high; they were very bitter feelings. I told two people that Johnson was going to get it: Lloyd Bentsen [U.S. congressman, later senator], of Texas, who said, "Abe, you're absolutely crazy"; and Scotty Reston [James B. Reston, columnist, the *New York Times*] who said, "I'd be a laughingstock if I went with that story." I always kid those two guys about it.

Ralph Yarborough   Kennedy could have carried Texas if he had put me on the ticket. When Kennedy got the nomination, Bobby Kennedy sent for me. I figured that's what they were figuring on, because they had offered it to Lyndon Johnson and he'd refused it, at first, because old Lyndon—he was a smart politician—he was making them beg him for it; he was playing hard to get. Shucks—a lot of people—old Sam Rayburn thought he didn't want it. It was beneath him, as majority leader. Lyndon fooled all of them; he started running. I didn't think he could ever get that nomination.

But after that first short visit up to Bobby Kennedy's office, Lyndon Johnson came over and the deal had been cut. He was going to be on the ticket, so they never spoke to me again at the convention.

Joseph Rauh, Jr.   The people who are in the running are Humphrey, Freeman, Symington, and Jackson; all four names are being batted about—the joke has always been that the bar in the headquarters hotel wasn't big enough to cover all the people who had been promised the vice presidency. I knew that Phil Graham was working for Kennedy for president and Johnson for vice president. I had my own delegation—the District of Columbia delegation. There were a great many blacks who were as violently opposed to Johnson as I was. The *Washington Post* said that once Kennedy is nominated, he will announce Johnson as his vice president. This was a terrible shock, for two reasons: One, I had a promise to the contrary, which I thought was a good promise; two, I had promised the delegation that it wasn't going to be Johnson. I grabbed the newspaper and headed for Kennedy's headquarters and asked for Bobby. I said to him: "Look at this, Bobby—this is Tuesday morning—what do I do with my delegation?" He said, "You tell them it's *not* going to be Johnson." I believe implicitly that he was telling me the truth. I don't think he was being shady, because I saw him two days later—on Thursday, after it was announced—and he was in abject despair. Some people say that the Kennedys wanted Johnson to turn it down, and then they'd have party unity, because they'd offered it to him; others say that Jack Kennedy wanted Johnson. I don't know. All I know is that if a political promise is worth a damn, I had a broken promise. Naturally, I felt pretty bad, and that was when I made the appeal on television to Jack not to do it, but he did; I knew it was hopeless [to make the appeal], but I don't mind being hopeless when I'm right. We did have a little battle, we had a few scattered votes against it, in Michigan and the District of Columbia. When they had the roll call, Texas nominated Johnson, and then Massachusetts moved to close debate. Governor LeRoy Collins [of Florida], in the chair, announced a vote and said that it takes two-thirds to shut off debate. There's a tremendous vote against it. But that's a gallery vote; poor Collins, Stevenson people had loaded the galleries. But on the floor, the regulars had the control. It was perfectly clear that they had the two-thirds needed for that vote. But Collins hesitated—he's standing up there and hesitating—and Sam Rayburn is shouting at him: "It's passed! It's passed!" So Johnson was nominated, and after a few drinks and a couple of friendly messages from the Kennedy people, everybody went for the ticket.

Why Did Johnson Accept the Nomination?

Ben Bradlee   Don't you have to take the vice presidential job? I guess not, but it seems to me that if the president of the United States asks you to take it, you can't really say, "No, I want to stay in the Senate and make life difficult for you."

John Seigenthaler   Who is going to be in the driver's seat for four years if they knock Kennedy off in this campaign? I think that is the train of thought: If we say no, they will never let us forget it. The liberal press will never let us forget it. Kennedy really put Lyndon in a bind. All of his advisers felt very much as Bob Kerr [Robert S. Kerr, U.S. senator (D., Okla.)] felt. I think that it made more sense for him to do it than not to. Maybe it is a close call, but how do you benefit more, politically? If you win, you win; if you lose, he loses, but do you lose? Is anyone going to blame you because the second Catholic didn't get elected president of the United States? There is a lot of work that could be done to build friendships outside the South during the campaign. If I had been an adviser to him, I would have said, "How can you not do this? What do you have to lose? If we win, what the hell have I lost? I am vice president of the United States."

Bobby Baker   When Kennedy offered the vice presidency to Johnson, instead of saying, "I'm honored; I'm flattered; we're going to win; I'm with you," he said, "I've got to talk to Mr. Rayburn and my friends, and I'll let you know." That thing could have screwed it all up. He couldn't make a decision right that minute. That was typical Johnson; he was always touching his bases.

He took the nomination because of the knowledge that if he was ever going to be anything but a senator, it was not bad for his image to be the vice presidential nominee. Kennedy had told me time and time again, when he was running, that the ablest man in the Democratic party was Lyndon Johnson, but with labor opposed to him, he could not get the nomination, the way the Democratic Convention was established, but that if he, Kennedy, did not get the nomination, he was going to support Johnson. There was never anything but collegiality between them; Kennedy was very respectful.

Jack Valenti, adviser to Lyndon Johnson   I was surprised because I was more naive than I am now. After the bellicosity of the campaign, it just never occurred to me that they would pick Johnson. I'd heard that people like Soapy Williams and Walter Reuther [president, United Automobile Workers] were anti-Johnson, to the nth degree, and I just did not think that the breach could be healed. I was quite astonished. Johnson wasn't surprised; he was an old pol. He realized very quickly that the mix was good: Catholic from Boston, Protestant from Texas; the baronial leader of the Senate against a backbencher. It was a perfect fit. People like Sam Rayburn told Johnson, "If they offer you the vice presidency, you can't accept it." Then Rayburn changed his mind.

Johnson looked at it in another way. First, he and Rayburn loathed Nixon from the McCarthy days—the way they treated George Marshall [secretary of state, defense, Truman administration] and others. So he figured anything he could do to help Kennedy win he would do. And he realized if you were going to carry Texas you'd better have Lyndon Johnson on that ticket. The second reason is—I get this from people around Johnson and his family—if you're majority leader and a Republican is president, that's one thing, but if you're majority leader with a strong, vibrant, popular president, that's quite another thing. And you aren't going to be as powerful as you once were. And I think Mrs. Johnson was delighted because she thought he would slow down if he was vice president.

He told me when he was vice president he thought no Southerner would ever be nominated for president in his lifetime. And he always believed he was going to come back to Texas after eight years, and he would have been sixty years old, so he was ready to come back to Texas and leave politics. That's what he said; now, did he really mean it? I can only tell you what he said.

Eugene McCarthy, U.S. senator (D., Minn.)   I was at a regional meeting in Albuquerque, and he came in and was passing out cowboy hats and pins, and people didn't know who he was. And this was in New Mexico, just across the border from Texas. He was big in Washington, but when he got outside, nobody knew anybody that looked like Lyndon Johnson. The only chance he had for the presidency was to do service for the party.

Najeeb Halaby, administrator, Federal Aviation Authority (FAA) My assumption has always been that he wanted to arrive; he wanted to be accepted. This poor boy from the salty Texas flats wanted to be one of the big boys. That was really driving him constantly. This was bigger and better than being majority leader. Who knows where it might lead? I can't have it myself; this is as near as I might get to it, so Lady Bird, let's go for it.

John Kenneth Galbraith, U.S. ambassador to India   I think that Lyndon, who was a very close friend of mine in those days—we remained close friends until we broke apart in the Vietnam War; we were of the same age and had something of the same rural background—saw the vice presidency as a step on to the presidency. He'd already had a long tour of duty on the Hill. He'd already exhausted the possibility. This was the logical next step.

Tom Wicker, correspondent, Washington Bureau, *New York Times* A friend of mine who worked for the *Baltimore Sun* was very close to Johnson. He told me that at one point Johnson turned to Lady Bird, who was lukewarm about this proposition, and—as I myself have seen him do—tapped her on the chest and said, "Goddamn it, Lady Bird! Don't you realize I'll be one heartbeat away?" That seems to me to be a characteristic story.

Norman Podhoretz, editor, *Commentary* He was thought to be the most powerful man in the country, in a way, as Senate majority leader, but he took the nomination for all the usual reasons: The party wanted it; he was a party loyalist. He might have seen it as a stepping-stone to the presidency, which, of course, it turned out to be. He certainly did not anticipate the terrible treatment he was to receive at the hands of the Kennedys. He was shocked and depressed by it. Of course, ever since Johnson took that job, it has been assumed by almost everybody that it is an excellent stepping-stone to the presidency. Now everybody who has a chance to get that job jumps at it, no matter what his previous position has been.

George Smathers I went down to visit with Lyndon, and Sam Rayburn and Bob Kerr and Lady Bird and the others were all there. And Lyndon was concerned—he wouldn't think of it—and said: "If I stay as majority leader, I'm going to be twice as powerful as Jack Kennedy. Jack Kennedy will have to deal with me. He can't pass anything unless he comes to me as majority leader, so why in the hell would I want to be vice president?"

I think that Lady Bird Johnson—there's ten thousand theories as to what changed Lyndon's mind—my theory is that Lady Bird, who of course was very much in love with Lyndon and was concerned about him—he had had two heart attacks—that she, knowing that the vice president's job was less tiring, less burdensome, and he had much less responsibility, nobody thought that Kennedy would not live out his first term—so she thought that it would be an appropriate place for Johnson to be, where he wouldn't have to work so very hard, where he'd be head of the Space Program—where he'd been in the Senate, that he'd continue that program—that would be about all he'd do, other than ceremonial functions.

Gerald R. Ford, U.S. congressman (R., Mich.)   I recall Hale Boggs [U.S. congressman (D., La.)] telling of the meeting at the Democratic Convention in 1960 when Kennedy won the nomination, and the question was: Who would be his running mate? Boggs related to me on more than one occasion how Sam Rayburn and he, and maybe others, talked Lyndon into being the vice presidential candidate. Apparently Lyndon wanted no part of it, and according to Hale Boggs, Rayburn sat Lyndon down and told him: You be the candidate. Hale said Rayburn engineered it.

Pierre Salinger   When he heard he was going to be the vice presidential nominee, Johnson called John Nance Garner [vice president under Franklin D. Roosevelt, 1937–41] and said, "I'm being offered the vice presidency," and Garner replied, "You shouldn't take it; it's not worth a bottle of piss." Johnson saw the vice presidency as a future for his career. Even if Kennedy had survived and gone eight years, Johnson would have been a potential presidential candidate, although Robert Kennedy would, perhaps, have been a more potential candidate. But Johnson wanted to be president someday.

Joseph Dolan   I have always felt that the vice presidency has been misinterpreted. It has been the easiest way to the White House; if you want your daughter or son to be president, tell them to become vice president. That's the way to get there. Johnson probably felt that Kennedy would give him a really significant position. Kennedy's nickname for Johnson was "Riverboat." He was a riverboat gambler. I think John Kennedy had a limited admiration for roguish politicians.

George Romney, chairman of the board and president, American Motors Corporation; governor of Michigan   I think he visualized a young president who did not have the experience he had and that perhaps he could exert more influence than it turned out he could. That is why I joined the Nixon cabinet. I thought I could have more influence on some of the national issues that I was concerned about by being a part of the team and having access to the top leadership. Johnson may have felt the same way.

Terry Sanford I had no question in my mind ever that he would accept it eagerly and, as a matter of fact, would fight to get it. I believe he would have gone to great lengths, and he did make some effort to get it, because it was the path to the presidency—the only path. It ultimately happened, but it gave him the chance to be the next in line, pretty much the way Nixon became the next in line after Eisenhower. Johnson had that illustration right before him that that was the path to the White House. There is no question that he was consumed with the desire to be president, so I never had any doubt he would take it. Actually the majority leader is not all that powerful, except in a small, tight circle.

THE CAMPAIGN

Donald Wilson, deputy director, United States Information Agency (USIA) At the beginning he was an underdog. It changed as a result of the debates and other events. I think he thought it would be close. I really think that right up until the end, he didn't know who would win. I never heard any lack of confidence; it was a confident crew. He and the people around him were upbeat and positive, but they didn't slap each other on the back and say, "Hey, we are going to win." It was very cold, hard, calculating stuff of how you make your way to the presidency.

Louis Martin, deputy director, Democratic National Committee We had a staff meeting—JFK was up in Hyannis Port. They wanted to issue a press release about the existence of this civil rights unit in the campaign. I was asked to work on one, but there were many prominent names, and I had to find out who was the most important. That was when I was cast in the role of a mediator; someone was needed to run the office and organize the troops. I was particularly concerned to organize the black preachers, because of the Catholic issue, so we sent the story up to Hyannis Port and JFK released it. That was the way we began.

A week later I saw Dawson [William Dawson, U.S. congressman (D., Ill.)] in Chicago. He was not excited about the Kennedys. Bobby was not the warmest type of person. It was like the good cop, bad cop: JFK was always full of syrup, and Bobby was full of vinegar. You had to know which one you were dealing with.

One day, during the campaign, Bobby came to the office and there was a very smart young man—very professional looking—with this diagram, sketching things, putting names down, and so forth. Bobby asked what he was doing. Someone said, "He is coordinating things and making sense out of the campaign." Bobby replied, "Well, fire that son of a bitch right now."

Terry Sanford   I came out for Kennedy in 1960. This was a considerable risk in political terms, because he wasn't all that popular in the South; he was perceived as being very liberal on racial fairness in the South, and for that matter, in the nation as a whole. He was a Yankee, so there wasn't any political advantage in supporting him, but I wanted to be a part of what I considered the new generation. I was also offended that in the South, we would go with candidates like Richard Russell [U.S. senator (D., Ga.)], who had no chance of winning. So I felt, Why don't we quit this business and join the rest of the nation?

I sat down with my campaign manager and said, "If we are going to begin this thing, we ought to be in it the right way. And the right way is to support the candidate we think ought to win." We did have a poll. John Kennedy was one of the early people to take polls. The poll showed I was ahead of my opponent with about 66 percent of the vote, but that Kennedy had only 32 percent. As it turned out in the election, I had 55 percent and he had between 50 and 54. We barely carried the state for him.

Philip Kaiser, U.S. ambassador to Senegal and Mauritania   I've been in several campaigns—I served as one of Byron White's [deputy attorney general] deputies in the Citizens for Kennedy operation, working mainly in the Midwest, Illinois, Michigan, and Ohio—and they were all a mess. But I must say that Bobby was the best campaign manager I ever saw. He was the candidate's brother, so he could take care of any personality tensions—people striving for status and positions. Everyone knew he had complete access to his brother. This is an invaluable asset, which he used very intelligently. He was also very open. Often people who run campaigns don't understand that people want to help, and they turn them off. He never turned anybody off. The Kennedys understood. They never cut anybody out. They knew that people felt they really wanted them.

Louis Martin I got into a fight with Bobby the first time I met him. I didn't have a title when I joined the campaign; I just had a typewriter and a desk. The whole campaign was run by members of the family. Sarge [R. Sargent Shriver, Jr., director, Peace Corps; husband of president Kennedy's sister Eunice] was in charge of women and minorities. I was one of his boys, but they didn't know what to call me. One day those of us in the civil rights division of the campaign—twenty-five of us—were told we should come over to Bobby's office. This meeting was supercritical, based on what people he had called told him we were doing. When he got to me, I told him what I was doing. I said, "The trouble is that you are running this goddamn thing. I don't think you guys are doing a thing." So Sarge says, "He's from Chicago," and he tried to explain me away.

After the meeting John Seigenthaler asked if I could stay after the others left. He wanted to know more. When we were alone, I began to tell him about black politicians, like Dawson in Chicago—who had spent their lives in this business. I said, "Whether you like them or not, at least they have some followers. Half of these people around here haven't got two votes. Why don't you use what's out there, rather than try to reinvent the wheel?" Seigenthaler was very nice about it, and Bobby said, "Maybe we ought to look into it." I said, "There's no point in looking into it. Why don't you meet Dawson? You count on [Mayor Richard] Daley to carry Chicago, and he counts on Dawson to carry the blacks." He said, "All right," he'd like to meet him.

So a few days later I put Dawson in a cab and took him over to the headquarters at 1001 Connecticut Avenue. He was an old-time pol, always wanting to make some deals. He wasn't happy about my being a witness to whatever he was doing, so I said, "You go in and talk to Bobby, and I'll wait out here." So they got together for a half hour or so, and then it was all over with.

Dawson never would tell me what they talked about, nor would Bobby. I knew Bobby had a rough reputation—that he bought and sold these characters. I didn't know what kind of deal he might have made with them. It turned out that Dawson wasn't enthusiastic about Bobby at all, and Bobby wasn't enthusiastic about him; they didn't get on a bit. I said, "I must have done the wrong thing."

Donald Wilson   During the campaign, Kennedy was all business. There was not a lot of socializing. He was moving on to the next stop or the next objective. There was very little time spent in small talk with the staff, or putting his arm around you and saying, "You did a good job." He was a man who, even then, and in the presidency, was not tremendously generous with praise for other people. If you ever got a compliment from John F. Kennedy, you treasured it. In the campaign there were almost no moments that I can recall—and I was with him constantly—of sitting down, relaxing, and schmoozing; it was all business.

On the other hand, it was fun to be in the campaign. There was such a contrast with Lyndon Johnson, who operated through fear. I worked for him for a year after the assassination, and there were times when you thought he was trying to scare you into doing something. There was not one iota of that in John F. Kennedy. It was really uplifting and fun to work for him. He had a remarkable personality. I've never come across anybody who had such a good one. He never put people down. He had some fools around him, but I never remember his embarrassing anyone in front of people.

Paul Samuelson, adviser on economic affairs   Jackie was pregnant during the campaign, and the candidate was told to make something of it, so at one of the meetings he started out to say something about it, but he didn't like it and he stopped toward the middle. He later said, "Hell. If that's what it takes to be elected, I'll lose. I am not going to mention pregnancy again." He didn't brandish her plain cloth coat.[*]

Arthur Schlesinger, Jr.   Kennedy was not a toucher, and he didn't like being touched; people from New England don't. One of the great differences between Texas and New England was that Lyndon Johnson was all

---

[*]On September 23, 1952, Richard M. Nixon, Republican candidate for vice president, in a nationally televised address answering charges of misuse of campaign funds, stated that his wife, Patricia Ryan Nixon, did not own a mink coat but possessed "a respectable Republican cloth coat." The address is known as the "Checkers" speech, after Nixon's mention of the family's cocker spaniel, Checkers.

over you—that was his way, but Kennedy was a very effective campaigner, and he enjoyed it.

Ralph Yarborough   I saw a debate they had on television in West Virginia; Kennedy was debating Hubert Humphrey. If the press asked a mean, tough one, Kennedy would look straight ahead but wouldn't jump in if the question were addressed to both of them, but Hubert Humphrey would jump in nearly every time and give them a straight answer, and give Kennedy time to give a less offensive answer. They asked about food stamps, and Kennedy reached down—he had long, slender fingers—and picked up a box of eggs and said, "With your food stamps, all you can get are these aye-ughs; you have to eat those aye-ughs all the time. When I'm president, you'll have something to eat besides aye-ughs." He just slaughtered Hubert Humphrey on things like that. On the next question a black man wanted to buy a coat, and they refused to sell it to him. He asked, "What would you do if you were the proprietor?" and Hubert gave him a long lecture on civil rights, and what was fair. And they asked Kennedy for his answer, and he said, "I'd sell him a suit."

Tom Wicker   I never quite understood the transformation: Somewhere in the middle of the 1960 campaign, Kennedy suddenly became a matinee idol. Remember Kennedy's speech in Los Angeles right after he was nominated? It was not a good speech; it was not well delivered. He only got to be a great candidate by early October.

Pierre Salinger   It was an interesting campaign in terms of what we did behind the scenes to prevent both parties, and both candidates, from going down dirty tracks. Herb Klein, Nixon's communications director [and campaign aide], and I decided that if we discovered anything behind the scenes that was going to be a dirty shot, we would tell each other and keep it down.

Lloyd Cutler, adviser to the president on Cuban prisoner exchange   In the winter or spring of 1960, I did a little volunteer investigative work about Bebe Rebozo [confidant of Richard M. Nixon], along with Bill Baggs, who was the editor of the *Miami News* at that time and a friend and supporter of President Kennedy.

At that point, Bill Baggs, who was a friend of mine, was especially interested in the weekend parties that Richard Nixon used to attend at Bebe Rebozo's house in Key Biscayne, which had gone on for a long time. Bill had found some girls in Miami who claimed to have been there, at these parties.

It was all going to make a very good story about Richard Nixon until we learned that among the people who were frequently in the house was Senator Kennedy, so we dropped that story. We never did find out whether Mr. Nixon had gone upstairs.

The Debates

Roman Puchinski, U.S. congressman (D., Ill.) The first debate was held in Chicago, and there were only three people allowed in the control room: Mayor Richard Daley, his wife, and myself. Jack came out first and took his position at the lectern. Nixon came out second, and when he walked out onto that stage, Daley said, "My God, they've embalmed him before he even died." They had done a horrible makeup job on Nixon; he looked absolutely horrible.

When Jack went to the lectern, he seemed confident, and he held this confidence. Nixon looked very nervous, heavy sweating—this makeup—and there were people in this country who would have bet every dollar they had that the guy who made Nixon up was a Kennedy supporter; that was a rumor in the studio right after the debate. From the control room we could see both men. When Kennedy spoke, Nixon was cracking his hands.

I talked with Kennedy after the debate and he was very pleased. He said, "I came out better than I thought I would." He was elated with the makeup because even *he* saw what they had done to Nixon. He said he was glad they had not put makeup on him. He was on cloud nine.

Donald Wilson I was in the outer reaches of the studio during the first debate. I remember very clearly that I thought he had demolished Nixon. Afterward we were exultant. There was no question about it. People in the campaign thought he was a real victor.

I had had a lot of exposure to Nixon: I was on his campaign train in 1952, I covered him during the whole period leading up to the Checkers speech, and I had gone to Latin America with him—one of only five journalists on that three-week trip. I believe that Nixon thought he would demolish Kennedy. He had eight years of experience as vice president; he was a very accomplished debater. He had a hell of a good mind, but I think he underestimated Kennedy. He assumed that—without question—he would take Kennedy in the debates.

John Kenneth Galbraith   Nixon was extremely cooperative in those television debates—with Kennedy looking young and handsome and Nixon—particularly in the first one—looking very bearded and too much like Richard Nixon. I don't think you can underestimate Nixon's capacity to lose. I think if John F. Kennedy had been up against Dwight D. Eisenhower, as Eisenhower was in 1952, the outcome would have been very different. There is always the problem of counting the votes on the other side.

Archibald Cox, solicitor general of the United States   Bowles [Chester Bowles, undersecretary of state] and I thought the president should not take anywhere as near the aggressive position against [Fidel] Castro [president of Cuba] as he did in the first debate, where he set out to be tougher than Nixon. We thought it would be far better to deal with the problem in a softer way.

Gerald Ford   I always assume elections are going to be close. I knew Jack Kennedy was a formidable candidate. I always understood certain potential liabilities that Nixon had. It was quite a contrast. Kennedy presented a warm, friendly public image, Nixon had a totally different public image. You never knew how the public was going to accept him.

The debates did have an impact. Particularly the first one. I suspect that was the turning point. I recall vividly the night of the first debate I was campaigning out in a rural area, and I was driving from Coopersville, Michigan, to Grand Haven, or Holland, and heard it on the radio. I thought Nixon did very well. Then I got home that night and the next morning there were all these stories about how badly Nixon looked on television. My impression was totally different. Because on radio Nixon sounded very persuasive. So television for the first time had a major impact on a presidential election.

Tom Wicker   I think that Kennedy intimidated Nixon a bit. I have always felt that the first debate was a classic example of that. Here is poor Nixon—he has been sick, his short collar doesn't fit, the beard shadow, he's sweating. The door opens and in walks John F. Kennedy. Nobody could be more urbane and handsome, and if Kennedy lost the election, he's just going to go off cruising in the Mediterranean with beautiful girls. If Nixon loses, he's lost everything. I think that intimidated him.

I watched the debate on television and didn't have anywhere near a strong impression that Kennedy was the overwhelming victor, as turned out to be the case. I guess I was listening more closely to the literal exchanges rather than watching the images. I didn't see much difference, frankly. I went back to the Museum of Broadcasting in preparing my Nixon book and watched that debate all over again, and I still don't see much difference between them. But there is no doubt—when you watch the debate with many years of watching television—that Kennedy was so smooth and calm and cool, and here's Nixon. Well, no wonder he lost.

I was in New York, traveling with the Lodge [Henry Cabot Lodge, Republican candidate for vice president, 1960] campaign, and the next morning, when I went down to get in the bus, I found the Lodge people were just downcast, acting like they had been killed. They knew Nixon had lost.

Norman Podhoretz   That famous debate. I remember it very well. There was this charming, handsome, rich young aristocrat. There was a certain amount of boredom with the Eisenhower years. Nixon carried the burden of the recent recession. In the culture, there was this stirring of a new spirit—people looking for something exciting, innovating. Yes. A New Frontier. So Kennedy was able to do better than he might otherwise have done.

Adlai Stevenson III   I remember watching a Kennedy-Nixon debate and feeling my father's frustration. I knew he was thinking to himself—in fact, he said it a couple of times—he would have handled it differently, and therefore better, than Kennedy. I have to speculate—I guess I would have to speculate—that my father, as totally opposed to Nixon, would have great difficulty understanding what charms he could offer anybody, let alone a majority, how anybody could vote for that man. It would be a little difficult for him to grasp.

The King Phone Call

Morris B. Abram, general counsel, Peace Corps; member, UN Subcommission on Prevention of Discrimination and Protection of Minorities The genesis of the call from Senator Kennedy to Coretta Scott King [wife of Dr. Martin Luther King, Jr.] was a telephone call I received from Harris Wofford [campaign aide; White House aide]. Harris, at the time, was Sargent Shriver's assistant in the civil rights division of the Kennedy campaign. The object was so they would be able to claim credit for King's release. The vote was extremely close, and the black vote was important. I told Wofford that I couldn't go to see Mayor [William] Hartsfield [of Atlanta] because I had a date with my daughter, who was then nine. He said, "Take her with you." So I took her down, and she spent twelve hours with me in the mayor's office as we negotiated to get Martin out of jail. I even went at eleven in the evening to Dick Rich's [Richard Rich, owner, Rich's Department Stores, Atlanta, Ga.] house to try to get him to drop the charges. This was extremely difficult to accomplish. There also had been some Klansmen arrested, and you had to let them go, too.

Sometime during the day Bobby Troutman, my old friend and college roommate, who was running much of the Southern campaign, heard about our efforts and came rushing to see Bill Hartsfield, to say that if the mayor—in the name of Kennedy—did something for this fellow, King, then Fritz Hollings would desert the campaign. Nevertheless, we did get the charges dropped, but Martin [Rev. Dr. Martin Luther King, Jr., president, Southern Christian Leadership Conference] refused to leave the jail. The slogan was "No jail, no bail." Finally, the president of Atlanta University persuaded him to come out of jail. The Klansmen were also released.

The reason Martin didn't want to come out of jail became obvious thereafter: he was put on probation for a driving license violation from the neighboring county. He had been put on probation by a Judge Mitchell [Oscar Mitchell, judge, De Kalb County, Ga.], who was a notorious antiblack, and Martin feared that something would happen as a result of this, if there were any kind of failure to live up to the terms of the parole.

Indeed, something did happen. He was then brought before Judge Mitchell and sentenced down to that terrible place—the prison at Reidsville—where he was in great danger. I was in touch with the civil rights division of the Kennedy campaign. We were very concerned. We didn't know what was going to happen. In any event Shriver did it by speaking, impulsively, to Jack when he was in Chicago. He picked up the phone.

I've always said of Shriver—and I still say it—he's a secular priest; he is a deeply devout Catholic. I think he really does have a motivation to do good all the time. I seriously doubt that other than a political motive would have impulsed any of the Kennedys, but it certainly would have impulsed Shriver.

R. Sargent Shriver, Jr., director, Peace Corps   With due respect to everyone else, I am the only one who knows what really happened. I was in Chicago, running the Kennedy for President operation in Illinois, when I got a call from Harris Wofford, who was in the civil rights headquarters in Washington. He said, "Sarge, I have been thinking about the situation involving Martin Luther King, Jr., who is in jail in Georgia. I think it would be a marvelous idea if we could get the candidate to call Mrs. King and express his sympathy. He doesn't have to do anything more than that; he doesn't have to make any kind of political commitment."

Kennedy was in Chicago, and I was in charge of his visit. We had held a breakfast for local leaders, and then Kennedy went back to a motel near the airport where he was staying, and we went into his room. There were people there—talking about the breakfast—and someone said, "The plane leaves at about ten o'clock; we have to pack." So everyone else left, and I remained with the candidate, who began to pack his bag. It was miraculous, because I had not wanted to bring up the idea of calling Mrs. King with the others there, because I knew it would precipitate a debate about the call's pros and cons.

I said, "Jack, I have an idea that might help you in the campaign: Mrs. Martin Luther King is sitting down there in Atlanta, and she is terribly worried about what is going to happen to her husband. I have her home telephone number; I suggest that you pick up the phone, say hello, and tell her you hope that everything works out well."

There was a silence of ten or fifteen seconds, and then he said,

"That's a good idea; can you get her on the phone?" So I picked up the phone near the bed, and dialed her number, and she answered. I said, "Mrs. King, this is Sargent Shriver"—the King family knew me—"and I am here with Senator Kennedy. He would like to speak with you; is that okay?" She said, "Fine," and I handed the phone to Jack.

He spoke for a maximum of three minutes. All he did was to express his sympathy and interest—as a citizen and as a political leader—over the plight of the King family, and then he hung up.

I said, "Thanks, Jack. I think that will make a big difference to a lot of people."

Jack then went on to Michigan, and then to New York, landing at the Marine Terminal at La Guardia Airport. He was immediately asked about the call to Mrs. King, and shortly after that, I got scorched out by officials of the Kennedy campaign. They asked who the hell I thought I was, getting the candidate to make such a call without consultation with national campaign headquarters. Thirty-six hours later, they changed their tune, and started saying how important the call had been.

Did the King Phone Call Have an Impact on the Black Vote?

Rev. Fred Shuttlesworth, secretary, Southern Christian Leadership Conference (SCLC); president, Alabama Christian Movement for Human Rights I would give the phone call great significance; it was, indeed, a turning point, which helped many to make up their minds that Kennedy would be concerned, at least, about what Dr. King was talking about—trying to get justice for the black people.

Julian Bond, member, Student Non-Violent Coordinating Committee (SNCC) I remember thinking that it was nice that he called, but so what? That was the first time I voted for a president—we could vote at eighteen in Georgia*—and I voted for Kennedy, but I don't remember being particularly impressed by the phone call; I think others were likely to have been more impressed by it. We were kind of cynical young people—cynical and romantic at the same time.

---

*The Twenty-sixth Amendment, ratified in 1971, gave the right to vote to all U.S. citizens eighteen years of age or older.

John Lewis, chairman, Student Non-Violent Coordinating Committee   A guy like Daddy King [Rev. Dr. Martin Luther King, Sr., pastor, Ebenezer Baptist Church, Atlanta, Ga.] had some problems, some concerns, about John F. Kennedy. I don't know if they were just based on the fact that he was this liberal Democrat out of New England, or whether it was because he was Catholic, Daddy King being a devoted Baptist. But after that telephone call, he said, "I now have a suitcase full of votes for Mr. Kennedy." That telephone call sent a strong message, and it traveled through the black community of this nation like wildfire.

The Daddy King Endorsement

Morris Abram   They called me from the Kennedy headquarters and wanted me to get an endorsement of Senator Kennedy from Martin Luther King, Jr. His father was a client of mine, and in my office about this time, and I asked him about his son endorsing Senator Kennedy. He said he appreciated all that Kennedy had done for his son, but he said, "My son runs a tax-exempt organization and he can't do that." It just occurred to me to say, "Look. Why don't you do it? Who in the hell will know the difference between 'Martin Luther King' and 'Martin Luther King'?" He said, "I can't do it." I said, "Why?" He said, "Because he's a Catholic and I'm a Baptist." We talked about that for a few minutes, and he said, "Well, after all he's done for my son, I'm going to do it. You have the press down at the Ebenezer Baptist Church, and I'll have the congregation there, and I'll say that I'm going to deliver Senator Kennedy a bushel basket full of votes," which he did.

The Religious Issue

The issue of Kennedy's Roman Catholicism emerged as the most vexing problem in his quest for the presidency. While the issue was primarily raised by Protestant fundamentalists, some mainline Protestants and Jews also voiced concern over the potential impact of Kennedy's religious affiliation on policy formulation. There is also evidence that some of the more egregious criticism of the candidate's religious beliefs came from his political opponents.

Kennedy formed a special campaign unit to deal with the religious issue, and his aides met with a wide range of religious leaders to reassure them that the candidate was a vigorous proponent of religious liberty and pluralism.

Pierre Salinger   The religious issue was very important; we realized it from the very beginning. In the period before the nomination, we tried to put together a committee of Protestant leaders. They didn't have to come out for Kennedy, just to say that this was not a religious issue; people should make up their minds based on other factors.

Ralph Dungan   While we didn't have a strategy on the religious issue, except to talk about it up front and not hide it, we were very careful about getting a line that would meet orthodoxy with the Catholic church, and would, at the same time, provide a reasonable basis. Rev. John Courtney Murray [Roman Catholic theologian] was a great contact and friend. Later I maintained a liaison with Bishop Hannan [Rt. Rev. Philip Hannan, auxiliary bishop of Washington, D.C.], in Washington. President Kennedy felt comfortable with both of them, particularly with Hannan, unlike Cushing [Rt. Rev. Richard Cardinal Cushing, archbishop of Boston], because Cushing was not a very subtle guy; he was not the kind of guy you could sit down and talk this issue out with. Murray was very helpful in giving us an intellectual base consistent with our political objectives. Kennedy himself was illiterate on any of the philosophic, intellectual bases, but he was a quick learner. You could give him essential things, and he would internalize them very quickly and articulate them very well.

I don't think Kennedy took many attacks on the religious issue very seriously; he was used to that kind of stuff. He was no hotshot Catholic by a long shot: On birth control—like many Catholics in those days—he rejected the Church's teaching; he would go to mass on Sunday if somebody was watching, but he was not orthodox by any stretch of the imagination. He really didn't understand some of the attacks; he saw them as politically motivated, not based on any ideology. The Kennedy attitude was that you take that stuff in stride; you assume that it is going to happen; you get mad if you see real evidence of it, but you have to live with it. He was extremely pragmatic in things like that.

Eugene McCarthy   He used me on the religious issues. I spoke on a number of college campuses. At the University of Washington, somebody said, "Will Kennedy send an ambassador to the Vatican?" I replied, "I don't know if he will or not, but if you ask me, I would give him about twenty other places where he ought to get representation before he worries about the Vatican. I'd try First Boston and New York City Bank and General Motors. After he'd used up twenty ambassadors in those major corporations, he could send one to the Vatican if he had one left over. The corporations had more power and influence."

Ralph Dungan   The Catholic politicians were rascals. They were so apprehensive about the religious issue; as far as any of them had to deal with it, they would duck it. Religion wasn't an issue at other levels of the body politic, only at the presidential level. Many of the Catholic politicians were conservatives. They didn't like Kennedy and would be pessimistic and, indeed, negative. Their thought was: No Catholic ought to run; we don't need another Al Smith [Democratic candidate for president, 1928] situation. Let's not stir it up. Don't rock the boat.

I had spent a lot of time on the religious issue. I was interested in the church-state issue, and I used to read *Christianity and Crisis*, which was edited by Reinhold Niebuhr [Protestant theologian].

Rev. William Sloane Coffin, Jr., civil rights activist; consultant to the Peace Corps   I remember talking to Reinhold Niebuhr, and his reaction was, Well, I never thought I'd be voting for a compulsive adulterer, but he certainly has a better grasp of the situation than Nixon. It wasn't his Catholicism that bothered Reinhold Niebuhr. Now that's a pretty sophisticated response from a highly intelligent theologian. In 1960 I said to the Catholic chaplain at Yale, "We'll take up a collection for the Little Sisters of Charity, and you take up a collection for some Protestant charity." He shook his head and said, "We could never do that." When I think that was the atmosphere at Yale—in the country as a whole—there was still deep-seated suspicion of Catholics. We tend to think that the Roman Catholic church is much more monolithic than it is.

Gaylord Nelson   The Catholics in Wisconsin did not vote a religious prejudice; the Protestants did.

Theodore Hesburgh, member, U.S. Civil Rights Commission; president, Notre Dame University   Kennedy was the first one through the gate, and that makes an enormous difference. It wasn't as vitriolic as the Al Smith time. I think what people miss is that there was something called Vatican II going on in the early 1960s. By the time that it concluded in 1965, this whole animosity between Protestants and Catholics that I knew as a kid growing up in Syracuse, New York, was changed; today, you'd have to sit up all night to get a fight started. Kennedy put to rest the whole question of whether a Catholic could be president. I think the same thing has to happen for a black, a Jew, and a woman. I think it will, one of these days.

Philip Klutznick, U.S. ambassador to the UN Economic and Social Council At the beginning I didn't think Kennedy had a chance; the odds were against him. But as the campaign developed, it was clear from the way he handled himself and from the mistakes the other side made, that the issue of his being a Catholic was not going to be that important. I personally was surprised at Kennedy's maturity; I think he exceeded the expectations of many of those who supported him. It was fortuitous that he had Nixon as an opponent. He was probably the best candidate you could have chosen to give Jack a chance. He might have had a tough time with Lodge or another Republican.

Ralph Dungan West Virginia certainly was a big factor in terms of undermining those Democratic delegates who thought the religious issue to be an impenetrable obstacle. I think that was the real significance of West Virginia; it would have been much, much more difficult in the convention if we had lost there.

Adlai Stevenson III Right after the convention, Bobby Kennedy's first stop was a rally in my father's home of Libertyville, and I can't remember what exactly were Bobby Kennedy's words, but I do remember it was an impassioned plea for an open mind and, "Don't hold his Catholicism against him." That's kind of hard to imagine now, but at the time, it was seen, at least in the Kennedy camp, as a major obstacle that had to be overcome. I really don't know now, to what extent concerns about a Catholic president hurt, or helped, or what the net effect was. This was 1960—eight years of Eisenhower and good feelings—and there wasn't any great discontent in the country. I can't believe that Eisenhower was very enthusiastically supportive of Nixon. He tried repeatedly to dump him, but still, he was the candidate of the Eisenhower party. The country wasn't yet at war, or suffering economically. A young Catholic running for president—one without a very strong record in the Senate?

George McGovern, director, Food for Peace Program; U.S. senator (D., S. Dak.)   The religious issue was a big factor in South Dakota; no doubt about it. On the closing weekend of the campaign—and even at the polling places—some of the Republican organizational people were distributing just frankly anti-Catholic literature. There was a fellow running for Congress named FitzGerald, who was a devout Catholic; Kennedy was at the top of the ticket, and I was running for the Senate. They distributed this card saying "Preserve America's Time-Honored Separation of Church and State; Vote No on Kennedy, McGovern and FitzGerald." I wasn't a Catholic—my Dad was a Methodist clergyman— but they figured: What the hell! His name is McGovern; he must be as bad as Kennedy and FitzGerald. I think it was effective. I never saw Nixon's hand in it, but it may well have been. I wasn't quite as paranoid about him then as I am now.

James Wine, campaign aide; U.S. ambassador to Luxembourg and to the Ivory Coast   I think that because of the insidiousness of the attacks—such things as a direct line to the Vatican from the Oval Office—Kennedy recognized the seriousness of it from a political standpoint, but it was a little bit like Butch Cassidy and the Sundance Kid. Who are these guys? Who are those people? And we found some very interesting things.

There were huge pockets of money and great wealth, for example, in California. They engaged people to write anti-Catholic tracts, which we ultimately discovered were printed in Long Island. They were trying to avoid a paper trail. What was interesting to me was who was doing it. We knew that after a while they were not anti-Catholic; they were anti-Kennedy. They were looking for all kinds of ploys to use to attack him and weaken his candidacy, and that happened to be one.

I don't recall that we ever documented a link to Nixon. But names would pop up; associations would pop up; and this convinced us, because many of them were people who were Nixon's real supporters when he became the candidate and were very much in his camp. And every now and then we would read names in the newspapers, of people who were doing this or that and were supportive of Mr. Nixon.

I remember an instance in Iowa where there was an epidemic of tracts. It was quite easy in that instance to find out who was really involved, and I had one discussion, I can't remember the man's name, in Des Moines. When the facts were in, we knew pretty well where these things were coming from.

Of course it was denied outright. I said, "You can deny all you want, but we know the source." It didn't recur in Iowa after that.

Jack Valenti   I wouldn't put it past them. They were Neanderthals from the word *go*. But I don't see smoking guns. They were troglodytes in politics, so I'm sure they would have tried if they could. I suspect they did, but I can't prove it. They almost didn't have to. This was one of those issues that was so inflammable you didn't have to prod anybody on it. And you're talking about the Bible Belt when you're in East Texas and along South Texas and in the West Texas area, this is fundamentalist country. I was a Catholic boy growing up in Texas. I know all about the Bible Belt.

Bobby Baker   I would doubt that Nixon was involved in any of the anti-Catholic stuff; Nixon's too smart; there are a lot of conservative Catholics who vote Republican, especially the Italians.

Tom Wicker   I am not among those who attribute all aspects of evil to Richard Nixon—most aspects, but not all. In this case I don't think Nixon was involved in the religious issue. That would have been self-defeating; I don't necessarily claim that Nixon was too good for that, but that he was too smart for that.

Bernard Boutin   We were very concerned about the religious issue in New Hampshire because of the *Manchester Union Leader* and its impact. It was the only statewide newspaper, and it played hardball. There was nothing very praiseworthy about some of their political shenanigans. Also, there was a very strong "Protestants and Other Americans United" organization in New Hampshire. I remember a trip when I went with Kennedy to Dartmouth College for a speech. The hall was jammed. There was polite applause when he came in. The audience went right for the jugular—right for the religious issue. This was, of course, before the Houston Ministers Meeting. But he was so adept at communicating with people that by the time we left, the students were on their feet, cheering. I saw the identical thing happen at the University of New Hampshire. He had to win over these people.

James Wine   Our assessment was that Billy Graham [Rev. Dr. William F. Graham, evangelist] wasn't going to openly endorse the proposition that there should be no religious test, on the one hand—the reason being that it might be offensive to some parts of his following in the South—and on the other hand, he wasn't going to get out on the stump and carry any black banner of negativism. It was a neutralizing effect, as I recall.

I personally met with Norman Vincent Peale [Rev. Dr. Norman Vincent Peale, pastor, Marble Collegiate Church, New York City]. I had the feeling that I got nowhere, but I did with Mrs. Peale. And that discussion was very positive. And continued to be. And she did not see it the same way that Norman Vincent did. And when I say see it, I mean did not perceive the total picture of fearfulness of a Catholic in the White House. She looked at it like the rest of us, I guess.

I think it just came out over a cup of tea. We were just talking, and she said that she didn't share the views of a lot of others and felt very strongly about religious liberty.

Louis Martin   The Catholic issue was a phony issue. The only real Catholic was Sarge. He would go to mass every morning. I was a Catholic also. When Bobby heard I was on the staff and he was told I was a Catholic, he said, "You mean you got a son of a bitch in here who is a black Catholic? That's the last thing we need."

Drew Pearson [syndicated columnist] had an item in his column that the old man Kennedy had talked favorably about Hitler. I got Phil Klutznick, then president of B'nai B'rith, to make a speech—I wrote the speech—answering Drew Pearson: The old man came from Boston. He had been excluded by the Brahmins, not the Jews. I never heard JFK or LBJ make a remark about Jews. It was the last speech of the 1960 campaign that was broadcast.

The Houston Ministers Meeting

The climactic moment in the debate over Kennedy's religious beliefs came on September 12, 1960, when he addressed the Greater Houston Ministerial Association. There, through his speech and the question-and-answer period that followed, Kennedy was finally able to defuse the religious issue. This neutralization of the Protestant clergy proved to be the turning point of the campaign.

James Wine   I went to Houston and made all the arrangements. The Houston meeting was a pure fluke. The senator asked who beside the presiding officer of the association would chair the meeting? He wanted no one else on the platform; he wanted to stand alone. He wanted to make a ten-minute presentation. And there were two problems. One was that Johnson said he ought to be on the platform too, since he was in Texas. And the ministers said they didn't want him to make a statement; they wanted him to answer questions.

Ten minutes before the meeting, I said, "The senator is going to make a statement, and then these fellows can ask questions." So we never did resolve it; we just did it. Some of the questions were pretty dumb, and some of them were read from index cards. The only thing I was concerned about was whether we could pull it off from the standpoint of Lyndon Johnson, because the senator felt very strongly about that—he wanted nobody on that stage except himself. In modern political language, it was handled: Bill Moyers's role was to keep Lyndon out; he understood.

Ralph Yarborough   It went marvelously. They wouldn't let any of the staff in there—Kennedy had to be in there by himself. Maybe one aide. I walked down the hall, and a door opened up. I couldn't see in there and I never heard the questions, but I heard Kennedy's answers. I marveled at his intelligence. I thought: My God, if somebody asked me my religion, what on earth would I tell them? He was supreme intelligence. He didn't convert all of them, but he converted enough that he won on that issue, put it to rest.

Eugene McCarthy   I didn't really approve of the full text of his Houston speech. I thought he had gone too far, even in going to talk to the ministers as if they had a right to pass judgment on him. It may have got him elected. I don't think it did. But to say ministers can set themselves up and say you can come down here and justify yourself, I thought, was a concession that wasn't warranted under the Constitution. If the bishops had said to some candidate, "We want you to come and talk to us," I would say they had no right to do it. What he said in his statement was all right, but I thought he was saying that the ministers should have accepted, anyway; he didn't have to go in and make a kind of confession. He had done all right in the primaries without having to make any statements to ministers. I could be a little pure about it, but he couldn't because he was a candidate. I think his people thought it was a positive influence on the election.

Jack Valenti   Kennedy came out of the back room by himself—no aides around him—and strode confidently, but not arrogantly, with an easy stride, to the rostrum. No one was there to guard him; no one was around him. It's as if he said, Okay, you bastards. You want me—here I am. Take a hack at me and I'm going to come right back at you. By that one single gesture, by that simple act of one lonely man ready to take on the hordes, he threw the first punch, and it was about as brilliant a performance as ever I've witnessed, as a clinical observer.

I was in front with the technicians. I did not attempt to consort with the candidate. If he had asked me, I would have suggested that these guys were ripe for the plucking; they were overconfident. Just take 'em on, head on, and hit 'em hard, right from the beginning. And that's precisely what he did, so he didn't need my help.

If there was a turning point in that issue, it was there. I know that in Texas there was only one issue; it was religion, and from the northern tier along the Red River down to the Rio Grande border, from El Paso over to the Sabine River, the Protestants were laying in wait for Kennedy. Johnson knew going in that that was the only issue. He thought it was very important that this be tackled head-on. To give you some idea of how deep this issue cut, Kennedy carried Texas by 36,000-plus votes. In the next election, Johnson carried it by almost two million. So you can see the paucity of that margin and how poverty-stricken it was. It was a terrible issue. That's why Johnson and Rayburn and all of the great Texas politicians were roaming up and down that state and saying, You don't believe I'd be with this Catholic boy unless I believed he was going to be a good president and not a good Catholic. And so he won it. No Democratic candidate has ever won the presidency without carrying Texas [until Bill Clinton in 1992], and my guess is that Texas and Illinois were the two key states. Without either one of them, Kennedy would not have been president. Lyndon Johnson had an organization in every one of the 254 counties. The Johnson political organization was strained to the snapping point, and as Johnson used to say, "We're going to shove in our stack because this is it; this is Armageddon time." But even so, with all of that muscle exhibited over Texas, you had to quash this Catholic issue.

Theodore Hesburgh   I think he almost had to do that. I don't agree with everything he said, from a strictly theological point of view. He made a fairly attractive case, and I am sure he believed what he said. There is something about bigotry you have to face head-on. You have to say: "I have as much right as you have. I am an American; you're an American. I fought in the war. You judge me on what I say I will do."

Tom Wicker   It was extremely important. In fact, the way the Kennedy campaign approached that whole issue was, I thought, exceptionally clever and shrewd, politically. At the outset, they made it disreputable to be anti-Kennedy on religious grounds. And then, they quite shrewdly exploited the Catholic vote so that, in the long run, the Catholic issue helped Kennedy rather than hurt him.

I don't think the religious issue was the key one. There was always a debate as to whether there really was enough anti-Catholic sentiment to beat someone as attractive as Kennedy.

Bobby Baker   I can never forget how enthused Lyndon was after the Houston meeting—so was Sam Rayburn. For the first time Rayburn felt that Kennedy had defused the religious issue.

James Wine   When he finished, he stepped down from the podium and was off and back to the suite. The first fellow I ran into was Scotty Reston, who had been standing at the back of the room. He said: "The senator won this one."

Throughout the campaign there was considerable speculation concerning Senator Kennedy's health.

Roman Puchinski   He loved to campaign, but he was uncomfortable. There are those who say the reason for that had nothing to do with his attitude; it was the brace that he wore that created great agony for him. People didn't realize that the brace made him look like he was uncomfortable.

Abraham Ribicoff   It was raining like hell that night. We reached Waterbury about three in the morning. People were standing out in the plaza in front of the City Hall. And from the crowd you knew Connecticut was going to go for Kennedy. After he finished speaking he went on to Boston to close the campaign. Early the next morning I had a call from him. He said, "Jesus, Abe, the bag with all my medications, we can't find it." He had a medical kit with him; he had a lot of medical problems. He said, "I don't want anybody to find that bag and see what's in it." So I called the superintendent of the state police and told him that somewhere in the state there is a black bag and please find that goddamn bag. Well, the next day they found the bag, and I called Jack and told him I had it. He said, "Keep it, don't send it. I don't want anybody to see it."

Joseph Rauh, Jr.   On June 9—that was before the convention, of course—Senator Kennedy was speaking at a fund-raising luncheon for George McGovern that I was running, then left to go back to the Senate. I had nothing further to do; I was just standing on the side or sitting somewhere and he saw me and he motioned to me to follow him. So I went. He said, "Would you ride back to the Hill with me?" I said sure, we got a cab in front of the hotel and went up to the Hill. And, very concerned and agitated, he said to me, "Your friend"—he had good intelligence—"your friend Jimmy Wechsler [James Wechsler, editor, *New York Post*]"—one of my best friends—"is going to kill my presidential nomination tomorrow." And I said, "Gee whiz, he's not against you." Kennedy says, "Well, they're doing a medical story on my drugs," and I said, "Well, is the story they're doing true?" He said, "No." But he said it in a way that what he really meant was, It's slanted, not that there wasn't anything there at all, and then he told me exactly what the medical situation was and what the doctors had said to him. He was not on drugs that in any way would affect his ability to be president, and he made this very explicit. I knew that this was an important discussion and I said, "I will call Jimmy." I didn't want to say what I was going to tell him, because I wasn't sure; I had to make up my mind when I went back to my office.

Election Day/Night

Louis Martin One day before the election, I was riding down Connecticut Avenue with Ralph Dungan. He turns to me and says, "Louis, suppose we win this thing. What the hell are we going to do?"

Donald Wilson I was in Hyannis on election night. The Kennedy family was out at the compound. The press headquarters was downtown, in a large building. Most of the staff was situated there. I did have one conversation with the candidate that night, at about ten-thirty P.M. The election was fairly close. A Western Union man came up and handed me a telegram. It was a telegram of congratulations to Senator Kennedy for winning the presidency, from Dwight D. Eisenhower. I, at least, had the wit to know that this was awfully early for the president of the United States to be congratulating his successor, so I called out to the compound and reached Pierre Salinger and Ted Sorensen [Theodore C. Sorensen, special counsel to the president]. To their credit, their first instinct was to be cautious. They told me to call Jim Hagerty, Eisenhower's press secretary. I had a tough time tracking him down; he was at some party. I told him I had gotten this telegram at ten-thirty, and Hagerty was dumbfounded and furious that there had been a mistake. The thing was prepared and ready to go, but it had not been authorized for release. Frankly the situation gave me great pleasure, because when I was a correspondent, there in the second Eisenhower term, there was the usual confrontational relationship with the president's press secretary, although I liked Jim Hagerty. He was one of the best press secretaries there ever was. Anyway, Hagerty was pleading with me. He said, "Please don't put that out; please talk to Senator Kennedy." So I called back to the compound and said I had talked to Hagerty, and they said, "Hold on." Senator Kennedy came on the line and he said, "Don't put it out. Call Hagerty back and tell him we won't put it out until they authorize us to put it out." Well, Hagerty was beside himself with gratitude.

Ralph Dungan On election night Kennedy was pretty calm. The rest of us weren't. He went up to bed, and most of us did, too; we really couldn't do anything more at that point. Bobby was absolutely going around the walls—he was something else; the Bobby of that period was not the Bobby of 1963 or 1964. He was a different animal in those days. He was always pugnacious and aggressive and, I personally believe, somewhat unfair in many of his tussles. He was headstrong and would push issues strictly on the basis of the force of his personality. There was a remarkable change after the assassination. I didn't see much of the evolution during the Kennedy administration.

John Patterson, governor of Alabama   We carried Alabama for the Democratic ticket. Unfortunately we had a Dixiecrat movement at that time in Alabama. It was this group that had supported Johnson for the nomination. We elected eleven electors, and out of the eleven, six were Dixiecrats. When they met at the secretary of state's office in December to cast their ballots—my God!—six of them voted for Harry Byrd [U.S. senator (D., Va.)] and Kennedy got five votes. The next time I saw him he kidded me about that. We had gone through all that trouble and all that hell for him and wound up getting only five of the eleven electors.

Donald Wilson   We stayed up all night. At first it was exhilarating, because it looked like he was going to win. Then it began to go the other way. It was exciting; it was a very interesting night. In the early hours of the evening, I became convinced we were going to win, and I never lost that conviction. Of course, the following morning it was totally exhilarating. It was really over. I spent a good part of the day at the compound. We arranged for pictures of the family, and the Kennedys were quite relaxed; they were throwing around a football. The senator was on the phone all day long, being congratulated by everyone he ever knew and by world leaders.

2

The Kennedy Appeal

John F. Kennedy was noted for his charismatic personality, which, to some observers, overshadowed his performance as president.

KENNEDY'S PERSONALITY, CHARM, AND CHARACTER

Rev. Fred Shuttlesworth   I certainly was impressed with this young man, John Kennedy. He seemed to offer a breath of fresh air to the stale American scene.

Norbert A. Schlei, assistant attorney general, Office of Legal Counsel   I had started out being a Stevenson supporter but at some point swung over and became a Kennedy partisan. I came to the conclusion that Stevenson, although a wonderful man, just didn't have the executive qualities, the leadership qualities, to run the country, and Kennedy did. And I think I was absolutely right.

Adlai Stevenson III   Kennedy was very bright and very charming. He was an intellectual himself. There may be nobody more pragmatic than a converted intellectual or academician, given the chance to be a politician. That's true, with a relish that exceeds the capabilities of the politician; sometimes they've learned that they know about politics from reading books, and it becomes much more a game of pragmatism and expediency than it really has to be. They wanted to win, and they wanted to be near the seat of power, and not only near the seat of power, but to exercise—to fill the seats of power, and carry over much of what they had developed and supported during the '52 and '56 campaigns to the New Frontier.

Ralph Yarborough   He was basically a shy person. He wasn't effusive, like Johnson. Johnson would grab everybody and put his arm around them. Kennedy resented anybody putting their hands on him. Of course, he had that sore back and he didn't want people back-slapping him. The worst thing you could do was come up and grab his hand or his knee. He resented being called Jack; he resented anybody putting their hands on him. He didn't even let Bob Kennedy call him Jack. Bob Kennedy had to call him Mr. President. He was Mr. President, and everybody else had to understand it too. I admired the fellow greatly.

Abraham Ribicoff   Strange as it may seem, he was a very introverted man. He kept a lot of things to himself, and he only exposed different facets of himself to different people. It becomes very obvious that very few people knew Kennedy. I remember when Bobby was nominated for the Senate in 1964, I happened to be in Palm Beach and I remember that Bobby and I had his father's yacht and we took a five-hour sail around Palm Beach. And I was reminiscing about certain things with Bobby that he never even knew. If Bobby didn't know it, believe me, no one else knew it.

Norman Podhoretz   I met Kennedy once in the White House with a small group. He was quite overwhelming. He was the first president I ever met, and that may account for the impact he made. I've never been able to decide in my own mind whether the power of his presence had to do with any of his personal qualities or the sheer fact that he was president of the United States. He was very good-looking and charming, and that must have helped. In those days, I was not politically sympathetic to the administration; I was a critic from the left. I was quite taken aback by my reaction to shaking his hand and exchanging a word with him. That was true of several of the people who were there that day.

George Wallace, governor of Alabama   My impression of JFK was that he was very affable, very intelligent and easy to get along with. When I ran for governor in '58, he wrote me a letter, just before the election, saying: "I understand from my good friend, Ed Reid, that you are going to win the Democratic nomination—which is tantamount to election—and when you are in Washington, will you please come by my office to see me?" He wanted to talk about organizing delegates in Alabama for him. John Patterson beat me. He was for Kennedy anyway.

Roman Puchinski   Jack never carried any money around. When he arrived at the Sheraton Hotel, he needed to go to the washroom, but he had no money to tip the attendant. Luckily I had some change.

Jack was so well liked. There was a sort of regal air about him. In my district, there were all ethnics, people from Poland and Italy, where the master of the plantation was in charge. These people had a strong feeling about his aura. You would be surprised at just how many people wanted to kiss his hand. His wealth never bothered anybody. I never heard anyone say, "Oh, he's rich." I did hear people say his father made millions smuggling scotch.

Roger Hilsman, director, State Department Bureau of Intelligence and Research; assistant secretary of state for Far Eastern affairs   Everybody thinks Lyndon Johnson is the best politician we have had in a long time. President Kennedy was a better politician in that he had a longer view, in that he surrounded himself with people who told him things he didn't want to hear—and that is a better politician, in the long-range sense, than one who is just good at manipulating people. Johnson was better at manipulating people, but Kennedy was a better politician in the long-range sense at this point of history. He was very sensitive, a quick learner. He had a broad sense of the political forces around. He taught me a lot about things that I had a Ph.D. in.

Claiborne Pell, U.S. senator (D., R.I.)   He was exceptionally bright, attractive, and alert. I didn't know him intimately then. Ours was a strange relationship, in that I saw him more *after* he became president; I used to go up to the family dining room, and we went sailing together. He was great fun to be with—full of jokes. He loved to hear the latest gossip. The conversation centered on politics, in a humorous way.

Wayne Fredericks, deputy assistant secretary of state for African affairs   As the president of the Ivory Coast departed, the president turned to Governor Williams and said, "Mennen"—he always called him Mennen—"I always have difficulty understanding French, but for some reason I can always understand your French. Why is that?"

Paul Samuelson   I thought one of the admirable things about him was his wry sense of humor, so different from Nixon's fake piety. He told me that after the West Virginia campaign, after one of his speeches, a man came up to him and said, "Senator Kennedy, I want you to know that I'm with you all the way. If there are two things in this world I cannot stand, it's a nigger and a bigot." When Jim Tobin [James Tobin, member, Council of Economic Advisers] came to meet him, he said, "You look familiar to me." Tobin said, "Yes. I was in the class of '39, between your brother Joe's class and yours," and he said, "Dammit. I am trying to get away from Harvard; I thought I had a Yale man, but it turns out it's Harvard after all." Another story he told about the campaign was, he went to a big gathering in Oregon and Nat ("King") Cole was to introduce him. When Cole came on the stage, the crowd went wild, and Nat said, "Wait a minute, I ain't him."

Ralph Dungan   He could get angry—usually quick flashes of anger. He didn't hold it. The one thing he couldn't stand—and which was not usually forgiven—was lying. Anybody who would tell him an untruth and knew it, would find himself kicked upstairs someplace. Some were able to lie to him and he never knew it, but lying really drove him up the wall.

Sargent Shriver   Kennedy was one of the most astute, sensitive political personalities I have ever met. He knew people extraordinarily well; it was almost like a sixth sense. He knew people's strengths and weaknesses; he knew whom to trust and not to trust. But he was not a person who harbored grievances or who was bitter or selfish.

Donald Wilson   He had a steely core. I don't remember any occasions where he was cold, but I can remember many occasions where he was strong, and even abrupt, in making decisions; he was not polite all the time. I cannot think of any example of cruelty. God knows there are lots of examples of cruelty as far as Lyndon Johnson was concerned, so it isn't as if this doesn't exist in political figures and presidents.

Lee White, assistant special counsel to the president   Kennedy generally had a "good guy, bad guy" attitude. If you were a good guy, you were a *good* guy; if you were a bad guy, you were a *bad* guy. Most of us feel the same way, but we have a little more shading.

Esther Peterson, assistant secretary of labor for labor standards He never talked down to anybody; you never felt that he was up here and you were down there. Johnson was a little bit above us.

Yuri Barsukov, Washington correspondent, *Izvestia*   I would say many Russian reporters who were working in Washington at the time were under the spell or influence of the John Kennedy personality.

Viktor Sukhodrev, interpreter to Soviet premier Nikita S. Khrushchev   During the very lengthy discussions—he was never a smoker. I'm told he would have a cigar after dinner, let's say. But this was a very lengthy conversation. I'm a smoker; my counterpart on the American side, Alex Akolovsky, used to smoke too. Khrushchev didn't smoke. As two hours go by, it's a very nerve-racking job. We sort of made eye contact with Alex Akolovsky. He drew out his pack of cigarettes and put it on the table; I drew out mine and we decided to smoke. And Kennedy started taking Alex's cigarettes. He smoked several in the course of the discussion, again saying, "Look, I don't usually smoke, but can I have one of yours?"

I liked Kennedy immensely. He was verbal. He was able to put people at ease. You never felt that you were in the presence of royalty. He was a very, very normal, down-to-earth person who had been by force of circumstances elevated to the position of the top leader and he retained his naturalness. My experience told me that a lot of people change when they are elevated by force of circumstances to an exalted position. They change, they start playing the part. Kennedy was not playing the part. He *was* the part—unlike many others that I have seen before and since.

Sergei Khrushchev, son of Nikita S. Khrushchev   When they met in Vienna, my father told Kennedy, joking, "Mr. President, I also voted for you."

Bui Diem, member of the South Vietnamese opposition to President Ngo Dinh Diem I had quite an admiration for Kennedy even before he was elected president. Deep in my heart, I wished that he would be elected president. I remember going to the USIA office in Saigon on the night of the election; it was a rainy night. When he was elected, I was really elated.

Claiborne Pell Kennedy had a frothy appearance, but he had a mind like a steel trap: I went to him once with three problems—at dinner. He never wrote a word down, but he solved all three problems within a few days.

George Ball He was not a deep abstract thinker. If you asked him, "How will this look in five years' time?" he would say, "Tell me, George, how will this look the day after tomorrow?"

Bobby Baker The youngsters loved Kennedy; he had a magic about him. And I want to tell you, I loved him—more than I did Johnson. If Kennedy liked you, he was a fun guy. He was not mean; he was thoughtful. He had a zest for living. He had a very good relationship with Goldwater. The Republicans did not hate him the way they did some of the other people.

Walt Rostow Kennedy had charisma; it is a mysterious quality. People felt that what he was saying to them was what he was saying to his staff, or his wife, and that was true. He'd be talking to a group of us, and Kenny O'Donnell would say, "They're assembled in the Rose Garden," and he'd go out there and put his hands in his pockets and talk to them just the way he talked to us. He wasn't a glad-hander, but you thought, What I am hearing is what the fellow feels.

Mordechai Gazit, deputy chief of mission, Israeli Embassy, Washington, D.C. Kennedy was very impressive, intelligent, and open-minded. I met with him when Shimon Peres, who was deputy minister of defense, came to Washington. We waited in the Oval Office and the president came in. I was very impressed with the figure of the man. He sat down in the rocking chair. He asked, "What will happen if King Hussein disappears tomorrow?" Peres was so awed by the president that he whispered his replies. I could hardly hear his answers.

Louis Martin   What really sold me on JFK was the reaction of people to the man. He had tough old newspaper guys who don't like anybody admiring him, but they didn't know why they admired him. I don't think there is any explanation for that. It was the legend of the man: the daddy, the money, his charm, his good looks, his talk, his warmth. He was a new kind of political animal. It was almost like reading in a storybook about some Prince Charming. Nobody could ever explain to me how that guy could affect people.

Ralph Dungan   I have sometimes speculated that he was really an adolescent in terms of sexual relationships. He was emotionally immature. All of this stuff was casual—as if he were in high school—hijinks. And certain aspects of his married life would suggest that also.

Edward McDermott   The president was very aware that his staff were making personal sacrifices in order to work for him—that they would have to spend considerable time away from their families. From time to time the Kennedys would invite children of staff members, of different age groups, to come to the White House for a social occasion. Once, the group was made up of children five to ten years of age. The president came in and spent a few minutes with them and told them how much he appreciated the fact that their fathers were working in his administration, and how much he appreciated the fact that the children were making a sacrifice to enable their fathers to spend so much time working.

Ralph Dungan   I joined him at the behest of Ted Sorensen. One of my first assignments was to go up to a B'nai B'rith meeting with Kennedy in Baltimore. I'll never forget it. I said to my wife, "If this guy is going to run for president, I don't know how he is going to do it; I can give a better speech than he gave that night." It was on foreign policy, too. He was awful: awkward and gawky. But the interesting thing is that he improved every day. He absorbed a lot of information, but he also observed other people. Of course, he turned out to be a magnificent speaker, but in those days—that was 1957—he was not a very prepossessing person. He was good, one to one, but in a group situation he was not effective at all.

George Smathers   Jack Kennedy evolved from a shy, bashful, nonambitious, nice, always nice, nice man, charming man who had a hard time telling his name—he was nonaggressive—into a very, very motivated, well-spoken, good-looking, determined fellow. I never in my life have ever seen a transformation like that. Exactly why—I couldn't tell you why.

Edmund G. ("Pat") Brown, Sr., governor of California   I had made some disparaging statement about something he did, and when I walked into the office, there was the president holding something in his hand ready to throw it at me. I can't remember what it was, though. But then he sat down, and we were very, very friendly.

George Smathers   He got married, and as he used to remind me, "You were the only politician I invited to be at my wedding." And I *was* the only politician, at that time. One time I said, "I was the best man at your wedding." He said, "Yes, you were," and later on, I heard several other people say they were, and one day, I accused Jack, and I said, "What the hell! Don't you know I was your best man?" And he said, "Look, everybody I talk to, I tell them they were the best man."

Lee White   The president decided he was going to make a speech after the Birmingham church bombing. It was a big deal. Sorensen was writing the speech. He was dictating to a secretary thirty yards from the president's office. As he was dictating, she was typing. Somebody was taking the sheets from the typewriter and handing them to the president. So Sorensen was writing the speech as the president was delivering it. But all of a sudden Kennedy was talking faster than Sorensen could dictate and the secretary could type, so he ran out of sheets. But you could not tell where the script ended and where the president began to take off with his own words. The guy was that spectacular.

Louis Martin   The president was scheduled to make a speech to a meeting of black sororities shortly after he took office. O'Donnell called me and said, "Make sure that the president is briefed," so I worked like hell and prepared six pages of notes. On the day of the speech, I called O'Donnell and said, "I'll come over to brief the president." He replied, "There is no time. You ride in the car with him and brief him on the way." So I get into the limousine and sit on the right side. O'Donnell comes along and says, "Get over on the other side, stupid; you are in the president's seat." The president got in, and I gave him a folder with my notes. He takes it and very rapidly goes through the six pages. I said to myself, I've done all this work, and he's hardly looked at it.

When we get to the hotel and he makes the speech, I can hardly believe my ears. He has all the dates right, all the facts. I still don't understand how he could have digested all that material in so short a period; he had it down pat. I was stupefied. I couldn't believe that anyone could have that quick a mind.

Harry D. Felt, admiral, U.S. Navy; commander in chief, U.S. Armed Forces in the Pacific I first met President Kennedy in January 1962. I went to the White House with the chairman of the Joint Chiefs of Staff and McNamara [Robert S. McNamara, secretary of defense], to ask the president to give greater support to our Military Assistance Program. The chairman of the Joint Chiefs spoke up, and then I said, "May I show you some flip charts, Mr. President?" He looked, listened, and said, "I will take care of that." I don't know whether it was the next evening, but President Kennedy went on television and used flip charts to show what the situation was—to tell the public what the situation was—and apparently, told the public that he was providing more support.

John Kenneth Galbraith He was an omnivorous reader. He was enormously interested in the ideas associated with government and politics. He loved it. If that makes an intellectual, I suppose he was. In terms of intellectual competence, if you put Ronald Reagan at one end, I think you would put Kennedy at the other.

John Patterson The first time I met him was at a convention in Birmingham in 1955. Subsequent to that, we would correspond with each other, and then he would invite me to his office, and then to his home in Georgetown for breakfast when I would be up in Washington—and I was up there frequently in those days because we had so much litigation in the United States Supreme Court because of the racial situation. I thought he was a fine personality, a lot of charisma. He was smooth and easygoing, likable; the kind of fellow it was easy to sit down and talk with. I always thought he used too many four-letter words, but I liked him personally.

Robert Komer, senior staff member, National Security Council I was the most junior man on the White House staff who had the authority to see the president. They usually put me last on the list. So after all the others had gotten in by seven o'clock, I was allowed to go in. And usually he was pretty tolerant. Frequently he was playing with the two children. And I had the wit to get down on the floor and play too. He had trains and trucks and all that sort of stuff. So here was the president pushing all these things around. Poor John-John [John F. Kennedy, Jr.] didn't get much of a chance with them. I took a truck and I pushed it around and crashed it into the president, and that gave John-John a big thrill, but it didn't give the president any thrill. But John-John thought I was super, so he said, "Give it to me," and he banged it into the president.

Harry Felt   *On a presidential visit to Hawaii, where Admiral Felt was headquartered:*

John F. Kennedy's naval aide showed up to make the arrangements, and Catherine [Mrs. Felt] had fixed up the guesthouse, assigned a steward to take care of him, had put her best sheets on the bed. The aide looked all this over and said, "He must have white sheets." This was of a Saturday, so we sent somebody rushing downtown to Sears to buy white sheets. Then he said, "He must have a television." We didn't have a television in the guesthouse, so someone along the road lent us one. Then we were told that he wanted Hawaiian songs—records—so someone provided some of those old-time, wonderful records. Along with the president, as usual, were his security people.

After the president vacated that guesthouse, we went over, and security people had apparently gone in and cleaned out all the remaining booze—and those records were gone. So I wrote a letter—to whom, I don't remember—and the president's steward went to the president and said to him: "Mr. President, I'm in trouble; Admiral Felt says I stole his records." Well, I got a check from President Kennedy. I should have pasted it to the wall.

Victor Krulak, major general, U.S. Marine Corps; special assistant for counter-insurgency and special activities, Office of the Joint Chiefs of Staff   *Recalling a World War II episode in the Pacific, where, as a naval officer, John F. Kennedy commanded PT 109:*

When Kennedy was elected president, I was assigned to duty at the Pentagon, which involved spending some time at the White House, and frequent contact with the president. One day, I said to him, "Mr. President, you probably don't remember this incident in the South Pacific,"* and he replied, "I remember it very well; I recall pulling kids out of the water." I said, "Do you remember that I told you I had a bottle of whiskey that I would give you?" and he replied, "Just vaguely." I said, "I have a bottle of Three Feathers in my briefcase." He answered, "Well, after the meeting, let's go up to my quarters." We did, and he sent for some ice and a couple of glasses, and he said, "Let's have a drink of this stuff."

Alexei Adzhubei, editor, *Izvestia*; son-in-law of Nikita S. Khrushchev   I once came to interview Kennedy, but had nothing to wear; so I bought in Paris a dark blue suit and nice American shoes. When the president saw me, he began to laugh, because he was wearing the same suit and shoes.

David Bell, director, Bureau of the Budget; administrator, agency for International Development (AID)   There was always a glint of humor in him. I saw him mostly in small groups. The meetings were businesslike, but they were also easy. One time—it must have been on a weekend morning—we were all sitting around the cabinet table in a large, formal meeting, and the door to the Oval Office opened, and Caroline [daughter of John F. Kennedy] came in—she was three years old—and said: "Daddy, Mommy wants you." Every father in the room vibrated to it. The president laughed—we all laughed—and then he told her to tell her mother he'd be along in a minute, and we finished the meeting.

Angier Biddle Duke, chief of protocol for the White House and State Department   We got down to the wharf at Wexford [during Kennedy's visit to Ireland] and the president got up on a barrel on the wharf and introduced his staff—Larry O'Brien and Kenny O'Donnell—and he said, "There's one fellow, I'm sorry to say, who hasn't got one drop of Irish blood and that's my chief of protocol, Ambassador Duke." Honest to God, I felt so humiliated.

We went to a farm one afternoon, and there was a young man there—about twenty-three or twenty-four, who was—I'm not making it dramatic when I tell you—he was shoveling manure. And there was the most striking resemblance between this young Fitzgerald and JFK. It

---

*Major General Krulak was involved in the rescue of sailors from the torpedoed PT 109.

was really quite striking, and so, of course, Kennedy saw it and stopped to talk to him, and said, "Now wait a minute. Let's get it straight. Who's your grandfather?" Well, they figured it out that his great-grandfather and Kennedy's grandfather were brothers, and you couldn't help but think—you're looking at these two young men, one twenty-four, the other forty-two or forty-three—that if the two grandfathers—the two brothers—had both gone to America ...

Alexei Adzhubei   Once we were in the White House with Jacqueline. It was very late, around midnight—he apologized because he was very busy and free only at that time—Salinger and the Soviet journalist who published *Soviet Life* were there, and Kennedy told everybody to take off their shoes, so we went barefoot, all of us. He told Jacqueline not to take off her shoes. We sat at the table, drank tea, and discussed different things. I will remember that evening for my whole life. A little girl ran in in a nightgown; that was Caroline. She woke up scared and ran to look for her father. He took her into his arms and they went to her room, and [he] put her into her bed, where nearby there were a Matrushka* and a cross. He told his wife that my father-in-law says, "'Your children will live under Communism,' and I have put near my daughter's bed a Russian Matrushka and a cross; it seems to me that the children must choose themselves."

Victor Krulak   There was an interesting incident on my trip to Vietnam. We had a KC-135 aircraft—a big jet tanker—there were just the State Department gentleman and myself flying. When we got to the airport in Saigon for the trip home, a man came up to us, introduced himself, and said, "I'm from the United States Information Agency; I'm wondering if you could give me a ride to Washington." I said, "Sure. We'd be delighted to take you." When we were in the air, I asked someone, "What is that orange bag over there? It looks like a mail sack." The USIA man said, "Well, that's CBS film; they asked me to take it back for them, in order to avoid the censor." At that time in Vietnam, there was martial law and they were exercising censorship over the media. I said, "Look, this is President Kennedy's airplane and the Vietnamese are a friendly government. What you and I are now doing is—in effect—violating the laws of a friendly government, using as a vehicle President Kennedy's airplane, and

---

*Russian wooden nesting doll.

that's no good." He said, "There is no quicker way of getting the news out." That was true, but it bothered me. So when we stopped for fuel at Elmendorf Air Force Base, in Alaska, I said to the gentleman from the USIA, "Now here is the way we are going to play that orange bag; either you and it get off, or it gets off. Either way I am going to arrange that the commanding officer of the air force base send it by ship to CBS." I didn't think any more about the incident, but it became a cause célèbre and was brought up at a White House meeting. The president asked me, "Did this really happen? Is that what you did?" I said, "Yes, sir. That is what I did," and he said, "That was the correct thing to do."

Angier Biddle Duke   The president would pull the unexpected—for instance, in Paris on the French visit. On the first night we stayed at the Quai D'Orsay. President de Gaulle was to come at ten P.M. and by golly, I have never seen such a downpour. It was really raining, simply terrible. At one minute of ten, de Gaulle presented himself at the door in a very heavy black raincoat and a rainhat, under an umbrella. And I took President Kennedy to the door and he said, "What kind of car are we going in?" and we looked out the door and there was a very smart little French four-seat convertible. And it was, as I say, raining like the devil, and the president said, "Well, I don't think we can go through the streets of Paris without people seeing us. Don't you think we ought to have the top down?" And de Gaulle said, "In the rain?" And Kennedy said, "Well, I think we owe it to them, don't you, General?" Well, they pushed a button and the roof went down, and the president said, "Let's go." And then de Gaulle said, "But your raincoat?" And Kennedy answered, "Oh, I never wear a raincoat." So, with great—I mean *great*—reluctance, de Gaulle takes his raincoat off and the two of them get in the open car, and they drive through the streets of Paris absolutely drenched. He would do things like that.

August Heckscher, adviser to the president on the arts   He was most interested in history, and he conceived of history as an art. He was interested in all of the arts, more from the point of view of the discipline and the search for excellence which they embodied than he was in what might be called more purely aesthetic forms. He couldn't listen to music. I don't think he liked music. Sitting on those little White House chairs in the East Room was really physically painful.

There was a wonderful relationship with Robert Frost, as far as poetry goes, but the relationship with poetry didn't go much further than that. I saw a lot of Frost, because Kennedy wanted him to come around to the White House all the time. When Frost said that politics was poetry and power, that appealed very much to Kennedy.

Walt Rostow   He had a wonderful capacity to understand ideas. When you explained an idea to him, the odds were ninety out of a hundred he had already heard about it and thought about it. He'd say, "What do you want me to do about it today?" Ideas were totally operational for him at one level—his working level. But there was another level to him in which ideas were terribly important. He had a great sense of history. To have a sense of history is a very different thing from being a historian; a lot of historians I know don't have a sense of history. Harry Truman [thirty-third president of the United States] had a sense of history; he read a lot in an amateur way. I don't really think Eisenhower had a great sense of history; he was a very shrewd man and had a quick mind; he was a good politician. Kennedy's sense of history consisted, in good part, of a sense of the scale and timing of the problems he confronted, versus the capacities even of the United States. It was a proportioning of what he was doing, and could do, versus the scale of the problems. That's why he said, when we got the test ban treaty, "A journey of a thousand miles has got to begin with a single step."

Another very powerful idea to him was that life was really unfair. I think that came out of his personal life—his family. His sister, who was mentally deficient; his favorite sister, who was killed young; and a brother who was killed. Death was a very real thing to him. Joe Alsop [Joseph W. Alsop, syndicated columnist] and I both felt that one of the reasons he ran in 1960 was that he felt his life would not be long. He had received extreme unction in the mid-1950s. He carried pain all the time.

Another idea which was very powerful in the way he behaved with other people was the Greek definition of happiness, which he paraphrased out of Aristotle: "Happiness is the maximum expression of a man's capacities, set against standards of excellence." He really meant that.

3

Kennedy's Political Philosophy

Joseph Rauh, Jr.   He believed that government could function to the benefit of all the people, and that's the real reason that I still look back on the Kennedy administration as a real success, which would have been a greater success had he lived through a second term, which I think he would have won by a landslide. But the anomaly is that while he wanted government to do these things, he was held back until he died by the narrowness of his election, by feeling he had to hold back on divisive issues, but he still accomplished a great deal. And with all of my feeling that he held back on civil rights too long, he did start the ball rolling.

George Romney   I thought at that time, and I still think now, that President Kennedy began the trend that has accelerated in enlarging the federal role and bypassing the states to a considerable extent, because he placed a lot of emphasis on direct relationship between the federal government and the local government. I think the entitlement programs have grown tremendously as a result of what he didn't complete because they weren't fully developed when Johnson took over. But Johnson went on and developed them.

Clark Kerr, president, University of California   I would classify Kennedy as a centrist. On domestic issues I would put LBJ to his left. On foreign issues I would put LBJ to his right. I never looked upon him as an ideologue or a radical. I sometimes thought of him as an enthusiastic Edmund Burke. When some things had to be done, it was better to take charge and to do them early, rather than to wait around until it was too late, or somebody else took over. I thought that Kennedy saw the necessities. He was responding more to the longer-run necessities, as he saw them, and giving enthusiastic leadership to the tendencies he thought were proper than anybody who came in with some ideological vision. There was some idealistic vision, but not ideological. I never looked upon him as an ideological leftist at all.

Gerald Ford   Jack's orientation, once he got to the White House, was a global one. I never felt that Jack Kennedy had as deep an interest in domestic affairs.

James Tobin, member, Council of Economic Advisers   President Kennedy is the man who introduced the idea of a war on poverty; he had read Michael Harrington. He talked to Walter Heller [chairman, Council of Economic Advisers] about these problems, and the response was to generate some kind of concerted campaign through a series of measures to do something about it. The idea was in the president's message to Congress in 1963. At that time he was beginning to feel more comfortable with his popularity in the country.

Lee White   On the domestic side the president was purely pragmatic. I don't think he had any terrific, particular enunciated goals that he was going to achieve. He had a relatively classical liberal attitude about human rights and civil rights and all of that. He would not have been happily fond of Pat Moynihan's [Daniel Patrick Moynihan, assistant secretary of labor for policy planning and research] phrase *benign neglect,* but it was clear that the president, if anything, was overly sensitive to the fact that his victory was narrow.

George Romney   He came to Michigan, but he never bothered to talk to the governor; he talked to the mayor of Detroit. I was quite aware he was more interested in the mayors than the governors. Local government is the creature of the state, and bypassing the states became a very unfortunate thing in Kennedy's administration.

Joseph Rauh, Jr.   Civil rights was always a moral issue for him, and that's what made him so unhappy and unresponsive when I held him to the fire at that meeting in 1961. I think those must have been unhappy years for him between February 1961, when he made his decision for no legislation, and 1963, when he made his decision for legislation.

Najeeb Halaby   I think he regarded big business as a challenge. These guys had feet made of clay. They were a lot of stuffed shirts, and he could penetrate those shirts. He knew he needed them, and he would try to persuade them, but if he couldn't, then he would confront them. He knew many of them personally, through his father, and through his congressional days.

Henry Fowler, undersecretary of the treasury   I don't think he was given to economic philosophy. He reminded me of one of my teachers at Yale Law School, who used to say, "Don't ever trust anyone who is too much of a philosopher." President Kennedy had strong views, but he also had an open mind. He was the kind of person who would listen to his father, or a friend, or people with whom he was in contact.

George Wallace   I liked Kennedy; he was more conservative than most people believe at that time. He wasn't outright a raging liberal, but Kefauver [Estles Kefauver, U.S. senator (D., Tenn.)] was, and the Southern folks thought he was so liberal, and voted against him. I remember a fellow from Tennessee who told me: "I wish I could vote against Kefauver, but the people at home might not like it," so they went and voted for him.

I don't think JFK was soft on communism. I don't think that Hoover [J. Edgar Hoover, director, Federal Bureau of Investigation (FBI)] had anything on the Kennedys.

Claiborne Pell   There were those streaks of conservatism that both John and Bobby had.

Lloyd Cutler   I think Jack was a hard-liner in his time, and for good reason. Khrushchev was a step forward from what we'd had beforehand, but still, he was a pure communist, running an imperial system.

Bradford Morse, U.S. congressman (R., Mass.)   His views, in general, were not unconventional for the time. He would have been a cold warrior of the Harvard stripe. That was probably where he would have come down.

William H. Sullivan, special assistant to the undersecretary of state for political affairs; UN adviser, Bureau of Far Eastern Affairs   Kennedy was prepared in international affairs to be far more flexible, to take more chances, to look for more reciprocity. When you look back, for example, to the rigidities of [John] Foster Dulles [secretary of state, Eisenhower administration], there is a significant gap—even though they may both have felt concerned by the Soviet menace and be considered historically as cold warriors. Certainly John Kennedy as cold warrior is a far different character than Foster Dulles.

Philip Kaiser   With Eisenhower and Dulles neutrality wasn't good enough: You were either on our side or not. Kennedy made it clear that neutrality was fine.

Richard Helms, deputy to the director for plans; deputy director for plans, Central Intelligence Agency (CIA)   Robert was certainly very anticommunist and the president himself probably equally so, but less outspoken on this subject. But we never had any sensation that we were dealing with a "liberal" in the sense of foreign policy—that everything the Soviets did was fine, or everything the communists did was fine—not at all. We had the sensation that Kennedy was very conservative in his views when it came to the cold war.

Ray Cline, CIA station chief, Taipei, Formosa (Taiwan); deputy director for intelligence, CIA   I felt that Jack Kennedy—he was a contemporary of mine; he was a year older than I was—was rather naive and optimistic about dealing with the Soviet empire. He talked to me all the time about the fact that Khrushchev was being friendly to him, and I think I was the only person at the CIA who got the Khrushchev letters. I also saw the drafts that Kennedy sent back. I felt that Khrushchev was deceiving Kennedy, but he didn't think so; he really felt that he was doing the right thing.

Marcus Raskin, member, Special Staff, National Security Council; staff member, Bureau of the Budget   Bundy [McGeorge Bundy, special assistant to the president for national security affairs] once said to me, "You know, there are only two pacifists here in the White House: you and Kennedy." I used to think it was a big joke, but maybe I want to take it more seriously than I should. In any case there were people who did not see it the way I did. Most people saw it as a crusade against communism. It was American triumphalism, all of that stuff.

William Colby, first secretary, U.S. Embassy, Saigon; director, Far East Division, CIA Kennedy was a liberal who was intent on fighting for freedom, too. Pay any price, you know. He goes back to my era, when the liberals were internationalists; when the conservatives were isolationists. The whole Vietnam War reversed that. We are now still struggling with it. But Kennedy was formed out of World War II and the buildup to that war.

He felt there was a communist tide running in the world that had to be stopped, in Latin America, Southeast Asia, and Europe.

Norman Podhoretz People on the left in those days—it was just beginning to be called the "New Left"—thought of the Kennedy administration as conservative in its policies, and to the extent that it had liberal impulses, it was either too timid politically or too cowardly to follow those impulses, particularly in the field of civil rights and in foreign policy. The two main areas in which people on the left were attacking the Kennedy administration had to do with blacks and the pace of reform, and the cold war: negotiations with the Soviet Union, arms control, and the test ban treaty. The general feeling was that the Kennedy administration was fundamentally concerned with shoring up its position—guarding its right flank in the South, and that Kennedy himself had brought in Schlesinger and Galbraith—in India—and a few other people who were sort of apostles to the liberals, and whose job it was to persuade them that Kennedy was really on their side. But most of us did not take that seriously.

From my present perspective I have a better opinion of the policies of the Kennedy administration—not the actions—than I did then. I think it is fair to say that Kennedy himself was no liberal by any definition, Robert Kennedy even less so. Of course, in later years Robert Kennedy moved to the left. But Jack Kennedy was a fairly conventional Massachusetts machine pol. He had conspicuously avoided opposing

McCarthy [Senator Joseph R. McCarthy (R., Wis.)]. We used to joke about *Profiles in Courage:* He managed not to be present in the Senate when the censure vote on McCarthy took place.* He was very hawkish on issues of foreign policy. It always astonished young people—by now Kennedy is like George Washington: ancient history—but some years back you could always get an astonished response out of somebody who wasn't alive in those days by telling him that in the 1960 campaign, Kennedy attacked Nixon for being soft on communism. He was harder-line than Nixon, at least in his rhetoric, but he also meant it. He talked about a missile gap, which people later said was mythical. It wasn't quite mythical. But whether it was mythical or not, he was calling for an increase in defense spending—much more aggressive policy toward the Soviet Union, in general, than the Eisenhower administration had pursued, so that was certainly not what people later thought of as liberal.

Paul Samuelson   One of the problems for me as a Stevenson man was whether John F. Kennedy and Robert Kennedy, the sons of the son of a bitch Joe Kennedy, were liberal elements in American life. Joe Kennedy had been an appeaser of Hitler and a manipulator. He was at least somewhat widely known as an anti-Semite; a general son of a bitch. When I was asked to give informal advice to the senator from Massachusetts, I said, "I'm not for you, I'm for Stevenson." I was told, "Nobody is asking you to be. We just want the best advice that we can get." So I did it on that basis, for the country. Then I finally decided that whatever John F. Kennedy or Robert's roles had been in the McCarthy congressional days, John had cast his lot with the liberal cause and would be an effective president.

Tom Wicker   Stone [Oliver Stone, director, *JFK*] in his film alleges that Kennedy was killed because he was soft on communism, which I think is a farce. But Kennedy wasn't a flaming liberal; he was the old man's son, and Robert's brother—the guy who didn't vote against Joe McCarthy. We are not talking George McGovern here.

---

*On December 2, 1954, the U.S. Senate voted 67–22 to censure Senator McCarthy for actions related to the operation of his Senate investigating committee. Senator Kennedy, recuperating from back surgery, did not participate in the vote.

4

The Kennedy Family and the Presidency

AMBASSADOR JOSEPH P. KENNEDY'S INFLUENCE ON HIS CHILDREN

John Seigenthaler At the convention in Los Angeles, Bob asked me if I would take a leave from the newspaper and come to work as his administrative assistant, so I covered the convention and went to work for him afterward. The second day I was there, Bob asked, "Is there anything I can do for you?" I said, "Yes, as a matter of fact, there is. Can you get me an interview with your father?" His face got that look he had when he'd heard something he didn't want to hear: The mask came down; his eyes veiled. He said, "You know, my father is not giving any interviews." I said, "I didn't think you would ask me if I wanted something that was easy to get." He didn't smile, but he picked up the phone and called his father. He said, "You remember John," and you could tell he was getting some argument from his father, who didn't want me to come. But Bob finally talked him into it.

I went out to where he was staying the next day. We sat by the pool and he made it absolutely clear that he did not want to talk to me. He moved the umbrella on the table so it covered him, but I was sitting in the sun. This was his message: that he wanted this over quickly. I made up my mind if I could get him to talk about his children I could be there as long as I wanted. Sure enough, after a while, he moved the umbrella so it covered both of us. He thought his children were wonderful. He ran down the litany of their names. It was clear they were stars in his eyes, and his eyes twinkled every time he mentioned them. I asked him about Rosemary, the daughter who had some problems. He said, "Who knows why one child is as bright as the sun and another is as dull as a dollar." And I thought, Here is one of the richest men in America, and he thinks dollars are dull; he had given his whole life to making dollars.

Cartha DeLoach, assistant director, Federal Bureau of Investigation (FBI)   I think some of Bobby and the president's personality may have come from old man Joe Kennedy, who didn't mind bowling people over. He got his wealth the hard way; he assumed great positions in life as a result of his wealth, and I am sure—of his ability. He had many escapades which would have embarrassed a normal man or upset a normal relationship. He loved the usage of power, and so did the president and Bobby; Bobby, I think, more than the president.

Pierre Salinger   Ambassador Kennedy was pretty much eased out during the campaign—and once Kennedy won the presidency, he didn't want people to have the impression that he was being monitored by his father. Once we moved to the White House, his father would call and say, "Did you see this story? Do something about it!" But he was not calling his son.

Bradford Morse   Simply because he was Joe Kennedy and John Kennedy was his son, there can be no doubt that he played a major part in each of the Kennedy campaigns. However, he was smart enough not to let himself be seen: He was invisible as a force in any of the Kennedy campaigns. There were those who would seek to identify with some of the positions Ambassador Kennedy had taken in the past, particularly in the late 1930s, but they weren't particularly successful.

Theodore Hesburgh   It was a very lively dinner table. Joe Kennedy was constantly challenging those kids on ideas and political action. It was a free-for-all. During the meal, he would chase them around the table, at least verbally. He had an enormous impact on Jack and Bobby and his daughters also.

John Seigenthaler   There is absolutely no doubt that Joe wanted Bobby to be attorney general; there is absolutely no doubt he wanted Ted to run for the Senate. But Bob had decided he did not want to be attorney general. He said to me the night before he and Jack finally talked about it, "This will be tough for Dad." I rarely heard Joe Kennedy's name mentioned. He was rarely in contact with his son, the attorney general of the United States. Rarely. If he was, it was some obscure call about a matter that did not have anything to do with anything. That is from day one. I see television docudramas that create meetings that never took place. In my considered judgment, as well as that of those who worked after I did at the department, this question of the influence of Joe did not exist. I think they were very respectful of their father, and there is absolutely no doubt they loved him and were loyal to him. There is no doubt in my mind that if he had wanted to impose himself, they would have listened to him. I am not saying that they didn't get together occasionally and that there weren't times when they sat down together, and that when they talked together, inevitably, the issues that were on their minds must have come up. But nobody I know who was close would see any credence in the idea of influence by Joe.

Ralph Dungan   Bobby was brought into the administration because of that strong Kennedy family thing. I wouldn't be surprised if the old man put the arm on JFK to appoint him; it represents the "all hang together" business. It turns me off. I mean, I'm for strong ties, except that the Kennedys take them to the extreme.

I'm sure Joe Kennedy was involved in job selection in the postelection period, but not, however, below the cabinet level. I'm certain at the cabinet level there were discussions within the family group at Palm Beach.

Roswell Gilpatric, deputy secretary of defense   I was told that he passed on many of the appointments. I was told by a good friend of his, Morton Downey, Sr. [entertainer], that Joe Kennedy asked Downey to check me out. I don't know how much weight that carried. I think probably my own past record and Lovett [Robert A. Lovett, secretary of defense, Truman administration] and Symington made more difference. But I certainly had the impression, in the early days, that the ambassador was tuned into everything that went on and was checking up on every-thing. I used to see him in Palm Beach, and Jackie took me to visit him several times, particularly as his health began to fail.

McGeorge Bundy, special assistant to the president for national security affairs   I am not sure any one of those people he brought in would have been his father's choices. The ambassador was certainly an influence, in the sense that he was very important to his son. He didn't, at least in my experience, call up other people and say, "Now you ought to do A or B or C"; I never recall hearing from him. I think his influence was primarily in what he said to the president of the United States, who is, of course, the person most people want to talk to when they want to influence an administration.

John Seigenthaler   When I arrived for the interview, Joe was listening to a little transistor radio he had on the table. He was following the news that Jack had agreed to accept an invitation to appear with Lyndon John-son before the Texas delegation. I asked him what he thought about that. Joe said, "He shouldn't go near it; he should stay the hell away. We've got this thing locked up. Bobby can give you the vote count." I said, "Is he going to call you and ask?" He replied, "He won't call me. If he does call me, I'll tell him what I think, but it won't make any difference." I said, "What do you mean?" He said, "He will go over there. I know he will." While we were talking, his daughter Jean [Jean Kennedy Smith, wife of Kennedy campaign aide Stephen Smith] came down for a swim and said, "Oh, Daddy, have you heard? Lyndon challenged Jack to a debate. And what do you think?" He said, "He ought to stay away from it." She said, "Daddy, he challenged him." She went in for her swim, and Joe said to me, "You'll see, he'll be over there. That's the way they are."

Ben Bradlee   I didn't get to know John Kennedy until the late 1950s. I think that the ambassador's role was certainly important financially and was certainly important with certain people. Jack told me that the deci-sion was under discussion in Palm Beach whether to go into the West Virginia primary, and old Joe had been very adamant that he should not go in because he was scared of getting licked in the Catholic thing, and Jack saying, "We've heard from the ambassador; now let's decide what we do. I say we go."

Paul Samuelson   I never heard John F. Kennedy say, "Okay, my father is a son of a bitch, but he's my father." But I did observe that Joe Kennedy thought that he was having more influence than he was having. For example, I was once asked during the campaign a very uncharacteristic request: Would I go and talk to old Henry Morgenthau? He had been Roosevelt's secretary of the treasury and had gotten the taste of battle again and wanted to let the candidate know that he was available. So I was told, "Just go talk to him; just soft-soap him. He's nothing, but he's got to be humored." I thought that was the way John F. Kennedy was handling his father. His father was putting up money, but there was no influence that I could see of his father's more conservative economic opinions on his camp and his thinking.

Louis Martin   That old man was really something. He would call up from New York and Sarge Shriver would talk to him, but sometimes Jack and Bobby wouldn't talk to him. They tried to keep him out of their business. I remember once in the campaign headquarters, I picked up the phone. It was the ambassador. I told Bobby, "The ambassador is on the phone." He said, "Tell him I'll call him later."

George Ball   The ambassador played a role in a rather interesting way: There was great concern in the administration at that time about our balance of payments deficit. I got into a feud with the Treasury Department; my position was that this was a political problem. When I would try to urge that position on the president, he would say to me, "George, I have to go to Hyannis Port this weekend. How the hell can I ever explain this to my father?" He was really very concerned about the fact that the old man thought the government was going to hell because we had a balance-of-payments deficit.

John Kenneth Galbraith   Ambassador Kennedy's influence was greatly exaggerated. I knew Joe Kennedy very well; I was halfway in age between Jack Kennedy and Joe Kennedy. By the time Jack Kennedy became president, the sense of authority had all passed to him. I remember a long discussion in 1960 on economic policy, followed by other discussions, later, where I had the backing of Joe Kennedy and where JFK in a greatly amused mood said, "I would like to know what handhold you have on my old man."

I wouldn't attribute technical economic views to Joe Kennedy. His was an expression of a mood rather than an expression of a detailed policy; that is a very important distinction. As an expression of mood, he was certainly critical of the business community from which he had emerged—both in Wall Street and generally. That expression of his in 1961 when you had that insane action of the steel companies was not surprising. I heard that before in other contexts. Most of us had.

Cartha DeLoach   The two Kennedy brothers loved their father just as they loved and respected their mother, who obviously is a saint; she'd have to be. But despite all their father's eccentricities and many faults, they still looked upon him as a very driving force and the patriarch of the family. Mr. Hoover and Joe Kennedy were very good friends. They had been good friends for many, many years and continued the friendship. After Joe Kennedy had suffered a stroke and was confined to a wheelchair, one day the president called Mr. Hoover and said, "My father will probably not be around much longer, and he can't talk. It would give him great comfort if you would come over and sit with him and talk with him for a while." And Mr. Hoover did. There was great respect between the two men. They were peers, and they had a long lingering relationship as far as correspondence was concerned.

I don't think Joe Kennedy prevailed too much on Bobby and Jack. Maybe they got their sexual proclivities from him, but I doubt seriously that he ruled the roost insofar as telling them what to do in such things as the steel matter.

John Seigenthaler   In 1959 I took an extended leave from the newspaper and went to stay at Hickory Hill and helped Bob with the first draft of *The Enemy Within*, which went to number two on the bestseller list. When the contract was signed, Robert and I had dinner one night with his father at Pavillon.* Joe gave me a lecture on taking the credit for writing his son's book. You could tell right away there was a little hostility on Joe's part toward Ted Sorensen. In effect, he was saying, "Look, Sorensen takes credit all the time for writing *Profiles in Courage*." I didn't believe that to be the case, but I was certain it would not happen with Robert and me, and I told Joe Kennedy that. But he still gave me

*An expensive Manhattan restaurant, no longer in existence.

the lecture. After the book was written and went on the bestseller list, we had another dinner to celebrate. His father was really excited and said, "The reason is, you fellows told that story so well; it just came alive; it read like a novel." He never could get my name right. He said, "This fellow here." Before we went to the restaurant that night, Bob had given me an autographed copy of the book. He said to me, "Show Dad what you have there." So I showed the book to Joe, and it said, "To John Seigenthaler, who wrote my book for me, from Bob Kennedy." And Joe said to Bobby, "You're a goddamn fool; this will be in the *New York Post* in three weeks." Well, I hadn't written the book. Robert Kennedy wrote every word of the first draft on yellow legal pads. The process was that he would write and I would edit.

Bobby Baker   Old man Joe Kennedy had an unusual influence with Bobby; he did not have the same influence with Jack. Jack would listen to him, but he was not a one-hundred-percenter.

Abraham Ribicoff   I don't think Joe Kennedy had as much influence as he thought he had. He was a domineering and dominating bastard.

JACK AND JACKIE

Angier Biddle Duke   I played a rather odd role in the relationship between the president and Mrs. Kennedy. He asked me to do things that helped me understand the marriage and helped me understand what was happening. The first thing he said to me was, "Would you find out for me, and lay down some guidelines, some rules for the appearance of the first lady? Would you go over this with her and work out an arrangement for her public appearances?" Now this is new to me, and I'm just on the job. I knew Jackie quite well, but naturally, as soon as she became first lady, she was Mrs. Kennedy to me.

I made an appointment to see Mrs. Kennedy, and I said, "Well, my job is to find out if we can't work out some programs that are good for the president, good for the country, and good for you. Now what is your idea of when you should appear?" And she said, "Well, let's start right away with that—as little as possible. Let's start from that point of view. I have young children; I've got responsibilities to them and they, as a matter of fact, come first as far as I'm concerned. But I will do my duty, and

I will do what is required of me." So I pointed out that if a head of state brings his wife to Washington on an official visit, protocol says that the president's wife must attend official functions. Jackie then said, "Can you fix it up with the ambassadors as much as you can to tell the heads of state not to bring their wives?"

August Heckscher   Jackie wanted to impress the French at the evening for André Malraux, the French author and minister of culture. Unfortunately, he was a man who was extraordinarily hard to understand. He had a kind of tic. And although my understanding of French is normally quite good, I had great trouble talking with him. As we left that night, my wife said to the president, "We had a very interesting time. Mr. Malraux was giving my husband advice on what the arts policy of the United States should be." In typical fashion the president asked, "What did he say?" Well, my wife is French, but she had a very hard time understanding what Malraux had been saying. Kennedy had that persistence of inquiry which was sometimes exhausting. I think he really listened to the answers; he really wanted the knowledge.

Edward McDermott   Mrs. Kennedy wanted to invite the composer Frederick Loewe to the White House for a small dinner, but she was concerned as to whether he would accept the invitation. She did not want it known if she invited someone and they refused. I knew Mr. Loewe, and I called him. He asked, "Are they inviting me for a social occasion, or do they want me to play? Because if that is the case I am not interested in coming." I assured him it was to be a social evening, so he accepted.

After dinner Mrs. Kennedy turned to the president and said, "Oh, Jack, could you get Mr. Loewe to play something?" And the president responded, "Well, he's Ed McDermott's friend; he'd better ask him." I was on the spot. We went into a room with a piano and I said to Mr. Loewe, "Let me ask you this, Fritz; what comes first: music or lyrics?" And, in response to the question, he walked over to the piano and started playing something, and he played the piano for about an hour and a half, and while he was playing, the president came over and sat on the piano bench with him.

Angier Biddle Duke The presidency is very demanding. All these little girls would scamper around. But there wasn't time for all of that, and I think that the president was growing up. He was managing his life better, and his and Jackie's relationship was a lot better. The Kennedy marriage would have flowered and prospered and grown stronger. I could see the relationship between them growing. I also saw that he had a wonderful sense of priorities. He knew what was important and what was not important, and if the girlfriends got in the way, they were expendable.

Bobby Baker Kennedy said, "I get a migraine headache if I don't get laid every day." He was very much like his father. I think the sexual things were a lark. I think that he selected Jackie to be his wife like a stockbroker decides to back a new company. He was smart enough to know that if he wanted to be president, he had to be married. He had this guy Charlie Bartlett [syndicated columnist] introduce them. It was like a business deal; he never loved Jackie, but once he had those two children, he became a caring, loving person. The two children changed his whole perspective. I don't think he ever would have changed his cheating habits, had he lived to be one hundred. I think that Jackie had so many hurts. To marry that Onassis [Aristotle Onassis, Greek shipping magnate], she was sending a message: "I'll get even with that guy!"

THE BROTHERS KENNEDY

The extraordinarily close relationship between John F. and Robert F. Kennedy had a major impact on the workings of the administration. Robert Kennedy's role went far beyond his specific duties as attorney general and involved him in a wide range of foreign policy and domestic issues. To some observers he was the president's most influential adviser and the driving force in the decision-making process.

Decision Making

Ben Bradlee On all of those tough decisions—the civil rights decisions—they sure as hell wanted Bobby at Jack's side; certainly in the missile crisis—yes, but I don't think of Bobby as having much of a role with Khrushchev, or much of a role in the State Department. They were very, very different. Jack was an easier read than Bobby; what you saw was what you got.

Dean Rusk, secretary of state   Bobby was in no sense the decision maker as far as JFK was concerned. JFK was the dominant member of those three brothers. He kept himself under control at all times. He, I'm sure, would listen to Bobby but would not be unduly influenced by Bobby if Bobby's ideas seemed to cut across President John F. Kennedy's thinking, and also, President Kennedy had the advice of myself, Secretary McNamara, the head of the CIA, and others in the administration that tended to counterbalance anything that Bobby Kennedy might have put to him.

President Kennedy had told me when the matter came up through Bobby Kennedy that I didn't appreciate that I should be reasonably sympathetic to Bobby Kennedy's interest in foreign policy, but that if he ever got in my way, I should come to President Kennedy and he'd straighten it out. So I had no feeling that if it came to a crunch that Bobby Kennedy would undercut me.

I mean, for example, Bobby Kennedy came up one time with the idea that we should organize American businessmen in foreign countries to lay on demonstrations in support of the United States on political matters. Well, I thought that was a very bad idea because it's not the business of business to undertake that sort of thing, and American business in foreign countries would be thrown out of the countries in many situations if they had tried to do that, and it was just not an appropriate thing for businessmen to try to do. I knocked that down, and we heard no more from Bobby Kennedy on that idea.

Nicholas deBelleville Katzenbach, assistant attorney general; deputy attorney general   Maybe Bob Kennedy had more influence in foreign policy decisions than he should have.

Terry Sanford   I think they probably were both driving the engine and relied on one another. They didn't have to discuss who was going to shoot the ball. They had worked so long together. I didn't feel that Bobby dominated John Kennedy, and I didn't think that John treated Bobby as a subordinate. I think they were pretty much equal.

Julian Bond   In hindsight, and from reading all these books, you now think that Robert Kennedy was erecting a wall of protection around his brother. But, of course, I think his brother probably wanted it to happen. It was the one hand washing the other. We thought that John Kennedy was creating policy and that Robert was just the instrument to carry it out.

William Y. Smith, major, U.S. Air Force; special assistant to Gen. Maxwell Taylor   Bobby Kennedy got to start some initiatives. I think that in certain areas, the president wasn't that interested, such as counterinsurgency and some of the early things in Vietnam. I think Bobby was speaking for the president, and the president wasn't that engaged. But on most key issues, such as the Berlin crisis and the Cuban missile crisis, there was never any doubt in my mind that the president was making the decisions. He was getting a lot of advice and listened to Bobby, but I never thought of him as just a front man for Bobby Kennedy.

Lee White   I had worked pretty closely with Bobby on civil rights and on other matters and had been in meetings where there were only the two of them, but it was clear who the president was.

James Farmer, national director, Congress of Racial Equality (CORE)   I had the feeling when we, the civil rights leaders, were in the White House, and Bobby and Jack were there at the same time, that it was Bobby who was doing the thinking and leading, and Jack who was following.

Burke Marshall, assistant attorney general in charge of the civil rights division   The president was the president; he made the decisions. He relied on Robert Kennedy for advice. Robert wasn't afraid to do things; if the president didn't know something, he'd just do it.

John Patterson   I think Bobby was making a lot of decisions, but I don't think he made the most important ones of the administration; I don't think that Robert overrode the president. Jack always struck me as being his own man. But Robert was something, I've got to tell you. He called me up one night at the governor's mansion in Montgomery about two A.M. and told me we didn't have enough police on Dexter Avenue.° I said, "God almighty, Robert, that's not any of my business, or yours, either." I had to ask him to quit calling me.

°A street in Montgomery, Alabama, near the State Capitol.

Bobby Baker   Bobby was very influential, but I've seen President Kennedy overrule him. President Kennedy called me and said, "Bobby, we are being destroyed daily by our inability to pass anything. The one thing that's a must is my tax bill; your friend, Senator Kerr, is killing me. Find out what I must do to get his support." So I went to Senator Kerr and said to him, "The president would really like to do business with you, and he desperately needs your support for his tax bill, and the key to it is a ten percent investment tax credit." And the senator said, "Bobby, I like the investment tax credit. But you tell your president— he's your friend; he's not mine—that there will not be any tax bill until that stupid brother of his sends down my recommendation for Ross Bohanan to be a U.S. district judge in Oklahoma."

So I called Evelyn Lincoln [President Kennedy's executive secretary] and gave her the message for the president to call me when it's convenient. She said, "He's right here. You can talk to him." I told him, "Mr. President, I can get the senator to support most of your tax bill—he loves your ten percent investment tax credit—but he's got a judge Bobby's sitting on, and he's said that there will be no tax bill until that judge is approved and you sign the appointment." He said, "I've never heard of him; let me call Bobby." So he called Bobby—he's on the speaker box—he said, "Who the hell is this Ross Bohanan?" Bobby said, "Mr. President, the American Bar Association says he is the least qualified man in the history of the Bar Association; over my dead body is he going to be named judge." So the president said, "Well, I just made a deal; I've got Bobby Baker on the phone over here, and Kerr will not support my tax bill unless Ross Bohanan is confirmed. Send down his nomination," and hung up.

Bobby was mad as hell, but within four hours that nomination was before the Senate Judiciary Committee, and we got him confirmed, and the president signed it, and we got our tax bill.

Bernard Boutin   They were as different as night and day. That led to strength in the relationship. Bobby was very quick to defer to the president; he had no illusions as to who made the decisions. The president listened to him, knowing that he would get Bobby's advice without prejudice. Bobby would give him his best advice, and he could do with it as he wished, which is exactly what he did. Bobby was much more combative than Jack was; he was a tough guy. Jack was tough minded, but he was not a tough guy.

Tom Wicker   I don't think the president said, Whatever Bobby wants to do is all right. He probably tried to smooth the rough edges off Bobby. I think he thought, This is a man I need, I trust, and who is also exceptionally able. Robert Kennedy didn't hesitate to cut somebody's throat if necessary. He was a tough guy, he really was. All that was valuable to John F.: The president thought that his agenda was Robert's agenda. It's typical of administrations, in general, if you have something like the James Meredith [civil rights activist who integrated the University of Mississippi] matter, the president is going to be alert to that, and is going to be on call, but he is not going to be micro-managing the situation. That was what Robert was doing.

Louis Martin   You really had two presidents. There was nothing Jack did that Bobby wasn't in on. He respected Bobby's fire, his loyalty, and in some ways, his experience, even though Bobby was much younger.

I remember that when Teddy returned from a trip to the West, he came into the office and Bobby chewed him out; he cussed him. I was shocked the way he talked to his brother. He said, "I want you to go to Africa and join a group of senators who are visiting there." He called me in and said, "I want you to meet with Teddy and fill him in on Africa." So the next day I get a call that Teddy will be in New York at Ambassador Kennedy's office. I hop on the shuttle. When the plane lands, I hear my name on the loudspeaker, and at the gate there are some people looking for me. There were three goons; they looked like gangsters. They go out to the parking lot to a big limousine. I didn't know what the hell was happening.

They took me to the ambassador's office on Park Avenue, where there is another bunch of goons. They ask me, "What do you think Teddy should have for his trip?" So I say, "Get him a camera, and here are the names of some books he should read." An hour later, they come back with this stuff, but Teddy hasn't arrived. So I go out to the airport to meet him.

He really didn't want a briefing, and I didn't know what to say to him, anyway. But I called a friend in London and told him that the next president's brother was going to Africa and stopping over in London, and asked him to take care of Teddy—to keep him out of trouble. Teddy decided to hold a press conference at the airport before he left for Africa, so I talked to him for about an hour. At the press conference, he was a pro. I was shocked; I didn't think he was as bright as his brothers. When the reporters asked him about Africa, he talked as if he knew all about the subject. I told Bobby, "Don't worry about this guy. He may be crazy, but he is smart."

Edward McDermott   I think the president relied as much on Bobby's advice as he did on anybody else's, with the possible exception of technical experts. I think he would defer to the director of CIA on intelligence evaluations rather than Bobby, because the director of CIA is supposed to know. I think he would rely on the secretary of defense about any matter of the military, in Vietnam, or whatever. Bobby, because of their long relationship, was the key adviser to the president. And I think many decisions the president made were discussed with Bobby, but I was under the distinct impression that the president made the decisions.

William Sullivan   I suspect Bobby probably forced the president to take decisions at times when the president would have preferred to defer them; Bob was always looking for decisions rather than letting things ride for a while.

Richard Helms   I think the attorney general had influence, and I think the president listened to him carefully and admired his judgment, probably, but I don't think that he was making these decisions for him. In fact, I never saw any evidence of that.

I think that he depended on the attorney general to handle a lot of difficult matters for him, and, in the parlance of Washington, the attorney general was the president's wire brushman. In other words he was the one who took on the nasty chores, telling people that they were wrong, or firing them, or getting them fired, or doing something of this kind, so the president didn't have to do it. Every president has somebody like that, and in this case, it just happened to be his brother, rather than some other influential individual. I think they were very close and worked in considerable harmony.

Roswell Gilpatric   I saw a great deal of them both and was with them a great deal. My characterization of their relationship was that they just operated as a team; they both recognized each other's qualities. You knew perfectly well anything you said to one, the other was going to repeat. I had an experience sitting with the president in the Oval Office, and the attorney general came over, and the president said, "Do you mind if I talk to Bobby?" And I got up to leave and he said, "No, stay here, I want you to hear this." Bobby came in, and the point was whether or not to bring a criminal, as well as a civil, antitrust proceeding against two San Francisco newspapers that had worked out some kind of a printing arrangement. Bobby wanted the president to know that when this hit the fan, there would be a big hue and cry to bring criminal proceedings against the newspapers. So, when they got through with the discussion, the president turned to me and said, "Ros, what do you think?" And I said, "Well, Mr. President, you know, to sustain a criminal indictment, you've got to have very positive evidence of intent. And I haven't heard from this account that we have that evidence." And the president said, "Bob, what about that?" And Bob said, "I've got to check that out." Well, they never brought the criminal proceeding. But, that's the kind of a thing that they would work together on. And particularly when we got into something called the Counterinsurgency Group. Both the president and his brother felt that the U.S. military, in the way that they were approaching the whole conflict in South Vietnam, were following tactics that they developed in World Wars I and II, and they taught in the command staff schools in the military academy, and that they weren't open to new ideas on how to fight guerrilla-type warfare. So they set up a group called the Counterinsurgency Group, of which Max Taylor [Gen. Maxwell D. Taylor, military representative of the president] was the chairman. Bobby came to every meeting, and one of the ground rules was, you couldn't send a substitute. You either came yourself, or you were not represented. My opposite number, [U.] Alexis Johnson [deputy undersecretary of state for political affairs], was on it; John McCone [director of CIA] was on it. We had some very interesting discussions. You knew that once the meeting was over, Bobby was going to go across the street to the White House and tell his brother everything that had happened. So you know, in dealing with them, there was this closeness. Bobby never purported to speak for the president, but you knew perfectly well that he had a great influence. That was apparent, above all, during the Cuban missile crisis.

Pierre Salinger   Bobby was the one who led the National Security Council down the right track as far as the Cuban missile crisis was concerned; he prevented what many of the people on the NSC wanted: an attack on Cuba; he came up with the idea for the naval blockade; he saw the possibility of attack as another Pearl Harbor and the possible outbreak of war.

But remember, there was something about the Kennedy administration that was different from other administrations: There was no locked door into the Oval Office; there were ten or twelve of us who had access into that office any time of day. We didn't have to go through somebody to get permission to see him. So Robert Kennedy wasn't the only person advising him. He was a powerful adviser, but there were others.

George Smathers   That's a generation younger than me and Jack Kennedy who's saying that Bobby made all the decisions. I don't believe that at all. That's Bobby's friends who're saying that. I haven't heard anybody at Jack's level who said that.

I don't think I've ever heard Dean Rusk say anything like that; don't think I've heard Bob McNamara say anything like that; I hear a lot of Bobby's friends say that. But that's not true; they're putting Bobby at a level he was not ever at.

That's not to say that he wasn't close to Jack; that's not to say that he did not know everything that was going on. Yes, but as far as Jack Kennedy listening to Bobby, Jack Kennedy was ten times smarter than Bobby.

Eugene McCarthy   I don't know about decision making. I think Bobby was the enforcer.

Bobby as Attorney General

Courtney Evans, FBI liaison with Robert Kennedy; assistant director, FBI   In Hoover's mind Robert Kennedy was an ineffectual attorney general, mainly because he was pushing things that Hoover did not want pushed. He wasn't really properly deferential to the director. When Robert Kennedy would go to a city, he would regularly meet with most of his agencies: the U.S. attorneys, the marshals, Immigration, the FBI. He probably spent more time in the FBI offices than anyplace else, and the agents loved him. It was the first time in their whole careers that they had even seen an attorney general up close, and here they got an opportunity to talk to him on a one-on-one basis. Hoover didn't like that. He felt that the agents should report to him and nobody else, and that he should be the one to decide what the attorney general should know about the bureau.

John Patterson   He didn't understand the state and federal relationship or even the state-municipal relationship. He'd get involved in things that were none of his business whatsoever, that would create all sorts of difficulties for local law enforcement people.

Cartha DeLoach   Mr. Hoover expressed great outrage when Bobby came over one day and briefed him concerning the use of organized crime individuals for the purpose of getting at Castro. Mr. Hoover said that it was the wrong thing to do—many of these same people were the people we were investigating, particularly Sam [Moe] Giancana in Chicago.

I would think that the CIA had a great deal to do with setting up a liaison with the organized crime elements and the Kennedy administration, insofar as the Castro matter was concerned. There was a relationship with Frank Sinatra; there was a relationship with other individuals; and, of course, the Kennedy brother-in-law Peter Lawford, who is now deceased, had a close relationship with Sinatra and others. I think it was a matter of expediency when the Kennedys decided to use them. On the other hand, the investigations into various heads of organized crime on the part of the FBI continued. I know of nothing that was ever said by the Kennedy administration or the attorney general which would have stopped those investigations. To the contrary, they encouraged them mightily, sometimes much to our sorrow. The desire of the attorney general to investigate organized crime caused the FBI to do certain things. For instance, the matter of placing microphones on leaders of organized crime in Las Vegas.

I think the president had a great deal of respect for the FBI. I think Bobby had respect, but felt in his own mind that he could do a better job, and as a result he set up his own investigative force in the Department of Justice. He conducted many investigative activities through that force, through his cronies, over the years. That would reflect a possible lack of respect for the FBI, or it might reflect ego, or pride, on Bobby's part that he thought he could do something better and wanted his own people, loyal to him, to conduct those investigations. That was true not only in the Teamsters investigation, involving Jimmy Hoffa [president, Teamsters Union], but others as well.

George Ball   Bobby was primarily interested in rather recondite things. He believed in covert operations and in counterinsurgency, which I thought was totally obnoxious. He had his following. He was interested, as far as the State Department was concerned, in getting them to approve all kinds of CIA operations, which I thought were for the birds. There was a committee set up to approve prospective operations. My deputy, U. Alexis Johnson, would bring in recommendations to me before each meeting. And we would go over them. I must say 98 percent of them were absurd. They were dangerous and contrary to American principles. So the State Department position was against practically all of them. On counterinsurgency it was Robert who was driving the president. It appealed to him as an adolescent fantasy.

Courtney Evans   He was very intolerant of incompetency or what he regarded as a wrong philosophical approach. I went to judicial conferences with him. He was very deferential to the judges. His relationship with his own people—the United States attorneys, the marshals, the Immigration Service people—was friendly, and yet he left a message with them that you had to work hard and you had to produce. He wanted to know facts in the greatest detail. When he traveled he wanted to sit in the front seat of a standard bureau automobile; he didn't want any limousines or big cars. He wanted to be able to talk to the agent who was driving, and he never wasted a minute from the airport to where he was going. He was always making these inquiries. He would ask a lot of questions, mostly the right ones; he was always learning. In the little over three years that I was associated with him when he was attorney general, I never saw a man mature more, and grow more, than Robert Kennedy did.

I know that the president changed in those years, not to the extent that the attorney general changed, but he soon found out that it was an entirely different thing to be president than to be a United States senator. One time I mentioned something to him about the presidential helicopter, and he said to me, "Courtney, I pay a big price for those helicopters"—meaning that his responsibilities were very demanding and that the helicopters were a small item.

Cartha DeLoach After a meeting with the president, several steel company executives immediately announced an increase in the price of steel. Bobby called over to Courtney Evans—the FBI liaison with the attorney general—and indicated there would be a meeting at the White House at eight o'clock the following morning, and that he wanted the FBI to go out and conduct interviews with the presidents of the steel companies and with members of the press who had attended the news conferences across the nation where the rise in steel prices was announced. Evans indicated it would be dangerous to wake up reporters in the middle of the night, or presidents of companies. He had in mind, and appropriately so, the knock on the door by the police, which carries a very heavy stigma. Mr. Hoover was very much against that, but Bobby told Evans that the attorney general would take the responsibility. Well, the FBI went out and conducted the investigations and got considerable facts and had them ready in report form for the meeting at the White House the following morning. But then all hell broke loose. Reporters started screaming "Gestapo" and "middle-of-the-night tactics," and "secret police," and the inquiries were referred to the Department of Justice, where the attorney general was supposed to indicate his responsibility. But he did not indicate his responsibility. To the contrary, he tried to dodge the issue, putting the onus back on the FBI. That caused a rift, and there were many things like that.

Robert Komer Bobby had his own kind of charisma. I had lots of dealings with him. He horned in on foreign policy. He was willing to listen to anyone's story. Once Bill Douglas [William O. Douglas, associate justice, U.S. Supreme Court] told him a story about how the Iranians were muscling in on a local tribe. Douglas said he had this from a very reliable source. He wanted us to support the tribe rather than the shah. This was a familiar story to me, as the tribes tended to be antishah. The president said to me that Bobby had complained to him about the matter. And he said, "I see there are two sides to this. But I want you to go over and straighten Bobby out about this." I went over to the Justice Department. The attorney general's office was the size of the Sistine Chapel, with murals on the ceiling. At the floor level there was a whole series of tables piled high with briefs. I walked into the office and couldn't see anybody. Suddenly out of the side of the room came the biggest bear I ever saw, and he jumped on me. Well, by this time I realized he was a big, furry dog. He licked me all over, especially on my face. Then I heard a voice, somewhere to the left, saying, "Down, Brumus." I walked over to the window, and there was the attorney general. He greets me, "Hi, Bob. What's this glop you're telling the president?" I told Bobby, "We have a lot of contrary evidence." He listened to me and said, "That makes a lot of sense. I'd appreciate it if you would go over to Bill Douglas and tell him the same thing. Tell him the story he got from the Iranian is half-assed." Well, I had great admiration for Bill Douglas, and I didn't know how I was going to tell him his story was half-assed.

Alexei Adzhubei   I came to America when Robert Kennedy was attorney general and registration of Communist party members was announced. That put me in a difficult situation: You are in touch with the Kennedy family and you are a communist, and they are starting a new anticommunist campaign. When I was leaving, Khrushchev asked: "Are they doing it on purpose? Who wants to put me in an awkward position?" On my own initiative I went to see Robert at his office. It was a large office—a personal room, with drawings by his children on the walls. There was also a sofa, and I realized that sometimes he spent the night there. The registration was abolished; it didn't take place.

Ralph Dungan   Frankly, I thought that lots of things he did as attorney general were wonderful. But in other areas, especially the foreign affairs field—although JFK relied a lot on him—I thought Bobby's judgment was not very good.

I was just never really taken with Bobby. I didn't like the style—the Hickory Hill bit. Bobby had a lot of influence; he could at least pick up the phone and chat, or come into the office late in the evening. Bobby and Kenny O'Donnell were very close, and Kenny was the door watcher. But even Kenny—sometimes looking at it from JFK's point of view, which he did, because his loyalties were clear—would rebel against Bobby's attitudes. Bobby and I never really came into conflict, and by and large I think he did very good work. It was really his brusque manner—he came on terribly strong—that I thought was quite unnecessary. It turned people off, which is not generally helpful in human relations.

Bobby's Personality

Angier Biddle Duke   I found him difficult to get along with; he was prickly.

Edward McDermott   Bobby was tense and intense: all business and very little levity, very little relaxed kind of conversation. Very little small talk. It was all business, and he had a capacity to master the relevant facts and remember them and associate them and correlate them.

Esther Peterson   Bobby would just lean toward people, people who were in need. I'll never forget. When we were working during the campaign, and we'd be up until two or three o'clock in the morning, Bob would say, "Let me send out for some sandwiches." He would be the last one to go.

James Meredith, civil rights activist   I was on "Meet the Press." Someone asked me if I had been to the White House. Then there was a call from Bobby Kennedy inviting me.

Ralph Dungan   There was a rumor that Bobby was going to be made secretary of state; it may have come from outside. That would have been terrible—he was too much of a hip-shooter; we didn't need that.

Robert Komer   Bobby really moved the government. When he got mad, all the guys could think of was, God, he's going to call his brother tonight and our bosses are going to get in deep diddle. So people listened. I generally thought he was a little excitable, but he was doing a good job in pushing around the bureaucracy.

Donald Wilson   One of the highest tenets of Robert Kennedy's faith was loyalty. Whenever the subject of Senator Joseph McCarthy came up in the campaign, my recollection is that he didn't put him down, or trash him, or say nasty things about him. In fact, one had the impression that he had a warm spot in his heart for him.

Wayne Fredericks   To many in the State Department, Bobby Kennedy was a source of freshness and support; to others, he was an irritant. I have the sense that he was probably an irritant to Secretary Rusk; he supported positions the secretary did not support.

Robert Manning, assistant secretary of state for public affairs
Bobby was quite impatient with the State Department. He thought they ought to get those guys off their asses over there. He was very impatient with suggested prose for foreign policy sections of the State of the Union Address. The kind of person he most respected in the department was George Ball, but he and George didn't get along very well.

Bradford Morse   I knew Bobby reasonably well when we were both functionaries on Capitol Hill. He was younger then, and worked for the McCarthy committee—which wasn't one of my favorite repositories of justice. He certainly was an aggressive fellow, and a fellow who got things done, but I never credited him with great intellect.

Harlan Cleveland   Bob Kennedy was to make an appearance in Syracuse. I went over to Auburn, where he gave a talk on foreign policy, and drove him to Syracuse. I had provided the campaign with a rather long memorandum on foreign policy. What Bobby said didn't track very well with my recommendations, so in the car coming over to Syracuse, I undertook to suggest a different way of looking at foreign policy in the campaign. When I was midsentence of making this argument, he reaches out his hand and turns on the transistor radio full blast so it was impossible to have a conversation. I thought to myself, Hey, I am trying to get his brother elected president; he doesn't have to do something like that. He was undoubtedly the rudest man I have ever encountered in public life, and I am surprised, in a way, that he got as far as he did. I think he probably would have been a very dangerous president.

Donald Wilson   Murrow [Edward R. Murrow, director, USIA] had first come across the Kennedys when he was in London and Joe Kennedy was U.S. ambassador. He thought Kennedy was on the wrong side of the fence. During the McCarthy period Murrow was the principal speaker at a banquet honoring the ten most outstanding young men of America. One of them was Robert F. Kennedy. When Murrow got up to speak, Robert F. Kennedy walked out of the room. Then, as recently as 1960, Murrow had lunch with Teddy White [Theodore H. White, author] and Arthur Schlesinger, and he carried on at some length about how he thought Kennedy was a young whippersnapper who didn't have the experience or the background to be president. He even went so far at that stage, just five months before the election, to say that John F. Kennedy was the kind of man who—if McCarthy were still alive and it was in his benefit to support McCarthy—would do it in a minute.

Edwin Martin, assistant secretary of state for economic affairs; assistant secretary of state for inter-American affairs It was not easy to travel with Bob Kennedy. He did not communicate well. You never knew quite what he was thinking or what he was going to do next.

William Trueheart, deputy chief of mission, U.S. Embassy, Saigon Bobby came out [to Vietnam] once—in the middle of the night—just at the airport. I didn't come away with a very warm feeling for him. It was—I thought—his total preoccupation with the domestic political aspects of what was going on. He may simply have been discouraged that he didn't get the feeling that we knew how we were going to finish the war.

Joseph Rauh, Jr. I look back happily on our relationship despite the fact that Bobby Kennedy once said at a dinner where he was speaking in my honor in New York: "The Kennedy administration always thought Goddamn-Joe-Rauh was one word." But we were friends, although there were tough moments.

John Patterson If you were out having a drink of whiskey with Robert Kennedy, he was just a hell of a fine fellow. But every decision that he made about anything was based upon what was best for them politically. He didn't consider the fact that you had a career and had a political agenda yourself.

Edmund Brown, Sr. Bobby was a tough guy; he was a much tougher human being. He came out to me in the primaries in '60 and damn near demanded that I support Kennedy. I said I was going to support Kennedy anyway, but I wanted to do it in my own way; I had to put all these delegates together, and I tried to explain it, but he wouldn't listen. So he and I never really got along. We never had a fight, but I never felt close to him.

George Ball   I knew Bobby because we took him on the airplane to the convention in Chicago in 1956. My impression was that Bobby was a very surly young man. He was annoyed that people all thought of him as John's brother; he thought he was somebody in his own right, and it was a blow to his vanity. He wasn't doing any good for Adlai. I don't know why we had him along.

Victor Krulak   There was a special Counterinsurgency Group that met in the Executive Office Building. I was the alternate for Mr. McNamara, but I went to just about every meeting. On one occasion, we were talking about a police advisory problem in some Latin American country. There was an adverse report on some individual's performance, and Robert Kennedy turned to Murrow, the head of the USIA, and said, "Find out who this fellow is, and fire him"—just like that.

Joseph Rauh, Jr.   When [Felix] Frankfurter resigned [from the Supreme Court] they had a meeting in the Oval Office, and the president proposed that it was time to name Paul Freund [professor, Harvard Law School], an adviser who was recognized as the greatest constitutional lawyer, to the position. Bobby said, "Not on your life. When we asked him to be solicitor general, he turned us down. We can't do this; if the person's coming from Harvard, it's going to be Archie Cox." Bobby was angry. He had been designated as attorney general but he hadn't been sworn in yet. But he had taken that lousy train up from Washington to Cambridge, Massachusetts, to see a professor in a dingy Harvard Law School office, and offered him the solicitor generalship and was turned down. I think he would remember that for a long time. The Kennedys remember old slights.

Harry Felt   Robert Kennedy came out in a commercial airplane. As soon as the door was opened, they scrambled out of the airplane; left their coats, magazines, books—everything—on the seats, in the airplane. I, of course, met them and took them to the guesthouse, which was right next door to my quarters, and he said: "I want to go swimmin'." So we brought him down to a beach we used; that was fine. He adopted that beach—sort of. The next day Catherine went down to take some lunch to the beach to Robert and Ethel [wife of Robert Kennedy], and Ethel said, "Shhh. He's asleep. Don't wake him up." While he was down at the beach one day, he saw that over at Hickam Air Force Base they had a sailing club with some little sailboat, and Robert Kennedy decided he'd sail one, and he tipped it over, and everyone cheered.

The worst thing that happened though—it was the first night they were there—I have a custom, when people fly a long distance, and then go to work, instead of throwing a dinner party ashore, I take them out in the fleet's big boat and serve them supper. Well, I invited a bunch of my civilian friends—I thought it would be nice for Robert Kennedy to meet them. So there were my civilian friends—Catherine and I were sitting and waiting. Here comes Bobby. He rushes right through the cabin, on to the fantail, and does this [gestures], and then come all of his press people, and he said, "They're my guests." So I had to feed the press people. He was madder than hell that they were fed down in a hold, instead of where they had tables set up, in a cabin. No. I didn't like him very much. It was personal.

Ben Bradlee   I think that Bobby was changing enormously—if you read his campaign speeches, he went from a McCarthy acolyte way over to the left; he was really a radical with the things he was saying in California, just before he was shot. They were thrilling to me. But he was a tough guy to get in touch with. I had all sorts of difficulties with him. I think he resented the fact that Toni Bradlee and I were friends of Jack's, and we had some silly fight: I picked Bobby up at Hickory Hill one morning at five-thirty or six and I spent a fabulous day with him—we went all over the country—and I sat next to him with a long yellow pad, taking notes, all day. The result of that was what *Newsweek* used to call an "inside cover," about Bobby's wanting the vice presidency under Johnson. It created a minor stink around here because people suspected he'd never said it, and here I was, quoting him. He left, before *Newsweek* came out, to go to Poland, and from Poland, they issued the denial of the story, saying they'd never talked to Bradlee. They came to me about it, and then they said it had all been off the record. And that's the most terrible thing you can say to a reporter: that he's broken that trust. But it was so ridiculous, and it took us a year to patch that up, if not longer.

Yuri Barsukov   In 1960 I went to the Kennedy campaign headquarters on Connecticut Avenue. I wanted to interview Robert Kennedy on campaign issues since at that time he was campaign manager. I saw a secretary first, and she introduced me to John Seigenthaler, who was RFK's assistant, and I told him that I would very much like to interview Robert Kennedy. He asked, "What kinds of questions would you like to ask?" to which I responded: "My major questions concern Soviet American relations and what his policy toward the Soviet Union will be if he is elected." John replied that it was too early to discuss these issues, but that "maybe we'll talk about it later on." But he said that he would talk to Robert Kennedy and "let you know his reaction." Of course, Robert Kennedy was very busy at the time, but I did get a call from Seigenthaler telling me that Robert would talk to me when he had the time. I did get my interview in November, after the election.

I had visited Kennedy headquarters several times before that, and John would tell me: "Today he's in Ohio; tomorrow he will be in Minnesota; then he will come to Washington, but only for a few hours." So I waited patiently. Then the election was over. I called the Kennedy headquarters two days after the election, asking for John Seigenthaler, and was told by the secretary that everybody was on leave for two days. I explained that I had discussed with John the possibility of interviewing Robert Kennedy, and she said, "Mr. Kennedy's in his office." I asked, "Could you connect me?" She did, and then I heard his voice.

We had a very good talk. Of course, I didn't discuss with him any big issues on Soviet American relations. I didn't have the impression that he was antagonistic, but I would say that sometimes he was a little suspicious—even toward a reporter like me. It seemed as if he were discussing everything openly, but there was some resentment, some distance between us. There was not a sense of a close, personal relationship; it was just official.

John Seigenthaler I was a reporter on the *Nashville Tennessean* and had done a long series of stories on corruption in the Teamsters Union. I had been unable to get the authorities to act in a way the community or the newspaper thought was effective. I went up to meet Robert Kennedy as a result of an interview Sargent Shriver arranged. It was an abrasive, unfriendly initial meeting. When I came in, he was preparing to go out. I was ten minutes early for the appointment; he insisted I was twenty minutes late. Angie Novello, his secretary, supported him in that.

I then produced a note from Sarge saying that the meeting was at the hour I said it was to be, so that I was ten minutes early, and he quipped that Sarge operated on Central Standard Time because he was from Chicago. In effect he walked out, and I was furious; I was outraged. I left there thinking he was a rich little snot and if I ever saw him again it would be too soon.

Subsequently I wrote a memorandum at Kennedy's administrative assistant's suggestion and brought it to Washington. I walked into the office in the Old Senate Office Building and asked to see Kennedy. His secretary asked if I had an appointment. I said no. At about that time, he walked out and walked right by me, looked through me, and shook hands with a reporter who was standing there and took him into his office. This absolutely rubbed salt into me. So, seething, I gave the memorandum to Robert Kennedy's assistant. I went back to Nashville and thought, I don't know what he's about, but I hope he fails. He had been rude and uncivil. I guess my Southern manners were offended by his brashness and insensitivity.

Six weeks later I am in my office and the telephone rings. It is Robert Kennedy. He said, "I've had a chance to read the memorandum and I would like to ask if I could send some investigators in to see you." Then we had a thirty- to forty-minute conversation in which every question he asked was right on the mark: incisive, perceptive. He had grasped the whole scheme of things.

I then began to go to Washington to cover the hearings, and by that time we were close friends. This lasted until he died in 1968.

Donald Wilson   My initial impression of Robert Kennedy was of a rather impetuous, not particularly thoughtful person who, of course, was totally devoted to his brother—and to his brother's cause. I felt he was a somewhat unsophisticated person, particularly internationally and world-wise. We became very close friends, and my view of him changed as I thought he changed. But my first view was not terribly favorable. I liked his brother at the outset, because I thought he was a much more sophisticated person. Like everybody else I found John F. Kennedy a charming person, delightful to be with. Robert Kennedy was more down-to-earth. He was less stimulating, but he was pretty damned interesting, too.

Jack Valenti   I remember the first time I ever saw Bobby Kennedy; it was some weeks after Johnson became president. A cabinet meeting was called and I came out of my office, which was right next door to the president's, and Bobby was walking down the corridor with Mike Feldman [Myer Feldman, deputy special counsel to the president] and he turned on me and said, "I'm getting tired of you spreading these rumors about me!" I didn't know what he was talking about. I was so green to Washington I didn't even know what a leak was; I thought that it was a hole in your roof. That really disturbed me. I talked to the president. I said, "Bobby Kennedy has accused me of something and I don't know what he's talking about."

Now later on, thanks to other people like Charlie Bartlett, I got to know Senator Kennedy. The more I got to know Bobby Kennedy, the more I got to like him. I think it was finally sealed about three months before he died. I had left the White House, and the president appointed me to the board of the Corporation for Public Broadcasting. I went to a Senate hearing to be confirmed. And because my commission said District of Columbia, there was no senator accompanying me, so Bobby Kennedy came forward and said, "Mr. Valenti does not have a senator to escort him, and I'd like the honor of commending him to this panel," which I thought was a very loving thing to do.

I went to his house after I left the White House several times. He had a party for [W.] Averell Harriman [senior State Department official in the Kennedy administration] on his seventy-fifth birthday, and Ethel and Bobby invited my wife and me to come. So I'm pleased to say at the end of his life I'm comforted by the thought that we had become friends. But in the beginning it was not so. And I'm of the belief that a lot of this was done by aides who corrode relationships by passing along gossip.

Norman Podhoretz   I found him quite acerbic and difficult to deal with. On the other hand, my wife found him very easy to deal with. I found him much less attractive a personality than Jack was. On the other hand, he later inspired almost fanatical devotion; I have friends who still swear by him. I have never been able to understand it. I never saw whatever it is they see in him. There are people who think if he hadn't been assassinated in 1968, he would have been elected president and everything would have been wonderful in this country—all the problems we have would not have developed. And people who think this are not stupid. I found Bobby Kennedy difficult to talk to. I didn't think he was all that bright, to tell you the truth, by which I mean, he rarely seemed to get a point you made in conversation that was not totally expected and conventional. If you said something even slightly subtle, it would puzzle him or bother him. I thought his mind operated almost entirely in clichés. Sometimes the clichés came from a different universe of discourse than they had two years earlier, but they were always bearing some form or other of conventional wisdom. In fact, anything outside that narrow framework he would be unable to listen to or understand.

The Relationship Between Jack and Bobby

Joseph Dolan   Robert Kennedy knew that John Kennedy was president. He had a phone on his desk that connected the president to him, but not him to the president.

Louis Martin   I never saw two guys work in more unison; even Kenny O'Donnell couldn't get between them. They reinforced each other. If there was something serious, you would see JFK and Bobby go out together to the Rose Garden. I don't think Bobby would ever have won it by himself.

Angier Biddle Duke   You cannot seem to get from people in responsible cabinet positions what they really think. I don't know why. But President Kennedy found this out pretty soon, and Bobby was the only person who would really say to him, "Mr. President, that is a terrible idea." Now, the president might not accept that advice. He might say, "I'm gonna go for it." But at least he would get an honest point of view from someone who was willing to say, "That's a terrible idea."

I think some people get that kind of advice from their wives. Sometimes a wife is so identified with her husband's work that he can try ideas out on her, and he knows she will give him advice that is in his best interest, although he may not act on that advice. I think Bobby played that role.

Victor Krulak   He was a task man, doing tasks set out by his brother. He did things far removed from his duties as attorney general because his brother wanted him to. Robert Kennedy's role was keenly important, and not just because of his entrée to his brother. In all of that hierarchy, Bobby was the most impatient; he wanted things done, and when his brother declared that he wanted a course of action followed, Bobby pursued it with a real aggressiveness. He was a results-oriented personality with very, very little patience, for which I do not condemn him; indeed, I applaud him.

Tom Wicker   It's probably true that Bobby was a little more of a killer than John F., but John F. was not a weak sister by any means; he could wield the knife too. It is certainly true that at that time, at least, John F. was more of a charmer. There is no doubt that Robert was totally devoted to John F.

John Seigenthaler   Bob used to say, "Don't get mad without a reason, and don't go into a meeting if you don't know how it is going to come out." Those were rules that the president probably also followed. If you watched them together, or listened to them on the telephone—which I did a hundred times—there was a question and answer that went on. One would start a sentence; the other would finish it. They could talk about somebody for five minutes on the telephone without mentioning the name. They had some code word for a given person. There was a connection between them that transcended passion. I think it was as close to one heartbeat, one pulsebeat, as you could get.

Louis Martin   People today talk about Jack and Bob's sex life. But they were Irish: They liked liquor and they liked women. You'd say, "How do you like those ladies?" The reply would be, "I like them prone."

Jack, Bobby, and Teddy

Lee White   The three Kennedy brothers that I've known had the ability to grow after reaching adulthood. They really did have the capacity to change. Most of us have a little bit of expansion built into us, but we're not much better at age fifty than we're going to be at age thirty-five. I think the Kennedy brothers did have a capacity for change and for growth, so the Bobby I first met back in 1954 was really not the Bobby who was assassinated. One reason, of course, was his own searing experience with his brother's assassination. It had a dramatic impact on him.

Gerald Ford   My impression is that of the three brothers, Jack was not as intellectually smart as Bobby, but he had a much nicer personality;

Bobby could be harsh and mean and tough. I never had that impression of Jack; he was friendly and gregarious. Teddy is sort of halfway between: not nearly as attractive as Jack; not nearly as smart as Bobby. But he's got other, personal problems that, as far as I know, neither Jack nor Bobby had.

Bobby could be very decisive. Jack could be too, but you had the feeling that Jack would try to accommodate a little more than Bobby. In my experience if Bobby had a goal, he wouldn't adjust very much.

Paul Samuelson   My judgment is that John F. Kennedy was the smartest of the three brothers. I would say that Richard Nixon could be a professor at a law school—like the University of Arkansas or maybe Duke; he would be a better academic than John F. Kennedy, because that wasn't where Kennedy's mind was. But John F. Kennedy was very quick, and he read quickly, which is a tremendous advantage. Someone like Eisenhower, who just can't read, is blinded. Truman was a reader. Kennedy was the most balanced and the brightest of the brothers. In the end, I think, Bobby was the most idealistic of them, which I had not expected.

Edmund Brown, Sr.   Teddy never impressed, you know—his speeches were not impressive. He just appeared as a nice guy. Jack was the strength of the trio.

Ralph Yarborough   I don't think Teddy had the charisma or the sensitivity of John F. Kennedy—or the brashness of Bob Kennedy; he was a different Kennedy, but he was an intelligent Kennedy.

Ben Bradlee   Jack thought Bobby was very smart, and I think he must have envied a certain compassion that Bobby had. I don't remember—it didn't stand out with Jack—Bobby was terribly sensitive to people. He had a sort of St. Francis dimension to him that was totally alien to Jack. And Teddy was the little brother; nobody had a sense of what he had—whether there was real strength there. Jack sure wanted Teddy to run for the Senate.

George Carver, Vietnam analyst, Office of National Estimates, CIA   When I was in college at Yale, we had a crew coach who arranged a boat race in Palm Beach, to be held on New Year's Day. The race was two thousand meters. We were all glad it wasn't two thousand and one, because the good burghers of Palm Beach were extremely hospitable, and their daughters even more so, and I doubt if we could have made that extra meter. I met John Kennedy and his two younger brothers at a party given by Marjorie Merriwether Post [society figure and philanthropist]. Frankly, if you had told any of us at the time that this fellow was going to become a sainted president, and his next younger brother would become attorney general—highly admired—and that little brother over in the corner, who was being generally obnoxious, was going to become a distinguished senator—also held in great esteem—we would all have accused you of smoking something other than tobacco.

Angier Biddle Duke   Ted Kennedy cannot be compared to Robert or John F. Kennedy—I don't think you could put Ted in there at all. It irritates me, this word, the *Kennedys*. It was John F. Kennedy—he was the president of the United States and was *the* Kennedy—and the others were midgets compared to him.

5

Was There a Dynasty in the Making?

Arthur Schlesinger, Jr.   Joe Kennedy, Jr., was a rather extroverted, gregarious, back-slapping fellow; very charming. John and Robert Kennedy were much more inward and introspective types. I think that after the war Jack Kennedy thought for a while about becoming a newspaperman. He had some assignment at the San Francisco Conference,° but also he had his own views on public affairs. His father thought that politics and government were far more important than business. He had been through business and made a lot of money, and he didn't want his sons to waste their time in doing that. The war was, in a certain sense, a disorienting experience. People changed a lot in the course of the war; whatever they had planned to do before the war very often seemed irrelevant to them afterward, and the opening of that congressional seat seemed to be a reasonable thing to do rather than go to law school.

George Smathers   Joe Kennedy was snubbed by the social people in New York and in Boston, and he just decided that this Irish family was going to be the number one family, and he was going to eliminate this stigma of being Irish Catholic. So he was going to use his sons to do that, and he did.

Pierre Salinger   The family put it on Jack's back. If Joe had not died in World War II, then Jack might not have gone into the political world. Or,

°The San Francisco Conference (April 25–June 26, 1945) was the founding conference of the United Nations.

if Joe had gone into the political world, Jack might have been in the same situation as Robert; he might have been number two. Jack was already writing books; he might have had some idea of what he was going to do in life, other than politics. But once Joe died, there was no question that the father was very eager to have one of his sons go down the political path.

Robert Manning If you look at everything that has transpired since, you get the sense that there is an impulse in the Kennedys to think in that direction. I've always had the feeling that Teddy did it only because he felt he had to. Bobby took on true ambition, but I wouldn't say he had dreams of becoming president himself until his brother was killed. There sure was an impulse beaten into those kids by their father. A fellow I know told me of being in Hyannis Port when Bobby had some friends with him in a sailing race. They came back for lunch with Joe Kennedy, and Joe asked Bobby how the race had come out. Bobby said, "We came in fifth." His father looked at him, pounded the table and knocked his glass over, and said, "Lunch is over."

Frank Moss I am sure it was a dynasty in the sense that old Joe Kennedy planned and put his finances and everything he could into seeking political power for Jack, and he was very glad to have Bobby in there with him, too. But I think he began to recede a bit in his power to shape things. Teddy had got started all right, but after Joe died, he never got beyond good placement in the Senate. By that time he had other problems.

John Seigenthaler If you are going to talk about a dynasty, you cannot ignore the fact that here is a man who made all the money in the world and wanted his children to be independent, so he gave each of them a certain amount of money to make them independent. But at the same time, both he and Rose Kennedy—she should not be ignored in all of this—ingrained in them a sense of public service. If you hear Eunice Shriver talk today, she sounds like Jack. All of those children in some way speak exactly the same about public service—the high calling.

I can be very cynical about it and say if Jack Kennedy hadn't run for Congress, what the hell would he have done? Where would he have found a job? Who would have hired him? Politics was made for them. They had two options: Go into the family business and help build the millions into billions, or go into public service. I don't see any middle road for them. Well, they could have taught in a college, and Bob really thought about it. His dilemma—and that of the children today—is, what do you do if the stamp of fame is on you? Joe Kennedy was a dominant figure in American politics in the Roosevelt administration. What do you do? I guess you can run the Merchandise Mart.° But it's a big family, and it's a crock of gold, as they call it. How many Steve Smiths can you have out there running the crock of gold? The whole issue of the dynasty is there because it happened.

All of them had politics in their genes. I think the women did also. Maybe it goes back to some warrior in Old Ireland. Who knows where it comes from? I don't agree that there is any evidence that there was a concerted conspiracy to create a dynasty. They believed politics was the highest calling; the most honorable profession. Sure, Joe put a little pressure on Jack to run for Congress, and when he did well, to run for the Senate and then the presidency. But he didn't have to put on much pressure; Bob wanted it; he loved it. He absolutely enjoyed politics and government and public service. It was the most he could do with this life. He was consumed with it; in the same way that guys on Wall Street are consumed with the market; in the same way his father was consumed with money. It was part of his fiber and being. It is the same way with the children. I talked to Kathleen [Kennedy, daughter of Robert F. Kennedy] when she ran for Congress in Maryland. Listening to her talk was like listening to her father talk or her uncle talk. The political speeches they make are sometimes different on the issues, but the theme and thrust and content is basically the same: You have to give something back.

Burke Marshall   Both Kennedys were delights to work with. President Kennedy enjoyed being president; the attorney general loved public service. This notion that their father had roles for them? It's difficult to believe that they wouldn't have ended up in public service on their own.

Ralph Dungan   I never saw or heard anything from JFK that suggested his interest in any dynastic business; he was not that kind of guy;

°Chicago-based business enterprise owned by Joseph P. Kennedy and managed by his son-in-law R. Sargent Shriver.

he didn't think that way. The old man did, but JFK didn't. Teddy's coming to the Senate was probably the old man's scheme; it was clear that he was being groomed. It's hard for me to think of JFK as a dynastic plotter—first of all, he was a good enough student of history to know the danger of dynasties. But there must have been somebody plotting it, and he certainly was a willing instrument of the plotting, so maybe he was part of it.

Bernard Boutin That was not in anybody's mind at all. When Teddy decided to run for the Senate in 1962, the president was very unhappy with that. I think he felt there were enough Kennedys on the scene at that point. His advice was no, and his hope was no, but when the answer was yes, then he was a Kennedy. I did not feel in any way, shape, or manner that the president thought Bobby would be his political heir. I don't think that thought would have crossed his mind. Bobby only ran very reluctantly for the Senate from New York; he was a very reluctant tiger.

I don't think that during the life of John Fitzgerald Kennedy, the thought of a dynasty ever entered his mind.

Joseph Dolan Teddy said to me once, "You know how I got that seat? The president wanted Torby [Torbert McDonald, U.S. congressman (D., Mass.)] or Boland [Edward Boland, U.S. congressman (D., Mass.)]. They couldn't decide, so the president said, "Why don't you flip a coin?" and Boland refused. So the president picked Benjamin Smith [U.S. senator (D., Mass.)] as a seat-warmer." And that opened it up for Teddy. Teddy came close to moving to Wyoming. I remember one time we were on a plane flying into Cheyenne, and John Kennedy looks out the window and says, "Teddy, Teddy, you want to live here?"

Bradford Morse I think I could have beaten Teddy for the Senate in 1962; I would have won on the dynasty issue. George [Cabot] Lodge, on the other hand, couldn't, because he couldn't raise it. I recall being at the White House a night or two before the Bay of Pigs and having a brief conversation with the president. He asked me if I were going to run, and I said something smarty like, "I can beat your guy if I do." He walked off.

John Kenneth Galbraith I don't think that Kennedys ever sat down and planned it out. But I think that the president saw his brothers as part of the natural process. They were all very, very close and strongly supportive of each other. I would be surprised if Kennedy had ever thought of Bobby as his natural successor at the end of the second term. That would be going a bit far. But certainly this was a greatly supportive family.

Tom Wicker   I don't think it was a conscious plan; it may have been in the old man's head. I don't think John Kennedy moved to set up a dynasty; I do think he moved to take care of his family. But Bobby, as we saw later, was a very able, tough manager, and John F. knew that—more than most of the rest of the people did. I have no doubt that if John had lived and served his two terms, Bobby would have sought the nomination in 1968. But was that Kennedy's purpose in making him attorney general? I doubt that very seriously; I don't think that John consciously had this idea of building up a dynasty. I expect that it occurred to Bobby.

Ben Bradlee   Some of the people around Bobby would say, "If Jack doesn't shape up, we're going to run Bobby."

Eugene McCarthy   Certainly after Jack was killed the concept developed—the right of continuity: The unfinished work will be fulfilled with Bobby. The inner crowd saw this as the wave of the future. There is more of a myth about Bobby now than there is about Jack. There is a sort of Bobby cult; Jack is in a secondary position. The Kennedy supporters thought they had a right of succession. I think that the idea of a dynasty was present before the assassination.

I felt when Teddy said he had to do it for the family, or for Jack, this was true. When Bobby said it I felt he was quite willing to do it for himself. It was sort of like a Greek tragedy in a way, because Bobby's campaign was actually a campaign against Jack; his opposition to the war that Jack had escalated. In a way he was also running against failure to do anything about civil rights. A big part of Bobby's campaign had nothing to do with civil rights or with me. It was a campaign saying you had to do more about civil rights. Bobby was quite willing to exploit the failures of Jack's administration.

Harlan Cleveland   I don't know that they saw themselves as a dynasty, but certainly Bob Kennedy was throwing his weight around in a very raw way at Los Angeles. I thought the people he had appointed, and he himself, were extraordinarily rude. These people were, after all, trying to get his brother elected president. I was chairman of Citizens for Kennedy in central New York, and I had a couple of run-ins with Bobby Kennedy. In fact, my appointment was slightly delayed by the fact that he opposed my being nominated for the State Department job. Rusk had to insist on it and get Bobby overruled.

Whether he thought in terms of succeeding his brother as president, I have no idea. But that he thought that he and his brother were going to run the country together was clear, even during the campaign.

Tom Wicker Bobby might have won in 1968, but I don't think he ever would have been nominated. It is a fallacy that if Bobby Kennedy hadn't been shot, the Democrats would have nominated him for president and he would have won, and the whole history of the world would be different. I analyzed that very closely. Robert Kennedy never would have been nominated in 1968. Had he been nominated, I think he could have beaten Nixon. In other words, he would do better in the country than within the Democratic party.

Joseph Dolan John Kennedy used to give out these plastic cigarette cases as souvenirs or Christmas presents. He gave Bobby one that said, "After Me, How About You?" It used to be out on the table at Hickory Hill.

Nicholas Katzenbach Until JFK died, the last thing Bobby wanted to be was president. Bobby didn't like government. JFK wondered what he would do after a second term. He used to talk about going back to the Senate. Bobby saw it as picking up the mantle—to fulfill his brother's promise, and probably in his own mind that was overstated. He would not have been happy staying in the Senate. People only care about what senators from New York say, not what they do.

Teddy is happy in the Senate. His presidential ambitions were also in picking up the mantle, but he didn't feel it as strongly as Bobby did. Events have certainly closed it for him. I don't think he's totally unhappy about it. As far as Joe Kennedy is concerned, I don't think he was spinning it out. He was too old. Rose didn't think about it.

Arthur Schlesinger, Jr.   The Kennedys were not great planners; they were marvelous improvisers. Robert Kennedy did not want to be attorney general, but the president wanted somebody in the cabinet he could fully trust. There were a number of members of the cabinet he hardly knew, including his secretaries of state, defense, and treasury. But he didn't expect Robert Kennedy to become president in 1968 and Ted Kennedy to become president in 1976. You live from day to day in politics. Long-term planning is impossible.

Edward McDermott   There was never anything said in my presence by the Kennedy sons that would suggest there had been this specifically programmed thing. However, they were all fairly ambitious people, and I'm not so sure that that might not have worked out if Bobby hadn't been assassinated, and if Teddy hadn't run off the bridge.

John Kenneth Galbraith   John Kennedy felt he was picking up the legacy of young Joe, but I wouldn't have thought that was on his mind every day; he was his own person.

Donald Wilson   They knew American history and knew how unlikely it would have been to have a dynasty. I believe if John F. Kennedy had lived for two full terms, it would have been absolutely astonishing if Robert Kennedy had been nominated for president in 1968. I think it would have turned off the American people, wholesale.

When Bobby ran for the Senate, he wanted to pick up the mantle. He probably, down the road, wanted to run for president. I think he knew he was getting nowhere in the Johnson administration. He wanted to get out from under that, but he wanted to have some independent power, and I am sure that somewhere deep down, he wanted to challenge Lyndon Johnson. I think that probably—very unfairly—he came to see Johnson as a usurper.

Norman Podhoretz   I don't have any doubt that there was an effort to create a dynasty. They say there still is—you have a whole new generation coming up the pike. I think America is finally growing bored and disillusioned with the Kennedys, but you've got about three of them active in politics, and I think we've yet to hear from John junior. Then there are these courtiers around them—some of them getting old, like

Schlesinger, who in effect put themselves at the service of one Kennedy after another, up to and including helping Teddy Kennedy write that mendacious speech after Chappaquidick.

The people we are talking about have, in one form or another, Potomac fever; they want to be in power. They are not content with writing books or being professors or foundation presidents; they want to run the country from Washington, and in this, the Kennedys presented themselves as a vehicle: If not one Kennedy, then another. These were the stars to whom they hitched their wagons, and without the Kennedys they had very little hope of getting back into paradise—which they tasted for such a brief time. They never were able to get over it: First it was Joe—and then Joe got killed; then it was Jack—and Jack got killed; then it was Bobby—and Bobby got killed; then it was Teddy—only Teddy couldn't hack it.

There is obviously some sort of hunger here for a royal family, and the Kennedys have been treated as a royal family. I have to say that— compared to other political dynasties in American history—they are a very second-rate or third-rate crew. If you compare them to the Adamses, it's a joke; or even to the Lodge dynasty. I thought there was something cheap about the Kennedys. It was this wedding between two very glamorous worlds—the world of political power and the world of high café society. Without the wealth you can be sure that none of this would have happened. Money is a very crucial part of it. I even think, in the old days, the aura of eroticism was a part of it. Now, of course, it's very unfashionable: Kennedy is put down for being a womanizer, because of feminism. But it was a sort of an unspoken element within the glamour—a lot of sex around it.

6

Cabinet Appointments

ROBERT KENNEDY'S APPOINTMENT
AS ATTORNEY GENERAL

Abraham Ribicoff The first person Kennedy sent for after the election was me. I came to Palm Beach. He offered me attorney general, and I turned it down. He was shocked and surprised, and he said, "Who should I take?" and I said, "Take Bobby." He said, "You're crazy; the country wouldn't stand for it." I said, "Look, Mr. President, I've known you two people intimately for so long, and whenever you have been faced with a crisis, as to a decision, you automatically turn to Bobby. You come out of the same womb. The first and most important person to you is Bobby. You're not going to be able to run the presidency without Bobby's help. The worst thing you could do is, when you need Bobby, to have him come around the back door. When you see Bobby, he has to come through the front door. In front of the public, so they know it, so the press knows it."

I also said to him, "Civil rights is going to be a big issue, and there's going to be hell to pay. But the worst thing that could happen is that you have a Catholic president use a Jew as attorney general, to push the blacks down the throats of the white Protestants. It would hurt the presidency; it would hurt you; and it would hurt the civil rights cause."

Pierre Salinger I think Bobby's appointment as attorney general was a JFK decision. Of course it was controversial; there was a lot of argument inside the group about it, but the decision to name his brother was 100 percent Jack's. If you had watched them working together on the Senate Labor Rackets Committee, where Jack was a member and Bobby was chief counsel, there was some logic in making him attorney general, as they had worked in a political, legal situation before.

George Smathers   I know he was scared to death of Joe, all the time. After he got to be president, one day—I think it was a few weeks after, maybe a week after, the election—we were in Palm Beach. He had invited me to spend the night, which I did, and in the morning, we were talking about who he was going to put in his cabinet. And Jack kept saying: "What the hell to do with Bobby?" Nobody knew Bobby particularly at that time—Bobby was just a guy who was along. Bobby did not have the nice personality Jack did, so Jack came to me and said: "What am I going to do with Bobby?" So I came up with the idea this morning we were at Palm Beach, to make him assistant secretary of defense—he likes the military; he's a macho guy; he's a bottom-line fellow, the military and all that. He could do that for two years and then be appointed secretary of defense. To be secretary of defense is the biggest budget in the government by far. He'd travel to every country in the world and have the head of that country come out and blow smoke at him. And in a short period of time, he would be the secretary.

And Joe Kennedy, Sr., said: "Did Jack Kennedy come down to the pool and suggest that?" I said, "Well, Mr. Ambassador, not really." I said, "It was my thought." He said to his son, "Jack, I want to tell you something: Don't you ever, ever, for one damn moment, get the idea that Bobby's going to be anything but attorney general. Bobby has given his blood for you; he's given his time for you; he's given his life for you. He wants to be attorney general, and he's going to be attorney general. I don't want anybody like this Smathers to come around and express anything else." I think it was Joe wanting it for Bobby.

Sargent Shriver   Bobby was not Jack's first choice for attorney general. Now, Bobby was not agitating for the job, but there were people who were. It was a difficult decision for Jack because of the nepotism factor.

I understood this, firsthand. I was in the White House one day when Abe Ribicoff said to me, "I am going to ask the president to make you my undersecretary at HEW." At that time I was president of the Chicago Board of Education, so I knew something about the subject.

Abe called Jack over and said he'd like to have me as undersecretary, and Jack turned to me and asked, "What do you think, Sarge?" I replied: "In light of the extraordinary heat you have taken about Bobby's appointment, it would be extraordinarily difficult—and politically unwise—for you to appoint me, because they would then start screaming about nepotism, and you would have it from two directions." Jack said, "I think that you are right," and he turned to Abe and said, "I don't think you should do that."

Bobby Baker John Kennedy did not want to name Bobby as attorney general. When he was in Palm Beach, he called Clark Clifford—Clifford was his personal attorney [and policy adviser] when the papers had some of those sex tapes about Kennedy that would have ruined him—Clifford always went to the *Star* and the *Post* and said, "I'm going to sue you for libel"—that was before *Sullivan* v. *New York Times*,* and the papers were scared of it—so president-elect Kennedy told Clifford: "Call Papa Joe and see if he'll take you to lunch, and explain to him that it would be the worst kind of nepotism to name Bobby attorney general." So when Clifford went up there and said, "Mr. Kennedy, I am of the opinion that it would do irreparable harm to the president if he were to select Bobby to be attorney general," Old Man Joe said, "It's not negotiable. If you want to talk about anything else, do so. Otherwise, the meeting's ended."

Old Man Joe Kennedy said that there were only two jobs—in addition to the presidency—worth a damn in Washington: attorney general and director of internal revenue. He picked Bobby to be attorney general, and Bobby picked his professor at the University of Virginia, Mortimer Caplin, as director of internal revenue.

Najeeb Halaby First, there was nepotism. Second, he didn't have experience for the nation's highest law office. Third, there was his role with McCarthy. I had to testify before McCarthy while I was at the Pentagon. There was Bobby—of course he was on the minority staff, but there he is—alongside Roy Cohn and G. David Schine [aides to Sen. Joseph R. McCarthy]. So those of us who thought of ourselves as honest-to-God liberals held that against him. Why on earth would a nice kid like that work for a son of a bitch like McCarthy? All of those factors were against Bobby.

---

*Libel case in which the U.S. Supreme Court redefined the legal concept of defamation.

But with the intense loyalty in the family, the feeling was, I have to have somebody in that job that I trust. And there is old J. Edgar underneath there, and Bobby is probably the one guy who can control J. Edgar. At about that time Hoover had just terrorized the place, and nobody could touch him. He would get Walter Winchell [syndicated columnist] and others like that to go after people he thought were encroaching on him, so all of that persuaded Kennedy that the risk of appointing a brother to that job could be taken and would be worth it.

John Seigenthaler   He wanted to be attorney general, but he reached a conclusion it was not something he should do. He struggled with it and finally decided that it was not a wise thing to do. The nepotism issue had been raised. The reaction to his appointment was nothing like what I expected; it was basically from the liberal community. The truth of the matter is that an awful lot of people in the country had come to admire Bob Kennedy as a result of the hearings. So, though some in the liberal community—particularly those who did not think they would become part of the administration—raised their voices; it was nothing like the firestorm I had anticipated.

I remember the day Robert made this series of visits to Senator Paul Douglas [D., Ill.], to J. Edgar Hoover, to the incumbent attorney general, to a half dozen senior citizens he had known and respected—from the ultra-liberals on one side to the ultraconservative J. Edgar Hoover on the other. All of them except Hoover told him not to do it. He decided that night not to do it, but at breakfast the next morning with the president-elect, he finally decided to do it. At that meeting, Jack made it impossible for him not to do it. He said, "I've known most of the people who are going to be in my cabinet for twenty minutes. I think they will all tell me what I need to hear, but I *know* you will." He had called Ribicoff and asked him to be attorney general. I spoke to Abe about this after Bob agreed to do it. He said, "You know, John, you are from the South. You know where it is ultimately going to come, and Jack does not need a Connecticut Jew doing this."

Cartha DeLoach   Bobby went to see Mr. Hoover when the president asked that he serve as attorney general and Bobby did not want the job. Mr. Hoover told him he felt he owed it to the president to take the job as attorney general. He said the president needed someone in his cabinet who would give him 100 percent loyalty. Mr. Hoover later regretted giving that advice.

Carl T. Curtis, U.S. senator (R., Nebr.)   I thought the Robert Kennedy appointment was a mistake. Bobby Kennedy was my favorite among all the Kennedy boys. We got along pretty well on a personal basis. We didn't always agree, but we respected each other. But Bobby had no experience at all. He told me that he had talked to a group of students after he became attorney general, and a young man had asked, "How do you get to be attorney general?" Bobby answered, "The first thing you do is get your brother elected president."

Sam Yorty, mayor of Los Angeles   I didn't support Jack. I think Bobby always held that against me. And I didn't think he should be attorney general under any president because he didn't have the background for it and wasn't qualified. He'd been a McCarthy stooge.

Adlai E Stevenson III   I think my father would have been horrified at the nepotism. Plus, there wasn't much love lost in the Stevenson camp for Bobby, though I think some members, later on, became avid followers of Bobby. But in those days he had been kind of a camp follower. He became suspected of this vendetta against Stevenson—I'm not sure anybody was conscious of that in '60—I can only guess that the thought of putting young Bobby Kennedy, the brother, in that sensitive position, would have really shocked him. There were plenty of people better qualified—and it was nepotism.

Maurine Neuberger   Bobby was different in many ways from his brother. He was stubborn and determined. Even though he had come in with a bit of a cloud from the McCarthy days, I thought he was a very effective senator. I defended his appointment as attorney general. I felt that any cabinet member has to work very closely with the president—nobody can be president of the United States single handed—that being his brother was an asset. But you had to defend that.

Archibald Cox   I wasn't only surprised, I was shocked at Bobby's appointment as attorney general. I came to admire the job he did as attorney general, but there was nothing in his record to suggest that he was possibly qualified. At the beginning I said, "My God! What are we doing?" At one point, when we were developing labor legislation, John Kennedy asked me to talk to Bobby about it, and I did not come away with a strongly favorable impression by any means; I didn't think he understood the problems. He very quickly labeled people "white hats" or "black hats," but he had a great capacity for work and had very able people working for him. He also had what I would describe as quite a knack for seeing key legal issues and putting them into human terms, somewhat similarly in that respect to Hugo Black [Supreme Court justice], who had that—second to none.

Joseph Dolan   At the 1960 convention, Byron White and I were floor advisers on rules. He became head of Citizens for Kennedy-Johnson in Washington, and I worked with him.

After the election I became the assistant to the deputy attorney general, Byron White. The bottom line on that was that I thought that Robert Kennedy was the worst possible appointee for attorney general of the United States that could have been imagined. I thought the country needed to be protected from him. It turns out this was an error of judgment on my part.

Lloyd Cutler   I think at the time I had a negative reaction because he was appointed before Byron White was selected. It was a surprise to me that he would first pick a relative, someone that close to him, and second, pick someone who, at least in the professional legal sense, was as inexperienced as Bobby was at the time. He turned out, I think, to be a very good attorney general.

Bobby Baker   Senator Russell had the votes, between the Southerners and the Republicans—to defeat Bobby Kennedy's nomination as attorney general. It's never been written, but Lyndon Johnson put his prestige with Richard Russell on the line, saying: "I need to start off good if I'm going to be of any help to the South with our new president, and I'm making a personal plea that you call off the dogs in your opposition to Bobby." Russell made the agreement to agree to a voice vote; he did not filibuster, and Bobby would never have been attorney general in his life if it had not been for Johnson's intervention, and Jack Kennedy knew that.

DEAN RUSK AS SECRETARY OF STATE

Dean Rusk   In that first meeting we talked about various names to be secretary of state. The president-elect had about three or four on his list, and I had two or three names that I added to the list. And there was no discussion whatever about my taking the job.

And so I went on back to the Rockefeller Foundation in New York and told my colleagues up there that I would be staying with the foundation and they could forget any of this press speculation that they had seen. The next morning Mr. Kennedy called me and said he wanted me to take the job. And I said, "Hey, wait a minute, there are a lot of things that we ought to discuss before you make that decision." So he asked me to come down to Palm Beach and spend the morning with him. And I did, and we got a lot of business done during that morning, including telephone calls to Adlai Stevenson to persuade him to take the UN job, and to Chester Bowles to take the undersecretary's job. So he finally proceeded to make the announcement to the press outside. I had not campaigned for the job; I had not asked anybody to write a letter on my behalf or speak to him on my behalf. I was not really an applicant for the job.

John Kenneth Galbraith   Kennedy wanted somebody who would bring a freshness of view. If I had been asked, the person I would have hoped he would put into that job would, of course, have been George Ball, who was a gleam of light in the orthodoxy of the cold war.

The serious possibilities for secretary of state were Fulbright [J. William Fulbright, U.S. senator (D., Ark.), chairman, Senate Foreign Relations Committee], who was passed over because he had signed the Southern manifesto°—and there was an exaggerated view on what the effect of that might be on the new African world. Actually, this wouldn't have been a problem. Fulbright had an infinite capacity to accommodate himself to what was right. Or Chester Bowles, whom Stevenson thought was a bit too didactic. And Adlai Stevenson, who would have been probably the best but had his own constituency. There was perhaps some personality problem between Stevenson and Kennedy; they weren't on

°A document signed by most of the Southern senators and ninety members of the House of Representatives pledging to resist integration.

the same wavelength. So he reached into the Rockefeller Foundation to get a relatively unknown bureaucrat who had the virtue of not making any waves but had the difficulty of accommodating himself to all of the conventional cold war clichés.

Walt Rostow   It was a good choice and just what Kennedy wanted. I think he thought Rusk was loyal—which he was. He had a good relationship with the Congress; he was a thorough professional; and he had a reverence for the office of the president. Kennedy understood fully why Rusk didn't debate the presidential aides around the cabinet table. There had never been a man in public life who had so little ego. He was a disciplined officer in the mold of George Marshall. Officers do not have morale problems—only enlisted men. When I became national security adviser in 1966, I told my staff, "I don't want any more memorandums that say 'Rusk,' or 'McNamara'; it is 'Secretary Rusk'; 'Secretary McNamara.'"

Joseph Sisco, deputy assistant secretary of state for international organization affairs   I was not particularly surprised by the Rusk appointment. I had known Dean Rusk both in his prior capacity at the State Department and as president of the Rockefeller Foundation. There was really no doubt in my mind that he was fully capable; he had tremendous background and experience. I was surprised in the sense that he was obviously not the visible figure Adlai Stevenson was.

Rusk was exceedingly good—in the sense that he never stood on ceremony or raised up his shoulders that he was secretary of state. Rather, he understood and appreciated Stevenson's stature and role. The relationship between the president and the secretary was very professional. I think that President Kennedy had a great deal of respect for Rusk as a competent, knowledgeable secretary of state. There were others in the White House who were more critical. The story got around, and is factually correct, that on occasions there were some thoughts being given to replacing Dean Rusk. But in his sheer articulateness and his loyalty to the president—as well as to the country—this was one of the finest human beings you ever wanted to meet. He patterned himself after George Marshall. He was dedicated to the public service. Once he took that oath, he was not the kind of man who would engage in the usual kind of talk that one finds within the bureaucracy. It is no secret that Bobby didn't think as highly of Dean Rusk as the president did.

Adlai Stevenson III   It's a cliché, but Kennedy wanted to be his own secretary of state; he couldn't be with Stevenson. Two, it was hardball: Kennedy's style—he did reward Stevensonians—but Stevenson had his chance; he was going to have to take his lumps, and he didn't make the deal. It was too late. There were the little resentments—the 1960 convention, especially, and finally, he may have thought that Stevenson, who wrongly, was looked upon by some around Kennedy as a threat and a rival, would be a greater threat and rival as secretary of state than as the representative to the United Nations. And there probably was a legitimate concern there: As secretary of state he'd be attracting a great deal of attention, some of it, perhaps, away from the president. As it was, he got a lot of attention at the UN, but still, that is not an office that can compete with the office of the secretary of state. I can understand why he could have, very understandably, had reservations—he wanted to be his own secretary of state. Stevenson would have had his own views on foreign policy. Also, Stevenson in that position would have been a real magnet for international attention. I hadn't really thought of it before, but when the chiefs of state came to Washington, they'd be having a better time with Stevenson than with Kennedy. They were on a first-name basis and were more or less contemporaries. Stevenson would have been—in that context in Washington and abroad—he would have been a rival for the president—a conspicuous figure on the world stage. To put it crassly: There'd be some fear of the secretary of state upstaging the president. I think anybody in Kennedy's position would have probably had some concern along those lines.

Arthur Schlesinger, Jr.   I think Kennedy felt—even apart from the irritations of Los Angeles—that Stevenson would bring a lot of baggage into the office of secretary of state. There would be a lot of resistance and mistrust on the Hill, and he wanted a secretary of state who would not draw the antagonism of the Hill. Also, Stevenson was a figure in his own right, and Kennedy wanted to make his own foreign policy. Therefore, he got what he thought to be a rather neutral figure in Rusk. Actually Kennedy's preference for secretary of state was Bill Fulbright, but he was dissuaded from appointing Fulbright by Robert Kennedy, who felt that Fulbright's position on civil rights would make him unacceptable to certain nonwhite parts of the world, and by the Bowles people, who were hoping that Chet Bowles would get it.

Walt Rostow   There is no question in my mind that Kennedy wanted somebody who was basically tougher than Stevenson. He felt Stevenson didn't like tough problems, and the world was going to be filled with tough problems—where rhetoric wouldn't suffice. The cold war was a very real thing at that time. He asked me about the secretary of state position just before he went down to Palm Beach, where he eventually made the announcement of Rusk. I said, "Well, you wrote a brilliant piece for the *Saturday Review of Literature*"—he began smiling, because I wrote it for him—"and you said that the most important thing about a secretary of state is that the president be comfortable." He said, "You know, it's a little bit like getting married." There were three people on the final list, but Stevenson wasn't on it.

Adlai had been in public service, and I don't think he minded at all working under a boss. He complained about Washington, but basically I think he was glad not to have that responsibility.

Joseph Rauh, Jr.   I think we made a mistake when we opposed Fulbright for secretary of state. He was Jack's first choice. Why did we oppose Fulbright? Well—civil rights. I mean, if you had said to me, "Joe, what's the most important thing in their constituency?" I'd have said, "Civil rights—that's going to be the big issue for liberals in the Kennedy administration," and so we fought Fulbright and won, but I think the whole Vietnam situation might have been totally different if we hadn't done that. But I don't want to do a mea culpa, because Fulbright had been so outrageously anti–civil rights down in Arkansas, that what else could you do, except oppose him for secretary of state—the symbol of our country?

He would have been good on civil rights once he was in the cabinet, so I think we made a mistake. I once was at a party at Charles Roberts's [correspondent, Washington Bureau, *Newsweek*] house, and I bumped into Fulbright and said, "Thank you so much," for what he was doing on Vietnam. He looked at me and said, "Joe, are you sorry you fought me on civil rights so hard? Didn't you realize I had to do that to be reelected?" I said, "Well, that's too Solomonic a question for a cocktail party," and

I've never answered it yet. But we did beat Fulbright, and it was a mistake.

ROBERT McNAMARA AS
SECRETARY OF DEFENSE

Ralph Dungan   We didn't fool with the cabinet selections. The president was making them—with some assists from anybody who thought they had access. My understanding of the way McNamara was selected was that Sargent Shriver read the *Time* magazine that had McNamara's face on the cover at about that time, and that he must have gone to the president and said, "Gee, Jack, here's a guy who looks terrific." That's how McNamara came along. Some of the others, I think, were obviously selected on a political basis—like Stewart Udall [secretary of the interior].

Tom Wicker   I have a high regard for McNamara, even including the Vietnam period. I think that his appointment was a good choice. I don't know on what grounds Kennedy made it, because McNamara's record at the Ford Motor Company had not been that outstanding.

Adam Yarmolinsky   McNamara was the first of the cabinet officers with whom we met. I had known him very slightly through the Ford Foundation connection. I was reminded by a friend, then the *Economist* magazine correspondent in Washington, that in August of 1960, I had said to him that a long-shot candidate for secretary of defense if Kennedy wins this election is this vice president of the Ford Motor Company, whom I've met in Ann Arbor, out at Dearborn. I'd forgotten all about it. The fact that I did suggests that I am not the primary source of McNamara's name. It came from Bob Lovett and I, of course, reinforced it vigorously when it came out.

Kennedy sent Shriver to Michigan to talk to McNamara. Then they had to do a sudden flurry to see if he was McNamara or *M-a-c* MacNamara, because if he was a Catholic, there couldn't be another Catholic in the cabinet. He was not an *M-a-c* MacNamara. Then he met with the president, and his appointment was announced very shortly.

J. Strom Thurmond, U.S. senator (D., S.C.)   A high-ranking naval officer told me a few weeks ago that Henry Ford said, "I've got the man ..." because Ford really wanted to get rid of him.

C. DOUGLAS DILLON AS
SECRETARY OF THE TREASURY

David Bell   Douglas Dillon was, and is, a very complex person who came out of an investment banking background. He is very intelligent, very cultivated, sophisticated—even in those days he owned vineyards in France—and easy to get along with. But his views were significantly more conservative than those of the members of the council [of Economic Advisers], or mine. My speculation is that the president was looking for an able man with government and business experience who would, to some extent, be reassuring to the business community. He must have looked at alternatives to Dillon—I don't know who they were—and concluded that there was nobody who filled the bill who was a Democrat.

John Kenneth Galbraith   I was serving with Sargent Shriver on a committee dealing with economic appointments; it was very informal. It was taken for granted that we had to bring in people who would give us a foothold in the center and larger business community. Douglas Dillon certainly filled that bill, apart from being a serious and intelligent man.

James Tobin   We thought Dillon would be a problem, but from our point of view, he was about the best we could have hoped for: He was fairly open minded about economic policy. We had our problems with him, but we always had good relations. I think it was important for the president to have appointed somebody like Dillon.

Arthur Schlesinger, Jr.   Douglas Dillon, whose appointment I did my best to prevent, turned out to be a first-rate secretary of the treasury. McNamara was an excellent secretary of defense, though I think he was badly wrong on Vietnam. He was—in a sense—betrayed by his own system: Information he received by the military in Vietnam misled him and gave him a wrong sense of how the war was going, but he is an admirable man. Robert Kennedy was first-rate as attorney general. People like Orville Freeman [secretary of agriculture] and Stewart Udall were excellent. Rusk is a fine gent, but he was much more conservative than Kennedy—much more conventional establishmentarian and cold warrior. I liked him in many ways, though I'm quite critical of him. Arthur

Goldberg was a first-class secretary of labor. Bill [W. Willard] Wirtz, his successor, was very good. It was a first-rate cabinet.

ADLAI STEVENSON'S APPOINTMENT AS U.S. AMBASSADOR TO THE UNITED NATIONS

Ralph Dungan   As far as selection of the secretary of state goes, several names were up for consideration. Stevenson was one, but that would have been impossible: Kennedy and Stevenson were not on the same wavelength at all. Kennedy considered him, in the modern jargon, a bit of a wimp. Stevenson's personality would have made it very difficult for him to have worked that closely with the president. I think that it really would have been a disaster; they were just so different in terms of temperament. I think Stevenson always would have thought: "I should be sitting here." He was brought in [to the United Nations] because there were a lot of other supporters—Mrs. Roosevelt, for one. Stevenson had a fantastic following; he had caught the imaginations of a lot of people in 1952, including mine. I think that Kennedy felt that Stevenson would add something in terms of his strength in the Democratic grouping. There were a lot of people who had reservations about having him up at the UN; the Irish Mafia didn't cotton to him at all.

Adlai Stevenson III   Sometime after the election, we were at a dinner party in Lake Forest, and a call came through from the president-elect for my father, in which Kennedy asked him to serve as representative at the United Nations. Of course I didn't hear the conversation, but I can still hear my father afterward. He was very upset. Next to being president, being secretary of state was the position that he sought, and for which he was ideally equipped. In fact, he said, "If I was qualified in the spring, why aren't I qualified now?" I remember he said, "Well, who will be my boss? Who will the secretary of state be?" And Kennedy said that that decision hadn't been made. So my father said, "Well, how can I make my decision until I know who my boss is going to be?" which is not a very gracious but nonetheless rational response.

Philip Klutznick   Kennedy called me and said, "You and I know that Adlai wants to be secretary of state, but he isn't going to be. I would like to have him be our representative at the United Nations. Isn't that a natural place for him? Can you talk to him about it?" I think the UN job fit Adlai's talents more than secretary of state, although he felt the UN post was a downgrading of his talents.

He did like the apartment at the Waldorf and the opportunity to entertain. I will say that at the UN he was very highly regarded. He did a first-class job of representing the United States. He had an advantage: He didn't have to prove himself; everyone knew who he was. What's more, they all thought he had more authority than he had.

Harlan Cleveland   Kennedy was very anxious to keep Stevenson happy. Here was a man with enormous worldwide prestige who had run twice, with great elegance, for president of the United States and who, in effect, had the affection of what you might call the lefthand side of the Democratic party. If he had defected from the Kennedy administration, this would have been an enormous political disaster for the administration. So in making sure that Stevenson was well serviced, and even keeping in touch with him on matters that weren't strictly UN affairs, such as Berlin, Kennedy assigned Arthur Schlesinger to make sure that Stevenson was reasonably happy. They would clear judgeships in Illinois with him from the White House.

Why Did Stevenson Accept the UN Position?

George Ball   I think I was more responsible than anybody for Stevenson's accepting the UN post. I spent an entire night talking to him. I simply said, "Look, Adlai, you are accustomed to being in the public eye, and to being a public figure. You have got to have some kind of a base if you are going to do that. I know from your experience at San Francisco that you have a very good idea of the limitations of the job. Nevertheless, you are going to be acutely unhappy if you don't take it. You won't have a base to express your ideas."

Adlai Stevenson III   Duty. I can't think of any other reason. I guess he didn't want to be on the outside, looking in. He did have strong feelings about the importance of the UN; he was at its birth in San Francisco, and then later, at the Preparatory Commission of the UN, and issues which he addressed throughout his life, including the gap between what he's called the "haves" and the "have-nots"; the developed and the less-developed world. He probably knew that he was ideally suited for the position: There just never has been an advocate for the United States like he was. He was a real hero to the rest of the world, most of which never understood why he wasn't president. His travels were triumphant; he knew the world's leaders on a first-name basis; and it was a very fortuitous appointment but it ultimately killed him. He knew what he was getting into. He took it seriously: Instead of making policy, he was out there on that cocktail circuit—umpteen receptions to attend—every night, and it was frustrating, especially as we got deeper into Vietnam.

Harlan Cleveland   He was of two minds, at first, about taking the UN job. After all, he had wanted to be president, to be secretary of state, and here was being offered an ambassadorship. He had quite a negotiation with the president-elect about it. He drew up a whole list of conditions, one of which was that he would be on the National Security Council and a member of the cabinet and be consulted on all matters of foreign policy, not just UN matters.

Philip Klutznick   He loved the UN, and given the opportunity to represent the United States there, why wouldn't he take it? He believed in the UN thoroughly. He and I were probably the only two in Illinois who did. He would have found it impossible to turn the offer down. It was an exciting post for a man like Stevenson.

Joseph Sisco   I'm from Illinois, and in 1948—when Stevenson ran for governor—I was a young college student, and I pushed doorbells in his campaign. In the course of his being ambassador to the United Nations, I got closer to him. He was dedicated and devoted to public service; he was a politician; he had absolutely no stomach for practicing law on La Salle Street in Chicago, and therefore the UN gave him a substantial amount of visibility. That vantage point gave him an excellent platform not only for continuing as a national figure, but also offered him a place from which he could influence American policy.

Norman Podhoretz   The job at the UN was better than nothing. The UN job—on certain occasions—has been a very good platform; on others it's been a backwater. I think that in those days it was still regarded as a fairly important position. After all, Johnson talked Arthur Goldberg into leaving the Supreme Court to go to the UN.

Eugene McCarthy   If Stevenson had asked me, I would have told him not to take it, but he didn't. He was unhappy there. They isolated him. If he had had a cabinet department, he would have been there every day, but being in the UN was like being in the provinces. So he was isolated from having an independent position, and also from having a role in policy-making. I could see why they didn't want him in a cabinet department, and why they didn't want him to be a free agent. He took it because there was nothing else to do. He may have thought he could have had more influence than he actually had.

Joseph Sisco   The feeling was—and I don't say it is justified—that Adlai was indecisive, able to look at all sides of the question and, therefore, insufficiently tough. This was being told to President Kennedy by all sorts of people in the White House, hence the perception. When a president sends an additional individual to sit alongside your ambassador to the UN in negotiations, it is indicative that this perception is the basis upon which the president is operating.

He was not entirely happy in the job, particularly as the months rolled by. At one point he felt that he'd had enough. He said to me, "What would you think if I decided to run for the senate in Illinois?" I said, "Adlai, you've been a presidential candidate; you are endeared worldwide. Have you really thought through what it would mean, even if you win, to be the junior senator from Illinois?"

Abraham Ribicoff   After Kennedy was elected, Stevenson had such a big following he wanted to be secretary of state. He ended up with the worst possible job, ambassador to the UN. And he was humiliated; he was a very unhappy man. He wasn't used. They threw him away. I think Adlai Stevenson died of a broken heart because he felt he was neglected and no one paid too much attention to him. He was thrown away because he didn't make the deal. Because of that conversation at Yale. As far as Kennedy was concerned, that was it. Stevenson wasn't going to get anything of value.

John Seigenthaler   I was sure that the president was sore when Adlai decided at the last minute to have his name put in nomination. But he thought it was a pathetic gesture. In my judgment, if Adlai Stevenson hadn't done that, he would have been secretary of state. Anything that Adlai Stevenson did at the convention was not to promote himself but to promote Lyndon Johnson. I never felt there was any deep-seated hostility. It's just that Adlai made a decision: He chose not to go with Jack Kennedy for president, and we are in a political world. Why in the world would he ever think of making him secretary of state when he wanted to be secretary of state? I mean, if he had wanted to be ambassador to the United Nations, they would have found some way to knock him down from that. It was the way the game was played. Adlai had no chips to offer at that point, no hand to play for himself, and so he had made himself vulnerable, which, according to Robert Kennedy, was exactly typecast.

When Adlai blistered the Russians at the UN during the missile crisis, he was so eloquent, so tough, what you got suddenly was the Adlai you identified with: tough, hard nosed, unyielding. This was Adlai acting as the Kennedys would have acted themselves. I remember one night walking with Bob in Georgetown, and we ran into Adlai and Marietta Tree [close friend and political associate of Stevenson's]. We chatted, and Bob was just effusive in his praise for Adlai's work during the crisis.

7

Sub-Cabinet-Level Appointments

Adam Yarmolinsky   We were not primarily involved in helping to select cabinet officers, but sub-cabinet and agency presidential appointments.

We collected lots of names. Actually I think that we were somewhat more reasonable in the quantity of names we collected. When the Carter administration came in and ran their talent hunt, they went overboard, so they had so many names they didn't know what to do with them.

People who sent in their own résumés didn't get much attention. In fact, the easiest way not to be selected was to be a candidate. If you were interested, you got somebody else to suggest you, which is the case in any important job that you really want.

Arthur Schlesinger, Jr.   Sarge Shriver and Ralph Dungan played very important roles in the recruiting process; they were both very imaginative. In foreign affairs Chester Bowles made excellent ambassadorial appointments—Galbraith in India and [Edwin O.] Reischauer in Japan, and a lot of the appointments in Africa were very imaginative.

Joseph Dolan   The thing that upset the early Kennedy people around the country the most was that, of the first one hundred jobs, about half of them went to Stevenson people. He apparently submitted some kind of list.

Adam Yarmolinsky   We discovered that if you want somebody, you don't worry about the problem of availability, and generally you ask people and they say yes. Now that was not true in later administrations. But there was something exciting about the New Frontier. On the other hand, there were occasions when we were enthusiastic about somebody, we brought him in to look at—and in the world of 1960 it was mostly him and not her—and we looked at him and said, "That was a big mistake." And we said to the person, "Thank you very much and glad to get to meet you."

Walt Rostow   Kennedy had different types of people on his staff because he had different jobs. If it weren't now a terrible thing to say, because of the feminists, he had a feminine sense of people—of how the world looked to them, and what they were good for, and what they shouldn't do. There was a hardness, but there was an empathy for other human beings. I think it was that, rather than the Harvard-MIT gang versus the Irish Mafia. We each did what we thought we were good at.

Adam Yarmolinsky   Louis Martin, good old Louis, was on the prowl for minority candidates. I remember he called me up once and said, "I've got just the person for the Defense Department. He's got a Ph.D." And I said, "Gee whiz."

At one point, Shriver, who had a number of friends in the business world that Wofford and Martin and I didn't have, asked Tom Watson of IBM to lend us somebody to advise us, because they do a lot of talent hunting. They lent us a young man named John Opal, who later became CEO of IBM, and John Opal came and sat with us for a day or two and watched what we were doing, discussed it with us, and at one point, said, "Maybe you could work out some formula based on how fast people have advanced in age versus salary in the private sphere," and finally he said, "I don't think I can help you; I think you're doing as good a job as you can. I don't think I can give you any advice that would improve your process."

HOW APPOINTEES LEARNED OF
THEIR SELECTION

Glenn Seaborg, chairman, Atomic Energy Commission (AEC)   I had a close association with McGeorge Bundy and Jerome [B.] Wiesner [special assistant to the president on science and technology] as a result of my service on Eisenhower's Science Advisory Committee. So when Kennedy was looking for a scientist to head up the Atomic Energy Commission, these people brought my name to his attention. He called me on January 9, 1961, and asked me if I would serve as AEC chairman. He said he wanted a strong candidate.

The first time I met him was in the reviewing stand in front of the White House on inaugural day. Bobby Kennedy spotted me. We talked, and then he brought his brother John over to meet me. John Kennedy's first words were that he would like me to find another scientist to fill a vacancy on the five-man AEC. He left the selection pretty much up to me.

Archibald Cox   I learned about my appointment from Anthony Lewis [correspondent, the *New York Times*]. There came to be a certain amount of strain between Ted Sorensen and myself; the senator knew there would be when he asked me to help during the summer. Toward the end of the campaign, he asked if I would be available to help during the transition. I was a bit disgruntled at the time and gave an answer that showed a lack of enthusiasm. My guess was that, at some point, I would be asked to go on the National Labor Relations Board, which I did not want to do. On the other hand, I had been writing speech material about public service, but I wasn't looking forward to having to do something. It never entered my head that he would ask me to be solicitor general. Well, Tony rang me up one day and said, "Have you been called yet to be solicitor general?" I said, "No. What are you talking about?" He said, "He will soon."

Well, the president called, but I was not in my office; I was driving across the snowswept roads of New Hampshire. I stopped at a pay phone and returned his call, and he did ask me. There wasn't any doubt in my mind that it was the best job for a lawyer there is—bar none. In fact, in some ways, it is even more fun than being on the Supreme Court.

James Tobin   Kennedy and I had been contemporaries at Harvard College. He was a year behind me. We first met at the Carlyle Hotel° in December 1960. At the time he was appointing people to his new administration, and he was sensitive to not appointing too many Harvard-associated people. Walter Heller, the incoming chairman of the council, was from Minnesota. That was very good from this point of view.

°On Madison Avenue, New York City.

I was now at Yale. When he saw me, he said, "Haven't I seen you before?" We hadn't been friends at college. He remembered my face.

August Heckscher Arthur Schlesinger called me up and said, "You are going to be getting a letter from Kennedy." The letter said he had been considering the need to establish in the White House an adviser on cultural affairs, so I went down to meet him.

It was on the front page of the *Times* that the president had appointed an adviser on the arts. A lot of people immediately asked my opinion on different matters. One of the first things I was asked was whether I thought the old State Department Building ought to be torn down. I was very rash, but I was also conscious of the fact that if I wasn't right on this, I wasn't going to be right on anything. I said, "I think it would be a crime not to preserve that building." Well, fortunately, that was the president's position too, but I hadn't checked with him.

Esther Peterson I handled the labor desk during the campaign out of the Washington headquarters. I remember, either Ralph Dungan or somebody else after he won, said "Esther, what do you want?" It never occurred to me that I was doing this for a job. I said, "Well, maybe the Women's Bureau," because I had always been concerned with the problems of the working woman getting the short end of the stick. I remember one of them saying, "Esther, wouldn't you like to go to the United Nations?" At that time my husband was very ill with cancer, and I didn't think that I wanted anything like that; I was very upset at that period. But, I do remember that little nibble, which always pleased me. At least my name was considered.

Roswell Gilpatric The first word I got of my impending appointment was from Clark Clifford, who was advising President Kennedy on the transition from the Eisenhower administration. He called me up—I remember very well—one Friday night in the middle of December and said, "You're going to get a call tomorrow from someone who wants to see you." It was very mysterious, but sure enough, the next morning at about five A.M., McNamara called me and we arranged a meeting in Baltimore the next day. That was the principal inkling I had that—in view of my work as the undersecretary of the Air Force during the Korean War, in the Truman administration—I might be considered in the Kennedy administration.

That was an interesting encounter: McNamara was exactly ten years younger than I am. He had burst upon the scene quite recently, when he was elevated to the presidency of the Ford Motor Company. I didn't know too much about him until his appointment as secretary of defense was announced about a week before I was approached, but we hit it off right away. I could see that his concept of the way the secretary of defense and his deputy would work made sense: We would share a number of responsibilities, and at the same time, he would delegate to me other activities which he felt could be carried on by one of us, rather than the two of us. He also indicated that he intended to treat me, in effect, as a junior partner and bring me to all meetings at the National Security Council, with the president, and so I was very favorably taken with his concept of how the Defense Department would be run. And after talking with my partners here, and my family, I told him the following Monday that I would be willing to serve.

Then I got a call the next morning from the president, who was in Florida with the vice president, and that was the beginning.

I picked up the phone and the president-elect was right on it—he was a great user of the telephone, as I found subsequently—and he said, "I understand that you're willing to come down to my administration and serve as McNamara's deputy. I'm delighted, and I'd like to have you talk to Lyndon Johnson and also to Pierre Salinger, about the wording of the announcement."

Johnson got on the phone and recommended to me that I immediately call on the senior leaders of the Armed Services Committee. I'd already expected to, but Johnson underscored the importance of doing it. And then Salinger got on the phone. He had a draft of the press release, which he asked me to correct, and I made some corrections. Then I wanted to add a sentence about my involvement with Nelson Rockefeller [governor of New York]—I was on a Rockefeller study group from '56 to '58, and I helped write up the section on National Security. Well, they weren't interested in putting anything about Rockefeller in the press release.

Adam Yarmolinsky   I was the person, I suppose, who worked most closely in helping McNamara to select the secretaries of the Army, Navy, Air Force, and the deputy secretary and the assistant secretaries, and then he asked me to come in as his special assistant, which I did.

After we had discussed a number of names, McNamara decided who he wanted. It wasn't for us to agree, but we discussed it. The decision was his; the recommendation was his; it was not a joint recommendation with us.

After McNamara had decided that Gilpatric was the person he wanted, he called the president–elect and said, "I'd like to pick Gilpatric; I'd like you to name Gilpatric as a presidential appointment." The president-elect said fine. There was an interesting story about the selection of John Connally as the secretary of the Navy. We came up with Connally's name because he had been in the Pentagon in a lower-level presidential appointment. We checked him out and he checked out well. McNamara said okay, and he called the president—at that point, the president-elect—and he said, "I found this John Connally, and from everything I know about him, I'd like to have him be secretary of the Navy." Kennedy happened to have Lyndon Johnson with him at the time, and this is the kind of joke that Kennedy really appreciated. He said, "John Connally? I think the vice president-elect knows him. Why don't I put him on the phone?" And, of course, everyone assumed that he was the vice president's person in the Defense Department and that he had been nominated by LBJ, but he wasn't. LBJ had nothing to do with his being named. I suppose if LBJ had said, He's a political enemy and don't do it, it is at least conceivable that the president would have had second thoughts about it. He might not have, or he might have done it anyway.

Phillips Talbot, assistant secretary of state for Near Eastern and South Asian affairs   I didn't even know how I came to the administration until later. The story seems to have been that there was some question as to who should be assistant secretary for the Near East and South Asia, because of the question of a person's prior position on the Near East. A decision was made to look for someone who really had broad experience with that area. Both Dean Rusk and Chet Bowles knew that I had been working mainly in the subcontinent for quite a few years, at that point, and they apparently recommended to the president that somebody with South Asian experience be appointed. I was in India for that year, so I knew nothing about this until a telegram came to the embassy in New Delhi, and I was asked by Ellsworth Bunker [U.S. diplomat] to come in to talk, and then was asked if I would agree to be considered for that post. I had not known President Kennedy. I had not been involved, particularly, in politics. My background had been very much, first, in newspapering and then on the university side, basically related to South and Southeast Asia, and not the Middle East, although I had been in the Middle East briefly as a reporter for the *Chicago Daily News* at the end of 1947, when the issue of Israel's emergence was on the griddle.

Robert Manning   I joined the administration in the spring of 1962. I got a call from Ralph Dungan, who asked if I would be interested in joining the administration. I was then Sunday editor of the *New York Herald Tribune,* which was like taking care of some of the deck chairs on the *Titanic.* The administration was looking for someone who would coordinate better between the State Department and the White House in the information function, which Kennedy—particularly in foreign affairs—took very seriously.

After Dungan and I talked, he suggested that I go over and talk to Secretary Rusk. Rusk had been part of a group that misled me years before on U.S. policy having to do with the partition of Palestine to create the State of Israel, so there was something between us. I am not sure he remembered this, but I did. I told him that I knew people in diplomacy were very leery of publicity, but at the same time, I was being asked to be a spokesman, and I asked what kind of access I would have. He said, "Would you be prepared to lie for your country?" I said, "I don't think that is necessary, Mr. Secretary; one can always say 'No comment,' or say nothing. You don't have to lie." After a long conversation, I left feeling he would play fairly. I also left feeling I would have to keep repeating my comments on access.

William Sullivan   One or two of our ambassadors were not of high quality. The president designated someone to Switzerland, and the Swiss rather stuffily turned him down, so he said, "Get me the worst dog you can get." They sent an awful one out there, but the Swiss couldn't do it twice.

Loy Henderson was in charge of administration in the Department of State. Loy had established a policy that no one could be a career minister and, ergo, could not be appointed as an ambassador from the career service until he was fifty years old. The president, being forty-three, thought that was ridiculous. I think I was about thirty-nine at the time, and he wanted me to go as ambassador to Taipei. I said, "That would be an insult to the Generalissimo [Chiang Kai-shek]." He was in his seventies, and I was pretty junior. The president said, "All right. Find a post you feel you can take, and talk it over with Ralph Dungan." So I went to Ralph, and we agreed on the Dominican Republic. At this stage I was working for Ave [Harriman], so I told him, and he said, "What a banana republic! You're wasting your time. I'll take care of that. I'll tell the president not to do this."

Lucius Battle, assistant secretary of state for educational and cultural affairs   Ball felt I was not being used adequately, and he offered me several jobs that I just didn't want to take, including the ambassadorship to Morocco. I said, "I don't think that's my post." You're not ever supposed to turn down an ambassadorship. I said, "My French isn't very good. I've just gotten to town and I like it in town. I don't really want to go." Then I was offered the job of deputy secretary for management, and I said, "I have had enough of that sort of thing. I really don't want it. I would rather have the cultural post." He was surprised that I wanted the cultural job, but I thought it was an exciting time to do it. I had been very interested in education and cultural things for years, and it was a natural move for me, and so I spent the next couple of years in that job, and was there when the assassination of President Kennedy occurred.

Norbert Schlei   I came into the administration on the recommendation of Nick Katzenbach. He had been a professor of mine at Yale Law School. One day, I picked up the phone and he was on the line and he asked me if I would take his job [assistant attorney general, Office of Legal Counsel] if he could get it for me. The last thing I was looking for was a new job.

I went to Washington the following week and met Robert Kennedy for the first time. When I came back, I did not think I would get the job because he was very concerned about my youth; I was thirty-two at the time. But in June Katzenbach called me and said, "The president is all ready to go. Come to work."

Bernard Boutin   Two days after the election, I was back in my own business office, and my secretary started waving her arms, saying, "Mr. Boutin, Mr. Boutin. It's the senator on the phone!" So I picked up the phone and it was Kennedy—no secretary—he had dialed right through, direct. He said, "Bernie, what are you doing?" I answered, "I am trying, after all these years, to make some sense out of my own business and get things in order." He said, "No. Sell it. I want you to come to Washington with me." I was flabbergasted.

I remember going home and telling my wife about the call and saying, "Well, we are going to Washington." I didn't know what for or doing what. Again, I had such confidence in him. In December I learned that I was going to be deputy administrator of GSA. It wasn't very reassuring, because the week before, Drew Pearson had characterized GSA as the biggest mess in Washington. I started work the afternoon of the inauguration.

Burke Marshall   Mine wasn't a very productive interview. Robert Kennedy was very intense and somewhat intimidating to someone meeting him for the first time. He knew I was an antitrust lawyer. Some of my friends suggested that I was being interviewed for the Civil Rights Division; he was looking for someone who had a reputation as a good lawyer, not one who was identified with the movement; it was very young in 1961. He called me a couple of days later and asked, "Do you want the job?" To a lawyer at that time, civil rights was very much on the legal—the constitutional—agenda.

Angier Biddle Duke   The president-elect called me after the election and before the inauguration. We had a couple of meetings and at the first one, he asked, "Would you become chief of protocol?" I took a deep breath. I had been doing a lot of work for Bob Kennedy in Central America and I had been chief of what we call intergroup relations—that was the old Nationalities Division of the Democratic State Committee in New York—and I was really bucking for an embassy in Latin America. The president-elect called and asked me to be chief of protocol, and I stumbled around on that: I didn't say no, and I didn't say yes, but I wasn't enthusiastic, and he said, "Think it over."

On the second call, he said, "How do you feel about it?" and I said, "I'm a little ..." He said, "What's wrong with it anyway?" and I said, "Well, the name is wrong." He said, "Well, go and talk to Dean Rusk and see what you can come up with. But I want to tell you something else: I have an idea about that job. I think you could be very useful because you've been a foreign service officer; you've been stationed abroad. After each visit, you could give me a memorandum on anything substantive that was discussed with you or with others and you could give me an evaluation of character, summations, observations on personalities and characters which could be very helpful to me, and I would like to con-

sider that job as an extension of the White House Oval Office and relationship with the world leaders."

Well, that was pretty gratifying, but I went off to lunch with Dean
Rusk and we spent most of the lunch fooling around with how you could
call this job something else. It ranks with assistant secretary of state, so if
it is assistant secretary of state, why not call it that? we said. Well, assistant secretary of state for what? Assistant secretary of state for diplomatic affairs? We tried that. Assistant secretary of state for ceremonial
affairs? We came up with one thing that was reassuring to me—chief of
protocol with the rank of ambassador. That had never been part of the
title. When Rusk and I came up with that, I got word back to Kennedy
that we had worked out an arrangement, so that was it.

George McGovern   He called me up just three or four days after the
election. He was with his father at their home in Palm Beach, and he
said, "George, I think I cost you that race in South Dakota." I cut him off
at that point. I said, "I don't think that's true, Mr. President; if I had won,
I wouldn't have given you credit." He then asked me to come and see
him, which was good news to me because it was quite clear he was thinking of some sort of appointment. I went after the agriculture job in the
cabinet. I talked to Bobby about it, and he said that it was realistic to try
for it, so I did. I think it narrowed down to a choice between me and
Governor Freeman of Minnesota. But I was delighted when he turned
to the Food for Peace appointment, because it actually had more sex
appeal than being secretary of agriculture.

He wanted Food for Peace to be an interdepartmental program; he
didn't want to give it entirely to the department of agriculture, or to state,
or to treasury. He thought that it cut across departmental lines, which it
did, so he felt it was better to put it at the presidential level. I was actually
in the Executive Office of the President, right across the street from the
White House. I functioned there for about a year and a half. What the
president did, in effect, was to put Food for Peace somewhat on the level
of the Peace Corps, as a kind of quasi-independent agency.

My view of Food for Peace—which was supported by President
Kennedy—was that instead of seeing it as a kind of surplus disposal
operation where you get rid of unwanted, burdensome surpluses, you
instead shift the emphasis to seeing this as an enormous U.S. resource
that no other country had, and that we had a moral obligation—and a

political opportunity—to use it as a constructive tool of American foreign policy, so that's where the shift came. Suddenly, instead of a troublesome burden, that we had to figure out some way to unload food surpluses, it became an asset to utilize with intelligence. We expanded the uses of it; we found ways of using it to pay the wages of people working on roads and water systems and housing abroad. They got part of their pay in the form of wheat, cornmeal, milk powder, flour. We expanded the school lunch programs overseas in the same pattern as they were structured in this country. The program expanded our foreign policy interests, but we never used it as a club.

Sargent Shriver   One night the phone rang at my house in Chicago, and it was Jack. He spoke to my wife for a few moments. Then I got on and he said, "Sarge, I want you to come down to Washington and run the Peace Corps."

We then had a lengthy conversation—at least, lengthy for him—and I told him that I was very happy in Chicago, but he kept insisting that I come, and if the president of the United States asks you to do something, you have to respond, so I told him that I would help him get the organization started.

Adam Yarmolinsky   I remember doing a panel discussion session on the talent hunt, and I described the process, and somebody, not unkindly, who was commenting, said, "You ended up with nine out of ten graduates of Ivy League colleges and New England boarding schools." And Christ, we did. It was the eastern establishment, only slightly leavened. Because it was an old boy network. If you look at it now, when Lyndon Johnson became president, you saw a lot of Texans; and when Jimmy Carter became president, you saw a lot of Georgians; and when Richard Nixon and Ronald Reagan were president, there were a lot of Californians. This was an even wider net, but it was a tighter net too.

William Sullivan   Half of Cambridge came down. There was much more of a sense of ideas, which had been repressed, just welling up in an effort to try to get to the president. There was a feeling that the president had an open mind and would not rigidly lock himself into preconceived ideas, but was always willing to listen to something else.

Adam Yarmolinsky   When Secretary Ribicoff was designated, and we had a meeting with him, we had a chart with all the key positions—we had collected two or three names for each position, and he looked at the chart and said, "I want this one, this one, and this one, and the rest you can put in stiffs." And we said, "Senator, that's not the way we do things around here. You can have anybody you want, and we're here to help you and suggest names to you." So that was the process.

PRESIDENT KENNEDY AND THE STAFF

William Smith   Kennedy really changed the nature of how the White House staff functioned. Until then staff had been primarily involved in organizing things for discussion by the president, as formulated in the departments. Under Kennedy the White House staff began to take a much larger role in initiating action, so they became the center for a lot of ideas, and for asking other agencies to do things, rather than being responsive. This allowed them to get into a lot more things than some less competent people would have wanted to do or could have done.

Lucius Battle   There's no confirmation process of White House staff. They have such authority as the president wishes to give them, but only in the president's name. There's no such thing as the White House; it's the president of the United States, period. And that was a lesson that the White House staff didn't really get.

Arthur Schlesinger, Jr.   We were all attracted to Kennedy; we all got along very well together. I still see Ted Sorensen and Mac Bundy all the time in New York. It was a very congenial staff. This great expansion of the White House staff came under Nixon. Our staff was small. Kennedy used the Roosevelt model. Kennedy was accessible to the staff. I can't believe it when I read how so-called presidential assistants have to make appointments to see the president weeks in advance.

Adam Yarmolinsky   The appointees proved excellent. And a lot of people stayed on through the Johnson administration. There was a good cabinet and then a first-rate group of people. There were a few bad actors.

8

President Kennedy's Administrative Style

President Kennedy's keen interest in the workings of government, and specifically of the presidency, were in part responsible for his unorthodox approach to his office. He created an executive staff considerably smaller than President Eisenhower's, and smaller still than the White House staffs of the 1970s and 1980s.

In terms of key personnel, the Kennedy White House consisted of disparate elements, including the so-called Boston Irish Mafia, former Senate aides, and intellectuals. In similar fashion, the cabinet consisted of individuals who had achieved success in a varied area of disciplines, including elective politics, business, and diplomacy.

Ralph Dungan   The staff handled a lot of things that he never even knew happened. I always likened myself to the maid that must have picked up his towel in the bathroom; he didn't attend to detail that he didn't need to. He would never plan how the White House staff was to be structured. I remember, just after we were sworn in, O'Donnell turns to me and says, "What do we do now?" It was awful.

Edward McDermott   Once, when I expressed some reservation about my ability to supervise, he said to me, "I have confidence that you can do the job; that is why I appointed you. I want you to make every decision you can make, and I will support you. If you think it is a decision the president must make, then you come to me and we will make it." Now some of the people he told that to misinterpreted the comment and used it as an effort to have more frequent access to the president than they would otherwise have. Some of these people were doing this so they could stand around at Washington cocktail parties talking about having met with the president this afternoon. Those people who abused the right of access were the first to leave the Kennedy administration.

Najeeb Halaby   He was a man who trusted his lieutenants and let them have their head until they goofed up. At that time the Federal Aviation Administration reported directly to the president. One of the things I had learned from previous government experience was to make sure I had the opportunity to see the president. He promised to see me whenever I thought it was essential. Then I conned him into letting me become a member of the White House mess. I would see his staff there frequently. I don't think we've since had as intelligent and devoted and unified a group of people as those so-called best and brightest. He not only wanted intelligent people around him but cherished and used them. I think he found them stimulating. Other presidents would have been terrified by people brighter than they were.

Eisenhower as commander in chief operated through some key generals around him and his chief of staff. It was a remote kind of trickle-down operation. I was deputy assistant secretary of defense during his administration, but I didn't see the president more than three times a year, and usually on some very narrow issues. I don't think that President Eisenhower did his homework the way Kennedy did. When you went in to see Kennedy, he would know the right questions to ask. It was kind of a pompousness versus a youthful, dynamic, "it-can-be-done" personality.

Donald Wilson   In our broadcasting on the Voice of America, Murrow was absolutely adamant that all news broadcasts be equivalent to American news broadcasts. They would tell the news as it was, no matter what it said about the United States, which meant, in those days, a lot of news about terrible race problems in the South. Kennedy was very supportive of the agency. Murrow sat on the National Security Council, and the agency was given a prominence it had not had before.

Robert Manning   Kennedy wanted an information operation he could be proud of—one that was forthcoming. The president's interest was what really made the job work. He would call up in the middle of the night, or in the early morning, asking, "What tone of voice are you going to use on Berlin today? I don't want any of that cold war tone."

Adlai Stevenson III   The genesis of the New Frontier was the campaign of 1956. There were some new ideas, like the Peace Corps, of which my father had some skepticism, but most of the ideas which came out of that campaign and were the product of the intellectuals, their articulation was the work of my father in the election carried over. It was a way for them to continue what they wanted to do, to serve the country, with their ideas implemented.

Ralph Yarborough   Kennedy said he was going to have equal rights for women. Two or three years later, the women's organizations said that it had no effect on wages. He said, "That doesn't apply to wages; that applies to civil rights, hotels and things," and Kennedy got on his high horse—when he wanted to pass something, he would pass it—and got a bill passed in '63 providing that equal rights for women meant equal wages for equal work.

There weren't that many women with the preliminary training, in my opinion, to serve in the administration, at that time. I don't think that Kennedy was deliberately passing them by; I think he was looking for the most experienced people.

Bradford Morse   I can't imagine John Kennedy having any great devotion to having a woman in his inner circle. I think it went back to the family tradition—the relationship between his mother and his father.

U. Alexis Johnson, deputy undersecretary of state for political affairs   One of Kennedy's problems was that he came to the presidency without any real experience in the executive branch. He came from an environment in which he'd get people assembled. A number of people around him would hold a seminar on a problem, exploring all different points of view. McNamara and Rusk were averse to this. Both of them, particularly Dean Rusk, were reluctant to debate policy in front of people who didn't have responsibility for it.

Ben Bradlee There was this tiny little Irish Mafia walking around the White House. Utilization of the Irish Mafia and the eastern establishment figures was part of the dichotomy that was the key to understanding John Kennedy. I always felt that he was half this urbane, charming intellectual and half this little street mick whose dad made a lot of money. Bobby was even more like that; if you shut your eyes, you could see Bobby with his shirttails out, the snot coming down his nose, just having been beaten up or having beaten someone up. You didn't see so much of that in Jack, but he loved those Irish stories of his Irish roots. He felt very comfortable with the Irish crowd, because they were so devoted to him. It went all through his life: He would say, in one breath, you haven't really survived unless you've run for office, and the other side of that coin was that it really wasn't very dignified.

Donald Wilson I suspect that the Kennedys felt that an administration made up only of brains and intellectuals would be a little too far removed from the people, and from the political side of things, so they built a balance in there with the Irish Mafia. Maybe that is giving them too much credit; maybe they owed a lot of jobs to these people from Massachusetts. But the Kennedys were attracted to the Galbraiths and the Schlesingers—the intellectuals. I personally found them much more attractive people than the Irish Mafia. I had my troubles with Kenny O'Donnell. Who didn't? He was a tough guy; a real tough cookie.

In retrospect this is not a bad combination, because the two groups kind of played off against each other and gave the president two very distinct points of view—neither of which became dominant. God knows, if that administration had been dominated by the Irish Mafia, I think it would have been terrible. On the other hand, I think it would have been ineffective if you were going too much with the professors and the intellectual side.

Thomas Mann, assistant secretary of state for inter-American affairs; ambassador to Mexico The people around Kennedy were full-time publicists. They advertised him as a commodity—that everything in the New Frontier was new, and that nothing had ever been done before. I just think this is amusing.

Lee White Muggsy O'Leary, the driver, was from the Capitol police force. You had to hope nobody, but nobody, ever needed him to help them. But Muggsy was just a good old guy. And the president, when he was a senator, liked Muggsy. He liked him when he was president, because he was a good guy. Muggsy didn't want anything, and the president was not suspicious of Muggsy's motives—or Dave Powers's [David F. Powers, White House special assistant] either. It's nice to have people like that around; it lifts your spirits. That's what Dave did—and did it handsomely. He swam with the president frequently. Everyone loved Dave. You couldn't help but love him. He knew every statistic about the Boston Red Sox and had a rich store of stories; you just couldn't help but like the guy. But he was no adviser.

Adam Yarmolinsky   The Kenny O'Donnells, Dick Donahue [White House aide], and Larry O'Brien were not policymakers. They solved political problems. They were doers. I don't mean to suggest they were errand runners. They were powerful and effective and very knowledgeable. But they were not policymakers.

Philip Kaiser   I brought in the president of Mauritania to see Kennedy. He had been dying to meet Kennedy. This was about two weeks before the assassination. The meeting was scheduled for one hour, but it lasted for two hours. When I walked out of the president's office, I met Kenny O'Donnell, who had a delegation from Illinois waiting to see the president. He said to me, "There aren't any votes in Mauritania."

Louis Martin   Once Arthur Goldberg called O'Donnell's office. The secretary told Kenny he was on the phone. Kenny asked what he wanted. The secretary said he wanted an appointment with the president. Kenny answered that he had seen the president for an hour a few days earlier and told him no and to go to hell. Kenny was a rough character and threw his weight around. Once he got mad at Pierre Salinger; the press briefings are piped in so the president and staff can hear the briefing. Well, Pierre made some statement Kenny didn't like. Kenny called him in and said, "Listen, you son of a bitch, I'll put you out on Connecticut Avenue with a tin cup." You never heard language like that spoken by these guys from Boston. They were terrible—you talk about street language.

Ralph Dungan   I straddled all the groups in the White House—the Bundy group, for example, which was egghead, Republican, Harvard.

They had a very difficult time initially. Later O'Donnell—who was really the key guy—found it much easier to deal with Mac. But in the initial stages—particularly after the Bay of Pigs—he was really suspect to those who considered themselves true blue and loyal sons of the sod and JFK's great supporters. Those relationships were difficult to work out, and I don't think they [the Irish Mafia] would have ever completely cottoned to Stevenson.

I often use the analogy of the spoke and the wheel—you have the hub and all those spokes; we are the spokes—to describe the functioning of the Kennedy White House. Thus, essentially, anybody who had a significant responsibility was in a direct relationship with the president. There was very little of the subordination and hierarchy that you have had in recent years; a lot of people had direct access to President Kennedy.

Adam Yarmolinsky I was the minister without portfolio. I did all the things that didn't fall clearly into anyone's domain. I did write speeches for McNamara, although he delivered so few speeches that that was a very small part of my job. But at various times I had the responsibility for civil defense and civil rights. There were a number of military-political crises in which I drafted papers. I was deeply involved in the Skybolt crisis,* the steel price rise, the Studebaker contract, the TFX,† and the congressional backlash against that contract award. I had a lawyer who worked in my back office for months drafting a brief, in effect explaining why the decision had been made the way it was. This was a decision in which Lyndon Johnson had no role, although it went to a Texas, rather than a Seattle, Washington, contractor.

David Bell The president was not well served in his relationship with Congress. He had a couple of people who had worked for the War and Navy departments, and they kind of walked around the Hill and kept track of how things were going up there, but they were not really competent to advise on substance. Kennedy's staff for congressional relation-

---

*The Skybolt crisis resulted from the Kennedy administration's decision to cancel an agreement entered into in 1960 by President Eisenhower and British Prime Minister Harold Macmillan, to provide the Skybolt missile, a bomber-launched two-stage missile, to Great Britain.

†A controversy over the Defense Department's decision to give the General Dynamics Corporation, rather than the Boeing Company, a contract to build a new fighter plane, the Tactical Fighter Experimental (TFX).

ships—headed by Larry O'Brien, and with Dick Donahue and several other excellent people, they were mostly Irish and they were first-class people—were very able. They were not simply political messenger boys to run back and forth to the Congress.

Gerald Ford   He or his staff didn't conduct the best relations with Congress. They were sort of disorganized. He could charm the Congress, but he didn't work it. Lyndon really knew how to manipulate the Congress. Jack's focus was different. And it was true when he was in the House and in the Senate. I guess it's hard to change.

Maurine Neuberger   Kennedy was building goodwill in the Congress, especially with the Southerners. He had to overcome some of the opposition to the Catholicism. I think Johnson was able to follow through because of the groundwork that had been laid. I didn't find Congress hostile to Kennedy. But it took a long time for Senator Russell and others to come around.

Frank Moss   He had difficulty in getting his legislative program through, largely because of lack of leadership in the Congress. Mike Mansfield [D., Mont.], who took over as majority leader of the Senate, was more of an umpire than an active, pushing man. Rayburn was sick; he had lost his edge in the House.

Sam Yorty   I think Kennedy's relationship with Congress was pretty good, because he had such a good press, and the Congress have their fingers up to see which way the wind's blowing. They're not a very bright bunch, taken as a whole. There are a lot of good congressmen, but there are a lot of 'em who shouldn't be there, and they don't know what's going on.

August Heckscher   I remember one day at lunch in the White House mess—Kennedy had been defeated on an issue in Congress—and somebody turning to me and saying, "Why the devil are you the only one ever getting good publicity for this administration?"

Richard Bissell, deputy director of plans, CIA   On the whole I was comfortable with his decision-making process. I was a little concerned that decisions weren't written down and their terms defined with care; I feel that a better record of the process should have been kept.

Orville Freeman   He didn't use the cabinet very well. Neither did Lyndon Johnson. He didn't really get into basic issues where he drew on his people and tried to call on them as part of the overall decision-making process. It was more a question of telling what he was doing and saying, and making reports to others, outside of the Cuban missile crisis, when he did share and really discuss and call on some of the cabinet.

Having been on quite a number of boards over the years, I knew that to really use a board effectively is hard work; it takes quite a bit of preparation, and he didn't do a particularly good job of using the cabinet. But he was very responsive in the sense that when you were up to doing something, he didn't meddle with it. He knew what you were doing and he followed it closely, and he was very alert. This was quite a difference from working with Lyndon Johnson, because when you were up on the Hill doing something you were supposed to do, all of a sudden you found out the president was up there changing it and didn't get around to telling you. Well, nothing like that happened under Kennedy.

Roswell Gilpatric   Many times McNamara and I saw him together. There were also a number of times that he would deal directly with me, as he did with other people who were subordinate to cabinet rank, and we developed a very good rapport. I was with him on a number of trips, particularly in Florida, and I saw him socially a good deal, because I had formed a friendship with his wife and I used to go over to small dinners at the White House.

He was always very inquisitive; he always wanted to learn more about whatever subject interested him. In my case, the subjects that came up more frequently were politics and the business community. I had been a business lawyer all my career, a corporate and financial lawyer, and I knew a number of people Kennedy had some problems with, including Roger Blough, the head of the U.S. Steel Corporation; he was a classmate of mine, a friend of mine at Yale Law School. So when they had the clash over the steel price increase, Kennedy brought me into that. He had never really known what I would call a typical businessman. His father certainly wasn't typical, so he was always asking me: "Why do businesspeople do this? What are their choices?"

And he constantly spoke about Nelson Rockefeller. They obviously had much in common: They both came from wealthy families; they both were moderates in their political spheres; they both loved the girls; and they were both very ambitious, and it was my clear impression that Kennedy expected that in the 1964 election he would be running against Nelson Rockefeller, whom I had quite a close tie to: I was on Nelson Rockefeller's State Defense Commission; I was chairman of the Democrats for Rockefeller when he ran against Harriman in 1958.

He was also giving me an education in politics—practical politics. He would say, "Now, Ros, you spend as much time as you can with these senators because they're very important. I know they happen to like gin rummy, and why don't you take them on," implying that I should lose some money, which I did. He had that sense of the importance of political ties. He was constantly urging me to cultivate an association with the principals, not just the individual congressmen themselves, but also with their staffs. And he urged me to cover the staff while McNamara was covering the chairmen. It was very good advice. We in fact worked both sides of the street. If Lyndon Johnson was there, we went over the whole gamut of characters on the Republican side or the Democratic side.

David Bell   The Kennedy style, which was just like Truman's—I attributed it to their military training—was to assign a staff job. Then you went away and did it, and brought it back when it was finished. It was a very compatible, comfortable, happy way of relating. Lyndon Johnson— who, of course, came out of a very different background and learned his management style up on the Hill—would give you a job to do; you'd go to do it; and half an hour later, he'd be on the phone, wanting to know how much you had done, and he'd have six more ideas about who you ought to talk to and what you ought to say, and "be sure not to do this; be sure to do that." He smothered you; he was on your back all the time. He would have loved to do it himself, if he'd had the time.

The first major meeting with the president-elect on substance that I was involved in took place in Palm Beach in December 1960. Sorensen, Elmer Staats [comptroller general], and I took along a long list of issues that were going to arise, and indications of whether they would involve legislative, or other action, as well as recommendations as to how he should deal with them. Douglas Dillon was also there. The meeting went on for hours. The president was laying out a system for getting information. On some things he wanted the Budget Bureau to prepare a paper; on others he wanted Sorensen or someone else to prepare a paper.

Esther Peterson　He was a politician. You made a case, he would accept it. That's one thing that I liked about him. And he could ask questions: "The people who were opposing—how strong are they?"

Phillips Talbot　He had this extraordinary ability of having a telephone conversation, of reading a newspaper and listening to some lackey in front of his desk, all at the same time.

I remember being in the White House one day, as we all so often were, trying to figure out some angle. So I led off with what I thought would be a plan that could break through the stalemate. And the president looked at me and said, "Phil, that's a very good plan indeed." But before I began to preen, he said, "There's only one problem," and I said, "Yes, Mr. President?" He said, "You never had to stand for election." So that ended the conversation.

Archibald Cox　In dealing with staff, Kennedy was very aware of Roosevelt's style. I complained once and asked for a clearer definition, and he said, There is no clearer definition. I assume that he thought that to some extent, friction and interplay are creative.

Walt Rostow　He had exactly the obverse of a Franklin Roosevelt approach of how to get things done. He came in and found that the Congress elected in 1960 was actually more conservative than the one it succeeded, so the scope for acting in the directions he wanted to move was limited. On civil rights everybody urged him initially: "Use the executive; don't try to get it through Congress, because it will obstruct everything you want to do." That was the advice from liberals, until Bull Connor [T. Eugene ("Bull") Connor, commissioner of public safety, Birmingham, Ala.] opened things up for him. The crisis in 1963 permitted action. His idea was: "I will incrementally educate people about Medicare and other issues. Then I will get elected with a bigger majority in 1964, and then I will have freedom to do these things."

Paul Samuelson　This was a president as different from Eisenhower and Reagan as you can imagine. Eisenhower and Reagan really did not know what was going on in most parts of their own house, most of the time. Through Bobby and Sorensen and Heller and Dillon, the president was informed on everything and was making White House judgments.

Phillips Talbot   The president was very direct in his communications, and before too long—he'd obviously had my briefings on this issue or that issue—he would telephone if something came up and say, "Phil, what is all this about?"—whatever it might be. I found that, immediately after responding, I had to get through to the secretary's office to tell him what question I had been asked and what I had replied, so if the president next called Dean Rusk, the secretary would know something of the prior conversation. It was a style very different from Lyndon Johnson's.

Johnson worked through the secretary and undersecretaries. He would talk with them and they would generate the response.

Richard Helms   The president received regular material from the agency in different forms. He received a daily digest—I forget what it was called in those days. He received all kinds of material that flowed through the hands of McGeorge Bundy, Dean Rusk, and others, but I don't know whether he had specific briefings. I was not working in that part of the agency in those days. The briefings were done on the intelligence side. I was on the operations side.

Ray Cline   I met Kennedy a number of times in the summer of 1962. One of the things he always said, especially at formal meetings of the National Security Council—I always sat in the back row—was "Well, what have we got to decide today?" Presidents never want to make up their minds on anything. Occasionally that is a mistake. But mostly, it's probably wise, politically, to keep decisions at arm's length. Most of the council members didn't ever press him to do anything, and I think that is why Kennedy was sometimes ill served.

Angier Biddle Duke   Now one of the things the president really despised was when someone would say, "Go ahead, Mr. President," and then go outside the meeting room and say, "I had my doubts all along about that policy." And Chester Bowles was one of these persons. Bowles had given the president the "yes" treatment on the Bay of Pigs, but afterward he leaked to the press that he had been against the operation all along.

The president called me and said, "I want to get rid of this guy, and I want you to give him the best ceremonial farewell. We've got to figure out some way." Well, Rusk thought up a job for Bowles, he decided to make him ambassador-at-large to the developing countries. Well, we always swore in this type of ambassador at the State Department, so I said, "We will have a ceremony that will make him look great. We will have it at the White House, in the Blue Room or in the Oval Office. We'll have the diplomatic corps and we'll decorate the room with the flags of the nations to which he's accredited." "Oh," the president said, "that sounds great. We'll do all that." So anyway, that's what happened to Chester Bowles. We kicked him out with a flourish.

Pierre Salinger   The announcement that Bowles was leaving was made at midnight in Hyannis Port so that it wouldn't attract any front-page story the next day.

A DAY IN THE WHITE HOUSE

Ralph Dungan   The president would read his intelligence briefing in the morning, and if there was nothing extraordinary that would have required waking him in the night, he probably would have a meeting with Sorensen, most likely on the substance of legislation or on a speech Sorensen was working on. The president would probably have met earlier with Bundy. Then there would be a Rose Garden group of one sort or another. A group of congressional leaders might come in. Then there would be lunch with Jackie, followed by a swim in the pool—oftentimes, Dave Powers would join him. Sometimes the president would stay in the private quarters for a bit, reading, or whatever he did. Then he would come back to the office and work until seven-thirty or eight, or later sometimes.

Lee White   Kennedy, when he left at seven or seven-thirty P.M., went home. If some crisis would come, he'd be there, but he could cut that off. He had a group of friends he felt comfortable with in a social sense.

Marcus Raskin   The word would come down that the president was going to make a speech on a particular subject and he was looking for ideas, and it would come to my desk. I wrote a memorandum for a speech, saying that the major problems of the time were moral and political; they were not administrative and technocratic. If you go back and read the speech, you will see that it says the major problems of our time are technical; they are not political. I don't know how that transformation occurred, but occur it did.

Lee White   We would be involved in going over a proposed special message to Congress. Our way was to commit to send a presidential message on various programmatic areas. One of them might be on natural resources. We had not discussed the environmental issue in the same sense that it's identified today, although—to his credit—Senator Gaylord Nelson, of Wisconsin, came and pounded me on the head, explaining how we were missing the greatest damn bet ever for politicians. He had ridden that wave in Wisconsin as governor and then as senator. Anyhow, we had a message on natural resources; we had one on housing; we had one on civil rights; we had one on foreign economic assistance; we had one on military activity—and every other damn thing in the world. It was in the process of preparing those messages for the president that an awful lot of the program was refined, developed, and reformed.

Without trying to be overly modest, no human being could have done all of those things well. We did some of them probably very well, some fairly well, and some of them half-assed, but that is the way we were functioning then. We relied heavily on the Bureau of the Budget, now the Office of Management and Budget; we relied heavily on the departments and agencies. One break that Kennedy did have over some of his predecessors and successors was that virtually everyone who worked for him in the White House had worked for him before, so that he knew them and they knew him, and that did facilitate things quite a bit. That exercise of putting together a special message on housing, for example, would pull in all the people who were involved, and pull in the Council of Economic Advisers, who, under Walter Heller, played a very significant role.

Heller concluded that President Kennedy was one of the better students and that he had an excellent mind. He was very quick, and a plodder like me, who likes to go from A to B to C to D to E, was a little bit discomfited. His mind worked that way.

Another part of the day would be devoted to phone calls from the Hill, or other places in the executive branch. People outside have quite a bit of haziness about how the White House functions. I could call some-body up in a department or agency and ask and request something and they didn't know whether I had come out of the president's office with a special mandate, or whether, in a conversation with one of my col-leagues, I'd decided to do something, or whether my grandma in Omaha had made a request.

I remember going home and telling my wife the first day I was there, "It's tough to understand, but suddenly everyone in the world is seeking my opinion." I wondered if it worked in reverse when you left, and I can tell you now that it does. There were an awful lot of people who wanted to get "word" from the White House. Most of them could not get through to the president. Most of them could not get through to some of the other assistants. But if they got ahold of me, or somebody else, then we were their window into that apparatus.

Part of the day would be spent working with Larry O'Brien and his group. Once a piece of legislation was formulated, or even a special mes-sage was formulated, we had to see if it would sail, so there was what was called "touching base." There is no better definition of touching base than touching base. It means informing somebody of what you plan to do, without asking for their comment. And if they wanted to give you their comment or give somebody else's comment, they could, and they then couldn't say they hadn't been given the opportunity to. We did a hell of a lot of touching base and, initially, the Democratic Committee chairman had a hell of a time realizing that there was now a Democratic administration: They had all served while Eisenhower was president, and they were used to beating up on the administration. It was so much more fun that they forgot we were us, and not them.

One of the benefits of the staff was that I could get quite a bit of work done just by walking into the men's room and standing next to Mike Mantos, who was Larry O'Brien's liaison with the Senate.

William Smith   General Taylor had a very sumptuous office on the third floor of the Executive Office Building. The rest of his staff had very modest, bare, and perfectly adequate offices down the hall. When I came in, the Southeast Asia Committees were beginning to form, and the question of reorganizing the army was taking some of General Tay-lor's time. But when I first got there, I certainly didn't walk into a buzz saw of excitement, where everyone was working twenty-four hours a day.

We used to work fourteen to sixteen hours, but that was considered normal. But with the Berlin crisis in the middle of August, things picked up quite a bit.

General Taylor's duties were to watch what was happening in the Department of Defense, and particularly the Joint Chiefs of Staff. He got involved in some reorganizations that the Army was interested in, but events focused his attention, because in April of 1961, there was trouble in Southeast Asia and in Laos, and the president began to seek some advice on what to do in the region.

At the time of the Laos situation, the president asked the Department of Defense what we should do. He did not only want the views of the Joint Chiefs, he wanted the views of the Secretaries of Defense, of each of the service secretaries and each member of the Joint Chiefs. He got nine different answers, and he decided, "I have to have something better than this." General Taylor wasn't there very long before he and Walt Rostow made that first trip to Southeast Asia. Then, in mid-August, the Berlin Wall went up, and that also shaped what General Taylor would become involved with.

Another item for his activity was counterinsurgency. There was a great interest in this, and Taylor was put in charge of a group looking at that subject from the White House point of view. Then there were clandestine, or special, operations, and there was a group looking at those activities, and Taylor had a role in that.

Lee White Assignments and my own activities would shift with whatever was important. To me it was very interesting to be able to read in the newspaper either at home or on the way in, to try to figure out what I was going to work on that day. A lot of it depended on just what was going on. We were both reactive in the sense that external events created things that you had to respond to, and to some extent we were sort of pro-active, in that there was a Kennedy program; there were things he wanted to do, partly because he had committed himself in the campaign, and mostly because, Why does an individual run for that office except to accomplish things? There are people who think you run for office because it's there; it's a lot of fun. There's a classic joke about a fellow who wanted to be governor in the worst way, and it turns out he was. Kennedy did have some things he wanted to focus on, and I believe that most of them were in the area of foreign affairs, foreign activities.

The equivalent of what is now the Domestic Affairs Council was the Office of Special Counsel, in which Ted Sorensen was the special counsel and obviously had a very unique and special relationship with President Kennedy. Initially, Myer Feldman and I and Dick Goodwin [Richard N. Goodwin, assistant special counsel to the president] constituted that whole office, and when you realize today that they've got committees and groups—and God, there's got to be thirty-five to forty people who can honestly say that they are in the White House Domestic Affairs Council—it's baffling.

THE ATMOSPHERE

Angier Biddle Duke   He wasn't one to sit around and crack jokes. He was one to pick the brains of his staff. On *Air Force One* he would handle government business, and then it would be time to sleep. He would take a sleeping pill, and bang, he'd get his six hours, eight hours—or whatever it was. But it was all a very well-organized use of his time. No wasting of time.

He had a wonderful manner and he was never rude, but he could be abrupt and he could turn things off. He knew the value of time and the use of time, and he wasn't going to waste his time with fools.

Robert Komer   Kennedy treated me like a contemporary. I have never seen a president who was more relaxed with his staff and more relaxed as he got settled in the presidency. He called me Bob. He'd call me up on the telephone and ask me a few silly questions. I'd say, That's silly, Mr. President, but he was terribly polite, terribly decent.

Kennedy was very decent to his people. When I arrived, although I was not an assistant, I was given White House mess privileges, which I adored. They had the best of Navy messes over there, and good food, and you don't have to walk out of the building. Kennedy never came down to the White House mess. LBJ came down about once every two months and sat down and told jokes.

Adam Yarmolinsky   If the common people didn't canonize Kennedy, at least they beatified him. He had the common touch in the way that an aristocrat has the common touch. He didn't invite those people to dinner.

When I was campaigning for Robert Kennedy, we would go from one town to another—advance people had arranged for us to stop off for a bite or something along the way—and you got treated very specially by these people, but they did not see themselves as social equals.

Angier Biddle Duke   Soapy Williams brought the first African ambassador into the White House—the ambassador of Somalia. Soapy had been quite a figure in the Kennedy campaign, but this was the first time in the White House, the first time in the presenting of credentials, and we were a little green on how to present credentials; we didn't have the thing down pat yet. We sit down, and the assistant secretary of state says, "Jack, I want to tell you about this ambassador. He is the greatest guy." And the president turns to the ambassador and says, "Well, I want you to know about his excellency. His excellency the governor is one of my most valued members of the team. Now, Governor Williams, would you, so on and so forth." He addressed him as "Excellency" and "Governor Williams" for the rest of the interview, and Soapy never called him anything but "Mr. President" after that. That's the way the president handled that kind of being off base.

Adam Yarmolinsky   He was not a ditherer. In an unconscious way, the fact that he lived in a world of rich people must have affected his judgment. One of the ideas that I would have pressed on a Democratic administration—that I would press on a Democratic administration if we ever have one again—is: Get rid of the military aides in the White House. I know it's very convenient to have all those people and they're free manpower, just to stand around and run errands. But use civilian volunteers.

I'm not saying that John Kennedy was a prisoner of the military at all, but he was, to some extent, influenced by the fact that he moved in a circle of eastern establishment rich people. And while his inquiring mind and his openness to new experience made him able to listen to old New Deal economists, he was not as at home with those people as with the establishment people.

Esther Peterson   He would get the opinion of all the people there. I was the only woman. Once Arthur Goldberg came in, and we were all sitting around there and deciding something, and the president said, "I can't make up my mind until I know what Esther says." It was terrific. I don't mean to say that because I'm bragging, but the point is he didn't care who it came from.

Edwin Martin   I recall a meeting on the mess-up in the operations of the Agency for International Development, where it got down to Kennedy's saying, "If you can't hire enough secretaries to do the work, here is a good temp organization you ought to go to."

Dean Rusk   He was an incendiary man who set most of the people around him on fire, and it was really fun to work with him.

For example, one morning around seven-thirty, he called me at home, and he was still at home, about a piece he had read in the *Washington Post* on page twelve or thirteen. He gave me hell about that leaky State Department, and he said, "Now I want you to go down to the department, find out who leaked that story, and fire him."

Well, I went down there and called in the reporter who had written the story, and in a very unconstitutional way, I said, "Look, you're going to have to earn your living around this department. If you think you're going to do so with any comfort, you've got to tell me who gave you that story."

And he did. I called back President Kennedy and said, "I found out who leaked that story, Mr. President."

He said, "Yes, who?"

I said, "You did, yesterday at four o'clock." It's fun to work for a fellow like that.

ACCESS TO THE PRESIDENT

Lee White   Access, really, I think, depends on how the president functions. Kennedy didn't like the notion of a chief of staff. But that didn't mean the people on his staff were equal, or had equal access. I never complained about mine. In fact, I could have had my head blown off once. It had to do with another one of those calls that came in at five-thirty. I knew damn well that Adam Yarmolinsky in McNamara's office can't get hold of anyone else, so he gets ahold of me. He says, "We have a problem out in Rapid City Air Force Base. The question is, can airmen who are off duty engage in a demonstration against some federal activity?" "Well, what are the rules?" "Well, we don't have any." "Well, what are you guys going to do?" "Well, I don't know. That's why I'm calling you." So we discuss it a bit. I say, "As long as they're not on active duty, as long as it doesn't interfere with discharge of their duties, I don't know why they can't." Well, that was one of fifty phone calls that day. About ten days later, I got a call from the president. He said, "Did you tell the Defense Department that?" I thought, Oh, shit. I want to hide and I try to explain how it came about. He wasn't interested; he had a perfect squelcher. He said, "Why didn't you ask me?" and he was right.

Wayne Fredericks   The president liked to meet with his ambassadors when they were back in Washington. This bothered a lot of people who had been in the system and were accustomed to chains of command. One always wondered what went on in these meetings—whether any secret protocols were reached. Also, if Kennedy wanted to know something, he might call someone in the bureau, down on one of the desks, without informing the assistant secretary. I accepted this as part of his thirst for information, so it bothered me and didn't bother me. Many of these ambassadors were friends of his or had worked in his campaigns, so it would be natural that he would want to talk to them without other people present.

Ralph Dungan   Kenny O'Donnell was on one door, and Evelyn Lincoln was on the other one, at the entry to the Oval Office. She would drive Kenny crazy, because he would stop someone, and they would go around and come in through her door. She would never stop anybody; an assassin could have walked in that door.

Cartha DeLoach   Because of the relationship of the two brothers, Mr. Hoover felt it an obvious necessity to go through the attorney general when Mr. Kennedy was president, because to do otherwise would have been wrong. I think Mr. Hoover would have been glad to have greater access to the president. Courtney Evans was given the job of liaison with the White House and the attorney general. It was due to Mr. Hoover's feelings that Evans had greater closeness with the Kennedy family and therefore would be of greater value to the bureau. Courtney Evans knew

Bobby Kennedy when he worked for the McClellan [John McClellan, U.S. senator (D., Ark.)] committee.[*] They struck up a friendship.

Ralph Dungan   I don't think the president was isolated by his staff, not because the staff wouldn't have wanted it that way, but that wasn't the president's style of operation. We only isolated him when we knew that he didn't value very highly advice he might be getting from so-and-so. Either the guy was a fool, or the president had made up his mind on the issue and didn't want any more palaver about it. A couple of times Stewart Udall was hot on some conservation issue, which basically bored Kennedy—he was no Theodore Roosevelt—and when the decision was made, he didn't want to hear any more pleadings. I think—on the whole—the staff did well by him, both on what they did and how they sifted it. There were lots of people who felt the "Mafia" kept them out. But that was because they knew that either explicitly or implicitly, the president didn't want to see them.

Pierre Salinger   There was something different in the Kennedy administration: There was no locked door into the Oval Office; there were twelve of us who had access to that office at any time of the day. We didn't have to go through somebody to get permission to see him; we walked in. So Robert Kennedy wasn't the only person advising him; there were others. Sometimes we would say things to the president that he did not agree with, and he would argue back strongly. But we had the right to say what we wanted to say; it was not an administration where the president's staff had to figure out what his position was before they went into a meeting and then make sure they followed that line. In a way, I was the outsider in the inside group: I was not a Harvard man, and I was not Irish—but that was never a problem. The essential thing to being on the inside team was to have gone through the campaign with the president.

THE PRESIDENT'S ASSOCIATES EVALUATE THEIR COLLEAGUES

Chester Bowles

Ralph Dungan   The Bowles appointment was controversial—kind of like Stevenson's. I happened to be a strong proponent of Bowles; I liked

---

[*]Robert F. Kennedy was chief counsel of the Senate Select Committee on Improper Activities in the Labor and Management Fields, chaired by Senator McClellan.

him and thought he was good for the State Department. That was given to Rusk, and I don't think he was very enthusiastic about it. I know it was a negotiation; again, my "Mafiosa" friends were opposed—the Massachusetts suspicions of liberals.

John Kenneth Galbraith   Bowles was a man with fresh ideas—a bit didactic in their statement—coming into the highly conventional world of the State Department and the military. He was basically very inconvenient. I was off in India by this time. The liberals in the administration, those who sought to have a fresh view of foreign policy and had doubts about our involvement in Indochina, for example, did not accord Chet all the support that he should have had. I think the Washington community could have done better by him than they did.

Walt Rostow   Chet's problem was an extraordinary one. The secretary of state would go out of town and would say, "Chet, these are the issues; here is our position; here is the president's position." And he would say, "Yes, yes." And then he would go and do something else; it was as though he was deaf—all he could hear was his own little drummer, and that wasn't quite the drummer of the president. It was a relief to have someone like George Ball, who was a lawyer. He understood precisely what policy was, even if he disagreed. He was an effective agent. That is what you have to be in that job. You are not in business for yourself as undersecretary of state.

George Ball   As far as Bowles was concerned, we were on the closest terms. But he was a man who was totally lost in abstractions of his own; he paid little specific attention to what went on in the department. Gradually Rusk turned to me and pulled me into political things. It became an established fact that the secretary and I worked together on political matters. It finally reached a point that was rather absurd. I was really functioning as the deputy secretary.

McGeorge Bundy

Robert Komer   Bundy, a firm Europeanist, had never bothered to learn about India and Pakistan, so I educated him as well as the president. But he never interfered unless he saw that I was advocating a policy that would cause trouble to the French or British or Italians. Mac was terrific to work for; he delegated everything to me east of Suez. In fact, east of the Atlantic. I had all of North Africa, including Tripoli.

Tom Wicker   I found McGeorge Bundy rather intimidating. He had a high reputation, and deservedly so. I lacked the intellectual confidence to deal with Bundy; I wouldn't now, but I did then. To some extent that was true of Sorensen, too. But you had to deal with him more often than with Bundy.

William Sloane Coffin, Jr.   Kennedy was sorely impressed by these Ivy League types like McGeorge Bundy and McNamara, who got him into a war his instincts told him he shouldn't get into.

McGeorge Bundy and Roger Hilsman

Victor Krulak   Bundy and Hilsman. I was never keenly moved in any direction with those fellows; they were doing the best they could with what they had in the way of background, intellect, and conviction.

Averell Harriman

William Colby   Harriman had a thing about dictators. He just hated them. He considered them all upstarts. He got along with Stalin as an opponent, but he couldn't stand these tiny little countries standing up when they were dependent on American assistance.

William Sullivan   Harriman was about seventy-five at the time, but he had expended all of his political opportunities when he couldn't win the governorship in New York. He was feeling very much out of things in the Eisenhower period; he wanted a piece of the action and it didn't much matter to him where he got his foot in the door. He ran one of the most interesting stag dinner salons for the period of the Kennedy administration—he had everyone there—and many of the ideas of the Kennedy administration, whether foreign or domestic, were formulated—or at least fermented—in Ave's house in Georgetown. He wanted to be in, and when he got in he made the most of it.

Roger Hilsman   He was right to promote Harriman. Everybody said Harriman was an antiquated, senile old man. He wasn't at all. He was just exactly the right guy to send to the Laos negotiations, and did very well as assistant secretary—very well as an undersecretary.

George Carver   Harriman played a fairly active role in the Department of State. He did not suffer fools gladly and made no secret of the fact that he felt occasionally surrounded by them.

Angier Biddle Duke   There is a certain allure to Harriman. First of all, Harriman was a tremendous sport. They were testing him. He'd been in Franklin Roosevelt's cabinet as secretary of commerce, ambassador to Great Britain, and ambassador to the Soviet Union, but they made him assistant secretary of state for Far Eastern affairs. I mean, they sent him to the back of the class. Well, Averell gets in there, and as history would have it, the world turned, and his area of the world became damned important. And his word on what was happening in Vietnam and in the Philippines became front-page stuff, and Harriman swam back into prominence. He was a very capable politician, and he was very ingratiating, excellent with the press, and although he was two generations apart from the smart, young guys in the White House, he made it his business to get along with them. He was very good with them, and he started up the ladder again, and he became an insider.

Gen. Maxwell Taylor

George Ball   I was initially enormously impressed by Maxwell Taylor. He was the most sophisticated military mind that I had encountered. He was a very cultivated man; he spoke four or five languages.

When we got into the Tonkin Gulf business in Vietnam, I thought Johnson was a bloody fool. He brought a general officer in who was known for his moderate views and for the fact that he was not the typical general. He thought Taylor would give him very modern advice. In a sense that is true, but the advice was still bad advice. Max was the defender of that great idea that if you slowly move the bombing line north, there would be a time that they would cry uncle. I was still fond of Max Taylor. I admired him, but I felt that in that case he let the side down.

Robert Komer   I had a few problems with Maxwell Taylor. He had some weird ideas: He said, Let's do a list of every country in the world marked first, second, third, fourth priority. But let's cover every country at least once every eighteen months. I said, "Good God, that's no way to do business." He wanted to set up an interagency group chaired by State. I said, "This won't work. It's going to be like the Eisenhower administration. You've got a board which is charged with investigating how the State Department executes foreign policy. State will be totally defensive and try to kill all the reports which are honest. What's the point? They are master evaders."

Evelyn Lincoln

Ralph Dungan   When you think of someone as being secretary to the president, she was off the wall. Nice but unsophisticated. She had been that way up on the Hill, too. What she was good at was to have a few dollars in the drawer to hand the president as he was flying out. Probably she knew so much that the president wouldn't dare to fire her. Kenny [O'Donnell] knew how to deal with her.

Robert McNamara

Ralph Dungan   We went over to the Ford Suite in the Wardman Park Hotel. We lasted about five minutes. McNamara said, "Thanks very much, gentlemen." He had his three-by-five cards and was rapidly putting his names together and let us know in no uncertain fashion that he didn't want any White House assistance in staffing the Defense Department.

Ben Bradlee   McNamara was really the most interesting figure of that time; he thought that everything was susceptible to high-tech solution.

Pierre Salinger   He became a much tougher defense secretary under Johnson than he had been under Kennedy.

Victor Krulak   McNamara was—if nothing else—obedient. He wanted to do what his boss told him to do without respect to his own ambition.

Harry Felt   McNamara was a pretty good listener. As a matter of fact, he outsmarted me: At that very first meeting, where the problem was creating infrastructure and we needed money to do it, McNamara said, "Heck. I've got a fifty-billion-dollar budget. Sure. I feel for you." I later found out that he took the money out of another one of my pockets. As I later viewed McNamara, he was a dove. He thought money could buy anything.

Roger Hilsman   McNamara had no international political sense and would just brush aside anything that you couldn't quantify or put into statistics. He didn't want to hear about it.

Carl Curtis   I thought the weak one was McNamara. He would come back from the war zone and make a rosy prediction. A few months later he had to make another prediction.

Ray Cline   I know McNamara very well and I like him, but he was not a strategic thinker at all. The president had high regard for him. Kennedy's father was a businessman and, after all, McNamara did the Edsel. It wasn't very successful, but he was the president of the Ford Motor Company, so President Kennedy thought McNamara is a pretty bright guy. I went on a trip with him to Vietnam. I was impressed with him, but I didn't think he had any strategic goals. He said every year, in '62, '63, and '64, We are going to polish this all off; we don't have to do any more; it's fine. But he ended up with five hundred thousand troops in Vietnam.

Roger Hilsman   I have come to believe that McNamara wasn't as good as I thought he was. I knew that McNamara was no good at international politics, but I did think he was doing something really great about the strategic things—the war plans; I thought he was knocking the Pentagon's heads together. I am now coming to believe, as evidence comes out, that it was not as successful as Kennedy thought it was—as we thought it was. We thought McNamara, with all of his faults about international politics and his bull-in-the-china-shop stuff, was worth it, because he was at least getting the Pentagon together.

Strom Thurmond   McNamara was the sorriest secretary we ever had.

Walt Rostow

Roger Hilsman   Walt Rostow is a special case. Eugene V. Debs Rostow and Walt Whitman Rostow; those names were chosen by their mother, who was a communist, or at least, an extreme socialist. And I always thought—I always used to say to Kennedy—Rostow is just living his name down. He isn't really the right-wing ideologue he appears to be. I was wrong. He was the right-wing ideologue he appeared to be. He wanted to be director of the policy planning staff from the beginning. He ran for that office for many years. That also says something about Walt, because that is the least important position on the sixth and seventh floor of the State Department. Its only real influence has been as a pool of talented people to throw into an emergency, but it is nothing; it is a nothing. It is not a line job, and they end up writing thoughtful papers, which they could do at Cambridge or at Columbia.

He kept writing memos, and every time there was a mission somewhere, like to Vietnam with Taylor, why, he was always there, clamoring to go. Kennedy called him "the air marshal," because every time anything happened in Southeast Asia, he wanted to bomb Hanoi.

Paul Samuelson   Walt Rostow had no very extensive influence on economic policy; what he did espouse before 1959 was a general set of principles of price control that, in broad outline, were similar to the guidelines that Heller, Tobin, and Gordon espoused.

Dean Rusk

Phillips Talbot   My guess now would be that Bobby was the one who found Rusk not the man he wanted to see there, and that it was Bobby who was pushing, although I have no evidence of that.

It seemed to me that the president and Rusk got on really very well on the basis that Rusk really was a servant of the president. And they were obviously in constant communication. But I never had any evidence of this anti-Rusk campaign.

Of course, after Kennedy's death a lot of the Kennedy people walked out; they wouldn't stay with Lyndon Johnson, and made a number of scornful remarks about him when they left. But one of the most scornful of Rusk was Ken Galbraith, and Ken had been a teacher of John

Kennedy. I think he felt that his message was not getting through, that Rusk was unimaginative and unresponsive, all this kind of thing.

My sense was different; my sense was that the president was not above playing people against each other, and that he was delighted to have Ken Galbraith in Delhi rather than in Washington, which I think was originally Ken's hope. But Ken in many respects was contemptuous of Rusk; their minds are quite different indeed, and Ken, I suspect, did not lose many opportunities to convey this to the White House.

Nicholas Katzenbach   Bobby and Rusk did not get along. He didn't have a lot of respect for Rusk—not as much as Rusk deserved. Bobby was a very direct, outspoken person. He did not think Rusk was. He thought Rusk wouldn't give advice until he knew how the president wanted to act.

Phillips Talbot   George Ball had supported Adlai Stevenson, and Rusk seemed to have some hesitancy in their communications until, at someone's behest, they started to have a drink together at the end of the day. And I think they came to work very closely with each other, and came to develop a very high respect. Rusk was a man of absolute integrity in everything he did in service to the president. There is a story which I believe is true, that when the Vietnam issue became really heated and Ball got quite upset about the policy, the two of them settled down and had a really vigorous discussion, at the conclusion of which Rusk said to Ball, "George, Vietnam is so important that the president should hear your views as well as mine, so when I go to talk about Vietnam in the White House, you'd better come with me." I just can't imagine a Dean Acheson [foreign policy adviser; secretary of state in the Truman administration] saying that; I can't imagine, obviously, a Henry Kissinger saying that, and my sense was that the president respected this. I have no doubt that the president went to other sources and said, "For God's sake, Rusk is telling me this. What's your view?" but it seemed to me that the derogation of Rusk came from somewhere other than the president himself.

Thomas Mann   I never did get along very well with Rusk—I guess for human reasons. I was over at the White House and Rusk said to me, "I would be ashamed to have lobbied for the ambassadorship to Mexico." He was speaking to a career foreign service officer. I said, "Damn you. I have never lobbied for a job in my life; that is an insult. I will be in your office in the morning to demand an apology." And the next morning I went in to see him and asked him what the basis was for what he had said, and that it affected my honor. And he backed off.

Eugene McCarthy   We didn't know much about Rusk. He was actually sort of a continuation of John Foster Dulles in terms of his whole approach, which, I guess, Kennedy didn't really want to challenge because it was consistent with his approach to foreign policy and the communist thing. It turned out he was a bad choice. He was an ideologue on that issue; he was almost worse than Dulles. He was sort of like Calvin's Cromwell. He perpetuated the whole ideological thing Dulles had set up, so that in any controversy where you could draw communist and noncommunist lines, there was no question what Rusk would recommend, whether it was Vietnam, Cuba, or whatever.

Robert Manning   I came out of the government with tremendous respect for Dean Rusk; he was a true patriot. But he never understood my function. There was a constant strain between us—not hostility but tension. He would ask, "Why do I have to do that? Why does the press have to know that?" I would travel with him and he would ask, "Why are you here? Why aren't you back doing your job?" Of course, my job was to be with him.

Harry Felt   Rusk came out to the Pacific in those days. Rusk was great. One time we were in Bangkok and I was sitting up in the front seat, alongside of the driver; Rusk was in the back seat, and he started to laugh and said, "My God! Look at that; I've got a full admiral as an aide." I think that Rusk was correct in making a statement that our role in South Vietnam is supportive. I think that was absolutely correct until we made another decision later on—not me, we.

Morris Abram   He is one of the finest men in public life. As Shakespeare says of Brutus, "He is an honorable man." I think he is a technocrat; I don't think he has the vision. He worked as a very competent foreign service officer. Now that is not to degrade him, because foreign service officers are sometimes people of great quality—as he is. But he was not a great voice.

Ralph Dungan   I used to do a lot on ambassadorial appointments. Rusk was terrible at that. Once he said to me that my job was to give him the best career officers for ambassadorial posts. I said, "Mr. Secretary, we see our job as to find the best person for the job—wherever he comes from." And he refused to come up with a noncareer name. I thought that was terrible.

Robert Komer   I had two run-ins with Dean Rusk. On both occasions a presidential letter had been sent over to him in advance by an assistant secretary for Rusk's sign-off before it was sent to the president. Well, the assistant secretary called me and said the event to which this letter is addressed is taking place tomorrow. So if the president doesn't sign the damn letter tonight, there is no point in sending it. I said, Surely you have told the secretary of state that. He said, I can't get to the secretary, he's too busy. It must be sitting in his in box. So I went to the president and told him, The secretary hasn't gotten around to this matter. Well, the president signed the letter, and the next morning Rusk saw it mentioned in the cables. He called me up personally and blew his stack. I said, Mr. Secretary, I believe the letter and a cable draft are in your in box. According to your staff it's been there for eleven days. And Rusk said, "Goddamn it, I don't care what the substance is. When I don't approve a letter, it doesn't go out. It doesn't go to the president for his signature." He cussed me again. He was a very good cusser. And he said, "Never do this again."

Pierre Salinger   There were two Rusks: the Kennedy Rusk and the Johnson Rusk. The reason for that is that Kennedy tried overwhelmingly to control foreign policy himself, and so Rusk did not have the same power with him that he had with Johnson.

Richard Bissell   Rusk is quite intelligent and quite competent. I came to admire him a great deal, in considerable measure because of his steadfastness and loyalty to the president—to two presidents.

Roger Hilsman   Rusk would just keep quiet, and you never knew whether he would slip into the president's office afterward. The idea was: "I will tell you what I think. This is the State Department view, but I will tell you what *I* think."

The point was that Rusk was very much out of sync with Kennedy, and very much in sync with Johnson. They would chatter like schoolgirls. They were both poor WASP Southern and respectful of the military, like Truman. And they had a Southern sort of simple patriotism that was not very complicated.

The pattern in those days was: Here is a reasonably bright boy, the son of a preacher; there is that college that they send them to in the South—I have forgotten the name—it's down in Georgia. But anyway, this is what happens to poor preachers' sons. The Rhodes [Scholarship] people wanted a black and desperately looked for one. They wanted a Southerner—they hadn't had a Southerner for years—and so Rusk got to be a Rhodes scholar. My theory about Rusk is that he was good, but not really that good. As a consequence he developed a kind of defense mechanism, where he concealed what he thought until he was damn sure what was the right thing to say.

Alexis Johnson Rusk could never talk in front of Schlesinger. He knew Schlesinger was sitting there writing his book. And this violated, in a sense, the way business should be done. So he'd wait and see the president alone, or with McNamara.

Angier Biddle Duke I think the president enjoyed the fact that Rusk was a bureaucratic figure, and he enjoyed poking a few pins in him. I think it made him feel good to pick at him a bit. They all did. The White House staff all made fun of Dean Rusk. They thought he was a ponderous, somewhat pompous bigot. He's not, but they liked to think he was.

McNamara was the "in" kid at the White House. Rusk was out. It was very embarrassing sometimes. We would have cocktails up in the Yellow Room on the second floor—just the principals—let's say, a foreign leader, his wife, myself, my wife, and Dean Rusk and the ambassador—just to get to know the inside group that's visiting. You have a cocktail, or whatever it is, up there before dinner, and Mrs. Rusk was hardly ever introduced. They just wouldn't bring her into the conversation. She would stand—so my wife would make a practice of taking Mrs. Rusk and introducing her to the visiting first lady and pushing her into the conversation. Otherwise nobody paid any attention to her. But those are the dynamics of social situations that reflect the sort of standing that Dean Rusk had as a bureaucratic figure.

Yuri Barsukov He was very competent, very democratic, very available for foreign reporters. Once Rusk had a briefing exclusively for foreign reporters. I have a high opinion of Rusk, and I think his State Department was very good.

Pierre Salinger

Alexei Adzhubei I knew Pierre Salinger very well. Kennedy was supposed to be interviewed by me in Washington. Adenauer [West German Chancellor Konrad Adenauer] was there then, so the interview was postponed. Salinger informed me I would have to go to Boston. I told him, "We are working people; we are only paid what is necessary. I don't have the money to buy my ticket." Pierre said, "You can borrow the money and then pay it back." There was a telephone call for me at the hotel. It was the president. He said, "Mr. Adzhubei, Pierre told me something. You can give your ticket back; my personal airplane will take you. Do you understand me?" I said, "Yes. But in the planes of American presidents stewardesses don't serve booze. Is it possible to take some along with me?" He replied, "Tell them I allowed it."

Arthur Schlesinger, Jr.

Richard Bissell I like Arthur Schlesinger, but I often disagree with him. He certainly is a bright man.

Ralph Dungan Schlesinger's role was as gadfly; he roamed about. He was great. He sat in on the Bundy meeting every morning, as I did. It turned out that what the president really wanted him to do was keep a book—a record—of what was going on. None of us knew about the recording machine at the time—none of *us*. Dave Powers knew, and he told me that the problem was that Evelyn Lincoln never knew when to turn it off, so you had a lot of babble.

Ben Bradlee Arthur Schlesinger was the liaison, but Arthur was under great suspicion at the White House from all the big shots, who didn't know what the hell Arthur was doing there. They were not natural allies. Probably Sorensen and Bundy had some better understanding of why he was there, but no great sympathy for why he was there.

Dean Rusk   One has to take account of Schlesinger's lack of influence in the Kennedy administration. I was with President Kennedy once when Arthur Schlesinger came in and made some rather outrageous proposal about some foreign policy matter, and Kennedy thanked him, and Schlesinger left the room and Kennedy looked at me and said, "Arthur can be very interesting sometimes in the Rose Garden." Kennedy liked to chew on ideas and liked to have around him people who had ideas, and Schlesinger was one of those who had ideas—sometimes good, sometimes bad. So he was not a mainstay of the Kennedy administration as far as policy was concerned.

Norman Podhoretz   He had Arthur Schlesinger, Jr., as his court historian. I've often said that you can't buy that kind of talent if you are looking for a PR man, and Schlesinger did, indeed, repay the appointment and the intimate contact he was given with the Kennedys by becoming a very effective and widely read apologist for everything about the Kennedy administration and the Kennedy family.

I suppose it was the presence of the Ivy League people that was responsible for the reputation of the Kennedy administration as an intellectually vital administration. Certainly, as compared with the sort of people in the Eisenhower White House, there were professional intellectuals involved. On the other hand, many people—including me—came to believe, as a result of the record of many of those people, that—as Bill Buckley has notoriously quipped—"We would rather be ruled by the first two thousand names in the Boston phone book than by the combined faculties of Harvard and MIT." The record of that administration was not exactly a brilliant testimony to the capacity of academics to govern.

Tom Wicker   Schlesinger's role in the White House was typified by the fact that his office was in the East Wing rather than the West Wing. I never have understood exactly what Arthur did. He is a very good friend of mine, and I have a high regard for him, but at that time, I didn't know what his role was. You could talk to him and get a general picture of what was going on. But whether he had any actual influence on things, I couldn't tell you.

Ted Sorensen

Paul Samuelson Kennedy had two absolutely loyal team members: He had Robert and he had Sorensen. Sorensen often acted in the name of the president, but I never saw a case where he acted other than where he thought the president would want to act. During the 1960 campaign, Galbraith—the old, experienced hand on campaigns—said, using his 1952 and 1956 experiences, "I can tell you one thing; before this campaign is over, everybody on the staff is going to be second-guessing the candidate and be disloyal." And Ted Sorensen said, "I know one who won't be."

THE "WISE MEN"

Ralph Dungan Kennedy was a curious combination: He was a New Frontiersman, but in foreign policy he really went for the gurus. I have a hunch that Joe's influence might have been significant there, not in the case of Harriman, but with Robert Murphy [former senior State Department official], quite likely. Kennedy thought of Harriman as being a really wise fellow, which he was. I didn't agree with a lot of things. I remember that special committee on Vietnam. I sat in with them a couple of times. Krulak was on it. They all became superhawks. I believe that what happens is that people like Harriman and Taylor begin to reinforce one another, and they begin to take in their own washing, and all of a sudden something becomes a policy which really started out as a glimmer or as a prejudice in one mind. I have a feeling that there was a lot of that "follow the leader" stuff, and the leader can change in a group.

Joseph Dolan Robert Kennedy used to say, "Don't forget we are political geniuses by 119,000 votes." The Kennedys were aware that the general perception of them on the part of a hell of a big segment was that they were new, brash, young, not old government types, not with a lot of international relations experience, so they were sensitive. They were also sensitive in the first year to what Eisenhower said about Kennedy. So if you talked to people whom Eisenhower respected, you were consulting the great, wiser heads. This makes your lines more solid. You don't have to listen to them, but it appears to the public that you are interested in everybody's view.

McGeorge Bundy   One has to say about most of the people that he called on in the older generation that they were well aware of what their role was and was not. Acheson had been so much in government that he knew very well the difference in being a senior adviser and being the secretary of state. Harriman was different. He came in and had a full-time job—a set of them, actually. Lovett was different again because he came in and out, although he may have been the one who Kennedy was temperamentally the closest to.

Arthur Schlesinger, Jr.   Kennedy had a great historical sense of continuity. He rather liked the idea of getting people into his administration who had experience. Those who succeeded the most—like Harriman—succeeded because they made allies with the young fellows. We all regarded Averell as a contemporary. He was a remarkable man. Some of Harriman's contemporaries—like Acheson—were just out of sync with the administration, but Kennedy liked to hear what Acheson had to say, because he knew that Acheson would make the strongest possible case for some course of policy Kennedy did not propose to pursue. But he wanted to hear what that case was; he liked to hear all sides.

George McGovern   I was always surprised when he leaned on Acheson the way he did. It seemed to me that was a throwback to an age that we were beginning to move out of. It was too rigid, too hard-line, to fit the Sixties. Harriman was more flexible, and he did bring a certain wisdom and experience that I think Kennedy found attractive. But the McCloys [John J. McCloy, foreign policy adviser], the Achesons, the Clark Cliffords, and some of the others, were pretty much from a different era—a more rigid and less imaginative one in terms of foreign policy and national defense. You know, we had this military-industrial complex speech by Eisenhower, and it seemed to me this group were the advocates of the military-industrial complex—and had been since World War II. He should have been looking at a somewhat broader direction—even bringing in General Taylor, as much prominence as he had, was a kind of throwback to a harder-line approach that I thought was a little bit out of sync with historical circumstances at the time.

It always seemed to me that things like the Alliance for Progress, the Peace Corps, Food for Peace, the nuclear test ban treaty, were at odds with the Acheson, Taylor, McCloy school of national security and foreign policy. Kennedy took a harder line on foreign policy than I did, and it's maybe that he felt more comfortable with them. I would not have felt comfortable taking advice from Acheson, Harriman, and some of the others that Jack seemed to think so highly of.

Ben Bradlee   You have to talk to your statesmen. If you're forty-three or forty-four years old, you can't settle for the advice of your peers. You have to go to McCloy, to Harriman—to the old farts. Some of them still had some clout: Bob Lovett—he had tried to get Lovett to join his cabinet. Averell? I don't know whether Averell was worth talking to; Averell was a gut fighter and, I think, would have been interested in that sense; McCloy was still a powerful figure in the establishment; I never knew Acheson very well, but I suspect he thought that nobody could be secretary of state just as well as he could. I think that Kennedy's policy of calling in the "Wise Men" was a good cover-your-ass political decision. I have a suspicion that they were being contacted by the staff on an informal basis at all times.

Lloyd Cutler   I think it's very sensible, especially in a government like ours, where people come and go. I urged doing that in the Carter administration, when we had our little confrontation about the Soviet brigade in Cuba, that we did bring in about exactly that same group—of course, all of this was in the middle of the SALT II consideration in the Senate, which I was involved in—but it turned out the Soviet brigade was not a new brigade; it had not just been introduced. It had been there since the 1962 missile crisis, in exactly the same place, with the same brigade number, and the intelligence agencies had simply forgotten its existence. We went back and we found statements by President Kennedy and by Secretary McNamara at the time of the Cuban missile crisis, that in addition to the aircraft which were there, and the missiles which were about to be brought in, that there were three or four combat brigades, which were there to protect the bases. And we identified them, and we insisted that they be removed, along with everything else. And when the Russians took steps, when the ships turned around and they removed the planes and the missiles that were in Cuba, we kept on saying, "You still have to get rid of those brigades." And 1962 finished, and 1963 went on, and they didn't move them, and we just stopped talking about it. And then we just stopped watching. And then, at the time, the

Soviets resumed various forms of activity in Cuba, including alleged construction of a submarine base. I guess it was true. Senator Stone, of Florida [Richard Stone (D.)], insisted that we resume surveillance, and we did. All these assets had been turned on Vietnam and Iran, and everything else that was there. And we rediscovered the air traffic relating to these brigades. That's what happened. But we called in a group, essentially the same group of "old boys" from Eisenhower, to consider what to do. They were, among them, the ones who reminded us all of what had happened before.

TENSIONS

Walt Rostow   The actual tension hinges on how the president runs his business, and what the personal relations are that develop under the president's guidance. Both Kennedy and Johnson were, unambiguously, personally in charge of policy. In no demeaning sense, they understood they were the only elected officials, and we were all meant to serve the president. What strikes you if you are in the middle of it is how small the U.S. government really is; it is the president and very few human beings. If the president creates the right kind of setting for it in terms of policy and human relations, it is not hard to hold it all together. But if the president is uncertain, as Jimmy Carter was—Brzezinski [Zbigniew Brzezinski, national security adviser] is up there on the Afghan frontier with a Sten gun, and Vance [Cyrus Vance, secretary of the Army] is trying to push arms control—the place is going to hell in a hack. You do need a president who doesn't stand for that, who doesn't encourage that kind of a schism.

Pierre Salinger   The one place Kennedy criticized was the State Department. He could ask for things and felt he wasn't getting them fast enough. I can remember a number of times when he asked the department to do something and it was now a month and a half later, and it hadn't been done.

Lucius Battle   I rejoined the Department of State at the request of Dean Rusk and to become executive secretary and special assistant to the secretary. The first day that I was there, Rusk said to me, "Luke, please try to get the White House under control. They're all over this building—staff members are all around the building." So I got in touch with Mac [Bundy] and he and I, in time, worked out a fairly good and airtight system: We had two sets of channels to the White House. One was Battle to Bundy, or Bundy to Battle, which didn't mean that we would be the actual person in either case, but we would shepherd whatever the document was. And anything that I sent over, signed by me, had had clearance, and was State Department position. Other than that, nothing was supposed to go over. The staff at the White House was most aggressive; it was stimulating, it was exciting, but it was aggressive, and it was hard to control. There were just all sorts of dangers of having people play around in the department when an act is thought of as a presidential directive when it isn't. There were a few instances which were pretty bad.

Martin Hillenbrand, deputy director, Berlin Task Force, U.S. Department of State; director   Part of the tension between the White House and the State Department was over the Berlin crisis, obviously in the way it was handled, and the policy recommendations that the State Department was making. I exclude McGeorge Bundy, who I think really was above that sort of thing. But I think there were other people in the White House, some of the Harvard types who came down other than Bundy, who really were sort of uncontrolled: they leaked, they gossiped, and they were too much involved on the Georgetown cocktail party circuit. They really were not disciplined as an efficient White House staff has to be disciplined.

Ted Sorensen was a good speech writer when flowing or glowing rhetoric was essential, but when it came to drafting more mundane pieces, the rhetoric sometimes ran away with the practical use of language. There were problems sometimes in the writing of presidential speeches where we thought a more modest and less rhetorical approach was desirable. I would exclude Sorensen generally from the people we thought were gossips and not capable of keeping the kind of discretionary privacy to affairs that are being handled that involve national security.

So there was tension, and of course this tension came to a head during the summer of 1961, after the Vienna summit meeting. Dean Acheson was brought in to draft recommendations, and he was generally regarded as a former secretary of state as somehow or other speaking for the State Department because he had his office there, and so on. His recommendations—not all of which were accepted by the secretary of state, nor were they ever embodied in formal recommendations by the State Department—did arouse the concerns of the people in the White House.

Adam Yarmolinsky Presidents always find the State Department unsatisfactory, because foreign policy is the president's natural long suit. People who are not experts are never willing to concede expertise. And I think it happens in every presidency.

The State Department sees its function as that of an adviser. That's a dangerous role for a bureaucracy which wants to be an effective adviser, because the Defense Department is in the business of managing the largest business in the world. It hires, feeds, clothes, transports, trains more people than any other business in the world. Let's think of it as a business, apart from its business of killing people. In the State Department, everybody suffers from what I've described as heliotropism. The secretary doesn't want to run the department because he wants to be the president's chief adviser. The assistant secretaries think they want to be the principal advisers to the secretary, and nobody runs the store.

Phillips Talbot Mac Bundy's idea was to get the departments to resolve their differences wherever they could and hold NSC as sort of a court of appeal, perhaps not the last appeal, that would go to the president. But Komer was certainly active in opposing this and opposing that, and I'm sure that the people at Defense talked to Komer as much as I did, to persuade Komer of our lines of thinking. In those days, of course, there were differences between Defense and State; they had different briefs. But the differences in our area were not terribly severe, because we were not dealing so much with adversaries as with area disputes; there wasn't much ideology in dealing with area disputes.

Dean Rusk There were occasional clashes with White House staff people, but not between me and President Kennedy. President Kennedy, by the way, found that I was the only cabinet officer that he always called Mr. Secretary; he never called me by my first name, as he did other members of the cabinet. Jacqueline Kennedy once referred to this as a neighbor at dinner and said that it was very significant that the president did that, but she didn't add any comment as to why he did it, and I didn't ask her why, so that remark remains a mystery to me, but it suited me very well to have a certain arm's-length relationship with the president.

I learned that from George Marshall, who managed to create an arm's-length relationship between himself and everyone who worked under him and everyone who worked above him. Because I think that it would be the duty of the president to replace me on a day's notice, that there ought not be any mixture of personal relationships and official relationships in a matter of that sort. George Marshall was very stern on that point, and I learned a good deal from him on that situation. For example, Franklin Roosevelt once referred to General Marshall as George, and he interrupted and said, "It's General Marshall, Mr. President."

George Ball   I think there was feeling in the early days that the "Mafia" was a little too close in their control of the president's movements and schedule. But that was overcome very quickly.

Adlai Stevenson III   I don't think there was any animosity on the part of Sarge Shriver. He was from Chicago, and we'd known the Shrivers, or our family had, for a long time. But there were others: the Irish Mafia, as they were called, who harbored resentments. A couple of episodes to illustrate: One, the Kennedy inauguration in 1961. Two vignettes: Right after the ceremony, limousines pulled up in front of the Capitol for the members of the cabinet. But there was one limousine too few, and that was the limousine for my father. So he ended up walking behind the limousines, down Pennsylvania Avenue, which was a stupid thing on the part of whoever it was, because it was embarrassing to the new administration. The parade route erupted in cheers for the walking, newly designated representative at the UN, which, of course, was a cabinet position. Then, at the White House, there was a small reception for members of the cabinet and families, and I can remember watching Kennedy— somebody came up, delivered a message, and he immediately, of all the people, including Rusk, motioned for my father to come over. He had just received news that the Russians, as a gesture, were going to release the downed RB-47 pilots.* And I was kind of struck at the time by the

---

*On July 1, 1960, the Soviets shot down a U.S. RB-47 aircraft over the Barents Sea. The two crew members, Capts. Freeman P. Olmstead and John R. McKone, were released in January 1961, arriving at Andrews Air Force Base, Maryland, on January 27.

ambivalence: On the one hand, he had been pushed aside in an unfortunate way at the Capitol, but when it came to making what was the first administrative decision after the inauguration, namely, "How do we respond to the Russians?" he beckoned to my father.

The other, best-known example was during the Cuban missile crisis, when my father suggested that the United States consider withdrawing obsolete bases in Turkey in exchange for the Russian withdrawal from Cuba. There was a leak immediately. My father was portrayed as a "dove," as the one weak link in the administration's united front—the one who was prepared to capitulate. It wasn't until years later that Dean Rusk acknowledged that my father's proposal had become, in fact, the administration's position. Who those individuals were, I really don't know. The finger of suspicion always pointed at Bobby; I don't think it ever pointed to O'Brien. I don't mean to suggest that the relationship between my father and Kennedy was intimate—by any means—they were of different generations, and I think that my father, while always respecting Kennedy himself, had some reservations, owing to the old man, Kennedy's father, for whom he had no use whatsoever, nor did any other people.

There was a little tension, owing to the difference in generations, and, I think, the feeling among some of the Kennedy supporters—or the inner circle—that Stevenson was a kind of a latent threat, or a rival, and that may have been owing partly to the 1960 convention. I don't think Kennedy could ever understand my father's attitude, and certainly, some around him didn't. He came to Libertyville sometime during the primaries of the spring of 1960—I don't remember exactly. I was there, and en route from the airport, [he] asked Newton Minow and Bill Blair if he should offer Stevenson the position of secretary of state, in exchange for his support. I believe they told him no, that my father wouldn't be influenced by the offer, and therefore, it would really not be helpful to make it. And he campaigned—my father campaigned very hard for Kennedy—throughout that campaign.

George Ball   There were some problems in how functions were allocated between the State Department and the National Security Council, but these sorted themselves out very quickly, largely because Bundy is a fellow of considerable understanding, and he understood the importance of the State Department in giving advice to the president.

McGeorge Bundy   There is always some tension between the NSC and the State Department—tension, stress. One person or another, either in the department or in the White House, might not be tactful, or might not share information at a useful point, and there is likely to be something that will go wrong as a result, and then it has to be sorted out. But in the main, it became clear to the two sides that they couldn't get along without each other, that the president had to have a staff—a President who was himself actively interested in foreign policy problems had to have people who would help him. And the department was an indispensable source; you couldn't very well tell the president yourself what the minister in a country thought unless you checked with the department and checked back with the assistant secretaries about what they thought of their ambassador. I think basically that Rusk and I understood it and tried to see to it that the rest of our people did.

Marcus Raskin   Mac [Bundy] is a very gifted, brilliant man. The intellectual character of the National Security Council staff was high. It was a very smart group of people. The problem in that period was that a great deal of energy was given over to action—often the wrong action, in the sense that it was not necessarily linked to wisdom and judgment. The president came in with a great handicap in the sense that it was basically a coalition government. He had won by a very narrow margin, so he was always aware he was a centrist.

Bundy's task was to get to the president a variety of opinions within a relatively limited frame of reference. The staff saw itself, and certainly Rusk felt this way, as competitive to the Department of State. I had nightmares every night, which were related to the development of a basic national security policy—which I thought then, and still believe, was disastrous: There was an extraordinary increase in defense spending. There was a very great increase in counterinsurgency forces, and an enormous increase in strategic weapons, so that every step of the violence scale was being increased in armaments. The theory behind that was that the United States should have the capacity for a flexible response, and I saw that as mistaken, because I viewed that as an instrument for continuous intervention and war.

David Bell   The State Department fought bitterly the thought that AID should report directly to the president, and the compromise was that the legislation was written to give equal status to assistant administrators of AID and assistant secretaries of state, and to have the AID administrators report to the secretary of state and the president. In my day I did not take any issue to the president personally. But the conception was a good one, and a strong one. It's been watered down since, to the loss of integrity and coherence in the foreign assistance program.

John Kenneth Galbraith   I only communicated directly with the president, to Dean Rusk's great dissatisfaction. He once asked McGeorge Bundy to stop my communications, on which I would put "Eyes Only: For the President," knowing that that would mean they would be circulated widely in the State Department. My communications were somewhat disturbing to the cliché-ridden community, the people who did not want any disturbance from thought. I, of course, saw the president whenever I was back, which was often. I continued my concern for economic matters, either directly with the president, or through Walter Heller, and met with Dillon, also, so I was a somewhat privileged figure as an ambassador. I don't think the ambassador to London or to Paris had quite as much access as I did. There was concern that sometimes my views were at odds with the accepted Washington view. I was very much opposed to the tax cut when it was under discussion in the autumn of 1962. The Council of Economic Advisers, with the State Department, established what was called the GEW Line, the Galbraith Early Warning System, so they would know when I was coming back and not schedule too many meetings that I might attend.

Kennedy was afraid of a secretary of state who had a constituency of his own, which Stevenson obviously had. He wanted somebody who would be passively his own figure. Rusk, a fairly colorless bureaucrat, fitted into that picture. I know that Kennedy didn't realize how committed Rusk was to the cold war clichés. In one of the last conversations I had with him in 1963—just a few weeks before he was killed—he told me that he was going to change his secretary of state in the next administration; he said he would have McNamara, except that there was a special problem: He needed McNamara to keep the military in line. Dean Rusk was an honorable man, but not exceptional, and he had a strong commitment to the clichés of foreign policy, to the State Department bureaucracy and to the attitudes of the cold war.

Dean Rusk   A president cannot be his own secretary of state. One must realize that the mass of business in foreign affairs is such that no one man can grasp it or handle the daily procedures, the daily work. Some three thousand telegrams went out of the State Department on every working day to our posts and to governments all over the world. On every working day some dozen international conferences were held somewhere, including subject matters ranging from the control of nuclear weapons to the control of cholera.

Now, the business can't be done unless there's a considerable amount of delegation. A secretary of state necessarily must delegate, but he cannot abdicate responsibility, so that everything that was done in the department was my responsibility, and everything that was done in the department was the president's responsibility as the head of the executive branch of the government. So the processes by which you inform hundreds of officers down the line who have to send out telegrams signed by the secretary of state as to what policy they should follow is a very subtle, pervasive process and requires a great deal of thought and attention on the part of the secretary.

Harlan Cleveland   Shortly after the beginning of the administration, we were engaged in some very interesting and difficult operations at the UN. One was the Congo issue; another was Angola. Cuba was already bubbling, and there was a lot of business up there. At the same time Stevenson was appointing four ambassadors to be his deputies. There was a lot of news about Stevenson.

At that time the *New York Times* tended to cover the UN almost as if it were local news, so you would have a situation where there would be three stories on the front page about what Kennedy was doing in Washington and another three stories there about what Stevenson was doing in New York. I began to get rumblings from Mac Bundy and others in the White House, saying that the president was not happy that he hadn't known how we were going to vote on Angola yesterday and had to read about it in the newspapers. As a result, at the end of each day, at about eight or nine o'clock, I would write a one-page memorandum about what we had done in the UN that day, with a special view to those things that were likely to have created some news. I would send these memos directly to Bundy, and he would put them in with Kennedy's nighttime reading.

Paul Samuelson   There were leaks, and the president hated leaks; all presidents do. As it was said, the ship of state is like no other ship: It leaks from the top. But there were persistent leaks. Stories would be published telling what had happened at a meeting. The president said, "The council is leaking," and the council said, "The treasury is leaking, we know that it wasn't here." Well, it was the council. It was actually an assistant to Walter Heller.

Lucius Battle   *On feelings in the State Department about Robert Kennedy's input into foreign affairs issues:*

Oh, God! Was there resentment!

In the late fall of 1961, President Kennedy, expressing uneasiness with the structure of the White House staff—and perhaps the manner in which the State Department was functioning—made major personnel changes in the administration. These came to be known as the "Thanksgiving Massacre."

Arthur Schlesinger, Jr.   The State Department was not working out, but Kennedy couldn't fire Rusk. That would have been to impeach his own judgment too much. He was fond of Chet Bowles. He agreed with Chet's policies, but Chet was given to philosophical expositions, including telling people a lot of things they already knew. Kennedy may have found that not so much trying as time-wasting. Kennedy had high regard and personal affection for Bowles and felt badly about it. He wanted to find some honorable alternative for him.

The president felt that Rusk was not an administrator. Rusk had not taken command of the department. The undersecretary should have done so, but Chet was not succeeding in this. The president felt that George Ball might be better at it. Sending Rostow and Goodwin over was part of a general attempt to try to get control of foreign policy.

I feel more sympathy now with the State Department than I did then. The Kennedy administration in foreign affairs was overactivist and felt that we should be going around trying to improve things around the world. I am now more skeptical of the capacity of one country to improve another. I think the State Department is more attuned to reporting than activism, and there may be something to be said for that.

McGeorge Bundy   Goodwin wasn't part of the massacre; he was part of the reinforcements. I think every one of the changes that was made at that time quite often has a quite personal complex history to it. There are things that Kennedy wanted to do, things that Rusk wanted to do, things that both of them wanted to do. The Rostow example was a very good one. The initial notion was that he would go into the State Department as head of policy planning. That was before I was ever involved in coming to the administration. Rusk didn't want to do that. The president said, "How would you like Walt as your deputy?" and I said fine; we were old friends. But when it came time to play musical chairs in the fall of 1961, Rusk no longer had those objections, and the reasons for wanting Walt as the policy planner had not changed in the president's mind—so there it was.

Lucius Battle   I don't think, at that point, that Rostow was regarded with as much horror as Goodwin. Ed Martin, who was assistant secretary of Latin American affairs, came up to see me, and he said, "What's the answer on this Goodwin thing?" I said, "Well, frankly, Ed, if I were assistant secretary for Latin America, I'd rather have him over here as my deputy than to have him over there."

He said, "Do you think we could manage him?" I said, "We could manage him better over here than we can over there." Goodwin would do unbelievable things.

Lincoln Gordon, U.S. ambassador to Brazil   I saw it happen, and I was a little perplexed about this assignment. One theory was that Kennedy was fed up with having Goodwin as a loose cannon in the White House, but on personal grounds didn't just want to fire him. So he put him in this job, knowing that Ed Martin would keep things on the rails. I really have no basis to evaluate whether that is a proper construction or not. There are obviously pro- and anti-Goodwin factions in this particular business. But I do know that Ed Martin felt that he was spending an awful lot of time and energy, unnecessarily, dealing with problems that Goodwin was creating. It was not the kind of relationship one wants with your right hand—your assistant secretary.

Edwin Martin   Goodwin was a superb speech writer and a very energetic person. He had done a lot of work on Latin America. He drafted most of the Alliance for Progress speech. Kennedy just thought there wasn't enough publicity and noise coming out of the State Department on the Alliance, and that Goodwin could do that. My problem with Goodwin was that my idea of a deputy is somebody who can deal with routine problems, but can stay informed on things so that if anything happens to me he can step into my shoes. Well, Goodwin was a special projects man; he was very good at that. We had another problem, in which he was scheduled to be on a Sunday morning television program with Carlos Fuentes, a Mexican author. Mann heard about it because Fuentes had asked for a visa. They had a copy of his communist card. Under the rules, communists were only given visas with permission of the Justice Department, and we didn't like to do it more often than necessary. So I took the matter up with Rusk, and he thought, as I did, that it was not necessary or desirable to give Fuentes this opportunity to appear on U.S. television. Goodwin was very unhappy about this. He went to the White House. On Saturday morning Kennedy called me to ask about it. I explained the situation to him. Later on Goodwin was replaced.

Lucius Battle   I got deeply enmeshed in the very unpleasant situation over Chet Bowles. I was fond of Chet Bowles, and in a different kind of situation it might have worked, but not the way it was.

Dean Rusk was spending most of his time over at the White House in the early part of the administration. Chet Bowles was locked in a room most of the time, trying to figure out where to make, and how to make, appointments, and Chet never understood that the policy was not something made, generally speaking, in an abstract way. I'd walk in the door and Chet would say, "Gosh, I'm glad to see you, Luke. I really want to talk with you about this problem." And we would sit there. I would say, "But I have something that's going out; the answer to the shah of Iran's request for something or other." An hour later, he had an appointment pending with somebody, and he would say, "Well, you go ahead and do whatever you think ought to be done." I'd say, "But it's about so-and-so." "Well, do whatever you think ought to be done." Well, what we were doing was that we were theoretically discussing issues that weren't immediate. There might have been an important discussion, or could have been, and we were ignoring the more immediate things that had to be dealt with.

Joseph Sisco   Most of us who were on the inside were not surprised by what happened to Chet Bowles. He was out of step. He was much more oriented to what I would call, very loosely, a Third World approach. He was not an experienced operative in the organizational sense. He was an intelligent man, but insofar as how he viewed various problems, there was a sharp contrast between him and Dean Rusk: Rusk was an eminent practitioner who knew how to do these things and was much congenial to Kennedy's approach; whereas Chet Bowles was out there looking at the world primarily with a view to extending American influence.

Angier Biddle Duke   Dean Rusk was anxious to get rid of Chester Bowles because every time Dean Rusk went to an international conference and Chester Bowles was acting secretary of state, he would appoint new ambassadors and promote his people in the department, and work on his agenda. When Rusk came back, he had to face a reshuffling of the deck.

Archibald Cox   I think the president tended to see Bowles as more of a soft-headed liberal than he actually was. I think Chester's style was a little bit imprecise.

Adam Yarmolinsky   That was a question of chemistry. Kennedy and Bowles just didn't get on. They were both fine people.

Kennedy was the pragmatist, and Bowles was an idealist. And Kennedy's pragmatism was tempered, and Bowles's idealism was tempered: Bowles was the Platonist and Kennedy was the Aristotelian.

Robert Manning   I had a feeling there was relief that Bowles was no longer in a major position. The main thing his departure did was to raise the stature of George Ball. Ball was a tough pragmatist; he was not a knee-jerk liberal. I don't think that Goodwin was sent into the State Department with the expectation that he was going to exert any tremendous influence. As a matter of fact, I've never been quite sure, but I think it is entirely possible that he was considered an inconvenience in the White House. Rostow didn't exert much influence in the State Department on day-to-day operations. His office did produce an avalanche of position papers, some of them brilliant.

William Smith I thought it was to move Rostow out of the White House where a competition with Bundy had developed, rather than to help State.

George Ball As far as getting rid of Walt Rostow and Dick Goodwin is concerned, I think that the president rather liked to have someone of his own in areas he was particularly interested in. Goodwin was a very facile writer; that's the best I can say. Rostow was a theorist, and getting into the job of policy planner was fine. Nobody paid any attention to any of the planning, I might say.

Harlan Cleveland I don't think that Walt [Rostow] and Kennedy were on the same wavelength. They weren't the same kind of people. Walt is a very bright and very comprehensive mind, a strategic mind. Asked for advice in a meeting, he would give the whole story. Kennedy was exactly the opposite kind of person. He didn't want to know about the whole story. He would ask very pointed and specific questions. You didn't give him a long dissertation on where it had all come from, historically. You just gave him the answer to his question. He was Mr. Pragmatic.

Walt Rostow The president wanted me to have the job of heading the State Department Policy Planning Council from the beginning. That is the job I thought I would enjoy, and I did. I had four glorious years in that job. At the beginning of the administration, Rusk wanted someone closer to him as a counselor in planning. An awful lot of people in the State Department were appointed by the president; they were his pals. They wouldn't have been the people Rusk would have wanted, so he felt he was owed somebody. And he knew George McGhee. He wanted me to be McGhee's deputy, and I said no. I liked George; we were Rhodes Scholars together, but the president wanted me; we had worked together for three years, so I got this deputy's job on the National Security staff. But it was quite explicit that I was deputy to the president. So Mac Bundy and I split the job.

By the fall of 1961 Rusk and I had worked together on a whole series of crises, and we had gotten to know one another. In fact, when the president called me up and asked me to take the job at State, I called Rusk and spoke very frankly with him. He said, "We have worked together; it will be okay." And we did get on very well. We would meet on Saturday afternoons. This was the day when we could both go to the office in slacks, without a tie. At the end of the day, we would sit and talk for a couple of hours, quite often, and have a drink.

Ralph Dungan   The president didn't want or need his people in the State Department; he had them. He wanted to get rid of them. Walt [Rostow] was a bloody bore—he talked too much; he'd get in there and he'd beat Kennedy's ear, and Kennedy didn't like that; he wanted it quick. I think Walt was getting on everybody's nerves. I never heard Bundy say it, but I can imagine he would just as soon have had Walt off the premises. I felt that way about Dick [Goodwin]. The only reservation I had about his going over to State was how he was going to foul up the Latin American bureau, which, indeed, he did. They were both kicked upstairs.

9

Lyndon Johnson

John F. Kennedy's surprise selection of Lyndon Baines Johnson, the Senate majority leader and his chief rival for the presidential nomination, to be his running mate was generally considered a wise, if controversial, political decision. Yet, once in office, the president kept Johnson outside the loop of major decision making.

Bobby Baker   Sam Rayburn said, "I've been there since Woodrow Wilson's administration, and no president, in all these years, has had a good relationship with his vice president."

Pierre Salinger   I think the Kennedy-Johnson relationship was going pretty well. The vice presidency is not really a job; you are just sitting there waiting for something to happen. In most cases nothing happens; in this case it did. The president and vice president would have breakfast or lunch together once or twice a week. Kennedy wanted to give Johnson some power to do things—like NASA.

Paul Samuelson   Johnson, to my great surprise, figured for nothing in the Kennedy presidency. I think it was his temperament. I had figured that they would use him as a point man to control Congress.

Tom Wicker   He was very much the Colossus of Rhodes; he was all over the place. His campaign plane was an Electra, with the circular seat in the rear. He would gather the reporters back there for hours on end. You dared not leave, not only for fear you would make him mad, but you might miss something. He never breathed, or said, that it ought to have been him who had the presidential nomination. He never disparaged Kennedy. Whatever else he was, he was loyal. He also understood that it would be bad politics.

Henry Fowler   At meetings Johnson was very quiet. He never interjected anything unless the president asked him. When the meeting was over, it was very obvious that the president and LBJ would walk into the Oval Office together. We didn't know what would happen then, but the assumption had to be that LBJ was reserving anything he had to say till he got together with the president on a one-to-one basis. He did not want to be in the position where something he said would put him in a different tangent from the president. He was very respectful of the office of the president. He felt in a similar way about Dick Nixon. I remember once calling him to say that I had accepted an invitation to meet with Nixon administration officials on a fiscal matter. He didn't hesitate for a minute. He said, "Joe [Fowler's nickname], you are doing the right thing. Whenever the president is doing something for the good of the country, support him. We'll have plenty of time to take care of him in November 1972." He would not tolerate anyone cutting up the president, because he had a great regard for the presidency.

Ray Cline   Johnson was a congressional man; he became vice president only because he had been in Congress. He was a congressional manipulator, and that is the way congressional politics works. I don't think he was a real presidential thinker. He was always playing politics. He accepted McNamara and these huge military forces in Vietnam because he wanted to protect South Vietnam. He wanted to destroy the North Vietnamese, but he was never able to do it. I met Lyndon when he came to Taiwan in 1961. When he was in Taiwan, Johnson said, "Look, Eisenhower was fired on for 140,000 rounds in Quemoy when he visited here in 1960." I said, "That was just a gesture from the Chinese Communist military to show they didn't like Eisenhower's being there." Johnson replied, "Are they going to fire on me?" I said, "I don't think so." He said "Anytime they fire at Quemoy, you tell me, because I want to talk about it." He was so vain.

Harlan Cleveland It was interesting to watch him as vice president: He was very low key and very loyal. He didn't rush around the country trying to be a premature candidate for anything. In the meetings of the National Security Council—which I attended quite frequently; I was a briefcase carrier for Rusk—it was notable that, in the discussion, Kennedy would always call on Johnson for his views. It was also notable that what he always addressed himself to was the domestic political implications of whatever was being discussed. On questions of political practicability and domestic experts, he was clearly a first-rate expert, and people listened to what he said.

Although I was in a number of meetings with him, and a couple of private meetings, I never saw the sort of profane arrogance that I later saw several times when he was president. It was a kind of character change. When somebody asked me how I liked my job after Johnson appointed me ambassador to NATO, I said, "I have the best job in the administration. I'm three thousand miles from the White House and ten thousand miles from Vietnam." I was told that comment got back to the president and he was not amused.

Donald Wilson I am inclined to believe that Johnson did more than we are aware of—on the telephone. Otherwise, what the hell did he do sitting there? Larry O'Brien was choreographing activity with Congress, but I think he was choreographing Johnson, too.

FROM THE PRESIDENT'S PERSPECTIVE

Tom Wicker Kennedy didn't particularly want to have Johnson take the credit for things which Johnson would have done. Johnson, I think, didn't want to pull Kennedy's apples out of the fire. He, as president, used to boast as to how he rescued Kennedy's civil rights bill and Kennedy's tax bill. They may have respected one another, but they weren't all that close.

Ralph Dungan Jack Kennedy was not really interested in having any kind of a partnership with him. Their personal relations were stiff. Kennedy never liked him. When Senator Kennedy and Sorensen used to go out on those forays two or three years before the convention, I was left holding the floor, trying to save us from embarrassment when Johnson, as majority leader, did everything in his power to schedule votes on Thursday and Friday afternoons when Kennedy was away, just to point up that he was an absentee senator. Johnson was no pal, and Kennedy had no affection for him. He had respect in the sense that Johnson was a power wielder—a great conniver—but no affection.

Tom Wicker I think there was the feeling that Johnson was a potential rival. Also, the Kennedy people were very urbane characters. They thought Johnson was a crude frontiersman. In many ways he was. But they made him feel that way; they didn't recognize that he was an exceptionally able man. He, in turn, had tried in Los Angeles to spread the word that Kennedy had health problems. He had let fall some uncomplimentary things about the old man, which is fatal in the Kennedy circle. Also, Johnson got a lot of credit from a lot of people for having helped win the 1960 campaign. They didn't like that.

It became clear, when Johnson became president, that there was a whole crowd of Democrats—Truman, party-regular, Johnson Democrats—who really didn't count for very much in the Kennedy administration. They came into their own when Johnson became president. Every president brings in his own crowd, but Kennedy did this to a remarkable extent. Nobody in Washington had dealt with Larry O'Brien, and people like that, before Kennedy brought those people in. And a lot of the old-line Democrats, who had been close to Johnson and probably had supported him in 1960—before Kennedy was nominated—just did not have much of an in at the White House.

Ben Bradlee Kennedy treated Johnson with deference. He liked anybody who'd run for office; he had a certain respect for anybody who'd run for office. He'd say: "It's a tough thing to put yourself out there on the line." He occasionally made fun of Lyndon's margin of victory that first time, but he wasn't the only person in town who was calling him "Landslide." They were not natural friends. Lyndon Johnson was a "good old boy"; he liked "good old boys." Jack liked a small dose of "good old boys."

Lee White The relationship between the president and the vice president wasn't bad. I wouldn't say they were big buddies, but it was the people who were around Kennedy who really didn't have a high regard for Lyndon Johnson as vice president.

I think part of it is the difference in growing up in Massachusetts and going to Harvard, and growing up in Johnson City and going to San Marcos State. I always thought that Johnson was way, way overly sensitive about his educational inadequacy, but he wasn't inadequate; he was one of the smartest minds I ever bumped into. He was really, in some ways, a genius. Certainly he was a legislative genius.

William Sloane Coffin, Jr. I always liked what Halberstam [David Halberstam, correspondent, *New York Times*] said about Johnson: he did not suffer from a bad education; he suffered from the belief he had had a bad education, so he didn't trust his instincts, which were a lot sounder in many ways than Kennedy's.

George Smathers They didn't like him because, well, first, Johnson was not an easy guy to like in many ways. He was so strong. He was a nice fellow in a way, but he was so very crude, and very rough, and he did not have all the advantages the Kennedys had grown up with in Boston. He was a rural guy, a country guy—didn't get to go to a big college, didn't have the opportunities that Jack had, or even that I had. So here is a rude guy from the country, just by dint of his guts and courage and drive had made himself a very powerful man. I've said many times— and I don't hesitate to say it—he's probably passed more legislation as majority leader, and as a president, than anybody in history. He was probably, in many ways, the least liked in Congress, because he could run all over you. I was his assistant leader for two years, and it in effect broke up my first marriage—he was so insistent that you work all night long; that you don't come home for dinner; that you go with him, where he was; he called all during the night, at any time; you had to be here when it was Christmas—with the family in Honolulu.

Bobby Baker After Kennedy was elected president, he sent for me and said, "You know, the toughest job in the world is the vice presidency, because under the Constitution, he's only got one job, to be president of the Senate. I will send Lyndon all over the world as my representative to keep him busy."

Robert Komer Kennedy decided in August 1962 that he was under too much pressure from foreigners for visits, and he was unable to get away.

He had to stay in Washington and keep an eye on Congress and on the legislative process. So he did what all presidents do: He asked the vice president to go. Well, the vice president wasn't eager. He said, Mr. President, I'll do anything you want me to do. But let me tell you, I went to the East in February with a State Department adviser and this guy gave me very, very bum steers. I do not want any more State Department advisers.

George Smathers   Jack's relationship with Lyndon Johnson was miserable, and I claim a lot of credit for sending Johnson on that trip to India, because Kennedy used to say to me: "I can't stand him."

Cartha DeLoach   Vice President Johnson was treated more or less as an orphan by the Kennedy administration; he was more or less a tool. He was deeply hurt that he didn't get the nomination. He took the second-best opportunity he could to assuage his feelings and pride. He had more or less divorced himself from his duties as majority leader. He would soon have to run again in Texas and had narrowly escaped defeat the last time he ran for office, so he decided the best thing was to take the vice presidential nomination, knowing he would be treated as an orphan; knowing that he would have abuse dumped on him by the Kennedys; but nevertheless he would have the title.

Frank Moss   Kennedy's close advisers, particularly Bobby, were suspicious of Johnson and shut him out whenever they could. Johnson felt it and resented it quite a bit. It was a difference in philosophy: Kennedy came in with the attitude of an Easterner and Johnson hadn't fully shaken off being a Southerner. After he assumed the presidency, he became a progressive.

Terry Sanford   I don't think the president liked the vice president, and consequently I don't think the vice president liked the president. But they got along. The staffs of the two were more hostile to one another than the principals. Kennedy was always very gracious to Johnson. To some extent Johnson viewed Kennedy with admiration of his ability, and with some jealousy that Kennedy was the person who was sharp and attractive and getting the attention.

I turned out to be a very strong Lyndon supporter before it was all over. I came to admire what I thought were his real good traits, without being diverted by the other stories coming forward now in these biographies. But Johnson, with some justification, resented not being brought into the Kennedy inner circle. He despised Bobby.

Ralph Yarborough Kennedy didn't like him very much, but Johnson stayed at that White House like a sick kitten hanging on to a hot brick.

Louis Martin I think that JFK felt he needed Johnson to get some of that Catholicism off him. He needed him in the beginning. LBJ was loyal most of the time. It was a marriage of convenience, with no love lost either way.

Norman Podhoretz I think the Kennedys were a little bit afraid of Johnson, but in part, I think they were contemptuous of him. There was sort of bigotry in it toward a loud, stereotypical Southern politician of a kind that all supposedly enlightened people were supposed to feel superior to.

Walt Rostow Whenever I saw Kennedy with Johnson, it was exactly as he had talked to me of him in 1958; he had great respect for him. He knew it was very tough for Johnson in that job. He had come from being head of the Senate to this job. He tried to give him some things of substance: He gave him the Space Program and other things.

He wanted his advice. I remember once, on Laos, the president said, "Where's the vice president? We are meeting in the Cabinet Room." Someone said, "He's circling Washington; the weather is bad." Kennedy replied, "We will take some other item up, but I want him here when we discuss Laos." And he would find times to see him alone.

A lot of the negative stuff came from Kennedy people, who didn't like Johnson. They thought: He isn't like us or the kind of people we admire. It's almost as if these people had never dealt with anyone from the South, or someone you wouldn't meet in New York or Boston. Some of my colleagues found him a little indigestible. But Kennedy was very, very considerate of the vice president. I remember once I was up there and I was waiting. I played the piano for Caroline; it was Christmastime. This old senator from Arizona [Carl Hayden] was with the president. It was late, and the president came out and said good-bye to the senator, and he turned to me and said, "Walt, I hate to do this, but I must see the vice president. He is waiting. Would you mind if we talk tomorrow?"

THE ANIMUS BETWEEN LYNDON JOHNSON AND ROBERT KENNEDY

John Seigenthaler   Before the president was assassinated, it was Lyndon disliking Bobby. There was no reason for us to worry about Johnson; he was sort of a likable adjunct to the administration. He was over in the Executive Office Building, he had good staff, all of whom knew him well and didn't want any trouble with anybody. Lyndon was basically self-conscious about Robert Kennedy's closeness to the president. I don't think he looked upon Bob as a competitor eight years from now: I think he just disliked him. In the same way that I thought he was a snotty little bastard, I think Lyndon thought to himself: He's a snotty little bastard. He certainly didn't want me to be vice president. He had come down and told me there would be a floor fight, and Jack overruled him, so he's not a friend of mine.

Lyndon's feelings about Bob were not returned, at that point. I recall a conversation with Bob the night after he and Lyndon had attended a dinner party. He said, "Do you remember what Lyndon said about Dad at the convention?" I said, "I sure as hell do." Bob asked what it was. I replied, "Lyndon said that his father never carried Neville Chamberlain's umbrella." He said, "That is why I never liked him, and why I didn't want him to be vice president." But again, Lyndon was no impediment to his functioning as attorney general. Their paths would rarely cross.

Ralph Yarborough   I went to see Bobby Kennedy—that was after Kennedy had been in nearly three years. I said, "I can't appoint anybody, in any department, anywhere—not even a secretary—if Johnson blocks it, or if the White House blocks it. I've got no patronage, nothing. I can't get anything." And Bobby Kennedy says, "Well, I can't go over to the White House and interfere; I've got to be attorney general. Johnson's over there every day, and I can't go over there." To judge from that, I wasn't the first person who'd made some complaint, and he made a suggestion: "You go see every cabinet officer—see them in person—tell them you have a personal reason—and you state the problem and ask them if you can get fair credit on this patronage for your state." I told him I would. This was just three weeks before Kennedy's assassination, and I never had a chance to put it into operation. But I judge from that

that the relationship between Bobby Kennedy and Lyndon wasn't very friendly.

John Seigenthaler There were occasions when Bob would talk to the president about Lyndon's unwillingness to get involved with legislative problems where he could have been helpful.

He did go out of his way to accommodate Lyndon when Sarah Hughes [U.S. district court judge] was appointed a federal judge. Sarah Hughes had known Sam Rayburn, and he and Lyndon came over to Bob's office. Lyndon said he was there because Mr. Sam wanted this lady named a judge. He said, "The president and I have an understanding that I will have a say in all patronage matters involving Texas. But," he said, "I consider the Justice Department off limits, Bobby, and I know you have your strict standards." Lyndon was assuming that, because Sarah Hughes was too old; there was no way Robert Kennedy would agree. He looked upon Robert Kennedy as rigid; unyielding; unwilling to bend. In Lyndon's eyes, Kennedy was not about to break a rule which said "we will not name a sixty-five-year-old person a judge." Mr. Sam said that day, "I don't know why you people even ask the woman's age."

When they left, Bob called Whizzer [Byron White] and said, "I want to name her if she's qualified." Byron didn't like it; "We had a commitment to the ABA—and to ourselves." But Bob said, "Well, she is a woman, and we haven't named many women, and you can't find that many. And beyond that, Byron, the vice president of the United States has been over here and asked me to make an exception, and we will make an exception."

The next day Bob told Lyndon, and after the conversation, he came into my office and said, "You won't believe what Lyndon said. He said, 'Those were Mr. Sam's nickels we had spent'; they weren't his." And the interesting thing is that she swore Lyndon Johnson in after the assassination.

Pierre Salinger Johnson was always outraged at Robert Kennedy, saying that he had tried to prevent him from becoming the vice presidential candidate. I kept arguing that it had been exactly the opposite—that in the first discussion we had on the vice presidency, it was Robert Kennedy who had put forward his name, but he had a hatred for Robert Kennedy, based on his view that Robert Kennedy had tried to sabotage his nomination as vice president. Before the 1964 convention, Johnson said that no member of his cabinet could be a candidate for vice president. He wasn't aiming at anybody except Robert Kennedy.

Bobby Baker   I've never seen two human beings hate the way Lyndon Johnson and Bobby did. Bobby had Lyndon's telephone lines tapped. When [Shimon] Peres came to town, a guy on his payroll called and asked if I'd do him a favor and get Johnson to see him. So I went to Johnson and said, "This guy has been very kind to us; he's a Jewish friend, and he's raised a lot of money for us, and he's going to be embarrassed if Mr. Peres sees that a big Jewish leader can't see somebody in this administration, and the president won't see him, so will you, unofficially, be gracious and meet this man?" So he did. Within fifteen minutes after Johnson had seen him—'cause Bobby had his phone tapped—they arranged a meeting for the president with Peres. Johnson was paranoid once he knew his phones were tapped. Nobody in the world knew about this meeting, because I took Mr. Peres in through the back door.

Najeeb Halaby   My impression was that people like Bobby and his associates at the Justice Department felt that civil rights was their territory. They all kept Lyndon at bay. I've never felt Lyndon was totally enthusiastic about the issue in the beginning, so that was another reason for not using him too much. When he became president, then there were a horse and saddle there for him to ride. Like a lot of us who grew up in the South, there was a mixture of compassion and guilt about blacks and how we treated them.

Jack Valenti   There were antagonisms that might have been spurred on by aides. I know that after Johnson became president, Charles Bartlett, who was very close to John Kennedy, he and I would conspire as to how we could bring together Bobby Kennedy and the president, and I remember one time one of Johnson's close aides came in, in the morning, and we were up in the bedroom, conveying some gossip about what Bobby Kennedy had said about Johnson. I got riled and I said to the guy, "You know, you weren't there. You're just passing along some gossip." I said, "What happens, Mr. President, is I'm sure people around Bobby Kennedy are saying, 'Boy, let me tell you what Lyndon Johnson said about you the other night.' We don't know this, and I think Bobby's people are pouring poison in his ear, just like some of us are pouring poison in your ear, and that's a shameful thing to do."

Walt Rostow On April 4, 1968, five days after Johnson said he wasn't going to run, Bobby Kennedy asked to see him. He brings Ted Sorensen with him. The only other people in the room are Charlie Murphy [Charles Murphy, associate of Lyndon Johnson] and me. The meeting was a very interesting and healing thing. The last time they had talked, it was an awful time. This time it was basically Bobby coming in to ask: If he ran for president, would Johnson knife him? The president said he would not; he didn't believe a former president should determine who should get the nomination. He referred to Truman's awkward effort to try to get the nomination for Averell Harriman in 1956. It didn't work and was demeaning for Truman. Johnson said, "I might support Humphrey. He has been an A-plus vice president. I was a B-minus or C-plus at the best." Then he said, "Senator, you and I were not made to be vice presidents." Then he spoke about how President Kennedy had understood his position and had always treated him with the greatest consideration. And it was true.

Bobby's relationship with Johnson was more complicated than you are led to believe. It is true there were elements of real cross-tension. On the other hand, there are letters in which Bobby wrote how he understood the burdens Johnson was carrying. He offered to be ambassador in Saigon. Johnson did not want Bobby to be vice president, but he felt he had a duty to help him get elected to the Senate, so he went up to New York and campaigned with him. And Bobby wanted this.

JOHNSON'S UNHAPPINESS AS VICE PRESIDENT

Lee White The president decided to have a whole series of meetings with labor leaders, business leaders, clergymen, and educators. I was the staff guy and Kennedy said to me, Be sure that Johnson comes to all these meetings, plus Bobby and the assistant attorney general, Burke Marshall. I would put the list together. I would have a memorandum of who they were and where we got the list. If it was labor leaders, we would have gotten it from the Labor Department. There were five or six points to be touched. Sometimes he used all of them, sometimes none of them. Johnson was always invited. This was before the day of Xeroxing. I wanted to, but I didn't always give a copy of the memo to Johnson. The president had fifteen minutes before the start of the meeting. Here's this six-foot five-inch vice president standing over my shoulder, reading a carbon copy of it, saying, "You think I could get a copy one day?" I said, "Yes. It slipped my mind."

One time he wasn't invited to a meeting. He was very sore. It was an asshole accident. The problem is that when you're working for the president, everybody else is sort of subordinate. He got very upset one time because he knew the Turkey River project,* which was very controversial in Texas, had come through the Budget Bureau and was sitting on my desk. He got me on the phone: "Lee. They tell me you've got this thing. I want to take you back and give you the history." The man had fantastic recall, and also discriminating recall: He remembered the things he wanted to remember. He had now taken me back to about 1909—he'd go all the way through until about 1930. Now he's got me to 1930 or '38—something like that, and I'm thinking to myself, What a damn shame my father isn't alive to know that his little boy is sitting here and talking to the vice president of the United States, trying to figure out how the hell to get rid of him, 'cause I've got to write a memo for the president. I had to break in and tell him I had to get something done, and get back to him, which I did. I didn't have any animus toward him, but others loved to tweak him, and the crowd must have driven him nuts. I don't think the president himself was a party to that. The president may have burlesqued his backslapping and a few other things, but I never saw any evidence of his abusing or maltreating the vice president.

Burke Marshall   I wouldn't agree that the vice president wasn't used as much as he could be. He was a difficult man to understand: You could never tell whether he was telling you what he was thinking or saying something for another reason.

Richard Bissell   During the time that I was in the CIA under President Kennedy, I never saw the vice president involved significantly in matters that seemed to me to be of primary interest to the president. Obviously, when you're in the CIA, the State Department, or the Pen-

---

*An incorrect reference to a major hydro-electric project on the Trinity River in Texas.

tagon, you're dealing with outward-looking business, not the domestic affairs of the presidency, and it may be that Johnson was more active and consulted on domestic affairs than on international affairs. But, I repeat, I never saw any indication of this involvement, even less than of Nixon's involvement in the Eisenhower years.

Ralph Dungan   The idea was to give Johnson things to do so he wouldn't give us trouble. It was a question of finding useful things for him to do. Kennedy didn't want him mucking around, looking over his shoulder on the day-to-day running of the government. He would have been nuts if he had.

Johnson was a pain in the ass on all those trips he took. I had to make arrangements for a couple of them, and he was always whining and crying; he had to have a limo, and this and that. The logistics of his travel, from the staff point of view, were terrible. He was always demanding more. He didn't do any harm on these trips; I guess he did some good. The idea was to get him out of your hair.

Abraham Ribicoff   I remember riding out to Virginia to dedicate a hospital, and Lyndon Johnson came, representing the president. He and I had a long talk, and I told him I was contemplating leaving the cabinet and running for the Senate. And he said, "Boy, that's the best job in politics. I've never been so unhappy as now as vice president." When I told Kennedy, he said, "The best job of all is being a United States senator. When my second term is up I'm going back to Massachusetts to run for the Senate."

Cartha DeLoach   I have never mentioned this to anyone. I went over to see Mr. Johnson one day and told him that I wanted to leave the FBI—that Mr. Hoover and I were having differences of opinion, that Mr. Hoover always won those differences of opinion, and that I was approaching the age of fifty; I had seven children, I needed to get them off to college; I couldn't do it on my salary as Mr. Hoover's deputy. I felt that I had a chance for an excellent corporation job. I told Johnson after he became president that I thought Mr. Hoover was going to stay on forever; that I felt I should move on before I was aged out of the market. He looked at me and said, "Don't do that; stay in office. Your time will come. I always told myself that if I were to accept humility and hurt pride, my time would come, and it has come. Yours will too."

10

Foreign Affairs

During just his first year in office, President Kennedy met in the United States with more than twenty leaders of other nations, ranging from Britian's Prime Minister Harold Macmillan to the prime minister of British Guiana (now Guyana). He visited Canada, Colombia, England, France, and Venezuela and held a summit meeting with Nikita Khrushchev in Vienna. In addition India's Prime Minister Jawaharlal Nehru, the shah of Iran, West Germany's Chancellor Konrad Adenauer, and Israel's Prime Minister David Ben-Gurion all had lengthy private discussions with the president during his first year in the White House.

Dean Rusk   President Kennedy had a very good grasp of foreign affairs, tempered by the thought that he was the first president born in this century, and he felt that a new generation had come to power, and that caused him to be ready to challenge conventional wisdom in every respect and to look at the whys and the wherefores of traditional policy.

Willy Brandt, mayor of Berlin; chancellor, Federal Republic of Germany   Kennedy belonged to those who at an early age looked beyond the boundaries of Western Europe. I remember when he came to Berlin in '63, especially in the speech in the university to professors and students, he spoke about a future which would include the other part of the continent—the other part of Europe—the bringing together of parts of Europe, at least thinking about the future, which would have to deal with Europe as a whole. This would not be possible if one excluded Germany from that process. It was a key to both processes, for the near future of bringing about West European unity and then, in addition, to envisage a future which would have to deal with Europe as a whole. I think he had the right feeling of these interdependencies.

KENNEDY'S RELATIONSHIPS
WITH FOREIGN LEADERS

Angier Biddle Duke   A chief of state like Tito or the shah got walked through the White House to the door, the car door closed, and you stood there on the curb and he drove away. If it was the head of government, the prime minister of Canada, prime minister of England, you took him to the door of your office and an aide walked him to the car. Those are the little things that go on. President Kennedy didn't mind that; he caught on to that. But what he said to me was, "I think we ought to do something in this hemisphere to create a club of democrats—the good guys. They ought to feel that they are in the inner circle of influence and power—have the right to come to me at any time, or I to them. We ought to set up a way of communicating and of closeness and I'd like to start with you. Would you devise a way of treating them differently?"

I wrote one of many memorandums to him and said, "Well, I think you have an extraordinary opportunity because your father's house is there in Florida. The twenty-one guns, the format, and the formulas of the state and official visits would have to be strictly maintained. Whether a dictator comes or the president of Costa Rica comes, they've got to be treated exactly the same in Washington. But after the visit is over, why don't you fly down—take him in *Air Force One*—to Palm Beach and have a barbecue around the swimming pool that evening, just the family—his family, your family, and anybody else you want— and have a really relaxed evening, and then, perhaps, as a special mark of respect, take him off to the airport and say good-bye on the following morning."

He loved it—Just thought it was great! Thought it was a wonderful idea, and sent it over to Tom Mann, who was the assistant secretary of state for Latin America, who, of course, shot it down at once, saying that this would create disharmony in the hemisphere and that this was the sort of thing—exactly the sort of thing—that the State Department had been fighting for years.

Charles de Gaulle (France)

Pierre Salinger   The relationship with de Gaulle started out exceedingly well; the Paris meeting of 1961 was very positive. De Gaulle admired Kennedy. They talked about some tough issues, particularly Vietnam. There was some collision between them, particularly on creating the military troika of the U.S., the U.K., and France; de Gaulle was against that, so they had some tough conversations over the telephone. But there were two dramatic examples of de Gaulle's fascination with, and respect for, Kennedy: De Gaulle was the first European leader to step out and say, "I'm with Kennedy all the way" during the Cuban missile crisis when Kennedy sent Acheson to Paris; and de Gaulle was the first public leader to say that he was coming to Kennedy's funeral.

John Diefenbaker (Canada)

Angier Biddle Duke   Traditionally Canada always called first; in this case, Prime Minister John Diefenbaker. It was my first experience taking a head of government into the White House. He was awkward. We stood awkwardly. I think it was I who said, "Let's sit down" or something. They sat down, and the conversation did not go smoothly—did not go well. The two men were nervous with each other. So, to break the tension, President Kennedy did something that really, really destroyed the whole thing. He said, "I've got something I'll show you that will interest you, Mr. Prime Minister. Come over here." We got up, and the president said, "Would you take a look at that," and he pointed at all these little holes in the parquet floor. He said, "That's Ike and you, when you came in to play golf with the president." And then he went on to say that Ike would come to his office in golf shoes and, in between appointments, would walk out and knock off a few balls in the garden, out onto the South Lawn. Well, instead of breaking the ice with Diefenbaker, it made him more nervous. It pointed up to his relationship with Ike, and the poor man was so uncomfortable. Well, I don't know how he terminated that, but it was one of the most awkward interviews that I ever sat in with President Kennedy.

Nikita S. Khrushchev (USSR)

William Smith   I think his personal feeling about Khrushchev changed over time. At the time of Berlin, everyone thought that Khrushchev was volatile and dangerous. I think the president shared that view. That began to change later, but what really changed it was the Cuban missile crisis. After that there was a common understanding of the responsibilities of both of them that exceeded the responsibilities that they wanted, and therefore, they both wanted to find some way to ease the tension a little bit.

Ralph Dungan   I don't think Kennedy and Khrushchev would ever have danced together. Khrushchev may not have been as impossible as Kennedy had thought after their initial meeting, but the atmosphere of that meeting was so tough, and Khrushchev so inflexible and unyielding, that I don't think Kennedy ever would have trusted him.

Sergei Khrushchev   My father understood that Kennedy made his own foreign policy. He had everything in his own head. He never went to his advisers on how to answer Khrushchev; he liked to talk eye to eye. My father said he realized that Kennedy was a young but clever president.

Harold Macmillan (United Kingdom)

Angier Biddle Duke   There was a wonderful relationship with Harold Macmillan who was—God knows—thirty or forty years older than the president. And this marvelous, old, distinguished parliamentarian always called him "Sir"—recognized the difference between a chief of government and a head of state. And he [the president] called him "Uncle Harold," and they got along extremely well.

Denis Greenhill (Lord Greenhill of Harrow), deputy chief of mission, British Embassy, Washington, D.C.   Prime Minister Macmillan was on very close terms with Eisenhower. He had served with him in the war. Kennedy asked Ike what sort of a man Macmillan was, and he replied, "The sort of a man worth listening to." Macmillan didn't know Kennedy. In this country the Kennedy name was not in very good odor, except in very limited circles. As far as we were concerned at the embassy in 1960, neither Kennedy nor Nixon was really fancied. But when Kennedy was elected, Macmillan was very anxious to meet him, particularly because he had been involved with Ike on nuclear defense matters. It was a blow to us that a new administration was going to come in just when the nuclear weapons discussions were being advanced. And also just when we were in favor of having a meeting with the Russians to discuss the whole issue. So Macmillan was very anxious, if possible, to get on terms with Kennedy. But he didn't know quite how to do it and was very concerned by the discrepancies in age and experience between them.

Eventually it was arranged that Macmillan should come to Washington in April 1961. We were all looking forward to this meeting. Before the meeting, Macmillan entered into correspondence with Kennedy. He struck the wrong tone, and it was soon quite clear that [the letters] didn't go down well in American circles. In March Macmillan was flying to Jamaica for a holiday, and the president proposed that his plane should stop at Key West, and that they should meet there.

The president's purpose in bringing this forward was his concern for the situation in Laos. He wanted to know if the British would supply troops. Kennedy came with McGeorge Bundy. He spoke first and did a very brilliant presentation on why it was desirable for us to send troops. He did what I call "the boy wonder" act. He had statistics out of the air and that sort of thing. When he finished, Macmillan made a speech, which was really his life story from the First War. He was in France and took part in the historic Battle of the Somme, in which British losses were catastrophic—five figures on the first day. Macmillan was wounded himself and lost many friends. He was very eloquent. He told how, when he came back, many of his friends were gone. And then he dealt with the question about troops for Laos, and said he would have to consult the cabinet.

The main thing was that the two hit it off. The prime minister admired the way Kennedy had done his bit, and it was perfectly clear that Kennedy was enormously impressed with Macmillan. The prime minister then ceased to worry about whether he could get on terms with Kennedy. There started a rapport which was very successful. The same sort of thing was repeated at the Nassau meeting, when Polaris° was agreed. The majority of the American delegation were opposed to giving us Polaris, and Macmillan did the old sort of Somme business again, and the president overruled his people. And we got the deal.

Jawaharlal Nehru (India)

Angier Biddle Duke   President Kennedy got along well with democratic leaders, but there was one he didn't get along with, which was not

°A guided missile fired from a submarine.

his fault. It was Prime Minister Nehru, who had a very negative and skeptical attitude toward Kennedy. Carol Laise, the director of the State Department's Bureau of Indian Affairs, later to become ambassador to Nepal and to marry Ellsworth Bunker, was sitting in on the meeting. She and I were both amazed at the coolness and the almost rudeness of Nehru. I don't quite know why that was. I think it was partly skepticism on Nehru's part about this young man. Secondly, I think he was anti-American in a particularly English sense. He was an Oxford Blue, Nehru was, and he had a certain arrogance about the lesser colonials, as he would class the Americans. He took a very superior attitude toward us that was reflected on Kennedy, and Kennedy was puzzled. He's so good at handling people, but he couldn't handle him well at all. That was a disaster, that interview.

John Kenneth Galbraith Kennedy had some difficulty in adjusting to Nehru's style, which was to listen to a comment, listen to a plea, and just be silent; most of us who knew Nehru were accustomed to that. I had warned Kennedy about it, but still it didn't lend itself to easygoing communication. For some reason or another, Jackie could talk much more easily to Nehru than her husband could.

THE ISSUES

Robert Komer Kennedy was, in my view, remarkably flexible and broad gauged on foreign security policy. He was as interested in what was going on in India and Pakistan as what was happening in France and Germany, though he recognized that our interest in Central Europe was much greater.

He was very tough minded. He was the best president on foreign policy we've ever had; he was outstanding. I had a measure of how tough he wanted to be and how well he knew when to compromise. But let me tell you, he was never tough with the Israelis, he was never really tough, nor was any other president, to my reflection, since 1947. But my feeling of how Kennedy handled issues—after all, I dealt with everything from Morocco to Burma—I found him remarkably flexible.

David Bell One of the first things that caught my eye about John Kennedy—long before he was a presidential candidate—was his extremely good speech, while in the Senate, on Algeria. It showed that he really understood what was going on in those countries. The president saw the situation of the Third World in a more accurate and broad-spectrum way than anybody—I thought Mr. Truman understood it quite well—including all those since his administration. Foreign aid has frequently been seen in Washington as simply a matter of the cold war. Mr. Kennedy never oversimplified it.

Africa

Wayne Fredericks   In the Eisenhower years African policy continued to be made in the corridors of the Western powers. The people in the White House surrounding Eisenhower had not given much, if any, thought to Africa. The national interest was viewed as sticking to colonial powers as long as one could.

I kept making the point that in the Democratic platform of 1960 there ought to be a plank on Africa, because in the 1960s there was going to be an explosion of independence. My feeling in the late 1950s was that Senator Kennedy, like many people at that time, was only beginning to become aware of Africa.

Harlan Cleveland   Kennedy, and the people who came in with him, generally felt that the Republicans hadn't given nearly enough attention to Africa and that giving attention to it was important to black voters in the United States. There were both substantive and political reasons to give the matter attention, reflected in the fact that the president-elect appointed an assistant secretary for Africa before he even appointed a secretary of state, which was constitutionally a little grotesque. Governor Williams came in as a committed advocate of Africa, in effect, within the administration. He was supported strongly in that by Chester Bowles and got into quite a lot of tangles with the European Bureau of the State Department and with the White House staff for pushing the African cause at the expense of various other aspects of our foreign policy.

The administration couldn't go all the way with the sort of pro-Africanist view; on the other hand, it also couldn't let Africa be dominated by the European colonial past. So it became important to squash those two views together—as a former mentor of mine used to say—to make a mesh of things.

Wayne Fredericks While Africa was nowhere near the top of President Kennedy's agenda, he did provide openings for us to create sensible policy—to open up new relationships. His youth and vitality had an indelible impact upon nearly every African leader he met. Almost all of them would tell me, after an Oval Office meeting, "It is incredible how much he knows about Africa. How did he learn all of this?"

Lucius Battle Africa was overwhelming us at that point. Seventeen nations had been created.

Ralph Dungan He was interested in Africa in a geopolitical way; he wasn't interested in black people, as such. All of these guys—Bush is the same way—get interested in international affairs because they are remote and can be dealt with on an intellectual level, because they don't really have to grovel. It's a tough problem to deal with Newark or Detroit; it's hard, long work.

Wayne Fredericks My impression is that from the beginning the president had an enormous curiosity about the African leaders I took to meet him. One of the most interesting visits was that of President Nyerere [Julius Nyerere, Tanzania], in July 1963. His visit came about as a result of a visit from the president of the Ivory Coast earlier that year. When that visit ended, President Kennedy said to me and to Governor Williams: "I very much enjoyed this visit. I have a place on my schedule for another African leader later this year. Can you send me a suggestion?" I blurted out immediately that it ought to be President Nyerere, and President Kennedy said fine.

As we were going back to the State Department, Governor Williams asked me why I had suggested Nyerere. I told him I thought Nyerere would be the African leader who could most help President Kennedy understand the importance of unfolding events in southern Africa—in Rhodesia,* and in South Africa, so that the visit of Nyerere would be more than just the visit of the president of Tanzania; it would be a genuinely philosophical and political examination of the problems in southern Africa. What resulted from that meeting was the American arms embargo against South Africa in 1963, in advance of the UN's taking action.

---

*Now Zimbabwe.

On these visits with African leaders, it was perfectly clear that the president had read his briefing papers; it was clear that he had read more than the executive summaries. His questions indicated he had probed more deeply than the one-pager that was on top. There was always a lively exchange of views. Normally the African leader, who in many cases represented a rather small country, would say to President Kennedy, "I must not take too much of your time. I know the level of responsibilities you have as the greatest country in the world." Every time except one that I can remember, Kennedy would say, "But I have some questions I would like to ask you." He would then proceed to prolong the conversation.

Angier Biddle Duke   The president of Tanzania, Julius Nyerere, was visiting Washington. Blair House was going into renovation and restoration, so there was no official guest house, and I offered my house. So the Secret Service came out and rewired the whole darn thing. We had to leave, of course; the whole house was just a shell. President Nyerere came over with staff and security and everything else, and they stayed there for a few days, but in the protocol of state visits, one of the acts in the drama is that the visiting chief of state entertains the president where he stays. At the reception that Julius Nyerere gave for President Kennedy, he invited Martin Luther King, Jr. I knew that Martin Luther King and the president had been talking—there had been accounts of their talking—but to my great personal surprise, they had never met, and there, on the terrace of my house, I introduced President Kennedy to Martin Luther King. They immediately withdrew to another part of the terrace.

The Congo

Wayne Fredericks   The Congo situation, which ranked with other world situations, was leading to some sort of crisis with Belgium, the UN, and with the Soviet Union, so almost at the beginning of the administration, we were involved in a very major crisis.

I remember saying to Rusk and to the White House, "If we don't have a Congo policy, we don't have an African policy. The Congo has all the classic components: a secessionist issue in the South; and a strong appeal to the American right wing, who would like to see Moise Tshombe [leader, Katanga Province, Belgian Congo] win in Katanga, if not in the whole of the Congo."

I argued that to support Tshombe was to set the stage for similar situations in southern Africa: The white racist forces in Rhodesia would be encouraged and would tend to support throughout southern Africa a whole series of impediments to democratic and nonracial governments. There was also at stake the issue of the unity of countries in Africa. For us to have supported Tshombe would have meant that we would divide ourselves from the general wave of opinion in Africa. There was also an attempt to portray this as an anticommunist Tshombe against a procommunist. This simply was not true. The leaders in Léopoldville may not have been the most competent people to run a country as big as the U.S. east of the Mississippi, but they were by no means communists.

In the end game the president was on the side of supporting the integrity of the Congo. There were pressures against this from all over the administration. Throughout Washington the Congo was quite divisive. In the Congress Hubert Humphrey was very supportive of our policy. On the other side of the issue was Senator Thomas Dodd [D., Conn.]. So there we were in the African Bureau, sitting in the midst of all of these pressures.

South Africa

Wayne Fredericks   As I observed the president, I tended to get the picture of someone who was under pressure from both sides—from black America and from the kinds of forces represented by Senator Dodd, some business interests, and other, much more conservative people. I don't know how the president weighed those forces from a political sense—if he did—in arriving at certain foreign policy decisions on Africa.

Our view in the bureau was that we couldn't be in favor of civil rights in the United States while supporting the status quo in South Africa. What could you do about it? It was a sovereign and strong country with lots of friends in Washington. There were business and military people in the United States who had lived and worked in South Africa. We put some task forces to work to figure out what things we were doing which we should stop. We cut back on military attachés there with McNamara's assistance, and we were able to have NASA move a major tracking station away from South Africa. These were messages to the Pretoria government. We discussed the issue of sanctions, but we did not have the support of the other Western nations.

Bobby Baker   It's a small world. Maurice Templesman, the guy who's Mrs. Kennedy's companion now, a diamond merchant—he's a dear friend of mine—when Kennedy was president, was close to the South African government, and we needed uranium. The price was very high. The former chairman of the Atomic Energy Commission had a deal that we would swap, say, a billion dollars' worth of wheat for a billion dollars' worth of uranium, so Maurice Templesman was involved.

John Lewis   He had a number of African guests, and you could see these young African leaders coming to Washington, and seeing John F. Kennedy and Mrs. Kennedy standing there—with the African leader and his wife—that sent a message. At the same time, some of the South African students at campuses in the South were saying that the whole of Africa would be free before we can get a hamburger and a Coca-Cola.

Connections between Black Americans and Africans

Wayne Fredericks   Early on I told Governor Williams that in my travels in Africa I had met a number of very capable young career foreign service officers, and a number of people in private life, in the academic world, and in business, who had lived and worked in Africa. I suggested we take a look at this range of people. This interested not only Governor Williams but Chester Bowles as well, so rather early in the game we started to select people who knew something about Africa. We made a good number of changes in personnel there.

We were also very conscious of the strong connections between Africans and black Americans. At that point there were very few blacks in positions of importance in the African Bureau. Soapy, having been a key figure in the civil rights movement as far back as 1948, moved on that very quickly, and we began to recruit black Americans.

We formed an advisory council to advise the African Bureau. This brought a number of black Americans into our work. As a result of this, I helped to organize the American Negro Leadership Conference on Africa, which consisted of the six major civil rights leaders at the time. I met with them every couple of months, so early in the game, we tried to move on the human front, the black front. Soapy tried to bring more blacks into the foreign service. It was not exactly a closed corporation, but there were not very many blacks in key positions or anywhere.

Problems of Black Africans in the United States

Angier Biddle Duke   That was a time when it wasn't safe for black people to travel in the South. I remember having an experience with Vice President [William] Tolbert of Liberia. He was here unofficially. But he wanted to drive through the South informally, and he said that he didn't want any security people and he didn't want this and he didn't want that. He just wanted to go down to Atlanta, and he wanted to drive to Washington. Now, it's a terrible thing to say, "You can't do it—it's not safe." So I called Terry Sanford, who was the governor of North Carolina at the time, and I said, "We have a vice president of a country. We'd like to see that he gets through all right. Could you discreetly watch him, monitor him, assign security, intelligence people to pick him up and see that he gets through?" Well, we got him through. He never even knew that he was being followed the whole way and things were made easy for him. He never had any problems.

We were going into Knoxville, Tennessee. There was an old hotel, and I called ahead and said, "I'm bringing the prime minister of Nigeria. Are we going to have difficulties of any kind?" "No, none at all." Just for the heck of it, I said, "The prime minister is a great swimmer; how about the swimming pool?" He replied, "Oh, no. Not the swimming pool." I said, "Yes, the swimming pool." "Oh, please, sir," he said. "We'll drain the pool." I said, "You keep that pool open or else we'll do two things: Number one, we won't come, and two, I'm going to see to it that you are sued under civil rights acts." "Mr. Ambassador, bring him." So that was the last little whimper I got on that field.

Wayne Fredericks   We worked a lot on the issue of African diplomats traveling between New York and Washington, both with the Africans and with the communities where incidents took place. We tried to respond to almost every incident. At that stage of the game, the wives had all sorts of problems: Coming from some obscure point in Africa to be the wife of an ambassador in Washington, how do you entertain? How do you handle household problems? Here the wives of members of the department, headed up by Mrs. Rusk and Mrs. Bowles, played an important and helpful role.

Angier Biddle Duke   Let's say that the Cameroon ambassador would arrive in Washington with his family, with language problems, and no place to stay—with all the covenants in the real estate section along Kalorama Road in Georgetown, nobody would sell to blacks, and they couldn't get a decent residence in the District of Columbia, nor could they set up office space; none of the office buildings in Washington would rent to blacks. It became my peculiar, strange duty to see that the diplomats could exercise their missions in our country. So I set up a special mission of the protocol office. We called it Special Protocol Services, and I got a very bright, aggressive, intelligent young man called Pedro San Juan to head it up. I had a lot of other things to do, but we did set this up, and we went at it pretty systematically.

We called for a meeting with the Real Estate Board of Washington, and the head of it was Morris Cafritz, who was a reasonable man to whom you could explain: "We've got these nations arriving here. The real estate people won't sell to them. Now what is it that's necessary? What do we have to do to bring our country in line with civilized behavior in the rest of the world?" And Morris Cafritz got it—in one afternoon, and with almost a stroke of a pen, he called a meeting of the Real Estate Board and asked me to present my case to them. They came right around. They said, "Sure, you bet we'll cooperate." It was amazing how Washington fell in place.

There were just a few agencies in Washington that had to be sold. That was the easiest one, the one that Morris Cafritz did. Then there were some others that required a bit more convincing, and a bit more arm-twisting, and we got some congressional leaders to work with us on that. It was interesting work but quite amazingly productive. Within a few weeks, we got Washington, D.C., the federal capital, and then, of course, the restaurants—the Restaurant Association, so that there was no possibility of anybody being embarrassed by going out in Washington. The clubs were tough. I had to resign from the Metropolitan Club, for example. But they've since come around.

We were able then to at least assure dignified residence and work space for the incoming ambassadors. Then, of course, there was the issue of housing their staff, their secretaries, and so on, who didn't necessarily live in the District of Columbia. That meant Virginia and Maryland. And then, some of the poorer nations couldn't afford to have ambassadors in both New York and Washington. They would accredit them to both places. We didn't like that. We discouraged it.

The Greek-Turkish Question

Phillips Talbot The president shared some of Jackie's enthusiasm for the Greek islands. In fact, we had a situation that was somewhat awkward—in which Jackie had gone off to Greece. The Kennedys knew Onassis, who had invited Jackie on his yacht to do some touring. We heard belatedly that the itinerary was going to include Istanbul. Well, for the wife of the president of the United States, at a time of tension, to visit Istanbul on a Greek yacht would have had repercussions. When this was laid out to the president, he caught it immediately and she didn't do that. It was clear that she had no great interest in Turkey. It was just that the yacht was traveling. Greek yachts always liked to touch Turkish ports because this makes the cruise international, and they get tax exemption from all the stores they buy in, whereas if they're only in Greek waters, they have to pay Greek taxes—I'm not suggesting Onassis couldn't pay his taxes.

The foreign lobbies that were the strongest in Washington in those days were the Israeli and the Greek lobbies. And both of those lobbies tended to have strong connections with the Democratic party, so that was a substantial consideration. Nonetheless, Kennedy was prepared to spend political chips in efforts to resolve some of these problems.

India

John Kenneth Galbraith There was always the problem with India as to whether economic aid was for good, compassionate purposes—which it largely was—or to recolonize India on behalf of the Americans after they got rid of the British, which was the view held not by Nehru but by a certain number of Indian intellectuals and publicists. So one was always contending with that ambivalence.

Phillips Talbot President Kennedy was interested in India—probably the first American president who was. He had Ken Galbraith out there, and he was intrigued. He and Nehru didn't get on too well together; they were intellectually quite different types; but the idea of an emergent

India appealed to President Kennedy, and so he paid attention. It was a time when we could be somewhat open handed in our aid programs and he was very much hoping that the subcontinent could quiet down, and that India and Pakistan could be reasonably good neighbors, because he felt it was an important part of the world.

There was a feeling that Pakistan in the 1950s, in the Eisenhower administration, had been a little unduly built up. India, quite clearly, in its conviction about nonalignment, refused to join any group with the U.S. Pakistan said, "Yes. We'll join." Pakistan offered geography really for U.S. activities. We had communications facilities there, and were eavesdropping on the Soviet missile range—that kind of thing, which the Pakistanis gave us in a relationship which had been fairly close, based upon different assumptions and expectations. The Pakistanis did this—as a junior country in the subcontinent—to have an American ally to give them more weight to balance the relationship with India. The Americans thought the Pakistanis were anticommunists and were resolutely going to help in anything against the Soviet Union. And later, when the collisions came, it was in part, I think, because of misunderstanding.

The Indians resented U.S. policy toward Pakistan. In the Kennedy administration, we emphasized India a bit more and Pakistan not so much, which caused some difficulties too. And then President Ayub came from Pakistan. That relationship, which started out fairly cool, warmed up to some extent. Also, in those days, as in other times, the Pentagon was very strongly insistent that we keep those facilities. We had the feeling that once we got satellites, we wouldn't be so dependent on these bits and pieces of real estate around the periphery of the Soviet Union. But until the satellites were ready, they were desperately important, so the whole question on the part of the Pentagon was to keep the relationship with Pakistan. The result, as in the case of Greece and Turkey, was that neither India nor Pakistan was happy with our policy, and we kind of bumped along with both.

Latin America

Edwin Martin Kennedy felt quite strongly that Latin America was much more important to the United States than previous presidents had recognized. He was keenly interested from the development standpoint, but he was also keenly interested from the Castro-Cuba standpoint. He would not have gotten the congressional and public support for his program if Castro had not been in Cuba. In his campaign against Nixon, he had denounced the Republicans for letting Castro take over. He had a real personal interest, but also a major policy interest. He felt the major encouragement of communism in Latin America was poverty.

Lincoln Gordon In the northern part of South America—we didn't go to Central America or the Caribbeans, just to ten countries in South America—there was tremendous interest and excitement. I'm speaking of Venezuela. Castro, of course, had tried to assassinate Betancourt [Rómulo Betancourt, president of Venezuela] and had very nearly succeeded. Betancourt had burns all over his hands and still had bandages at that time from the assassination attempt. I think they did kill somebody in his entourage with one of these car bombs.

But we found as we went further south, that the interest in Cuba was smaller and smaller. Down in Uruguay and Argentina and Brazil, the important problems were those of the big countries; that was their general frame of mind.

On the way back we cooked up a written report, rating the people that we met and what we thought was their order of priority, cooperativeness, and ability. When we got back to Washington, Adlai Stevenson and I went to report orally to the president as well as giving him the written report. He had a bad cold, so we talked to him in his bedroom in the White House. It was really a severe cold, I remember. But he was very interested.

One big question was, Should he promote a summit meeting? Adlai had waffled back and forth on this question, in the way that was supposed to be characteristic of him; he was described, characterized, as a Hamlet who never could quite make up his mind to act, and there were some other evidences of that, although he was a wonderful man. We got to be fast friends. I saw him after that every time I was in New York. I had come to the conclusion that a summit meeting might be useful at some place down the pike, but at this stage, it was not really a particularly good idea. The report, in fact, had leaned that way. Adlai had finally, sort of, come around to agreeing with us on this.

But we talked about the pros and cons with Kennedy. Obviously Stevenson was doing the great bulk of the talking. I mean Stevenson and Kennedy were doing the great bulk of the talking; I was essentially a listener. Once or twice Kennedy asked me something, or Stevenson asked me to comment on some particular people.

Kennedy was fascinated by the personalities. He asked us a lot about the individual presidents; what they were like, what their strengths and weaknesses seemed to be. It was a pretty long session, if I remember correctly. And I guess it ended up with some business about how the public relations aspects of it were to be handled. Stevenson was very good at that.

Brazil

Lincoln Gordon   Kennedy obviously couldn't have taken the same degree of interest in every country in the world that he did in Brazil; it would have been impossible. He obviously had some priority. I think he did something like this for India. India and Brazil were the two great aid recipients of that time.

The president invited me to be ambassador to Brazil. On a visit to Washington, the president and I cooked up the idea of a visit to Brazil by his brother if it wasn't possible or desirable for the president to go, and we decided we should get Bobby invited.

We had to have a flimsy pretext for Bobby to give to Goulart [João Goulart, vice president, and later president of Brazil] a firsthand message from John Kennedy. The essence of that message was: "We got along very well when you were here in April, but as I read the press and read the reports from Brazil, and learn from Ambassador Gordon, things have taken a very questionable turn. Maybe it's all in connection with your efforts to get back full presidential powers, but it also could be construed as an anti–United States, indeed, anti-Western turn in the road." He wasn't accusing Goulart of being a communist but of being very nationalist and not at all interested in collaborating under the Alliance for Progress. And the essence of the Bobby Kennedy message—it was not an ultimatum—was: "The United States has great regard for Brazil as a country and would like to help in its development in removing many of its problems. We have developed this Alliance for Progress—many of the ideas of which came from your own people; they played a very important part at Punta del Este in drafting the charter—but we know now that by then a plebiscite had been arranged for January, and everybody knew that Goulart was going to win it. We know you'll have full presidential powers and at that time you really must make up your mind whether you want to cooperate with us or not. And if you do, there are all these things that we would like to help you with." There was no threat, but the notion was that obviously, if they didn't cooperate, we wouldn't be cooperating, and that would be unfortunate. Goulart listened to all of that, and half responded.

Costa Rica

Edwin Martin We were almost persuaded not to go to Costa Rica because of the student problem, and that certainly he must not go to the university. Kennedy insisted that he wanted to go out to the university. They did arrest one student, but I had to join the Secret Service agents to protect him from the students who wanted to shake hands and wave to him, so that we could get him to the helicopter.

Cuba

Manuel Ray, member, Cuban Revolutionary Council; former minister of public works in Fidel Castro's government We started the relationship with Castro at the time of Batista [Fulgencio Batista, president of Cuba, 1952–59]. It was the struggle of the decent people of Cuba against a corrupt government. I became head of the Havana organization. Our task was to eliminate human misery. I knew that the United States had been in communication with Batista, and that some companies had connections with his government, but I never thought that the United States had a commitment to Batista. As a matter of fact, in the underground we had had contact with the American Embassy in Havana. We found there some people who understood our program. Some others did not. We felt there had been a shift in U.S. policy toward Cuba—that there was an attempt to put some distance between the U.S. government and Batista.

Thomas Mann I think if it had not been for the military power of the Soviet Union, we would not have been so preoccupied with Castro. But there were missiles with atomic warheads there pointed directly at the U.S. I considered Castro a puppet of Soviet military power who controlled territory ninety miles from the U.S., and I wasn't wrong.

Manuel Ray In the fall of 1959 I was in Havana, working in the underground against Castro. I received a call from the ambassador of Brazil to Cuba. He was willing to meet me underground. This was a risk for him, and quite unusual. We met and he told me that he was passing on a message from the American ambassador, Philip Bonsal, that the United States government sympathized with us and would try to help us. I told the Brazilian ambassador that we appreciated the offer, but we felt we would have to do most of the work ourselves, as we had done in Batista's time.

In the spring of 1959, when the Havana baseball team was still in the International League, there was an important game in Havana. We were having a cabinet meeting when Fidel said, "Let's go to the game." So we went to the ball park. That was the time of the climax of the popularity of Fidel. We came through the center field, and as we went to our seats, everyone was cheering Castro. Then we sat down, and some minutes later, it was announced that Mr. Philip Bonsal, the American ambassador, had arrived. It was the same thing; everybody stood up, and there was applause. The next day in the cabinet meeting, Fidel said, "Did you notice how the people reacted to a nation like this?"

Eugene McCarthy They say Castro was scouted by the New York Giants; that they offered him five thousand dollars to sign, but he wouldn't take it. He was also scouted by Clark Griffith, the owner of the Washington Senators. He brought in a number of Cubans. He scouted three pitchers, and the third one was Fidel. One of the reports was that they tried to get him with a baseball that was a bomb—that he would play catch with. When I saw Castro a number of years ago, I said, "I am really ashamed they tried to get you with a baseball." He told me, "We have a great shortstop here. They want him in the majors. But I can't let him go." I asked why not. Castro replied, "Ideology."

Manuel Ray Che Guevara [Ernesto ("Che") Guevara, key associate of Fidel Castro] came to see me in February 1959. He wanted the Ministry of Public Works, which I headed, to design a road to the top of the hills in the Sierre Maestre. It would be very costly to build this road and it did not seem that it would add to the development of the country. He said to me, "It is not meant for development; rather, it is to be a military road."

He also asked that we build some underground bunkers, because, he said, in a few months we would be fighting the United States. It seemed strange to me at the time, but he was sure there would be war.

Lincoln Gordon Goodwin was really playing games. At Punta del Este, he got involved in a private meeting with Che Guevara. I think he thought he was going to make up with Cuba. I remember Guevara gave him a great box of cigars with a lovely inscription on it. It was megalomania. I mean, he had grossly exaggerated views, and he really was extraordinarily innocent of understanding about what Latin America was all about. I felt something of a neophyte myself, but at least I'd been working on it for several years.

Manuel Ray When I left Cuba in November 1960 and went to Miami, I was troubled by the kinds of people the CIA was bringing into their effort. Many of them were conservatives; some were corrupt and completely against our principles.

We planned an uprising for November 26, 1960, on the Isle of Pines. We had the cooperation of several officers stationed there. I was going to fly from Miami to the Isle of Pines. Our policy was to ask assistance from the United States agencies only when we really needed it. We were prepared to act ourselves and felt we could do everything ourselves, but we did need some antiaircraft weapons to succeed. We were denied these weapons by the CIA operatives; we were told they were planning their own operation. I believe we would have been successful at the Isle of Pines if we had been given these weapons.

Mexico

Thomas Mann Kennedy's visit was magnificent—the only visit, I would have to say, in my time in the foreign service, where the gain outweighed the risks. It was tremendously successful. I have never seen anything like it, before or since. Jackie made a speech with a few sentences which she had memorized in Spanish. There were tears in the eyes of her listeners. Kennedy conducted himself very well. He and López Mateos [Adolfo López Mateos, president of Mexico] discussed a tract of land near El Paso, Texas. I had worked on this question ten years before, and became convinced that this was really Mexican territory.

Edwin Martin   On the Saturday afternoon before the Thursday the president left for Mexico, in June 1962, I got a call from the White House saying, We want you to meet with people from CIA, the Pentagon, and the State Department who are involved in security for the trip. I was also told Bobby Kennedy wanted to be with me, so I called Bobby, and he suggested we meet in my office. He came to my office at State, with his dog, to meet with all these people, and we decided it was fair risk that the Mexicans had done a good job. President Kennedy never got a warmer recognition any place in the world than he did in Mexico; the people were overwhelmingly enthusiastic, and Mexico had not been overfriendly to the United States. Immediately afterward, the political leaders were all busy telling each other, "We've been wrong about America." I think his personality, more than anything, influenced the Mexicans. On one occasion, he told a large audience that he and Jackie had had their honeymoon in Mexico, and that was how much they loved the country. They also broke tradition and went to the cathedral.

Thomas Mann   I was always opposed to visits by any president to any foreign country, especially in Latin America, because I think the dangers of being shot outweigh the temporary benefits of public relations. The dangers are very real. When I was in Mexico for the president's visit, I spent all my time in my office monitoring FBI and CIA reports. The Mexican government rounded up hundreds of people as a favor to themselves and to us. There was a real danger; Castro was there. Kennedy and President López Mateos rode in an open limousine from the airport, through the center of the city to the embassy. Anybody on top of a building, or in a window with a rifle, could have shot him.

Venezuela

Edwin Martin   When Kennedy was planning to visit Venezuela in December 1961, there was a lot of concern about the security situation, and particularly regarding students. The authorities, recognizing that when students are in classes they can get together to do things, advanced the Christmas holiday by about ten days.

The Alliance for Progress

Edwin Martin   The genesis for the Alliance for Progress was Milton Eisenhower [president John Hopkins University; brother of Dwight D. Eisenhower]. In 1953 or '54, President Eisenhower sent him to take a tour around Latin America to see what the problems were. After the Nixon visit—after the vice president got in trouble in Venezuela—the president sent Milton Eisenhower down again. His reports of what needed doing became the basis of the Alliance for Progress. Furthermore, in 1959, the president of Brazil, [Juscelino] Kubitschek, announced an Operation Pan American program, which was similar, although it made the mistake of saying that it was the Marshall Plan for America. The president really believed in the alliance. He, and many of us, thought that its aims could be achieved in ten years. The question is, Would it have happened better if Kennedy had had a second term? Johnson never took any great interest in the alliance; he never visited a Latin American country.

Lincoln Gordon   Ed Martin had participated actively in developing the Alliance for Progress. Then he was moved over from being assistant secretary for Economic Affairs to being assistant secretary for Latin America, and had to bear the cross of having Goodwin assigned to him as deputy assistant secretary. That was like oil and water; they didn't get along. And Goodwin was always running off the reservation, trying to make policy more or less on his own. It made life difficult for Ed Martin.

In spite of this considerable confidence that the powers that be had in me, I never strayed off the reservation. I was always reporting properly, keeping everybody informed, and generally speaking, providing policy advice that was accepted. And occasionally, I felt sufficiently confident about its character so that I would do something and get it ratified afterwards. I wasn't playing any games.

Thomas Mann   The Alliance for Progress was a propaganda ploy and, to a certain extent, a domestic political propaganda ploy. There was nothing new in it as compared with the Act of Bogotá, except for the spelling out of goals. Economic progress is essentially a self-help process. What will work in Western Europe may not work in Latin America; there is a great difference between Bolivia and Paris. We cannot control internal political developments in another country. That is the first lesson you learn in the first grade in foreign relations. I think Kennedy understood the real world. He was making political noises.

Lucius Battle   At the time of the Alliance for Progress, I talked to a number of people who were old Latin America hands, and they said, "It's too good to be true; we will not have the follow-through. We will never get the money. We'll be building up expectations that are not going to be forthcoming, and we're better off not building them up than we are letting them down."

Lincoln Gordon   My first return to Washington was at around Thanksgiving, because the AID, in its first work on cutting up the Alliance for Progress, had proposed an appropriation for Brazil that the AID director and I thought was too small.

Kennedy spoke no foreign language. That, incidentally, was why it was called the Alliance for Progress instead of the Alliance for Development. The first idea was to call it Alianza para el Desarrollo, which in Portuguese would be paro o Desovolomento. But Betancourt said he'd heard Kennedy try to pronounce foreign words a couple of times and he had a wooden tongue, and *Desarrollo* would obviously be beyond him, so let's think of something that pronounces the same in English as it does in Spanish. And *Progreso* was chosen—I believe they actually had a bottle of Progresso olive oil or something on the shelf at this time. This is the story Betancourt tells of where the name came from. It was a wise choice.

Goodwin didn't know the Spanish grammar. And in the original speech it was called Alianza para Progreso without the *el*, which is bad Spanish; it wouldn't be bad in Portuguese without the definite article. That finally got cleared up. Goodwin never could understand it. He'd say, "Why do they want to say 'Alliance for *the* Progress'? It doesn't sound well; it doesn't ring well."

The Middle East

The Kennedy administration attempted to establish ties with moderate Arab leaders, sought a solution to the Arab refugee problem, and in a break

with precedent, sold Israel major weaponry, including the Hawk missile.
Kennedy, who visited Palestine in 1939 and Israel in 1953, developed his
Middle East policy within the context of the traditional fiscal and electoral
support given the Democratic party by the American Jewish community.

Dean Rusk I would have to play down the Middle East as a matter of deep concern to President Kennedy.

Yuri Barsukov The Middle East was part of the problem in Soviet-American relations at the time. We asked questions on the Middle East, especially at the State Department briefings. This problem was discussed I know through diplomatic channels by Mr. Gromyko [Andrei Gromyko, foreign minister, USSR], who paid his regular visits to the UN General Assembly.

Phillips Talbot Kennedy didn't like the Saudi princes very much, especially after one of them cooked a little food in Blair House. A rug got burned. But he had respect for Faisal [crown prince of Saudi Arabia; King, 1964–75] as a serious person.

Working with Nasser

Robert Komer Kennedy was determined to have good relations with Israel without sacrificing relations with the Arab states. In fact, he bought my proposal that we try to get on a better basis with Gamal Abdel Nasser [president, United Arab Republic], which I had gotten through up to the Eisenhower National Security Council—and John Foster Dulles had peed on it. He said, "This is absolutely ridiculous. This guy is a Communist." His brother, Allen, didn't tell him he wasn't.

Mordechai Gazit It wasn't until September 1962, with the situation in Yemen, that the administration realized they had misread Nasser. And U.S. Ambassador Badeau [John Badeau (United Arab Republic)] helped them misread him.

Phillips Talbot We worked with Nasser in a variety of ways during the early period, and became increasingly conscious that Nasser, who was an ambitious man, was trying to assert his preeminence in the Arab world and was involved in efforts to establish his presence, not only in what was then called the UAR, the United Arab Republic—a joining of Syria and Egypt—but also in the Arabian Peninsula. And the problem that really led us to turn away from that effort, I think, was Nasser's determination to go into Yemen. We recognized Nasser, of course. We did not immediately, overtly oppose him on it. But when it became clear that he was pushing very hard, and when Faisal and the Saudis were getting increasingly nervous about this, it was clear that the relationship with Nasser was not going to work out as we had hoped.

The Israeli-Arab Impasse

Dean Rusk   I don't think Kennedy had any original ideas about the crisis between Israel and its Arab neighbors. I bear many scars from aborted efforts to find a solution. Had I known where the solution would lie, we would have solved that problem twenty-five years ago and not have had it drag on all this time. But I can't remember that Kennedy had any fresh ideas about the Middle East crisis. As a matter of fact, the Middle East was fairly dormant during Kennedy's years. It was not until the June 1967 War, during the Johnson administration, that things heated up a good deal.

Norman Podhoretz   He had no original ideas; I am not sure he had any ideas at all. What we know now—what I was not aware of then—is that Dean Rusk was violently anti-Israel. I assume he always had those feelings—maybe not as outspoken as today, but he sounded recently like a typical State Department Arabist of those years, and he was the secretary of state. But the Arab-Israeli conflict was not that salient in those years; nothing very big was going on. I don't remember it coming up all that much.

Mordechai Gazit   Rusk is a man who will get low marks in Israel's history because of his behavior in 1947 and '48.[*] He was dealing with United Nations affairs. The United States in 1948 changed its policy from partition to something phony, called trusteeship, and Rusk had very much to do with that, so he, Loy Henderson [former director, State

---

[*]In 1947–48 Rusk headed the State Department's UN desk. He opposed the UN partition plan for Palestine that would have set up two separate states and favored a binational state as the best solution to the conflict between the Jews and the Arabs.

Department Middle East Desk] and Robert Lovett were really not in our good books. Let's be open minded: In that period there were problems with Britain, so Rusk was laboring under difficulties. But when you meet with him, you encounter, again, this poker face, and the lack of real interest and warmth. I think Harman [Israel's ambassador to the United States, Avraham Harman] felt this.

Dean Rusk   It's ironic that the Palestinians are now demanding an Arab state in Palestine; they could have had an Arab state in Palestine had they accepted the partition resolution in 1947, which provided for an Arab state in Palestine and for a Jewish state in Palestine. But they went to war to prevent any part of the partition resolution from taking effect, including the creation of the state of Israel.

In a sense the Arabs have needed a good lawyer at times to tell them how to act to protect Arab interests in a timely fashion. There are many illustrations of that: In the session of the General Assembly which was considering the partition plan, in the American delegation we had counted noses in the assembly and we realized that if the Arabs made a simple motion to adjourn, that they had the votes to adjourn the assembly without a decision. Mr. Chamoun [Camille Chamoun, Lebanon's UN ambassador], the floor leader of the Arab side, went to the podium and made a motion to adjourn, but then, to our astonishment, he added the creation of a committee or commission to do x, y, or z. Well, that turned his motion into a substantive motion—an important motion which required a two-thirds vote. And he failed to get the two-thirds vote; had he just stopped with the motion to adjourn, he could have adjourned the assembly without a decision. So he needed a good lawyer on that occasion.

Israel's Special Relationship with the United States

Mordechai Gazit   Some months after the Kennedy administration began, Abba Eban, who was then Israel's Minister of Education and Culture, came to Washington. This was the same day that Golda Meir, the foreign minister, came, so our ambassador, Avraham Harman, was busy with the foreign minister. I was the number two, so I had to accompany Eban. He was staying at the Mayflower Hotel, and there, in a private room, we had Walt Rostow and McGeorge Bundy with Eban, certainly three very brilliant people. I distinctly remember my impression from that conversation, and it was a very optimistic one—that everything was open; everything could be reconsidered; there was no fixed or set mind. Under Eisenhower the feeling was that everything was terribly frozen.

Robert Komer   If I wasn't getting anywhere with the Israelis, I wrote a letter to Ben Gurion for the president to sign. Ben Gurion would call in Golda Meir and say, "Listen, we want to maintain good relations with the Americans. Now do it." He was a very independent guy.

Phillips Talbot   And years later, I got the impression, actually from the Israeli side, that the conversation involved Kennedy's acknowledgment of his dependence on the help he received from the Zionist community here [the United States]. And he was apparently reassuring the Israelis that he wouldn't go too far.

Mordechai Gazit   They always suspected us of exerting pressure on the administration—they were so well intentioned, and we were exerting pressure. Now, in those days we were not exerting too much pressure at all. We said, "This is no longer the Eisenhower administration. It's new; let's give them a chance." Also, we knew that without the massive Jewish vote for Kennedy, he would not have been able to achieve this very small plurality in the popular vote. I remember distinctly a conversation with Mike Feldman, when he was angry after Roscoe Drummond [syndicated columnist], in two lines in a five-hundred-word column, said that the balance of arms was tipped to the Arabs and had to be redressed. Feldman thought we had planted this. I said, "We didn't plant this. But let me tell you, if, indeed, you are concerned with the arms balance, it can only help you if a columnist tells you there may be a problem there."

Robert Komer   Mike Feldman could go in directly to the president, and the president, being a superb politician, was always very conscious of the fact he had won the 1960 election by only one hundred thousand to two hundred thousand votes. So he listened to Mike. He was calculating the impact upon domestic politics.

*Magazine published by AJC.

Norman Podhoretz   I had just become the editor of *Commentary* in 1960, and I remember how shocked I was when I heard that Mike Feldman had a meeting in the Oval Office with some American Jewish Committee leaders, where Kennedy complained about some critical articles in *Commentary*° about the administration. Of course, these AJC leaders—most of whom didn't read *Commentary*—were quite startled to hear this and didn't know what to say, and I remember thinking it was typical that the Kennedys would complain to the publisher without ever thinking that there might be such a thing as editorial independence.

Dean Rusk   Undoubtedly there was this steady, continuing pressure from the organized Jews in this country, some twelve Jewish organizations, to keep the United States in support of Israel. There was a foreign policy reason, however, for the same thing, because we recognized if American support for Israel seemed to falter, then the Arab price would go up and they would wind up demanding the extinction of the state of Israel. And so we had to keep that very much in mind.

Mordechai Gazit   On one occasion we went to see Harriman. We were meeting on the water question,° and after we had explained to him what we had come to see him about, he said, "Look, I don't understand." This was after we had discussed this problem for many months at lower levels. He said, "The Jordan River doesn't flow in America, so what does this have to do with us?" I thought this was a terrible thing. He was undersecretary at the time. This could destroy everything we had done. So I was so angry. I said, "But Mr. Secretary, there *is* a Jordan River in the United States. It is near Salt Lake City."

There was the beginning of a realization that we could not be easily intimidated diplomatically. I recall a conversation with Robert Komer in 1963 when we were interested in purchasing some tanks. This was like asking for a hydrogen bomb then. He said, "Why do you want tanks? Buy helicopters and you can attack tanks from the air." This tactic was, of course, developed later. So I said to him, "Look, the Israel Defense Forces need tanks. I am not going to talk them out of it. Maybe you can." He replied,

°An issue between Israel and neighboring Arab nations concerning control of the sources of the Jordan River.

"Why don't you discuss this with the State Department?" I said, "Because they will throw me out of the room." He said, "Have they ever thrown you out of the room?" I had a reputation of being tough.

Robert Komer   The Israeli ambassador [Harman] was a pain in the neck. He had been president of Hebrew University, and they made him ambassador, and I want to tell you—he wasn't a very good ambassador. In the first place he was very emotional. When he got excited about an issue—about how his country was being mishandled—he would cry. And goddamn—to have an ambassador weeping in your office! I said, "Leave that for the State Department; go over and cry on the State Department's time." Well, he was a decent guy. He said, "I get emotionally involved." His deputy, Mordechai Gazit, was one hard case. Apparently he and the ambassador regarded me as a hard case. They would come to see me with the damnedest stories you ever heard.

Mordechai Gazit   Bundy told me some years ago that he dealt very little with the Middle East; it was Komer's baby. This may explain that, on the one hand, there was an open mind, but it wasn't put to use. Bundy was interested in Europe. There was the Berlin crisis, and gradually there was Vietnam. Whenever Bundy had to deal with the Middle East, it was because he was put into an angry mood. Then he was angry with us. Israel had a role from the Middle Ages: Whenever the king was angry, there always was someone he flogged or whipped. So that was Israel. I remember one day Bundy phoned. The ambassador was away, so he talked to me. He was so angry, impolite, and discourteous in his remarks: "What do you think you are doing?" And we really had done nothing.

When Kennedy met with Golda Meir he said, "Madame Foreign Minister, let me tell you, we have a special relationship with Israel." Since when did we have a special relationship? Only when he opened his mouth at that meeting in December 1962. So the special relationship was born then and there. Then he said, "We will have the will and the capacity to come to Israel's assistance, if attacked."

Mordechai Gazit   If I look back at the many contacts I had with Bob Komer, he was not an easy customer. He thinks I was not easy either. I think I was easier. I did have the feeling that essentially he was open minded and that I could persuade him. I did not even discuss the Hawk with Feldman once, but with Komer I discussed it ad nauseam. I had a feeling that he was not that negative.

Robert Komer   Mike Feldman dealt with the president, and the first thing he asked for were the Hawk missiles. We had not given Israel any military aid; we gave them money and told them to buy from the British, French, or Germans. I found about the Hawks when, very late in the exercise, Kennedy asked me—when I was in his office on other business— "What do you think of the Hawk sale to the Israelis?" I said, "The Israelis have a pretty good case. They used to get military aid from Germany under Adenauer." The Israelis argue now that they have no more German aid; they need to ask somebody else. Kennedy said, "I'm not going to turn Mike off, but I will keep you clued in, and if you differ, you can send me a memo." So I became, in effect, the White House Arab, and Feldman the White House Jew, which was not fair, because I called them as I saw them, but he was simply a tool of the Israelis, going straight into the White House.

After a while the Israeli ambassador came to see me. I said, "If you have anything that is bothering you and you want to get it to the president, I recommend that you try through me, because he has a great deal more confidence in my objectivity and knowledge of the situation than he does in yours." Well, Mike didn't appreciate that; it was an insult, so he never told me anything unless he felt he had to.

Mordechai Gazit   Feldman did not engineer the Hawk himself; the State Department was very involved. At the last moment Britain offered us the Bloodhound system. But we did not want Bloodhound; we wanted the U.S. to get involved. We had France; we didn't need Britain. We wanted the U.S. for more advanced weapons. There was no formal announcement of the sale; the administration leaked the news to the *New York Times*.

Dean Rusk   We wanted Israel to have a military capacity to be able to defend itself without the introduction of U.S. forces, and so we sold Israel a fair amount of arms, including some sophisticated arms to put them in position to fend off any attacks. That of course upset the Arab side, but again, had we not done so, the Arab price would have gone through the ceiling; their demands would have been outrageous.

The Arab Refugee Problem

Robert Komer   In my opinion our lack of leverage on the Israelis, more than anything else, made it impossible to achieve any kind of Arab-Israeli settlement. We put up a proposal on the Arab exiles from Palestine and said if they wanted to go to Israel, we ought to start with about one hundred thousand and we will find the funds. The State Department insisted that most Arabs living in Saudi Arabia, Egypt, Libya, or Syria were not going to come back. They had established lives there, had families, and careers, and they would have to give up all of this if they came back. We said to the Israelis, "You can easily handle fifty thousand of the first one hundred thousand; we don't think that number will come at all." Well, the Israelis flatly disagreed with us. They thought all one hundred thousand were going to come to Israel and start a war. I said, "Look, they don't even have weapons." They said, "They'll steal ours." Well, we never convinced them. I must say that in 1961–62 the only person approaching JFK on Arab-Israeli matters was Mike Feldman, and Mike simply retailed the Israeli story without having a clue—or any other evidence—pro or con.

Phillips Talbot   President Kennedy had on the White House staff, quite outside the National Security Council staff, a gentleman named Mike Feldman, who made himself the person who, if you will, would give the other side of the story from the establishment's, the bureaucracy's, and who would constantly point out the risks and dangers of policy lines that were probably making the Israelis unhappy. I'm sure that Kennedy listened to him. Indeed, it was he, I believe, more than anyone else, who persuaded the president to call off the effort on the Palestinian refugees, because this was getting too costly for him. I thought that Mike Feldman went too far in trying to change the balance of foreign policy efforts because of domestic political considerations. Mike and I had a reasonably friendly running argument through most of that period.

Mordechai Gazit   My general feeling in that period was that if we could only talk to President Kennedy privately about the conflict, it would help. But the reality is that relations were such that we could not hope for this.

We warned Ben Gurion that Kennedy would raise the refugee question with him. We told Ben Gurion the best way to answer is to suggest setting up a technical committee to outline the parameters of the problem. He could have said, "Mr. President, do you realize what you are proposing here? I am sure you have the interests of Israel at heart. Do you really think that in a democratic government, I can pull this through? This is an election year. How can I do that?" But Ben Gurion didn't listen to us.

Phillips Talbot   We were contributing a lot of money for the [refugee] camps because the camps were better than what the alternative would have been if there hadn't been a settlement, but the arrangement was that the schools in the camps were run by refugees, and there's no doubt that they became indoctrination centers for the refugee families, and that the infection would grow and grow and grow. We had a plan that would have offered every refugee family a choice between taking a financial settlement, which, obviously, we would have had to provide, and going off into the Arab world, or anywhere else in the world, or returning to Israel. Now this is what scared the Israelis. The conditions we put on this we thought would keep most of the Arabs out. They would not necessarily get their prior lands back; they'd get some compensation for them. They would have to submit to Israeli law and become Israeli citizens with full obligations, including military. We thought that most of the Palestinians would not accept that; that they'd move in another direction. But David Ben-Gurion, among others, was very anxious then that Israel as a Jewish state would be diluted by Arabs. He'd be spinning in his grave if he knew how many Arabs were in Israel now, but that's another question. He felt that he couldn't afford to take the chance. His people would admit the logic of our arguments, but logic wasn't the controlling force at that time.

Robert Komer   I think that Arab-Israeli relations, which are often characterized as one of the great failures of American foreign policy, are actually one of the greatest successes; we actually managed to carry water on both shoulders. We increased our aid to Israel, increased our aid to the Arabs, and maintained tolerable relations with both. That was pretty surprising; it was not easy.

The United Kingdom

The Skybolt Missile

Adam Yarmolinsky   Skybolt was a classic case of failure to communicate between the military and the civilians: Here you had our military telling the British military that they didn't think there was much of a problem, and the British military not alerting their civilian masters, and then McNamara making a cost-benefit decision to cancel this project, and not realizing that the effect on the British was that they would lose a system which was critical to a position of the party in office. And when we offered them something called Hound Dog to take the place of something called Skybolt, McNamara did not at the time appreciate the rhetorical difference, which was a crucial political difference.

When the president was brought into it, he realized that there was a problem, and he fixed it. They met in Barbados or wherever it was and negotiated the agreement which gave the British something which the French subsequently resented so much that, I'm oversimplifying enormously, de Gaulle decided to take France out of NATO and NATO out of France, as things unraveled.

Herbert York, member, General Advisory Council, U.S. Disarmament and Arms Control Agency   There was a meeting in the Cabinet Room in February 1961, where President Kennedy went over large items in the defense budget, particularly those involving strategic questions. There were half a dozen of us, including McNamara. He decided to double the rate for producing certain missiles, but to reduce the actual numbers. He also made it clear he was going to cut the Skybolt, but not then. He said, "I need the Skybolt in order to cancel the B-70." He couldn't do both at once.

When he was in the Senate, Henry Jackson was his principal adviser on these issues. Now that he was in the White House, Bob McNamara was also new, but others, like Bundy and Jerome Wiesner, were familiar with strategic questions. Now, instead of relying on one senator, he had the benefit of staff.

I had told the British, "There is not going to be any Skybolt, fellows." I told that to [Lord Louis] Mountbatten, but they were just so caught up in it. But other people told them there would be one. The whole U.S. Air Force was pushing this. I looked at it from a technical point of view; it was premature. I told them there would not be a Skybolt in this decade. It was a flap and got a lot of publicity. Perhaps the publicity outran the reality. The British were counting on it.

Denis Greenhill There were two competing ideas: the submarine, using the Polaris; or the air, using the Skybolt missile. The RAF, of course, was keen on the Skybolt, because it could be linked with our own bombers. We reported from the embassy that it was unlikely we would get the Skybolt. But most of our air people in England had served in Washington, and they said, "If the American Air Force wants Skybolt, they will get it." So when McNamara scrapped Skybolt, it caused great trouble here. The American delegation went to Nassau with the intention of not helping us; it was the personal choice of the president to help. Macmillan thought, quite justifiably, that that was the dividend from the trouble he had taken to get on terms with this young man.

Middle Eastern Concerns

Robert Komer One day I got a call from Mrs. Lincoln. She says, "The president is going to be talking to Prime Minister Macmillan at six P.M. on the secure phone and he asked that you be present." Hell, I had never been present at any discussion between a president and a prime minister, and God, it must be something. Well, the president called later and said that the main thing Macmillan wants to talk about is Germany, and then he wants to talk to me about Yemen. I knew the Brits were going to say that we shouldn't recognize the Republic of Yemen for a while. So I gave the president a one-page memorandum with six reasons for our position.

I was there at six o'clock, and he was already there. After all, he lived and worked in the same building. He was sitting there smoking a Havana cigar. He smoked the best damn cigars I have ever smoked or tasted. He only smoked one or two a day and gave the rest to Pierre Salinger.

The conversation was to be on the secure phone with just the president and the prime minister, and no one else listening in. They required that; otherwise the CIA would listen. They got through the discussion on Germany, and then Macmillan said, "I want to talk about Yemen. The Foreign Office tells me you're planning to recognize the republic. That's a very difficult thing to do. These guys are army officers and they are no more going to be democratic than the man in the moon." Kennedy replied, "I understand your position, but let me give you ours." And then he gave my six points, verbatim—just right off the top of his head.

This guy got about a thousand memos every night—one half of them he threw in the wastebasket—which Mrs. Lincoln returned unread. Of the five hundred he decided to read, Mrs. Lincoln put those dealing with foreign affairs at the top.

Well, Macmillan wasn't listening and gave the same arguments again. At that point, the president said, "Look, you and I don't know much about this issue. I have my Yemen expert here, and I want to put him on the phone with you." And he hands me the damn phone. Well, I've never been handed a secure telephone by a president of the United States, before or since.

I said, "Mr. Prime Minister, I'm the Middle East expert on the president's staff." Well, Macmillan went through the same drill as he had with the president. I said, "Wait a minute; I think you have it wrong." He was very surprised not to be talking to the president. The president had scored one on him. Poor Macmillan said, "I don't have my Middle East expert here." I said, "Even if he were, he's running against policy." The president said, "Thanks a lot, Bob," and left the room, still smoking his cigar.

We were actually in the Situation Room, which was right next to Mac Bundy's office. They had put Mac in the basement of the White House, in a little office for someone who was really the most influential man there on policy. So I dropped by Mac's office and left him a message, which he got that night. Thank God he got it before the president called. I got home at about seven-thirty, and my wife gave me hell for being late. I said, "I've been talking to Prime Minister Macmillan." She said, "How the hell can you do that? He's in London." I didn't want to tell her about the special telephone, so I said, "You're not privileged," and that made her mad all night.

The next morning, I got in at my usual late hour. By the time I arrived at nine-thirty, Bundy had called four times. He said, "The president asked for you." I said, "Well, we've been communicating by phone and memo for some time." "Well," Bundy said, "you have made your number with the president. He knows your name; he links the name to the personality, and he links the personality to the substance. From now on he's going to call you directly. You may now send your memos directly, but send me a copy. Deal with the president directly on anything in your field."

USSR

Walt Rostow   On the Sunday after the inaugural, we had a meeting with the president. The first question he put to us was, Should he initiate a meeting with Khrushchev? I had read a biography of Khrushchev, and I pointed out to the president that Khrushchev was a gambler. He was boss of Moscow when they were building the subway. The engineers came to him and told him they had run into underground water they hadn't expected. They said there were two things they could do: one was to route it another way, or to put the piles through and pack them and minimize the likelihood of the water seeping through and damaging the subway. He said, "How long would it take to reroute the water?" They replied, "It would take eighteen months." He had promised to deliver the subway before that. He said, "What are the chances if you don't reroute?" They said, "About fifty-fifty." He said, "Go ahead and put it through." I said to President Kennedy, "So you see what a gambler he is. You have to be aware of that."

Ray Cline   I am pretty sure that we did a profile of Khrushchev; we did a lot of profiles, but they were mostly done by psychologists and psychiatrists, and I don't think the president ever paid much attention to them. We didn't have the facts. If we had had the real clear-cut view of Khrushchev, I think that the president would have paid attention to it.

William Smith   He was very concerned about the Soviets; it started with Southeast Asia. You had Khrushchev talk about the wars of national liberation. Then you had the president's trip to Vienna, where Khrushchev pushed him around a bit. The president put all those things together and felt: I'm under a big test here. He felt: That is what made the Berlin situation. He was confronted with a dilemma; he didn't want to start a war, but he didn't want to appear so weak that Khrushchev could decide to move into West Berlin. He was very suspicious, and very concerned, about Khrushchev; he thought Khrushchev was trying to take advantage of him.

He was concerned about Soviet military domination—if they achieved it, what they might do. He didn't like communism, not in terms of being anticommunist in a sense of always talking about it, but in looking at it more as the Soviets as a military power who threatened some of the values of the United States, and as what they might do in wars of national liberation. I think his feelings were like those of most people I dealt with: We didn't like the Soviets; we didn't trust them; we were concerned about them; we had to deal with them; they had a system we didn't think would work, and we wanted to defeat that system, and the way to do that was to be prepared to fight if we had to.

Ralph Dungan   Kennedy was a cold warrior; I think we all were. What the hell alternative did we have? We were cold warriors in the Kennan [George F. Kennan, U.S. ambassador to Yugoslavia, 1961–63] sense— the containment sense,* not an aggressive sense; not even to play some of the games the CIA guys were constantly doing.

Norman Podhoretz   At Vienna, Khrushchev was struck by how weak Kennedy seemed. There was that weak response to the Berlin Wall; he thought he could get away with it because Kennedy was not acting the way a man with his power should have acted in relation to a less powerful opponent. The Russians always played by the rules of the power game. They knew that they were not even entitled to mount a challenge to our superiority, given the disparities of power.

Khrushchev

Alexei Adzhubei   When I said good-bye to Khrushchev when I was on the way to the U.S. to interview Kennedy, he suddenly began to talk, and said, "Go and have supper with Kennedy's advisers one day before the interview. Tell them that besides *Izvestia* we have *Pravda,* and if there is something in the interview which we do not like, there will be trouble from *Pravda*." In this way Khrushchev was trying to tell Kennedy that things were not easy for him. He was asking in that interview not for confrontation but cooperation. The people invited to that supper realized what they were invited for. And Kennedy also realized it.

---

*As a foreign service officer serving in the U.S. Embassy in Moscow, 1944–46, Kennan filed reports giving his views on how to resist Soviet expansion, which came to be known as "containment" policy. They were published in the July 1947 issue of *Foreign Affairs,* under the name "X."

Yuri Barsukov Adzhubei had an official interview with the president—the first time that an editor of a major Soviet newspaper had such an interview. It was a general discussion. Adzhubei wasn't part of the diplomacy, so to say, although he had good contacts with the administration. During his later visits to the United States, as far as I know, he never saw President Kennedy; he only saw Robert Kennedy. Maybe he had some messages for the president, but he told them to Robert, not to the president himself.

Alexei Adzhubei When he was interviewed by me, Kennedy forgot his cigarettes—he smoked little black cigars—he asked me three times for a cigar; he used to talk very fast, but he paused, and said: "Adzhubei, I've smoked all my cigars." I answered, "I forgot my cigarettes in my coat." He replied, "Get yours and I will smoke them." I smoked awful cigarettes; very cheap, and the package was ugly. I thought, "How can I give them to Kennedy?" Kennedy realized what I was thinking. He said, "Put your cigarettes here." He smoked one, coughed, and must have thought, Only Russians can smoke these.

Yuri Barsukov I usually accompanied Adzhubei on his visits to Washington. My sense is that Adzhubei wasn't involved in exchanging messages, or in diplomatic practice; that was done through Ambassador Dobrynin [Anatoly Dobrynin, ambassador of the USSR to the United States], on that level. But Adzhubei did visit usually to have some exchange of views—he had good contacts with Pierre Salinger. He came regularly to the U.S.—usually once or twice a year—and met with Robert Kennedy, Pierre Salinger, and with newsmen such as James Reston. With Robert Kennedy and Salinger, he didn't discuss issues which couldn't be discussed at the ambassadorial level. There were no concrete problems, but rather, how to organize better contacts among journalists, how to change the propaganda on both sides.

Alexei Adzhubei Three days after I returned to Moscow, one of Khrushchev's advisers—he's now the ambassador to China—told me, without referring to Khrushchev: "You know, one of your questions was not very good, and Kennedy got you." Which question: "Mr. President, you are an officer of the American Army—the commander in chief—and I am an officer of the Soviet Army. What would you feel, if you were a former Soviet officer after the capitulation of Germany, when Germany started the arms race again?" President Kennedy's answer was good: "I wouldn't worry, if I were you. Why are you so worried about the arms in Germany? She has seven or eight divisions; her arms are limited." By this response Kennedy broke our propaganda stereotype that Germany was speeding the arms race.

Salinger's Meeting with Khrushchev

Yuri Barsukov   My guess is that Pierre Salinger was invited on the recommendation of Alexei Adzhubei, since he was his Washington contact. Since Pierre wasn't an ordinary man in the Kennedy administration, Khrushchev invited him to his dacha; it shows that Khrushchev was inclined to play every key on the piano.

Alexei Adzhubei   When Salinger came to meet with Khrushchev in the country, Khrushchev was taking to Kennedy through somebody very close to the president—almost like the president. All those contacts, Pierre's visits, were a sign that Khrushchev found a common language with Kennedy. Khrushchev had a very special attitude to Thompson's [Llewellyn E. Thompson, Jr., U.S. ambassador to the USSR] family. They were the only ambassadorial family who visited Khrushchev's house. No other foreign ambassador was treated like this; Khrushchev respected Thompson very much.

Pierre Salinger   When I arrived in Moscow, I was told as I got off the airplane that the whole schedule had been changed and that I was going to see Khrushchev. He wanted to do the same thing for me that Kennedy had done for Adzhubei. He did much more, because I ended up spending sixteen hours with him, in head-to-head conversation, which was absolutely amazing at that time. On the first day we talked from eleven until lunch, and then again until five o'clock. At that point Khrushchev asked Adzhubei—who had just arrived—"What plans do you have for Pierre tomorrow?" Adzhubei answered that he was going to take me along with him, and Khrushchev said, "Cancel all that; we are going to have another meeting."

They enlarged the second one to include Gromyko and the American ambassador. There were very specific issues to talk about: This was the time when U.S. troops had been deployed to Laos. I wasn't negotiating, but we talked about all the issues. When we talked about Kennedy, Khrushchev said that he was very impressed with him, that he had talked with other presidents, and when he had talked with Eisenhower, Khrushchev would ask him a question and Eisenhower would turn to one of the others around the table to respond, but that Kennedy would answer questions himself.

The first night of our talks, a car picked me up and took me to our embassy, where I wrote a long memorandum to Kennedy. I sent a message also on the second night from the embassy's secret room. After the first message Kennedy responded, telling me not to enter into negotiations—that he was getting messages from Adenauer, who was worried about my meeting with Khrushchev. The first day Khrushchev and I drank an entire bottle of vodka, but I didn't get drunk, because you just eat—a lot of caviar and smoked salmon. The next day Khrushchev told me his doctors had caught up with him, so he couldn't drink, but that I should have some vodka.

Viktor Sukhodrev   It was a discussion Khrushchev-style, no agenda, therefore no holds barred. For Khrushchev, again, Salinger was not part of the bureaucracy. It was a favored way for Khrushchev to do business, to talk to those that he thought were closest of all to the president, that he had the president's ear, not going through all the channels. It was, again, the next best thing to sitting face to face with the president.

The discussions—if you could call them that—they were conversations rather than discussions—were across the board. But it would be hard to pin anything down, even as food for some future accord. They were very wide ranging. The general tenor was that these two great countries should endeavor to work together rather than confront each other. But it was not something, I repeat, that could have led up to anything really material.

I don't know for sure whether or not Kennedy had any prior knowledge that Salinger would actually meet Khrushchev. However, it was very typical for Khrushchev to act on the spur of the moment. I was just called out and was given the task of going there and being the interpreter; I didn't have any advance notice of this. I knew that Salinger was coming, ostensibly at Adzhubei's invitation.

It came as a surprise for me when I was ordered to go. But it was very typical; I can surmise that it would have been typical for Adzhubei to have told his father-in-law, "Look, I've got this guy and he's very close to Kennedy." Whether he really had the kind of trust or whether Kennedy had the confidence in him as a negotiator, I don't know. But Adzhubei could have told Khrushchev that this was so, and Khrushchev could have jumped on it.

The whole meeting was very informal; it was at the dacha, out in the country. There was clay-pigeon shooting and all the rest of it—the long walks and all that sort of thing. It was not a sit-down, table, office sort of negotiation. These were conversations. It was meant, although he didn't think in those terms—his mind didn't work that way—more as Khrushchev trying to project his image, an image which Pierre could take back to Kennedy. It was, I think, a buildup for a future get-together, a future face-to-face.

11

Kennedy's Knowledge of, and Policy on, Various Issues

ATOMIC ENERGY

Glenn Seaborg   Eisenhower and Kennedy were not very different in their views concerning atomic energy. Eisenhower met rather regularly with his advisory committee. He didn't focus on atomic energy, but he was interested in the role science played in weapons. I would say that Kennedy, more than Eisenhower, had more of a technical grasp. In my first meeting with Kennedy, during the first week in February, he suggested immediately that he would like to visit the AEC headquarters. That was unprecedented for a president. We set a date, February 16, and flew out there by helicopter.

I gave him a thorough briefing on atomic and nuclear structure, and then, with the AEC staff, we had a thorough briefing on the entire program of the AEC—the peaceful applications as well as the weapons applications. He was supposed to be there for only an hour, but he was there practically the whole morning. He was very interested and a very apt pupil.

The president visited the Los Alamos Laboratory in December 1962. I flew out there with him in *Air Force One*. The next day, he went out to the Nevada test site. He asked to fly over the site in a helicopter. I accompanied him, and we flew over a crater that had been created in conjunction with a program we had for the peaceful uses of atomic energy. The crater was half a mile across and maybe several hundred feet deep. He said to the pilot, "This is very interesting. Let's land in this and look at it more closely." Of course, the pilot and I were horrified at the possibility of doing this, and we talked the president out of it. It was illustrative of his interest and his enthusiasm.

DEPRESSED AREAS

David Bell   There was a lot of concern over depressed areas—like West Virginia—that had been highlighted in Kennedy's campaign. That was an issue—so to speak—that the president brought with him. He had made promises about it, but the important thing was that he had seen how significant it was for the country's future, so a task force on the issue was created and there was legislation.

ECONOMICS

George Romney   A president is basically influenced in his first term by what his predecessor has done. Kennedy was very fortunate that Eisenhower had followed a very sound set of economic policies. Eisenhower even refrained from what Nixon and others have done, namely, undertaken to stimulate the economy ahead of the election in 1960. Nixon tried to get Eisenhower to do that, but he didn't succeed. The result is that Kennedy took over the last really good economic situation that we've had.

James Tobin   When Kennedy came into office, there was hope that there would be a change from the Eisenhower economic policies, and half of Kennedy favored that, but he was afraid of offending two establishments: the conservative Democrats in the Congress and the wider financial establishment. He had been a junior senator, and in the minds of many of the older Democratic committee chairmen, he was an upstart. Those of us at the council were disappointed by his caution at the beginning of the administration. We were trying to persuade the president to be more audacious in economic policy.

David Bell   I was favorably impressed with his knowledge of the workings of government in the Budget Bureau. Of course, I wasn't surprised at his knowledge; I had watched him closely during the cam-

paign. I was surprised when—in the early days of his administration—
he ran into an area which is very pertinent today, recession, and the
question then was the appropriate fiscal policy. Walter Heller and I
argued—in the standard Keynesian style—that it was the proper time
to have a modest, by today's standards, deficit, as a stimulus to economic recovery, and we ran into opposition from Douglas Dillon, who
was secretary of the treasury. Then the president was very uncomfortable about it and turned the idea down. I had not known the president's background on economic issues, and gradually it came out. He
was a very smart man, and ready to listen to and think about new ideas.
We did persuade him to accept a modestly unbalanced budget. Ted
Sorensen was very keenly interested in how it was presented. I learned
a lot from that first episode.

Paul Samuelson   Before the president was president, he really knew
little about economics. I recall one of the first meetings that Archie Cox
arranged at Hyannis Port. It must have been immediately after the convention. I drove down with Ken Galbraith. Seymour Harris [economic
adviser to Treasury Secretary Dillon] was there, as was Cox. It started off
with Seymour Harris briefing the presidential candidate on economics.
And Archie Cox said, "Wait a minute, Seymour. You're talking a mile a
minute. Make it 'Ec A.'" And Seymour said, "Jack had Ec A." Then
Kennedy said, "Yes. It's true. I had Ec A and I got a C in it." He learned
about economics in the course of the first two years. I think he was persuaded by the council on what the general direction of things turned out
to be, but he had a very strong sense of feasibility.

   Henry Brandon [British journalist, author] wrote a book suggesting
that the Kennedy dynasty might almost be a fascistic threat to the U.S.
Well, that was extremely different from the Kennedy I knew. The
Kennedy I knew was a very cold mind and was a very cautious mind. He
always tested the ice in front of him. If I would say, "You ought to fight
the good fight; even if you lose it, you have fought the good fight," he'd
say, "That's vanity. I'd pay for it later. Why should I?" So I didn't think of
him as a bold person. His entourage was lawyers, of which Sorensen was
the most important. The lawyers knew nothing about economics and
were the most surprised people in the world to be told by the economic
teams—of which there were at least three—that you don't get the country moving again by rhetoric, you get it moving by policies, and it's going
to involve d-e-f-i-c-i-t-s, because the Federal Reserve Board won't do

your bidding. We took office with an overvalued dollar and a very serious balance-of-payments constraint, and a constraint of being forced off the gold standard.

John Kenneth Galbraith   John F. Kennedy had been a student of economics—and particularly of Russell Nixon. He was a contemporary of mine at Harvard, and by all calculations, the leader of the left. It was one of the jokes that Kennedy loved to offer that when he didn't understand something, he'd say, "Why didn't Russ Nixon teach me that?" He was not only a student of economics, but he set himself to learn the economics of any issue; he wasn't content to take advice, or rely on advice; he wanted to understand himself. This was something we all came to understand. I recall somewhere a memorandum with a statement on the balance of payments problem, as it was then deemed to be, in somewhat exaggerated form, asking me for my comments on it in a page or two. At the bottom of the page, the president scribbled, "Remember, I'm pretty good at this; I was a student of Russ Nixon." That was in 1963, not long before his death.

Walt Rostow   Kennedy was, from the beginning, at cross purposes with his conventional Keynesian economists on one absolutely fundamental issue. The economists were all focused on demand, consumption. What Kennedy saw, which his economists did not see—they thought we should cut taxes—was that they should worry about gold. His aides thought it was prompted by his father, who was in New York and who knew that gold was flowing out. Kennedy understood the politics of the gold issue, but he also understood what underlay it, which was that the American competitive position was no longer one which was automatically going to churn out these big surpluses which we could use for military purposes or foreign aid.

George Romney   His father was never really in business. He was in the liquor business, but he was more of a dollar manager and a distributor than really a big businessman. He cleaned up; he made a fortune as a result of getting a monopoly on scotch when Prohibition ended, but he didn't really have an understanding of business. There are four levels of management, and the people who have the least understanding of what it takes to run a manufacturing organization or a major industrial organization are people who just manage money.

David Bell   The president was in no sense an economic or fiscal conservative. I suppose he was accustomed, in his household, to hearing from his father of the inequities of budget deficits and the necessity for balanced budgets, all concepts which we were challenging; we considered ourselves modern economists.

In the case of the military budget—the Defense Department budget is the largest—not only the budget staff, but Mac Bundy's staff and the president's science adviser's staff, were all interested in the review—from the policy point of view. I can only remember one case in which the Budget Bureau and the Defense Department did not agree, and we took the issue to the president. It had to do with $250 million—which is peanuts today but was a lot of money then—related to production of the Titan missile, which was being phased out. The essential question was: How fast should it be phased out? The president took the Budget Bureau's number rather than McNamara's. There was nothing of enormous significance in American history riding on it, but it was handled properly.

Paul Samuelson   Ken Galbraith was at the meeting where the question was: What are we going to do about gold? We had lost gold during the campaign, when it looked as if Kennedy was going to win; gold started to flow out, and there were all kinds of rumors. The legal reserve limit on the issue of federal reserve notes and the backing for federal reserve advances for member banks was not at the edge, but was getting worrisome, so we discussed whether we should ask for legislation to abrogate the debt limit. I think that the sense of the meeting was that was what we should do. At this point Galbraith pounded the table and said, "No. That is the worst thing you can do; everybody thinks the president is an unsound money man. Everybody over fifty will be writing letters to the editor." To my amazement that argument carried the day, and it turned out to be just right, because we weren't at the limit. Six months or a year later—on a quiet afternoon when nobody was looking—Congress passed a law changing the number, so that time Ken was on the beam.

Lincoln Gordon   When I had quarrels on AID matters and wanted to come back and get them straightened out, I must say—in general—if I insisted, things tended to fall my way. Dave Bell was a good friend of mine.

James Tobin   Our only powers were "the impeccable logic and correctness of our arguments" and the fact that the president took us seriously. If the president doesn't take the Council of Economic Advisers seriously, nobody else in Washington will.

Paul Samuelson   I recall that on inauguration afternoon—after the speech, but while people were still celebrating—there was the first official meeting of the new team. Heller and Tobin were there, and the decision was made at that time that we should aim for a twelve-billion-dollar deficit. That was the largest deficit we had ever had in any period, and it was thought the traffic would bear that. The council would have welcomed a larger figure if it had been feasible.

James Tobin   We were trying to get unemployment down from 7 to 4 percent, and we were trying to keep the Fed from raising interest rates. The president and Ted Sorensen both asked us this question: "Seven percent unemployment? That's ninety-three percent employment. And four percent unemployment? That's ninety-six percent. When we went to college, ninety-six was A and ninety-three was A-minus. Why should the president use political capital to improve your grades as economists from A-minus to A?" That was a good question, so we responded by showing how much that difference in employment meant to gross national product. Three points of unemployment meant ten points of GNP, and that meant all kinds of other things.

Paul Samuelson   When the president and his team were told, between the election and the inauguration, You should have a tax cut, he said, "Well, I have met with the Speaker of the House and the majority leader of the Senate, and I have promised them a balanced budget." I can tell you, that was a sick moment for the economists. We had hoped he'd lie a little. Later it was said that the budget will be balanced in the sense that only if there is a recession, which throws it out of balance, will that be tolerable. And then the president said, plaintively, "Look, my campaign didn't take off until that day in Detroit when I said, 'Don't ask what your country can do for you, ask what you can do for your country'"—a slogan which he used again and again after that because it met with a favorable response—"how can I ask the American people to sacrifice and take a tax cut?"

THE ENVIRONMENT

Gaylord Nelson   As governor in the early 1960s, I was trying to get the environmental issue into the political mainstream. I spoke on it a good deal around the country. Suddenly it dawned on me: If I could get the president to do a national conservation tour, that would focus the whole nation on the issue, because no president had ever done that. So I went to see Bobby Kennedy. He decided that this was a good idea. He talked to the president, who agreed to do the tour.

The problem was that no one around the president understood the issue; he didn't have any environmentalists close to him. I joined him on the first leg of the tour. We flew to Duluth and then in a helicopter over the Apostle Islands.* We landed in Ashland, Wisconsin, and the president gave a speech. I had sent the president a five-page, single-spaced memorandum on what I thought he should talk about. But he didn't make the comments I suggested, and the tour did not accomplish what I had hoped it would.

THE SPACE PROGRAM

The Eisenhower administration attempted to deal with the shock of the Soviet Union's successful launching of the Sputnik rocket by establishing a space exploration program. President Kennedy, early in his administration, made crucial decisions related to manned space flight, culminating in his administration's determination to place a man on the moon by the end of the decade. This determination intensified as of April 12, 1961, when Soviet cosmonaut Yuri Gagarin spent one hour and forty-eight minutes in orbit around the earth. Becoming increasingly interested in the space program, President Kennedy established personal relationships with the seven Mercury astronauts and acquired an informed layman's knowledge of the technology involved in space exploration.

Robert C. Seamans, Jr., deputy administrator, National Aeronautics and Space Administration (NASA)   As far as President Kennedy and the space program are concerned, he didn't really get his mind around it until Gagarin went into orbit. And I guess you can say that

---

*In Lake Superior.

President Kennedy also went into orbit. He was really upset. So he wrote a memorandum to the vice president, who was the head of the Space Council, which, in effect, said: "As president of the United States, I am sick and tired of having the Soviets out there in front, taking advantage, as if we had no science and technology capability, stealing a real march on us. What can we do that stands a reasonable chance of showing the world that we are preeminent in science and technology, and that we can do better than they can?"

This led to a series of meetings with the vice president and then a meeting between Mr. Webb [James E. Webb, director, NASA] and Mr. McNamara that I participated in, on a Saturday—the day after Alan Shepard [Mercury astronaut] had flown suborbital. The following Monday morning we—being McNamara and Webb—submitted their report to the vice president, and in the report there was a recommendation that the United States is going to land men on the moon, and the vice president submitted this to the president.

Glenn Seaborg   Johnson was very businesslike; he came in with an agenda. He would sit down and read remarks, and took it very seriously. He had a very central role in convincing the president to undertake the Manned Landing on the Moon project. Johnson was very oriented toward the space program.

Robert Seamans, Jr.   Three weeks later the president gave his State of the Union update and he told the Congress that we should go to the moon. A copy of the speech was sent over to our office. The speech said we were planning to send men to the moon and return them safely in 1967. We felt, however, that we should not nail the United States to that specific a goal. We were going public, while the Soviets were doing everything in secret. So we suggested, "Why don't we soften it by saying we are going to the moon within the decade?" And President Kennedy agreed to that change.

Herbert York   Eisenhower saw the space program as consisting of two parts: civilian and military. He recognized they were coupled, but he wanted that coupling to be kept to a minimum. Therefore, we ran the defense side, and NASA ran the civilian side. Kennedy essentially continued that. He took the step of saying we were going to the moon—a step that Eisenhower avoided. The reason had nothing to do with the difference in vision; it had to do with the fact that Eisenhower had been stung very badly by people making promises of what we were going to do and then failing to do it. So when Kennedy did say we are going to the moon within the decade, Eisenhower did react negatively to the statement because it was so contrary to the way he had been handling the publicity. But he also thought we were going to the moon sometime in the next ten to twenty years. So Eisenhower and Kennedy were both persuaded that there was real merit and value in space, both military and civilian.

Robert Seamans, Jr.   After Kennedy was elected, but before he was inaugurated, there was a lot of discussion, and there was actually a study carried out by Jerry Wiesner and others of both the missile program and the space program, and it was somewhat derogatory about NASA. There was even talk that, possibly, the Kennedy administration might be considering moving NASA back into the Department of Defense. It turned out that we didn't have an administrator of NASA when Kennedy was inaugurated, and we didn't have one for about six weeks, I think. Then Jim Webb came in, and he invited me to come in. I didn't know if I'd be sticking around or not, and we had quite a long talk in the morning, and he said, "Well, maybe it's time to go out to lunch," and I said, "Fine. Where will we go?" And I said, "Well, Mr. Webb, you've been in Washington longer than I have." He said, "Would you like to go to the National Democratic Club?" And I said, "That's fine, if they're willing to accept a Republican there for lunch."

David Bell   President Kennedy made the inspired choice of naming Jim Webb to run NASA; he was an absolutely magnificent federal administrator and manager, and very creative in the way that NASA was set up. Of course, they did get to the moon before the end of the decade. Most of us didn't believe it when the president said that in June of 1961.

Walter ("Wally") Schirra, astronaut, Mercury Program   I would suspect that Jim Webb and probably [Wernher] von Braun and [Robert] Gilruth* and others had some pretty good rap sessions and agreed this

---

*The German scientist responsible for the development of the World War II V-2 liquid fuel rocket, von Braun later worked in the U.S. space program and in 1970 became deputy associate director of NASA.

Robert Gilruth, an engineer and administrator, was a NASA official involved in the Mercury astronaut program.

could be done. They then took it to the president. He became quite enthused with it. We always kidded that you needed something like that to wipe out the Bay of Pigs.

I thought it would be possible, but that it would be a difficult task. We realized we had a lot of things to do, not to invent, but to proof-test, to get working on. We had the commitment before we even orbited. With that we had to create a total new project when Mercury was going on—that was Gemini; a transition program to do all the tasks that were required to go to the moon and back. Whoever wrote that series of remarks for President Kennedy was brilliant, because he said to the moon and back. He knew the ramifications of it and knew that it was obviously a major step. It was a commitment that the nation would have to make, and it did. That was the fascinating part of it. Many people try to bring the space program back into that framework again and it is impossible.

Robert Seamans, Jr.   We were racing the Soviets to be preeminent in space; the specific goal was going to the moon. We had evidence that they were trying to go to the moon, too. Of course they knew we were trying, because it was announced by the president and they could see what we were doing—everything was extremely open. We knew that they were building a rocket that had about twice the lifting power of the Saturn 5 that we used to go to the moon; it was a very large rocket. We could observe through our overhead satellite photography their building of a large launch complex, and we actually could observe them moving this great big rocket. It was towed out to the pad, and then it blew up. Then they built another one, and it got up a very short distance and blew up. At that point they pretty well gave up. But they also had a program to try to get a lunar sample back—even unmanned—before we got there with a man to bring back a sample. We felt they were going to use that to try to denigrate what we were doing and to say that they were risking lives to do something we didn't have to risk lives to do. So there were all kinds of skirmishes, you might say, along the line, as to whether we were doing the right thing or not.

Donald ("Deke") Slayton, chief astronaut, Mercury Program   What Kennedy did with the moon program was to pick a goal people could relate to. It has to be something under ten years; if you give people a thirty-year goal, they won't waste time thinking about it; it's too far away. My recollection is that there were some other people talking about it for a year or more before he announced it.

Walter Schirra   The Russians definitely wanted a flight before Shepard went, and they topped him beautifully by orbiting Gagarin. Then, as we started coming along with our Mercury flights, they flew a woman for more publicity. They were not as safety conscious as we were. Our crews were test pilot engineers, whereas the Russian cosmonauts were not. That was quite evident when we met with the cosmonauts in April 1991. They talked about Gagarin as a saint—about how he was a perfect Russian—a three-generation Russian from peasant stock; good looking. He did fly an airplane but did not have the qualifications we had. They were trained to go aboard a spacecraft for the ride—much like a chimpanzee. They were totally secretive about their missions. To my knowledge no Soviet citizen—other than those on the team—saw a launch. Of course, millions of Americans saw all of our launches.

They were competing with us very hard to go to the moon. In recent years, we saw a lunar module that they had built for one person to land on the moon, take off again, and come back.

Manned Flight

Donald Slayton   Some of the members of Kennedy's Science Advisory Committee were pretty anti–manned flight, although Kennedy, personally, wanted it. They thought there ought to be a lot more money going into pure science—the unmanned things as opposed to the manned flights; the manned flights were high visibility. My personal opinion is that if you hadn't had the manned flights with the high visibility, you never would have gotten the money to do other things, to begin with. They were doing all kinds of coattailing on the manned program for financing. James Van Allen, the inventor of the Van Allen belt,° was very anti–manned flight. He still is.

Robert Seamans, Jr.   The reaction after Glenn's [John H. Glenn, astronaut, Mercury Program; U.S. senator (D., Ohio)] flight was stupen-

---

°U.S. astrophysicist James Van Allen interpreted the discovery by the Explorer I satellite, launched in 1957, of the existence of two belts of radiation, which sometimes merged into one, outside the earth's atmosphere.

dous. One of the things that we always had to contend with was all the political forces to go grab that man with this great achievement. But we had a definite procedure for debriefing, so we're sure we get all the information for the next flight, so John Glenn was incarcerated for a very short while for the debriefing and was then flown to Cape Canaveral. Meeting him there were not only NASA types like myself, but both the president and the vice president, which is very unusual. More damn press than you can possibly imagine just converged on this place.

John Glenn became a great hero—a national and world hero. We'd do things like have John participate in an Oktoberfest in Germany. Crowds of Germans would try to get in to see him, and one time he ended up leading a German band, or something. Thousands of people would tend to crush in to the point that we had to use special security people to whisk John out the back before his clothes were torn off.

President Kennedy liked the Mercury astronauts, as did Bobby Kennedy, as did Lyndon Johnson. They were very engaging individuals. They had derring-do and they were attractive, proficient, and articulate—some of them more than others. The president, Bobby, and Lyndon Johnson saw them as very likable people—as human beings, and they obviously wanted to be sure that we weren't doing something to jeopardize their lives. They were also politically motivated: They knew damn well that the astronauts were very much in the public eye, and perhaps Lyndon Johnson, more than anybody else, loved to be sitting in the back of a car with one of the astronauts as the cameras flashed. President Kennedy had somewhat less opportunity, but when he came in, there was real concern—this is before Gagarin went into orbit—as to what was going to happen when men went into space. There could be the acceleration on the rocket, and maybe a lot of vibration and weightlessness, and there was a question of whether we had done enough animal tests. There was a decision that we had to run one more chimpanzee test before sending Alan Shepard up. If Alan had been on that flight, we'd have been ahead of Gagarin, not in orbiting the earth but at least in being in space. That was looking at things from a conservative standpoint. Then, after Gagarin flew, there was a geopolitical question, not just the life of Alan Shepard. Supposing we had to abort the flight and it wasn't successful. Even if Alan was okay, how would we look in the eyes of the world if they'd gone around the world and we only tried to take a little potshot—a few hundred miles—and we'd failed?

Walter Schirra   We would visit in the private quarters of the White House on occasion. I recall doing that after Alan Shepard's flight, after mine, Cooper's [L. Gordon Cooper, astronaut, Mercury Program], and Glenn's. We got to know the president socially, and I could detect his great sense of humor.

Once I was en route to the Oval Office accompanied by Robert Kennedy. My wife and two children were already there. Robert said to me, "Commander, we know you have had a very good space flight. We would like to know what kind of political considerations you have." I said almost immediately, and rather brusquely, "Mr. Kennedy, I wish you would realize that I am an engineer—something of a scientist—and politics is a totally different world. I find when I make a decision it is based on fact. The transition to politics would be impossible."

About three or four months later, we went back to the White House after Cooper's flight, and President Kennedy greeted us coming into the upstairs private quarters, and he said, "Wally, I understand that you base your decisions on facts." Just that fast.

Robert Seamans, Jr.   Alan Shepard, his wife, and his mother and father were all at the White House to receive the medal, and on Kennedy's staff there was also a Captain Shepard, and he made a joke out of that, wondering if his own staff person would be as proficient in space as was Alan. Then, in pinning on the medal, the president dropped it, and picking it up, he made an analogy to the way Alan Shepard had gone right from the ground on up, and here was this medal that had dropped down and he was picking it up to pin it on. He handled it, as was his custom, with a lot of grace and humor. He was obviously enjoying himself, and he was obviously most attracted not only to Alan, but to Alan's family, a New Hampshire family.

Just a month after he'd been shot, there was a tremendous emotional feeling amongst the NASA people that they owed a great deal to Kennedy's support, and they wanted to put Kennedy's name on a rocket. We didn't want to have people going up and writing on the rocket. We had to have guards to make sure it didn't happen. I was in the blockhouse—in those days you had to be very close to the rocket to launch it, and to be safe you had to have a blockhouse with a couple of feet of concrete reinforcement and steel doors in case the thing blew up—and after it was successfully in orbit, there were about two hundred people in there, and I think I was congratulating everybody on the successful launch, and somebody yelled out, "Why don't we call Mrs. Kennedy on the telephone and tell her it's been successfully launched and how much we appreciate the former president's support—her husband's support?" I said, "Mrs. Kennedy's been through an ordeal that no human being should have to go through and I don't think that would be at all appropriate, but I will, if you want, try to let her know in a more measured way how you all feel." And they agreed to that.

I got back to Washington and called Walter Sawyer, our general counsel, who knew Mrs. Kennedy, and he said, "I don't think that's a very good idea after all she's been through, but I'll call her," and he called me back in five minutes and said, "She'd love to have you come over. It can't be today. Come on over tomorrow, and have tea."

So I went over there with Walter and I took along a model—it wasn't a scale model, it wasn't quite that big—and I took along some pictures, and I explained it, and her first comments were, "Now I'm beginning to understand what Jack was so excited about," or words to that effect. And then she said, "Would you mind if Caroline and John-John came in to see the pictures?" And I said no. She said, "Have you had chicken pox?" and I said yes. And they came in. John-John went right for the model, and she said, "No, you can't touch it."

Later on, I sent over a few plastic models of things for him, and I arranged to have the model we showed her go to the Kennedy Library, and I got a lovely note from her telling me what the space program had meant to Jack.

THE PEACE CORPS

Sargent Shriver Hubert Humphrey had used the term *peace corps* in a piece of legislation; others had suggested similar initiatives; then, according to some, General James Gavin [U.S. ambassador to France, 1961–62] suggested something like the Peace Corps. I never paid serious attention to these claims or counterclaims.

In campaigning in Michigan, Kennedy had asked students how many of them were prepared to go overseas and work in the Third World, and he got a terrific response. So the truth of the matter is that it didn't matter who suggested it; this idea would have gone nowhere if

Kennedy hadn't made a public reference to it, and if there had been no response.

Once the Peace Corps was established, the president always did what we asked him to do; if there was an important meeting, he would attend.

You have to realize that if the president of General Electric calls you up and asks you to run a division of the company, he is not going to expect you to call all the time, asking about details. So I had the feeling that Kennedy had a tremendous amount of things to be concerned about—more than any human being could take care of. I didn't need continual contact with him to prove that I was close to him. After all, I was his brother-in-law.

Lincoln Gordon My first important business from Washington after settling in the embassy was meeting with Sargent Shriver, the head of the Peace Corps—and he and I, together, negotiated the first bilateral Peace Corps agreement. In fact, we had the first contingent, a few weeks later, of the Peace Corps anywhere in the world—a 4-H Club bunch of guys and girls up in the northeast of Brazil. And Kennedy was obviously enthusiastic about that.

William Sloane Coffin, Jr. Sargent Shriver wanted to set up a training camp in Puerto Rico, and he was told, There is only one guy to direct it, but you'll never get him—he's the chaplain at Yale. I went to see him, and I was very taken with him right away, and he got permission for me to be absent from Yale for a summer and a couple of months beyond that.

Lucius Battle The Peace Corps, I think, was a great success. I thought so then.

I didn't know Sargent Shriver at all before then. I've gotten to know him better since. He was very wise in a number of respects: He would not let the CIA get anywhere near the Peace Corps; and I, also, was determined that I was going to keep them out of my educational and cultural programs.

William Sloane Coffin, Jr. I don't think the Peace Corps had an imperialistic impulse, although there was such an impulse in the administration but we were not cognizant of it at the time. My main feeling was if we didn't do positive harm, what the volunteers would learn would be invaluable for the nation as a whole.

I imagine that in some of the presidential circles—where cynicism was highly valued—there probably was a lot of mocking of the Peace Corps. But I thought it was a terrific idea when I first heard about it. I liked Shriver enormously; he had a kind of boyish enthusiasm and great intelligence, and he surrounded himself with a very fine group of people—Bill Moyers and others. They were all a combination of St. Paul and St. Vitus: You could never get any work done; everybody was in everybody's hair. That's why you had to stay late at night to do your work. But I found the enthusiasm and the efficiency very impressive. Shriver was just the guy to set it up. That was a big plus in my mind for Kennedy. I have a lot of minuses, but that was a real plus.

Lucius Battle   I told the administration and others that the Peace Corps—I was thinking of the young people, not the older ones—was a very good recruiting place for the State Department: If you liked the life you led in the Peace Corps, you'd find the State Department world a different one but a very pleasant one. And if you could live in these remote places, you could take some of the remote assignments. It was a good training ground and it would restore confidence of the administration in what the foreign service was all about.

Very few of them wanted to go into the State Department—the striped pants and the "cookie pushing," as they referred to it. I never owned a pair of striped pants in my day. The natural training ground seemed to me to be a very logical one. And I still think it was not a bad idea.

William Sloane Coffin, Jr.   My main disappointment has been that the volunteers were so silent when they came back. They never got organized; they were never a voice against the Contra wars and such, where they presumably could have been, in saying that this is not a way to do business in the Third World countries.

Lee White   The Peace Corps is still alive and well. Whether Hubert Humphrey thought up the idea first or somebody else did is really irrelevant.

THE STEEL PRICE RISE

James Tobin   The steel companies and labor had reached a wage agreement. No sooner was the ink dry than U.S. Steel announced a price increase. They didn't tell the president or Secretary of Labor Arthur Goldberg in advance. Roger Blough of U.S. Steel asked for a five P.M. appointment with the president. At four forty-five, the price increase was announced to the press in New York, and when Blough came to the Oval Office he gave the president a copy of the press release. The president was pretty angry and dealt with his anger, and that precipitated the confrontation. The business community was angrier than ever, after a while, as they thought about this affair. This reinforced the president's feeling that we had to be more friendly toward them.

Roswell Gilpatric   He felt he didn't understand the psychology of the businessman: what made him tick, what were his motivations. He was particularly baffled with Roger Blough. It was basically a misunderstanding. Blough didn't deliberately mislead the president; it was just a failure of communication, and afterward—after the administration bore down on the steel industry and forced them to rescind the price increase—he wanted to talk about it and find out how it came about, why they acted and what the relationships were between the heads of the various companies.

Paul Samuelson   Everybody gets very excited when there is a missile crisis or a Berlin Wall. In the confrontation with Roger Blough, everybody was trying to calm the president down, and I think Kenny O'Donnell said to Walter Heller, "You don't understand; he doesn't want to be calmed down. He's got his Irish temper up." That is when he said, "My father always said all businessmen were sons of bitches." I knew Roger Blough. He never recovered from that confrontation; he was a broken man. It is a very hard thing when your president crucifies you before the American people.

William Sloane Coffin, Jr.   Shriver came to Yale and was going to speak at a couple of colleges around Connecticut. I spent the day with him; I drove him around, and he said, "We've got to get a newspaper." And there was Blough's picture. He was looking pale as a sheet. Shriver was cursing him up and down, and then Shriver said a very good thing:

"If any steel company behaves decently, it will be Inland Steel, because they're Jewish." I remember saying, "Well said for a Catholic; proud to be driving you around, Sarge." He was reflecting Kennedy's mood.

THE TEST BAN TREATY

Glenn Seaborg   As a result of the missile crisis, both Kennedy and Khrushchev had a better idea of the potential for nuclear war. I hesitate to use these terms, but they "got religion"; they were both strong supporters of a test ban from that time on. I believe if Kennedy had lived and Khrushchev had remained in power, we would have had a comprehensive test ban.

Robert Seamans, Jr.   It had become recognized that whenever there was a major nuclear explosion in space, it did all kinds of things to communications as well as releasing radiation, and if you happened to have somebody in a Mercury capsule orbiting around the earth at that time, it wouldn't necessarily be very healthy: They would not only lose the communications, in all probability, but they might get an overdose of radiation. What they were trying to plan was a way of terminating those airborne tests, so I was there to represent the astronauts, you might say, in space testing. Glenn Seaborg was there as head of the AEC. He wanted to carry out eleven tests before the ban went into effect, which had been agreed to with the Soviets. Kennedy was very good at trying to get from Glenn Seaborg why these eleven tests were important, and Glenn, I think, made a mistake at some point in talking about the morale of the people in the national laboratories who had been working, getting ready for these tests.

There's a lot more at stake in nuclear testing than a few thousand people in a laboratory, and Kennedy got that point across very well by the way he interrogated Seaborg. They finally agreed that they would eliminate five of those eleven tests, and only ran six more. That was all negotiated right across the table, in my presence, in about half an hour.

Glenn Seaborg   Kennedy was almost obsessed with the necessity for a test ban and undeviating in his attempts to achieve it, and personally monitoring what we were doing every step of the way. In fact, he kept in touch with Averell Harriman on a daily basis during the ten days of the negotiations on Moscow. This was unprecedented; no president has ever done this before or after.

He felt that the main reason for a test ban was to slow down and prevent, to a large extent, the proliferation of nuclear weapons. That was very high on his agenda. He was dedicated to this. It was just like a religion to him. I met with him time after time, sometimes on a daily basis, in the various contexts. He kept his finger on the pulse.

There were some pretty subtle reasons for each of those tests which were also discussed. It wasn't just a question of the morale of the troops. Then the question was: how about Wally Schirra, who was about to go up in the Mercury capsule, and it was agreed that it would take a little time for them to get ready to run the tests. I think we ended up with something like six weeks to get off that flight, or we were going to have to put it off for I don't know how long—a year, or something like that.

Roger Hilsman   Kennedy was afraid that the Soviets would sabotage the nuclear test ban treaty if he wanted three on-site inspections and object to their insistence on five. But Kennedy didn't figure on being killed. He thought there would be another test ban treaty, where he could get the inspection.

Denis Greenhill   There was correspondence between Khrushchev and Macmillan on the test ban treaty. There was a final message from Khrushchev, and the legend is that Kennedy said, "This is the end; we are not going to get anywhere," and Macmillan pointed out something in Khrushchev's message which he identified as the door still being open. He was right, and the negotiations continued.

Viktor Sukhodrev   I must say that the British were very passive during those talks in Moscow. I continuously had a feeling that they were in principle in favor of the treaty, but they wanted to sit back and let the two superpowers hammer it out. And they didn't much sort of care about the details. They were letting Harriman do most of the talking.

The British contribution was when the British representative said there was something wrong about the title, "The Treaty Banning Nuclear Weapon Tests in the Atmosphere, in Outer Space, and Underwater." And underwater—the Americans had prepared the English text—was written together, in one word. And Quintin Hogg [Lord Hailsham, minister of science, United Kingdom] said, "You see what happens if you look at it this way, it means in the atmosphere, in outer space, and actually in underwater, so we should make those two words instead of one." That was I think the most memorable contribution the British made to the actual text.

The negotiations would have gone on whoever the American representative was. But the fact that it was Harriman I think played some part in the overall attitude and approach. Khrushchev, like many in Russia, had a special feeling for people who had been somebody during the war. It was a kind of nostalgia.

That was one of the reasons that Eisenhower was so popular prior to the U-2 incident of course; that was a great disappointment. Perhaps erroneously, Eisenhower was seen as being a person for whom that wartime friendship, collaboration, cooperation had left a lasting impression, as it had on people like Khrushchev. And Harriman belonged to that team. He was there; he had been instrumental in his many meetings with Stalin, for instance. Those memories were very fresh in Khrushchev's mind. So I think that basically he was well pleased with the fact that Harriman had been chosen as the chief negotiator for the American side. The negotiations would have gone on, whoever the American representative was. But the fact that it was Harriman, I think, played some part in the overall attitude and approach.

Sergei Khrushchev   He really, all the time, wanted to stop the tests. He thought it would be possible to find agreement to stop underground testing. My father thought it would be cheaper for us.

J. William Fulbright, U.S. senator (D., Ark.); chairman, Senate Foreign Relations Committee   The only time I thought we were really doing something significant was the meeting with Khrushchev on the test ban treaty. It looked as though JFK had changed his mind. Originally he was going to tell the world how to act; we were big dogs. I thought that in the test ban treaty he had accepted the idea of working with the Russians to have a mutual understanding. I felt then that Kennedy was on the right track.

John Kenneth Galbraith   The partial test ban was extremely important. It lifted the whole question overnight. I think Kennedy in the

American University speech° was really at home with himself. That was the Kennedy of the partial test ban, not the Kennedy of the Bay of Pigs or the Berlin wall. In the Bay of Pigs—and at the Wall—he was yielding to the cold war pressures. He was himself at the American University and in sending Harriman and Carl Kaysen [deputy special assistant to the president for national security affairs] to negotiate the test ban.

Carl Curtis   I thought it had been presented as a cure-all against war, but it wasn't that. I didn't think it would abolish the nuclear threat, which it didn't.

Norman Podhoretz   The American University speech in support of the test ban treaty was the bones he was throwing to his own left. I don't think he thought you could end the cold war—that the Russians were ready to end the cold war. I think he took the correct hard-line anticommunist view of the cold war. The overwhelming evidence is that those were his convictions, and those were the standard convictions of people like him in those years: that the Soviets were out to dominate the world; that it was an evil system; that the United States had a responsibility—both in its own interests and for the sake of the West—in preventing that from happening—in containing them.

William Sloane Coffin, Jr.   The only thing he did was the partial test ban treaty.

And then Kennedy—with his great intelligence—mused: Why did it take us so long? as if all good things in the world are only rational in retrospect, which they are. You could say, How did it take us so long to give women their rights? How did it take us so long to get rid of slavery? But that was very typical of Kennedy, to make a very good philosophic remark like that. Then that stopped.

Eugene McCarthy   We really were agreeing not to radiate ourselves; it didn't have to do with the Russians radiating on us, or we on them— you could have done it on your own, to say: We are going to stop radiat-

°On June 10, 1963, President Kennedy delivered the commencement address at American University, Washington, D.C., on the subject of world peace. He announced that the United States, Great Britain, and the Soviet Union would soon begin discussions on a comprehensive nuclear test ban agreement.

ing our own people and our own cattle. We were lucky the air currents were in the right direction. We were radiating our people while they were radiating theirs. If it had been the other way, we might not have come to an agreement. It was a good thing, but I thought the substance of it was minimal.

I think any administration would have had to have stopped testing in the atmosphere.

Glenn Seaborg   After the signing of the treaty, Kennedy stumped the country to assure grass-roots support to the Senate for its ratification. It was finally ratified by well over the two-thirds majority that was required.

12

J. Edgar Hoover and the Kennedys

Cartha DeLoach   When John F. Kennedy announced for the Democratic nomination and he started gathering considerable strength, Mr. Hoover had Clyde Tolson, who was the associate director at the time, call me to his office. He said, "I want you personally to review the files on John F. Kennedy and let us know what is in there. I think I know him pretty well. I don't think you are going to find anything that I don't know already." So I pulled all the files on John F. Kennedy—there were no central files; there was cross-referencing—and his name was mentioned, for instance, the Inga Arvad–alleged German espionage investigation, where he was associating with her, considerably, and having sex with her, particularly in Charleston, South Carolina. There were other things cross-referenced in the various files, so I wrote a summary memorandum and took it into Tolson, and he sent it into Mr. Hoover, and they both called me and said, "You have the wrong Kennedy. You got the one that was killed in the early part of the war." I said, "No, I haven't." They said, "Yes, you have. You go back and review those files again, and you will find out that you've made a mistake." And I said, "I have not made a mistake." So finally, I produced proof that it was John F. Kennedy that was cross-referenced in the files, and I remember Mr. Hoover's exclamation, "Well, I'll be damned!"

Mr. Hoover and Mr. Nixon had always been very close since the time that Mr. Nixon came to the Congress, and John F. Kennedy defeated Mr. Nixon, and that caused, I'm sure, a feeling in Mr. Hoover's mind.

Mr. Hoover had to show compatibility because the president and

Bobby were his superiors. He had to do this through necessity. But on the other hand, Bobby and JFK showed compatibility through necessity also: the matter of Bobby paying a courtesy call on Mr. Hoover; the matter of JFK, prior to his election, being asked by a reporter, "Will you reappoint J. Edgar Hoover?" and JFK indicating, "That will be one of the first appointments I make." Of course, that time he needed votes and he felt that Mr. Hoover had great popularity in the United States with the rank and file out in the boonies, and so he made that answer. On both sides there was compatibility through necessity.

I think Mr. Hoover felt, as did many people in the United States, that it would be very difficult for Kennedy to gain the presidency, particularly against Nixon, who had been vice president for eight years, so he didn't think much about it in the beginning days, and later on he felt—because of his relationship with Ambassador Kennedy—that he'd have no difficulty getting along as he had with many other presidents.

Courtney Evans   Much has been made of the Hoover–Ambassador Kennedy relationship. I don't think it was ever anything of great depth.

The director had a minimal kind of relationship with President Kennedy, whose views came to us through Robert Kennedy. There was a docudrama about Kennedy and Hoover wherein an actor portrayed my role. He had me telling Robert Kennedy that things in the bureau were getting to be awfully rough: Hoover was accustomed to dealing with presidents in the past, with the exception of Truman, and couldn't Bob do something to help the situation? In the docudrama Bob picked up the phone and said, "The president would like to have lunch with you next Tuesday at one o'clock." Essentially that portrayal was true. Periodically I would say to Robert, "It is about time that he [Hoover] went over for lunch." Sure enough, within two or three weeks, he'd be invited to the White House for lunch.

Hoover—in his usual fashion—would go over armed to the teeth with all of the facts with regard to the major events that he wanted to present to the president, and the president was very cordial, but I don't think made very many commitments.

John Seigenthaler   In theory and in practice, Hoover was a law unto himself. Robert Kennedy went in there believing that he could work with Hoover, whom he truly admired—I hate to say it in retrospect—but truly admired. He thought Hoover ran one terrific investigative agency. His father once tried to hire Hoover for one hundred thousand dollars a year to run the security interests in the Kennedy empire. Robert Kennedy told me that at a time when we were hearing complaints from former FBI agents who were literally sneaking into the office at six o'clock in the morning to tell me that he was a tyrant.

Burke Marshall   Mr. Hoover didn't like having Robert Kennedy as attorney general because that meant he had someone between him and the president; he wanted to deal with the president directly.

Courtney Evans   Mr. Hoover wasn't available on many occasions, for one reason or another, and when he wasn't available, I got the calls from the attorney general. In later years he didn't bother to call Hoover. I got the calls.

In the beginning both the attorney general and Mr. Hoover made every effort to develop a cordial working relationship. That didn't work out, for a variety of reasons. Mr. Hoover was obviously old enough to be Robert Kennedy's father. He had known Robert since he was a small boy, at least casually, through Ambassador Kennedy, so there was some tendency on Hoover's part to regard him as a junior kind of person. On the other hand, Robert Kennedy was out to make a name for himself as attorney general—as he had up on the Hill—and he was rather demanding of work that the FBI should do, and he was a little reluctant to go along with Hoover's priorities on the assignment of manpower to certain types of cases. They just drifted apart.

Trying to mediate between these two very strong personalities was the hardest job I've ever had. Their principal issues of disagreement were organized crime, civil rights, employment of minorities, and too much emphasis on internal security-type investigations on the part of the bureau. Each had his own ideas as to what the bureau should be doing; the pragmatics flowed from that.

Hoover didn't believe in the existence of the Cosa Nostra to the extent that he felt that the bureau should not be expanding its manpower in what he regarded as essentially a problem for the local authorities. He and Mr. Anslinger (Harry Anslinger, director, Bureau of Narcotics, Treasury Department) didn't see eye to eye, by any stretch of the imagination. He didn't want to dissipate his resources to investigate organized crime. He lived and died before congressional appropriations committees by his statistical record; he was out to maintain it at all costs, and that he did.

Cartha DeLoach   Certain members of organized crime in the various casinos would have the casino where the gambling took place and then they would have a counting room where the Internal Revenue people would count the take for the United States government. But there would be a room in between where they would take so much off the top before they took it into the IRS. But we had a microphone in the room in between and one also, in one instance, in a restaurant of one of the casinos where the leaders of organized crime who had ownership in some casinos would gather once a week for breakfast. They would say so much for this person here, so much for this person in Chicago, so much for this person in Los Angeles, and so on.

The president's name came up as a result of a microphone usage in Chicago, where the mobsters indicated that the sum of $25,000 had been given to the Kennedy campaign for the presidency. Of course, Mr. Hoover advised the attorney general and the president about that.

In the matter of the president seeing Judith Exner, who was the companion of Moe Giancana, I don't recall if that ever came up through a microphone usage or not.

In today's society many writers who have attempted to butcher history through distortions and slanting of articles and books have indicated Mr. Hoover's purpose was blackmail. But having known the man and seeing him every day, and discussing things with him, that was the farthest thought from his mind. He did furnish that information to the Kennedys as a matter of courtesy. Any time the president's name came up, or anything concerning the administration came up, he furnished it to the attorney general and the president, but not for the purpose of blackmail. He was forthright in doing that. Opinions to the contrary—particularly in today's society—Mr. Hoover was a very deeply religious man who had his faults—and many eccentricities—who probably stayed in office too long, and who sometimes—when he thought the FBI was being unfairly criticized—leaned over backward to rebut such criticism; but nevertheless he was a great stickler for law and order, and when any agent would step out of line, he would cause immediate disciplinary action concerning the agent. I think that he felt the Kennedy administration—the Kennedys, although very sophisticated, intelligent, a wonderful education, a great family—nevertheless was very naive in many respects, particularly Bobby. He thought they were very naive as far as society was concerned. Also, Mr. Hoover, having been raised in a Quaker family, being a deeply religious individual—an elder in the Presbyterian Church—when he saw individuals more or less desecrating the law, in his opinion, or individuals in high places who acted improperly and didn't do anything about it, I am sure felt they were doing very wrong.

Bobby Baker   Hoover almost blackmailed Bobby to continue his illegal tapping of Martin Luther King because Hoover had taps of President Kennedy and that German girl. A good friend of mine was the wing man for President Kennedy when he was a congressman and a senator; the girl was supposed to be his date, but she was really Kennedy's date; he used to go all over the world with Kennedy. So when he became president he put my friend on the payroll at $100,000 per year, just to protect his flank; he was the one who got all the girls for Kennedy. I was at a cocktail party, and this German girl was there with a friend of mine, and my friend came up and said, "Who's that good-looking son of a bitch?" and I said, "She's a German; she's married to a sergeant in the German Embassy, but she likes to have a good time." And he said, "Do you think she'd have dinner with the president?" And I said, "Call my secretary, and she'll arrange it for him," and she did.

Bobby probably had more friends in the press than his brother did, and they kept saying that all these sex things had been going on and Jackie was going to file for divorce, and they knew about it. My friend took this German girl down, and Hoover had a tape of her being there, and you see how Hoover blackmailed Bobby to let him continue taping Martin Luther King. He had tapes of the girl where she made the phone contacts. So they deported her, and Bobby sent one of his former staff members from the Senate Investigating Committee with her, and they paid her; she's never talked. I've written to her recently to tell her I'd been informed that she could be paid at least a million dollars for her story. I wrote to her—she had not heard from me in twenty-seven years. She said everyone had been after her and that she was living a very quiet life and didn't want to talk. That is one of the reasons they couldn't get rid of Hoover. They would have in a second term, because he wouldn't have had to run again.

Bernard Boutin   They should have fired Hoover—Eisenhower and Truman before Kennedy, and Johnson after Kennedy. There are some who say that he had so much on everyone that they couldn't afford to fire him. He also had a public image as the great G-man. After Dillinger, what the hell did he do? Look at him with Joe McCarthy. The guy was a first-class bastard. Bobby just never did anything about him.

Courtney Evans   It is well known that in his bachelor days President Kennedy [had a reputation] for paying particular attention to the fairer sex. Hoover knew this, but it was also widely known among those concerned with the political picture in Washington. I've never seen any evidence that there was anything of substance that would cause any undue influence by Hoover on the president. I don't think there was something that if Hoover released it, was going to be devastating to the presidency.

Today there are all kinds of rumors and innuendo about Hoover himself. I have no information about this; no way of making a judgment. There weren't many facts to support it.

Pierre Salinger   The president wanted to get rid of Hoover but was finding it difficult to do. But I am convinced that if he had been reelected in 1964, Hoover would have been gone. Hoover was a very anti-Kennedy person: He didn't like Bobby because Bobby had started the whole team looking into the Mafia—that was something the FBI had never done before, and it angered Hoover a lot. My own relationship with Hoover was bad because just before I took over as press secretary, he leaked some misinformation to a newspaper that my mother was a communist.

Courtney Evans   I kept the Kennedys from firing Hoover. They were incensed at him from time to time. They felt he was wasting his manpower investigating national security cases. As President Johnson said, they were wary of Hoover's influence with powerful committee chairmen up on the Hill. Hoover was concerned about their desire to fire him. That was the reason for my downfall. There was no credible evidence that I was going to replace Hoover—none whatsoever, but the mere fact that the rumor got out was enough. I surmised their strategy to be that they would wait until after the 1964 election, when Hoover would reach his seventieth birthday, the mandatory retirement age, and they expected the law to take its course.

Ralph Dungan   There was no plan to retire Hoover, but everybody would have loved to find a way to do it—nobody would dare take him on. Hoover was a vicious son of a bitch. Some of that stuff that was coming over was pure garbage. People who had any contact with the president—they would send these little messages; there was a guy coming over from the FBI all the time, dropping these little billets-doux on O'Donnell's desk—anything from straight security clearance stuff to gossip about Martin Luther King. Some of it was terrible, with absolutely no foundation: "A qualified informer, blah, blah, blah."

Nicholas Katzenbach   Firing J. Edgar Hoover—Jesus Christ!—let's go back to those times to realize what that meant. I seriously question whether President Kennedy could have made a firing stick; he'd have been in a brouhaha for months.

They did plan to get rid of Hoover on his seventieth birthday. It was almost amusing. They would have the Marine Corps, Army and Navy bands, and the Air Force would fly over the White House steps. He wouldn't have been fired but would have reached mandatory retirement age. Of course Bobby's idea was: You flatter Hoover into doing things.

Richard Helms   Nixon was the only one I knew who definitely wanted to retire Hoover. That the Kennedys might have wanted to retire Hoover I don't question. Bobby didn't have a very good impression of what the bureau was doing when he was investigating the Mafia and Hoffa, and felt the bureau was doing nothing about these issues, which was true. They weren't.

Roger Hilsman   Every president from Roosevelt on wanted to fire J. Edgar Hoover, but none of them dared. A president could have, but the political costs would have outweighed the gain. It was better to go on and live with him. Kennedy was pissed at him and wanted him out. So he said, "What we are going to do is this: We'll have the Army Band walk down one side of the Mall playing 'The Star Spangled Banner,' and the Navy Band at the other side. The Air Force Band will parachute, playing the national anthem as they descend. From a platform in the middle of the Mall, I will present Hoover with the Medal of Freedom and every other medal we can possibly think of. Then I will whisper in his ear, 'You are fired.'" But he couldn't touch him.

13

Civil Rights

_____

The burgeoning civil rights movement was the most pressing domestic issue confronting the Kennedy administration. The sit-ins, Freedom Rides, and mass demonstrations met with white opposition in Congress and on the streets of scores of Southern cities and small towns.

The Kennedy approach to civil rights favored executive action rather than legislation. This policy grew out of the political calculation that Kennedy could not garner enough votes in Congress to pass meaningful legislation, and that even if such legislation were possible, its very adoption would embitter the South, resulting in disastrous political consequences for the president's 1964 reelection bid.

The White House did introduce civil rights legislation in the fall of 1963, but only after extensive media coverage of violent demonstrations and bombings in Birmingham, Alabama, had brought the black struggle for equality into American homes.

John Patterson   He would occasionally ask me questions about the situation in Alabama—what the status of litigation was. I never asked him, in all the time I knew him, for a commitment on anything. I had enough sense to know that nobody could be elected president of the United States on a segregation ticket. But it seemed to me his interests—his primary interest—lay in equal opportunities for blacks and the right to vote and participate in the political process. He seemed to shy away from the school situation, which was so volatile at that time. It seemed like he was primarily concerned in pushing the rights of the blacks in the field of equal opportunity, equal employment, and equal political participation.

I felt that he understood the problems we were having down here. If he had to put his foot on us, he'd put it on us lightly; he'd work with us. If you have somebody who is friendly, and who is understanding of the problem, then it is easier to work out from under the difficulties that we were having. Nobody down here with any understanding of the Constitution could conclude other than that we would ultimately lose the segregation battle. Legally we couldn't win. I knew that when I was attorney general. What we were doing in Alabama was fighting a delaying action legally—above board—to try to give people time to adjust gradually to change without violence. This was the policy I pursued for eight years, and largely successfully. We had very little difficulty till the Freedom Rider situation, where I fell out with Robert. I never got invited back to the White House again.

Joseph Rauh, Jr. I had been designated to deal with civil rights for the ADA [Americans for Democratic Action], so I started in, "Mr. President, we came here to urge action on legislation on civil rights." We also proposed legislation on voting rights extensions, and I made a full litany of proposals. He was not at all happy with my presentation. He didn't say that he would go out and build up support; he didn't say anything like that. He was very stern on this, unusually so for all the times in my life that I had seen him, and he said no—he was very firm—"I'm not in any position to do what you ask; we can't get it through. What I have done is to make a number of black appointments, and there will be more, and Bobby will bring some voting lawsuits." And he was saying to us, That's what there is going to be, and no more. He didn't want people—and I was one of them—going around saying, He's not for civil rights. That, he felt, was bad politics. But he also had a certain guilt feeling on this issue. He didn't change until June 1963, two years later. It was political pressure that changed him, but the great event that changed him was King's march in Birmingham; there's no question about that.

Robert Moses, director, Mississippi Council of Federated Organizations Kennedy represented a new generation to take power. He called forth the sense that this country was going to embark on a new course. That was not spelled out in terms of internal policy. But it fed into, and was part of, this general revolution of rising expectations that was sweeping the world. So young black people may have moved into that energy in quite an unexpected way: This is a new generation which is going to exercise some power; it's going to take some steps on its own. It's going to answer this question of, What can I do for this country? in a very unexpected way. I don't think Kennedy anticipated that his words would touch people who were looking for new expectations from this country.

John Lewis   John F. Kennedy's very election ushered in a sense of optimism—of great expectation. In Kennedy, you had a young, likable, exciting president. It was also the things he said: He was asked, "What do you think of those who are sitting in?" and he said, "By sitting in, they're standing up." There was something about the Kennedy presidency— about the man—that touched the black people immediately.

Norman Podhoretz   I think the mainstream civil rights movement in the pre-1965 period, and the people in the Kennedy administration— including those who were very sympathetic to the civil rights movement—shared a fundamental premise, which was that the problem was external barriers, discriminatory barriers, and that they were worse in the South but they also existed in the North. If you knocked down those barriers and you would establish equality of opportunity which had been denied, this would lead—as it had in the case of the Jews, for example— to economic and social advancement, and everything would be fine; it was just a matter of fighting discrimination. The argument was over how fast you could move in fighting discrimination; it wasn't over the objective; it wasn't over whether there were other factors that had to be taken into consideration, or whether there were other problems that were more serious than external discrimination. That came a little later. So it was always a question of the pace at which he was willing to go, especially in the South—in fact, almost entirely in the South.

Later you had the rise of a body of sentiment, both among blacks and whites, that said that external barriers of discrimination are the least of it—that there were deeper problems inside the black community but also in the hearts of whites: institutionalized racism, as it later got to be called. Thus more radical measures were needed. It was not a problem of individuals facing discrimination, which was the perspective in the Kennedy years; we now had to deal with it in terms of groups. You couldn't deal with it as a matter of trying to establish a level playing field, as Lyndon Johnson put it, in the first affirmative action speech—that blacks were handicapped, therefore they needed a little extra help. That was all foreign to the thinking of people like Roy Wilkins [executive director, NAACP] and other mainstream black leaders, and was certainly foreign to the thinking of people in the Kennedy administration, who, I think, would have been quite outraged by any such idea.

Ralph Dungan   The Kennedy administration was not rushing into it, but they were being moved into the mainstream. The movement was growing, and there was nothing anybody could do to stop it. They were moving into it—or being moved into the mainstream—and there was no question, on an intellectual level, where they would have come out.

Nicholas Katzenbach   Harris [Wofford] didn't get the job he really wanted; the feeling was he could make a lot of political difficulties. He wanted Burke Marshall's job. The White House operation on civil rights was not a power center. Bobby was a great admirer of Louis Martin. He did have a great influence, probably greater than anyone gave him credit for. He played an important part in the Civil Rights Act: what should be in the act—not in the drafting but in what the black community wanted. Bobby did not know many blacks. The president did not know many blacks, coming from Massachusetts at that time.

Fred Shuttlesworth   The Kennedys would not go out voluntarily and crusade for change. But since change was coming, and since this thing was moving up, and since there was a moral right, and since this had the eyes of the nation, I believe they began to get the feeling that they were there to really see to it that the law begins to mean the same thing for everybody.

After Birmingham the Kennedys began to move against the state and local officials. They were shocked by the violence in Birmingham; they had believed the people were not so brutal. But they didn't reason that the Klan itself, the core of it, is violent—violence against white people, as well as black people, against Jews and everybody else. I think that at first the Kennedys believed that a mere enunciation of the law and the promise of the government would naturally quiet people. They believed that everybody had a basic respect for law. But segregation did not respect law.

George Wallace   I met with John Kennedy in Mussel Shoals. He wanted me to hire some black clerks, but I had already hired some in Birmingham. I talked to a bunch of businessmen up there; I asked them to put on another black clerk or two and they said, "We've got three; we'll hire one more."

Theodore Hesburgh   As an intellectual endeavor Kennedy did understand the issue and what needed to be done about it. During the campaign he criticized Eisenhower on housing and promised to deal with discrimination in housing with the stroke of a pen, yet he was in office for two years without that stroke of the pen taking place. On the other hand, he did things that were rather unusual. On the morning after he was inaugurated, he called up the head of the Coast Guard Academy and asked, "Was that your outfit walking down Pennsylvania Avenue yesterday?" The admiral said, "Yes, sir." The president said, "I didn't see a single black. You'd better get some blacks in there, and do it quickly." Things like that he could do, but he was very chary of stepping on the toes of the Southerners, who were very sensitive on this issue.

William Sloane Coffin, Jr.   I never was impressed that Kennedy did very much on the home front for the civil rights movement. I don't think he understood it. I think privilege requires a certain measure of ignorance, and he was a very privileged guy. It was a very moving thing that Bobby Kennedy broke through and went down to Mississippi, where he met Peter Edelman [aide to Attorney General Robert F. Kennedy] and Marian Wright [civil rights worker], and I felt that Bobby Kennedy had really caught on to what the civil rights movement was all about. But I remember well calling Harris Wofford from Montgomery, Alabama, on a Freedom Ride: Just before I got arrested that night, I was hanging around Ralph Abernathy's [Rev. Ralph Abernathy, secretary-treasurer, SCLC] house. There wasn't much to do, and there was a phone across the street, so I put a dime in and called the White House, collect, and I got McGeorge Bundy out of bed, and he was not pleased. He said, "Oh, our peripatetic chaplain." I almost said, You get into your trousers one leg at a time, McGeorge, too. But I decided that was true, but not helpful, as the shrinks say, so I simply said to him, "Why doesn't Kennedy make a speech the way de Gaulle did about Algeria? This is a great moral issue; he could pick the country up and really deal with it." And

Bundy was totally unimpressed. I think he expected his information to come through channels, and not through a Montgomery telephone booth. But I got Harris Wofford, who understood exactly what was going on, and he said to me, "Bill, I couldn't agree with you more; but it's going to be well over a year from now before Kennedy ever takes a stand on civil rights." I think Kennedy was just a real pol at that point who didn't understand basically what the civil rights movement was all about. And Bobby Kennedy didn't understand it then either, I think. It took a while; not many people did, and certainly very few in positions of power did.

Norbert Schlei   We had the feeling we were getting a tremendous amount of flak from people we thought would see us as their allies in trying to achieve the same goals. There is an expression—a good turn never goes unpunished. We thought we were going as fast as we could.

Terry Sanford   The natural tendency is to up the ante; the more you give people freedom, the more they want—which is all right. You just need to understand that. They are not going to appreciate a quarter of a loaf if they feel they are entitled to a whole loaf. I was in a position of wanting to give them the whole loaf—to know that if I did, that they would never get it, and I would be gone. And it wouldn't be any great deal that I was gone, but what would be in my place wouldn't want to give them a quarter of a loaf. So you had to play that as much as the traffic would bear. Kennedy was doing that.

Archibald Cox   You're very seldom doing everything that one extreme thinks you should be doing. For example, in the case of the sit-ins, civil rights lawyers wanted the government to take the position that any prosecution of criminal trespass of a civic demonstration was a violation of the Fourteenth Amendment. There was a real question as to whether the Supreme Court would buy that, so I set about to find some narrower ground on which we could get each and every conviction reversed. And the Good Lord was kind to us. I'm inclined to think that if I had not taken these—if you will—legalistic grounds, following the theory of slicing off as little as you have to at one time, that they might well have lost in the beginning.

Nicholas Katzenbach   There were times that civil rights issues preoccupied the president. The problems were hard to resolve and certainly occupied a great deal of Bobby's time. Therefore the president spent more time on them, and they would talk a great deal about an issue that was on Bobby's mind. Yet I think other things were far more important. He was really interested in foreign policy and wanted to be involved in it. This caused problems with State; he wanted to be his own secretary of state.

He was always conscious of the closeness of the election, I always thought too conscious. He didn't feel he had a mandate, didn't feel he would succeed. In truth he didn't like working with Congress, even though he was a former senator and congressman. That's why he had Larry O'Brien, as opposed to LBJ, who reveled in working with Congress. Kennedy was inhibited about civil rights; he had all these demons going— the sit-ins, Meredith [James Meredith, the first black to attend the University of Mississipi], Wallace. He wanted to get other things done.

Morris Abram How much time did Jack Kennedy have to give to this? He was doing a hell of a lot of things we didn't know about. He was carrying on an enormous number of affairs. Foreign affairs was a preoccupation; this was an irritation. This was a volatile thing. He couldn't win. The Democratic party controlled the House and the Senate, and the lords of the party were all Southerners; there was no win for him. Now Burke Marshall's heart was in it; Wofford's heart was in it; Shriver and Seigenthaler also, and in a certain sense, Bobby was in it, because he was the guy who ran the department Marshall and Seigenthaler were in. The question was: How to contain this thing and keep it from damaging the party and the presidency? It was a hell of an irritant.

You know, every time people say in these riots now, "Oh, America is a racist society," they ought to have lived through those days. There was no black mayor of Chicago; no black mayor of New York; no black mayor of Detroit; no black mayor of Los Angeles; no black governor of Virginia; no thousand black sheriffs and other officers in the South. You have to put it in perspective; things have changed. I have always said that race is a dominant factor in attitude. Lyndon Johnson knew that you could not change attitudes very well, but you could change public attitudes, and I always say, "The day the blacks got the vote in South Carolina you saw Strom Thurmond referring to them no longer as 'niggers' but as 'our beloved brethren.'"

Bobby Baker I don't think John Kennedy really cared. Politically, he knew he had to be out front, but he didn't want to call Mrs. King. They had to put a lot of heat on him. People in the South have a totally differ-ent relationship with blacks than Northerners do; we were raised with them. Kennedy, in his whole life, was never around blacks.

James Farmer   He didn't move on the stroke-of-the-pen promise [exec-utive action on discrimination in housing] for two years, so he wasn't going to do anything unless he had to. Politicians respond to anxiety, and Jack Kennedy was no exception. Furthermore, Jack Kennedy was particularly ignorant on civil rights in particular and blacks in general at the time he became president. He had had no contact with blacks. The late Jackie Robinson [Republican activist; first black to play on a major league base-ball team] said, and I guess this can be taken as truth, that during the 1960 campaign Jack Kennedy said to him, "Mr. Robinson, I don't know any Negroes. Would you introduce me to some?"

Joseph Rauh, Jr.   I think he resented civil rights pressure because it was hard for him. Look, here he is a Catholic president who has barely made it; has lost all these seats in Congress in 1962; and here we come asking him to do these things which would really have been divisive. I think he should have done it, but one can certainly understand the feelings he had when the civil rights thing was really thrown in his face. I mean, they didn't understand the depth of this thing. But they were sympathetic. The Kennedys were somewhat academic in the depth of the liberalism and the depth of their civil rights views, but they grew. I always thought the Kennedys were like flowers, you put water on them and they bloom, and that's what happened to all three Kennedys in Washington.

Ralph Dungan   I'm really sorry to say that on the civil rights side, we were not very good. We never asked ourselves the question "What's right?"

There was a guy who worked for Sarge [Shriver] who was really pushing on the civil rights thing. He used to come around often to see me and to urge me to try to get things on the issue into speeches. He helped the president a lot; he had direct relations with the president. He had a very difficult time trying to advance the civil rights issue—to push it up on the agenda; it never got there, really.

William Sloane Coffin, Jr.   Progressives do much better when you have a liberal fellow in power, and then you have to push him a little further. I couldn't say if we would have done the same with Nixon as president. As far as black leaders were concerned, they felt they had a massive educational job to do. Kennedy had to uphold the law. He couldn't allow Governor Patterson to make a fool of him any more than Faubus [Orval Faubus, governor of Arkansas] could be allowed to make a fool of Eisenhower. Kennedy had to move in against John Patterson to uphold the law of the land; it was a matter of order, far more than law, and I don't think that King or Abernathy or Fred Shuttlesworth felt that they had real boosters in government. By the time of Birmingham, when Burke Marshall came down, they felt he was a lot friendlier than in 1961. Don't forget that in 1961, what Kennedy was being told by Bobby and Burke Marshall was that we need a cooling-off period. King and Abernathy were very clear that they couldn't call it off until there was some promise of change. And the change was going to have to be forced by them, because the president wasn't going to take any initiative.

My feeling all along was that we didn't look to the Kennedy administration for much; we looked to the Supreme Court. The Warren Court was called controversial only because the lower courts wouldn't do their job. I remember that during the Freedom Ride, we went up before Judge Marks [Alex Marks, County Court, Montgomery County, Ala.], and he gave us a little talk: "When in Rome, do as the Romans do, boy." And he sentenced one of us with something he wasn't even charged with. And when one of the prosecutors, who was as rednecked as you could be, said, "Judge, I don't think you can do that," Marks leaned over and said, "Son, I just did." In doing the right thing, the Warren Court was called controversial by people who showed how far removed from real controversy they were.

James Farmer I got to the Oval Office on time, a couple of minutes early. The president walked in a few minutes later, maybe five minutes later, which is quite all right, no problem there at all. I was seated, so I stood. The president walked in, head down. He had a sheaf of papers in his hand, and he nodded briefly to me and then sat down. Well, I just had forty-five minutes with him, and he continued to look at these papers, making notations, signing, initialing, crossing out, and speed-reading. My time was ticking away; the clock was ticking, and he hadn't looked up at me. I decided I'd better start talking or my time would be gone. So I started talking. I thought: Maybe then I'll get his attention.

But he continued working on his papers. So I went on talking. Finally I said, "Mr. President, if you are too busy for this meeting, I'm sure it can be rescheduled at a more convenient time." He looked up briefly and said, "No, go right ahead," and went back to his papers. Well, I was insulted, you know. When the time was up, I said, "Well, Mr. President, I see my time has elapsed, so I won't impose further on your time." I then stood; he stood, shook hands and sat back down with his papers. He was essentially giving a message to me that I was a no-no; I was the "bad boy," the uncompromising one, the one who would not halt when they had said, "Halt the Freedom Ride."

Well, later, I was at Aspen, Colorado, moderating one of those Institute of Humanistic Studies seminars for corporate leaders. When it was over, Joe Slater, who was then president of the Aspen Institute, came to me and asked if I could stay another week. He explained that the attorney general was coming in for a seminar with foreign students and that many if not most of the questions would deal with civil rights. I said, "Well, I'll get back to you this afternoon; I will have to readjust my schedule." So I called him back that afternoon and said, "Joe, I can do it. It will take a little maneuvering with my calendar, but I can do it." He then said, "I'm embarrassed, but I am going to have to withdraw the invitation." I asked why and he said, "Well, I called Attorney General Kennedy and told him I might be able to get you to stay for his seminar and he said, 'If that son of a bitch Farmer is going to be there, I'm not coming. Cancel him, or I cancel. I'll bring Thurgood Marshall [U.S. circuit judge, Second Circuit Court of Appeals; later associate justice, U.S. Supreme Court].'" So I was cancelled and packed my bags and my wife and I went home. Thurgood didn't know about this, I'm sure. That was the attitude the Kennedys had from the Freedom Rides on.

On one occasion at the White House when there was a reception, all the members of the Kennedy family were there. I remember Jackie was there, and so was Joan Kennedy, Teddy's wife at the time. She had on hot pants or a miniskirt, and that struck everybody's attention. This time, when I walked into the White House, the president seemed rather cordial. He smiled, shook hands, and said, "Mr. Farmer, come right in." Jackie Kennedy shook hands too, rather warmly. This, however, was very shortly—if memory serves me right—after I had had a debate with Malcolm X [Black Muslim leader] on a network in New York, where the nub of the argument was on the Kennedys. Malcolm referred to the president as that Ku Klux Klan president, which set me off. I said, "I've had my problems with the Kennedys—and probably would go on having problems—but to call him a KKK president is the height of absurdity. It just so happens, Malcolm, that the speech the president recently made, the second speech after Meredith tried to get into Ole Miss, was the strongest civil rights speech of any president in American history, including Lincoln." And then Malcolm and I went at it. I recalled that at the next CRIAL° meeting, Stephen Currier [president, Taconic Foundation] was all smiles and shook my hand: "Oh, you did great," and then shortly after that, at the White House, Kennedy seemed more cordial. That was in late 1963, though.

Louis Martin   I scheduled a lot of the meetings with black leaders, and sat in on some of them, but it didn't matter what went on in the meeting. What you had to do when the meeting was over was to go into the Oval Office, where JFK and Bobby were, to find out what was really important.

When we would do something on civil rights, Bobby used to kid me, "Now you lost me the South; what else are you going to lose?"

Robert Moses   During that time, I had no thought really about either of the Kennedys. We were dealing with John Doar [Justice Department aide, Civil Rights Division] and Burke Marshall, and we were trying to work out the ways in which we could eventually interface with the Justice Department in a way which would help us to do our work and would help them to do their work. On the one hand there was a lot of media hype—which went back and forth—where people were sending out press releases saying "the Justice Department didn't do this or that," or "the department should do this or that." That was one kind of activity, but on the other hand there was real work going on. As we carefully documented cases about voter registration denials and violence, we were passing them on to the Civil Rights Division people in the Justice Department.

Julian Bond   I remember this awful feeling of frustration at these people who had earlier promised—and then acted as if they'd never promised—or repudiated the promise. I'm in the office in Atlanta—pretty safe and secure; nobody is bothering me. But these are my friends who are getting

---

°An ad hoc group of leaders of major civil rights organizations.

shot at, beaten up, put in jail. And we know these people could protect them if they wanted to. There's no reason they couldn't, except to get along well with Senator Eastland [James Eastland, U.S. senator (D., Miss.)]. They thought that was more important than saving my friends' lives.

John Doar and Burke Marshall represented the Justice Department to us. That they were readily accessible, we thought, was a positive step. Our field staff could call them at home, collect; could call them at the Justice Department, collect. But they wouldn't do anything, so you had access but not protection—no assurance if you called and said that a mob was outside your building; you had the security of knowing that the last person you spoke to on earth would be an official of the Justice Department. Oh, yes. We had access to John Doar and Burke Marshall, and they had access to John and Robert Kennedy. We were calling employees, and they were calling the chief. But then, of course, we didn't need to call the president; we needed to call Burke Marshall, because Burke Marshall was in the Civil Rights Division of the Department of Justice; that's what we were doing. They needed to call the president, because that's what they were doing. I'm not saying that we didn't resent their access, but it wasn't anything we expected to have—we were, after all, students; we didn't expect to be on a telephone basis with the president of the United States or the attorney general. It was pretty good for us to be able to call Burke Marshall, collect.

Burke Marshall   Robert Kennedy said that when he became attorney general he didn't know much about the civil rights problem. I think that the Kennedys looked at the problem—as politicians of both parties did—as one of the interest groups. President Kennedy's knowledge of the issue had to do with the 1957 and 1960 Civil Rights Acts. It became clear to me that under John and Robert Kennedy, civil rights would be handled aggressively—in the Justice Department, not in the Congress. They were acutely aware that a Little Rock–type problem might arise. Kennedy realized that the votes weren't there. The question was not whether he would get legislation, but whether he would make the gesture; he was not a man *not* to do things seriously.

Morris Abram   The fact is that they were entirely political. I was involved in the campaign to cause the president to sign the fair housing thing. He said he would accomplish this by the stroke of a pen, but it was hard to get him to strike that pen. I understand it. Hell, he had a Southern-dominated Senate and House, and he was very chary of this. He was also very loath to damage his credit with the black community. I remember being outside the Oval Office with Harry Belafonte [entertainer; confidant of Martin Luther King, Jr.], Rostow, and Harris Wofford. We had just left the president's office, talking about civil rights and urging him to do what we thought he should do. And somebody, I think it was Harry Belafonte, said something about what he had said about the situation, and the president heard him and followed us out and stopped and said, "Dammit. All you've read is the headlines. Why don't you read the whole statement?" So, even in the early days of the administration, he was very conscious of the fact that he didn't want to be painted as not doing what he said he would do and not being seen as sympathetic of the civil rights movement.

Theodore Hesburgh   Robert Kennedy looked upon this as his private domain, and he was very cautious about backing the Civil Rights Commission on anything, because he wanted the Kennedy administration to get credit for any progress that had been made. On the other hand, the moment Johnson was in there, he had the commission come over and he sat us down and told us he wanted to do something about poverty. He wanted that to be the keynote of his administration. That was very forthright, and in a matter of months he had a much tougher civil rights law even than the one we were trying to get the Kennedy administration to put up. He pulled out all the stops, and I think you have to say that the 1964 law changed the face of America.

John Patterson   I might have been a problem to him. He never indicated that. He was always friendly and courteous toward me. And I think he understood our situation. Every time I went up to the White House—or even went up there to visit him—and it got out in the press that I had done that, Martin Luther King and all those folks would descend on him and say, What the hell are you doing with a fellow like Patterson? I was somewhat of a liability. I understand that.

One of the great problems we have had is that Alabama has been deprived of its right to participate in national political affairs, and to have influence in these affairs, because of the race issue. That's held us back. It made it very difficult for us to work with people in Washington in terms of common interest, simply because of the race issue. At that time in

Alabama you couldn't be elected governor, or be elected to any office, unless you were considered to be a strong segregationist. If you were perceived to be weak on that issue, then you would be wasting your time; you might as well go on home and forget it. That's the pure and simple of it. I got elected primarily on law enforcement. But before I'd been in my race six weeks, race had become the primary issue. That's all anybody was interested in—all they wanted to talk about. George Wallace at that time was perceived to be weak on that question, believe it or not.

James Farmer The Kennedys were opposed to civil rights legislation and until after Birmingham, told us so. What they said to us—the two Kennedys—in the White House, with the heads of civil rights organizations there, was that they did not think that new civil rights legislation was either necessary or feasible. In terms of necessary, I guess it's self-apparent: There are laws on the books—the Constitution and the other civil rights laws of the past—which can be dragged up and enforced. In terms of feasible, the question of the solid South, keeping the coalition together—here we didn't have a consensus—but after Birmingham, and this was the beauty of many of King's demonstrations, the media were drawn in in full force. SNCC started things in Birmingham. They brought King in somewhat reluctantly, but it was important that King be brought in, because where King went, the media went. If King issued a call, then the nation's people of goodwill would respond to that call and come.

Birmingham happened when Bull Connor played into their hands by turning the police dogs loose on little children, and the firemen turned their hoses on the crowd, with women rolling down the streets with their skirts flying. People—decent people, most people are inherently, the Judeo-Christian tradition—all over the U.S. sat in their living rooms, just finishing dinner or eating dessert and drinking coffee, and watched those abysmal scenes. Those scenes are horrible; those little children—they haven't hurt anybody—those women. Bull Connor's a beast, we have to get rid of him; we have to put an end to this thing. This is not American. Give us some laws; let's have laws. Laws that can be enforced and get this problem behind us. Well, the Kennedys saw that. The pollsters were also telling them that the nation's public opinion was swinging to the civil rights side: After Birmingham, the majority was with us; their consensus had arrived; the Kennedys were told the consensus was in favor of new civil rights legislation. New civil rights legislation was introduced, but I doubt if Kennedy could have gotten it passed. It had to wait for a Southern president—Southern accent, a back-slapper and arm-twister—like LBJ to get it through. I sat in Johnson's office, and he was on the phone twisting senators' arms, threatening them, cajoling them, lining up votes for the Civil Rights Act. I doubt that Kennedy could have done that. But he was going to give it the old college try—get the legislation introduced. And who knows whether his getting the legislation introduced had something to do with his death. Future historians will tell us.

Bradford Morse   He had a major legislative victory the first day of Congress, with the Rules Committee vote. He did not make a strenuous effort on civil rights, but the Rules Committee fight was perceived as a civil rights issue. It would seem that civil rights legislation would have been worth a far stronger shot than it got. The Rules Committee victory let you get measures to the floor. If they were delaying because of the closeness of the 1960 vote, and with an eye on 1964, that's not defensible. If a person is elected president of the United States, he is elected to be president; he is not elected to be a candidate for reelection.

Norbert Schlei   It was clear to the Kennedys that if you sent a civil rights bill up to Congress, the result would be a two-year debate, which you would lose, and that nothing else would get through. You couldn't get it through the House, and even if you did, in the Senate it would be filibustered. The president was interested in getting through a tax cut which he thought would help black people more than a civil rights bill. Obviously, a civil rights bill was good for the soul, but the tax cut and other economic measures would do more good—at least in the short run.

The thing that really changed the situation was Birmingham. The president and the attorney general got that message very quickly. The next weekend they had us in there, in the Justice Department, to have a big meeting to draft a civil rights bill. People say that Johnson got it through, but meanwhile, he had defeated Goldwater and had a margin in the House of 135 votes. He could have sent the telephone directory up, and they'd have passed it.

Arthur Schlesinger, Jr.   Legislation was not possible until the dogs lunged at the peaceful marchers in Birmingham in 1963. Kennedy had sent up a civil rights message the month before and it had gotten nowhere. He could not even get Thurgood Marshall appointed; he had to accept some Confederate judges in order to do that. He tried to get a Department of Urban Affairs established. Robert Weaver [administrator, Housing and Home Finance Agency], a black economist, was to be appointed. He couldn't get that through. The resistance in Congress to any kind of civil rights legislation was intense. He could have done more by executive order on housing.

I think we all underestimated the moral dynamism that the civil rights movement was acquiring by the early 1960s. It wasn't until the spring of 1963 that we began to understand that. Robert Kennedy, who as attorney general was more involved in the enforcement of federal court orders, had sensed this earlier. The great argument in the spring of 1963 was whether the administration should put itself at the head of the fight for civil rights. Lyndon Johnson didn't feel that, politically, this was the sensible thing to do. Robert Kennedy was very strongly for it. So was John Kennedy. That speech he gave in June—one can look at it in the sense of recent events in Los Angeles—where he defined racial justice as a moral issue and a top priority—was remarkable.

Kenny O'Donnell was a strong liberal on most things, and on its merits, he would have been strongly for civil rights. But, as I recall, he thought differently politically. He was right. Kennedy's approval rating, once he got involved in the civil rights fight, fell by fifteen points or so, from seventy to fifty-five. That fall was mostly in the South. Kennedy felt he had to do it both because of the merits of the issue and to hold the country together.

It was a movement whose time had come. It was the kind of thing de Tocqueville described about the French Revolution: that revolutions come not when people feel themselves without hope; revolutions come when things begin to open up—when they have shown moderate improvement. When people feel, If they have made it this far, why can't they go farther, and faster? That was what was happening. The Supreme Court decision in 1954, the Civil Rights Act of 1957, all this awakened hope. It gave black America the thought that maybe they could claim the constitutional rights to which they were entitled as American citizens. They brought the pressure, and a few whites, like Joe Rauh, Paul Douglas [U.S. senator (D., Ill.)], and Hubert Humphrey, understood this. They had been fighting for civil rights since 1948, so it had been a long fight. More and more, the blacks themselves were playing more assertive roles.

Louis Martin   JFK said he had no muscle. He said, "I can't get a Mother's Day resolution through that goddamn Congress." We came back to him and said, "Let's put some blacks in important jobs." The argument was that in putting blacks in nontraditional spots, we were giving a new power to black leadership. Robert Weaver was the top person. He was a very professional-looking guy. He was first head of an independent agency of color. This showed we no longer had to sit at the elbow of a white-power person whispering in his ear.

John Patterson   If you base it on what he said, and what he tried to do, I guess you have to conclude that Bobby Kennedy's civil rights sympathies were deeper than his brother's. I am not so sure about his motives. I *don't* have any doubts about the president's motives. My impression of President Kennedy was that he wanted to do everything he could for the blacks, for the minorities. He wanted to integrate them fully into our society. At the same time he recognized the political ramifications of that, and the necessity in some areas for not going too fast. He never said anything to me that I could put my finger on; this was my feeling about the matter. Now Robert just wanted to do it overnight. But I don't think the Republican leadership ever felt toward the minorities as the Kennedys did.

Bobby Baker   Bobby Kennedy had some strong people working for him, but I came away with the impression that he was a weakling with George Wallace and all those guys. He had people on his staff who were courageous—he had Nick Katzenbach and John Seigenthaler; they were the people who risked getting killed down there. Harris Wofford was a courageous guy, too.

Ben Bradlee   Jack Kennedy came late to a sensitivity and recognition of race problems in this country. The day he gave his Howard University speech—about all the inequities—we saw him that night, and he shook his head and said he wondered why it had taken him so long to confront that. I'd like to bet he had never met a black person in his life. I didn't— and I was on the WASP side of the same street—meet a black till I was sixteen. I think that Bobby—St. Francis—felt that there was deep moral inequity, and I don't think that Jack felt that instinctively.

Walt Rostow   The full stature of John Kennedy is not yet appreciated, the seriousness of it and how much he did get done. He laid the basis for civil rights. It was an uphill climb. Johnson was very helpful here. You can't really understand quite how important Johnson was, and how seriously Kennedy took him, unless you look at what he did on civil rights. In the summer of 1963, Kennedy got a draft of a civil rights speech he was to make from Ted Sorensen. What he would do with a draft when he wanted a change was say to Ted, "Let's give it to X, and see what he thinks." On this one he said, "Ted, give it to the vice president."

We have the transcript of the telephone conversation between LBJ and Ted. It's fascinating. It is typical of Johnson on the phone: at great length—going around in circles but very rich. The point he was trying to make—and did drive home—was, if you want to carry the South on this thing and break the filibuster, there is only one appeal you can make: It is the right thing to do. You must appeal to morality, to their attachment to the Bible. Johnson went up to Gettysburg before President Kennedy made his civil rights speech to show him how to do it.

Julian Bond   By the end of 1963, I began to feel that Bobby Kennedy had reached over the gulf and closed it. But I didn't feel that way about John Kennedy. There were so many distances between us. He seemed older than Martin Luther King, so there was that distance. He was this wealthy, wealthy man. He was up there; we were down here. There was this enormous cultural difference. He went to Harvard, we went to Morehouse or Alabama State. I remember liking him and thinking how neat he and Jackie were. But I didn't think he and I could talk together.

George Wallace   I think that Robert Kennedy developed a passion for civil rights; I developed a passion for civil rights, too, because it's in the best interest of the country to have integration.

During the Birmingham crisis in the spring of 1963, Robert Kennedy and Burke Marshall flew to Montgomery, Alabama, for a meeting with Governor Wallace.

Burke Marshall   It was out of Kafka: the attorney general and I got there in an FBI car. The steps of the State Capitol were lined with police with very fat stomachs, so we had to go single file. The governor turned on his tape recorder; the attorney general made his speech. It went downhill from there. It was not a conversation; it was an event.

George Wallace   I enjoyed meeting with Robert Kennedy during the crisis. He was so nervous—and sweating so. I said, "Mighty hot, isn't it?" Kennedy came to see me, and then he tried to con me. I wouldn't talk to him because everything he said to an official in Mississippi, he recorded it and quoted it. I was sincere, and every man over there was trying to make it look like he resisted them, but he didn't. He talked about all the things he had said, so I wouldn't talk to him. I talked to him when he came to see me. Bob put on a recording thing, and we agreed that if we ever released it, we'd both agree on it. I released it once, and he wrote and thanked me for getting his permission.

Cartha DeLoach   I think that the civil rights movement was a bubbling cauldron, an exercise of our constitutional rights and privileges that had to burst forth. Now, some expedient individuals may have used it for the purpose of enhancing their own prestige and influence, but it is something that would have come forth anyhow; it could not be hidden; it could not be swept under the rug any longer. It had to come forward, and it did come forward, and there was considerable bloodshed as a result of it. It was a phase in our history that we can't be proud of, but nevertheless it was a cleansing phase.

Robert Moses   I don't think that the Kennedys were champions of civil rights. They grew into the movement as they were confronted with it. It was an issue that wouldn't go away. Kennedy was interested in foreign policy—that was his major thrust—but this issue of civil rights was connected with Africa and the United Nations, and it wouldn't go away. You want people in such higher offices who have the capacity to grow to meet the challenges that they can't really anticipate when they take office.

I am sure that they did not think that this issue would have to take priority over how they were going to have to deal with Russia and other affairs of state. That's what happened.

In an effort to promote dialogue, Robert Kennedy asked for a meeting with black writers and entertainers. The session was arranged by Harry Belafonte and was held in Joseph Kennedy's apartment in New York.

Nicholas Katzenbach Bobby was devastated. He really thought he'd done a hell of a lot for civil rights, and he was suddenly just absolutely denounced. I was surprised they did it to Bobby Kennedy. It really was maddening, because these were the people who, hopefully, would be the beneficiaries of this law, opposing you at virtually every step and making it far more difficult to get it enacted. It was difficult to take: Being denounced for things you won't do—would be crazy to do—because it would hurt the act. Joe Rauh fought us every inch of the way. It was tactics. Their idea of how to enact a civil rights law was to go as far as you could go, then to give in to get it through. Our strategy was to get support from the Republicans, thus it had to be nonpolitical. LBJ was helpful in this, but the trouble was that, like most vice presidents, people forgot about him until the last minute. I remember one meeting on this. We were all sitting over there. Kennedy said, "Didn't anybody ask the vice president?" Of course, Bobby and LBJ were not exactly warm friends. LBJ wanted to be helpful, but it just wasn't possible for Bob Kennedy and Lyndon Johnson to work together on civil rights. I don't think that Bobby even trusted him on civil rights, and he should have.

William Sloane Coffin, Jr. As with parents, so with politicians: Gratitude may not be a profound emotion, but the expectation of it most certainly is, and Kennedy'd never gotten a good black rap. I remember the first time I got a good black rap. It is a compliment; they don't do it for people who aren't going to do anything for them. But it was a real shockeroo for Bobby to hear Baldwin [James Baldwin, author] sound off like that, because Bobby hadn't been down to Mississippi yet; he hadn't seen what was going on. And there were no blacks advising him at a high level.

Robert Moses It wasn't all the people; it was Jerome Smith [civil rights activist] of New Orleans. He was a young man out of the student movement. Of course Jerome is acting out of his knowledge and deep experience, confronting this issue down on the firing line, and he's not going to be listening to polite talk. So it's like saying, Hey are you for real, or are you going to sit here and just give us some kind of political hogwash, or are you calling us together to really understand what's going on? It was the intensity of Jerome's feeling. Jerome's telling Bobby Kennedy he wouldn't fight for this country was an awakening. Is the country producing a corps of young black people who are not prepared to fight for it? So the celebrities backed Jerome; but they couldn't do less than that.

Louis Martin   He called me up right afterward. I gave him hell: I said, "You go out and make your own appointments without telling me. I could have told you what would happen." I think Bobby felt that they didn't have an appreciation for his own sense of rectitude. He felt the was a straight shooter. His integrity was impugned there in a way he was not accustomed to. I think Bobby also sensed that most of the blacks were on the make themselves. They were looking for a place in the sun. He was thinking of them like the Boston Irish in the old days—like Honey Fitz—they were always scrambling.

Arthur Schlesinger, Jr.   He called me up when he got back. He was particularly shocked when this fellow said he wouldn't fight for his country. But his later reaction was that it was a good step in education. He got a sense of the rage and the despair from that meeting that enabled him to widen his understanding of the problem.

Tom Wicker   I think Robert didn't realize the depth of black feeling. These guys were from Massachusetts; they didn't know anything about that. They didn't campaign very much in the South. I saw James Baldwin later that night. That meeting was very important, because they opened Robert Kennedy's eyes, not only to the seriousness of the matter but to the depth of feeling in the black community. Baldwin at that time was a very intense, charged-up guy, and when I saw him he was angry. If you had a white skin that night, he was going for you.

John Seigenthaler   I think that was naïveté. It's: Don't go into a meeting unless you know how it is going to come out. Bobby looked on that visit as an opportunity to challenge the black intelligentsia to be better than they were; to have more sensitivity and compassion and more of a commitment toward performing as role models for young black people in the South. In effect he was saying to them: You and I are one, and we have it, and let's give something back. That was his mind-set when he went up there.

What he found initially was a reaction that said: You are not me, and we are not you; and you don't walk in my shoes, and you don't know the shit that I have to walk through. It was just about that blunt and candid. I think that took him aback. Then this young man, Jerome Smith, hits him with what—for him at the time—was the ultimate slap in the face: "I wouldn't fight for my country." It was such a radical statement, from his perspective, and he is thinking: Sure to God, these people who have made it in this society understand that there comes a time when you have to stand up and fight for your country. And he counterattacks, and then each of them—Jimmy Baldwin and Lorraine Hansberry [playwright, author]—their perception was, This kid is saying what we really think and never had the guts to say. And they go after him.

When I talked to Bobby, he was really down about it. This was a few days later. He was mad at himself, not at them; he was absolutely angry—furious at himself. I don't believe, after that, that I ever visited his home for anything larger than a party of a couple or three couples when there was not a black present. It wasn't spoken that there had been a change, but there was a heightened sensitivity that hadn't been there before, in my view.

I don't think the president subjected himself to that sort of ordeal. I don't want to deny the president the capacity to feel in the same way that Bob felt, in the absence of the experience—remember, Robert experienced the death of his brother, and after that tragedy he experienced something that is impossible to measure: At some point he became willing to be vulnerable. I am not sure the president ever did. An awful lot of that has to do with the sort of experience you are willing to tolerate.

Given the same set of circumstances, I think that they both would have come to the same conclusions on matters of politics and character; I think they had the same hand on the same rudder. But I do think that Bob, over his career, had more opportunities to expose himself to more situations in which there was a chance to evaluate him as a human being. And the president, because he was relatively isolated from many of the situations to which Robert Kennedy subjected himself, isn't seen in the same way, and you don't know for sure how he would react.

Ralph Dungan   We had a meeting just before the president left for Dallas, in the Cabinet Room with key staff, to talk about the 1964 campaign. It was the first group discussion on the campaign. There was definitely the tone: Win it in '64, and then we'll go for broke. I heard that same thing, particularly in the civil rights area, from the president in discussions with small groups of inside people: "After '64, we will do it the way we want to do it."

Lee White   We were reacting to circumstances. I think the president's plan was to move, but not at breakneck pace until the second term. Then he would do what he wanted to do. I don't know if he could have done what Johnson did. First of all Johnson had the benefit, if there is such a thing, of Kennedy's assassination to use as a device, as a mechanism. He was so skillful at it. Then, secondly, he had the benefit at least of being, if not from the South, from the Southwest. That accent helped him enormously.

THE FREEDOM RIDES

On May 14, 1961, two buses carrying integrated groups of civil rights campaigners were attacked in Alabama. The first bus reached the Birmingham terminal, where a white mob beat the Freedom Riders in and near the station as the local police looked on. The second bus was pelted with rocks as it passed through Anniston on the way to Birmingham. This bus, when forced to stop for a tire change, was set afire. A photograph of the burning bus appeared in newspapers around the world and brought home to an increasing number of Americans the fierceness of white resistance to black demands for equality.

James Farmer   There was a book put out, I think in the early seventies, a resource book in the social studies. It said that the most exciting, dramatic, and possibly the most significant project of the civil rights movement was the Freedom Rides in 1961. The book said it is unknown how the Freedom Rides got started. However, it is believed that they were instigated by the Kennedys. I thought, That's a good one. My late wife was furious when she read it, and I told her she should not think about that;

just imagine the agony that the Kennedys must be going through if they were aware of what the book said. The fact is, they tried to get the Freedom Rides stopped; they tried to get them halted, unsuccessfully.

I had sent letters to the president, to the attorney general, to the chairman of the Interstate Commerce Commission, and to FBI Director Hoover, telling them about the projected Freedom Rides and giving them the itinerary and the dates of departures and arrivals. But they never got the letters. This was clear from what I was told, I think by Harris Wofford. He said the president had called a meeting of his staff after the bus burning in Anniston and had pounded the table and said, "How the hell could anything like this happen without our knowing about it in advance? We're supposed to have advance knowledge of these things." And nobody had enough guts to tell him that there was a letter.

Burke Marshall   They sent a press release; nobody in the Justice Department focused on it. Somebody in the Justice Department, maybe me, should have realized what would occur. The FBI did not communicate with me. What happened at Anniston was shocking; it's preposterous that that should happen to a group just passing by—I still find it shocking that white people would be so disturbed about black people and white people sitting together.

Nicholas Katzenbach   I don't know if there was a letter. I will say this: Bobby was enormously protective of his brother, and if he thought this was a matter in which the president shouldn't get involved, he would have so advised him. He would have said, "You never heard of it, for God's sake, don't get involved."

These things [the Freedom Rides] were seen as a pain in the ass. There really wasn't anything you could do. You could bolster the Civil Rights Division, but you couldn't get legislation; there were limits to what you could do.

John Lewis   There was a feeling: It is dangerous, but we have a new administration. I think we knew we were testing this new administration when we decided on the Freedom Rides. I think it was right to test this young president early. The people associated with Kennedy gave us a lot of hope; there was something about the man that was the embodiment of change. What made it possible for the movement to take great leaps was the sense that by moving—by agitating—someone in Washington would listen. We didn't have that confidence in the Eisenhower years. The night before we went on the Freedom Ride—the night of May 3, 1961—we went to a Chinese restaurant, and I remember someone saying, "You should eat well, because this may be the Last Supper." I was beaten in Rock Hill, South Carolina, with a young man from Cos Cob, Connecticut, by the name of Albert Bigelow. We had tried to enter a so-called white waiting room and were jumped by a group of young white men and beaten.

James Farmer   There were nineteen Freedom Riders, including myself. The training included lectures by lawyers on what our legal rights were—and were not; and what the legal status of the issue was vis-à-vis Supreme Court decisions and local ordinances and state laws in the South. Social scientists spoke to us about the customs, folkways, and mores of the areas in which we were going and what steps people were likely to go to to maintain the racial status quo. Activists, I think they were persons from the NAACP from the Deep South, spoke to us and told us what was really going to happen. And what they said was: "You're going to get yourselves killed." And we had sociodrama, role-playing, etc., half the group playing the role of Freedom Riders at bus terminals, sitting at lunch counters waiting to be served, and the other half playing the roles of hoodlums coming in to beat them up. They could be realistic, too; they knocked us off the stools and kicked us. The purpose was to teach us how to cover up and, hopefully, to avoid serious and permanent injury. We discussed the scene that had been acted out and then reversed roles and played it over again, followed by more discussion. At the end of the week, I thought everybody was ready for anything that might happen, including death, and we knew that was a possibility. So that was the genesis of the Freedom Ride. I took the group out to dinner the night before we were to board the buses. I told them they were not locked into this; this was a dangerous—and maybe even suicidal—mission that they were embarking on.

John Patterson   When the Freedom Riders started down here from Washington, of course, publicity preceded them. This thing was a hotbed down here; it was a volatile thing, and dangerous. And as they came on and got to Atlanta, my director of public safety, Floyd Mann, and I got together and we sent an undercover Alabama officer over to catch that bus, so we had a state officer on that bus when it was set on fire outside of Anniston. He drew his pistol and forced the crowd back away from the bus and saved people from serious injury.

We know now that shortly before the Freedom Riders got to Birmingham, there was a meeting between the Klan and the city of Birmingham officials, in which an agreement was made to give them thirty minutes' free time to beat up the Freedom Riders when they got to the bus station. We didn't know that. We also know now that in that meeting was Gary Rowe, an undercover FBI informant posing as a Klansman, who reported after that meeting to FBI officials in Birmingham as to what had occurred, and asked for instructions. He was instructed to go ahead and beat them up. The FBI never informed anybody about it. I can't hardly conceive of that. Now some people claim that Robert Kennedy didn't know anything about that—that it was Hoover. I don't buy that. Frankly I think Robert knew everything about that. How could he not know? That's a great problem for me. The purpose was to get what the Freedom Riders really came after. We played their game. If I had it to do all over again, I'd do it completely differently. I would ask Mr. Kennedy for instructions. I would ask him exactly what he wanted me to do. I'd round up everybody that had anything to do with it at all; I would go after that crowd—Klan and all—with everything I had, right at the beginning.

James Farmer   It later turned out that it had been a mistake to give the itinerary to Hoover. We learned several years later, from the testimony of FBI informants, that the FBI turned copies of our itinerary over to the law enforcement officials in Alabama whom they knew to be leaders of the Ku Klux Klan. As a result the Klan had a warm reception for us at every stop in Alabama, and several people almost lost their lives. The FBI files indicate that an informant, I guess not an agent, a black person, was sent to join the Freedom Ride. I don't want to speculate on who that person was, because they have their lives now, and some of them are doing great things. One of them, indeed, became a staff member of CORE and is one of our best staff members. It doesn't matter who the person was, but they knew about the Freedom Ride, the FBI did, and sent somebody along to inform them. They turned over copies of the itinerary to law enforcement officials in Alabama, where we were practically done in. So they knew about the Freedom Ride, but it seems the attorney general did not know about it until it hit the headlines.

John Lewis   Robert F. Kennedy, in his capacity as attorney general— but also as a concerned person—did everything to see that we were protected. That was the first time President Kennedy demonstrated that he meant business and would use federal power to protect the people. The president and Robert Kennedy were taken aback by the violence; I don't think they understood the climate of fear that existed there. I think maybe that is the reason Robert Kennedy sent John Seigenthaler down. I was very much involved in the Freedom Rides. I did not anticipate the level of violence that occurred, but I was prepared. Even before leaving Washington, the CORE people had sent a message to Robert Kennedy, and it was just put into his in box. From what I have been able to gather, he didn't know that the ride was moving along until an incident occurred. But after the burning of the bus in Anniston and the violence in Birmingham, it was Robert Kennedy who suggested there should be a cooling-off period—that the rides should end. Some of us felt different; that we had a right to travel. We were, in effect, testing a decision of the U.S. Supreme Court.

Burke Marshall   President Kennedy, when the Freedom Rides were evolving—and just prior to the meeting in Vienna with Khrushchev— met with Robert Kennedy, Byron White, and myself, and he asked about the timing of events. I don't think he was as concerned with what was going on as in being out of touch while he was in Vienna.

Arthur Schlesinger, Jr.   The Freedom Rides irritated him. This was at the time when he was going to Paris to see de Gaulle and to Vienna to meet with Khrushchev. He felt that his international position was weakened. But by 1963 he understood.

Fred Shuttlesworth   I became the central figure—more than the historians write about. I don't think the Kennedys encouraged the Freedom Rides. I was in church that Sunday when someone came to me and said to come outside. There was a young black man beaten up, bloody.

We went up in four cars to Anniston to bring the Freedom Riders to my house in Birmingham. This was the only safe place; no hotel would take them. Bull Connor called me and asked if I didn't have whites at the house. I told him it was my business who I had in my house.

Robert Kennedy called me to see what could be done. This was what made me know that the Kennedys, once they had to move, had the courage and the capacity to move. I said to him, "Well, you can help us get the buses rolling." The drivers wouldn't drive. I talked to Kennedy three times from the bus station. He said, "What can I do?" I replied, "Your brother said from the White House that people have the right to pursue their constitutional right to travel in this country." He said, "Well, I'll call you back." I think he talked to Bull Connor, and I think Mr. Connor cursed him out at first. But the Kennedys had the unusual ability to say the law is the law—you have to obey the law, and you have to protect these people's rights. So Connor finally decided to escort us to the city limits. Kennedy thought he had won a great victory. So he called me and said, "I have good news." I said, "What's the good news?" He said, "Mr. Connor is going to escort you to the city limits." I said, "Mr. Attorney General, do you realize it was at the city limits in Anniston that the buses were burned? So we must go beyond the city limits." He said, "Wait a minute, I'll call you back." So he called Governor Patterson, who also cursed him out. But Kennedy said, You have to do your duty or we will do ours. So he called me back and said, "The governor will escort you to Montgomery." I said, "We have to get farther than Montgomery." He asked, "Where are you going?" I replied, "Mississippi." He said, "Oh my God, Reverend, the Lord ain't been to Mississippi."

Joseph Dolan   In 1961, when King was in the church in Birmingham during the Freedom Rides, we had ninety guards from a federal prison, and every border guard from Canada and down, around to Florida. The borders were wide open. And we had the IRS. The toughest guys were the prison guards, and after that, the IRS, because they were from the Southeast region and were used to going into the hollows after moonshiners. They're combat ready. When we got the word to send them downtown, they were to ride in post office trucks. James McShane, the chief marshal, was out there at the gate, waving: "Go, go, go." After about five trucks went by, somebody said, "Shit, they're empty." When the last truck went out, Byron White turned to me and said, "I wonder which side they'll take?"

James Farmer   In Montgomery we encountered a mob—a riot; at least hundreds of white men in shirt sleeves were in the streets, beating up blacks. The Freedom Riders were in the First Baptist Church, where a rally was held. King had flown in from Atlanta; Abernathy was already there. The mob blocked my route to the church as we tried to drive there. We tried another route, and they blocked the car that time and tried to turn it over, so we tried a third route, which was to the other side of the graveyard. We left the car and walked through the graveyard so we could get to the back of the church before the mob completely surrounded that church. We walked through the mob, but that was not my courage; it was the courage of that pastor, Fred Shuttlesworth. Yes, he was a gutsy man—such physical courage I've never seen. He said, "Jim, I've got to get you in that church. Come on, we are going to walk through that mob." I said, "We're going to do what?" and we walked through the mob. Shuttlesworth was a little guy. He said, "Get out of the way, let me through." They looked at him and stepped aside—they were so shocked and surprised—and I was trying to hide behind him—big me—hiding behind little Fred to get to the church, and we got there.

The attorney general had sent in U.S. marshals to try to protect those of us who were in the church and to try to keep peace with this mob that was out there in the streets. Bobby called Martin, or Martin called Bob; I do not know who initiated that call. Martin was in the basement of this church and was talking to the attorney general right after I got there. The attorney general asked Martin to try to persuade me to halt the Freedom Ride and have a cooling-off period. Martin relayed that message to me. I told him, Cooling off will put us in the deep freeze; the Freedom Ride will continue.

Fred Shuttlesworth   I went to Montgomery and went out to the airport to pick up James Farmer. When we got outside Ralph Abernathy's church, it was getting kind of ferocious; the federal marshals were catching the devil. James Farmer was very nervous. I said to the crowd, "Move back," and they fell back, and I went right up to the door and went in. We could have gotten killed right there.

Burke Marshall   The Freedom Rides made it clear—it may have been clear before that—that events could not be controlled, managed, or timed; so in that sense, things were out of control.

John Patterson   When the Freedom Riders finally left Birmingham and headed for Montgomery, we had assurances from the city authorities that they would protect these people, and the authorities even asked us not to interfere with them; that they would take care of business themselves. But we escorted the riders all the way from Birmingham to Montgomery, and when they got to the bus station we didn't entirely trust the Montgomery people. We had brought in a lot of our own people; we had a lot of them stashed nearby, out of sight. But when the riders got to the bus station, a tremendous mob of about three thousand people materialized, and there were no city policemen. It turned out that the city police commissioner had made a similar deal with the Klan to the one that Bull Connor had made in Birmingham. We moved in there real quick and saved those people, but a couple of them got beat up before we got in.

John Seigenthaler got in that damn thing, and he was a fool for doing it. I really got on him about that. He came in after I said to Robert, "Let's quit talking on the telephone; send a man down here—somebody you trust to give you the straight information; somebody to work with me as a liaison person." So he sends John Seigenthaler. Now he arrives with a fellow named John Doar, and they check into a motel near the Capitol. The morning of the riot, they got up and put on some old clothes; left their identification at the motel; and got a U-Drive It with a Montgomery license plate on it, drove down to the bus station, got out, and got in that disturbance. And John got knocked down. And nobody found out who he was till he got out to the hospital, and he wouldn't give them his name, and that's when he wanted to call somebody, and he called Washington. Somebody at the hospital listened in to his phone call and found out who he was. He shouldn't have gone down there and got in that riot. He was the president's representative, and he did something very foolish. It brought a lot of trouble to us. Then Martin Luther King comes to town, and this made it hotter. The streets of Montgomery were full of all kinds of people. Rockwell's Nazis from New Jersey were here, and our plainclothes officers would talk to people on the street and ask them, "Where are you from?" "I'm from California"; "I'm from Texas." "Why are you in town?" "Well, I just come over here to see what was going on." It was a very dangerous situation.

* * *

Of course, that night, when they tried to storm the church where King was, again the city of Montgomery did not do its duties. But we had learned a lesson. They had brought in all these marshals, about eight hundred of them. These were not trained people in crowd control; they purported to be that, but they were process servers. They formed a ring around this church. We had brought in about a regiment of National Guard downtown, and we were ready for any eventuality. When nightfall came, a crowd began to gather. After dark this crowd rushed those marshals and ran over them. But by the time the crowd got to the door of the church, we were able to feed our people in there. I immediately declared martial law, and that was the end of the whole thing.

The afternoon before that happened, John Kennedy called me. The legislature was in session. I didn't take that call. The reason was, I found out that a company of infantry at Fort Benning had been alerted to move to Maxwell Field, and by this time I was mad. They were not cooperating with us at all, and we were looking real bad. I was very disturbed and mad about it, and I wasn't in a cooperative mood, and I figured at that time that he was going to ask me a question that either way I answered it, I'd cook my goose. One was: Can you guarantee the protection of these people? If I said, No, I can't, he would use that as an excuse to send in federal troops. The governor of Alabama admitted with his own mouth he couldn't maintain order. And I knew that the troops were on the way.

I wasn't willing to completely say that I could guarantee their safety. How can you guarantee the safety of somebody who won't do what you say? These people were not bona fide interstate travelers; they were professionals at what they were doing, and they would come into a town and get out and scatter out and go into places that were traditionally white places. They would create disturbances. Now, how can you personally guarantee the safety of people like that? It's a very difficult thing to do. If I had said, Yes, I can guarantee their protection, and one of them got hurt, then he'd send the troops in anyway. So I decided under those circumstances not to take that phone call.

Burke Marshall   The notion that John Patterson wouldn't return their phone calls was shocking to the Kennedys. The reactions to those bus rides made us realize that we were just at the beginning of a contest of wills. I can't believe that Governor Patterson would want the attack to take the form it did.

John Patterson It was a mistake for me not to take the president's calls. I was a lot younger then; impetuous. I've matured a great deal since then. I never got invited back to the White House again after that. I did hear from the president indirectly. Occasionally he would see a former member of my staff who he had appointed head of the Export- Import Bank, and he would ask about me and pass messages to me through him: "How are you doing? I hope you're doing all right."

THE INTEGRATION OF OLE MISS

On the late afternoon of September 30, 1962, James Meredith, a seven-year Air Force veteran, was brought by federal marshals to the campus of the University of Mississippi at Oxford. Meredith had initially applied for admission to the all-white school just after Kennedy's inauguration. His application became entangled in the state and federal courts and was staunchly resisted by then Mississippi governor Ross Barnett. As Meredith was escorted to a dormitory to await registration the following morning, the president, in a nationally televised address, appealed to the white citizens of Mississippi to remain calm. This plea went unheeded as a full-scale riot ensued, pitting nearly 25,000 people against a force of marshals, Mississippi National Guardsmen, and federal troops. The next morning, with two people dead and hundreds injured, James Meredith was registered and attended his first class.

Nicholas Katzenbach The Kennedys thought that the one bad mistake Ike made was to send troops into Little Rock. They were determined not to send troops in, so that was the reason they worked so hard on Barnett. Also, what you got from Barnett depended on the last person he spoke with. He was an idiot, a terrible man. No strength at all. The Barnett experience influenced the way we dealt with Governor Wallace. Since it didn't work with Barnett, we had less incentive to talk to Wallace. We did talk to him, but we didn't get anywhere.

Burke Marshall   Nobody thought that Barnett was very credible or trustworthy at any point.

Norbert Schlei   Barnett had walked into an airplane propeller; he was not playing with a full deck. You could make an agreement with him, and the next day he didn't seem to remember that he had made the agreement with you. There were many people in Mississippi who were ashamed of Barnett and who wanted change.

Najeeb Halaby   The FAA got involved in the James Meredith situation. It was the issue of whether Governor Barnett will come up from Jackson to Oxford and act like a state commander in chief. By coincidence, I was driving up to meet with the chairman of the House committee that controlled my budget. The president called on the car phone and said, "Jeeb, I want you to keep Governor Barnett out of the air. I don't want him to fly up to Oxford." I said, "Yes, sir. What is the problem?" He replied, "We have the National Guard going in there, and we are going to have a real scene if he gets up there. This is a matter of the next hour or so. You take whatever authority you have and keep him out of there." I did have the authority to declare an emergency over a particular airport, so we issued a one-line prohibited airspace. Then I called the guy who flew the governor's plane, and I said, "Jim, you can't do this; this is prohibited airspace and it will affect the whole future of Mississippi state aviation. You go see the governor and tell him just not to do it."

Julian Bond   Uncle Sam did about as well as he could have there in helping Meredith to get in. They probably should have realized that a riot would, or could, ensue, and should have been a little better equipped to put it down. From Kennedy's perspective I bet he really believed the speech he made that night, talking about Ole Miss, football tradition, a sense of goodwill and sportsmanship, and that he thought: People at Harvard feel that way, and I'm sure they feel that way at Ole Miss.

Joseph Dolan   I was in Mississippi with "I" James Meredith. That's what we used to call him because he was always, "I, I, I." I was told by the attorney general to go to the campus and arrange with Colonel Birdsong [Thomas B. Birdsong, Mississippi commissioner of public safety], to escort Meredith onto the campus. So I went there and met with Birdsong in the Alumni Club. He shook hands with me and said, "Let's sit down and wait." So we waited for about a half hour, without talking to one another. Then the phone rang. He talked for a minute and said, "All right, Mr. Dolan. Let's go."

We got into his car and went out to the airport. Meredith got off the plane, and Birdsong and I walked over to him and we took him to the dorm, about a half mile from the Lyceum. The mob thought Meredith was there, and they began to gather around the building.

Right after we arrived on the campus, Nick Katzenbach said to me, "Get a line to Washington right away." I looked around and thought, "We don't want to use the university phones; they might cut us off." I saw a phone booth and put a dime in and called the White House. I told the operator, "We want to keep this line open all night. No matter what happens, don't cut it off." And it was open all night, so that every time Cyrus Vance [secretary of the Army] tried to tell the president something, he would say, "Yeah. I know. Nick told me." The next day, when Nick and I went over to meet the Army general in command of the troops, he said, "You gentlemen have unbelievable, marvelous communications." Nick says, "Well, General, when you go out on something like this, you just gotta remember to bring a dime."

Nicholas Katzenbach   There were murderous people at Ole Miss that night. The outsiders who came onto the campus. The administration at the university was terrible. We brought in too many troops, too late. In retrospect, there should have been more decisive action. The Kennedys just didn't understand Barnett's weakness.

Burke Marshall   Nick Katzenbach, that high government official in the phone booth, was the only effective means of communication. His dime worked. Thank heavens for AT&T!

Norbert Schlei   I hadn't expected to go to Mississippi, but on Saturday morning the attorney general said to me, "Norb, why don't you go with them?" So Nick and I flew down to Oxford in this Jet Star. We deployed the force of marshals around the Lyceum Building, which was the administration office of the university. As a result of speeches by retired [Major] General Edwin Walker [U.S. Army, political activist], a tremendous crowd had gathered in Oxford, and as it got dark, things began to get ugly. Chief Marshal McShane decided to fire tear gas, and some members of the state police were hit with canisters and withdrew, and the war was on.

I was in and around the Lyceum Building. The whole area was suffused with tear gas; it was tremendously uncomfortable. The whole thing dramatically illustrated the difference between the Kennedy administration's approach to civil rights and that of the Eisenhower administration. In the Autherine Lucy [the black woman who attempted to integrate the University of Alabama] case, at the University of Alabama, the president had hardly been aware. But this president we had on an open line from the basement of the Lyceum Building all night long. He was getting a blow-by-blow description as things were happening throughout the evening and into the small hours.

At some point in the evening, the president called the Army to come, but he got angrier and angrier at the long time it took for them to get from Memphis down to Oxford. They finally arrived at dawn. It was a very dramatic scene. You could see the troops marching along in cadence, and this mob was milling around, off about fifty yards away from them. Somebody in the mob threw a Molotov cocktail that started in the streets in front of the advancing soldiers, and the bottle burst, and the flames burst up, and the troops just went clonk, clonk, clonk right through the flames. There was a collective gasp from this mob, and that was the end of it right there. They began to dissipate.

John Patterson   They handled it very badly. I'm not saying that I'd have done any better. I talked to Ross Barnett. I told him about my experience with them on the Freedom Riders thing. I told him about the phone call that I got. I said, "Ross, you're going to get one, one of these days." Sure enough he did. I sent some people over there to just observe so that I could learn some lessons. What happened was that when those marshals fired the gas canisters point-blank into the students, it infuriated that crowd and they turned on the marshals. When the day came in Alabama—the best example is Auburn—the president of the university called me one day and said, "Governor, it looks like we are going to have to take a black into Auburn. I want you to know I think I can handle this situation myself. We are going to obey the law and the court decrees." And that is exactly the way it happened.

Burke Marshall   You have no idea how ineffectively the Pentagon handled the Meredith incident. There was misplaced hope that there
wouldn't be a riot.

John Seigenthaler   I don't think Ross Barnett wanted to visit an invasion of federal troops on Mississippi. Why would he? Or even an invasion of U.S. marshals. We had demonstrated we were going to do what
we said we were going to do. I don't think Ross Barnett could ever have
doubted that the Kennedy administration was going to do what it had to
do to get integration achieved in the same way that Ike had called out
the troops in Little Rock, in the way we had to send marshals into Montgomery. It may seem naive now, but you would think if a thoughtful,
intelligent, sensitive governor—no matter how racist and no matter how
surrounded by racists—knew that he was going to lose, why would he
risk visiting that sort of torment on his state and the state university,
which was a proud school?

I think that too often, we look at it and we say, "Why didn't the
Kennedys?" I think it is fair to ask, "Why the hell didn't Barnett?" I know
that every time it came up, we trusted local law enforcement, because
they made the pledge, and then you said to yourself, why wouldn't they
live up to the pledge? I have absolutely no idea why John Patterson [in
Alabama] ran out on his commissioner of safety. Then you ask yourself,
why did Floyd Mann, the commissioner, stand up against the governor
and against the cabinet, against the whole state? You keep hoping that
somebody like Floyd Mann is going to represent most of the thinking; he
was raised in the same culture they were. If you had asked me the day
before violence broke out at Ole Miss, Did I think it was going to break
out? I would have told you no. And if we go back, there were damn few
people who thought it would break out.

That being the case, you want to go with a minimum amount of protection; a minimum amount of force. And when U.S. marshals start
falling, you think, Oh my God, what am I doing? How quickly can we get
troops there? We damn near didn't get them there at all.

James Meredith   In order to prevail, I had to get the federal government on my side, and that was the whole reason for making the maneu-
ver to put the Kennedy administration under the gun with their
promises. I was well aware of the contact between Ross Barnett and the

Kennedys. Between them I was always sure the U.S. government was going to win. Frankly, I thought the only two people who knew what was going on were Barnett and me. I think their strategy at that time was that the black race issue was Bobby Kennedy's, because they were still looking to get Jack [re]elected. My greatest fear was a deal between Barnett and Kennedy. I had no trust in either of them, and less trust for Kennedy than for Barnett, because the law barred Barnett from reelection, but I knew John Kennedy wanted to be reelected.

I didn't hear the president's speech; I went to sleep. I was not really aware of what was happening that night on the campus. It was not of any real concern to me. My job had long been finished; my job was to get the federal force on my side. I frankly didn't know what happened that night until they came in the morning to get me to go to register, and the car the marshals drove me in had all the windows shot out.

In 1963 the University of Alabama at Tuscaloosa was successfully integrated, but not before a confrontation took place between Governor Wallace and Justice Department official Nicholas Katzenbach.

Burke Marshall   Wallace was under enormous pressure not to let Ole Miss recur in Tuscaloosa.

George Wallace   Some people don't understand. I wasn't trying to block anybody from going to school, or to ban a court order. I tried to raise the question of whether we could set the timetable for integration. We already voted integration in '64. They said '63; we said '64. I brought the troops there about a year before. We were informed that we might have the same groups that had come to Alabama before: neo-Nazi groups, Minute Men, the Klan killed three people—hit our students with shotgun pellets, burned buildings and looted them. They destroyed our university. I had troops there in case they showed up; we would put them in every jail in Alabama. I was on the bench for six years; I had more sense than that. I knew the state couldn't take troopers and block anything. They were there for the purpose of keeping that crowd there—and they didn't show up, either. There was a girl in a dorm, on a street. We kept unmarked cars and people in the hedges at night. If someone shot off a firecracker or shouted an obscenity, we ran them down and put them in jail. I wasn't going to have any violence. The violence at Ole Miss was terrible—terrible. Two people got killed, and many were seriously injured; buildings were burned and looted.

President Kennedy dealt with it. Since he wouldn't raise the question, I tried to raise it with him. There wasn't anything to do but leave, because I wasn't going to block an entrance; I was going to protect an entrance.

John Patterson   The stand in the schoolhouse door at Tuscaloosa—well, I don't want to criticize Governor Wallace, but he got out of that thing exactly what he wanted: He got tremendous political publicity out of it, which catapulted him onto the national scene and caused him to run for president. But to tell you the truth, that wasn't badly handled, although there was a scenario; it was a planned thing, in my judgment.

Nicholas Katzenbach   Justice [Hugo] Black said to me one night, "The trouble is you and Bobby and Burke Marshall don't know a god-damn thing about civil rights." That was the Alabamian in him talking—"You don't understand these people." The Southern white boy, he would vote the right way; he was a leader on equal rights, but he was still a Southerner.

THE MARCH ON WASHINGTON

On August 28, 1963, an integrated group of more than two hundred thousand people assembled in front of the Lincoln Memorial in what was then the largest civil rights demonstration in American history. The March on Washington, as the rally was called, marked a watershed in the modern struggle for black rights and was supported by a coalition of labor unions; religious organizations; mainline and more radical black groups; local, state, and federal legislators; and grass-roots citizens.

The march caused considerable anxiety within the Kennedy administration, where there was fear for public safety and concern as to how the American public would interpret the event.

Lee White   There was a lot of antsiness. We'd never had 250,000 people here before, and our Washington police force was not as sophisticated as it is today. We had army units all over. The focal point of the operation was the Justice Department. John Douglas, the son of Senator

Paul Douglas, was assigned to coordinate activity. He was an assistant attorney general in the Civil Division, an absolutely sterling fellow. He was right there. The logistics were very difficult. You have to have toilets for 250,000 people. You have to have people who can get buses in and out. Remember that Washington in August is not the most pleasant place. So there was a lot of anxiety; a lot of it was, Let's get the damn thing over with and get everybody home without any interruption.

Ralph Dungan   I can remember when the rioters in Birmingham were going down the street and we'd say "When is this all going away?" as if it were a snowstorm. That was the feeling about the March on Washington.

Cartha DeLoach   The March on Washington was discussed with the bureau. There were many individuals who attempted to take advantage of such events to promote their own causes. The attorney general had a special committee who looked into such things and who furnished information to him and to the White House, insofar as possible, on instances that could arise. Anarchy that might have been promoted, and things of that nature. The bureau assisted in furnishing all intelligence it had concerning that potential event.

Fred Shuttlesworth   They were afraid of violence. There is politics in the back of it. They would rather have not had this possibility. But they had to recognize that this nonviolent movement was based on the Bible, and on what people believed to be morality, and what the country ought to be about. In 1963 the nation was disturbed and seemed to get a fresh grasp on its history and its idealism. The Kennedys had hoped the Birmingham settlement would be enough. Our business was to educate America, not only the Deep South but the North as well. We had the eyes of the nation. We were trying to get Americans committed to the idea of elemental justice. We were aware in our meetings that the president wished we would not hold the march.

The Birmingham agreement was reached in May, and we were trying to find a way to dramatize this victory, because this was the first significant victory over segregation. The Montgomery Bus Boycott was not as important as Birmingham, which was a complete victory where the segregationists gave in to us. As Kennedy himself said to us in Washington, "But for Birmingham we would not be here." Our position was that people have to feel that we can win a victory.

John Lewis The president wanted to do the right thing; he wanted to be on the right side. I don't think the administration tried to stop the march; they learned they couldn't stop it. There was concern on Kennedy's part that if there was an outbreak of violence, you wouldn't have a chance for legislation.

Louis Martin The problem was that the business community in Washington had gotten to the administration and told them it was dangerous. Joe Califano called me one day from the Pentagon and said, "You have to come with me." He picked me up in a car and we met with the chief of police. The whole discussion was on the March on Washington. Bayard [Bayard Rustin, civil rights leader and organizer of the march] made an eloquent account of the precautions that had been taken by the civil rights groups to make sure this would be a serious and orderly situation. I didn't know what was in the minds of some of the guys in the White House. Some of them were more skittish than others, but I never got the feeling that JFK and LBJ were afraid of it.

Their problem was: How much should they be personally involved? I decided I should get involved. I got someone I knew in New York to become an aide to Roy Wilkins. He would sit in on the meetings of the leaders in New York, so I got a direct fill-in on everything that was happening. I told the White House people—and Joe stood with me—"This thing will be under control. These damned merchants are scared of everything. There is not going to be any riot."

One thing we worked out with Bayard was to coordinate the buses. There were several hundred buses coming in. They had to leave at a certain time. We worked it out so there would be no loitering. The last issue to be resolved was whether the White House meeting would be before or after the march. Kenny O'Donnell wanted the meeting with the president before the program. The guy I had inside the committee who organized the march said there was no way to convince King and Roy Wilkins to meet before.

I wanted the meeting afterward because I knew they would all be on their good manners; they wouldn't want to screw up a positive day. They were all very PR conscious, and they were on the spot. When we got to the Cabinet Room, Walter Reuther said to me, "Louis, I want to see how much power you have. I want a cup of coffee." I called down to the mess, and they sent up a pot of coffee. The day worked out beautifully, and whatever fears they might have had vanished. By seven o'clock every bus had gone. I greeted King and brought him into the Cabinet Room. JFK told him, said, "I heard your speech," and he congratulated King.

Julian Bond   I thought the march was great. I enjoyed it. I loved King's speech. You know, we had this cynical thing toward King. On the one hand, we thought it was clever to denigrate him, and his style and his preacherisms and so on. And on the other hand, I think all of us really liked him and were moved by him and entranced by him. I wish I had souvenirs and had gotten signatures and autographs and had taken pictures. I was there; I was one of the 250,000 people who were there. There are only 250,000 people who can say that. It made a big difference to the people who were there, an enormous difference. To me it was a cataclysmic event.

William Sloane Coffin, Jr.   It was a great march. There are a lot of interesting angles to it when you think back on it. Bayard Rustin said, "This is for jobs and freedom." He was beginning to understand that legal equality is supposed to promise some greater measure of economic equality, and it hadn't delivered, and that votes don't change the power structure, so he was already thinking about jobs. King's speech never mentioned jobs. Rustin must have had a fit. But King's speech, which I heard parts of many times before—you never tired of hearing those great metaphors—was so terrific, and the march was such an outpouring and so nonviolent that it was very impressive for the country as a whole. The administration thought it was going to be violent; they didn't think there would be that many people. It was a very impressive demonstration. But I don't know what Kennedy was planning to do.

To me, the march enormously enhanced the stature of King. He was seen to be the great hero of it all. He made the final speech. He shook the world. I was in India the following year. They all knew about that speech; they all wanted to know about King. In every miserable little hut that I visited in India, they had a picture of both King and Kennedy. The mythology was very much alive.

Julian Bond I remember the archbishop [Patrick A. O'Boyle, Roman Catholic archbishop of Washington, D.C.] raising a fuss over John's [Lewis's] speech,* and I don't remember things the way they are recounted in a great many books. I remember the speech changes as having been made on the podium that day—last-minute changes—and that other changes had been made beforehand. I remember distributing copies of both speeches; I was the press guy—Henry Lee Moon of the NAACP was the senior person and I was the junior person. I remember saying to the press people: "Look at the difference." There was an understanding among us that you couldn't say there was a difference or what had happened, and I was really irritated that not as many people as I would have liked said, "Oh my God! He's changed his speech."

John Lewis Some people saw copies of the text and said we'd have to change it; they didn't like for me to use the words *revolution* and *masses*.

Julian Bond John F. Kennedy knew how many people were there. The people who needed to know, the people who count—and I mean who count both in terms of their importance and who know how to count—knew how many people were there and how many potential votes they represented.

John Lewis After the march was over, we went to the White House. The president was very pleased. He was proud. He was acting very relieved that it had been peaceful. I don't know if it ever came up to invite the president or the vice president to speak at the march. I don't remember a single ranking member of the administration attending it.

Robert Moses The question is, What is the political fallout of this going to be? Are you going to be able to stage such a march so that it has positive political fallout for the president? Because he is clearly closely identified with this event, so if it had negative political fallout, it is going to fall out on him. The question then is, Can you control the march? Can you control who is in it, and how it is presented, and what ideas are presented to the nation? It's high drama, high politics.

---

*The archbishop was troubled by some portions of the draft speech submitted by John Lewis, one of the major speakers at the march. In the draft Lewis promised a "scorched earth" policy to end segregation.

At that level what you are talking about is harming the presidency. That was the bottom line for the Kennedys. From their point of view, they are representing the expectations of a different set of people, because this is the first time the Irish population, the Catholic population, the underdogs of Europe, are taking control of the presidency. That is a whole other struggle within this country. The bottom line is this is what is to be protected.

There was a response in the South to the march. We felt this in Mississippi in the winter of 1963–64. There was an increase in cross-burnings, churches being burned, and actual deaths. I recall that when the authorities went to dredge up the bodies of the three civil rights workers killed in 1964,° there was a report that some bodies had been found in one of the other rivers. These were young students who had been killed the winter before.

Nicholas Katzenbach   There was a feeling that something was achieved, but what was achieved should be separated from what was prevented. It was not violent. The speeches were good, the more militant ones were edited down, not by the administration but by the bishop. Looking back, there is much more reason to view it as a great occasion than we might have had at the time. I think relief overwhelms any other feeling.

THE FBI AND THE CIVIL RIGHTS MOVEMENT

Many civil rights leaders and workers were troubled by what they believed was the failure of the FBI to investigate civil rights violations and to apprehend and bring to justice the perpetrators of anti–civil rights violence.

Questions were raised as to why President Kennedy kept J. Edgar Hoover in office, and as to whether the FBI director was blackmailing the Kennedy brothers.

There was also concern that Hoover had a vendetta against Martin Luther King, Jr., who was emerging as the nation's preeminent civil rights leader.

°The bodies of three civil rights workers—James Chaney, Andrew Goodman, and Michael Schwerner—were found near Philadelphia, Mississippi, on August 4, 1964. All three had been shot, and Chaney, a black, had broken and crushed bones.

John Lewis   The role of the FBI at that time was to us the greatest disappointment of the Kennedy administration. Many of us, not just in SNCC, were very critical of the Department of Justice and the FBI, not only on protection of civil rights workers but on the civil rights issue. We felt that the administration could have done much more—they had very little influence with Mr. Hoover—and we felt that Mr. Hoover was in cahoots with the local authorities. We felt that in a second term President Kennedy would have been better in dealing with the FBI.

Julian Bond   Before we lost all faith in the FBI, we wanted their agents to make arrests. Our argument was: If an FBI agent was standing outside a bank and saw a gangster run out with a mask over his face, a gun in one hand and money in the other, they'd stop the man right there; and if you saw somebody violating civil rights, you should do the same thing. Of course the FBI never did it then, and they've never done it since.

Robert Moses   When I was knife-whipped in Liberty, Mississippi, and had some stitches in my head, they sent the FBI resident agent over from Natchez. And I knew from the questions he asked me what kind of report he was going to send. So I sent my own story to the Civil Rights Division, and they ended up with two contradictory stories. Now, this agent turns back up again to do the story over, and he looks at me dead in the eye and says, "You know, I could kill somebody if I thought that they were trying to mess with my career." So of course I write that down and send that on back up to the Justice Department. So a little while later, John Doar is in the area and he notices all these scars on my head. He has pictures taken—the FBI of course didn't even take pictures. Doar's position was, well, you can't fight the FBI. Clearly the Kennedy administration had no control; their control over the FBI was minimal. The attorney general theoretically had control, but those FBI people answered to Hoover, and if he didn't want them to do left or right, that was it; they were going straight down the chalk line.

Cartha DeLoach   Both the president and the attorney general were troubled by information they were getting from the bureau about Dr. King. They both talked to Dr. King at great length about that. At first Dr. King did not take any action. Later on, he did decide to take action and told the Kennedys accordingly. Contrary to public opinion, Bobby Kennedy first asked the FBI to put a wiretap on Dr. King. Mr. Hoover told Courtney Evans to go back and try to talk him out of it, because he realized the ramifications if it ever became public. Later on, when FBI informants gave further information on the communist associations of members of King's staff, the attorney general ordered a wiretap, and a communication was sent over, which the attorney general signed, approving the wiretap on Dr. King.

Contrary to statements that have been made, no one in the FBI, to my knowledge, ever offered to play a journalist the tapes on Dr. King. I never had possession of them; I couldn't have played them for a journalist if I had wanted to. Neither could Mr. Hoover have.

Nicholas Katzenbach While Hoover didn't do the telephone taps on his own, he did all the [hotel room] bugs on his own. I'm absolutely certain Bobby didn't know about them. If you are really objective, you would conclude Bobby didn't know about them.

Courtney Evans The record should reflect that the bureau was very interested in getting this coverage. They had tried at least once before and had been turned down, a highly unusual procedure. Ultimately the attorney general came to the point of view that he had better do this, just to prove once and for all that Dr. King was not being directed by or subjected to, communism. It was a reluctant decision on the attorney general's part, made with the proviso that it be reviewed in sixty to ninety days, before it should continue. In the meantime, we had the assassination. The attempt to get information on Dr. King's extracurricular proclivities was all done separately; I was not privy to this. There must have been a fear on the part of the director and some of his close associates at the top that if I knew about it, the Kennedys would know about it.

Theodore Hesburgh The FBI was enormously uncooperative. Blacks in the South thought the FBI was a federal organization and therefore could be counted on to back them up. We had one case where a fellow was being harassed—shot at—and his home blown up, and we called the FBI, and the next thing you know the local sheriff showed up. The fellow was put in jail at hard labor for nine months. We got that changed, but it was typical of the kind of lack of cooperation.

Cartha DeLoach   I think criticism of the FBI on civil rights is one of the great distortions of history. We had no jurisdiction to protect blacks. We had, at that time, about seven thousand agents, and for us to go beyond our jurisdiction to protect blacks in those times would have taken the entire work force of the FBI. At that time there were almost two hundred other matters we had jurisdiction over and that Congress insisted we handle. They included Soviet espionage, internal security, and revolutionary activities in the United States. But the claim that the FBI stood by and refused to protect blacks became a cause célèbre.

We gathered notes, particularly when we saw police brutality. We investigated the police, and in many instances, sent many of them to jail for mistreating blacks. So we would gather notes and information and investigate and refer to the Department of Justice for further investigation and/or grand jury action—and take further action ourselves, insofar as testifying as to the facts. That was the best thing we could do, rather than stepping in, as the U.S. marshals did at Attorney General Kennedy's instructions. Neither the attorney general nor the president ever asked us to protect lives. We did a great deal of good as far as protection of blacks in Mississippi is concerned. We investigated people who were burning churches and the people in Birmingham who caused the dynamiting of the church where four little girls were killed.* We brought those cases to the attention of the Department of Justice. There was much sacrifice there. I hate to tell you how many hours of sleep I lost on the case of the murder of the three civil rights workers in Mississippi. I am a Southerner, but it would never enter my mind that I should shirk my duties in favor of segregation rather than carrying out my responsibilities as an FBI agent. And it never came to Mr. Hoover's mind in that regard. If any FBI agent had ever shirked his duty and not thoroughly investigated a case, he would have been fired immediately. It was a very emotional time, and I think the FBI should be very proud in terms of its role in civil rights matters.

Norbert Schlei   The FBI was kind of an obstacle because the local FBI representatives were part of the community; they worked closely with the police. They were very much inculcated with the idea that they

---

*On Sunday, September 15, 1963, an explosion blew out the basement of the Sixteenth Baptist Church in Birmingham, Alabama. The blast, caused by sticks of explosives, killed four children: Addie Mae Collins, Denise McNair, Carole Robertson, and Cynthia Wesley.

had very limited functions: They weren't supposed to act like local police. They had this standoffish role where they could only deal with federal statutes and accede to the local police jurisdiction over normal criminal areas. They were very conservative folks. When you wanted to get them to do something that involved them in an alliance with street demonstrators and opposing local police, they were troubled.

Arthur Schlesinger, Jr.   Robert Kennedy did his best to get Hoover into the field of civil rights and to get him to appoint black FBI agents. There was a more principled problem that Burke Marshall had to struggle with: The civil rights workers, not quite unreasonably, wanted more federal protection than they were getting, against white violence. But the whole problem of federalism, the location of the police power, worried someone like Burke Marshall very much. The FBI is not a national police; it is a bureau of investigation. There was a genuine constitutional issue involved.

Burke Marshall   One cannot accept the fact that the FBI was grudging about doing anything about civil rights until 1964. They didn't have any agents who knew how to talk to black people in the South. There were bureaucratic reasons: They were trained to chase communists and find stolen cars. Mr. Hoover viewed the civil rights activists as lawbreakers. The FBI was worse than useless, given his mind-set. I would send them one-hundred-page memoranda telling them what to do; they didn't know how to do my cases. Mr. Hoover had enormous support from the public and Congress. I have no doubt that Hoover would have been retired in a second Kennedy term.

Courtney Evans   Burke Marshall told me and other people at the time that if you feel that the bureau has a duty to physically protect these people, then in effect, you have a national police organization instead of an investigating organization that makes arrests only when the prosecutor says you have a probable cause to make an arrest. Hoover was adamantly against the bureau's ever being a national police force. It wasn't until the advent of the bank robberies that he ever even accepted the power of arrest. It was his theory that the bureau had investigative responsibility and should have no concern with prosecution other than furnishing the facts developed in the investigation.

John Seigenthaler   Hoover's assertion that these were the limits to his authority were supportable. Congress certainly believed that, and in a real sense the administration believed that. I think the courts—up until that point—had pretty well upheld that. The reality was: We were a society that had but one court decision that overturned Jim Crow laws, and that had to do with the narrow context of education. And we had had but one confrontation, in 1958, in Little Rock: *Brown* v. *Topeka Board of Education* said, "with all deliberate speed." There were very real feelings that this was not a federal matter.

The time that Burke Marshall spent dealing with civil rights had to do with jurisdiction: Do we have the authority to do this? to do that? If you look at the whole issue of the demonstrations that were creating the need for protection, you are really talking about demonstrators who say, "We understand we are violating the law, and we are willing to go to jail because we think the laws are unjust." If you took all the FBI agents Hoover had working on communism and put them in the area of civil rights and sent them South, you'd still have about two or three FBI agents in communities where you needed committed police officers in forces of five, six, seven hundred to protect those who needed protection.

When I went to Alabama to get the first wave of Freedom Riders on a plane out of Birmingham to New Orleans, I didn't have anybody the FBI could call on, or ask for help. They didn't have any men to send out to the airport to protect those riders. When we got off the plane in New Orleans, the cops were the worst: There was this line of cops, and every one of them was giving us hell. The Klan had infiltrated the police departments of the South, and in the largest cities there, you had two or three FBI agents—maybe ten to cover a whole state.

And Hoover is saying, "I don't have jurisdiction to do this." There is a very real question as to whether he does. You have Congressman Rooney [John Rooney (D., N.Y.)], who says, "Continue to focus on the communist conspiracy, which is where the nation's interests are. The other matter must be determined by the courts." Of course, politically Kennedy is hoping the matter is going to be determined in the courts. There is a time warp that is almost impossible to understand unless you realize that a segregated Southern society was legal in the eyes of the nation, and that Martin Luther King and the demonstrators—in the eyes of most of the nation—were law violators who were trying to change the law. Most of the nation, for much of the time, was unsympathetic to that. Certainly, massive numbers of people in the South were unsympathetic to that, and most of the people in the Congress did not give a damn about that. So Hoover was not perceived, at that point, to be anything more than an administrator of an agency whose responsibility was to enforce certain federal laws, and the law on civil rights was not that clear. It was certainly clear that if you were going to desegregate a high school or a grade school, there was a responsibility to get them in there. But as Ike found in Little Rock, you couldn't do it with the FBI; you had to do it with troops. And if we tried to do it when the Freedom Riders expanded that part of transportation, it was assumed that segregation on buses would continue.

It is really difficult to suggest that anybody was focusing on Hoover as the center of the problem. To the extent that the problem was perceived at all, it was perceived by those who wanted to change as a problem that was vested in the governorship and the law enforcement authorities of the states and the cities across the South where the resistance was. And if it took troops to get black students into Central High School in Little Rock, if you are going to think about change, you are going to need substantially larger numbers of law enforcement officers than Hoover ever had to throw into it. If you had relied on FBI agents to get the students into Central High School, maybe the entire force of the FBI would have had to be sent into Little Rock. It had never been perceived that the FBI had the authority to enforce local law.

James Farmer   I did not think of Hoover as being a lone operator; I thought of him as being part of the administration; one whom the president would hesitate to get rid of because of his files, but nevertheless he was part of the administration. I thought if he were zeroing on King, as he apparently was, then the Kennedys must know about it. I thought that they did have the authority to call him off.

William Sloane Coffin, Jr.   Kennedy was scared to death of Hoover, I guess. Hoover, by that time, was getting to be quite sick. He was a real racist. In the many times I was in the South, we never looked to the FBI for anything but trouble. They were really part of the problem. The fact that Kennedy wouldn't do more with the FBI is another indication of his failure to come through. But one constantly has to remember what the ethos was: There were very, very few people at any high level who understood what was going on.

Lee White   Mr. Hoover didn't like blacks; he didn't like communists and tended to equate one with the other. So a lot of it was taken with a grain of salt.

I didn't know anything about the alleged romantic liaisons between Kennedy and Judith Exner, or Marilyn Monroe, or anyone else for that matter, or whether there was some concern on Bobby's part that Hoover held some goods on his brother.

Courtney Evans   There is no doubt that there were tensions between Hoover and Martin Luther King, Jr.; the public record is too replete with instances to think otherwise. He didn't have much regard for Dr. King. Hoover learned of some of Dr. King's extracurricular activities, and he thought that they were very demeaning for a gentleman of the cloth. After all, Hoover himself had given serious consideration to becoming a minister before he decided to be a lawyer. He had a whole history of close association with the church; of teaching Sunday school classes. He put clergymen in a special category. Another thing was the general reaction against the civil rights movement, and he thought that Dr. King was moving too fast, even in a nonviolent kind of way.

President Kennedy sent a civil rights bill up to Congress in 1963, but the legislation was not passed prior to his death. President Johnson had greater success in bringing civil rights legislation to fruition.

Burke Marshall   In 1963, when President Kennedy decided to send the Civil Rights Bill down to Congress, it was thoroughly discussed with the vice president. Johnson had some reservations about the bill— he told me that—but he wasn't going to tell the president not to do this.

Ben Bradlee   Jack Kennedy didn't have the mandate to get civil rights legislation through that Lyndon Johnson did. And Lyndon Johnson had to spend it all to get that bill through. The feeling of the country wasn't there yet, and the Congress didn't represent that part of American opinion; it represented the status quo.

Eugene McCarthy   We always had enough strength in the House to pass civil rights legislation from the time I arrived in 1948. After the election of 1962, we had strength in the Senate. It wasn't just numbers but a trend of public acceptance. But the Kennedys, in view of all the support they got from Southern governors in 1960, were really under pressure in the rights legislative fight until after the 1964 election.

John Lewis   One thing about both Kennedy and Johnson—I'm not sure this would have happened with Nixon—we were like players on a stage: We had roles to play; we had to make it possible for them to act. They were capable of listening and responding. It had to go the way it did. We could have passed some laws, but then you have to have the power to implement them. The way it happened was the best way to bring about lasting change. It had a cleansing effect on Americans, especially Southerners. Many white Southerners have changed; there has been a profound change. My greatest fear now—we no longer look to the federal government as referee—is that the Supreme Court will pull the rug out from under us.

Julian Bond   As far as civil rights was concerned, I developed over the years a rosier and rosier view. And it may be that Robert Kennedy had more to do with the changes in my mind than John Kennedy. I thought: "If the little brother did okay, then the big brother must be okay, too." Over the last few years, as all this information has come out, it hasn't affected me in any way or the other. I just wonder, in reading the next volume of Robert Caro's book, if there is going to be some awful story of Lyndon Johnson and John F. Kennedy telling nigger jokes together.

Tom Wicker   Wallace once said to me, "People don't understand the use of defiance." He made a career of defiance. He never accomplished anything; he didn't really preserve anything in the South. George just spoke defiantly. I felt the Kennedys had to take him on. That whole period was the time—the time of Dr. King, the time of the demonstrations. The power of the government and the presidency had to be thrown in. You couldn't sit back, as Eisenhower did for eight years. John F. Kennedy is revered today; you will find his picture and Robert's in black households that don't think anything of Lyndon Johnson, who you would have thought would be the great hero. Someone once told me the reason Kennedy's picture is up on the wall is because he was the first president to call this a moral crisis. And it was a moral crisis; it still is.

What these folks remember is that for the first time in American history a president said, "The way we treat blacks is a moral crisis." I think that was one of the defining moments of Kennedy's presidency. I could make a case that Lyndon Johnson was much more effective: the voting rights act, "we shall overcome" in Congress. But Kennedy was first on that score, and that is what people remember.

14

The Bay of Pigs

The ultimate objective of the American-sponsored invasion of Cuba—at the site called the Bay of Pigs—was the overthrow of the government of Fidel Castro. But the effort of the CIA-trained Cuban expatriate forces failed, due both to poor military planning and faulty intelligence, causing acute embarrassment to the Kennedy administration.

THE BACKGROUND OF THE BAY OF PIGS OPERATION

On March 17, 1960, then President Dwight Eisenhower directed the CIA to bring together Cuban exiles into a unified political opposition to Fidel Castro, and to train a force of Cubans to engage in guerrilla action within Cuba. This presidential directive resulted in the CIA's establishment of a secret training camp and air base in Guatemala.

John Patterson   The reason they didn't go may be that they were not ready. But I don't believe President Eisenhower would deliberately plan a thing like that and pull it off just before the election to affect the outcome. I don't think he was that kind of man.

Brig. Gen. Andrew Goodpaster, staff secretary to President Eisenhower   I remember talking with Eisenhower when he authorized the training of this contingent. I said to him, "There is always the danger that this will develop a momentum of its own." He kind of snapped back at me, "Not so long as I'm here." And I said, "Yes, sir. That's just the problem." I think that he covered this quite clearly with President-elect Kennedy. He had a card with five or six points of discussion listed, and I think he did work through all of those points during those meetings.

They were going to be trained with no decision to commit them. President Eisenhower reserved decision to see whether there was any prospect that they could be used effectively. He said, "The authorization is only for training. I will reserve to myself whether they will actually be committed or not." He made no decision on that.

President-elect Kennedy Is Briefed on the Existence of the Cuban Exile Force

There are varying accounts of when and under what circumstances the existence of an exile invasion force was revealed to either candidate or, later, to President-elect Kennedy.

On November 17, 1960, two weeks after the presidential election, during a briefing conducted by CIA Director Allen Dulles, President-elect Kennedy was told of the existence of the Cuban force in Guatemala. And in a second briefing, on November 29, Mr. Dulles told the president-elect details of an overall plan for guerrilla action in Cuba. He stated that a force of between 600 and 750 men would come ashore in the Trinidad area, on Cuba's south coast, and that the force would be aided by air strikes against the Cuban Air Force flown from bases in Nicaragua, and would be able to make its way from the beach into the Escambray Mountains.

President-elect Kennedy rejected the Trinidad plan, insisting that a new one be developed that would not require U.S. military intervention, and on March 14, 1961, Kennedy, having assumed the presidency, approved a plan for an action in Cochinos Bay (the Bay of Pigs), located about one hundred miles west of Trinidad. The new plan depended for its success on the initial assault's producing internal armed resistance from anti-Castro elements.

Manuel Ray The CIA did not want an uprising. We had given them a proposal called "Cuba in Flames." This was for a one-week period of sabotage. Then we would wait two months to see the effects of this campaign—to see how many people in the Castro government would get in contact with us. We gave them a list of twenty-five to thirty acts of sabotage that could be done. We knew this would work; it would attract the people who were not satisfied with the revolution.

Andrew Goodpaster   The plan Bissell and Dulles presented to President-elect Kennedy went beyond what Eisenhower had approved. That's the way I read it. There is a background to this. Earlier in 1960 there had been proposals to land and destroy a power station, a sugar mill, and a sawmill, and things of that kind. That was reviewed by the group that vetted these proposed covert operations. I think that it came up at an NSC meeting, and Eisenhower said he did not want to get into anything piecemeal; he wanted to see a comprehensive, well-thought-out plan, and only then would he begin to authorize things. It is my understanding that the training was part of this comprehensive plan. That was approved but explicitly without obligation to commit the unit; that decision would be reserved. We were nowhere close to making that decision. There was no intelligence evidence to suggest that that time was near.

Richard Bissell   Allen Dulles and I went down together to the Kennedy house [in Palm Beach]. I think the whole conversation took place out of doors. I think Kennedy had obviously heard of the project—just how, I don't know, but that wasn't surprising; a fair number of people knew about it.

John Patterson   During World War II I knew and worked for General Eisenhower, first in his headquarters in London in 1942 and then in Algeria in 1942 and 1943. In early 1960, while governor, I was approached by a CIA official. We met at the governor's mansion. He brought along Major General Reid [G.] Doster, the chief of staff of our Air National Guard. What they wanted me to do was to let them recruit certain types of personnel out of the Alabama Air National Guard and out of Hayes Aircraft Corporation in Birmingham, to form a nucleus for assembling and equipping for a Cuban invasion force. They seemed to be having trouble getting people to do this, so I asked the CIA official if Eisenhower was aware of this, and he said, "Oh, yes, he has given his full approval to this." I said, "All right, I'll help you." So we recruited about 350 Alabamians—everything from cooks to bakers to aircraft mechanics, flight instructors, medics, and operational personnel—and we assembled all these old World War II–type B-26 bombers from all over the country that were still being used by the National Guard, and we moved it all down to Guatemala and set up a camp down there to train the Cuban invasion force, and this was to be the air arm of the invasion force. They were employed by a fictitious corporation, handsomely paid, and handsomely insured by Lloyd's of London, to test military equipment. Every few weeks, Reid Doster would stop in to see me on his way home to Birmingham to report what was going on. This was in 1960.

Now, in the meantime I got involved in the presidential campaign; I was very active in it. I loaned Kennedy some of my staff; we raised a lot of money in Alabama for him. And all the time that thing was cooking down there, very hush-hush.

About three or four weeks before the November election—it was looking close by then—Reid Doster stopped by my office and said, "Any morning now, you are going to pick up the newspaper and read about a Cuban invasion. It's going to be a tremendous success." Well, I got to thinking about that. Nixon was vice president; he was chairman of the National Security Council, and he was bound to be privy to that thing. If it came off on the eve of the election and was highly successful, he'd be elected president for sure; he'd claim full credit for it.

So I got on the telephone and called Steve Smith in New York. I said, "I want five minutes of his time; I have something to tell him that I think he really ought to know." So Smith told me to fly up to New York and check into the Barclay Hotel, and he said, "At ten o'clock on a certain night the senator will come to your room." Kennedy came—he had a guy with him—and I said, "I'd like to talk to you privately." So he had the guy wait in the hall. Then I told him exactly what I knew, and I said, "I want you to promise me that you are never going to breathe a word about this to anybody if you do not know about it, because there are a lot of lives at stake." I watched him very carefully while I told him, to see if he would indicate in any manner that he knew about it, but I couldn't tell.

The Eisenhower administration conducted periodic briefings for the candidates, but they never briefed him on that.

When I got finished, he thanked me and left. There is some indication that shortly before the election, he began to speak out that something be done for the Cubans. He began to tailor his speeches to recommend it, and Nixon apparently got disturbed about that and came out against any intervention in Cuba during the campaign. It seems to me that Kennedy might have used the information to tailor his speeches—just in case I happened to be right.

Terry Sanford   There were four people from Alabama having lunch in Bobby's office just before the Bay of Pigs. I was over there also. It was a tremendous office, and they were in one corner. They talked about the planes. That is all I heard. It was enough to raise my curiosity, but I didn't want to know any more then.

Richard Bissell   The president was a good listener. He asked a few questions, but not very many. Most of them were about the design of the plan, what prospect it had for success, and why we thought it had a prospect for success. He made it clear that he took it as a serious step and was concerned that it could have wide repercussions—as it did. I thought that he was studiously careful to express neither disapproval nor approval of the plan; he was not yet inaugurated and he was being very careful not to act prematurely as president. My recollection is that after the briefing, he and Allen went off and talked privately for a little while—I don't know what about; I didn't ask Allen.

Roger Hilsman   The original plan was to go north through Santiago, using American naval and air support. When General Lemnitzer [Lyman Lemnitzer, chairman, Joint Chiefs of Staff] and Bissell and Dulles presented the plan to President Kennedy, he told them, While I have been campaigning for two years saying Eisenhower made a terrible mistake letting Castro win, I would not use American troops to remove Castro. I would love to see you guys knock Castro off, but not with American military forces. If you can accomplish this with a Cuban brigade, you have my permission. So they had to cancel the original plan through Santiago and developed an operation involving the Bay of Pigs.

Andrew Goodpaster   I am not aware that Kennedy received the advice of the Joint Chiefs; I think there is a dispute on that. I heard General Lemnitzer say later that the advice of the chiefs was not sought. There is a significant point there. I had a bit of a feeling that instead of this being pulled in, at least in those early days, there was a tendency on the part of the president-elect to expect people to bring proposals to him.

When I came back to Washington as assistant to the chairman of the Joint Chiefs, I found that, going back into the early days of the Kennedy administration, the chiefs had been cut out of the act, where Eisenhower had insisted that they be drawn in and, in fact, required them to state their view, which oftentimes was something he would disagree with. But he did insist on their participation. I think, as was related to me by Generals Lemnitzer and Wheeler [Earle Wheeler, chief of staff, U.S. Army], that there was a gap in the early part of the Kennedy administration. Secretary McNamara took a more active, personal part. And there was that group that he had around him, the so-called whiz kids. There was some tendency, as reported to me by the uniformed people, to fence them out, and for those people to take over the running of the thing.

Roger Hilsman   I found out about the plan in a conversation with Allen Dulles. I then immediately went to see Rusk. I said, "Mr. Secretary, you and I are the two guys in the State Department with the most military experience, and we both know that landing on a hostile shore is the most dangerous military operation there is. I think these bastards are going to use that Cuban brigade to land at the Bay of Pigs and invade Cuba." Rusk looked at me and replied, "Roger, I am sorry. This is being too tightly held; I don't know anything about Cuba."

Lucius Battle   It was kept so secret that there wasn't a challenge to the accuracy of judgments and decisions throughout the process, which is absolutely essential to having a sound decision-making process. It's interesting to compare it with the Persian Gulf or Panama. It became a big issue, and at the conclusion we felt that the government had been run badly, and particularly the State Department. But then, certainly nobody had pulled together the agencies concerned with these issues—Defense, CIA, and all the others that were involved. So this led to the creation of an operations center, which I had advocated for some time.

It was based upon the notion that small, unknown bits of real estate around the world suddenly become the most important bits of a plan on the whole face of the earth—be it Panama, or Angola, or Vietnam. That suddenly you find a small country becoming the test of wills between the East and West, or the test of the direction in which the world is going for one or another reason. I said, "Any person that happens to be on the Congo Desk, and has absolutely no contact with the senior members of government, and the president of the United States, suddenly finds himself elevated because his bit of land is the hot item that week." We were simply providing a first-rate, small staff to back up the assistant secretary covering that area and to bring the expertise that existed on that Congo Desk—or wherever, to support it on an around-the-clock basis and carry it through that period. But not to make decisions. Decisions would be made in the same way they were always made. But all information available on that issue would be kept there, and all agencies of the government would be representing a set of issues and facts concerning it.

Richard Bissell   There were an awful lot of people in the media who knew that training was going on, and they didn't need hard evidence. They took it for granted that the organization was not only U.S.-funded but also U.S.-directed and -organized.

I don't think I had ever thought of limitations, such as no use of U.S. volunteer personnel, no training or basing on any U.S. territory.

Manuel Ray   I was told by the operation aide to Frank Bender [CIA organizer in Miami] that it was to be a military invasion. They would have the power to go straight to Havana. He said the invasion was being planned by the best military people in the world. He told me, "Once the operation starts, it cannot be stopped." I believe that was the idea they had to double-cross Mr. Kennedy.

The CIA man told me that the brigade commanders would be instructed to disarm and then detain those who might be participating in an uprising against the government. There was a special unit headed by someone who had been close to Batista, to destroy the underground network that had been operating against Castro. The goal was to take full charge of Cuba.

I personally feel we were betrayed by the people in charge of the Bay of Pigs operation. They had their own agenda. They told the brigade members they would get all necessary assistance from the U.S. government, and they told President Kennedy they didn't need any assistance. The actual betrayal was from these people to the people they were training. I believe this was their strategy: to tell Mr. Kennedy everything they needed to tell him so he would authorize the invasion. The CIA people believed that if things went badly, Kennedy would have to intervene—he could not let it fail.

[José] Miro Cardona [head of the Cuban Revolutionary Council] was very upset by Kennedy's speech before the invasion, that the U.S. would not put any troops in Cuba. Later he said that Adolph Berle [Jr., chairman, Interdepartmental Task Force on Latin America] had promised him ten thousand troops. But I never heard this promise from the Americans. All we were told from people in the administration was that we would win.

We had a meeting with administration officials to discuss the strategy of the council. We made a proposal to first develop as intensely as possible the underground against Castro inside Cuba; that would take one or two months; maybe that would be enough to accomplish the task. If not, then we can start some actions from outside. Finally, we can come with some landings in Cuba, which would be consecutive.

We knew Castro's strength. We knew that he had only two or three good commanders. We believed that there should be one landing, then two days later another landing at another place, and a few days later at another place—perhaps ten landings in all. Castro would not be able to cope with this. We signed an agreement on March 22 that top priority would be given to the internal struggle in Cuba.

Arthur Schlesinger, Jr.   He did cut it down. He had the CIA reduce the noise level. He made it clear that there would be no American participation. I think that it was foredoomed from the beginning: the notion that twelve hundred fellows come here to overthrow an army of two hundred thousand. Even if there had been a second air strike, the only way it could have succeeded was if there had been uprisings behind the lines and defections from the Cuban Army. The whole thing was a botch from the beginning.

The only way it could succeed—and this is what I believe Dulles and Bissell had in the backs of their minds—was through sending the Marines. They may have felt that once Kennedy got committed to it, if there weren't all these defections and uprisings, having involved U.S. prestige up to that point, he would have had to have followed up by the use of U.S. force.

The Decision to Go Ahead with the Operation

Richard Bissell   It was quite soon after his inauguration that the president decided to go with the operation.

Richard Hilsman   I said to Rusk, "One brigade can't take on the Cuban Army. They must believe the Cuban people will rise. Now I don't know much about Cuba, but it is not my impression that the people are going to rise."

Andrew Goodpaster   There was no intelligence evidence that there was any substantial dissidence against Castro—no evidence of an uprising of that kind.

Richard Bissell   I'm sure that there was a lot of conversation between the president and his brother. As I recall, Robert did not come to many of the policy meetings, but I'm sure his brother consulted him. The day before the operation, the president told me to go to Robert's office in the Justice Department to brief him. Robert was very poker-faced: His parting comment was that he hoped we were right in our belief that the operation could succeed, but he said it in such a way as to reveal some skepticism. He obviously was concerned about the wide negative reaction there could be, especially to an unsuccessful operation.

Cartha DeLoach   We were kept out of that situation until Bobby came over one morning just shortly prior to the Bay of Pigs incident and briefed Mr. Hoover concerning the matter. We had heard various vague rumblings about it, particularly the training of the Cubans, but we were kept completely out of it. Mr. Hoover listened to Bobby, but we were just strictly sidelined in that entire matter. I think the director was relieved that he did not have a role.

William Fulbright   His father had a place in Palm Beach; my wife's aunt had a place in Delray Beach about fifteen miles away. At Eastertime JFK asked me to go on his plane to Florida. A committee staff member and I had prepared a memorandum on Cuba, which I gave to him. I then flew back with him, and when we got to Washington, he asked me to go with him to a meeting at the State Department with about fifteen executive staff members. He called on all of them and they supported the invasion. I didn't.

Richard Bissell   McNamara was very much a listener in the Bay of Pigs briefings; I think that in that famous vote—going around the table—he voted yes. Arleigh Burke [admiral; chief of naval operations] was a supporter; he would have liked nothing more than to have been allowed on the last day to intervene. Rusk was basically opposed to the operation, but he was totally loyal to the president, and I think that he did not want to go against the president's intentions in meetings of that size. Nevertheless his recommendations to the president—especially on the cancellation of the second air strike—were influential and very important. Rusk had been in the China-Burma theater in World War II and had developed views about guerrilla warfare; his opinion was that the Bay of Pigs operation should have been organized—pure and simple—as guerrilla warfare and not as a miniature World War II amphibious operation. McGeorge Bundy also voted for the operation. He made a good effort as national security adviser to be a good staff officer—that is, instead of making up his mind what he thought U.S. policy ought to be and then urging that course on the president, he wanted to be sure that the president had all views presented to him.

Donald Wilson   One day in late March or early April, Tad Szulc, a reporter for the *New York Times* who I knew, called me and said he must see me immediately. He said, "I know that an invasion is about to be launched in Cuba by refugees supported by the United States government, and I think it is very important that the U.S. government set up an information office, in Miami or even on the island of Cuba, when the invasion takes place." I was sitting there stunned; I knew nothing about the Bay of Pigs.

I went right to Murrow and told him what I had heard. He was steaming. He picked up the phone and called Allen Dulles—his clout was sufficient that he could get Dulles on the phone. He said, "Allen, I am sitting here with my deputy, who has given me information pertaining to Cuba, which I think you should know right away." So Dulles told us to come right over. I then told Dulles the story, and he sat there and smoked his pipe and made no comment. When I finished, he said, "Thank you very much." Murrow didn't express outrage; he didn't argue with Dulles. He was sophisticated enough to know that Dulles had been told not to tell anybody.

When we got back to the office, there was a call from Mac Bundy, asking Murrow to come to the White House after lunch. Bundy then told Murrow the whole thing. Murrow blew up at Bundy and said,

"When I was brought into this administration I thought I would at least have a role in giving my opinion about some of the major foreign policy thrusts." Then he told Bundy it was a terrible idea. He blew his steam off and came back to his office.

Then the Bay of Pigs happened. Murrow was in a foul humor, but he was totally loyal. We did all we could to make it appear a reasonable venture, but of course it was a total disaster. Then President Kennedy, in a speech to the American people, took the full blame, and I remember after the speech, Murrow—with his eyes almost moisting over—said, "He did something wonderful."

Some of the Likely Reasons
Why the President Bought into the Operation

Angier Biddle Duke   He's in office ten days; is he going to call this thing off just because he thinks it isn't going to work? He didn't trust his own judgment at that time. He didn't have enough confidence in his own judgment. He respected the Supreme Allied Commander, the twice-elected president of the United States, and this venerable figure, Allen Dulles, who has conducted so many successful operations.

Bobby Baker   I think John Kennedy bought into the Bay of Pigs through lack of information. He was totally ill equipped for that kind of crisis that early in his administration. Look at his whole background in Congress: He'd never been on the Armed Services Committee. John Foster Dulles and Allen Dulles had a mystique he was deferential to. Both of them were ill equipped for their jobs. John Foster Dulles was an absolute disaster; he was pitiful; he didn't know what the hell it was all about.

John Seigenthaler   He bought in because the CIA told him there was going to be an uprising. That is what Bob told me before they did it. They were shocked that there was not that uprising.

George Ball   It wasn't Kennedy's plan; it was Eisenhower's. And Eisenhower told him in their final meeting that it was going well and said, "I am trusting you, as a head of state, to carry this through." Kennedy had just come to office. He was very in awe of Eisenhower, and, I think, he felt he had no option but to go through with it. You had all of these people assembled. What would he do with them otherwise? It was what is known as the disposal problem. That was a very big factor.

Roger Hilsman   Kennedy realized that Nixon knew all about the plan, and that if he turned it down out of hand, Nixon would use this against him on everything else he tried to do. So Kennedy was boxed in.

Andrew Goodpaster   I do not believe it was made clear to Kennedy that Eisenhower had never given the approval for actual commitment of the force, because I heard people say later, "Well, Eisenhower had approved all of this." I knew that wasn't so.

We leaned over backward to try to establish some kind of a viable relationship with Castro. I think some of our people thought that we allowed ourselves to be strung along for quite a long time by a man who, at a very deep level, had made a commitment to communism. I still don't know whether at that time he had done that. You know, he was a typical leader of that *caudillo* genre.° Whether he had made the commitment to communism, or whether that came after his break with the United States, we began to see it harden in the spring of 1960. Up until then, there had been some hope that we could work with him; we had worked with others who had a negative stance toward the United States: Kubitschek in Brazil, to some degree; Goulart, very strongly opposed to the United States, and many others. Eisenhower had no animus; he showed no emotion about Castro. He thought that a lot of this was showmanship and that it would be dangerous and not in the interests of the Cuban people. On the other hand, Eisenhower had no illusions about Batista, who had preceded Castro.

Roger Hilsman   The CIA had a terrible guilt feeling that it had let Eisenhower down about Castro; they had told him that Castro wasn't a communist. They let Castro win out of a kind of stupidity. Their guilt feelings led to the Bay of Pigs operation.

Ben Bradlee   President Kennedy looked around the table—it must have seemed to him that everybody who made him feel insecure was sitting there: all the admirals and generals, all the CIA people, none of whom liked him, and he knew that—remember, his mandate consisted

°A type of Spanish or Latin American political leader with his own military following.

of 104,000 votes—and he went around the table to each of them, and they all said, "Yes. Go!" I'm sure he was worried about the mandate and the charge that he was going to be a liberal, peacenik type. The Bay of Pigs came so fast after he assumed office, and Kennedy had not developed relationships with any of them.

Eugene McCarthy   Why would Kennedy do it? Maybe it could be explained psychologically: "We've got to do this because it is the way we can scare the communists forever." It could have been pragmatic, the influence of the old man, or proving to be decisive, or a cheap operation against communism. That might have been it. I think Rusk was capable of making that kind of argument.

There was pressure on Kennedy. The military said it would be easy, and Kennedy would prove his anticommunism and his competence to make decisions. It was so ridiculous. You had the whole damn Marine Corps down in Guantanamo. If you really want to take over Cuba, why do a Mickey Mouse thing?

The cynical explanation was that Kennedy, who always speed-read, was speed-reading from the digest of the plan prepared for Eisenhower. If you speed-read the digest, you are going to leave out some important details.

His record was pretty marginal on this whole anticommunist thing from the beginning, from his first congressional race. Then came the involvement with Joe McCarthy, which could have been pragmatic under the influence of the old man. Maybe the feeling was: If you do this against Cuba, this is a cheap operation against communism, and the Russians will be afraid of you forever.

Dean Rusk   At the time that he gave the order to go, I think that he thought that there was some chance that the brigade could succeed. After all, Castro had come ashore that way, with a handful of people.

Richard Bissell   There was nothing that the president wanted less than to seem, at the beginning of his term, to be soft in the face of a threat; to be unwilling to use strong measures if they held some promise of success. I'm sure that he had visions of being told in the press that he had lost Cuba in the first few weeks of his administration by throwing away a plan to retrieve Cuba from Castro.

Dean Rusk I don't think that when he made the decision that he thought it was a mistake. He was aware of a well-known hostility toward Fidel Castro—he'd campaigned on it during his presidential campaign—he certainly did not like Fidel Castro. But he had faced other problems and what would you do if you turned off this Cuban brigade and had three or four thousand highly vocal and highly dissident Cubans wandering around the U.S. being critical of the president?

He learned a good deal about the unreliability of reports from refugees; he was told all sorts of things by the Cuban refugees in this country that simply weren't true about units of the Cuban Army revolting and joining the brigade and a popular uprising by the Cuban people against Castro—things like that that just never happened.

Harlan Cleveland My interpretation as to why Kennedy got into the Bay of Pigs is that he had never been an executive before. The last executive job he had had before becoming president was to be commander of a PT boat. He didn't know that the executive executes mostly by asking questions. He didn't, in the Bay of Pigs, ask the people that he should ask what he should have asked them. I once ran into a former member of the Joint Chiefs on an airplane. I asked him why the Joint Chiefs never told the president that, from a military point of view, this CIA plan was for the birds. He said, "You won't believe this, but the fact is we were so in awe of this bright, young, charismatic hero, that we were waiting to speak when we were spoken to. We were old enough to be his father; and he never asked us."

Tom Wicker In 1964, when I was Washington bureau chief of the *New York Times,* we prepared a series on the CIA. I went to see Allen Dulles, who was then retired and living in Georgetown, and I got along famously with him. He told me the following story: He said, "I take full responsibility for the Bay of Pigs," which is more than he ever did publicly. "I should have known that President Kennedy would not go through with that thing wholeheartedly. He was reluctant about it from the start, until I finally said to him, 'Mr. Kennedy, are you going to be less anticommunist than President Eisenhower was?'" I think that story gets at the truth that Kennedy did not want to be less anticommunist than Eisenhower. And also, probably he wasn't self-confident enough to brush aside Dulles and Dick Bissell and say, I am not going to do this.

Arthur Schlesinger, Jr.   He had no choice. In their last meeting, the day before the inauguration, Eisenhower said this was U.S. policy and should go forward at all possible speed. Allen Dulles said to him, "If you disband this expedition, you are faced with a disposal problem. What is going to happen to these twelve hundred people down there that the CIA has been training? They will go all around Central and South America saying that they had been trained by the Eisenhower administration to overthrow Castro, and the Kennedy administration had then canceled this, and that would give Castro a great impetus in Latin America." And Allen Dulles didn't say it—but he didn't have to—that in the United States, the notion that a fellow who had been a lieutenant JG in the Second World War would overrule a plan agreed to by the commander of the greatest amphibious invasion in history would not have gone down. He was really trapped by what he had inherited.

Richard Helms   Castro was regarded as a Russian surrogate. And as a Russian surrogate, he was a platform for Russian penetration of this continent and was regarded as a very substantial threat, not only to the Monroe Doctrine, but to the national security of the United States. If he had been able to get away with putting those missiles in Cuba and have them sit there for all that time, I think it would have been regarded as a real coup for Castro, so this cannot be regarded as separating Castro as an individual target. It was in relationship with Moscow that this was important. Then, later, it became a personal thing with President Kennedy, with regard to Castro as a fellow who had challenged him. And the whole mess with getting the brigade out afterward, and all the rest of it, was very aggravating to President Kennedy. So there was no doubt about it that he thought he ought to do everything he possibly could to get rid of this fellow.

THE OPERATION
An Air Strike, a "Defection," an Emergency Landing, and Cancellation of the Second Air Strike

The first part of the operation involved an air strike by eight B-26 aircraft on three airfields in Cuba. As part of the initial phase, the CIA, in an attempt to establish the cover that the aircraft were flown by defectors from Castro's air force, had a ninth B-26 fly directly to Miami, where the pilot immediately requested asylum.

The raid itself was only partially successful, resulting in the destruction of five Cuban aircraft on the ground. In what proved to be a more unfortunate development, one of the attacking pilots was forced to land in Key West after his plane experienced engine trouble.

As questions began to mount as to the real identity of the Cuban pilots in South Florida, Ambassador Stevenson, engaged at the UN in a debate on the Cuban issue, was informed that the pilots were genuine defectors. Within hours, however, reporters in south Florida began to unravel the CIA cover story, leading President Kennedy to cancel a second, more crucial air strike—one that was aimed at providing support for the actual invasion force.

Richard Bissell   The news didn't turn bad till after we'd missed the chance of a second strike, and pretty soon after that, we did have permission to use all the aircraft we could get into the air. The trouble was that the next night, there were still a couple of Castro's T-33s armed, for which the B-26s were no match. The damage had been done, and furthermore we had begun to pay the price of having to fly from Central America, which cut by at least three-quarters the air arm's effectiveness.

Manuel Ray   If on the day before the operation began we had been told what they were planning, we would have said, "No, absolutely no. It is not going to work." As a matter of fact, in my worries before the operation, I told the CIA operations chief and Mr. Muñoz Marín [Luís Muñoz Marín, governor of Puerto Rico], in Puerto Rico, "It seems like something like an invasion is being planned for Cuba, and I believe it is going in a way that will be wrong." Muñoz Marín told President Kennedy. Later Kennedy called Muñoz Marín and said, "It happened the way you told me it would."

Ray Cline   I cannot understand why the Joint Chiefs of Staff decided to move the CIA operation from the Sierra Maestre to the Bay of Pigs. It was crazy. All they ever said was that it will be logistically a lot better if you go to the west end of the island. This is going to be a lot handier for us. I am sure they thought a military action would succeed if the Cuban brigade was failing. The original idea was for the CIA to infiltrate the Sierre Maestre the way Castro did. The Cuban brigade was supposed to drift up into the mountains, not invade anything. But the military guys tend to be a little practical, and formalistic, and they said, "Infiltrating the Sierra Maestre is not such a good idea; we have to have logistic support to do all these things." They had a World War II–type of landing. The brigade landed at the Bay of Pigs, but it got destroyed. One of the reasons was that no aircraft cover was provided. That would have been easy, but Kennedy thought that it was just a covert operation.

Harlan Cleveland   I went up a week before the operation with a representative of CIA who was assigned to tell Stevenson what was going on. It was not a very candid briefing; they didn't indicate what the timing would be. The extent to which the operation was CIA-directed and not a lot of freedom fighters whom we were helping on the side—the extent to which this was, in effect, a U.S. initiative—was not clear in that briefing. The fact that we were not told about the timing was understandable in that they wanted to keep this a secret.

But they brilliantly timed it for the day that the Cuban item, which was a charge that we were about to invade them resulting from a previous incident, was going to come up for debate in the General Assembly of the United Nations. So we were already in the General Assembly, and on the Cuban item, when they unleashed the Bay of Pigs operation. This, from a political point of view, was a rather questionable piece of timing.

The first big incident, and the one Adlai Stevenson was most unhappy about, resulted from a ploy prior to the invasion itself. A plane with Cuban markings came into Florida and landed in a swamp. The pilot said he was a defector. This plane had been prepared in Nicaragua. It flew over Cuba and then flew away, making it look like a defector. This was a psychological warfare thing to encourage them to rise against Cuba. As soon as I heard about this, I asked the Latin American Bureau what was going on. They asked the CIA, which provided us with a cover story which was, i.e., this was a defector. They didn't tell us the rest of the story. I then authorized Stevenson—it was my job in Washington to process instructions on missions involved in international organizations—to give the cover story, not knowing it was a cover story.

Stevenson's staff then compounded the error. The pilot had given an interview in Florida with the same story and it went out on the Associated Press wire. So just after Stevenson had followed our instructions on the story, his staff runs in to him with the tape off the ticker, and Stevenson tells the General Assembly, "I have just had confirmation of what I just told you." In less than twenty-four hours, some enterprising reporter in Florida had taken a close look at the airplane. He found paint scraped off the side and U.S. Air Force markings underneath. So the whole cover blew off. Particularly in the UN, Stevenson had egg all over his face. His great prestige, which was partly based on people feeling he was an honest and civilized person, his world credibility, had been used by his government, and he was fit to be tied. He was close to resigning, and it took a lot of effort by the president personally to try to recover from it.

Joseph Sisco Stevenson was critical of the Bay of Pigs operation. In the midst of the operation, a cover story was developed with regard to two airplanes. Adlai Stevenson, on that day, was scheduled to make a speech in the Security Council. The question arose as to what he was going to say. I got on the telephone and made contact with the CIA, and we were given a story, but were not told that, in fact, this was a cover story. I took what was told to me as fact, and I conveyed that to Adlai Stevenson as fact, so we were both duped. He made a public statement and then, several days later, found himself in an embarrassing position. I can tell you quite honestly that he wondered out loud—I heard it firsthand—as to whether he shouldn't resign. We all prevailed upon him not to do it. There would have been tremendous repercussions, not only domestically but overseas. The failure of the Bay of Pigs was bad enough, but to add to it the resignation of Adlai Stevenson?

George Smathers Bobby was the guy who came in and told us we were very screwed up because Adlai Stevenson was our United States ambassador to the UN, and here were the Fidel Castro people saying that we in the United States were getting ready to lend these airplanes to be used by the Cubans to defeat Castro. And Adlai Stevenson had stood up on the floor of the United Nations and said it wasn't true, and he was going to resign from his ambassadorship if that occurred, and nobody had told him that there had already been an okay for us to let the Cubans—the so-called "freedom fighters"—use the planes. So when Bobby came in and told everybody that Adlai was going to create a big stink, and resign as ambassador to the United Nations, that would have made the administration look so bad—that they had forgotten to clue him in—so that was actually the deciding factor against letting them use the planes.

The Invasion

On the morning of Monday, April 17, the invasion began. Cuban Army units were soon engaging the invasion force, and the Cuban Air Force sank a ship carrying reserve ammunition and communications equipment. By the next day it appeared that the invasion was in serious trouble: Castro forces—led by tanks—began to move toward the beach.

A B-26 air strike from Nicaragua was planned in order to protect the beach and to provide air cover for the operation. President Kennedy authorized an overflight of the area by six unmarked fighter jets from the carrier Essex. But due to a misunderstanding of the difference in time zones between Nicaragua and Cuba, the B-26s arrived over the beach one hour before the overflight of the Essex planes occurred. The B-26s were routed by the Cuban Air Force, resulting in the deaths of four American pilots who had flown in the mission.

At this point it appeared that nothing short of an all-out U.S. military action could possibly save both the Cuban brigade and the Bay of Pigs operation. Faced with this knowledge, President Kennedy decided not to move militarily, and the operation ended in the defeat and capture of the surviving members of the brigade.

Manuel Ray   We arrived at Opa-Locka airport at four in the morning, at an abandoned airport with guards all around. We did not know the name of the place; we found out it was Opa-Locka. At six A.M., we heard on the radio that the operation had begun. We were surprised at this news. We knew that they were planning some imminent action, but we did not know what, where, how, and when; the administration had never asked our views concerning the plan for the Bay of Pigs.

I found out from the CIA that some of the people involved in the brigade had been murderers for Batista. I told the CIA operations man, "If these people are taken prisoner by Fidel and put on television, it will turn the people against the operation." He said to me, "These people are anticommunist." I answered, "That is not the question; it is a matter of symbols. People have to believe they are fighting for something. You cannot make a murderer into a positive symbol."

There was a man called El Morto [Death]. He had been paid two thousand dollars by Trujillo, [Rafael Trujillo, dictator, Dominican

Republic]° to kill one of his enemies in Havana. El Morto was recruited and was sent to Guatemala. I told the CIA, This type of person helps Fidel; he doesn't help us. I got the impression that there was some thought in the planning of the operation to be known that it was directed by the old army that was able to come back and defeat the rebel army that had defeated them. But this was a mistake because it would only cause the rebel army to work together.

A person arrived who identified himself as a naval officer—perhaps a lieutenant commander. He told us the operation was having problems but that we should not worry because the president would give authorization for the U.S. ships offshore to fire on any Cuban aircraft that came over the beach. This conversation took place between one to two in the afternoon. That person had left Washington at about ten o'clock that morning. He winked at me and said that at six P.M. Kennedy would have a memorandum on his desk ready for signature, authorizing the use of the American military, so when this officer left Washington at ten A.M., the plan had already been prepared to put this memorandum on Kennedy's desk later in the day.

Yuri Barsukov The Soviet officials didn't expect that Kennedy would act that way about the men on the beach. And they didn't think, first of all, that Kennedy would support the invasion; that was a surprise for us. There was the feeling that it would harm relations, although Kennedy's actions were directed not against the Soviet Union but against Cuba.

Richard Bissell I was for the crucial forty-eight or seventy-two hours in my office, and slept in a neighboring office. The atmosphere was one of total gloom. On Tuesday evening Walt Rostow got hold of me and took me over to the White House. There was a big party going on. The president was in evening dress; Arleigh Burke was in his dress uniform, and Dean Rusk was there. That was when permission was finally granted for the one-hour naval air cover. As Walt Rostow said later, I was—in effect—the commander of an army being lost.

°Rafael Leonídas Trujillo Molina was president of the Dominican Republic, 1930–38 and 1942–52, but ruled as a dictator from 1930 until his death by assassination in 1961.

Ralph Dungan   I recall all the hubbub—people moving in and out, knowing there was something really hot going on, but not really knowing what it was. It was held very tight—O'Donnell didn't know about it until the disaster occurred. Then, of course, we all knew. That was a terrible day. It happened so early in JFK's administration. On reconstructing it later, I think he was terribly misled: Nobody was equipped to ask the right questions and—because of the security—Bundy was brand-new in that kind of role, and all those guys involved in its planning were his friends from Yale—and wherever.

Dean Rusk   The original plan for the Bay of Pigs had the landing occur in the far eastern section of Cuba. I took the view that as an alternative plan the brigade go in immediately adjacent to Guantanamo, and that if it succeeded, we could support it. If it failed, we could give it refuge. But that was turned down by the Joint Chiefs of Staff, who did not want Guantanamo to be compromised by this kind of expedition, and so it was moved to the Bay of Pigs.

But there was almost complete misunderstanding and miscommunication between President Kennedy and the leadership of the brigade in Cuba, and one must hold the CIA responsible for that. For example, undoubtedly the members of the brigade who went ashore thought that they would be supported by American forces if they got into trouble. We were told in Washington if the brigade got into trouble, it would melt away into the countryside and become guerrillas. Well, when we got to that point, we learned that the members of the brigade had had no guerrilla training whatever and were simply incapable of guerrilla action. So it was a bungled mistake, much of the bungling due, I think, to the people in the CIA who allowed deep misunderstandings between the president and the brigade to occur.

Richard Bissell   There was not a well-worked-out contingency plan. The responsibility for that falls directly on my staff and me. There was not either a well-worked-out plan for the latter phases if the beachhead had been secured and held successfully.

Richard Helms   Eisenhower, having been a military officer all his life and in command of vast armies, understood the military problems connected with an operation of this kind far better than Kennedy, who had never commanded any troops or had any particular experience with respect to military operations of this sort. Either he was inadequately briefed or he didn't understand the hazards involved and what he was getting into.

If there was a problem with the Bay of Pigs operation as such, it rested in the fact that the way this operation was designed under President Eisenhower and received, I believe, his approval, was a different kind of operation than it turned out to be at the end. Not that we weren't going to use this invasion force of Cuban exiles, but the idea as I understood it was to set up a sort of small government-in-exile in an enclave on the island of Cuba, and then, if they were going to be overwhelmed by superior forces from Castro, that Eisenhower was prepared to send in troops to support them or at least send some type of force to help this government-in-exile survive until they could overthrow Castro. This also applied to the air coverage for the initial landing—that the Navy was going to provide air coverage. The Cuban exiles didn't provide their own air coverage but if they got in trouble, the Navy was going to provide firepower and assistance to make the landing succeed. That was withdrawn, for whatever reason, when the operation actually began, so that there was no way of succeeding.

McGeorge Bundy   There was a real breakdown in communication between the White House and the people at the CIA who were in charge. The president told them as hard as he could that he wasn't going to have it turn into an American operation. But they really didn't believe him, as they later said. They believed if he once got as far in as the initial enterprise would put him, and then it was about to fail, he would change his mind and see the light from their point of view and put American forces in. They were simply wrong on that. That difference of approach between the people in charge of the operation and what they had heard but didn't really believe from the president is at the center of the problem, I think.

Richard Bissell   I was disappointed by some of the president's decisions; I regretted some of them. I wasn't surprised, however. He made his decisions in accordance with the policy he said he was going to follow: nonintervention. He did finally make the concession of authorizing a one-hour Navy air cover for resupply; it was a complete failure. I thought that if he was going to make that much of a concession, he might just as well have made a bit more of a concession. It was ridiculous, in hindsight, to have limited it to one hour.

John Patterson   On the last day of the invasion, it was failing. It was poorly planned and poorly equipped; Batista's government had received from us about fifteen T-33 jet trainers. Castro's people armed those jet trainers. The lumbering, old, World War II twin engine B-26s of the invasion force were no match for the T-33s. On the last day of the operation, a decision was made to make one last strike of napalm to try to save the beach. When they got ready for that strike, the Cuban pilots wouldn't fly, so the Alabama Air National Guard, against all of our agreements—we had an understanding that no Alabamian would be committed to the operation—flew the last strike. Four of them didn't come back—four fellows from Birmingham. The next morning it was all over, and everybody who could, ran under a rock: All of these people from Alabama are down there, and four of them are missing. Somebody had to go to Birmingham to tell their folks, and the Alabama folks were left holding the sack. What a mess! Our people had the understanding that they would be covered by carrier-based aircraft as they flew over the beach. When they got over the beach, the carrier fighters didn't go up. This accounted for our losses. It was later said that the reason was that we were in different time zones; they got the times mixed up.

Richard Bissell   Our experience with the Cubans was that they were incurably insecure, and we attached a great deal of importance to operational secrecy—maintaining real secrecy about the time and place of the landing—and I think that was achieved. It would have been preferable—from our point of view—if there had been a core group of Cuban politicians who really could have been trusted to handle the information with effective security, but that they were not able to do.

The attempt to maintain plausible deniability—that is, the attempt to keep the U.S. government in a position to disclaim responsibility, except for some funding—prompted limitations on the way the operation was run that proved to be extremely damaging and may indeed have meant the difference between success and failure. Almost everybody involved should have realized that it would be attributed to the U.S. government, regardless of what was said. From top to bottom—from Kennedy down to those of us in charge of the operation in the agency—all of us, in varying degrees, made the same mistake.

George Ball   It would have been very hard to do, but I think Kennedy should have stayed out of it. It was a cockamamie scheme. He had nothing but amateurs running the damn thing. The military were kept strictly on the sidelines. The agency was in charge. They were amateur soldiers; they were Ph.D.s in economics.

There was no good option once he started the damn thing. He couldn't pull back, and, if we had committed our own forces, then it would have been a big, imperialistic war against a little country. This was the last thing in the world he wanted to be involved in. Nixon did it to him; Nixon was the biggest promoter of the Bay of Pigs operation. That was the beginning of the downfall of Chester Bowles, too, because he went around telling people in town that he had always been against the Bay of Pigs.

John Kenneth Galbraith   I did not know legally about the Bay of Pigs, but I heard it illegally from Chet Bowles just a night before I left for India. I was invited with Rusk to a dinner that night for the prime minister of Sweden at the Swedish Embassy. I was so disturbed about it, I didn't get to the dinner until they were close to dessert. I stopped by to write a memorandum to the president. I had the problem that I was not supposed to know about it, so I wrote a letter—one of the better letters I ever wrote—protesting against a concept of adventurism in the Caribbean and South America. I am sure the president read the letter, but I did not get a response.

I had an enormous feeling that in some ways this was the best solution. It was a terrific lesson in the irresponsibility of the CIA—in some measure even to the military. It put the quietus on any such other adventures. At the same time, we got out of it with minimum military problems; we avoided an all-out war with Castro. I never look back on the Bay of Pigs without thinking, in some ways—I am not exaggerating here—that this was the luckiest moment of Kennedy's career, that we got out as successfully as we did.

Strom Thurmond   I thought it was terrible that the president withdrew at the last minute. I was told by somebody that Castro had a plane ready; he thought he would have to go to another country. I understand that Fulbright was one of those who had advised the president not to give air cover; I guess I'm tougher against communists than he was.

THE AFTERMATH

Arthur Schlesinger, Jr.   There was a certain amount of resentment as to the way the CIA handled the operation, and the way they handled the Cubans who were part of the Cuban Revolutionary Council. They were down in a safe house at the Opa-Locka airport in Miami. They were being used by the CIA.

Adolph Berle and I went down to Miami together. We decided that the way to contain the indignation of these people, who had been kept in this house and had not known what was going on—some of them had sons in the expeditionary force—was for the president to calm them down. So I called Kennedy and said that, and he replied, "Well, bring them along."

I think that the president was madder at the military because the Joint Chiefs of Staff had said—as he understood it—that these plans of the CIA were militarily feasible. Then later they began leaking stories about how they weren't responsible for it at all. I don't think he ever believed anything the Joint Chiefs told him again. Thank God! In that sense, it was a very salutary experience, because the Joint Chiefs were wrong in practically everything—even in strictly military matters. The only member of the Joint Chiefs the president really liked was General Shoup [David Shoup, commandant, U.S. Marine Corps], the Marine hero, who was an honest fellow.

Manuel Ray   Our group came back to Washington with Adolph Berle and Arthur Schlesinger to see President Kennedy.

On the flight from Opa-Locka to Washington, Berle asked me to sit by him. He told me that on that day the Soviets had mobilized their forces around Berlin, so that if the United States landed in Cuba, they would take over Berlin. They could do that very easily; it would look like a trade.

President Kennedy sat in his rocking chair and told us that before the invasion he had been told that the invasion had the capability of overthrowing Castro. He sent an officer to visit the brigade at the training area and the officer reported that the men were well trained. As we talked, some members of the council urged the president to send troops in. I remember his reply, which he repeated two or three times: "I cannot send Americans to kill Cubans." Later he said the same thing in another way. This made me believe that this was at the center of his reflections at that time: that he could not send Americans to kill Cubans.

I can still see his face when we came into the office. He was tense, he was serious—not in panic but worried. He tried to comfort us. We met again the next day. He mentioned that there had not been uprisings to support the invasion. He said that everybody had told him there would be uprisings. I told the president that nothing had happened there because it was not coordinated to happen. He then said, "Yes. But whoever would organize this could not be told the date it was going to happen." I told him, "There are ways to coordinate this without knowing the date it will happen, but nobody tried to coordinate that; nobody wanted that to happen. This was because the people planning the operation wanted to control everything."

Pierre Salinger   The Bay of Pigs was almost the end of my career in the White House. I didn't know anything about it until two A.M. the day it began, when Kennedy called me. After the operation was over, I went to see the president and said, "To have credibility, your press secretary has to know about everything; I couldn't handle that in the Bay of Pigs." The president understood that, and from then on, I was involved in everything.

Ralph Dungan   After the Bay of Pigs Stevenson was really suspect to those who considered themselves true-blue, loyal sons of the sod and JFK's great supporters. Those relationships were difficult to work out, and I don't think they would ever have completely cottoned to Stevenson.

Adlai Stevenson III   My father was misled and—to say the least—uninformed and innocent, but nonetheless guilty of misleading the United Nations. He was terribly embarrassed by that, and as it turned out, it was much more of an embarrassment for the president than it was for the ambassador. The representatives of the UN knew exactly what had happened—that my father never would have intentionally misled anyone—and so they all rallied to his support. I think after that, maybe, the relationship with the State Department and the White House improved a little, but it was never very close.

John Seigenthaler   In the Bay of Pigs Bobby emerged as such a strong force. Part of it was that finger in Chester Bowles's chest, saying, "Don't give me that 'we were all for it,'" which, incidentally, shook Bowles. I mean, his teeth hurt from that finger in his chest. He told me when I visited him in India that he would always remember that day. He asked me if Bobby held it against him, and I said no.

I really felt it was a disaster that was based on false intelligence, and I don't think the president ever trusted the CIA after that. I don't think Bobby did either. They listened to Dick Helms and a couple of other people. The interesting thing to me is that the first two or three appointments of his administration were Hoover and Dulles. That was to send a message to the world that the president had confidence in the intelligence community. If you look back on it, I think that the two agencies that failed him were the FBI, in civil rights, and the CIA, in intelligence, not only in the Bay of Pigs but in general.

Richard Bissell   The following day, there was a long meeting in the White House. It was a kind of ongoing, rather unguided conversation. By that time it was perfectly clear that the military operation had failed, and the discussion was of how to pick up the pieces. Adolph Berle told me that he had voted for the operation and said, "I think it should have gone forward. I think we are better off for having tried it than we would have been if we hadn't."

Walt Rostow   It was only that terrible last night, when at the White House there were all these people in white ties and medals—it was a marvelous demonstration of the limitations of power, the greatest power in the world, and this little operation fails—that he learned what he believed wasn't true: that is to say, that if it failed, they could get back up into the hills. He hadn't known they had switched the landing to a place on the beach where there was a swamp behind it. So he felt he'd failed because he hadn't pressed them hard enough. He was going to make damn sure that he and the staff were going to get to the bottom of things themselves and not rely on prestigious folks.

There was a meeting shortly afterwards. The president was called out to see an African political leader. Everyone was exhausted. Rusk pounded the president's chair and said, "This is the man we have to worry about." And Bobby suddenly turned on everybody and said, "All you bright fellows: You got the president into this. We've got to do something to show the Russians we are not paper tigers." It was outrageous but natural. It was a profoundly emotional time. I walked over to Bobby and took my whole relationship with the Kennedys in hand. But I thought someone should cool him off.

So I took Bobby outside and I said, "Bobby, when you are in a schoolhouse fight and you get knocked on your ass, you don't come up swinging wildly. That's when you can really get hurt. You have to dance around until your head cools. We will have plenty of occasions to show we are serious." He looked at me with those blue, hooded eyes. I didn't know whether he was going to slug me or what. He said, "That's constructive," and we walked out together.

Ralph Dungan   The Bay of Pigs made the president goddamn skeptical of the intelligence community and the Joint Chiefs. I had to create an ambassadorial position for the then chairman of the Joint Chiefs, who went very quickly afterward to Portugal. In one sense, it was a good thing to have experienced the Bay of Pigs very early in the administration, had it not been so tragic an experience. Sure it made him skeptical, perhaps not skeptical enough, when you think of the Vietnam conflict.

George Ball   I think there was a good deal of the sense that the CIA had goofed. I think that was what prevented Dick Bissell from going any higher in the government. In the early days there was some talk of his coming over to the State Department. That obviously didn't happen. I think what happened in the Bay of Pigs had a certain psychological effect on the president's response on the Cuban missile crisis, because he couldn't stand being put down by Cuba in two situations.

John Patterson   I know from having talked to him that Kennedy was terribly disappointed and sick over the operation, and that he never again trusted his generals. Of course, I don't blame him; I wouldn't either.

McGeorge Bundy   Certainly there was some feeling that he hadn't been very well served by the CIA people or by the Joint Chiefs. I thought myself that the case with respect to the agency was clear—that they really didn't tell it as bare and clear as they should have, because of the hope that once they got it started, he would change his mind about the use of American forces. I think his feelings that the Joint Chiefs hadn't helped him was not quite as strong and a little less justified, because what they were doing is what so often happens in a bureaucracy, where one element doesn't really like to criticize the other guy's product out loud. And if we had been more sophisticated and more experienced, we would have discounted things accordingly.

Richard Bissell I think that the published accounts have been a little bit more critical of the agency than it deserved; they haven't counted up all the operational restrictions—many of them imposed several months before the landing—and the cumulative effect of all this. I think that one part of the charge about misleading the president is correct, although it was not a matter of deliberately misleading him. I think that he was allowed to form an incorrect impression of the prospects for a guerrilla phase if the beachhead could not be held; I think he counted on that a great deal—more than I had realized. My own belief until very late in the game was that the seizure of the beachhead could be accomplished with a high likelihood of success, and that the really difficult problems would loom up in the later phases of the operation.

George McGovern The saving thing about it I've always thought is that the president took the full responsibility for it himself. That first of all struck a good note with the American public, and the national press corps, and the Congress. But it also indicated the possibility of political and intellectual growth. A professor friend of mine called me a few days later and said, "Well, you know those damn Kennedys. They're so educable; they're quick learners; I think the president will pick up something from this." And I think he did. I think from that point on he was more skeptical about nifty-sounding proposals than he had been before.

I think that a person with greater experience and grasp in dealing with Third World countries would not have gone in there.

Walt Rostow Gunnar Myrdal [Swedish sociologist, author] came to Washington in May 1961. We had hardly got the blood off our hands. He said, "Well, you have a great president." I said, "Yes. But I don't think we've done very much. Why do you think so?" He replied, "The Bay of Pigs; the way he handled it." If he had turned it down, he'd have been dead. He made statements in the campaign; here was all this *Profiles in*

Courage stuff. On the other hand, if he backed a failed covert operation by going to war, that would have wrecked his position in the world; that is something a great power cannot do, so he took his losses.

The president thought he shouldn't have taken their [Dulles's/Bissell's] words; he should have done it himself. That was when he ordered Mac Bundy out of the Executive Office Building and down into the White House basement. That is when we finally got the cables all sent to the White House—all the intelligence directed there. The Joint Chiefs had also let him down. They didn't like the operation, but they didn't say, "This is crazy."

Lloyd Cutler   One of problems at the end of the Bay of Pigs was to get back our prisoners—all of the expatriates that were in there. Bobby was determined to get them out as an act of expiation. I was counsel to the pharmaceutical companies; the Trade Associations and Lou Oberdorfer [Louis F. Oberdorfer, assistant attorney general, Tax Division] came to me with this idea of ransoming the prisoners, in effect, with gifts of medical supplies to the Cubans, and Bobby took a very direct part in that. I assembled a group of pharmaceutical executives and brought them down to the Justice Department, and Bobby exhorted them, and raised the antitrust questions involved. He needed a tax ruling that if we gave this stuff, its value would be deductible for tax purposes, and that the government was, in effect, blessing what today we would regard as the paying of a ransom. And Bobby just drove right through, and he got it done. He was an action person.

John Patterson   I learned a lesson: If President Bush called me up today and said, "Now, John, I want you to do something for me," I'd say, "What is it? Let's talk about it." It wouldn't have been, "Yes, sir!" I was at the White House some time after that, having lunch—Lyndon Johnson was there—and Kennedy said to me, "I hope I live long enough to some-day do something to recognize what those four boys from Alabama did for their country." But our government never recognized them.

George Wallace   Since they started it, they should have gone through with it, because they abandoned those people who got killed from Alabama. The Alabama National Guard generals went and did it.

I went to a funeral about five or six years ago of a man they kept in Cuba twenty years. They could have sent his body back before then. I don't think they [the Kennedys] should have backed down, since they committed them and helped get them all killed.

Ralph Dungan That was a terrible jolt for the president. Jesus—he took more personally than I thought he should the loss of those lives—both those killed and taken prisoner. We were down in Miami the weekend before he was assassinated—I happened to go along because Goodwin was writing a speech and the "Mafia" didn't trust Dick; they were fearful that he would write something that would go too far, so I was sent along to keep an eye on that one. The meeting the president had with the Bay of Pigs veterans was very moving: Even at that stage the president felt very strongly about it, and so did Bobby, because they really felt they were the responsible guys.

Manuel Ray I participated in the investigation that was held in May, concerning the failure of the operation. This was the group that included Maxwell Taylor, Robert Kennedy, and Allen Dulles. The amount of misinformation they discovered was incredible. I mentioned to them the case of the presence of the brigade of the murderers who worked for Batista; I mentioned the case of El Morto. Dulles asked me, "Are you sure of that?" I said, "Yes, I am." He told me, "Don't you believe they had him in jail before the operation and then put him on television and claimed he came on the invasion?" I said, "No. I knew when he joined the brigade, and I protested this as a Cuban." Imagine at that time, after the failure of the operation, that Dulles was still saying someone like El Morto had not participated in the invasion but had been in jail in Cuba beforehand—that type of misinformation, at that level.

Arthur Schlesinger, Jr. Taylor was a very effective military politician—a very nice man. He was brought in as a buffer between the president and the chiefs. After Taylor's time in the White House, Kennedy had confidence in him and made him chairman of the Joint Chiefs, but he didn't follow Taylor's advice in the missile crisis; Taylor wanted to attack the missiles.

The CIA was a somewhat different problem. He liked Dick Bissell; we all did. I had lunch with Dick Helms soon after the Bay of Pigs, and he, for the first time, made it clear to me how little the CIA had been brought into this expedition. Allen and Dick Bissell had held the thing so closely that even someone like Dick Helms, who was deputy director for plans, didn't know. The deputy director for intelligence was never officially informed. We did not realize it had been held this tightly at CIA. We assumed that these various branches of the agency had had their own chances to comment on the plan.

The president decided that the CIA had to be reorganized. He liked Dulles and Bissell, so he wanted to do that as gracefully as possible. He brought in John McCone, who was a top manager, and he brought in Clark Clifford as a member—and later chairman—of the president's Foreign Intelligence Advisory Board.

George Carver There was a great deal of scurrying, because it was not considered good form to let it get out that a reversal in the Oval Office, done for domestic political reasons and to protect Adlai Stevenson, had condemned the brigade to death. Therefore the word was that the military planning was awful; it was everybody else's fault. The fault was John Fitzgerald and Robert Kennedy's—by playing soldier and opting to switch things. The Oval Office makes a wretched command post. Whenever you try to use it as such, you usually engender disaster. That was one of the problems with the Iranian operation when we tried to pull the hostages out. You don't run an operation like that with a bunch of civilians playing war.

Sergei Khrushchev The Bay of Pigs was the defending of revolution—of the first socialist country in the West. It was the first victory in the West. It was heroes in the minds of all Soviet people. Castro was, of course, especially after the Bay of Pigs, twice a hero. He was given decorations of a hero of the Soviet Union. It was not only my father's decision but that of the Soviet people.

15

The Vienna Summit

President Kennedy met with Soviet leader Nikita S. Khrushchev in Vienna, June 3–4, 1961. The U.S.–Soviet summit took place approximately one year after a scheduled Eisenhower-Khrushchev meeting was derailed due to the downing by the Soviets of an American U-2 reconnaissance aircraft.

Martin Hillenbrand   It became evident fairly early that a summit meeting with Khrushchev was going to be on the agenda. We were involved in the preparatory work for that summit, and in connection with that I can recall several meetings in the White House to brief the president on what he might expect, although most of the briefing obviously was done in the form of memoranda which we drafted in the Office of German Affairs and then sent up to the secretary of state, and it was under his name that the memoranda would go over to the White House.

Dean Rusk   Secretaries of state generally are quite reluctant about summit meetings and usually insist on thorough preparation before you go into a summit. There's always some danger in having the court of last resort come into session. When the two heads of government meet, then there's no one to refer things back to, to get advice from back home. That creates a danger. I still shiver when I think of the possibility of what might have happened had Kennedy and Khrushchev met personally during the Cuban missile crisis. That could have allowed the situation to get completely out of control.

Viktor Sukhodrev   Nothing had been prepared, like a draft treaty or agreement, whether on arms control or anything else. Nothing had been hammered out prior. There had been no series of expert meetings, in short, leading up to the summit. So I don't think that really anybody could have—those who were in on the preparatory period—no one really expected any specific agreements to come out of that meeting.

Sergei Khrushchev   My father never thought it was possible to change the policy of the country in a large sense because there was a change of presidents, even if the president was weak, because it was the policy of the country.

He thought it was possible to talk with President Kennedy like a new person in the White House, like a president of the other party, because behind Eisenhower was not only the spirit of Camp David but was the U-2 incident. It now was easier to talk because you do not need to talk about what had happened in the past. He was disappointed though, because before the Vienna meeting the Bay of Pigs had occurred, and the Americans would not be talking as those who saw things from victory's eyes. He did feel it was possible to make decisions about Berlin, because from his point of view it was not a retreat for the U.S.—there were two German countries. Now you had to make the status quo. These two countries must have borders.

McGeorge Bundy   It was a very serious meeting, and it gave Kennedy a very real feeling that he had a crisis over Berlin that he would have to cope with; that was not exactly a surprise. It was a disappointment, because you always hope things will come out better than your average estimate.

Martin Hillenbrand   As we began to prepare for the Vienna summit, we came into more intimate contact with the president and the way he operated. I think we were generally impressed that this was not a man who was going to be a pushover for Khrushchev. And that's the way it turned out.

Yuri Barsukov   The meeting in Vienna was a surprise for Khrushchev. Apparently he didn't expect that he would find in John Kennedy such an inexperienced politician. Apparently Khrushchev didn't take John

Kennedy very seriously after their personal confrontation in Vienna, and that's why there was a period of some negative influence of that meeting on Soviet-American relations. That was some kind of surprise for Soviet officials.

Viktor Sukhodrev   Kennedy had narrowly won the election—won over Nixon, who was much more known as a personality, perhaps an evil personality in the eyes of some. But Nixon was nonetheless a well-known politician. Kennedy in the eyes of many was a kind of an upstart. There were many people in this country who wrote that he was too young, he was from this aristocratic family, that he couldn't really represent the man in the street in America or the less fortunate, coming from that family as he did. Of course a lot of that was reflected, written about, quoted in the Soviet press as well.

So there was that kind of a guarded attitude to this new, young, unknown man who had suddenly been elevated to the presidency. And Khrushchev was trying to measure him up, to take his bearings. So in any event, however, the entire tenor of the conversation was—they didn't raise their voices, it wasn't a slanging match, and that has to be, I think, understood from the very start. But at the same time there was no proper chemistry. They really didn't latch on to each other constructively.

Dean Rusk   They could have gotten into a slanging match. Khrushchev was a very impulsive kind of fellow. He was a dedicated communist. He was eloquent, vulgar. He used figures of speech frequently to make his point. For example, he once said that Berlin was the testicles of the West, and when he wanted to make the West scream, he just squeezed on Berlin. Well, that was, unfortunately, a rather accurate metaphor.

Kennedy was disturbed by Khrushchev's manner—his obvious feeling that he could somehow bluff or intimidate this young new president of the United States. That disturbed Kennedy as much as the substance of the ultimatum on Berlin. So he was quite disturbed about the way the summit ended.

Viktor Sukhodrev   When Khrushchev asked Kennedy how old he was, and Kennedy told him, Khrushchev rather wistfully said, "Oh, my son would have been that age, but he was killed in the war." Now a lot has been written about that particular exchange. Kennedy didn't like it. He thought that Khrushchev was looking down on Kennedy as a kid. But knowing Khrushchev, I don't think he really meant it that way. It was—I think the proper word to characterize it is wistfully. He was thinking about his son. He was not trying to downgrade Kennedy. There was no outward expression of disdain. In short, it was a very civilized get-together.

There was no chemistry in that, I think, again, from a vantage point of many other Soviet-American summit meetings that I attended, that this one was not properly prepared. Basically I would think that the reason for that lies in the personality of Khrushchev. He was a man who liked to do things off the cuff. He didn't like fixed agendas. He was not organized for that kind of work. He would go into—this applied to many other meetings—a meeting and just play it by ear.

Khrushchev always thought that he could do his sort of thing, that he could make friends and influence people. It didn't always work, but that's what he thought. Perhaps that was one of the reasons why he didn't like fixed agendas; he thought that was too bureaucratic, and he would leave that to the diplomats, to Gromyko to talk over technical things. He wanted just to have a wide-ranging discussion, and he would go off on a tangent, catching hold of a phrase uttered by the other man. He'd sometimes go off on a tangent which would more often than not just lead to nowhere. That was why there were no specific results from that meeting other than a general agreement on Laos.

Martin Hillenbrand The last meeting between the two principals was a private meeting with only interpreters present and the American delegation, as I remember very well—this took place in the residence of the American ambassador—we were standing around outside the door wondering what was happening.

And then Kennedy came out. I think his face was paler than normal. He obviously gave the impression of someone who was somewhat shaken. Then, of course, we quickly learned that in fact Khrushchev had threatened and said, "If you do that there will be war." Then Kennedy had responded, "I believe then there will be war." When he came out he said, "This is going to be a long, cold winter."

I think the idea that somehow or other the president had received a blow to his psychological solar plexus is a correct interpretation of his reaction. On the other hand I think we came to the conclusion that Khrushchev, who obviously entered this conference thinking he could bully a young, inexperienced American president who had already been involved in the Bay of Pigs fiasco, came out of this meeting much more impressed with Kennedy's ability to stand up to bullying and his ultimate firmness in that concluding session between the two. I and, I think, others there were impressed that the president had stood up well under this attempt to put him under intense pressure. But we also knew we were facing a long hard summer, even before the long cold winter came. Of course, at that time we didn't know the Berlin Wall would be going up within a few months after Vienna.

VIENNA'S AFTERMATH

Martin Hillenbrand   It was quite clear, I think, to all of us upon returning from Vienna that the president was now personally involved in the Berlin crisis in a way which made it the single most important item on his plate.

Viktor Sukhodrev   I think that Khrushchev thought that he could be a better judge of whomever he was meeting than any ambassador in the field—that he could size up a person in a much better way than any diplomatic bureaucrat could. So that's what he wanted to do, and I'm afraid that he came away with not too good an impression of President Kennedy. I don't think he thought that Kennedy could be a match for him. I think he came away with the feeling that the guy was inexperienced, perhaps not up to the task of properly running a country such as the United States. And I think that led to some, perhaps, wrong judgments in Soviet policies, subsequently.

16

The Berlin Crisis

The issue of the status of Berlin—located one hundred miles inside the then-Soviet-controlled region designated the German Democratic Republic—had been discussed at length by President Kennedy and Premier Khrushchev during the Vienna Summit.

At that time Khrushchev had insisted that the World War II Allies— the United States, United Kingdom, France, and the USSR—sign a peace treaty with East Germany. If the Allies refused to do so, he said that by the end of 1961, he would sign a separate treaty—one that would not guarantee Western access to Berlin.

President Kennedy rejected the Soviet demand, and the stage was set for U.S.–Soviet confrontation.

Willy Brandt   Berlin as a whole was under Four Power responsibility, and most of us—I have rarely had my doubts—most of my fellow citizens felt that this meant the Russians couldn't just do with East Berlin as they wanted. It was clear that since '48, under that roof of the Four Power responsibility, it had been stated that the sector commandants had the responsibility for their part of Berlin and the three Western powers had come together to a certain degree. Still, most of us found it difficult to accept that the Russians, in contradiction to the Four Power status, just could authorize the East German authorities to split off their part of Berlin and, in a way, this meant that the Russians had handed over responsibility to a factor that was not part of the Four Power agreement—the East German military and government. So from a legal point of view, the Western powers could have been authorized to say they took over a vacuum, but this would not have led very far. I mean, how far could they have moved? What kind of conflict could this have resulted in?

But what I felt was that this move on the Eastern side could have been used as an argument for bringing about a negotiation on what does the Four Power status for Berlin now mean. I remember rather a short time before the wall came up, there was a kind of summit in Paris of the three Western governments, and the Federal Republic was present there, and I tried to convince them to raise this question, to force the Russians into a negotiation about what the Four Power status would mean. The Federal Republic was against this, so there we are back at my observation from the earlier part of our conversation: The Federal Republic did not like it. This was one part of the background.

The other part had to do with wishful thinking on the German side and perhaps not enough clear expression of what the Western powers could do and could not do. You remember the NATO meeting in Norway in the spring of 1961, when it was said in rather clear terms that the Western Allies would defend West Berlin if necessary. On the German side, especially in Berlin, one didn't listen carefully enough to this. One lived still with the illusion that there was a kind of coresponsibility, not only on paper. This then led to a good deal of confusion.

Martin Hillenbrand   The crisis over Berlin had been going on since November of '58, and everyone knew that our conventional military position in Berlin—and that of our French and British allies—was indefensible against a major Soviet offensive against the city, so that the protective veil that the three Allies, particularly, of course, the U.S., hung over the city was essentially that if the Soviets initiated either an attack or brought Berlin under such pressure that it could not endure, the ultimate security of the city—and of what we had defined as our vital interest—lay in a nuclear response. That was always the hidden—perhaps not-so-hidden—premise of the American, British, and French position. The fact that you did have a danger of escalation, in my view, was the principal reason the Soviets, despite all of their verbal attacks on the city, and the threats and the ultimata and so on that they issued, ultimately were deterred from executing any of these threats, and they always accepted the delaying tactics we tried to impose as a better course than actually moving against our position.

Of course, they had had the previous experience of the attempted blockade of the city in '48 ... and the airlift that was mounted in '48–'49, so they knew that an attempt to fundamentally destroy access to the city could be deferred at least by another airlift, and we, of course, had over the years built up vast reserves of bulk items in Berlin, and they knew that, so that they couldn't in effect starve the city out in a short period of time, as they thought they could have done in 1948, if it had not been for the airlift.

Dean Rusk   One has to keep in mind the characteristics of Mr. Khrushchev; he was a very volatile man, a very unpredictable man. He was capable of impulsive action for the good or the bad. I mean he was the one who opened the way for the nuclear test ban treaty of 1963 by recommending a partial test ban treaty. But on the other hand, he was responsible for putting missiles in Cuba and for creating the Berlin crisis of '61–'62.

In April 1961 President Kennedy called on Dean Acheson, secretary of state in the Truman administration, to draft memorandums on the Berlin situation.

Martin Hillenbrand   The Acheson memoranda were never endorsed as such by the department. While he had his office in the State Department, he was not speaking for the department; he was speaking for himself as an individual asked by the president to make recommendations. But somehow or other there was always the confusion in the minds of some of these people as to what the two Acheson memoranda actually represented.

I personally had a great deal of respect for Dean Acheson. I used to have lunch with him at the Metropolitan Club from time to time to discuss the Berlin crisis—this was apart from his specific role in 1961. We did feel probably that Acheson was a desirable counterbalance to the rather soft attitudes that some people in the White House were taking, even though some of the specific recommendations that Acheson made in his two memoranda we felt were too aggressive.

Willy Brandt   I met Acheson when I was in the States for the first time in '54 before I became mayor of Berlin, and he, of course, was a most remarkable man. But he did not believe at all that during his time, and perhaps even for a generation following, that there would be any chance for a change in things as they were. So he regarded it—if I remember correctly—he regarded it being almost a ridiculous thing to believe that Germany could become one state again. He thought that this division would be something for much more than one generation, leaving open what might come in the distant future. So there was a different approach. Kennedy himself believed much more in possible changes, much more than Acheson did.

Martin Hillenbrand   Henry Kissinger was also brought down from Harvard for a brief period, but then left, and I think he would agree that some people in the White House—not that they were prepared to give away Berlin—were advocating a procedure which might very well have led, if not to the loss of Berlin, then at least to the collapse of Berlin morale.

On July 25, 1961, in a nationally televised address, the president told the American people: "Berlin has become the great testing place of Western will and courage."

In the early part of August 1961, thousands of East Germans fled to the western part of Berlin, and on August 13, the Soviet authorities in East Berlin erected a high wall—topped by barbed wire—dividing the city.

Martin Hillenbrand   We didn't expect it when it came. I was sitting on an island off the coast of Georgia. I had come back from Paris, and after two months of intensive activity I was pretty well exhausted. So I took off with my family. I received a phone call from Foy Kohler telling me to get back to Washington, that a wall had been erected in Berlin separating the Western sectors from the Soviet sector of the city.

I came back to Washington a couple of days after the wall had actually been erected, so I was not directly involved in the immediate reaction.

Richard Helms   We provided a lot of intelligence information about the Berlin crisis—the wall and all the rest of it. I picked up a book about the Berlin wall—a big, thick book—in which in two places the author said that I had underestimated what was going on and that I had been rather cavalier in saying, Why would anybody expect us to predict that they were going to put up a wall? That is nonsense. The decision to put up the Berlin wall was made from one day to the next, by Honecker, as I recall. Now, we didn't have any agent sitting in Honecker's lap, nor did we have anybody inside his head. I think it would have been very difficult to have found out about a decision he hadn't even made until he made it, and went ahead and put the wall up, so I don't feel any discomfort about that. God did not give me the gift of prescience, and anybody who thinks we are going to be able to run an intelligence organization inside the head of every chief of state in the world is suffering from delusions.

Willy Brandt   There was a good deal of fear in the city. People didn't realize that what was going on; it was terrible, from many points of view—one had the other part of one's family on the other isde and shatnot. But they did not realize that it did not mean that one had to expect a Russian or East German invasion into West Berlin. This was part of the thing.

Then there was the other element—that most people did not understand that within the decisions taken before, the Western powers could not move, so what could one do then? One could bring together a crowd of people, one of the biggest meetings we've had, on the sixteenth, in front of the city hall, and there one could say I've sent a letter to the president of the United States to express our concern. And if you look into that paper, the kind of proposals I make express what I call helplessness. This happens in a situation like this. You do something which looks like an action and in reality isn't much more than a piece of public relations.

Martin Hillenbrand   Willy Brandt's reaction was that somehow or other we had fallen short of taking the necessary steps to react against the wall. I discussed this with him on a number of occasions, years later, and I always had the impression that, somehow or other, his confidence in the U.S. was weakened and that some of the things he later did and said were partially attributable to his disappointment at the American reaction, even though, as I have pointed out to both Brandt and Egon Bahr [official in Brandt's government] on occasion, if they had read carefully the diplomatic exchanges, and particularly the president's speech after his return from Vienna, his first speech after the note—the response to the aide-mémoire—had gone forward: that we had never claimed that it was a vital interest of the U.S. to prevent action in East Berlin which was contrary to the basic Four Power agreements. We had always spelled out our vital interests as affecting our position and the position of the British and the French in West Berlin and the access to the city, and it was never our intention to move military force into East Berlin under any circumstances. So the idea that, somehow or other, we should, with our meager tank force and bulldozer equipment, have knocked down the wall—with twenty-one Soviet divisions in the neighborhood—would have been utter futility, in my view.

They could simply have rebuilt the wall. Had we knocked down a portion, they could have built it a hundred feet further in the rear. We would have been faced with an endless progression. That never made much sense to me, but I recognized that in Brandt's own thinking about the reliability of American protection, because after all we were the major nuclear power here, that somehow or other we had fallen short. This is a case where our planning and the logic of our position as specifically spelled out in diplomatic exchanges, and in the presidential speech, fell far short of what the Germans, and particularly Willy Brandt—I can't say the same of Adenauer—expected of us, although Brandt was never very specific at the time or subsequently in spelling out exactly what he wanted us to do.

Willy Brandt   Kennedy was absolutely right when he said—I don't remember now the occasion or the date—that nobody advised him to take military action against the erection of the wall. And when he said nobody gave him that advice, he included my name: "Not even the mayor of Berlin did," which is true.

Responding to the erection of the wall, President Kennedy sent fifteen hundred troops over the autobahn to bolster the U.S. garrison in West Berlin. The president also sent Vice President Johnson to the city to reassure its citizens of the American resolve that they should remain free. In addition, the president dispatched Gen. Lucius Clay, a hero of the 1948 airlift, as his personal emissary to the city.

McGeorge Bundy   The wall was a shock to morale in Berlin—to everybody from Brandt on down. We didn't respond to that overnight; it took us three or four days to send reinforcements—to send the vice president. But if some in Germany think we should have made war out of it, I think that's a lot of nonsense. And we did get there on time. It's worth noting that we were a little quicker in reacting than the chancellor of the Federal Republic, who might have been thought to have been closer to the problem. Certainly the citizens of Berlin did not hold it against Kennedy—as we all know from what happened when he went there.

William Colby   Khrushchev felt he could crowd Kennedy, so Kennedy had to stand up to him. That was what the mobilization in Berlin was all about. Khrushchev was a very elemental guy. He thought, If I just snarl at him, he'll get frightened. He did get frightened, and then decided he'd have to do something about it.

Richard Helms   I don't think that President Kennedy had any intention of trying to start World War III, and I think that it could have been very dicey if we had put a lot of troops in there to face the Red Army. They had a lot of forces in East Germany, and they could have put up one hell of a battle. Anything that would have brought that on would have been a big mistake, just as I thought that Kennedy was prudent in not bombing Cuba when the missiles showed up there.

Martin Hillenbrand   You know, after the wall was built, and after the foreign ministers' meeting in Paris, with the consent of President Kennedy, who agreed to calling up the reserves and augmenting the troops in both Berlin and West Germany and asking the Congress for more money for a military buildup, the State Department position—and obviously as secretary, Dean Rusk took this position—was that we should at the same time explore whether there was any possibility of meaningful negotiations.

And so, for over year, he conducted with Foreign Minister Gromyko, both in New York during the GA [General Assembly] sessions and also in Geneva, on a number of occasions he explored—the designated description of these talks was "exploratory talks to determine whether a basis for negotiations exists." Now this had seemed to me, and in the State

Department, the logical way to go about handling the thing—that this was one way of deferring any ultimative execution on the part of the Soviets. We gained time and eventually, after the Cuban missile crisis, even though threats to our position in Berlin continued, the Berlin crisis gradually faded away.

So the delaying tactics which Dean Rusk executed with Foreign Minister Gromyko turned out to be effective. But it is true that the White House, some of the people there and some of the people in the State Department who had come down with the Kennedy administration—and I exclude completely Dean Rusk from this category—were prepared to make major concessions in the course of the negotiations they were advocating, which I, Foy Kohler [assistant secretary of state for European affairs], and Dean Rusk felt would be giving away the store. First of all, these people were basically not well versed in what had happened during the Eisenhower administration, and they never came up with a detailed plan as to what our position in our negotiations would be. They were merely seeking negotiations in order to avoid what they feared would be a confrontation, and they were quite opposed to the recommendations that Dean Acheson made in his memoranda, which were, in effect, to test the Soviet will by running convoys through and so on. That whole summer of intense diplomacy, certainly from my point of view almost the most intense in which I've ever been involved, has never been fully recorded.

Alexei Adzhubei   Marshal Koniev [Ivan Stepanovich Koniev] came to see Khrushchev and told him that the Americans would succeed; the gun was loaded, and Khrushchev was scared. He was silent for a long time, and then he said, "Let our tanks go away." But Koniev said, "They will get through," and Khrushchev said, "I don't think so." The American tanks stayed for an hour more, and then they went away. Everybody had to observe the balance between the political structures. Kennedy had his generals, and Khrushchev had his.

VICE PRESIDENT JOHNSON'S AND GENERAL CLAY'S VISITS

Willy Brandt   I think Johnson's visit, under the given conditions, was a very successful one—again, more from the public relations view. Berliners got the impression that if the vice president comes, looks at things, discusses things, this means we can be sure the United States will not let us down.

Of course he was very able in making contact with people. The fact that the vice president was there in West Berlin, in a way to welcome the Americans when they came in on the autobahn, that he went to the big refugee camp that we had and spoke to the people who had just come from East Berlin and East Germany, was a most effective way of counteracting this feeling of uncertainty which was spreading during these days following August 13.

Martin Hillenbrand   This was something unprecedented internationally. I can't remember any previous situation which even vaguely duplicated the building of a wall to stop a massive outflow of refugees. Of course I think the initial reaction was perhaps not sufficient to meet the problem of Berlin morale. That's why Vice President Johnson was sent there to demonstrate great concern at the highest levels of the U.S. government. Other morale-building actions were taken in order to impress the Berliners that we still cared.

I think on the whole, despite some rather peculiar peripheral china-purchasing activities on the part of the vice president—who had an avid desire wherever he went to acquire china—apart from that, I think his visit did contribute to the partial restoration of Berlin morale.

My deputy, Frank Cash, accompanied Vice President Johnson on the trip to Berlin. I think the atmosphere was mixed. The overt expression was to condemn this iniquitous wall, which was totally inhumane, totally contrary to international practice, and so on.

But I think there was also a feeling on the part of some, which could not be expressed, obviously, because of the effect it would have had on Berlin morale, that the Berlin Wall, despite its iniquitous appearance and the iniquitous concept it expressed, did relieve some of the pressure, from the Soviet and East German point of view.

Willy Brandt   Sending Clay meant a way to signal a grand coalition on the question of defending West Berlin, and I think it was understood this way. Berliners loved General Clay in a way. He himself was a very communicative person, and in the eyes of Berliners, even Germans, he was the man who, one remembered, had organized the airlift. And a year later, he came back and brought the Freedom Bell to Berlin. A big crowd was there at the time. So he was in a way regarded as the man who had worked so West Berliners could survive.

Martin Hillenbrand   We felt concern that Clay was not the right man in the right place, even though we had a great deal of respect for Clay's performance as head of military government in the formative period prior to the existence of the FRG. I had been in Germany during the early years after the war and respected Clay. He provided the kind of leadership and firmness that we needed in those early years. But we also knew that Clay took certain positions then which, translated into the scene in 1961, might very well be out of tempo with the general approach which we thought was desirable—the Rusk approach, the idea of delaying talks, stretching out talks with the Soviets as long as we could in order to eliminate any ultimative threat.

Some in the State Department felt that this was not necessarily a wise thing to do, that General Clay might turn out to be somewhat of a loose cannon on an empty deck, which of course was not contrary to the way things actually turned out.

My own impression was that after Clay got there and went into action, the president quickly came to regret having sent him there, but could not really withdraw him without a decent interval of time passing, because Clay had been sent there as a morale booster, as a prominent Republican who was now enrolled in the cause of protecting Berlin, so there was no way of getting him out until Clay made the mistake of the tank confrontation, which not only worried Washington but also incensed General Norstad [Lauris Norstad, supreme commander, NATO forces] and General Bruce Clark [commander, U.S. forces, Europe]. They felt that Clay, without any military command authority, was attempting to use American forces, without even consulting the commanding generals.

On June 28, 1963, President Kennedy further demonstrated the U.S. government's commitment to Berlin by visiting the city himself and addressing a massive crowd in front of the city hall.

Martin Hillenbrand   By '63 I was already in Germany as deputy chief of mission. It was absolutely part of the required drill that the high-level visitor go to Berlin and repeat the American commitment to the protection of the city. Failure to do that would have been an enormous blow to Berlin morale, so it was automatically assumed that when Kennedy came to the Federal Republic, a visit to Berlin would have to be part of the visit.

Every subsequent president has been in exactly the same position. The problem that we have always faced—parenthetically, I might add this—with subsequent presidents was that Kennedy's visit to both West Germany and to Berlin was such a triumphal thing that subsequent presidents have always felt somehow or other they had to duplicate it at least.

Willy Brandt   I then called it one of the greatest days in the history of that city. I wonder if there has been any other occasion after the end of the war when so many people were in the streets and felt involved in this event. Today perhaps I would add November 1989. There was nothing in between which in a way had the same importance as far as the involvement of the people was concerned. The fact that Adenauer also came of course was important, even if it was a short time before Adenauer left his office here in Bonn.

Angier Biddle Duke   Berlin was so thrilling; it was one of the most exciting periods of my life. There was sparring between Willy Brandt and Konrad Adenauer over where each of them would sit in relation to President Kennedy. Under American protocol the most important person is on the right, and the next most important person is on the left, and the least important person is on the extreme left. Under German protocol you go: One, two, three. We were going to have to decide whether German or American protocol would be followed, and we weren't in Germany; we were in Berlin—in the American Zone. Willy Brandt said, "I am the mayor of Berlin and the number one person here, and I get to sit next to the president under American protocol." Somehow this got back to Adenauer. He said, "Fine," and it was quite amusing, because Brandt *did* get to sit next to the president, but five million people turned out—two and one-half million people on either side of the street—and Adenauer had two and a half million on his side of the street, the president had two and a half million on the other side, and Brandt, between them, was out of sight, so in winning he got lost.

We get to Checkpoint Charlie and get out a block ahead. We get out of our cars, and the press rushes up ahead, to the barricades—God, there must have been four hundred newspapermen!—and the president is to walk up to the tower of Checkpoint Charlie. As we get close to the end, there is a red-faced, enthusiastic guy in the press section—it was Bill Hearst [William Randolph Hearst, Jr.]—and he says, "Hiya, Jack!" and the president turns to him and says, "Why, it's Mr. Hearst!"

"ICH BIN EIN BERLINER"

Martin Hillenbrand The idea of the president's saying "Ich bin ein Berliner" was improvised on the flight up to Berlin, and there was some doubt as to whether Kennedy's German was equal to those four words.

Willy Brandt My own contribution to the speech was that before he went out—he was at my office at the city hall—he tried to get a reasonable pronunciation of the sentence, *"Ich bin ein Berliner."* Well, it was a moving thing. And he worked hard at it, at the pronunciation.

John Kenneth Galbraith When Kennedy went to Berlin and talked about himself as a Berliner, I thought this was unduly extravagant.

Martin Hillenbrand There's a tendency, obviously, when you have presidential visits which turn into media circuses, inevitably to attribute more historic importance to them than they necessarily may have ten years later. Certainly it seemed like the Kennedy visit was of intense historical significance in German American relations. Perhaps, in the light of hindsight, some of the consequences of that visit faded sooner in terms of German-American relations than we had expected at the time—of course we've had all sorts of crises since in German American relations. Nevertheless, of all the visits of American presidents that I've been involved with, either as a member of the American delegation or having been at the receiving end in an embassy, this was certainly the most spectacular, and perhaps—if spectacular is equivalent to successful—then it was also the most successful of presidential visits.

Willy Brandt Looking back at it now, of course it meant a good deal more than just Berlin. Especially his speech at the university which, in a way, took up the theme from his university speech of June 10, I think it was—his dealing with what he called the winds of change which went beyond the Iron Curtain—all this went a good deal beyond the question of taking care of West Berlin and was the source of a good deal of hope. Of course nobody then could know that he only had a few months more ahead of him.

ASSESSING THE MAGNITUDE OF THE CRISIS

Martin Hillenbrand   The Berlin crisis could have escalated if the Soviets had taken action to induce escalation in a way that could ultimately have involved a fundamental decision on the use of nuclear weapons. Fortunately it never came to that. The way it turned out, despite all the static coming from members of the Kennedy team in the White House, and a few of them planted in the State Department, it was handled in about as good a way as one could have expected. The decisions that the president made were part of a coherent process of decision making within the government, even though his style obviously was completely different than that of President Eisenhower, who provided a kind of reassurance that a man like Kennedy simply couldn't provide.

Yuri Barsukov   It looks like Khrushchev at that time was acting more decisively than John Kennedy, because there was a big risk that could lead to direct confrontation in Europe between the Soviet Union and Western powers. My feeling is that the risk was quite big, so that's why I think Khrushchev gambled.

But fortunately both leaders apparently realized that it was a very serious issue and found a solution.

Richard Helms   It was a very tense period; there's no doubt about it. On the other hand, I think the Cuban missile crisis was tenser.

17

The Cuban Missile Crisis

THE PRELUDE

Norbert Schlei The very first thing I was asked to do when I joined the department was when the attorney general called me in and said, "I want you to write a memorandum for the president about what the United States could do as a matter of international law if the Soviet Union put missiles in Cuba. As far as we know they don't have any, but there has been a lot of talk about it and we would like to make a warning statement. Before we make the statement, we'd better figure out what we could do if they disregard it. We would like to know what the lay of the land is." So I started to work on a memorandum. I am the originator of the quarantine concept that the president used, although *quarantine* was his own word. I did the memorandum during August, and it was circulated just before the Labor Day weekend. I met with Dean Rusk and Nicholas Katzenbach on Labor Day to talk about it, and in early September the president did make a warning statement to the Soviet Union.

A blockade is an absolute bar to traffic; you stop everything—medicines or food or whatever. It seemed to me that that was hard to justify; what we were justified in blocking was offensive weaponry. So I proposed a partial blockade that would only stop offensive weaponry and let everything else go by. I called it "visit and search blockade." I argued that this would be justified because the essence of self-defense is proportionality: you may do something that is proportional to the threat. So if someone is simply creating a threat by putting in missiles, it's hard to justify bombing, because you are meeting a potential threat by inflicting actual harm to the person who is presenting the threat. I also said that it would be infinitely easier to justify taking action if we did it in the name of the Organization of American States, so we would not just take a unilateral act. The president took that advice, and the quarantine was imposed by the OAS.

We had a meeting with the president in the Cabinet Room to discuss the warning statement. He said, "Why don't you get something together for me and I'll look at it." So Bundy took us all downstairs to his office and we sat around for an hour or two, kicking around the language, and eventually a statement was arrived at. Then Bundy took it to the president, who released it at his press conference later in the day.

On Sunday, October 14, 1962, a U-2 reconnaissance aircraft flown by Air Force Maj. Rudolph Anderson, Jr., over western Cuba, brought back photographic evidence of medium-range ballistic missile sites. This information was conveyed to President Kennedy by McGeorge Bundy on Tuesday morning.

Ray Cline On the afternoon of the fifteenth, I asked our staff to check the photo information out twice. I felt everything was going to hit the fan the next morning, so I asked the staff to make sure they were absolutely right. They called me late in the afternoon to say, "We are absolutely sure we are right. We don't have all the photographs yet, but by the morning we will have it all organized."

Strangely enough, I had a meeting with British, Canadian, Australian, and New Zealand intelligence officers; I was their host as the DDI.° So we had a big party—from about five to seven—in the CIA, at Langley. I managed to conceal all this information from them. The fact that we had this party caused me not to get home until about nine o'clock. While technically we could have called the White House on the secure phone, that isn't the way things work. I went home and called Mac Bundy. We did it very cryptically over the telephone, but he knew exactly what I was saying.

I had McCone's deputy tell McNamara, who was also at a party. I had two teenage daughters at the time, and they were listening to my call to Bundy, and one daughter came out and said, "Dad, where are

°Deputy director, intelligence, CIA.

these missiles? Are they in China or Cuba?" I said, "Don't say anything about it; they are in Cuba."

Bundy's reaction was to support the president. He felt Kennedy was going to get mad and get even. What I recall is that Bundy said he thought there might be a crisis over Berlin. He felt that if the Russians are putting missiles in Cuba, they want to change the balance of power, and they want to force us out of Berlin. Of course, this didn't happen, mainly because Khrushchev had to retreat.

Richard Helms The agency provided a constant stream of information about the sighting of missiles in Cuba and what was going on there, not only from agents but from defectors and deserters. We had a camp down in Opa-Locka, Florida, where we interviewed all these people that came out of Cuba, and then, after much persuading, the president permitted a U-2 flight* and located the missile site being built in San Cristóbal province. Then the analysts took the photographs, and they found a manual that we had gotten from [Col. Oleg] Penkovsky† when he was an agent of ours, and it was the manual for this particular missile; it had actual drawings of how they set up the missile sites. This information gave the president a few days to work out some kind of solution. I don't think the president would have dared to announce to the American people that there was a missile sitting in Cuba ready to fire on the domestic United States; they would have run him out of town. He would have had to send the Air Force in there to take out the whole installation, so these few days were very important to him. That piece of intelligence analysis was a very important turning point in the whole crisis.

Edwin Martin The Monday night that the photographic proof came in, I was giving a speech to correspondents at the National Press Club on Cuba-Soviet relations. I had cleared my speech very carefully with Defense and the White House. I said we did not think the Soviets, who had never put nuclear missiles in Eastern Europe, would do so way off in Cuba, where they couldn't really control their use. While I was answering a question, I was called to the phone. It was Roger Hilsman. He said, "We have seen those films, and there is a meeting in the Cabi-

---

*On Sunday, October 14.
†A Soviet military intelligence officer who, during a year and a half in the early 1960s, turned over key date to the CIA until he was arrested and then executed in the USSR.

net Room tomorrow at ten." Then I had to go back in and answer questions.

Ray Cline I insisted that Bobby Kennedy go out to our photo center. I said, "You must see these films. They are clear; you can blow them up indefinitely, but doing prints is not so good, so go see them." So he did. He came over to the photo center and he said, "Well, we weren't absolutely sure what the hell was going on, but you convinced us that we are doing the right thing." I think the Kennedys readily accepted the photographs because they were photographs. What we did in the photo center was to label things. We'd say "medium-range missile," but if you didn't see the label on the photograph, you wouldn't know what it was. In the photographs, the missiles looked like logs—all scattered around. Both Bobby and Jack said, "The CIA must be telling us the truth."

Raymond Garthoff, special assistant for Soviet bloc politicol-military affairs, Department of State In the politicol-military bureau we were involved from a point several days into the crisis, on the NATO side and evaluating the Soviet reaction. I was accidentally involved in it from the first day on because on the first morning, when the president was being told, I happened to be over at the CIA—the office of the deputy director of intelligence—helping them prepare material on Warsaw Pact forces.

In that connection Ray Cline had told me there was something new that I ought to see. So I told his executive assistant that Ray had just said there was something new in that I ought to see. The only thing that was new that he thought of were the photographs of the missiles in Cuba, so he showed them to me. I went back to the department, and the only person that I told was Alexis Johnson, who already knew, but he went pale when I went in and asked him if he had heard about the missiles. I wasn't supposed to know. I explained to him how I happened to know, and assured him I wouldn't tell anyone else, and I didn't. At about that time, I got a call from Ray Cline's assistant at the agency, asking whether I had told anyone. He said, "Don't tell anyone; you weren't supposed to know."

McGeorge Bundy I went over; it was the normal thing to do—you call up and ask, "Is the president awake?" and if you have something urgent, can you come over? You talk to the marine outside the president's door.

He asks the president, and he says, "Sure." I tell the president that the agency has told me that the U-2 pictures show missile sites. He says, "Well, what are we going to do? We have to do something." I think his first reaction was that we have to take them out. What does "take them out" mean? Some form of air attack. "But we're not going to decide anything right now. What we have to decide right now is what we are going to do. We will have a meeting, as soon as the agency people are ready." He tells me who ought to be in the meeting, and we're off on a terribly busy two-week course.

Norbert Schlei   When the Cuban missile crisis first arose, I was still down in Oxford, Mississippi. I came back late at night. I called the operator to see if I had any messages. I was astonished when she said, "Let me ring your office." The phone rang, and my assistant picked it up. I said, "Harold, what the hell are you doing in the office?" He said, "I can't tell you over the telephone." So I went into the office and he told me about the previous evening. They were at work on a revision of my original memorandum in relation to an actual rather than a hypothetical situation.

Gaylord Nelson   Bobby Kennedy was out in Wisconsin when this crisis was happening. We flew from Milwaukee to Green Bay to watch a Packer game. On the way there Bobby said, "What do you think about the Cuban situation?" I said, "As far as the public is concerned, the president is barely keeping up with the crowd. Public opinion is moving out ahead of him. The president should declare a belligerent blockade." Although he has been credited with supporting the blockade, he said, "No, no. It would be the worst thing you could do. The Russians would challenge it. What we really should do is make a strike—a huge strike, and knock 'em right out of business." In any event, that was Bobby's position at the Green Bay game before the president went ahead and put up the blockade.

The EXCOM

To deal with the crisis, perhaps the single event that best defines the manner in which the Kennedy presidency functioned, the chief executive convened an interdepartmental group of advisers and experts as a special committee of the National Security Council. This group, known as EXCOM—which met for the first time unofficially on October 16 and was formally constituted by the president on October 22—was responsible for the development and implementation of administration polity and strategy.

Roswell Gilpatric The president must have had in mind at the beginning how he was going to handle something like the missile crisis, because from all accounts and what Mac Bundy told me and others, when Mac Bundy woke him up Tuesday morning with the news of the discovery of the sites, Kennedy just reeled off the names of ten or twelve of us whom he wanted to come over to the White House that morning at eleven. He indicated to me that he was not going to get carried away with any feeling that this was a way to put the Soviets down—that we'd welcome a showdown. He seemed to be very cautious, very careful, and very deliberative. And he didn't, until the very end of our meetings, indicate what he was going to do. Whatever he may have felt inside, he didn't show his hand. He insisted until the very end on going through the ordeal of having to hear some of the military tell him that the only way to deal with this would be to bomb Cuba back to the Stone Age.

Raymond Garthoff I think the president was initially inclined to think that an air strike was necessary. After a couple of days he concluded one could apply some effective pressure through a blockade that wouldn't rule out escalating to an air strike and, if necessary, escalating beyond that to an invasion. The change in his thinking partly came about by the discussions in the EXCOM. While there were sharp divisions in the EXCOM, within a few days at least the alternatives were clearer, so I think his decision was influenced by the process. Now that doesn't mean that he ever intended to just abide by what a majority would come up with, and I think, as the process went forward, in addition to using it as a way of getting information and ideas out, that particularly through Bobby, he did in turn influence the EXCOM's thinking. He benefited from the exchange and hashing out of ideas, but I think a lot of it also was giving everyone a chance to vent his ideas and to feel he was participating.

Dean Rusk The president thought that it was well to let his principal subordinates—the secretaries of state, defense, national security adviser, people like that—meet on their own without his presence and debate these things among themselves as a matter of gaining a consensus among his chief advisers.

Ray Cline I attended most of the EXCOM meetings. I was not a member of EXCOM, but I was the chief intelligence officer presenting material to the EXCOM people. I could see, particularly in those first few days—we met in the State Department—that Dean Rusk was a little vague; he didn't seem to have very strong principles about dealing with them. Everyone changed their minds during the first few days.

Pierre Salinger President Kennedy created EXCOM because he did not want the American people to know about the crisis until he had made a decision, and also because he was involved in a political campaign, and if he had to leave Washington, it was useful to have the EXCOM continue to meet around the clock.

Walt Rostow The president had other things to do, but I also think he felt they should feel free to argue with each other. The process of EXCOM has not been well written up, because people's views changed: Monday was different from Tuesday, which was different from Wednesday. It was a dynamic human process. People worried, to different degrees, depending on how surprised they were that the Russians did it.

Richard Bissell Eisenhower was a great believer in having staff work done and problems packaged rather tidily and brought up to the boss to be resolved. In a way that's what Kennedy did, but the big difference between them was that Eisenhower liked to make it a tidy process; under Kennedy, there was more opportunity—and indeed, more incentive—for the individuals on EXCOM to say what they really thought, instead of trying to agree on a watered-down result. I think the procedure was a pretty good one.

Roswell Gilpatric He recognized from the beginning that there was this very basic cleavage, a split: what we referred to as the hawks and the doves. Initially, the hawks outnumbered the doves two to one; McNamara, Tommy [Llewellyn] Thompson, and I felt pretty lonely in the early days. I think the president felt that we all would express ourselves more freely and openly, and we'd be more likely to reach a common ground, if we had these brainstorming sessions without his presence. And since Bobby was there, not chairing the thing, not directing the discussion, but watching what everybody was doing—and I'm sure he kept a score on different people's attitudes—I think the president got the benefit of all he was looking for, which was a wide range of views. He may have made up his mind in advance on a particular subject, but he drilled himself— he disciplined himself—into listening to all these other viewpoints. That was particularly true in dealing with the uniformed people—the Joint Chiefs of Staff. There was a deliberate effort between the two brothers that we have these continuous sessions and try to reach a common ground, but that everybody's point of view be brought out, whether it was Acheson's—he was always a hawk; or Tommy Thompson's or Chip's [Charles E. Bohlen, State Department special assistant for Soviet affairs]. In the case of McNamara and myself, we both had the instinctive feeling that the minimum amount of military force that could be applied was all that should be brought into being. The idea of the quarantine or the blockade appealed to us because that was the lowest order of military activity we could envision as having the desired effect.

Richard Helms   You're always going to have something like an EXCOM. It comes under different names in different administrations; there is always an inner core of people who have to deal with these problems. In the Johnson administration, the people who made policy attended something called the Tuesday Lunch. In the Nixon administration, it tended to be Nixon, the chairman of the Joint Chiefs, Kissinger, and Haig, running the war in Vietnam. There's always a small group on the inside, for two reasons: One, the president wants to sit down with people day after day who know the facts; two, you want to have people there that you trust—and trust not to leak to the newspapers the minute they walk out of the office.

Ralph Dungan   President Kennedy probably didn't know what he was going to do until he had heard enough, particularly about the technical aspects. I do think that there was—with some of the guys—genuine consultation. I also believe—as is always the case in situations like that—you cover your arse; Johnson was a past master at that: in most decisions where he convened committees, he knew well in advance what the outcome would be, but he would cover himself. There was an element of that in EXCOM. And the president surely didn't want any of them going off the reservation later and saying, "Well, that wasn't *my* decision."

Donald Wilson   I got involved in the EXCOM the Thursday before the president's speech. Murrow was sick, so I was running the agency. There was a cabinet meeting, and I went in Murrow's place. Bob Kennedy came over to me and said, "Where's Ed?" I said, "Ed is sick; he is in New York." He asked, "When will he be back?" and I answered, "Probably not soon." So he asked me, "What are you doing this weekend?" I said, "I am going to visit my mother." He said, "Don't visit your mother; stick around." A couple of hours later I got a phone call to go see George Ball at the White House. He said, "Starting tomorrow, we want you to join the EXCOM meetings. The president is particularly concerned that USIA get involved, so that whatever action the United States takes will be understood by the Cuban people."

I was advised by experts on my staff that the way to communicate with the Cuban people was not to use shortwave but to get our message on radio stations in Florida and in the southeastern part of the U.S., which are heard very clearly at night. So we developed a plan that was approved by the EXCOM, whereby we would set up, unbeknownst to the ten radio stations in the southeastern United States, telephone lines directly from the White House to these stations. At five P.M., two hours before the president was scheduled to speak, Pierre Salinger called each of the ten stations, one at a time, and asked if we could feed in the Voice of America's Spanish-language translation. It was amazing. All the stations said yes. It was the power of a call from the White House.

Being involved with EXCOM was an incredible experience. It was the most meaningful experience of my life. The day after the speech, there was considerable skepticism in the European press. They didn't believe the president, apparently. The president was very upset about this, so I argued vigorously to release the low-level photos of the missiles—which had not been released, basically because the CIA didn't want to reveal the quality of the camera equipment. I said, "If we release the pictures worldwide, that will close the argument pretty fast." John McCone, the CIA director, didn't think this was a good idea, but the president did, and the pictures were released. It turned the issue right around. They were on the front page of every newspaper in the world the next day.

Ben Bradlee   I'm just thinking about the president's sitting around that table, having to stare at Arleigh Burke, who probably thought that he was a pipsqueak; to stare at Curtis LeMay [chief of staff, U.S. Air Force], who thought it was a goddamn disaster that Kennedy had been elected. They were not friendly to Kennedy; they were of the old school, and Kennedy—conservative as he was—represented a radical shift; he was a youngster.

Edwin Martin   A lot of the immediate reaction was for forceful action, particularly by some of the people brought in from the outside, like Dean Acheson: Bomb them immediately. The president kept looking for better answers. On Saturday afternoon Bundy said, "Let's start over and look at all the alternatives." And we did. Saturday afternoon was particularly difficult because we had gotten the second letter, with the Turkey business in it. We had talked to the Turks about five months before about pulling the missiles out, because the submarines were much better and the missiles were obsolete. It was a hard thing to get killed over.

I think we felt the conditions in the first message were much better, and logical. That was Khrushchev himself. It was much easier to answer.

There were some leaks. Finally, on the Saturday before the president's speech, the people who had the story were told that if they held it they would get a briefing in advance of the public briefing on Monday afternoon. George Ball, Alexis Johnson, and I gave that briefing to about four correspondents. These correspondents actually knew very little, just that there was a problem of some weapons in Cuba that we were worried about.

Roswell Gilpatric   The EXCOM grew from ten or twelve to about eighteen people. This meant that conversations got unwieldy, and we tended to break into groups. I was given the assignment of developing a scenario on how we were to go about closing the Jupiter sites in Italy and Turkey.

The president not only allowed, he encouraged open discussion. There was never any attempt to cut off interventions. He was particularly tolerant, it seemed to me, when it came to the State Department, where there were several points of view.

Roger Hilsman   If you are the Soviets, you don't probe the will of the West when you know the West realizes they are ahead in missiles. Once the EXCOM understood that, they began to behave in a different way. They talked about what was going on in the Soviet Union—that there must be an internal struggle for power going on, and the best thing for us is not to put Khrushchev in a position where his hawks could take over. So we were very careful. And Khrushchev behaved in a sensible way also.

Alexis Johnson   This was so unprecedented in Soviet practice. It was the first time they ever deployed any nuclear missiles outside of the Soviet Union itself. And the act was so irrational, that rational people would have great concern as to what was really the objective. It was only as we examined the alternatives to bombing that we worked out a plan that would give Khrushchev time to draw back. So we decided to start at the longer end of the scale, but if this did not work, we were prepared to up the ante.

Martin Hillenbrand   The Berlin Task Force was involved in discussions on the missile crisis because we thought that Khrushchev would react against us in Berlin as there we were in a strategically indefensible position. So we had a subgroup of the EXCOM—a Berlin planning group.

Dean Rusk   The United States had overwhelming conventional superiority in the neighborhood of Cuba, and we could have gone in there and taken out those missiles almost with the snap of a finger. But we knew that if we did that, this would force Khrushchev to take further steps, such as the seizure of Berlin or some other similar action that could have greatly enlarged the dangers of the crisis. For example, in one day Khrushchev could count sixteen American troop ships coming through the Panama Canal filled with troops, and we didn't mind that he was able to count them.

Ralph Dungan   Those of us outside the room knew there was something going on, but I didn't know the details until quite late that week. The group itself was quite disciplined; it is remarkable that they could keep it quiet for five days. I think you have to look at some of the personalities of the EXCOM participants: LeMay—I think that the president thought of him as some of the Germans thought of Göring in some of the bombastic statements on air cover he was going to provide. I think that the president didn't think much of LeMay; he didn't trust his judgment. I doubt if Johnson contributed anything, because from a political point of view, he would have wanted to keep his options open so he could slide either way. I don't think that Kennedy consciously used the old Rooseveltian way of playing one adviser off against another.

Edward McDermott   Bobby was very heavily involved. He and McNamara had this close personal relationship. McNamara, as secretary of defense, had the potential to be among the strongest on the EXCOM. His alliance with Bobby made them, together, that much stronger. There is no doubt that Bobby dominated that group.

Roswell Gilpatric   Vice President Johnson was there; he was called on. But he was very careful, in my judgment. He preserved his secondary, nonauthoritative role; he would rarely volunteer a comment. I don't recall anything he said that had a major impact upon the rest of us. You couldn't tell by watching him—he was very impassive—how any of these views struck him. But, like other occasions, the president wanted him brought in.

Alexis Johnson   The initial view of most of us, I think, at the time of the discovery of the missiles, was that we should bomb them.

The essence of the handling of the Cuban missile crisis was the ability to maintain absolute security on the problem. It gave time for us to think in the EXCOM; it gave time for us to deliberate.

And the president was magnificent on his handling of it in terms of enforcing strict security. Those of us who were engaged say among ourselves, no, this could never be repeated again, because there was an atmosphere at that time within the government of discipline that does not now exist.

Sergei Khrushchev   We had no agent in the EXCOM!

On the afternoon of October 18, President Kennedy met for two hours with Soviet Foreign Minister Andrei Gromyko, who assured Kennedy that his government was only interested in developing Cuba's defensive capabilities. In the session Gromyko did not mention the missiles.

Viktor Sukhodrev   Gromyko was tenser than usual. I think he was sort of steeling himself to the possibility that Kennedy might just come out with it. I really don't know whether or not Gromyko knew, or could know, that Kennedy had aerial photographs. I think he was steeling himself to being confronted with a direct statement. But Kennedy decided against it.

Kennedy, as I read subsequently, had those photographs in a drawer by his side and didn't take them out. Cuba came up as a subject only in general terms, in terms of Gromyko talking about the United States' aggressive attitude toward Cuba and Kennedy saying that the United States did not have any aggressive intentions vis-à-vis Cuba. It was a general, a broad-termed discussion, without the specifics of what was actually going on.

William Smith   The president never asked Gromyko the question. Gromyko phrased what they were doing in a way that one could say it wasn't an outright lie. But he did not tell the president what was going on, and he did this deliberately; he knew. He would have lied to the president if he had been asked the question. The administration worried that if they said something to the Soviets, then they would immediately get into a period of negotiations: The Soviets would say, "Let's negotiate all of this." The U.S. did not want to open the issue up to negotiations before a decision had been made on a course of action. That is why the president didn't say anything to Gromyko; he did not want the Russians to know that we knew.

Yuri Barsukov   I think it was quite possible that Gromyko didn't know about the missiles. At that time, he wasn't a member of the Politburo; he was just foreign minister. Foreign policy was formulated by Khrushchev. I could imagine that John Kennedy felt that Gromyko lied to him, but the tragedy is that Gromyko didn't know about the missiles.

Lloyd Cutler   There's no question that Gromyko lied to us.

The next day the president left Washington for a series of campaign appearances, but on Saturday he returned to the capital to confer with advisers and to order a quarantine prohibiting the shipment of offensive weapons to Cuba. On Monday the president briefed congressional lead-

ers in the late afternoon, and at seven P.M., in a nationally televised address from the Oval Office, he offered irrefutable proof of the presence in Cuba of Soviet ballistic missiles capable of bearing nuclear warheads and Soviet jet bombers capable of dropping nuclear weapons.

Roman Puchinski I flew with him on *Air Force One* from Washington to Chicago, where he spoke at a fund-raising dinner just before the missile crisis became public. It is certain that he did not have a cold. On the way to Chicago he was very friendly. He had a great sense of humor. He was in good spirits.

Gaylord Nelson He was due to come to Milwaukee for a speech. I went to Chicago to fly back there with him. We were at the airport, and he came out to the plane and shook hands with everybody. The story said that the president had taken ill. He looked perfectly fine to me. I remember going back to Milwaukee and saying, "He isn't ill at all; he looks in perfect shape. Something big is happening."

Pierre Salinger As we were flying back to Washington from Chicago on *Air Force One,* I said to the president: "You know you don't have the flu; you look perfectly well." He said, "That's true; you'll find out why I'm going back to Washington when we get there, and when you do, grab your balls!"

Angier Biddle Duke God knows what was happening outside!* But inside the Oval Office: "Why Mr. Obote [Milton Obote, president of Uganda], now let us go over your last trade figures. What was the export balance? Do tell me if we can give you preferential trade treatment." Why, for half an hour, we discussed—how in the world could you discuss Uganda–U.S. relations? I don't know—but, anyway, under those circumstances, I mean, it's breathtaking when you think of it.

I told President Obote that international tensions were occurring and that the president would be going on the air at seven o'clock to explain to the American people what was going on, and I asked if he

---

*President Kennedy's meeting with the Ugandan leader occurred only hours before the seven P.M. address.

would like to attend the press conference with President Kennedy—the president had told me that that would be okay—and I said, "This is an interesting opportunity; I think that President Kennedy would very much like you to come along." President Obote said, "Oh, that's a domestic problem of yours. I'm more interested in Uganda–U.S. relations, and I think I wouldn't want to mix into whatever problems you have. Could you arrange for me to see it on TV at Blair House?" I said sure. I was disappointed as hell.

Wayne Fredericks   I took Obote to see the president at four o'clock that afternoon. We sat there and talked. I knew what was taking place, but Obote didn't. But for thirty minutes the president talked to Obote about Uganda and about Africa. I hosted a dinner for Obote that night at Blair House, and he was quite stunned by this. By that time, we had heard the president's broadcast. Obote said, "I would just like to tell the people assembled here that today I got one of the most impressive experiences of my life: For thirty minutes this afternoon I had the full and undivided attention of the president of the United States of America, and I had not the slightest inkling of the problems he was facing."

Joseph Dolan   At about five o'clock on the afternoon of the president's speech, Bobby called about six of us into his office and he told us what was going to happen. He told us he wanted us to be able to go home to be with our families, and he said, "We think there is going to be some loss of life. The bottom line is, the least there is going to be is some loss of life; the maximum is that it's World War III." How did they know? They couldn't read Khrushchev's mind, and he couldn't read Kennedy's mind. I think Kennedy was very much affected by Barbara Tuchman's *The Guns of August.*°

Alexis Johnson   I remember that when we briefed the congressional leaders shortly before the president's speech, the CIA photo interpreter pointed to the photographs of the missiles and he showed us the azimuth being straight through the heart of Madison, Wisconsin. Senator Wiley

---

°Tuchman's book (New York: Macmillan, 1962) suggested that World War I had resulted from crucial misunderstandings among the leaders of various European nations.

[Alexander Wiley (R., Wis.)], was sitting there, half dozing, and boy, he really sat up. He said, "Where are you pointing?" The CIA man said, "To Madison, Wisconsin."

Viktor Sukhodrev We were flying with Gromyko over the ocean, and we landed at an airport in Scotland. And it was while we were flying that Kennedy made his statement. So when we landed in Scotland, the British papers had the Kennedy statement on the Soviet missiles and the embargo on the front page. So we were literally up in the air when it happened.

Why Did Khrushchev Put the Missiles into Cuba?

Dean Rusk We never really knew the answer to that question; we speculated about it a good deal. In his book *Khrushchev Remembers,* he claims that he put the missiles in there to defend Cuba against an attack by the United States. But my guess is that he recognized that putting a hundred missiles in Cuba which could knock out the SAC bases with a minimum of advance warning would have created a major change in the world strategic situation, and that if there were a 20 percent chance that he could get away with it, the chance was worth taking. But I think that the strength of the American reaction caught him by surprise. We caught him with his scenario down; he was obviously very distraught by the strength of the American reaction and seemed not to have his equilibrium with him. But we never knew exactly why he put the missiles in Cuba.

George Carver The seeds of the crisis lie in Kennedy's meeting with Khrushchev in Vienna—this great delusion of American presidents: Roosevelt thought he could deal with Uncle Joe—that somehow foreign leaders are going to be moved by the color of your eyes or the force of your personality to deviate one micromillimeter from the pursuit of their own interests. At Vienna Khrushchev thought Kennedy was an idiot who could be had and outbluffed. The result of this was the Berlin crisis and the Cuban missile crisis. Khrushchev's judgment was that Kennedy was a lightweight pretty boy who could be had.

Raymond Garthoff It is very unlikely that Khrushchev thought Kennedy was weak in the spring of 1962, when the decision was made to put the missiles in Cuba, principally because we had been through the Berlin crisis, where Kennedy and the alliance had been very staunch. Notwithstanding that there had been some criticisms about not doing something about the wall, certainly Khrushchev realized—and recognized that Kennedy did too—that that was just his own fallback in dealing with the defensive part of the problem in stopping the outflow from East Germany and was not a successful offensive move. On the contrary, he had repeatedly had to back down on his demands for changed status in Berlin and readiness to sign a separate peace treaty and turn over controls to East Germany; he had been stood down by Kennedy on that. And the United States was moving ahead with its military buildup. That contributed to his decision by making him feel a considerable need to bolster his thin deterrent in the period before he was able to field large numbers of ICBMs.

George McGovern   I think they were there as a possible deterrent to a Bay of Pigs number two. I think Castro was after something to stay the hand and, as a matter of fact, we know now that the administration was considering follow-up actions against Castro in some way or another. We certainly know they were attempting to assassinate Castro and he had every reason to fear another American military action, the next time, with all the firepower that was needed to knock him out. So I've always felt the missiles were not put there to attack the United States, but for the same reason you have missiles in the U.S. and in the Soviet Union, to deter the other country from attacking.

William Smith   It was not a clear-cut thing. If it had gotten to Monday or Tuesday and nothing had happened, there would have been tremendous pressure from the military, and from members of Congress and others in the American public, to launch at least an air attack on Cuba, to make sure those missiles didn't become operational. That would have been a very large attack.

Some people would argue: What difference did it make if those missiles were in Cuba or in the Soviet Union? If they could strike the United States from Cuba, they could do so from the USSR. So militarily it didn't make much difference. There is a certain logic to that, except in that case, it turns out they could not fire from the Soviet Union, so the missiles in Cuba gave them an immediate advantage. Also, there is the

Monroe Doctrine, and while we may not talk much about it, there was a difference that the missiles were ninety miles offshore.

Ray Cline I took the photographs up to Adlai Stevenson at the UN. He was very skeptical because he had been burned in the Bay of Pigs operation. I said, "We are absolutely telling you the truth; the CIA may have lied to you in the past, but they are not lying now." We did persuade Adlai. He let me write the paper for him, which he used that day when he was arguing with the Soviet delegate. We had a military person put all those photographs up on the easels. I didn't go to that session because I didn't want to be seen there.

Joseph Sisco I did a lot of shuttling between Washington and New York. My most vivid recollection is of being in the UN Security Council when the missiles were on the way to Cuba and the president had made it clear to Khrushchev that we would not permit those missiles to go to Cuba. The president had given UN Secretary General U Thant the mission of conveying the message to Khrushchev that he wanted to turn them back. Arthur Schlesinger, John Wilson, and I had been working for a couple of days on what proved to be a fifty- to sixty-page speech for Stevenson. We went over it on the night before the Security Council meeting—Adlai was one of those people who kept changing the text right up to the last minute. Shortly before the meeting, which was scheduled for three o'clock, Stevenson was ready to give this speech, where he would lay out all the information.

I got a call from Harlan Cleveland, the assistant secretary. Everybody was watching on television, the president included. Cleveland said, "President Kennedy does not want Stevenson to give the speech at this moment because we are awaiting a reply from U Thant, and if he gives that all-out speech, it might give the Russians a pretext for a negative response." Well, Adlai exploded—he was seated at the Security Council table—and he said: "The meeting is about to begin. I am going to give this speech."

There is a telephone booth just outside the Security Council chamber. I got on the line and called Cleveland to tell the president that Adlai refuses; he is going to give the speech, and that there is only one way the speech can be stopped: Namely, will the president get on the line, and I'll get Adlai on the line. Cleveland got the president. He says, "Joe, put

Adlai on the line." I go in and I say, "Governor"—Adlai used to love to be called Governor—"the president wants to talk to you." He turns to me and says, "Joe, I can't talk to the president. It is three o'clock, and the meeting is about to start. How can I go out there and talk to the president?" I said, "Adlai, you cannot refuse to talk to the president. In the meantime I will see to it that the meeting is delayed."

Well, I went to the president of the Security Council—who happened to be the Russian, [Valerian A.] Zorin. I said, "Mr. Ambassador, Ambassador Stevenson has been called to the telephone. He is taking a call from the president. Could you delay the meeting?" He said, "Mr. Sisco, I will not start the meeting until you give me a signal."

So the president and Adlai talked. In the meantime we had this sixty-page speech. I exxed out about forty pages of it while Stevenson was in the telephone booth. He came back, and I said, "Adlai, you can make a speech, but I have exxed out a lot of it." He didn't know what I had cut out. He made a fairly brief speech. By the time he ends the speech, I am called out of the Security Council chamber and the word is given to me: "We have heard from the UN Secretary General. The Russians have said to him that they are going to turn the ships back."

So I go back into the chamber, and I say, "Adlai, there is good news; here it is. Now I want you to call for a suspension of this meeting." He did so, and we went into a side room. This time we had all the photographs ready to go. We said to him, "Now you can give the speech; we will bring in the photography, and create maximum tension in this council." And he took the speech, and he really let loose.

But the record should show that when Adlai said that he would wait until hell freezes over—that famous quote—it was totally ad libbed; there was nothing like that in the text. The president was really calling the shots in the Security Council right from the White House as he watched on the television and talked on an open line into the phone booth. What a primitive way to communicate!

How Strict Secrecy Was Maintained

Edward McDermott   The president was very, very concerned that there not be a sense of panic created in the American people. I was present in the discussions that took place after his return from Chicago with the alleged cold, and that culminated in a Sunday afternoon meeting in the private living room quarters, on the second floor of the White House. About ten people were seated in a semicircle around the president. After the discussion, we went around the circle and asked each person what their recommendation would be. Then he got up and walked out onto the balcony. He was out there a few minutes it seemed like a few hours. Bobby, who was at the meeting, got up and went out on the balcony with him. The president came back in, obviously very concerned. It had taken its physical and mental toll, and he sat down and said, "I've made my decision, and I know each of you hope I didn't accept your recommendation." And then he went on and explained what he was going to do about the whole scheme. Now, he said that because he—and every president before— was constantly concerned about leaks from the National Security Council.

Pierre Salinger   I sat in on all of the NSC meetings, and afterward we would hold a session to decide what to tell the press.

George Ball   The *New York Times* had the information on the Bay of Pigs but withheld the story, and many of their staff were in an uproar about that. Then Scotty Reston called me on Sunday night—the evening before the president was going to tell the nation about the missile crisis. He knew in detail about American troop movements in the southern United States. I said, "Scotty, I am not going to touch this. You should call Bundy," who gave him a very dusty answer, and as a result Reston talked to the president. Kennedy appealed to Reston to hold the story, and he did, but there was a hell of a big row in the *Times* editorial staff about that. Since then we have had Watergate and this whole fascination with investigatory reporting.

Yuri Barsukov   I didn't have much information on how the crisis was being debated in the White House, and—as far as I can judge—other Soviet reporters didn't know what was going on. Even the contacts between U.S. and Soviet officials at the time; I found out about them much later.

McGeorge Bundy   It was held as tightly as we knew how and, at the same time, to be able to consult the people the president wanted to consult. It was done that way because he wanted it done that way. That was the reason I hadn't called him up the night before, because either he calls a lot of people out of dinner parties, or he has a lousy night alone. Neither one seemed to me the best way to begin. We all know we are running against some sort of a clock that's ticking down, because a secret of this kind isn't going to last more than a couple of weeks. A lot of subterfuges were used: people not saying where they were going to meetings; the president kept to his election campaign calendar. And we just about made it. As it was, he had to talk the *Times* and the *Post* out of printing it.

The relations between the president and the press were not the same thirty years ago. And I wouldn't blame anybody currently in the government for getting nostalgic about that.

Ben Bradlee   You can keep secrets in this town if everybody wants to, and everybody wanted to. There are more secrets kept in this town than you'd think.

PRESIDENT KENNEDY'S RESPONSE TO THE MISSILE CRISIS

Edward McDermott   I saw the president at the National Security Council meeting. He was harried, concerned, tired, and worried, yet he was extremely thoughtful.

Eugene McCarthy   The only time I ever saw Jack really kind of scared was the time of the missile crisis.

Dean Rusk   Fortunately, during the Cuban missile crisis, President Kennedy had ice water in his veins.

August Heckscher   At the time of the Cuban missile crisis, I had arranged with some care for there to be a reception in the White House, with the president attending, for the top poets in this country. Kennedy canceled it. I remember complaining at that time; I thought that was just the moment when the White House ought to be receiving poets—showing that we were a country of peace. But there was no consideration possible for anything except this terrible crisis.

Roswell Gilpatric   At times the president would appear distracted or depressed. He was visibly shaken on Saturday morning when the news came in that Major Anderson had been shot down.

Roger Hilsman   As I was walking past Bundy's office in the basement to go to my car, one of his aides grabbed me and said, "Your office is on the phone; it is urgent."

The guy in my office is talking with me on one phone, and with the Pentagon War Room on another. He tells me that one of our U-2s has taken a wrong turn over the North Pole and has crossed Soviet air space. This has caused the Soviets to scramble fighters. I run back upstairs to Mrs. Lincoln's office, where the president and Bundy were standing, and I tell them about the U-2. There is this long pause, and then the president, who was the calmest guy in the room, laughs and says, "There is always some son of a bitch that doesn't get the word." And he says to me, "Get to the Pentagon and make sure the Soviets realize this plane is a mistake." And as I turned to leave the room, I almost staggered or lost my balance. And Bundy says, "Mr. President, Roger hasn't been to bed for thirty-six hours. Can't someone else handle this one?" Kennedy looks at me and says, "Sure. Go home, Roger. Get a couple of hours' sleep and come back."

Ralph Dungan   The Cuban missile crisis was not without its interpersonal frictions. Rusk's performance, for example, was not good from JFK's point of view: He found Rusk irritating as hell. Rusk was not decisive, and he would waffle a lot. In circumstances like that Kennedy really appreciated crispness. The atmosphere was of great tension.

Dean Rusk   I met frequently during those thirteen days with Bob McNamara and Robert Kennedy: We built a consensus among the three of us that the quarantine should be the technique used in response to the crisis, realizing that that might not be more than a temporary move, because in the background was the possibility of direct military action.

Ben Bradlee   I think that Kennedy was more at ease during the missile crisis in his relationship with the Joint Chiefs. He'd been very unhappy with the Pentagon during the Bay of Pigs. I think that he was not at all at ease with his enemy; he didn't know who his enemy was; what kind of person he was; how to reach him.

Alexei Adzhubei   Khrushchev realized that the military were pressing Kennedy.

Richard Helms   You have to have confidence in the people making the decisions; there's no sense in your going around wailing and saying, "If there were only somebody else in the White House." That doesn't do a damn bit of good; it's counterproductive in the worst way. You go with this fellow and just hope he's right. But there were some tense moments there.

Rating President Kennedy's Response

Roswell Gilpatric   If you want to give star billing in the missile crisis, I think you rank the president first, then Robert Kennedy, then McNamara. I think you would put the attorney general as the president's alter ego in many ways. But McNamara was certainly responsible for persuading a number of the hawks—people like Bundy and Dillon—to change their tune. He could speak so clearly and easily and get to the point so fast. This appealed to the president, who had in mind promoting McNamara—making him at least number one cabinet officer in a second administration.

Richard Bissell   From the time the hard evidence was in, Kennedy handled himself very well. I don't know how many options he had open to him: with the hard evidence in, he couldn't simply dust his hands and say he didn't believe it, or that it didn't really make any difference whether there were missiles there or not. Some of the intimate participants in Washington really thought we were close to nuclear war.

Roger Hilsman   Most presidents that I have known quickly learn that the best thing to do is keep your options open until it either comes down to one thing that is clearly going to succeed or you can't let it go any longer. But in the case of the Cuban missile crisis, it very quickly became clear to Kennedy that it was his baby, and he became the desk officer; he could not delegate this one. So, boy, he was on top right from the beginning. And the idea of a blockade was his.

Ray Cline   Bobby was not as impressive as Jack was. I think he was really a vindictive fellow. I hate to say that, but I think he was really determined to put Castro out of business. Jack Kennedy would have made up his own mind, and he would have finally made the bitter decision to move against Cuba, because he knew that the Russians couldn't move against him. We had plans for maybe seventy cities to be destroyed in the Soviet Union.

Donald Wilson   President Kennedy did a terrific job; he was almost indispensable. The president wasn't in the room that much. This was purposefully done. Whenever the president is there it makes a hell of a difference; everybody is in awe of the president; it is very hard to differ with him. If he is not there, there is a much greater opportunity for free discussion. Without him, it is a level playing field, with a lot of powerful and articulate people playing. Without the president you were freer to express your thoughts, even though you knew whatever you said would get back to him.

Roswell Gilpatric   He must have had it in mind that he wanted to get a broad section of people—like Dillon, whose function in the government was quite different from that of the secretaries of state and defense, and the director of central intelligence. I think he had this preconceived idea that after the Bay of Pigs, in another crisis with Khrushchev, he would deal with it by bringing in a much broader range of advisers than he had had in the Bay of Pigs.

Roger Hilsman   My impression was that by Tuesday night, Kennedy had decided on a blockade, and that the rest of the week—where we met morning and night—was spent in making sure the government was unified, that the Air Force had the feeling that they had been given every chance to give the case for bombing and then failed to persuade.

Martin Hillenbrand   I think the president demonstrated in the missile crisis that he did have the capacity to make decisions, to choose one of four or five different scenarios and then to implement, without being distracted off-course by the fact that other people, on the right or on the left—hawks or doves—were saying, "That's the wrong course to take."

Alexis Johnson   We were conscious it was a very grave situation. We accomplished our purpose without ever firing a shot. Through political and military planning it meshed and was played out with complete security and discipline at every stage. I look back on it as a model operation. The whole purpose of having a military force, of course, is not to use it.

BACK-CHANNEL CONTACTS

On Friday, October 26, Aleksandr Fomin, counselor of the Soviet Embassy in Washington, asked John Scali, the ABC-TV State Department correspondent, for an urgent meeting. This session resulted in an unexpected back-channel communication, in which the Russian laid out possible terms for an agreement to end the crisis. The Fomin-Scali conversations, which took place in a hotel coffee shop, were viewed by some in the EXCOM as serious, playing a role in the resolution of the crisis, and by others as a Soviet ploy.

Roger Hilsman   The Soviets have used this sort of technique many many times over the last thirty or forty years: They make an official demarche, whether it is a public speech or a statement, or the ambassador goes in to call on the chief of state and makes a statement. They make it sound forthcoming. Then, through other channels, they will be more concrete, more specific. Here we are, and it is coming in from every direction.

So Scali comes in and says, "Look—the KGB came and said, can you—do you have a friend—can you get Hilsman to take a message to Kennedy?" I think that is what was said. And Scali said, "I think so." Well, the message was very simple: We will remove the missiles under UN supervision if the United States will make a public renunciation of any plan to invade Cuba.

Pierre Salinger   The Scali incident played an enormous role; it was the first message we received that the possibility existed for the withdrawal of the missiles in return for a guarantee of noninvasion of Cuba. I had come out of my office and seen Scali and tried to throw him out. Then Rusk came along and said, "No, no. He's working for us now." Back-channel activity was part of the Soviet mentality; they loved it. One of our problems during the missile crisis was that when we sent official messages, they wouldn't get there for twenty-four hours. In January 1962 I had proposed a hotline to the Soviets, but they had rejected it. They accepted a hotline within hours after the missile crisis.

Dean Rusk   It was unexpected, but it was, in effect, reassuring, because what we were getting from that channel helped us to figure out which communications from Khrushchev were real. We thought we had a clear contact with the KGB through John Scali's channel and as it turned out, it was a very useful confirmation. Now, it was not as central to the solution of the problem as Scali sometimes thinks. Nevertheless it was a very helpful and useful interchange.

Raymond Garthoff   It now seems quite clear that Fomin was acting on his own—that this did not have the significance that it seemed to have at the time.

Two Cables Come in from Moscow

Dean Rusk   The first message which came in—on I think a Thursday of that week—seemed to be Khrushchev *personally;* it was emotional, dis-traught. We were rather concerned about it because we thought the old man was losing his cool. But nevertheless, there was in the letter a sentence or two that seemed to offer a possibility of a peaceful settlement. About, for example, an agreement for the United States not to attack Cuba.

Well, then, the *next* day, Friday, came in a letter which was obviously a bureaucratic letter, a foreign office/State Department–type letter, rep-resented in multiple drafting, that sort of thing. Well, Llewellyn Thomp-son came up with the idea, which Bobby Kennedy picked up at the meet-ing, that we ought to ignore the second letter and respond to the first let-ter, and that proved to be the key that unlocked the whole situation.

Roger Hilsman   Bob Kennedy was the hero. He said, "Let's take out of the Khrushchev message and the Scali-Fomin conversation the thing that we want." It was brilliant. We called it the Trollope ploy, after the novel where a guy squeezes a girl's hand and she looks at him and says, "I accept your proposal of marriage."*

George Ball Bobby Kennedy picked it up. We were all sitting around. It was a time of great depression. We had been quite exhilarated getting the first message, which was a very earthy message. Somebody had told me that when Khrushchev wanted to write something like this on a personal basis, he sat in his office and faced the wall, and he had a male secretary sitting behind him and he just talked. If you read the message you could believe it. That was exactly the way it sounded.

William Smith The common wisdom at the time was that Bobby Kennedy had done it. It's later been said that Tommy Thompson was the first one who mentioned it. I bet if you went far enough, there would be some third person who mentioned it. That is the kind of thing that occurs. When Thompson said it no one paid much attention, but the one they listened to was Bobby Kennedy. My experience in most government works is, if you say something too soon, no one will pay attention to it. It might be the right thing to do, but people won't listen; they are not that far in their thinking.

Raymond Garthoff It wasn't Bobby Kennedy who came up with the Trollope ploy. Both Bundy and Llewellyn Thompson had earlier discussed it.

Victor Sukhodrev I think that that time there could have been no message that came from the foreign ministry rather than from Khrushchev. Everything went through Khrushchev. Everything. Khrushchev was very direct in his language; he was not the person who would sit down, take a pen, and write a letter, let's say, to another head of state. But he dictated a lot. He used his stenographers all the time. So he would sit down and dictate in plain words, sometimes earthy words, the gist, the idea, and it was then for the foreign ministry—for, let's say, Gromyko's team—to put that into the proper—to translate that, as it were—into the proper diplomatic language. There was never any question of the foreign ministry doing

---

*English novelist Anthony Trollope (1815–82); his novel *Doctor Thorne* contains a scene like the one described.

something that did not have Khrushchev's approval. That was out of the question at that time. He was the boss, period.

Khrushchev had his options. I mean he was the kind of person who could sit down and talk about various options. He was not always correct, didn't always have the proper historical perceptions. He wasn't a person well versed in history or historical precedents. His was a kind of gut diplomacy. But it was that gut feeling that led him to believe that Kennedy meant what he was saying and that it was time to do something before it was too late. That was the way his mind worked. He knew when to stop.

Yuri Barsukov   Maybe it's a bit unusual that the two messages came, but I think it reflects that there wasn't unity among the Soviet leaders at the time. But Khrushchev was in complete control. He discussed things with people who worked with him—Politburo members—but he was in control.

Alexis Johnson   I think that the Friday message was the foreign office—the bureaucracy—and the Saturday message was pure Khrushchev. My Soviet colleagues later told me that his messages went directly to the Central Committee and not to the Foreign Ministry.

Pierre Salinger   The first cable was a direct response to the Fomin-Scali conversation; the second had all kinds of questions, and we said to ourselves: "Let's forget about those conditions and just answer the first one." If we had understood Saddam Hussein's message in February 1991—when he had all kinds of conditions but said he was pulling out—if we had answered him the way Kennedy answered Khrushchev, there would not have been a war.

THE CRISIS ENDS

Pierre Salinger   It was not a case of "We won; they lost." That was Kennedy's strong point from the minute the crisis came to an end. He called me in and said: "This is not our victory; this is a joint victory of the two nations; we did it together. Don't let anybody go out and say this was America's victory."

Tom Wicker   I think the U.S. public and the world thought that Kennedy had won. But very shortly there began to be a backlash, led by Senator [Kenneth] Keating [(R.)], of New York, on the idea that

Kennedy had given up too much here and in effect had said that Castro could stay in power. Keating may have been technically correct that in order to avoid nuclear war, Kennedy had given Castro a free ticket on Cuba. But what could Kennedy do about that anyway? As far as public perceptions in this country were concerned, it was generally viewed that bold, brave John F. Kennedy had faced them down. Certainly by the time of his death, he was still regarded as victor of the missile crisis.

Raymond Garthoff   Essentially we won; the missiles were removed, and that was our objective, but it was certainly not as clear-cut and one-sided. There was the very delicately handled negotiation about the withdrawal of the missiles from Italy and Turkey, which we were, in fact, interested in removing and planning to at some point. But the precise move to get them all out in the five months after wasn't coincidental. What still isn't publicly known is that that discussion had actually started earlier in the week. It is also now clear that the president was thinking about other diplomatic steps he might have taken if Khrushchev had not responded positively.

William Smith   Dean Rusk said it right: The other guy blinked. And that is what world public opinion thought at the time. I think a lot of people at the time, including General Taylor, thought we could have gotten more. But we won; we got those missiles out of there—this had been our objective. We didn't get UN inspection or some other things, but the Soviets backed down, and there wasn't any doubt after that about whose prestige was higher in the world. In fact, that made the Kennedy administration; that really pulled it together. It gave the administration a confidence and cohesion it had not had before. I think we won both internationally and domestically, because it gave the Kennedy administration a respect it had not had among the American people.

We had already decided to take those missiles out of Turkey. They were not very good missiles. They were somewhat of a threat, because they could reach the Soviet Union. I don't think taking the missiles out of Turkey diminishes our success, although, I will admit, it was not known at the time that the administration had decided to take the missiles out. I did not know this, and I was pretty well informed. These discussions had started in May of 1961, so President Kennedy likely thought: Why in the world am I going to get into a fight over some missiles that I don't want there anyway?

18

Vietnam

In an attempt to bolster the regime of Ngo Dinh Diem, the Kennedy administration, in its early months, provided military and technical advisers to the Republic of South Vietnam. In the ensuing months some of Kennedy's aides believed that Diem was making progress on both the political and military fronts, while others were convinced that Diem could not successfully counter the communist challenge. The latter view was strengthened when, on January 2, 1963, at Ap Bac, fifty miles from Saigon, a Viet Cong battalion, though outnumbered ten to one by a force of South Vietnamese regulars, shot down five U.S. helicopters, killing three American advisers.

Marcus Raskin The Joint Chiefs believed that they were king of the hill. They would be able to move anyplace, anywhere, because there was no balance of power in the sense that it was defined at that time. The Soviets would back off; the United States would be able to move where it wanted to move. In my view this mistake in judgment helped to create the notion that the United States could go into Vietnam in a very big way without fear of response from the Soviet Union. That was a correct analysis. The problem with that analysis was that it never took into account the Vietnamese. So while the Soviets might not come in, the Vietnamese would have their own views, and their own capacities, as to how they would confront the United States.

William Sullivan It was not imperialism in the sense of wanting to have territory. It was imperialism in the sense that you were manipulating lesser breeds. Probably all of us were guilty of the hubris that carried from our success in World War II, and from several other arrangements that we had made around the world in attempting to order other people's lives in a way that we thought would be better for them and better for the world as a whole. I guess if that be imperialism, one has to make the most of it. I don't think that we as a nation have yet lost it—being better nannies. We seemed to know better what was good for people. That surely was pretty pronounced in the whole question of dealing with Diem and Nhu [Ngo Dinh Nhu, President Diem's brother and chief political aide].

William Sloane Coffin, Jr.   I didn't really catch on to what was going on in Vietnam until 1964. Then I remember initially thinking, Well, this is a perversion of American foreign policy. It took me a few more years to realize this was mainstream American foreign policy. This was standard operating procedure ever since the Truman Doctrine in Greece and the landing of the marines in Lebanon. The Bay of Pigs in 1961. This was standard American foreign policy since the end of World War II, to intervene, massively, unilaterally, sometimes by the CIA and sometimes by the military, to intervene in Third World countries.

Robert Manning   In the early period Vietnam was hardly on the minds of the people in the State Department. Rusk was preoccupied with Berlin, the balance of trade, and NATO affairs. The Pentagon was really the architect of Vietnam policy; they were pretty much running all the meetings. Rusk didn't pay enough attention to the potential of Vietnam. I think he can be faulted for that. Ball didn't want any part of it; he was a Europeanist, entirely. So there was no one in the State Department, except down at the bureau level, who was taking a day-to-day interest in it. The Pentagon was really involved, and we had General Krulak, this marine general, coming back and giving these rosy interpretations; you had the can-do attitude of the military.

Bui Diem   The Vietnamese in the early 1960s knew very little about American politics and American policy. They looked at Americans the way all Asian peoples looked at America after the Second World War: the Americans, according to our point of view, were the ones who intervened in Greece, who intervened in Korea, and so we considered the

Americans as the champion of freedom—perhaps naively—but anyway, that was our opinion. Later on, when President Kennedy sent the group of advisers to South Vietnam during the time of President Diem, we understood that the Americans were on our side exactly the way the Americans were on the side of the South Koreans in the 1950s.

Kennedy was seen as a new type of American leader—very idealistic. There were a lot of expectations in Saigon. The perception at that time was that Kennedy was a man who was strongly in favor of defending freedom and helping other people. We understood that he was strongly against communism. We saw the Cuban crisis and how courageous he was against Khrushchev.

Richard Bissell   Many people have forgotten that following Diem's early battle with the sects, mostly carried out in Saigon, there was a period of several years or more when things seemed to be going pretty well. It was, of course, only after Dien Bien Phu and the French capitulation that the U.S.-assisted transfer of mostly Christians from the North to South Vietnam took place. Most of those who left the North were anticommunist, so this significant population movement appeared to be strengthening Diem. Also, he appeared to have considerable charisma. I still remember the reports of public speeches and other occasions that he would mingle with crowds, somewhat to the despair of his guards. He was very popular.

Then came the decision not to hold elections. It was after that that the Vietcong began to be much more active in South Vietnam, and the South Vietnamese Army was plainly not able to contain them. This phase occurred during the Eisenhower presidency, and we began to put military advisers with the Vietnamese Army. I think that Kennedy faced a situation where we had a commitment—still very small, measured in troops and dollars—but still, if not a commitment to, at least an involvement with the Diem regime. And he came in at a time when the military news was very bad. In hindsight, it probably would have been better if we'd cut our losses and pulled out entirely. But that didn't seem to be a desirable course of action: We'd had a lot to do with the movement of population, with getting the agreement that ended the active fighting and getting the partition of the country, and it would have been a very major public relations setback if we'd had to pull out entirely and let it slide. I believe it was that set of pressures that led to a steadily deepening involvement.

William Sullivan   When President Kennedy met with President Eisenhower before the inauguration, Eisenhower spent almost the entire period on Laos, and how a collapse in Laos would mean a collapse of the dominos. Shortly after the inauguration Kennedy asked the Joint Chiefs to do a study of what would be necessary to stop the North Vietnamese from moving into Laos. They came back with a rather extensive paper saying, in effect, it would take a lot, and probably in the long run they might have to use atomic weapons to keep the Chinese out. This troubled Kennedy very much. He came to the conclusion that the military ideas on Laos were totally out of whack, and if any stand was going to be taken in Southeast Asia or old Indochina, it would be in Vietnam because the coast was available for logistics. The Vietnamese were reputed to be better fighters, and we weren't trapped into the jungles of Laos with all the long logistic lines that that entailed. So I would say the president had his own strategic ideas, and they were formed in part in discussions with people like Harriman, but also with people like Max Taylor and Dean Rusk and Walt Rostow and, of course, Bob McNamara.

William Smith   People forget that we went into Vietnam thinking we were doing the right thing. What has disappointed me more than anything else is the number of people who act like they were against it from the beginning. But at the time we were concerned with wars of national liberation—the threat from communism. We all had to draw the line somewhere, and this seemed the thing to do. We were trying to help the South Vietnamese; we had a government there under Diem that was as respectable as any other we were likely to get. I think that the president looked at it as the United States versus the Soviet Union rather than in terms of Vietnam per se, and I think that prism of U.S.–Soviet relations made us not as mindful of some of the consequences we had gotten ourselves into as we probably should have been. Over time the Soviet part of it was still there, but went into the background, and our problems of fighting that kind of war became more burdensome.

William Trueheart   In 1962 I accompanied the South Vietnamese defense minister while he was in Washington. He called on the president and all the top people in government. The meeting with the president, while a courtesy call, was really quite a substantive meeting—thirty minutes or more. I was very much struck by Kennedy's familiarity with what was going on there, with what we were reporting. All the telegrams and whatnot. I was really quite astonished. He struck me as being more familiar with it than any of the other people we talked with—Rusk or McNamara for example. He was a quick study, and no doubt he had had a briefing before the meeting.

William Colby I think he was, like all of us, caught up in the cold war, and that was an expression of the contest that was going on between the communist world and the free world at the time. Consequently it had to be met; the question was how. He had had a bad experience with the CIA in the Bay of Pigs, of course, but then he turned to the CIA very successfully in Laos. Also it began to perform fairly well in Vietnam, and then the situation became overmilitarized.

George McGovern We always talked favorably about the importance of a sense of history, but I don't think he had as developed a sense of history as one would have wished. He hadn't really understood the historical forces that were moving either in Cuba or in Southeast Asia—the passion behind these revolutionary movements and the difficulty of foreigners, even well-intentioned foreigners like the United States, trying to control events in these Third World areas. I've always felt that was a flaw in President Kennedy's approach to world affairs. He had too much faith in the power of arms and in the capacity of great powers to shape events and not enough appreciation for indigenous grass-roots forces that were moving in those areas after World War II.

Roswell Gilpatric I think the president was very uncomfortable with decision making in Far East matters. I don't think he had any real feel for it. And I don't think this country did. I mean, that's my own personal view. I don't think we ever understood what made the Vietnamese tick. We don't know their history or their culture or their psychology. I think he was at a loss. I mean, you get this conflicting advice. McNamara was always very sure of himself. He doesn't have any difficulty in reaching decisions. He was very forceful and effective in defending them.

Harry Felt Who made the U.S. policy in those days? I think the president did. Isn't that always true? The president's policy was pretty simple, I think: Deter war; defend the United States in case of war; help our friends in Southeast Asia. There was a policy that was carried on until too many mistakes were made in implementing the policy, like the counterinsurgency. Counterinsurgency covers a lot of things: it's not just killing Viet Cong. It has to be an integrated thing—what one could call "rural development." The biggest mistake, during my time, the only program—if you could call it a program—the South Vietnam Army had was to try to clear out a district; that was McNamara's concept. That's fine if, after you sweep it out, you take steps to hold it. That was never done. They'd sweep, kill, never hold. Westmoreland [Gen. William C. Westmoreland, superintendent, U.S. Military Academy; later U.S. Army chief of staff] was guilty of the same thing. His strategy was: Sweep and destroy. That business of destroying Viet Cong—we get into this business of statistics. That's where Krulak was involved—gathering all the statistics. In Saigon there was a briefing for me by Harkins's [Gen. Paul Harkins, U.S. Military Assistance Command, Vietnam] staff. A guy came up with all these numbers—My God! all these people were killed, and whatnot—and I said, "I don't believe it!" Well, Harkins got madder than hell. "If you don't believe what this colonel says—who's just come in from the field at my request to brief you—" I said, "What this colonel is telling me is what you want me to know. I have reason to believe that the figures you've been feeding in to me—and I'm passing them on to the Pentagon—are overblown." I should have parted company with Harkins right there, but my staff was back there cheering, and so was his staff. They knew this was true. A guy comes in from the field, talks to his district guy; the district guy wants a *good* report, and he's going to give him a *good* report. I don't know how much the president was concerned about Vietnam—Viet Cong casualties. But after all that's one criterion to use. Well, we got fooled on that.

Victor Krulak   I saw the president often during the Vietnam years. He was impatient; he wanted things to happen; he wanted progress to be made. He didn't understand the war any more than the rest of us did; we were all monumentally ignorant. My impression was then—and still is—that President Kennedy had a large view of what we were doing, as opposed to Lyndon Johnson, who had a parochial, political view of what we were trying to do in Southeast Asia. This is because Kennedy was probably smarter than Johnson—you only had to say something once to Kennedy and he would understand it. The president asked a lot of questions. He listened to anyone and everyone; he was clearly interested in learning. His advisers were not homogeneous in their evaluation of what was going on, but there were very few that were uncertain. I once commented that it was like an old county judge who says, "This court may be in error, but it is never in doubt."

There was no one who was prepared to make a scenario. I believe that Kennedy was no different from the rest in that regard. He wasn't sure—I am certain of that—any more than any of the rest of us were about how long it would go on, what it would take. In 1962 there was a real question of How do you know you are winning? It was that fundamental. There was some debate: Are you winning? If not, how near are you to the point where you will say you are winning? What will it take? How soon? But no comprehensive assessment.

William Smith   There were two different views on how to fight the war. Krulak thought he might become the next commandant of the Marine Corps. He knew that if he hoped to do that, he had to maintain good relations with the other people in the Joint Chiefs of Staff. He believed what they thought and took a harder line than the State Department did. They thought it could be solved with less use of force. But that was not only the State Department; that was McNamara—the civilian echelon with the Department of Defense.

William Sullivan   I think one of the reasons the president's advisers differed so much was that the military had very specific, concrete things that they were doing, and they sort of checked them off as they accomplished them. They had their checklists, mostly of what the Vietnamese were doing, and they were all pretty negative, because nothing was being permanently accomplished on nation building or moving away from corruption toward a resilient national fabric. So they were looking at two different aspects of the elephant, and clearly both of them had to be looked at, because one wasn't going to succeed without the other, as we later learned.

I think the president, in his own way, was able to draw the conclusions that he needed from the advisers. I don't say he took them with a grain of salt, but he certainly absorbed them through experience, which made him somewhat skeptical of the rather glowing military terms.

David Bell   The particular governments—before and after Diem— were not capable of understanding, and were not interested in really responding to the underlying difficulties. By that time there had been twenty years of history, of which most of us knew very little about. There had been a very effective development of an underground organization. Against that kind of situation, we were whistling in the wind. I don't mean to blame President Kennedy or the people around him, except in the sense that it was clear, early on, that we didn't know much about what was happening. I sat in meetings as AID administrator—two or three—in which the president was briefed by the military about the situation on the ground in Vietnam.

What the military was saying to the president was quite different from what we in AID were hearing from our civilian people on the ground, on the same issues. There was a rather awkward confrontation at one of those meetings, after one of Krulak and Mendenhall's [Joseph Mendenhall, State Department Vietnam expert] visits to Vietnam. I was there with a guy named Phillips, who was one of the civilians who worked for AID in Vietnam. I spoke up and said, "This isn't the way we are hearing about it." And Phillips countered what Krulak had just reported. That's not the way a thing like that should have been handled. Bundy and I, and the president's staff, should have known about that in advance, and should have organized the presentation, if necessary. There was nothing the president could do; he was simply given reports that the facts were different, and he didn't know who to believe. The meeting didn't go anywhere.

It should have been clearer to us at the time that this was a very complicated matter with a lot of local roots, and that we were—by and large—trying to apply very oversimplified paradigms, either from the Korean War or the Malayan situation—or whatever—and getting in deeper. The turning point, under Johnson, was an ill-considered one. But it wouldn't have been easy for President Kennedy to reduce the involvement. The president had not really encountered the fierce objections that he would have run into had he seriously tried to lower the level of involvement and taken out advisers and gradually backed away from it—after all, 1964 was going to be an election year; to do all that in an election year would have been very, very difficult. The president had learned at the Bay of Pigs, and otherwise, to be cautious about advice he got from the military. The president was killed, and Johnson came in and didn't know up from down on foreign policy; that was his Achilles' heel. That was a great tragedy.

George Ball   The people the president sent would be on the spot and could make an appraisal on the spot. Obviously what they were getting was from the people who were on the spot who had their own agendas. I have always thought this idea of personal envoys was greatly overblown. Kennedy gave me hell when I suggested that you get more by talking to the correspondents coming back. The idea that you talk to the press about anything was an anathema. He hated David Halberstam in particular. He worried about a fellow who had ideas that were so contrary to his own.

William Sullivan   When Kennedy came into office in 1961, the chairman of the Joint Chiefs was Lyman Lemnitzer. Lem was an old buddy of Eisenhower. He was pretty much a conventional warfare fellow. Maxwell Taylor had quit in 1959 or so and written his book *The Uncertain Trumpet.* Then he came into the White House in the extraordinary position as military adviser to the president, something that constitutionally or legally never existed. It was an ad hoc creation. Kennedy was turned off by the conventional military. As it turns out, the advice that Lemnitzer was personally prepared to give on Vietnam turned out to be sounder than the advice that Max Taylor gave. But Lem was never allowed to get it to the president. In fact, the highest he ever got was a briefing he did in Bob McNamara's office. I was there; Rusk was not. I guess Harriman was there. Mac Bundy was there, Max Taylor also. But what Lem proposed was militarily much sounder than the final plan that we followed.

He proposed a limited invasion of the southern two provinces of North Vietnam to cut off the Ho Chi Minh Trail. Belatedly, if you read Westmoreland's painful analysis, he suddenly discovered in the last of his years there that the Ho Chi Minh Trail was his weakness because they were funneling the stuff down the trail and he wasn't able to get at it. I won't say the president rejected Lem's proposals, because I don't think he actually ever heard them played out in the way Lem actually wanted to present them to him. Instead he bought Max's idea of counterinsurgency. By the time he was assassinated, he had come to the conclusion that this probably wasn't going to work.

THE TAYLOR MISSION

In October 1961, as the situation in South Vietnam deteriorated, President Kennedy sent Gen. Maxwell Taylor and Walt Rostow to Vietnam. They were accompanied by Worth Bagley, a naval officer on Tay-

lor's White House staff. The Taylor-Rostow mission resulted in a recommendation that U.S. troops be sent to Vietnam.

Worth Bagley, staff assistant to Gen. Maxwell Taylor, military representative of the president; lieutenant commander, U.S. Navy   Nineteen sixty-one was really the crucial year, at least from the standpoint of President Kennedy's decision to send General Taylor and Walt Rostow on their mission to Saigon. The months before this had been difficult for the president. The Bay of Pigs, the situation in Laos, the Vienna summit, and the erection of the Berlin Wall had created a feeling that international events were not going well. There was a sense that the president's ability to lead had been put into question. I think it is accurate to say that he began to explore what he could do to reestablish his credibility and that of the United States in a situation that seemed to be working against him.

Taylor was given a directive which essentially said that the president wanted his recommendations on the steps, both military and nonmilitary, that the U.S. might take to prevent further deterioration in Vietnam's security, and how, eventually, to contain and eliminate the threat to Vietnam's independence. There was also a second injunction, which was more ambiguous, which suggested that Kennedy was of two minds on what he wanted to do. He told Taylor by letter that the leaders and the people of South Vietnam had the initial responsibility for maintaining their independence, and that whatever options America might consider would have to be evaluated on that basis. Those two injunctions appeared on the surface to be inconsistent. But the president and Taylor talked about this, and Kennedy said quite clearly that he preferred to stand and overcome insurgency rather than to disengage from South Vietnam.

In Vietnam Taylor learned that the stability and control over the countryside was decreasing. He had evidence that the strength of the insurgency force was increasing, as was the flow of supplies and support from the North. Taylor had conversations with Diem and came away feeling that Diem was not very honest—that he had tried to mislead him about the political and military situation. Taylor felt that things were getting worse, that the populace had to be brought into the struggle against insurgency, and most important, the infiltration had to be stopped, so whatever the penalties would be if we went in, they would not be increasing the whole time we were there.

Taylor proposed that Diem be made to accept a personal envoy from the president who would coordinate joint U.S.–South Vietnamese activity. He also suggested that U.S. advisers or military units in increased numbers be committed only when we were confident of Diem's cooperation. The final proposal was that a plan would have to be developed to interrupt the overland and seaborne transport of supplies from the North. In addition Taylor proposed that one way to gauge the effect of a greater American presence on how the Viet Cong acted would be to make a gesture to help the South Vietnamese overcome the effects of one of their regular flooding season incidents. It happened that that year much of the Mekong Delta was flooded and many roads were impassable. Taylor's idea was to send in an unarmed army engineer battalion for a period of two to three months to help the village areas recover. This was communicated to the president in an "eyes only" message that was leaked by someone in the White House to the *Washington Post*. The newspaper then published an editorial which essentially said that Taylor was preparing an outrageous proposal to widen the war by committing American combat troops.

When the president met with Taylor, he was essentially unmoved. He did not accept Taylor's proposals, including the introduction of the engineer battalion.

William Trueheart   I must say I didn't know until long after I left Vietnam that General Taylor recommended that they send an engineering battalion—in other words, some American ground forces. That part of the recommendation was not approved by Kennedy. I knew that this sort of thing was being considered because for some reason I was sent out with one of the generals on the Military Assistance Group to look over the situation in the flood area. At that time there was an enormous flood on the Mekong, and the question was whether we could do anything about it in a humanitarian sense. But I realized they were also considering if some army engineer units could do something, so we would have a military presence there drawing out of this humanitarian operation. So the general and I—he was an engineer—flew all over the area in a little plane, and he said it wasn't like a flood on the Mississippi or anything like that. The water just came up and went down. The people were quite accustomed to this happening and just climbed in trees and almost took their cattle into the trees. In any case, he came back and said he couldn't see anything for American engineers to do and perform a useful service there. I certainly couldn't disagree with him. So it would have been a subterfuge if they had decided to do something like that.

George Ball   I think Kennedy's view was that he very much wanted to avoid getting in deeply in the war. At the same time he didn't want to be regarded as a coward.

What happened was that Rostow and Taylor came back from a fact-finding trip with a recommendation to up the present level of six hundred advisers and go on open-ended. They would not be there to fight but would have to be equipped to defend themselves. I told McNamara and Gilpatric that I thought the Rostow-Taylor report was a most dangerous document. They were going to involve us in a major war and we wouldn't be able to get out of it. It's the wrong kind of a war in the wrong place. Vietnam is hostile country, both politically and topographically. Well, they didn't agree with me at all.

The next couple of days, I talked to the president. I said, Mr. President, I think you would make an enormous mistake if you accepted the Rostow-Taylor report. You are going to have thousands of men in the jungles and rice paddies of Vietnam and you'll never find them again, because it's hostile country, topographically and politically. We are going to repeat the experience of the French. If you escalate at this point you will go on escalating and we will have three hundred thousand men there in five years. Well, I was quite wrong: we had five hundred thousand men in three years. He said to me, "George, I always thought you were one of the brightest guys in town, but you're crazier than hell, this isn't going to happen." I don't know what he meant by that. Whether he wouldn't let it happen or that wasn't the way events would move, I can't tell. I've puzzled about that in my mind. He would have had exactly the same people advising him who advised Johnson to push in. By the time of his death, we had sixteen thousand men out there. I can't imagine he would have brought them out. I know the real Kennedy-philes disagree heartily with me on that.

John Kenneth Galbraith   In the autumn of 1961 I was in Washington with Nehru, and Max Taylor and Walt Rostow had just come back with the Taylor report, which proposed putting troops into Vietnam as flood-control workers—a somewhat imperfect disguise. They would have defended Vietnam on the pretense of damming up the dikes on the Mekong River. I went to Kennedy and protested against that. Kennedy, knowing that I did not have an open mind, sent me to Vietnam so he would have another report so he could say, "Well, Max and Walt say this, but Galbraith says this." I went out to Vietnam—I must say I had some experience, more than most, on Oriental governments—but I was not prepared for anything quite as bad as Diem.

I met with the military, CIA, and AID. I must say that the level of confusion you got talking with the generals was as impressive as anything on that trip. I think at that time the military was finding its way in Vietnam and was divided between those who saw a real problem and those who had some notion that this was a small insurrection that could be rather easily put down.

You must not minimize the role that was played by the youthful and middle-aged adventurers who had a sense of the enormous drama of their situation and loved the idea that here they were in charge of the whole world, or, as it was called, the whole free world, and had a license for all kinds of activities which in a normal, civilized, law-abiding country wouldn't be permitted.

William Trueheart   The way it got put in the Taylor report, it said it was important to establish some ground presence in Vietnam, but Kennedy wasn't ready to go that far. I don't know who was advising him against it. I presume someone like George Ball. I am pretty sure that we at the embassy were not asked for comments on it. I'm sure that Nolting [Ambassador Frederick E. Nolting, Jr.] would have been opposed to it at that time. But out of that did grow the whole business of establishing the military command setup which we opposed very strongly. I think Nolting came very close to resigning over this issue. On the one hand it changed the relationship between the ambassador and the military people in the country; but more importantly we were convinced we had a political problem to deal with and this was the first step in deciding it was a military problem.

THE AUGUST 24 CABLE

In the spring of 1963 the situation took a dramatic turn for the worse when the Buddhist community conducted a series of demonstrations, including highly publicized self-immolations, on the streets of the capital. In August Diem's troops raided the Buddhist pagodas, roughing up and arresting hundreds of people. This action prompted a dissident group of South Vietnamese generals to contact the U.S. ambassador, Henry Cabot Lodge, Jr., to determine how the Kennedy administration would react if they were to launch a coup against the Diem regime.

On August 24, a Saturday, when many high government officials, including the president, were out of Washington, State Department officials Averell Harriman and Roger Hilsman, along with presidential assistant Michael Forrestal, drafted a cable to Ambassador Lodge. This cable has become the subject of significant debate as to whether the message sent a clear signal to the Vietnamese generals of American intentions regarding the Diem government.

Roger Hilsman   The generals came on a Saturday to our ambassador and said, "We have reason to believe, we have evidence that they are going to have us arrested. We may find it necessary to pull a coup to save our lives and our country. What would be your attitude on this?" It was a Saturday, so Mike Forrestal, Averell Harriman, and I got together and drafted a cable which was pretty much boilerplate: "The United States cannot engage in the internal affairs of Vietnam. This is an internal matter. However, we share a worldview. We will examine any new government, or a government that comes about by a coup, but we cannot participate in the coup. We cannot take a stand on this." That cable was then cleared.

Dick Helms, deputy CIA director, said, "Boy, it is about time. I couldn't approve more." Bob McNamara was out of town. Roswell Gilpatric said they couldn't approve more, and Max Taylor signed off. Max Taylor turned out to be the only coward, because he signed off on it without any question. Then later, he said, "Well, I thought it had all been agreed to." Now, that is bullshit. I wouldn't sign off on a cable that I didn't agree with without at least expressing my doubt. I think that was an abdication of his job, if he had any doubts at the time.

President Kennedy was at Hyannis Port. He had secure communications. Several drafts went back and forth to him. You didn't send anything like that without the president's signature on it. Not only did the president get the first draft, the president got subsequent drafts.

It is perfectly true that there were plenty of us who were hoping for a coup. But we just said, This has got to be a Vietnamese decision. We cannot come down on one side or another. We will examine any new government on its own merits. That was the original draft. Rusk added a paragraph that made us more committed to a coup, or to encouraging a coup, than did the original draft. Now, the interesting thing is that I am told by people who knew him that he denied it.

Now, one of the paragraphs in that cable was: "You must give Diem one last chance, so tell him that we have heard about coup plotting and tell him that we believe that the only way he can save his government is to revise his policies." Well, Lodge received the cable on Saturday, and on Sunday, we got a cable back from Lodge, saying: "If you make me do this, Diem will move. He will arrest the generals; he will kill the generals and you will have their blood on your hands." So Monday morning the NSC convened, and Kennedy came in and was mad that the cable was cleared. But in light of Lodge's cable, McCone and McNamara now added: "If I had been in town, I wouldn't have signed off on it." So his government was going to pieces; that was what he was mad about. I had never been in a meeting like this before. He was mad. Not mad at anybody in particular. He was mad because it went to pieces. He said, "Look, nothing has happened. Lodge has not done anything." He said we have three choices: We could go with the original cable; we could cancel the whole fucking business; or we could accept Lodge's revision. And then he did something I have never seen a president do. He said, "Mr. Rusk, what do you think?" Rusk said, "I will go with Lodge." "Mr. McNamara?" "I will go with Lodge." "Mr. McCone?" "I will go with Lodge." So it went around, and the revised August 24 cable was agreed to by vote.

Victor Krulak I was playing golf at the Chevy Chase Club when I got a call, which I took in the men's locker room. It was Hilsman, who said that they would like me to come down to the White House as soon as I could—that they had something to show me. When I got there, they showed me the draft of a cable; they wanted me to initial it for the Pentagon. I said, "No. I don't want to do that; it is not appropriate. The chairman of the Joint Chiefs of Staff is in town, so why don't you find General Taylor?"—I knew he was out shopping. That did not fit their time schedule, so I left without initialing the message. In any case, it went out—and we know the result. What the cable said to me was that if you are determined to change your government, we will not interpose an objection. I didn't want any part of it. The cable indicated that there was dissent in the highest echelons of government; there is nothing unusual about that, nor is it bad.

George Ball I didn't have anything to do with drafting the cable. That happened the one time in my life I decided I would go out and play some golf. All of a sudden when we got up to the eighteenth green, here was a big Cadillac with Averell Harriman and Roger Hilsman. And they had this telegram. I was acting secretary because Rusk had gone up to New York for the UN. The president was up in Hyannis Port and Bob McNamara was out climbing a mountain somewhere, and the place was just decimated. So they handed me this telegram and said, We want to send this. I said, "I am not going to send it on my own authority; this has to be cleared by the president." So I called the president and read him the telegram. He said, "Do you think it is a good idea?" I said, "I think the problems are getting enormous for us in Vietnam. We are associated with a regime that is behaving in an outrageous fashion and I would think this cable is sufficiently qualified so that there would be no great harm in doing it." So he said, "If you agree and Dean agrees." I said, "I haven't been able to reach him." Then I did reach Dean. And Rusk said, "If the president is willing to do this, and if McNamara is willing, I guess we might as well go ahead. If it brings the government down, it brings the government down."

Everybody by that time had lost faith in Diem. He was obviously a pleasant fellow, but he had this terrible incubus of this damned brother and sister-in-law. My secret feeling was perhaps this would collapse the war and we would get out. I couldn't reach McNamara, but I got hold of Roswell Gilpatric down at his farm. Actually the cable had no real effect. It wasn't until September that the president appeared on television and said, These fellows would have to shape up or we are going to have to help change it; we can't go on. I always thought that the incident was enormously overblown.

William Colby The cable represented disarray. Hilsman and Harriman put it together one Saturday afternoon. Lodge took it as a direct order to put on a coup. The cable clearly was a call for change. On Monday

Kennedy got everybody in a room and asked if they wanted to change their mind. Nobody quite dared to do that. I think there was a reluctance to think in terms of Diem's death.

Dean Rusk That telegram in August was sent out when President Kennedy, McNamara, and I were, all three, out of town. It was cleared by clear telephone—unclassified telephone. When it was discussed with me, I was told that President Kennedy had already approved it, so I gave my decision to go along with it. But when the three of us got back to town, we found that this telegram had gone much further than we wanted it to go in encouraging a coup in Vietnam.

It was not a "smoking gun," but it seemed to encourage Cabot Lodge to throw some influence in favor of a coup and that was too much for us, when Kennedy, McNamara, and I got back to Washington to see what the cable actually said. And so we pulled back on that pretty fast.

And so we found a way to pull back on the implications of that cable in communications that followed. Now I don't know what young CIA staffers might have said to what generals out there; there's no way to know that.

William Colby The fact is that the Americans had gone to the generals and said, We will continue support if you replace Diem; that's your green light. We scared the generals to death. They were afraid the word would get back and they would be punished.

Harry Felt On a Saturday somebody called me from the State Department and read to me over the phone a message which he had drafted, saying that the United States government wants brother Nhu out of the country, and asked me what I thought of that. Well, I agreed that we should get him out of the country, of course, so I tried to call the chairman of the Joint Chiefs—this was a Saturday. He was out of town. I tried to call McNamara; he was out of town. I said, "Oh, what the heck. The guy asked a question; I'm going to call the State Department and say, 'Yes. I agree.'" Well, on Monday, the chairman of the Joint Chiefs, and McNamara found out about this, and just hit the roof. And they immediately hopped over to the White House and asked President Kennedy to fire me. Roger Hilsman says in his book that the president just smiled.

William Trueheart   I am not sure Washington ever reached a point in deciding there had to be a change. The famous telegram which, in effect, kicked things off, in a way was not all that clearly approved. I think that right up until the very end, Washington was holding out the prospect that if Diem could send Nhu and Madame Nhu off, that might change the whole thing. In the end, I think, it is true to say that the Vietnamese military did take things in their own hands.

Angier Biddle Duke   Kennedy had an ambivalence about Diem. I was conscious of it because I had told him that I wanted to ambassador to Spain when I left, and he said, "Gee, a Catholic country." He thought of Diem, I think, very much like Franco. He was very, very careful of his own involvement with another Catholic chief of state. He was very sensitive to that and very conscious of Diem as a Catholic figure. Therefore, he wanted to deal with it as objectively as possible, to remove the Catholic issue from that entirely.

To illustrate my point, when we called on the pope, it was, of course, billed and arranged as a meeting between two chiefs of state. However, he did bring his family with him, and they wanted to be briefed, evidently, as thoroughly as all the rest of us were. When we got into the papal library for the presentation, the president gave the pope a firm handshake, and Eunice started to swoop to the floor to kiss his ring, and the president got her in a grip of iron and yanked her to her feet.

Alexis Johnson   Before Averell [Harriman] died, we were at a big cocktail party. Averell spotted me across the room and made a beeline for me. Averell said to me, "You know, there was plenty of time after that telegram for people to change it, or reverse it, if they wanted to." That's all he said. This was years afterward, you see. I'd never said anything to him about it. We'd never discussed it, and it was obviously preying on Averell's mind. I never forgot it. It was one or two years before he passed away.

THE COUP AGAINST DIEM

Ambassador Lodge and Admiral Harry Felt, who was visiting Saigon in his capacity as commander in chief of U.S. armed forces in the

Pacific, met with President Diem on November 1, 1963, the morning of the day on which the coup began.

Harry Felt   I had been in Bangkok at a SEATO meeting and decided on the way home: I might as well pop into Saigon and see my chief MAG [military assistance group], for just that purpose. When I arrived at the airport in Saigon, General [Tran Van] Don, chief of the armed services, was there to meet me, and right away, he said: "Are you going to see the president?" I said, "No, I hadn't intended to; I saw him not too long ago. I'm just going to talk to my MAG." He said, "I think you should see the president." Harkins was with me also. So Harkins and I thought about this, and I said, "We'd better go see the ambassador." Lodge listened to this, and I said, "A lot of rumors have been going around about coups. What about that?" And he said, "There is no general with hair enough on his chest to pull one off." But, he said, "I guess we'd better ask for an audience with the president." So he got on the phone and made the arrangements.

We went to call on President Diem the next morning. The first thing President Diem brought up was: "Are there any rumors around about coups?" "We don't know of any," said Lodge. And then Diem went into his usual hour to hour-and-a-half monologue, and after a while, an officer came in and said something to the president. It gave me an opportunity to interrupt, and I said, "What did he say, Mr. President?" He said, "You have to catch a plane at twelve o'clock." I said, "That's right; I'm supposed to leave at twelve o'clock." He said, "Oh, well, you'll catch the plane all right," and then he went on talking. But finally, he quit, and we departed—Harkins and I—Lodge remained behind with President Diem.

When we got to the airport, there was Don again, to see me off, and the press was there, and fired off questions. I passed some of them to Don; he'd take some of them; I'd take some of them. The ladies who were there watching said Don was very nervous—they'd never seen him chew gum before, and he was very nervous. The day before, when Don had met me on arrival in Saigon, I said, "Well, I'll come up to your head-quarters and pay my respects, General," and he said, "No. I'm going to come to General Harkins's and pay my respects." So I said, "General, I'm a visitor. That isn't the way it's supposed to be done. I'm going to call on you." He said, "Never mind. I'm going to call on you," which he did.

Westmoreland was there, waiting to take over from Harkins. I was in Westmoreland's office when Don came in. And I said, "Let's go into General Harkins's office." So we went in there, and immediately General Harkins said—looking up at the map—"There's a marine unit which is uncommitted—one of your big marine units." And General Don said, "Oh, it's committed. It's moving up-country." And Harkins pointed to another unit, and Don said, "It's committed; it's moving." Well, those were the two units that pulled the coup. That's probably why Don didn't want me in his headquarters. I've come to the tentative conclusion that Don was trying to protect me, or else using me as a front.

William Trueheart After he and Admiral Felt met with Diem, Lodge went home for lunch. I went to my house, and my driver went off for his lunch. But he came back immediately and told me the military were taking over the police station near his house. I thought this was clear evidence that the coup had begun.

The idea of what was going to happen to Diem personally did not arise during the twenty-four to forty-eight hours that the coup took place. I spent the whole time in my office in the embassy, and Lodge was at his house. The coup itself was a military operation with troops advancing on the palace, where we all thought Diem and Nhu were holed up. They were not there, but I don't believe anybody in the American community knew this. The first information we had, in fact, was when the military was trying to reach them in the palace.

Then, at about four P.M., Diem called the embassy from Cholon. He told Lodge that it appeared that a coup was under way and asked what was the position of Washington. Lodge replied, "It is the middle of the night in Washington; I don't know if they have any policy." Lodge expressed concern for Diem's safety, but he definitely did not say we will help you get out of the country.

The next thing I heard was that they had been assassinated. I've heard many stories about who gave that order, but I've never heard anything convincing as to who did what. I've heard that when Kennedy was told, he was quite visibly shocked. I was present when Lodge heard, but I don't recall him being visibly shaken by that—or by anything else.

William Smith I think there was a certain amount of impatience that led some to want Diem out. It was probably a little bit of escapism. They could see the logic of events and they asked, How can we change the logic? so they thought getting rid of Diem might be one way of doing it.

Once we started that course of action, we knew what would be the consequences. In a place like that, what are you going to do with someone? You might say you would exile him. I think once you started that, you knew what was going to happen. And you accepted it.

If I had been in Diem's position, I would have known at that time if something like this were happening, the United States had to be informed about—and at least know about—what was going on. And I would have said to myself—that being true—"I'm not sure the U.S. Embassy is the safest place for me."

Marcus Raskin   It goes to show the hubris of the period. The assumption was that you could get rid of somebody and do it in the way that you wanted, to get rid of them, that the people who were out in the field were not independent actors who had their own interests, their own animosities, their own purpose. So it stands to reason that unless a direct order was given, or the CIA, or a group within the CIA, wanted to do it, I imagine people thinking, Well, we will give this guy a safe conduct card out; we'll just get rid of him. That is the way we'll deal with it—much the way you might want to deal with a Latin American dictator—that these people are pawns on a chessboard.

There was this view at the time that if you had the right sort of guy in Vietnam, rather than this terrible Diem, that somehow it would all work out. That was currency of the realm of the liberal newspapers during that period. That somehow the right guy could make it okay. In September of 1963 there were reports on the Buddhist situation—the immolations—and there was this liberal notion that this was a corrupt operation. If you get rid of Diem, somehow things will fall into place.

George McGovern   I think we were involved—at least in looking the other way. I don't know to what extent the president was personally involved, but I've always felt that it would not have happened without at least our cooperation. I don't think we set it up, but I think we agreed not to intervene with what was a gathering storm inside the Diem administration. I know that McNamara and Rusk both came to regret that incident in the Vietnam period, perhaps because it wasn't an attractive and acceptable alternative.

Diem was a very difficult little man. I don't think the drafters of the cable or Lodge intended, or expected, that the two brothers would be rubbed out the way they were. Now that may have been naive, particularly in the light of the character of some of the people who were involved on the edges and the fringes of the coup. But certainly, I think all those on the U.S. side who sponsored this would have recoiled from it had they believed that it was going to be an assassination rather than a more gentle departure.

Pierre Salinger   Despite all the things that have been said, Kennedy was not responsible for Diem's assassination. He was aware that there might be a coup d'état, but he did not give instructions for the coup makers to kill Diem.

Norman Podhoretz   I don't have the slightest doubt that the Diem assassination was authorized—maybe not in so many words, but I don't have any doubt whatever that they decided to get rid of him and a blind eye was turned; tacit signals were given. I don't for a minute doubt that they knew and approved of the assassination.

Harry Felt   I don't think the administration ever wanted Diem out. I've been asked the question: "Was Diem good for the country?" He was. For a long, long time he was very good for the country. He was reelected, and then he became a mandarin-type guy; he got mixed up with the Buddhists, and as Dean Rusk commented, "He's fighting two wars now." I talked to Big Minh after that assassination, and according to him, he and General Don, and Kim, had decided that Diem should go. And so they called the president on the telephone, and the president angrily slammed down the phone. Big Minh said, "That does it. Let's go get him." According to Big Minh, again, they found the two of them in a Catholic church and put them in a covered lorry. And, according to this story, Brother Nhu pulled a gun. One of Minh's guards shot him.

Bui Diem   I do not see a kind of smoking gun behind the Diem assassination, but it is quite clear that without some kind of green light from the American side, the Vietnamese generals could not do the coup. From my personal point of view, I would say that even without direct involvement in the coup, the Americans somehow have to accept responsibility in the whole thing, in the sense that without the green light from the American side, the Vietnamese generals would be in a very difficult situation to start the coup.

The generals who planned the coup did not plan to have Diem assassinated. The assassination—if it happened the way it happened—occurred without the knowledge of many people inside the group who organized the coup. Even right now, among the Vietnamese, we try to find out what really happened; who gave the order to kill Mr. Diem and his brother. But even though we tried to find the answer, we couldn't find a definite one about this question. There are many many versions, but none of the versions can be entirely verified.

Roger Hilsman Maybe I thought it was riskier, and maybe I failed Kennedy in pointing out that there wasn't a damn thing we could do about it—you know, the schedule when it happened and Diem and Nhu escaped from the palace and went to the Chinese guy's friends in Cholon° and called Lodge. Lodge said, "I will personally come over to where you are and put you in my car and take you to the airport and put you on an American plane," and Diem would have none of it. I was surprised that he was assassinated. I guess half of me, or two-thirds of me, was not. On alternate Tuesdays I believed there would be a coup, and on alternate Wednesdays I believed there would never be a coup, no matter what happened. You can't push a piece of cooked spaghetti; I had very little confidence that the Vietnamese military were ever going to pull a coup. But I remember Maggie Higgins [Marguerite Higgins, correspondent, *New York Herald Tribune*] called me up in the middle of the night—hawk of hawks. But Maggie was a friend, and she asked, "How does it feel to have blood on your hands?" And I said, "God, Maggie, this is a revolution; people get hurt in revolutions. No way you can stop that."

Victor Krulak When Mr. McNamara and I were in Saigon, before the incident, we talked to a British expert about the prospect for a change in government, and he said that you must be careful, because what you would get might be worse than what you have. That impressed me. To say that the U.S. government had a role in the assassination of Diem is ridiculous.

°After escaping from the presidential palace in Saigon, Diem and Nhu took refuge in the home of a Chinese friend in the twin city of Cholon, where they had earlier established a communications center.

Nicholas Katzenbach   In a sense it was a terrible mistake, for as bad as Diem was—and he was terrible—you had no one to replace him; you had nothing else. It would have been easier to withdraw from Vietnam with Diem still in power than it was later.

Ray Cline   There was a smoking gun in the assassination. Kennedy signed the paper. Now, it was a little vague; it didn't say "assassination." What they said was that if brother Nhu *didn't* get put out of power, they would have to turn against Diem. Asian families are very powerful, and Nhu was not going to go out of business. Therefore, I felt it was a disaster for Harriman and Hilsman to say, We can destroy Diem. You see, everybody thinks something better will come along. But it didn't. Diem was destroyed by the military people, but this didn't improve anything. They went down the drain until Thieu [Nguyen Van Thieu] came along, many years later.* This is the kind of innocence that Americans have: something better will always come along. It seldom does.

The real problem was that McGeorge Bundy was all involved in this, too, and they thought somehow they could get rid of Nhu. That was their goal—and if they could get rid of him, then Diem could do a better job. But they didn't realize that if the military killed Nhu, they would also kill Diem; it was just natural. These families all hang together. If they get back in power, they will destroy the military people. Their family structures are just very tight; I don't think Kennedy understood that.

William Colby   Kennedy's decisions did not have a straight line in them. My complaint in retrospect is that he rather vacillated on the subject of Vietnam, and on the subject of President Diem. There was a big fight here in the summer of 1963 after the Buddhist situation erupted. Some of the people said, We have to get rid of Diem. We cannot win this war with Diem, he had been totally repudiated by his population. The other group, of which I was one, said, There is nothing better than him around, he's not as bad as all that, he represents some stability. So stay with him and try to help him improve. That argument went on among the president's advisers, frequently very bitter. The president would sort of take sometimes one advice and sometimes the other.

In Vietnam we made three serious mistakes. The first was the over-

*Thieu become president of the Republic of South Vietnam in 1967, remaining in office until the North Vietnamese takeover of South Vietnam in the spring of 1975.

throw of Diem. The second was overmilitarizing. The third was abandoning it. Curiously, the third came from the second, and the second came from the first, so the seminal problem was the overthrow of Diem. That created the confusion and chaos that Lyndon Johnson could only deal with with troops, and once you got them in there, you couldn't get them out. If we had left Diem in power in 1963 and not participated in the coup, he would have turned back to the strategic hamlets as his primary strategy, which it had been before he got diverted by the Buddhist thing, and gradually damped the war down over the next couple of years, or he would have failed. And the Communists would have won in 1965. Either result was better than what happened.

THE LODGE APPOINTMENT

In July 1963 President Kennedy announced that former senator Henry Cabot Lodge, Jr., would replace Frederick Nolting as U.S. ambassador to South Vietnam. Nolting had lost favor with both the American establishment in Saigon and with officials in Washington who felt he was too close to President Diem.

William Trueheart   There had been an effort the year before Kennedy came into office to force Diem to become a better politician, to govern the country in a better way. The leverage the previous ambassador used did not work. The conclusion reached in Washington before Nolting was selected was Diem was the best we were going to get, and we had to try to get along with him and hopefully improve his performance, but not to use any pressure. That was the brief Nolting had when he went out. He developed a good relationship with Diem, but I don't think of any reason to believe he convinced Diem to do anything in particular that was helpful. He had been there for about two years and he went on home leave. If he had had any understanding that he was not going to return for another tour of duty, I didn't know about it. He went on a long leave to Greece with his family. It was while he was there that this Buddhist crisis really developed. In the course of it the Kennedys had decided to replace him with Lodge. As far as I know he was not informed of this until he heard about it on the boat coming back from Europe to the United States. Of course I knew nothing about it. When I got the telegram saying Henry Cabot Lodge, Jr., I frankly thought this was his son.

They didn't send any information so I looked it up in *Who's Who* and found out *he* was junior.

William Sullivan   Politically it was a good appointment. Also I think Cabot introduced an independence with the military that a career man at that time could not have done. Paul Harkins, the head of the military advisory group, was something of a cavalier type, but he had also been somebody that Cabot had known for years, and Cabot wasn't very high on Paul. Among other things Paul used to smoke cigarettes in a long holder, and the smoke would blow in Cabot's face, and Cabot would get damned annoyed with it. But I think he was able to introduce his judgment, which was significantly more reserved than the gung-ho military, in a way that gave the president a better perspective. Cabot was not the hardest-working person in the world, but by and large he gave the embassy there a new sense of respectability and responsibility.

Ben Bradlee   I'm not so sure how noble Kennedy's motive was in sending Cabot Lodge to Vietnam as ambassador. Kennedy had beaten Cabot Lodge; Cabot Lodge was of the Boston aristocracy that had lifted its leg on the Kennedys for years, and he felt that Cabot Lodge would silence the Republicans. I thought that Jack just knew that it was a stroke of genius to get Cabot Lodge out there; he knew that Cabot Lodge—who was such a gent that they knew he would do it—would treat him seriously, unlike the others. He knew that there would be no funny business in the political area—Cabot Lodge wasn't going anywhere.

John Kenneth Galbraith   First of all it was a foothold in the Republican party; a foothold in the opposition. It meant that the Republicans were partly responsible for it. But Cabot was a very intelligent man, with a good political sense, and a good operator. I had a feeling that Kennedy felt that he was a stronger, more reliable figure than Fred Nolting, and less inclined than Nolting was to simply go along with the establishment view.

Lucius Battle   Cabot Lodge was a Republican. He was considered, I think, to be brainier than he really was. I never found him particularly smart myself. But he was a figure of some note in the country. It was the deflection of criticism that they wanted—the appearance of bipartisanism that may or may not have really existed at that point.

William Trueheart I thought Lodge performed magnificently in those first months there. He came in the middle of the night to a city under martial law. I've never seen anybody take charge of a complicated and difficult situation in a more commanding way. You must bear in mind that by the time he got there, the regime had already repudiated whatever commitment they had made to Nolting, raided the pagodas, and totally alienated the student population and just about everybody in town, so that Lodge was coming into a situation of great turmoil. I don't know if he had had an open mind before he left Washington, but I'm pretty sure it wasn't very open by the time he got to Saigon.

Lodge acted in a way that suggested he would be quite different from Nolting, he would be aloof to the Diem government. I don't think the decision to send Lodge in fact meant the decision had been taken to facilitate a coup d'état. I think the president had concluded the approach Nolting had been told to take would not work, and pressure would have to be applied to Diem even though it had been tried before without success. I think if Diem had made any reasonable efforts to resolve these problems, to broaden his government—and above all to resolve this religious dispute—things might have been different as far as our policies were concerned. In retrospect I doubt no matter what he had done, it would have been possible for him to put off the inevitable victory of the Ho Chi Minh [leader of North Vietnam] elements. They had too much going for them in terms of popular support, so much outrage at the colonial heritage.

COUNTERINSURGENCY

As frustration mounted with the increase in Viet Cong activity, the administration turned to counterinsurgency as a potentially effective means of countering the guerrillas. The counterinsurgency experts, Maj. Gen. Edward Lansdale and Sir Robert Thompson, were increasingly called upon to present their views. To some observers, the Kennedy brothers were fascinated by these heroes of World War II and by the techniques they advocated.

Worth Bagley The interest in counterinsurgency really did not develop until mid-1961. At that point people started calling in the Lansdales and Thompsons and all the experts from Vietnam and Malaysia.

Taylor himself was convinced it required centralization of authority and a great deal of initiative down the line. Both were incorporated in the conditions he set for Kennedy, but these conditions were rejected by the president and by Diem. In a sense Kennedy wanted to try to do something in Vietnam without the price required in order to do it. Thus there was no way you were going to improve the situation in Vietnam.

I had no evidence that Kennedy had a romanticized view of counterinsurgency. The evidence I had suggested a harsher strategic and political view of these matters than it had to do with the details or romance of counterinsurgency.

There were a number of points of view in the White House on Vietnam. One point of view was that the Soviets would not use force. The best way to deal with them was in a nonmilitary way. That point of view was refuted in 1962 in the missile crisis.

William Colby   He was interested in counterinsurgency. The military paid it lip service but was not very serious about it. He thought it offered an alternative to sending large forces. He supported the growth of the Special Forces. Counterinsurgency was very much on the front burner at the time among a lot of thinking people. The search for an alternative to the clash of major military forces. I was particularly interested in it, too. I had been a guerrilla in World War II.

On my first tour in Vietnam I generated a lot of experiments on how this could be done, using one of the Special Forces with training but basically in how to organize the people to protect themselves, so that their safety would not solely depend on soldiers. The strategic hamlets came out of our early experiments in arming local communities to defend themselves.

Certainly the communists began in 1959 what they call the People's War. When Diem developed the strategic hamlets, he had some success for about a year in stemming the tide, but of course he was overthrown, and the place went into chaos.

Walt Rostow   Kennedy got interested in guerrilla warfare because the Soviets were involved in this in Latin America, Africa, and Asia. It wasn't something he cooked up from some Russian verbiage; it was coming in over the cables very damn day. We had a study done which showed that guerrilla war is very tough if there is an open frontier. We faced an open frontier in Laos and Vietnam. I think it could have been closed by putting a couple of U.S. divisions across the Ho Chi Minh Trail in Laos. But it was never done. Arthur Schlesinger called me "Chet Bowles with a machine gun."

Pierre Salinger   President Kennedy understood very soon after he got involved in Vietnam that this was a guerrilla war and that you could not fight it in a normal Western style—that you had to have Green Berets and that kind of thing. He created the Green Berets organization at Fort Bragg because he understood that that was the kind of outfit we needed to be able to fight in that war. Having gone through the Berlin crisis and the missile crisis, he was trying to limit Vietnam as much as he could. To give it a low profile and not make it a major event that was going to touch the American people. I wouldn't say he was a pacifist at all; he was looking at the world in a global way and trying to balance out what he had to deal with. In 1963, while things were getting worse in Vietnam, they were getting better with the Soviet Union.

Ben Bradlee   Kennedy felt that something short of war had to be done, because the war decisions were so awful. General Taylor got Kennedy into the Special Forces and the Green Berets—and all that stuff that really didn't do America much good as it turned out; it didn't solve any problems. Lansdale was being hyped by Joe Alsop and all those people.

Ray Cline   From time to time I talked to Kennedy about what they called "the brushfire wars." He felt there wasn't going to be a general war, but that if South Vietnam got destroyed, then another domino move would take place. Kennedy had this concept that if we used special forces, we can stop wars fast and prevent the communists from making domino gains. I think he was right on this. He said, "We have to stop these brushfire wars." His object was to have guerrilla warfare, and he set up the Special Forces—the Green Berets. I think they are now pretty damn good; it took about twenty years to do it.

Victor Krulak   It was such a different war; the objectives were not hills and valleys, road junctions, towns and river crossings, but people. The president put his shoulder behind the counterinsurgency business. In terms of the structure: I was the person at the Joint Chiefs of Staff level;

there were Army, Navy, Air Force, and Marine Corps people, and others, in the various unified commands—sort of a Christmas tree. There was one wraithlike personality who crept in and out, named Lansdale. I was never sure where he'd been, where he was going, or why. He was a very secretive person who spoke in parables. He also had a few links with the CIA.

Ralph Dungan   Bobby was high on Krulak. I thought Krulak was a menace; I think he bamboozled Taylor. Bobby was very, very hawkish; he had no subtlety at all. He was unschooled, basically; he knew nothing of foreign cultures. I often thought he was a loose cannon.

Counterinsurgency was more Bobby, but there was a little of that in the president. That was show stuff. The president liked to go out and look at the Polaris submarine. And he had great admiration for people who were valorous, tough, quick and successful, as the Special Forces were. There was some of the little boy playing with toy soldiers in it—a romanticism that came from the Navy days. I always thought that Krulak was dangerous because I knew that Bobby was a sucker for that kind of stuff.

William Sullivan   The president was rather taken with counterinsurgency. Bobby became all enthused about it. He was always fascinated by the Green Berets and the Lansdale cloak-and-dagger sort of business. The president assigned Bobby to the Counterinsurgency Committee, which I served on for some time until I could gracefully squeeze off it. It was very much the "ugly American" sort of script that these fellows were following. And to some degree, although Max Taylor as a professional would deny that that at all was the premise of his attitude, to some degree he was swept up in it too. And we had a lot of bright young military at the time who all felt that was the way to go.

John Kenneth Galbraith   There was a mood; I think the Green Berets fitted well into that mood. Kennedy was not part of it, nor was Bobby. They had, unfortunately, to accept some of the responsibility for it. I was not part of it. One of my early activities in India was to get rid of the covert activities there, partly because I didn't believe in them; partly because they were so easily exposed, and I would be partly blamed for them. You couldn't have any of these activities without involving Indians. And any Indian, at any particular moment, could blow the whole thing. It was a risk I didn't care to run. After the Bay of Pigs there was a general clampdown on this activity. I was able to get out from under this whole burden of activity in India, partly helped by the Bay of Pigs.

Harry Felt Kennedy certainly didn't cause the secretary of defense to do anything that was workable. He may have gotten turned on, but he didn't know what it was all about. This is a paper I wrote in 1966, entitled "Subversive Insurgency—Power Factors: Ideology, Cadres, Leadership, Popular Support, External Support, Sanctuary, Intelligence." These factors form a framework for counterinsurgency actions.

The primary factors are cadre, ideology, leadership. Limit one of them to handicap the insurgent movement; destroy one of them to collapse the movement; military action can limit or reduce the insurgency, but can never eliminate the movement completely. No amount of military action can hope to destroy an ideology, nor eliminate a leadership which is regenerative, nor destroy a cadre which has infiltrated the masses.

The secondary, or material power factors—multipliers for the basic strength of the movement—are those which are vulnerable to military action. Applying sufficient force can deny use of a sanctuary, prevent matériel from the outside reaching the movement. Separate the insurgents from their ultimate base of support, the people, giving them security and gaining intelligence from them about location and identity of insurgent cadres.

What is required is a two-pronged attack: strong governmental leadership of reform, to correct existing abuses; countercadre campaign, aimed at discrediting insurgent leadership, paralleled by military attack on the secondary factors. Obviously the requirements were not met in South Vietnam.

The paper winds up by saying what's required: an integrated program, and we didn't have one. The South Vietnamese government itself did not have an integrated program. The only program they had—which is the one McNamara went along with—was to clear out a district at a time. It failed because the fault was that there was no follow-up, or immediate follow-up, to hold what they gained, and Westmoreland did the same damned thing.

How come Westmoreland was defeated—Tet was just one incident—how come he didn't do the job of clearing out the Viet Cong? A worldwide-known photographer—I can't remember his name—was in

Vietnam for some time and had an opportunity to observe from his point of view what was going on. He came back through here, and I said, "I'm going to pose a dirty question: Did General Westmoreland have any concept of rural development?" He said, "I'm sorry to tell you he did not." It all goes back to people—no matter where you go, it's people. These people in South Vietnam wanted only one thing, and that was to be left alone so that they could control their own affairs, in accordance with their own customs and traditions.

Throughout his involvement with the Vietnam problem, President Kennedy sent officials from Washington to Vietnam on fact-finding missions. Perhaps the most famous of these missions and the one that most closely suggests the difficulties the president had in sorting out the information the officials brought back was the visit undertaken at the president's behest in early September 1963 by Marine Corps Major General Krulak and State Department official Joseph Mendenhall.

Victor Krulak   There were often disagreements in the government about what was going on in Vietnam. At a meeting one day in the cabinet room, McCone said that he had information that the Buddhist crisis was causing defections in the ranks of the South Vietnamese Army, and that if these reports were true, the situation was very serious. President Kennedy replied that we ought to be able to know whether that was happening or not, not by asking the Vietnamese, who might not—for their own purposes—be telling the truth, but through our own advisory system. He turned to me and said, "I'd like you to go out there and ask them the single question: 'Is the Buddhist crisis causing defections in the Vietnamese Army?' How soon can you go?" I replied that I could go right away—it was then eleven o'clock—and he said, "How about one o'clock? We'll have an aircraft at Andrews [Andrews Air Force Base] waiting for you."

At that point, Rusk said, "I'd like to send somebody along; I don't know who it will be, but he'll be out there at one o'clock, ready to go." And he was. In fact he was there before I was, and we flew to Vietnam.

I had sent a message ahead that I wanted a small plane available to take me from one end of the country to the other, so that I could talk to the advisers. I also wanted to meet with the ambassador before I went on the trip and to report to him at its conclusion on what I had seen.

When I arrived, I was taken to the embassy, and Mr. Lodge came down to greet me wearing a dressing gown. I told him what President Kennedy wanted, and he said, "The place is yours; do whatever you want." So I went from one end of the country to the other. The upshot was that the Buddhist crisis wasn't causing defections; there were lots of other problems.

The State Department man who went with me [Joseph Mendenhall], a very nice, gentle fellow, took a different tack: While I went into the backwoods, he went to Saigon, and other cities, and we agreed to rejoin forty-eight hours later. I came back to Saigon and reported to Mr. Lodge on what I had seen. Then we left, and on the plane we compared notes, and it was quite obvious that we had been in two different parts of the world: I was out in the mud, and he was in the cities, talking to diplomats, politicians, and provincial authorities. He got a far less sanguine reaction than I did. It didn't bother me, because if we analyzed it, we got what we should have expected.

We arrived at Andrews at five A.M. and went to an eleven o'clock meeting at the White House. I made my presentation, and the State Department gentleman made his, and then President Kennedy asked his famous question: "Were you two fellows in the same country?" There was a lot of silence. Finally I said, "I think I can explain it to you: I went into the countryside and he went into the cities. But the war was in the countryside." The president got up at that point, went toward the door to the Oval Office, and stopped by my chair and said, "When this is finished, come in and see me." The meeting ended as soon as the president left, and I went to McNamara and said, "The president wants to see me." What I was really saying to him was "He wants to see me, and maybe you should come along." And he did.

The president was sitting at this desk, and he got up and came around it and said to me, "I just want you to know that I understand." And that was the totality of our conversation. It was very reassuring and reconvinced me that Kennedy could see beyond the moment—beyond the day—and that a lot of others couldn't.

19

The Assassination

"Shots rang out today as President Kennedy's motorcade rode through Dallas," the first wire service bulletin announced as the tragic story of November 22, 1963, began to unfold.

The assassination of President Kennedy has had a profound impact upon the lives of millions of people throughout the world. Even today, almost three decades after the event, many individuals are able to recall with great clarity where they were and what they were doing when they heard the news of the president's death. Now, nearly thirty years later, heated controversy continues to rage over the motive for the assassination and the identity of its perpetrator or perpetrators.

WHY KENNEDY WENT TO DALLAS

Bobby Baker I know that Johnson was opposed to Kennedy's going to Texas; Connally begged him not to go. The presidential advisers wanted him to go to Texas to raise money; they knew very well that to win, they needed to carry Texas.

Ralph Dungan On the same day we had the meeting to plan the 1964 campaign, before he went to Dallas, Kenny [O'Donnell] and I were talking with the president, and he said he had to go to Dallas. I suspect having the top down on the car was his choice. They had a tough time with him; he didn't like that confinement. I guess no president really does.

O'Donnell was the liaison with the Secret Service; he must have been getting some signals from the Secret Service about Dallas not being the place to go.

Bernard Boutin It was a real risk for the president to go to Dallas. Quite a few of us were opposed to the visit and hated to see him go; we couldn't see any logic to the trip. He felt he needed to mend some fences there. He was particularly sensitive to the loss of prestige that Johnson had suffered and wanted to do something to correct all of that. Of course, the trip—up to the Book Depository—was a smashing success. His speech in Houston at the Albert Thomas [U.S. congressman (D., Tex.)] dinner was tremendously attended and received.

Jack Valenti Johnson didn't want him to go, for a number of reasons. He thought it was a bad political time. The senior senator, Ralph Yarborough, was in venomous discord with Governor John Connally—I mean they loathed each other. And Johnson didn't know what was going to happen. He thought that the party was divided and this wasn't the time to go. But Kennedy cut a deal with Connally, and Johnson was out of the loop and had to accept it. Kennedy also wanted to raise a lot of money, because, if you recall, the last night—the twenty-second, the day he was killed—was the night this huge fund-raiser was scheduled in Austin, Texas. He could maybe pick up a couple of million bucks; he wanted to refurbish the coffers and the deal was cut. Johnson was opposed to it, not because he thought something was going to happen to Kennedy but because he thought the political moment was not right to do it.

Ralph Yarborough They were getting ready for the race of '64, and they had to think for '64. They called it the Boston-Austin axis. Johnson was telling Kennedy—suggesting that Kennedy would have a whale of a time being reelected. They had meetings at those two places; they had one first in Boston. It was tremendously successful; they raised a lot of money. And they had the next one in Texas, and Johnson was driving hard. Mike Mansfield told me, three days after Kennedy was assassinated, the reason he went to Texas was because Johnson was insisting he come to Texas; Johnson demanded it. Well, I didn't think Johnson demanded that he come, thinking he might be assassinated. Well, Johnson's henchman and flunky was Connally, and Connally was in the governorship. They were taking polls in Texas, showing that Johnson and Kennedy were running about fifty-fifty, and Connally was trailing, and I was leading the lot. The *Houston Chronicle* took that poll, and the editor had a dinner in the Rice Hotel the night before the assassination—the editor and maybe another officer—and Lyndon, Lady Bird, and Kennedy, and Jacqueline Kennedy, and I think two or three or four more I heard about, were at the dinner. The editor of the *Houston Chronicle* told me that they had taken this poll, and they were going to print it the next morning, after Kennedy was gone, because they weren't going to be discourteous enough to Kennedy to print it while he was right there in Houston. They were his hosts, and after he got out they'd print it. They modified it a little—they didn't make it as blunt as it was—after he got assassinated.

I think one reason Johnson was driving so hard—he was using Connally as his wedge—was to try to beat me; not running against me, but trying to weaken my position on all these bills I was introducing. Well, I think Johnson was driving hard to get the president into Texas to reelect John Connally. That was buttressed, in my mind, by the fact that Kennedy violated all protocol in Texas. He rode with Connally in that car. Protocol is, you take the highest-ranking Democrat. Next to governor, the highest-ranking Democrats would have been me and Albert Thomas, in the House. Albert Thomas was senior to Lyndon Johnson. Albert Thomas didn't like Lyndon Johnson. They had phoned me two or three weeks before, and Larry O'Brien says, "Well, when we get to Houston, we've scheduled you to arrive with Albert Thomas. Do you have any objections?" I said, "Not at all. I don't mind doing that." I was in about the seventh car back, so nobody would ever see me in the motorcade with him on television. My main object on that trip to Texas was: Don't rock the boat; don't cause any quarrel at any time.

Pierre Salinger   He did get considerable advice not to go to Dallas, but he made that decision himself. The day I left for Tokyo with the cabinet members, I got a letter from a woman in Texas saying, "Tell the president not to come down here, because he's likely to get killed." I told the president about it, and he was very relaxed about it; he said, "If somebody wants to kill a president, they can do it, but they will get killed themselves."

LAST CONVERSATIONS WITH THE PRESIDENT

Adam Yarmolinsky The last conversation I had with him was about the extent to which there was public concern about arms control and interest in it, about the extent to which arms control was a politically viable issue. This was before he flew off to Texas.

Edward McDermott The night before he went to Texas, there was a private party at the White House, at which Mrs. McDermott and I were present, which was primarily in celebration, as I recall, of Bobby's birthday. It was a relaxed and jovial evening, and there was considerable discussion of the president's intention to fly to Texas the next morning. Adlai Stevenson had been down there a week or so previously. They threw tomatoes and eggs at him, and he had recommended to the president he not go, that it wasn't worth it. He was very upbeat about it and insisted that there was just a little political problem down there within the party that he felt he could resolve.

The next morning he departed. My office, in the old Executive Office Building, was the former office of the secretary of state, Cordell Hull. I was at my desk when the helicopter came in and landed. And just as it landed, my phone rang. It was someone saying that the president would like to see you right away, for a minute. So I went immediately to his office, and Ted Clifton [Brig. Gen. Chester V. Clifton, military aide to President Kennedy] was standing over by the door leading out onto the porch. He had a briefcase and the black box and so on with him. The president was standing behind his desk with papers in his briefcase.

He said, "I just had a call from our friend, Phil [Philip H.] Hoff." Now, Phil Hoff was governor of Vermont, and Phil had been a friend of mine, had been active in the campaign, and was a personal friend of the president, and he said, "Phil says that they're having a very severe drought in Vermont and that it's dried up the ponds for the dairy herd, and the dairy industry, which is a critical element of the economy of Vermont, is suffering very badly, and he wants a declaration of major disaster so there can be federal assistance. Phil's a good guy. Will you fly up there tomorrow, check that situation out, see if it qualifies for federal assistance, and I'll talk to you about it when I get back." And with that, he got up, walked over to the door, and walked out to the helicopter.

Now, the last act that he did within the Oval Office itself was a personalized response to a request from a state governor.

Ralph Yarborough   I was on the plane with Kennedy. I had told Albert Thomas: "I'm not going to treat the president like Price Daniel [govenor of Texas] did, when he was here before on a trip. Price was with him, and when he got to Fort Worth, Price vanished—just like the earth had just swallowed him up; I looked around and I couldn't see him. He wouldn't go to Dallas; he knew that Lyndon was very unpopular in Dallas; he didn't go with him. And I said, "Now, I'm not going to treat the president like Price Daniel did. I'm going to warn him, when we get to Austin, that Connally's been bragging that I would not be seated on the stage; I'd be seated back with—and introduced with—the Texas legislature. They're bragging everywhere in Austin that that's going to happen. I'm going to tell the president."

I talked to him on the plane. He came back and said, "Well, I've seen the polls in Houston; you're doing well in Texas." And I learned then that Lyndon had told him I was dragging the ticket. The next morning he went out and spoke to a crowd; I was with him on the platform, and I was cheering and smiling; I was tickled to death. And Johnson and Connally were sitting there and glaring at the applause he was getting in front of the hotel that morning.

I flew with the president to Love Field. Before we went out there, up there in the room as we were getting ready to go, he said, "Ralph, I guess you've seen the papers, about the blow they've given us about your not riding with Johnson. I wish you'd ride with him." I says, "Well, Mr. President, that was just a misunderstanding earlier. I rode with him out at the Carswell Air Base last night, and I'll ask if I can ride with him. I'll ride over with him and be there." That was settled that morning. I passed it off as a misunderstanding. It was a misunderstanding—with Larry O'Brien and Lyndon. At Love Field they walked down the fence, shaking hands with people, with Connally, and I didn't walk down the fence with them. I knew Connally and Johnson would be mad as the devil.

Jack Valenti   I was working on a big dinner in Houston for Congressman Albert Thomas, who was chairman of a House Appropriations subcommittee. It was Albert Thomas who brought the Space Center to Houston, not Lyndon Johnson, because Thomas was a very powerful congressman. The key speakers were to be President Kennedy and Vice President Johnson, so I was very much involved in that. When Kennedy and Johnson arrived, I rode in with Kenny O'Donnell from the airport. He was overjoyed; crowds were huge and hospitable. Johnson, by this time, was elated with the way the trip was going, because the Kennedy people were ecstatic. He said to me, "Instead of you going on to Austin, come on with me to Fort Worth, and we'll go to Dallas, and then we'll go to Austin together." So I flew up to Fort Worth and spent the night with him at the Texas Hotel, and we chewed the fat and talked about politics, and then I flew with him on *Air Force Two* to Dallas.

"SHOTS RANG OUT"

Ralph Yarborough As we were leaving the airport—we didn't go very far before we had to cross a railroad crossing—we stopped; we couldn't see from the car we were in what was going on up there. I understood later that Kennedy had gotten out of the car and shook hands with people, and Johnson, in a rather irritated voice, had said, "Turn it on! Turn it on!" and had them turn the radio on—loud—and it stayed turned on all the way down to the hospital. This was just the regular radio in the car. You could hear the noise. If anybody had taken a picture, they would have seen him listening to that thing all the way to the hospital. It just shows how false it was; they knew by then there wasn't any way it could be disproved, and he gave Youngblood [Secret Service Agent Rufus Youngblood] a gold medal for protecting him and saving his life.

Jack Valenti I got into the motorcade, riding, as I recall, with Pamela Turnure [press secretary to Mrs. John F. Kennedy], Evelyn Lincoln, and Liz Carpenter [press secretary to Mrs. Lyndon B. Johnson]. At about the time we reached the grassy knoll, the car in front of us suddenly looked like A. J. Foyt [racing driver; frequent participant in Indianapolis 500] had taken the wheel. It sped off. We didn't know what was going on. Most of us dreaded to ask questions. Somebody concluded that maybe the president was late; he had a speech at the Trade Mart, so we dashed off from there, because the crowd started milling. There was a very strange, bizarre turn of events. We got to the Trade Mart. People were all in their seats, but there was no president. A Secret Service agent told us the president had been shot; the governor had been shot; they were at Parkland Hospital. Mrs. Lincoln, of course, almost collapsed. I commandeered a deputy sheriff, and he took us to Parkland Hospital, sirens keening. When we got there, I took Mrs. Lincoln up to the administrator's office because she was in a terrible state, and I wandered around in the basement, where the president was, in the emergency operating room, which had a stainless steel door.

Ralph Yarborough   As we got down, going down Main, those vast crowds—the people on each side—were packed to the wall and giving the president an enthusiastic reception. And we came on in the third car, and they hollered: "Lyndon! Lyndon!" and Lyndon wouldn't look at them, wouldn't respond. And I'd say: "Mr. Vice President, the people are cheering you, and you never looked over and responded." That's amazing to me. He may have been mad at me, because he got a bad press. I got a bad press, but he got one too, out of not riding with me. I got some letters saying: "I wouldn't have ridden with that old skunk anyway." That wasn't all loss.

I looked up one or two stories, where you could see people in those windows. There wasn't a smile anywhere; they were glaring. And I got concerned. I thought, "My goodness; what if somebody throws a pot of flowers on the president?" Some of the people nodded at me; I recognized a bunch of them; they came from the rural counties of East Texas, where I was from. When we got to the end of that street—I'm an old ex-hunter, and I've known the times, boy, when I was in the woods, and feeling not very safe, over in East Texas, and I see the end of a lane—I was getting out of those woods, up to the hills, to go home—I'd feel relieved I was getting out. When we got close to the end of Main Street, I felt that same relief, of getting out of that hostile place, of coming into the clear. And I was surprised when they turned right—turned right, and then back left—right on the buildings, where there's danger again. And they didn't go straight on down. Now, yes, I felt that concern then. It wasn't that I thought something was going to happen here; it was just not getting out of the woods. And I thought, "We're still not out of the woods." And then the shots rang out.

I knew that the first one was a rifle shot. And I knew that the third one was a rifle shot. And I was kind of dumb-fussing about the middle one, because there were three distinct explosions. That Warren Report that there were two was just a lot of bunk. The third one caused my confusion there. Immediately after the first shot the motorcade slowed up— slowed up to just nearly a walk. I thought it stopped. And I could smell smoke—gunsmoke—'cause it's coming down from that rifle right over us; we were in the back seat, behind it, that second shot, then it came. It was just like counting: one, two, three. I thought: My goodness. Was there a bomb? What's that smoke up there? And what are they all stopping for? Was I mistaken? Was that a bomb, instead of a rifle? And then, after the third shot, they took off.

Well, after the confusion of the second shot, I just assumed it was all in one place. I was very much concerned about that second shot, because I was smelling smoke. Somebody—one of the Lyndon Johnson men—was trying to discredit me; he said I was so excited I thought I smelled gunsmoke. I told the Dallas police later—I was by there later and saw them—and they said, "We all smelled that gunsmoke."

Let me tell you one thing that didn't happen: that cock-and-bull story he [Johnson] told about Youngblood pushing him down and jumping over and sitting on him. It's just plain—a fabrication. It didn't happen at all. Youngblood turned around. He had a little box—I guess it was an information box from the radio—and he leaned over. See, we had a small car; you couldn't have pushed big old Lyndon down there. So Youngblood leaned over and looked right in Johnson's eyes, and Johnson looked straight ahead and didn't look at anything.

The first time I talked to Johnson, I said, "They're cheering along here; they're cheering," and he didn't answer; he didn't respond. When they started going fast, when they came up on the other side of the underpass, that Secret Service man, Mrs. Kennedy's Secret Service man, had an arm over the seat, holding her in there, and the other hand—his face was turned toward us; he was beating his hand on that car in utter anguish. I felt they'd probably killed him [President Kennedy] by then. When they got to the hospital, the Secret Service left Kennedy and came down and circled around Johnson. One of them said, "Mr. President." They left President Kennedy in the car, and Mrs. Kennedy. Then they brought the stretcher out, and they put Connally on the stretcher and rolled off, and left Kennedy and Mrs. Kennedy. That woman's a great woman, in my opinion, whatever they say about her. She was leaning over his head and moaning: "They've killed my husband; they've killed my husband."

Jack Valenti I was going to wander back up to the second floor to see Mrs. Lincoln when Cliff Carter, chief political agent for the vice president, said to me, "The vice president wants to see you right away." Then he hesitated, and said, "The president is dead, you know." Well, I had to compose myself, because I started weeping, and I went to a room where Johnson had been sequestered. There was a lone Secret Service man there, named Lem Johns, who later became head of the White House detail.

Ralph Yarborough . The minute they ran back there and said, "Mr. President" to Johnson, I knew that the president was dead. Some of the press came up to me and asked me what happened. I thought it would be wholly inappropriate for me to announce Kennedy's death—they had to go in and have the priest and everybody; I said, "Excalibur has sunk beneath the waves."

JOHNSON IS SWORN IN AS PRESIDENT

Ralph Yarborough   I was in the hospital; I was not invited into the emergency room, and I wasn't going to barge in. The Secret Service took Johnson off in a separate room. If they thought it was a conspiracy, they had to be careful. I think that Henry Gonzalez [U.S. congressman (D., Tex.)] walked down there—into the room where the doctors were treating Kennedy. I stayed there. They told some wild tale that I had to have a sedative. A nurse came down and asked me if I wanted one, and I said, "I don't need a sedative," and she said, "You can sit in here."

In the meantime another exciting thing happened: Two men engaged in a most vicious combat with each other, without taking a pistol and shooting each other, that I've seen, right there in the hallway of the hospital. One of them was with the Secret Service, and the other one was FBI. They didn't know each other, and each one was suspicious of the other. They wrestled to the floor—each afraid the other was an assassin. But they weren't shooting; each was trying to control the other without having any gunfire.

The brigadier general in charge told me I wouldn't be going back to Love Field in the car in I came in; to get into this van. Several of us were put in that van; we weren't needed for the swearing-in. I didn't want to be at the swearing-in anyway. I thought it was horrible what they did to Mrs. Kennedy, having her come in with that blood on her clothes and standing there. Anyway, I got there, and they said, "You will not be riding back [to Washington] on *Air Force One; you'll be on *Air Force Three.*"

Johnson moved up to *Air Force One.* As I got there Judge Sarah Hughes was coming down the steps of the president's plane, with the Bible in her hand, and she said, "Well, I've just sworn Lyndon in as president."

Jack Valenti I went out to the airport with Lem Johns, and he put me on *Air Force One,* which I'd never been on before. On *Air Force One* you get on forward and you go aft. Midships is the presidential office. After that is the presidential bedroom, and after that is the galley and the back part of the plane, where President Kennedy's coffin later resided, flag draped. I remember that Johnson came out of the presidential bedroom while we were still on the ground, and he beckoned to me and said, "I want you on my staff. I want you to fly back to Washington with me." I had no idea what that meant. I was the first person he hired, within minutes after getting back to the airplane. I said, "Fine. Whatever you want, Mr. President."

My first official duty was to talk to a fellow named Katzenbach—who I'd never heard of—to talk about the presidential oath of office, because Johnson had determined he'd be sworn in in Dallas, which was a brilliant move, although Robert Kennedy and Katzenbach suggested he get out of there fast. But Johnson made two command decisions that, in retrospect, were so right. One was he wasn't going to leave without the coffin of the thirty-fifth president; number two, he wanted to be sworn in so that the picture of that swearing-in would be flashed around the world and the people of the world would realize that while the light in the White House may flicker, it never goes out. That is a symbolic thing that would be a powerful message to send to a gasping, anxious world.

I got on the phone with Nick Katzenbach, trying to find the presidential oath, and we couldn't find it. There was supposed to be a Bible, which we had to find, and the presidential oath. Finally, on around the second phone call, some bright young guy, who had been good in history, realized that the presidential oath is in the Constitution of the United States. We found something in the airplane. Larry O'Brien thought it was a Catholic missal; somebody said it was a Bible, but nobody knows, because whatever it was, it's lost.

Katzenbach called back and the oath was dictated to a secretary, and then I read it back to Katzenbach, and then we gave it to Judge Sarah Hughes, who had finally gotten on board. She read it off to the president, and that famous picture was taken that was flashed around the world. He'd asked Mrs. Kennedy to be in that picture, which was great, because what that picture showed was the linear connection of the president—not only to the birth year of the Republic, but to John Kennedy: His widow, the new president and his wife were there. Indeed, what Johnson wanted to show was that the Kennedy legacy will live on. Five days later, when he spoke to the joint session, he started by saying, "John Kennedy said, 'Let us begin,' and I say, 'Let us continue.'"

The second thing about that trip is that a lot has been written about the hostility on the airplane. If there was hostility, I didn't see it. Now General McHugh [Godfrey McHugh, military aide to the president] became out of control because he tried to get the plane airborne. The pilot said, "I'm sorry. The president—" and he said, "What do you mean, the president? I'm in command here. I want this plane to leave." Well, McHugh went out of his gourd. I said, "General, President Johnson said this plane ain't leaving till he says it leaves." It finally dawned on McHugh that he was no longer in power.

What I saw in O'Brien and O'Donnell, and those guys, was such numbing grief; such an avalanche of doom had flowed over them. Here you are: You're living in the golden sunlight; you're next to the president; you're the most powerful men in the world, and suddenly your leader is struck down, and where are you? I didn't see hostility; I just saw dumb, mute grief.

THE IMMEDIATE HOURS AFTERWARD

Edward McDermott When I got to the Situation Room at the White House from Andrews, the place was practically deserted. The cabinet was out over the Pacific, en route to Japan. Andy Hatcher, the deputy press secretary, had taken the day off to go to a ball game in Baltimore. It was very skeletal staff there. The first reports that we got were that Johnson had also been shot, and the question was, Was it fatal? If it was, John McCormack [John W. McCormack, Speaker of the House] was president of the United States. So there was a great, great scramble. And then it was confirmed that LBJ was alive and that those early stories were wrong. And then the next report, of course, was that LBJ was on the plane and had taken the oath of office. But there was that interval where there was uncertainty as to whether we had a constitutional president of the United States.

Julian Bond I remember the first thing we did was to call a friend who lived in Texas, and ask, "Who is this guy, Lyndon Johnson?" so I think we were less worried about who Lee Harvey Oswald was, or what was happening, even before you knew there was a Lee Harvey Oswald. Our big thing was: Who is this guy, Lyndon Johnson? What does he mean? And some friends, I remember—we were back and forth on the phones in the SNCC offices—they told us that he was tied to big oil money, but he'd been a New Dealer. And that reassured us. Well, we thought, if the guy was a New Dealer. . . . If I had read the Robert Caro book° then, I would have been terrified.

Edward McDermott I stayed at the White House nearly all that night. It was chaotic. The family immediately began the preparation of the funeral. It is interesting that in all the contingencies that the Kennedy family had dealt with, and the government itself had dealt with, no one was prepared for the assassination of President Kennedy in office, and there were actually no plans as to how the funeral would be handled. After we knew that we had a constitutional president, the thrust of all the attention was on funeral preparations.

The funeral represented the largest assembly of heads of state who had ever been in one place in history. We got word that all of these prime ministers, premiers, and kings were coming to Washington. And the protocol facilities of the State Department were overwhelmed. None of the usual protocol procedures could be followed. So every embassy was put on notice that they should deal with their own principal when he comes. Then the rest of the preparations went forward, in which Mrs. Kennedy played a remarkably active role.

James Wine The next morning, Saturday, as was customary down at the Chancery—at the embassy residence they have what they call an open book where they made courtesy calls—ambassadors and Cabinet

°*The Years of Lyndon Johnson*, vol. 1, *The Path to Power* (New York: Alfred A. Knopf, 1982).

officers of local government came to my residence. The others went to the Chancery. Well, they came in a steady stream all morning. And at midday things are shut down in Africa, and I was pretty well exhausted at that point. I walked up into the garden and looked around, and the driveway was a long half circle; in the center there is a flagpole. And there was an African standing there, and I didn't see any of the house-boys around, so I walked out, and he said, "Is this the American Embassy?" I said, "Yes, it is." And he told me his name, which I had for-gotten, and he said, "I am from"—he gave the name of a very small vil-lage about twenty miles away—"where I am a storekeeper. I came down on the bus this morning. I never knew President Kennedy; I never saw President Kennedy, but he was my friend."

Edward McDermott   The president was lying in this beautiful room where the Wednesday night before there had been music and dancing. The casket was in the center of the room, and in each corner of the room stood a representative of one of the four military services. There was a kneeling bench, and you came in through a doorway on the far side and exited through the other side of the room, and the mourners were lined up in order of protocol. So you went to the casket and knelt down, and you were alone with the president and the four military personnel, and then you went out the door.

Archibald Cox   One of the very moving things was when the Harvard football team, the night before the game with Yale, went down to where his body was lying in state at the Capitol, late at night. This was quite an extraordinary tribute.

Robert Manning   Once we were back, there was much to do. Johnson was very smart. He asked everybody to stay, and he made all sorts of demands on everybody. This was partly because he sensed that the more they had to work, the better it would be for everybody concerned. I felt tremendous sympathy for him—the way in which he took over. He said he didn't want to be there, and this was believable. God knows, he wanted to be president some day, but not under those circumstances.

Orville Freeman   The new president called a meeting at about eight in the morning, and we were all there, and the only one not there was

Bobby. LBJ was sitting in the president's chair; that almost seemed sacrilegious. We were all feeling pretty bad, and Bobby came in late, and he walked around, and he stopped, and he looked at the back of LBJ's head, and he was loathing with contempt and walked out. He just hated him.

THE PRESIDENT'S ASSOCIATES AND OTHERS LEARN HE IS DEAD

Burke Marshall   Hoover was cold about informing Robert Kennedy that the president had been shot—as if it had been the president of Tanzania, that was how Robert felt.

Cartha DeLoach   I think Mr. Hoover's reaction was like it would have been in any other incident: "What is the FBI's responsibility insofar as this matter is concerned? What is the principal thing the FBI should do at this time?" Contrary to many public reports today, Mr. Hoover did call Bobby several times to tell him the president had been shot. He was the first one to talk to Bobby and to call him again to tell him the president was at Parkland Hospital, and then tell him the president was dead. There was not any staccato abruptness. It was a matter of compassion and reporting to the attorney general, who was his immediate superior and the president's brother. Mr. Hoover's immediate reaction was, first, notification of the attorney general; secondly, What could the FBI do insofar as its jurisdiction was concerned?

You might call that expedient, but I think any good administrative head would think of things like that. Mr. Hoover's personality would indicate from time to time a sternness, an aloofness, but in this particular instance, I know that is not true. He did what he thought he should do. He thought he had an obligation to keep the attorney general advised, and he did it.

The president and Mr. Hoover spoke the following day. The president wanted to go all-out in the investigation, and he also asked him to appoint me as liaison to the White House.

I was on the phone constantly with Mr. Hoover the day of the assassination. He wanted to get to the bottom of it as quickly as possible. It was at his instruction that a special agent went to Parkland Hospital, where they were working on the president in the operating room, and saw the tracheotomy performed.

George McGovern I was in the Senate when it happened, and my impression was that Ted was presiding. I was sitting in the back row, and Mike Mansfield came into the Senate and motioned for me to come over. I went up and took Ted's place presiding, and Mansfield spoke to Ted and told him what had happened and then moved that the Senate adjourn. I walked back to my office, and by the time I got there, they announced he was dead.

Gaylord Nelson Ted Kennedy was presiding. I walked out into the hall near the ticker tape. One senator was looking at the tape and he said to me, "Hey! It says here that the president has been shot." I turned around and walked into the chamber with the intention of telling Teddy. Another senator had arrived a few moments before me, and Teddy was already walking out.

Maurine Neuberger I was talking on the phone to a friend in my office. My secretary burst into the room and said, "Senator Mansfield wants everyone on the floor at once." We were all gathered in the cloakroom, where the teletype machines were; everyone was standing there in disbelief. I remember the pall that came over us. We then went into the chamber. One of the very touching things was that Margaret Chase Smith, [U.S. senator (R., Maine)], who always wore a rose on her lapel, went over and put a rose on what had been his desk.

Pierre Salinger I was trying to find out what happened. When we first got the news, we were not getting the information that he was dead but that he had been shot. That is why Rusk asked me to establish communication between the plane and the White House; there was a lot of confusion. When we got the news that the president was dead, there was some discussion on the plane as to who could be responsible. Rusk thought it might be an international affair, and we sent a message to all U.S. embassies to see if they could find out anything.

Bernard Boutin I had had an early luncheon appointment and had barely gotten back to the office when I had a call from the Secret Service telling me that the president had been hit, but they didn't know if it was serious; they had no details. It was an alert call. I subsequently got a couple of calls from the FBI; and then another call from the Secret Service when the president was taken to Parkland Hospital, and then another reporting that he had died.

We, at that point, did not know if it was as major conspiracy, so as administrator of GSA, and being responsible for all the federal buildings, we had calls out to all of our security forces to secure the buildings and to be very much alert. Flags were all dropped to half mast. I stayed in the office well into the evening. I was busy and devastated. I couldn't believe that this man whom I loved so much, and had so much respect for, was dead.

Orville Freeman We were having breakfast. We were about a couple of hours out of Honolulu. We had just started eating, and someone came down and said, "The secretary of state would like to see you," and I said, "Tell him I'll go as soon as I finish my breakfast." He said, "I think he wants to see you right away." And I said, "What the devil could be important enough"—we've got an eight-hour trip—"to not let me be able to finish my breakfast?" We walked in, and he was as white as a sheet. He said, "The president's been shot." I said, "Where was he hit?" And he said, "He was hit in the head." And I said, "Well, he's all right; I was shot in the head, and it didn't kill me." This was in World War II. We didn't know whether he was alive or he had died.

Finally we did make contact with somebody who told the secretary. It came over the loudspeaker, and it said, "The president is dead, God save our country." You could have cut the melancholy in that plane with a very dull knife. Gradually different people drifted up to me because they knew that I knew Johnson much better than they did, and they asked me what kind of president I thought he would be; what would he do, and so forth. It was a long, long trip and a very sad one.

Robert Manning We took off from Honolulu in one of the presidential aircraft and were several hundred miles west of there. Several cabinet secretaries were with us, as was Pierre Salinger. I had been in the press, so I knew by the sound that there was a flash on the news ticker. I walked toward the communications area, and the sergeant had a piece of wire copy in his hand. He said, "The secretary [Rusk] will have to see this." It was a flash saying: "Dallas. President Kennedy shot." Then a bulletin: "Perhaps shot fatally." We took it to Rusk and he asked me to bring the cabinet secretaries to his compartment.

We immediately got on the phone with the White House Situation Room. They confirmed that something had happened and that the president had been rushed to the hospital. Rusk got on the public address system and told everybody we had some bad, unclear news: President Kennedy had been wounded, and we were going to turn back. Salinger got in touch with the White House and used his code name. He said, "This is Wayside. What word do you have on Lancer?" At the other end the fellow said, "Lancer is dead." Rusk then went back on the PA system and said, "I am sorry to have to bring you this grievous news, but President Kennedy has been killed. We now have a new president. May God bless our president and the United States of America."

The news then came in that someone named Oswald[Lee Harvey Oswald, presumed assassin of Kennedy], who had been in the Soviet Union, had done this. The news caused great alarm.

Rusk had allowed me to bring two or three correspondents on the plane as we headed back to Washington from Honolulu. They, Salinger, and three or four others of us got into this utterly reckless poker game: No one cared whether they won or lost. Others just stared into space or comforted each other. It was an endless trip; it really was a weird sensation. Here were seven or eight top officials of the most powerful nation on earth, complete prisoners in this aluminum tube.

John Lewis I was getting into a car on the Fisk campus when I heard President Kennedy had been shot. From time to time I had disagreed with President Kennedy. But the man! I adored him! For me, he could do no wrong. I was distraught. I wondered: Where do we go from here? We were robbed of something. If Kennedy had lived and been reelected, and if Martin Luther King had lived, where would we be as a nation? I used to disagree with my friends in SNCC who said, "We don't need a great leader." John F. Kennedy represented the best of our public servants.

Bui Diem When he was assassinated I felt this greatly in my heart, and I think many of the Vietnamese felt the same way.

James Farmer   I was, of course, stunned and shocked and walked around like a zombie. Though my relations were not good, the Kennedy mystique had affected me too. And I adored what he had done for the country, and the spirit of youth, and how he had encouraged our movement by his rhetoric. He hadn't intended to do that, I guess, but he had: "Ask not what your country can do for you; ask what you can do for your country." Ah, "What I can do for my country is to wipe out segregation," we answered. "I want desperately to get this country moving again," he says. "Oh, that is wonderful; such spirit of youth. We want to get it moving too; we're walking together, Mr. President."

There was a businessman's convention in the hotel I was in. I noticed a number of badges. I'd gotten on the elevator and was going down, and one businessman was saying to the other, "Ah, ah—they got the wrong damn Kennedy. They should have killed that Bobby son-of-a-bitch." You know, it was all I could do to keep nonviolent. Then I looked at them and almost flew at them. As the door opened—on a floor I hadn't intended to get out on—I got out and then asked somebody, "Is it true? Has the president been shot?" For weeks I walked around like a zombie.

Gerald Ford   I remember vividly where I was when I heard it on the radio. My wife and I had gone to Washington for an interview with a counselor with reference to the educational problems of one of our sons. We were in the automobile and heard it on the radio. I was saddened and shocked because of my long personal as well as political relationship with Jack.

Theodore Hesburgh   I was up on top of a mountain in Colorado looking at a site for the new atmospheric research center we were going to build for the National Science Foundation. We went down to Boulder, to the home of the president of the University of Colorado, who was going to have us for lunch. As I was getting out of the minivan, someone said, "The president was just shot." There were two radios in the house and half the group went into the front room to listen to one, and I went into the kitchen to listen to the other, and we went through that horrible half hour until it was announced that he was dead.

We had lunch, and as soon as it was over we started talking about the most mundane matters. After about ten minutes I said to the chairman, "I'm going home." I had a hard time getting back, but I got a flight to

Chicago that night and went to stay at a high school. Then I called my executive vice president, who was out in Iowa because we were scheduled to play the University of Iowa the next day. I said, "What is the situation?" He said, "I know where you're coming from, but they want to play." I said, "Well, they can play alone, but they are not going to play with us. Put the team on a plane tomorrow morning, and come home." He said, "Why don't we play the game and have a memorial service at half time?" I said, "Baloney. We are not going to play a football game as if it doesn't matter." He said, "What about the people who bought tickets?" I said, "Just put out an announcement that between us, Iowa and ourselves will pay anybody that wants a return ticket." I didn't think anyone would, but we returned ninety thousand dollars out of a total of about two hundred thousand that had been bought at that point.

We came home. I got a call from Ethel asking if I would come down to be with the family for the funeral, and I went to Washington.

Willy Brandt   I took the government plane to Hannover and came with another plane from there to Berlin in the afternoon. And later that afternoon, early that evening, I got a call about what had happened. I didn't believe it. Then I took a car to the American commandant to get the official news, and then I went to my city hall, where people started to come in great numbers. So I thought this was something which went very far. I mean a tragedy. As one reacts in things like this, to begin with, one just resists believing it.

Alexei Adzhubei   When Kennedy was killed, Khrushchev was very depressed. He learned about it in Paris. He cried. It was horrible news. It was a complicated time, because they had just started to untie all the knots. He sent a letter to Jacqueline. "If Kennedy had not been killed, Khrushchev would not have resigned," a friend of mine, a professor, told me. I think that there were three people: the pope, Kennedy, and Khrushchev; Kennedy was killed, the pope died, and Khrushchev was dismissed.

Viktor Sukhodrev   It came as a great shock to him [Khrushchev]. Of course his immediate reaction was to send the man at that time most suited to represent him, Mikoyan [Anastas Mikoyan, first deputy premier, USSR].

It was a very sincere gesture on Khrushchev's part. I think it was a sign of his personal feeling of sadness, his personal feeling of tragedy. And the response was immediate: to send a very, very high-ranking person, not just a figurehead but a person known for his ability to talk, to negotiate. That was, I think, a very important step, not just a gesture. He could have sent anybody else who would have been high in terms of figurehead, but no one in terms of talking to the new incumbent.

Pierre Salinger Khrushchev was absolutely stunned. He walked to the U.S. Embassy to be the first person to sign the condolence book. I am still very much in touch with his family, and we talk about those days, and it always comes out that there is enormous warmth for Kennedy.

Martin Hillenbrand I was in Bonn at the time of the assassination, and in one of those unhappy coincidences, the McGhees (George McGhee, U.S. ambassador) were celebrating a wedding anniversary, and he was having a white-tie dinner dance at the residence. With the time difference, the guests, including my wife and myself, in white tie and evening dress, were arriving at the residence when McGhee came out white faced, saying, "The president has just died." It was the first word we'd had of it, because when we were getting dressed, we weren't listening to the radio.

Obviously the party was off, but then we all sat around and said, What can we do; we'll presumably get some instructions, because the first flashes didn't indicate that Johnson was in a position to take over right away. So we spent the evening just listening to the news broadcasts, and then we did get some cables from the State Department. It was a rather ridiculous evening; we were all sitting around in white tie and evening dresses. Some German guests had come from out of town. Obviously, the dance was off—but we didn't even have a sit-down dinner, as had been planned. We just had a buffet out, and ate.

Of course, as is customary, the embassy put out a book to be signed by dignitaries, and Adenauer came in within an hour after the book had been opened and signed it. All the prominent German officials then came in within a day or so to sign the book.

James Wine There was six hours' difference in time. That day was the Lebanese national day. We were at the Lebanese Embassy, and we were standing out in the garden with the president of the country and some of his staff and chief of protocol. I looked up, and someone came right straight through the house, came out into the garden, and said, "The president wants to see you immediately." Good Lord, have mercy, I thought, what have we done now? We went up into the foyer of the ambassador's residence, and he took me off and he said, "Did you know that President Kennedy has been shot?" And I said no. He said, "I just heard it on the radio."

I said, "Is he dead?" and he said, "I don't know." My deputy chief lived directly across the street, so I went right back down and got ahold of him and I said, "Get all the staff together and bring them over to your house right away. And get out your radio." He did.

At that time, of course, the announcement was made, very succinctly: "The president is dead." It was one of the worst nights I ever spent. I did not want to discuss it. I wanted to be alone. My wife knew me well enough that just a squeeze of her hand was all that was necessary to communicate. I went back to my residence and went into the library, shut the door, and sat there, and then I began to replay the previous years, thinking of all of those moments, and asking that ever-recurring three-letter word: *Why?*

Ralph Dungan   I was having lunch at the Chilean Embassy—it was a big lunch; Hubert Humphrey was there, and a couple of journalists. Hubert got called to the phone and came back and whispered in my ear: "I think we'd better go. The president has just been shot, in Dallas." So I went back, and by the time I arrived at the White House, the president was dead. My office was where we all met, to decide who would get invitations to the funeral. It was a terrible time—a terrible weekend. Shriver was very much involved in the planning, but Jackie made most of the decisions; she had very clear ideas. Interestingly she knew about the history of the stuff. The military has a script for all this, so you basically modify the script. Jackie was great, and Sarge would liaison with her, and their good friend, the artist Bill Walton, who helped a lot.

Adlai Stevenson III   I think my father felt some responsibility; he'd been in Dallas not long before and had had an experience which really alarmed him. He'd had all kinds of experiences in politics: he'd been spat on, had stones thrown at him, and all the rest—but we endure. But something in the atmosphere in Dallas alarmed him, and I think he did try to urge the White House not to let Kennedy go to Dallas. Maybe it was a premonition, because no matter what he sensed in the environment down there, it really didn't have much to do with that lone—as far as we know—sniper-assassin. But he said something—I can't remember the words exactly—which expressed some feelings of guilt.

William Sloane Coffin, Jr.   I remember being absolutely heartbroken when I heard of his assassination. I called Joe Lieberman, now senator from Connecticut. I have forgotten why I wanted to talk to him—but they said, "He's gone back to his room; he's so upset." I said, "Upset about what?" and they told me. I recall hanging up the phone in the kitchen, walking out of the house, and just putting my head down on the top of the nearest car and just bawling. It just seemed an awful, terrible tragedy—a real, real loss. In retrospect, so far as the nation goes, I don't feel quite the same way. I think that Bobby Kennedy's death was the really, really tragic one, for I think he had seen the light and I think he would have gotten the nomination and won the election. It might have made a real big difference.

Martin Hillenbrand   There was no doubt that the assassination of Kennedy left its mark in Germany. It demonstrated the positive image of the president that most Germans had. But it also led, I think, to a feeling that somehow or other there must be a basic fault in a country that could have its young president assassinated as he was. Then of course, this was compounded by the assassinations of Robert Kennedy and Martin Luther King.

   I think we've never fully recovered from the reaction of Europeans to the successive assassinations that, somehow or other, America is a country of uncontrolled violence; that its social structure, or social fabric, is in the process of partial disintegration. I think many Germans wouldn't say that openly, but that's the conclusion which they arrived at in one way or another, perhaps not as precisely articulated as I put it.

WAS IT A CONSPIRACY?

Viktor Sukhodrev   Khrushchev never really could rid himself of the thought that it was a conspiracy. I don't think that he could ever believe that it was simply a one-man job. Not really. But American writers certainly gave enough food to keep that thought uppermost in his mind.

Willy Brandt   How could one know? When I went over for the funeral, I was on the plane from New York to Washington together with, among others, Jean Monnet [French economist], and there was a good deal of confusion—what will happen? When I came to Washington, a good friend of mine said, "You'd better get out of this place, because nobody knows what will happen." Then you looked at television, with the assassination of Oswald. I myself did not get any feeling that there wouldn't be an orderly transfer of power to the new president.

Richard Bissell   I tend to be suspicious of conspiracy theories because they always rest on the assumption that highly complicated activities can be carried out without any mistakes. I think that conspiracy theories have to be viewed with skepticism. It is not clear to me who had a motive in President Kennedy's assassination. I thought from the beginning that the Russians, an official communist organization, would not have done it; it is contrary to their doctrine and procedures. I don't think that the Bay of Pigs survivors had the skills and clout to organize a conspiracy of that sort, nor do I really think there was a motivation.

No doubt we did try to assassinate Castro—there is hard evidence in the Church Committee. It was ongoing. Beginning in late 1961, a new anti-Castro project was launched, propelled on the occasion primarily by Bobby Kennedy. Lansdale was initially in charge. He had an office in the Pentagon, but he could call on CIA resources, and there grew out of that what was later called Operation Mongoose; it went on right up to Kennedy's death. Castro had a motive for Kennedy's assassination, but I think that he would have seen the risks in such an undertaking as being absolutely overwhelming.

Cartha DeLoach   Mr. Hoover never wavered from his belief that Oswald was the lone assassin. All the evidence pointing to that fact is overwhelming. The ordering of the gun under the name of A. J. Hidell; the fingerprints left at the scene of the crime; the usage of the rifle and the ballistic evidence that the rifle killed Kennedy; Oswald's ownership of the rifle; the fact that he was placed through fingerprints at the scene of the crime, the sixth-floor window in the Book Depository building. Once he made up his mind and had all the evidence, he was very sure that there was no conspiracy involved.

Thomas Mann   Our intelligence agencies were in agreement that Oswald had been in Mexico City twice and had visited both the Soviet and Cuban embassies on both occasions. I did not see him in person. After the assassination, I told the department about that and didn't get any answer, and told them again. I was instructed, the only time in my career it ever happened, not to talk about those visits again and to quit talking to the Mexican government about it. Maybe there was a very good reason for that.

Viktor Sukhodrev   Oswald's Russian connection, of course, was troubling, and the Soviet side immediately provided the Americans with all the information they had available to them on Oswald's period in the Soviet Union, his marriage, his departure, and that was done very sincerely, very sincerely. Some of the material was still coming in while we were on our way, and it was passed on to Mikoyan at the embassy. He said that everything that existed on Oswald, every item that existed anywhere in the Soviet Union, should immediately be given to the Americans to dispel even the slightest suspicion that there could have been some kind of a Moscow connection.

Yuri Barsukov   That was a very disturbing report that Oswald was in the Soviet Union. I personally never believed that he could assassinate John Kennedy as a Russian agent. Despite all the difficulties which we had with the administration of John Kennedy, the feeling we had was that we were quite satisfied with the state of Soviet American relations, so I thought, "It's just absurd." I was very glad to hear later on that it was not the case.

Viktor Sukhodrev   I think that there was somewhere that thought that Oswald was a CIA plant. I mean this was such a tragedy happening in a country like the United States. This was no banana republic; this was the United States. Of course I think that that thought could not but have come into Khrushchev's mind. It was natural.

Alexei Adzhubei   Nobody suspected that Oswald was working for the CIA. In the 1930s people would have suspected him to be an agent; in the 1960s there was different thinking.

Robert Manning   From my experience in government, I don't think the CIA was capable of pulling off a conspiracy; it lies when it doesn't have to; it is the only secret service in the world that has its own press office. There is a character in the play *The Hostage*° who says, "I am in the Irish Secret Service, and I don't care who knows." Overseas everyone knew who the CIA people were. They were flamboyant about it.

William Smith   I was at the White House that day and was told that President Johnson, as he got on the plane in Dallas, said, "This is a communist conspiracy." Based on intelligence I looked really carefully over at the time, we felt it was a single person. In the military there was never great talk that reached any level of respectability at that time that this had been a conspiracy, or that the Soviets had done it.

Today I think there is probably more uncertainty as to Oswald and his schedule and his motivations. The Soviets said they had nothing to do with it, and I, for one, believed that; they liked Kennedy. There is the Mafia theory. Actually, I still think it was Oswald, but I don't think it with the firm conviction I did before. It is just harder to explain Ruby [Jack Ruby, assassin of Lee Harvey Oswald]—the fact that Oswald was killed. It looks more complicated now than it did at the time.

Cartha DeLoach   President Johnson asked me one day a simple, rhetorical question: "Do you think the FBI had anything to do with this?" I told him no.

Later on, when the Senate Select Committee on Intelligence got hold of all those files, one senator from Pennsylvania tried to get publicity. He asked me while I was under oath if President Johnson had made this statement. I said, "It wasn't a statement; it was a question." I said, "He just asked this in idle conversation and did not state whether he believed that or not." President Johnson did not think that. He was just asking a question—covering the gamut, so to speak.

°By Brendan Behan (1923–64).

Jack Valenti   Later on Johnson told me that he believed that the source bed of the assassination was in Cuba. He believed that Castro, vengeful and vexed that the Kennedys were trying to kill him, used Oswald as his instrument to kill Kennedy—no proof, absolutely none, but he just believed that. He couldn't figure out any other reason to murder Kennedy. This was way after the Warren Commission. Remember, the Warren Commission says Oswald was the lone assassin. Johnson never disputed that. But who was Oswald? What prompted him? Johnson believed that Oswald was a witting, or unwitting, instrument of Cuba.

Sergei Khrushchev   He [Lyndon Johnson] was from the right wing, and so maybe he was involved in all this—the assassination—maybe not. Maybe he knew something; not that he was one who knew something, but that he was a representative [of this thinking].

Robert Moses   For my money the FBI was at the root of Kennedy's assassination. I think one of the issues was, Where was the appropriate protection for the president? This protection lies with the FBI in coordination with the Secret Service. I don't think there was any real interest within the FBI in cooperating to do that kind of thing. I think the FBI hated Kennedy with a passion. We felt that on our end of the movement.

Sam Yorty   I think Ruby was permitted to kill Oswald because I think that Ruby was part of the mob. And I think Oswald was supposed to assassinate the president, then beat it down to Mexico or someplace and go back to Russia. But he got fouled up, went to a theater, and got caught, and then I think they had to get rid of him or he'd tell the truth, and so they had Ruby shoot him. It's ridiculous to walk into a police department and shoot a suspected assassin.

William Sloane Coffin, Jr.   We're such a country of crazies, and you know something about American history—how many times we tried to assassinate people in the past—but I certainly didn't buy into the conspiracy theory right away, though now I'm more suspicious. There's probably more to it than what's come out yet, in the same way as with [James Earl] Ray and the assassination of King. But probably not with Bobby Kennedy's assassination.

THE WARREN COMMISSION

Dean Rusk   Well, we subjected that issue to the most strenuous investigation that we were capable of, and we could not find any evidence of the involvement of a foreign government in the assassination of President Kennedy. That could easily have been a question of war and peace had we found some. I've not made a career out of reading everything that's been written about the assassination of JFK, but I've read a good deal of it and thus far I've not seen any hard facts that cause me to dispute the main conclusions of the Warren Commission. A lot of it is just fanciful speculation.

John Sherman Cooper, U.S. senator (R., Ky.); member, Warren Commission*   People write me about their ideas on the assassination. They have read about the Warren Commission. They weren't on it, but I was. I remember some of the people who served: Senator Russell, Hale Boggs, Gerald Ford, and, of course, Earl Warren [chief justice of the United States], who had been a judge. People are concerned because the president was assassinated, but they never talked to any of the witnesses. Senator Russell and I went down to Dallas and talked to Marina Oswald, and she told us when she heard about the assassination, she went to see where her husband's rifle was, and it was gone.

Gerald Ford   I am the only surviving member. I reaffirm the two basic decisions of the Warren Commission are as valid today as they were then. Those were that Lee Harvey Oswald committed the assassination, and secondly, our commission found no evidence of a conspiracy, foreign or domestic. Now, our staff, when they submitted to the commission the proposed draft of our report, said, "We should say there was no conspiracy." Our commission said, "No. We're going to change it and say we found no evidence," which we hadn't. And I don't think we have found any evidence to date that there was a conspiracy.

As a member of the commission, I had no feeling that President Johnson was directing it. The chief justice may have had that subjective feeling. I can't point to anything specific. But I don't think the commission had any prejudiced view, period. That was a very good commission. I

*Deceased.

happen to think we did a good job. And I resent and reject all these speculative stories and promotions. There has been no new credible evidence. People who have written books and produced television stories have taken whatever evidence we dug up and manipulated it to their own point of view.

Bobby Baker   I knew the people who served on the Warren Commission. If you were able to hoodwink that group of people, we're in terrible trouble. John Connally was there; Nellie [Idanell B. Connally, Governor Connally's wife] was there. I have to take their view as to what happened. Now, Johnson always thought that it was Castro; he thought it was a conspiracy.

Bernard Boutin   I never have accepted the conclusions of the Warren Commission; I don't believe they are true. I don't believe that Lee Harvey Oswald could possibly, as a single person without any help, have done what he is accused of having done. I think he was a party to it, but I don't think it was just Lee Harvey Oswald. I don't think it was international in terms of the communists.

I think that the FBI and the CIA were both derelict—absolutely, unequivocally derelict. By commission or omission. That is another question.

Richard Bissell   I thought it was a very astute and proper thing to appoint a distinguished commission like that. Allen Dulles was one of its members. I really never had any reason to doubt or question the commission's conclusions; I am not one of those who thought the commission did a poor job. As to a second assassin, I suppose you'd have to say that if there was one, it was indeed a failure of our intelligence, our criminal-control organizations, that the individual not only was never caught but that his existence has never even been officially admitted. There seems to be some hard evidence of the second man—the second gun, at least, so it is alleged.

Norman Podhoretz   I didn't believe the story, and I didn't believe the Warren Report, particularly. I didn't have any other theory. I just wasn't convinced. I still don't have any other theory.

Sam Yorty   I don't think the Warren Commission ever did a good job. I don't think most people believe what they found. I don't think the truth ever came out about Ruby and his connections. It came out later that Kennedy had wanted old Castro assassinated, but that was covered up for a long time. I think that was, in part, in back of the thing. I'm sure the Cubans were involved. Oswald had been down to the Russian Embassy in Mexico before he assassinated the president.

Ralph Yarborough   When Kennedy was assassinated, I was in the second car behind. The Secret Service car was next to him, and I was in the car with Lyndon Johnson and Lady Bird. They asked everybody to come and testify, and they never asked me. I wrote the Warren Commission a letter, and they never invited me—asked me—to come testify, and when the House reopened it, the same thing; I wrote them.

The Warren Commission created the impression that the president's car took off immediately. They didn't take off immediately. If they had, he might have been saved. I talked to the security man from the State Department. He came up to talk to me about that—one of the Secret Service men. He said, "Well, the drivers have instructions if you've got a dignitary"—they wouldn't say "a president"—"from a foreign country, head of state, or secretary of state—and shots are fired, you take off immediately. You don't take the time to find out where." Well, the Secret Service never did that. I saw them look back up. I wasn't going to turn my head around. I wanted to look and see where that shot was coming from. But the Secret Service looked up there, and they gradually, slowly, pulled out rifles. Well, they found out later, through the investigation, that they were being entertained until two or four o'clock the morning before, over in a nightclub in Fort Worth. They didn't respond rapidly at all; they didn't take off—speed off—until after the third shot.

Ray Cline   The Oliver Stone movie is crazy. The idea that the CIA and the FBI and the military could all cooperate together is nutty; no bureaucracies ever cooperate together. If the CIA had been trying to assassinate Kennedy, I would have known about it. I would have found out and I would have told him. I don't think there was ever any opportunity, or thought of the CIA's doing this deed.

The CIA did know a good bit about the Oswald exploit. He went to

Russia, he married a Russian woman, and then he came back. Unfortunately, in my view, the CIA wasn't able to do anything about it, although they studied him carefully abroad. When he came back, the FBI took charge. I think that J. Edgar Hoover made a big mistake: He tried to say that Oswald was a loner and a crazy man. I don't think that was true. I think that Hoover should have watched him more closely than he did. I still think it's conceivable that the Cubans had something to do with it. But we don't know. The evidence is not clear. The CIA understood a lot, but they were cut off from domestic affairs; the FBI had charge of this event. J. Edgar Hoover and CIA director John McCone were not too cordial with one another. Bureaucracies tend to be hostile to one another. Hoover, especially when he went on to his dotage, made a lot of mistakes. What he did in the Warren Commission was to try to cover up the FBI mistakes; there were mistakes.

Dean Rusk I do have one reservation about my part in the testimony before the Warren Commission. I was asked whether we'd had any evidence of involvement of a foreign government, and I proceeded with a statement that we had not found any evidence of such, and then I added a paragraph that I did not think that any foreign government had any motivation to be a participant in such a thing. Well, at that time, I did not know that the CIA was involved in various assassination attempts against Castro, and Allen Dulles was sitting in on the Warren Commission, and he did know about these things, and he didn't take me by the coattails and say, "Wait a minute, there's something you ought to know about before you add that paragraph." I have always been resentful that I was not informed about these CIA efforts to assassinate Castro in time to make a more straightforward presentation to the Warren Commission.

20

Camelot

────────

In the period immediately following the assassination, the Kennedy era came increasingly to be described as "Camelot," in reference to the legend of King Arthur, which was set in a magical period not likely to soon be repeated; characterized by grace, wit, and intelligence; and peopled by those superbly prepared for their brief but eminently successful adventure in governance. According to several Kennedy intimates, writer Theodore White was responsible for the Camelot characterization, which greatly facilitated the development of the Kennedy mystique and legend. It should be noted, however, that the president's widow and other Kennedy family members and close associates worked diligently to foster and perpetuate the Camelot legend.

On August 19, 1990, Senator Edward M. Kennedy, in commenting on the death of Stephen E. Smith, said: "There wouldn't have been a Camelot without Steve Smith."

Pierre Salinger   Camelot is a fraud; the word never came out during the Kennedy administration, but a week after the assassination in an interview with Theodore White. Now it has become *the* word; we're living in a world where the words *Camelot* and *myth* are attached to the Kennedy name. I constantly argue against this.

Arthur Schlesinger, Jr.   Camelot was, of course, unknown in Kennedy's lifetime. JFK himself would have regarded that with derision. However, he and Alan Lerner [Alan Jay Lerner, who—with Frederick

Loewe—wrote the musical *Camelot*] were very old friends. They had gone to Choate and Harvard together, and they traveled to Europe together in the 1930s. But that was not the way we saw ourselves. Those were romantic memories.

Roger Hilsman   Camelot was an invention of my good friend Teddy White, using Jackie's romanticism after the president's death. If Jack Kennedy had heard this stuff about Camelot, he would have vomited; it would have made him sick to his stomach. There was a widow, a romantic young widow, trying to express to Teddy White the magic that she felt. But that was a journalistic invention.

Dean Rusk   JFK would have kicked the idea of Camelot right out the window. He was a very practical, hard-headed, down-to-earth kind of fellow who would not have indulged in the sentiment of Camelot while he was alive. Camelot was started by a remark made by Jacqueline Kennedy after his death. In my judgment JFK would not have played around with that idea at all.

Nor would he have claimed that his administration was filled with the best and the brightest. We had no sense at all during the Kennedy administration that we were the best and the brightest. We had a hard row to hoe. We had major problems and dangerous problems, and we were working like hell to deal with these problems without an explosion. So we didn't look upon ourselves as the best and the brightest.

William Sullivan   All things are relative. The musical *Camelot* appeared at a time when there was a great deal of self-congratulation amongst the New Frontiersmen, and they sort of co-opted it for themselves. I remember being up at the UN with Chip Bohlen and there was a storm coming that night, so we were able to get tickets, and I had the impression that some of the staging on some of the role-playing may have been designed to resonate with the Kennedy administration: the caricature of de Gaulle in the figure of Lancelot. I don't think the whole gang did anything to discourage the view that they were Camelot.

Adam Yarmolinsky   Why is Camelot associated with the Kennedy administration? Because it's a natural. But you've got to remember the last scene, which is the key to the whole thing: It's just off the battlefield.

The battle is about to begin, and a young man runs onto the stage, and there's King Arthur, and the young man says he wants to join the troops, to enlist. And King Arthur says, "No, Tom. I don't want you in the battle. I want you, Tom, to go tell our story." The young man was Thomas Malory.°

It certainly seemed like Camelot at the time, and it seems like Camelot in retrospect. There's a bit of Oz in it too; if you went behind the scenes, you'd see somebody puffing and struggling and working the gears and levers. Kennedy was quoted as saying that happiness consists in the fullest use of one's powers in the pursuit of excellence, which I think is something out of a Greek anthology. And there were more people who believed that in the Kennedy administration than I have seen in any administration since. And pervading the administration was the sense that you could. It was true in the Johnson administration, but Kennedy started it.

There was a quality of youthful hope about the Kennedy administration, and the Johnson administration was struggling to accomplish things in the face of knowledge of mortality. The two sort of complemented each other.

Clark Kerr I was at the famous White House dinner where he invited all the Nobel Prize winners. It was an elegant occasion. The spirit was that new ideas made a difference and that people engaged on the frontiers of thinking were highly valued. There was a sense that intellectuals made a difference. I remember Linus Pauling [double Nobel laureate] walking around telling everybody, "I am the only person in the United States who can picket the president in the afternoon and be invited for dinner the same evening."

Edward McDermott There was such good feeling—the Bay of Pigs, the Cuban missile crisis, all of those things notwithstanding. There was the feeling that there was a new and revived America, that things could be different: The poor won't be so poor; the uneducated will get a better education. There was an exhilaration that a lot could be done and that this was a group of people collectively, led by the president, that could

---

°Sir Thomas Malory (d. 1471), author of the *Morte Darthur*, one of the sources on which *Camelot* was based.

inspire the American people to do things that they hadn't done before. It was Camelot.

Lincoln Gordon   I think the Camelot promoters overdo it terribly. And their denigration of Johnson seems to me utterly unnecessary. Somehow or other they seem to feel they can only glorify Kennedy by diminishing Johnson. And I see no reason to do that. It seems to me the Kennedy personality and record can stand on its own, and Johnson's can stand on its own. They're entirely different, but they both accomplished many things. Both of them made terrible mistakes. The Bay of Pigs was obviously a small mistake; Vietnam was a huge mistake. Kennedy, to some extent, was also involved in that in its early stages.

John Kenneth Galbraith   I have never used the word *Camelot,* but it was an exciting period in American history. As in the New Deal years, there was a feeling that what happened in Washington really mattered for the country as a whole—the commitment that was identified as the national interest, the national well-being. It brought to Washington a talented, committed group of young people. I was distant, being in India, and in a way not part of it because I was much older; it was in the Kennedy administration that I first learned that people were saying "sir" to me.

Ralph Yarborough   It was a special time; I was there. Lord, I've never had such a feeling before or since then. It was marvelous; without living it, you can't express it. It gave the country a lift; it gave the world a lift. People cried in the dusty streets of Africa when he died. This world hasn't recovered yet from Kennedy's assassination. He created hope in people. Reagan instilled hope in the rich, but who was going to take care of the poor? He'd let them starve. He was asked about those people who sleep on grates, and he said, "They like to sleep on grates."

William Smith   There was a glamour about the White House at that time. The president looked good; his wife was attractive; they had a young family; they had a lot of money, so they lived well; they attracted interesting people around them. If you put it all together, there was a difference from any other presidential style in this century.

Robert Manning   There is no question that the atmosphere in Washington when Kennedy took over was of a city suddenly becoming sophisticated. There was the feeling of youth and vigor—Pablo Casals [cellist] in the White House—that was exciting. It was a tremendous change from the Eisenhower period. Bundy once said, "Here is a president who leaves the room at the first crack of a fiddle, but he sure knew how to bring culture into Washington." If you look at the record collection that they had, they were all rock and roll stuff. Bobby Kennedy had a lot of young people around him, and there were a lot of bright young people at secondary and tertiary levels of the bureaucracy. Ideas were encouraged: Write a memo and send it to somebody.

William Sloane Coffin, Jr.   The Camelot image was just that; there wasn't much substance behind it. It was glamorous. We love celebrities in this country. We don't have a king, and suddenly, here's a very young, bright, funny guy; he could laugh at himself. His wife was gorgeous, and there was a great family behind him. Look at all the cultural luminaries who went down there—concerts in the White House. I remember Sol Hurok [impresario] telling me he'd met Eisenhower, and he was quite impressed being in the president's box. And Ike said, "Who was that great tenor you had from one of those Scandinavian countries?" and he said, "Melchior." And Ike said, "That's the one. God, could he ever sing 'The Star Spangled Banner.'" Culturally, you got that with Eisenhower. And then you had Pablo Casals playing away in the Kennedy White House. I think we were all quite bedazzled.

Tom Wicker   In the first year or two, there was great deal of glamour about the White House. It was very chic to get pushed into Bobby Kennedy's pool. I remember Ayub Khan [president of Pakistan] came, and they had that famous dinner at Mount Vernon. God, that was glamorized beyond belief! I remember that Kennedy, the patrician—one generation removed from bootlegging—decreed that the gentlemen couldn't wear white jackets; they had to be black. God, I remember thinking that these were the most glamorous people that ever lived.

Donald Wilson   There was a freedom, an openness, and a liveliness. It was open because Kennedy was; the president really sets the tone for an administration. There was the social side to it also: the dances, football, throwing people in the pool—things which were immature—but I felt it was stimulating. Camelot, maybe, is too much.

Norman Podhoretz   Camelot is ridiculous—just a pop-culture myth. There was real glamour surrounding the Kennedys—the glamour of café society combined with great political power. People, naturally, were flattered if they were invited into those circles. For many intellectuals and journalists, writers and literary people—who had never had any contact with the world of political power—it was a very heady experience to be recognized, to be treated with respect. For that alone, many people were bought off. They were simply intoxicated.

It was intoxicating if you were not used to it, and even if you were. I have been to many state dinners; it is always very flattering to be at a White House dinner. What always struck me as most fascinating was that even cabinet members—people who probably go to a hundred state dinners—are absolutely delighted to be there. You would think they would be blasé. Not at all. Some people would almost kill to be brought that close to the glamour and power. And to that glamour was added the slightly rakish, upper bohemian glamour of the Kennedys: a lot of beautiful women, a lot of—at least superficially—brilliant men. It's like the merging of two very seductive worlds.

Nicholas Katzenbach   I don't know about Camelot. I think it's a bum rap Jackie got for her parties—too excessive or not.

Ralph Dungan   Camelot is a creation of journalists. I'm sure that Jackie, in her kind of romantic, fuzzy way, thought that it was neat. She didn't understand things, mostly, and they didn't interest her. I think that probably contributed to the weakness of their marriage: For a while, I guess, it was nice to have somebody who didn't know anything about things—you didn't have to talk about them—but after a while, when you're living it, you really have to talk to someone. Jackie had good instincts about people. She had an interest in the artistic manifestations, which she did very well. I think that whole cultural thing in the White House was really great. Kennedy had very little of that, actually. He didn't like music and ballet. I don't know whether he liked Pablo Casals, but I thought it was the greatest thing ever; I got to go to that one. There is no doubt it was a special time; it impacted upon so many people. The Kennedy administration was going in the right direction—leave aside all the lacunae and that civil rights was an important issue that was not attended to properly.

Bernard Boutin   There is no question about it; it was a period of American history that has never been achieved again. You had the feeling of an appreciation for things of beauty, whether they were words, or buildings, or poetry. The events that occurred at the White House were spellbinding. The great artists were brought in in an atmosphere that was so conducive to enhancing their own performances. Kennedy loved that. I remember going to him and talking to him about historical publications—how we needed to do something to encourage people to create history—not the event but the word of history—to write history, to research history. With his sponsorship legislation was proposed and approved, providing grants to writers. It was a wonderful thing. I don't think George Bush would give that a thought.

All of it wasn't Camelot. The Bay of Pigs was a disaster, but it was part of his education.

Orville Freeman   It was a great period. Any number of people who were in it come up to me and say what a great period it was. It wasn't all easy; there were strikes and all kinds of problems with the steel people. It was never an easy job. That nuclear thing with the Russians, and then along came the Cuban missile crisis. The success of that one was, of course, a big step up. I think that he has earned his place in history. And all the stories of what a ladies' man he was—there's no evidence of that whatsoever. I've always said, Hell, he was too smart to do that—to take a chance at exposure in a job like that. You think he'd want to jump in bed with some doll? I haven't read hardly any of the books. I find it painful to read them.

Lloyd Cutler   It's a romanticization of the fact that clean-cut young people—when I say clean-cut I don't mean especially moral, but nice-looking, vigorous young people—were running the government, and that it was our ideas—of our generation—because it's been a long time since a forty-three-year-old became president of the United States.

Mrs. Kennedy contributed to the glamour. They were just an interesting bunch. And, as we've learned, exciting things keep happening to the Kennedys.

Ralph Dungan   A few marriages broke up. Some people suffered under the strain. Everybody paid. Kids paid; they didn't see their fathers. There were a lot of downsides to this lovely Camelot.

Adlai Stevenson III   This was not "Camelot." These were very practical politicians. My father became quite close to Jackie Kennedy. She'd escape this so-called Camelot by going to New York and to the theater with my father. Camelot is celluloid. I mean, it's just totally unreal, and I don't think it really did, or would have, come about except for the tragedy—the assassination. And then he became larger than life.

Camelot? The Kennedy administration wasn't all that successful; it had some wonderful, very bright, talented people in it, and many of them were my father's old friends: George Ball, Bill Wirtz [W. Willard Wirtz, secretary of labor], and many others. But Camelot was myth, created after the assassination.

Richard Helms   It's like a lot of the myths we have—it's a lot of rot. Imagine going back to the Middle Ages and then deciding this was what you had brought the United States of America to in the twentieth century! It really is kind of tawdry. Honestly, it never made any sense to me at all. Kennedy was a good-looking man; Jackie was a good-looking woman. They were good-looking and vivacious and young. It was great. I'm glad he was president. It was fine, but do we have to make this— because he got assassinated—into a kind of mythology?

After all, when you get into negotiations, Camelot doesn't play a large role. The Russians don't care about Camelot. They probably never heard of it.

21

If Kennedy Had Lived

_____

PROSPECTS FOR THE 1964 ELECTION

Bernard Boutin A small group of us—three or four in the beginning, and gradually expanded—started moving in early 1962 toward the reelection. We met regularly and set up an excellent communication, getting feedback from all over the country. I think he would have run away with the election.

Walt Rostow He told me that he thought he could defeat Goldwater [Barry M. Goldwater, U.S. senator (R., Ariz.)] in 1964 with 56 percent of the vote.

Ralph Dungan Johnson would have stayed on the ticket. Who could dump a vice president? I think that would have complicated the campaign, unless Johnson wanted out, but there was no indication of that. Where did he have to go?

Ralph Yarborough This is not based on anything anybody ever told me—it's my own surmise of the situation: It's pretty well known that Bobby Kennedy did not want Lyndon Johnson on that ticket for the second term, and John F. Kennedy never said a word. It was my opinion that he was going to put him on the ticket for a second term because to keep Johnson off was liable to outrage all those Southerners that had voted for him.

Terry Sanford I kept hearing, "Well now, in the next term." They were very cautious in looking at the 1964 election—much more so than I thought was wise.

Julian Bond Had Kennedy lived and run against Goldwater in 1964, we would have been forced to support him. But had Kennedy run against someone who had offered the slightest bit of competition on civil rights, I think we would have been enticed to look at that person, even a Republican—a Nelson Rockefeller—because none of us were, at that young age, tied to the Democratic party; we didn't have any history with the Democratic party—You know, we hadn't come through the New Deal; most of us had not cast our first votes in 1960. If you didn't live in Georgia in 1960 and you weren't eighteen, you weren't voting. Most of these people, if they were my age, didn't cast their first vote until the 1962 congressional elections, or in 1964.

James Farmer Against Rockefeller he would have been perceived, even by the solid South, as the lesser of two evils. Nobody would have the right of center to take from him. Against Goldwater I think the president would have been in trouble. I think Goldwater would have taken the center all the way right, and Kennedy would have been left with the left of center, with a lot of difficulties from that.

Adam Yarmolinsky If it had not been Barry Goldwater it would not have been quite the landslide that Johnson carried off, but probably some kind of a landslide. The Republicans really were committing suicide by nominating Goldwater, and I think they would have done it again.

I think, had it been Rockefeller, it would have been close, but he would have been the incumbent. I think he would have won.

John Patterson   Robert changed his tune about the Freedom Riders after they got to Mississippi. He began to coax them into going home. I think that Kennedy was planning to run for reelection, and they were trying to build a civil rights record that would be unequaled by anybody else. The more they pushed this thing down here, the more reluctant all of us would have been to get out and get openly involved in his reelection. Maybe they knew they were writing us off, and we didn't really matter.

The Electoral College has been both good and bad. With the migration of the blacks out of the South to the East and Midwest right after World War II, they all vote in a bloc. Truman proved in 1948 that you did not have to carry a single Southern state to be elected president. Maybe the Kennedys realized that if they carried the key states like New York, Illinois, California, he could be elected president without having to worry about these Southern states.

The president never said much, but Robert pushed the civil rights thing very hard, and he was alienating their former support down here very rapidly. He'd have had a hell of a time finding someone like me to stand up for him the next time.

Tom Wicker   I think he would have been reelected with Johnson as his running mate. They would have run against Barry Goldwater and Bill Miller and wiped them out, just the way Johnson did. Maybe not quite as much so, because Kennedy would not have carried the entire South.

Sam Yorty   I don't think he would have been reelected, because he was unpopular down in Texas and the South. That's why he went down to Texas, to try and mend his fences.

I think he would have *had* to keep LBJ on the ticket. I don't know what he would have done, but I think he would have had to.

William Sloane Coffin, Jr.   I don't think he made many enemies. People now had settled down on the Catholic issue; there was no black backlash; and I don't see why he wouldn't have won rather handily, as Johnson did.

Gerald Ford   A Rockefeller-Kennedy race in 1964 would have been a totally different campaign from Goldwater-Kennedy. That could have been an interesting political campaign. My own impression was that the early glamour of Kennedy, which was a factor in the election of 1960, was beginning to wear thin. He was losing a never-very-solid relationship with Congress; he never really had that relationship, because when Jack Kennedy was in Congress, whether the House or the Senate, he was never really a part of the establishment. So, when he started out, his relationship with the Congress was not what you'd call solid, substantial.

And as his administration proceeded, it didn't get better; it was beginning to disintegrate. If he had lived and gone to the public in 1964, he could not have talked about significant legislative accomplishments, because he didn't have this background, this expertise, this relationship with the Congress. I don't think most people understood that. Those of us in the Congress saw how he operated. He never really had a significant legislative record as president. Johnson had a much better record, because Johnson understood the Congress; he was part of the Congress.

Phillips Talbot   It's clear that Kennedy was already in trouble with Congress when he died, so my sense is that he would have been reelected quite easily, but that he would have been rather more preoccupied than he had anticipated, in getting the congressional agenda sorted out.

There was a conviction that if we worked hard, we could accomplish things, and there was also a conviction that if we were to solve the world's problems, he would be elected in a breeze in '64. There was a very strong feeling that Congress, which was getting restless before he was killed, would see what a substantial political lead he could give, and his influence with Congress—his ability to manage Congress—would be greater. His standing in the world would be strengthened, because people would no longer look at him as having just managed to get in.

Roswell Gilpatric   He was interested in finding out what kind of an adversary Rockefeller would be. I think he was appealed to personally by Rockefeller's personality. For example, when I was assigned responsibility for civil defense, McNamara wasn't interested in civil defense, didn't believe in bomb shelters—this was the president's decision, so I got the job running that phase of the Pentagon's activities. Nelson Rockefeller was very hipped on civil defense, and he would come down to get briefed on what we were doing on the national scale. He always came to see me in the Pentagon. I always got word from the White House to be sure that the governor came over to the White House before he left Washington. In other words, Kennedy was attracted to Rockefeller as a person, but at the same time was very wary about what sort of an adversary he would be if they were opponents in the 1964 presidential election.

Pierre Salinger   As far as 1964 was concerned, Kennedy knew that Goldwater would be his opponent, and he had a discussion with Goldwater as to how they were going to run the campaign together—they were very good friends—and they decided that the 1964 campaign would be debates across the country, like the Lincoln debates back in the nineteenth century. They would go from one city to another, and in each city, would debate one issue. It would have been a fantastic campaign. Kennedy was confident he could win—when he was killed he was very popular: He had a 62 percent positive rating in the polls, and he was getting more popular. He had had no power base when he was first elected; it all had to be created during his presidency. He was also at his most popular and influential moment with Congress when he was killed.

Lincoln Gordon   Kennedy was in terrible trouble with Congress in 1963 at the time that he was killed, and who can say what would have happened if he had lived? Whether he would have been reelected, what fraction of that legislation on civil rights and on the Great Society, as it came to be called, would have been passed? I just don't know.

Marcus Raskin   I have never allowed myself to think of what it would have meant had he lived. I think that there were very powerful forces unleashed in the society during that period, and it would have been very hard to put them back into the bottle; nobody could do that. So a president would have to ride those forces. In that sense Robert Kennedy was not that far away from Jack Kennedy; he rode those forces; he became part of it; he saw himself in that framework. In terms of makeup John Kennedy was a Whig: dubious, sardonic; he would make a correction here, a change there.

George McGovern   I think that Jack was a cautious, pragmatic, political figure. I think he never let idealism get the better of his pragmatic view of what it took to stay in office and get reelected. It was certainly no myth that he wanted to win; he didn't want to lose when he ran for office, so that I think he felt that a hard line on communism, caution on civil rights—those were realistic judgments that he had to make if he wanted to lead the country and stay in power.

As far as a second term, it would have been a pragmatic assessment that they could do it in the second term without fear of future elections. But I think he had the intelligence and experience by then to take more humanitarian, idealistic positions than he did in the first term. I think he would have opened the doors to China; that he would have tried harder for an arms deal with the Russians; that he would probably have pressed harder on civil rights. He knew those things were right, and I think he would have done them once free of the terrible tyranny of a forthcoming election.

William Colby   I suspect that the antiwar movement wouldn't have been what it was if Kennedy had lived; he would have been smart enough to defuse it.

If Kennedy had lived he might have had a more mixed reputation, because it was Johnson that got civil rights through. But remember, Kennedy was fighting the battles of Oxford, Mississippi; there was a commitment there.

One is just aghast at the personal behavior—every skirt for miles around, apparently. It is a great tribute to the Secret Service to keep their mouths shut, because they must have known about it. You just ask: How is that image compatible with those other images? It's a weakness. We all have weaknesses.

WHAT WOULD KENNEDY HAVE DONE AFTER A SECOND TERM?

Pierre Salinger   Had John Kennedy lived, he would have become the youngest former president of the United States. One day I said to him: "What will you do? You will have been president for eight years; what the hell do you do after that?" He said, "I'm going to buy a newspaper in Boston—you'll be editor—and we'll be reporting on Bobby's presidency."

Bradford Morse   I can't conceive, if John Kennedy had lived, of his heading up a Bobby Kennedy booster society for the presidency. I think

Bobby Kennedy, as he did, would have come into presidential politics, but he would have done it on his own merits, for the same reason that Joe Kennedy was never seen to be heading up the John Kennedy bandwagon: It just would have been bad politics. It would have given the opponents the dynasty issue, and the issue that he was not his own man.

Adam Yarmolinsky   He always said that when he retired, he would like to own a newspaper, edit a newspaper, write. In many ways, the world lost a great journalist when he became a politician. I think he was one of the people who helped to make journalists in Washington the aristocracy of Washington society, which they continue to be.

Ralph Dungan   I doubt that Kennedy would have written his own memoirs; he would let others do that. I would have thought after a second term, he would have gotten into some other active thing—writing probably wouldn't have been it. He might have gone off to teach. He might have gone off into something international. But he would have been a terrible general secretary of the UN; he would have been awful at that. He would have been poor at anything that demanded methodical administration; as happened in everything else, somebody would have been there to pick up the towel.

WOULD KENNEDY BE A
VIABLE CANDIDATE IN THE 1990s?

Pierre Salinger   I think that in today's climate—there has been such a change in the political mentality in this country; conducting investigations into the private lives of political leaders has become a major point—Kennedy would probably have a greater problem getting elected. This is a very Anglo-Saxon way of looking at politics. In the European countries it doesn't exist—the president of France has had fifty mistresses and named one of them to be prime minister; in the United States that would be the scandal of the century. I was only asked about Kennedy's private life one time as press secretary: A journalist came in to see me and said, "I am beginning to get information that Kennedy has got mistresses." I gave an answer then that I could not give today, because I would be thrown out as press secretary. I said, "Listen, this man is the president of the United States; he works fourteen or fifteen hours a day; he has to deal with international problems. If he does that all day long and still has time to have a mistress, what the hell difference does it make?" The guy laughed and walked out, and that was the end of it.

Edward McDermott   I don't think that today the media will permit such a personality to develop. We're committed today to tarnishing our public figures before they ever reach office so that they have no integrity or credibility by the time they get there. It's tragic, and that's the way it is.

Richard Bissell   I think he might well be a viable candidate today: He had the reputation of being tough—perhaps to a fault—on certain domestic and foreign matters, but at the same time of being liberal in most domestic matters. I think that's a combination of political philosophies that has worked pretty well in this country. I think that Kennedy would represent an alternative to Bush that many Americans would see as a desirable alternative, his having been brighter and more articulate. Now, I don't know how much his candidacy would be affected by all the books that are coming out, focusing on his personal morals. One has to qualify an answer about his being a good candidate by that fact—just as Gary Hart [candidate for Democratic nomination for president in 1988] ceased to be a good candidate.

William Colby   Today he probably would catch a great deal of what Clinton is catching; it would certainly come out. You go back to the old days when they never took a picture of Roosevelt in his braces or in a wheelchair. I think if some of it on Kennedy had come out, you would have gotten some more negatives about him. But even Nixon would not have used it, particularly; he wouldn't think it was right.

Marcus Raskin   Kennedy would not be viable today running on the same terms as he did in 1960. He would be viable because he was a very attractive man. He could use the phrase "get the country moving again." That would make a great deal of sense. A number of things that Clinton says are not so far from what I think Jack Kennedy would have said. Clinton is trying to do that. The first time it comes as a tragedy, the second time as a farce. At least that is the way it is beginning to look now.

Gerald R. Ford   His appeal on television was outstanding. Whether his philosophical views would be appealing today I don't know. My own impression is that Jack could be flexible enough so that if he were today a potential presidential candidate, he would adjust his philosophical views; he wasn't as ideologically pure as some other potential Democrats are. Yes, certainly from the PR point of view, he would definitely be a candidate; he would be more or less in the mainstream.

Donald Wilson   He could be elected in 1992, but with the tremendous caveat on his relationship with women. Otherwise he would be as damn near electable today as he was then. As a matter of fact, he would be winning the primaries today. He had the charisma, the brains. He had it all. It probably would be easier to beat Bush than it was to beat Nixon.

Joseph Sisco   Judging from what we know today, with the press playing an absolutely full-blown monitoring role, while he enjoyed excellent relationships with the press, I would doubt that his private life could have survived the kind of scrutiny that is so characteristic of our society today.

Adam Yarmolinsky   I suppose one has to leave a question mark for the consequences of his personal behavior. I think he had enormous potential, which was not realized. He accomplished more after his death than he did in office. But he had the equipment for it. He had the brains, and he had the judgment, and he had the heart. And he had the energy, which is one of the essential requirements.

Lucius Battle   He would still be a viable candidate. You'd have to change some of the slogans, maybe. They were not quite structured for this era. But he was an awfully appealing person: the voice, the manner, the charm just doesn't come along often. I wish he was still around.

22

The Kennedy Legacy

Richard Helms His inaugural address really inspired people; it was a feeling of renewal. That is what he should be remembered for. He made an effort to try to get some of those things started, but on the really important issues of the time, either he didn't have the time or the energy or the opportunity to bring them to fruition. For example, civil rights legislation was all Johnson. I don't think Kennedy could have gotten it through Congress the way Johnson did—not even in a second term. I don't think Kennedy could have talked to Richard Russell and the other Southern senators the way Johnson did. I think that was the whole key to getting the civil rights legislation through.

Clark Kerr Eisenhower had kind of a status quo administration, and when Kennedy came in, it was really like a breath of fresh air, raising new possibilities: a heightened interest in the arts and new ideas, generally. It particularly had an impact, as I saw it, on the social sciences. They became more important at about that time. It had an impact of seeming to open up people's expectations and minds to new ideas.

Aspirations were raised, and then they weren't fulfilled. What came after was not a new and better world but a lot of difficulties and disappointments. There was sort of a high peak of aspiration and of expectation, followed by a valley.

George McGovern   The president had raised the standard pretty high in his inaugural address—that business of bearing any burden and taking on any foe was great at the time, but looking back on it, I think it was really quite arrogant and extravagant in assuming that any one country had the right to do that.

Phillips Talbot   He was an exciting political personality on the world scene almost from the time he took office. His inaugural address had raised immense enthusiasm all over the place. This was true in India, too, but I don't think in any of the eighteen countries that I had to deal with there was any serious feeling, apart from the fact that it is marvelous, we have a president who recognizes what we today call the Third World—we did not call it that then—who understands that people in other countries have aspirations, who is supportive of them, who is trying to help, who doesn't take a military view of the United States in the way that the military president had done. So there was a very strong Kennedy movement all through these developing countries, and this was part of the joy for a person like me—working in that administration—as I traveled through that area, because I wasn't having to constantly defend the U.S. against unpopular positions.

Eugene McCarthy   There was no New Frontier on foreign policy at all. They really pushed the old frontier farther than it was under Eisenhower. On the domestic front there wasn't very much that wasn't inherent in the old New Deal. Even in civil rights, the Eisenhower administration had done in their own way just about as much on civil rights. There was no real breaking of new ground.

Esther Peterson   He made you feel good about serving your people, serving your country; at least to me it was that way. And as I talk to my grandsons—we talk about it a little bit—that's there. That's what I hope will come more in the future: that the young students coming up now will feel not just that they can serve in war, but that they can serve in all these other areas.

Willy Brandt   He was a great hope during the postwar time, with this remarkable ability to catch the imagination of young people by arguing beyond an existing situation, and also his ability to catch the attention of intellectuals, get them mobilized, get their thinking moving beyond things as they were. As a man—and then also as a president—he had not only the will but also the ability to break out of the narrow borderlines of bureaucracy and traditional diplomacy.

Archibald Cox   The single most important thing about him was that he was the last—not only president but public figure—that did strike a chord of idealism and commitment, in a high-minded way, to public service.

Burke Marshall   He was a president who was filmed, so people who weren't alive then still see him. He was a tremendously attractive person to the people who worked with him. There were three generations of people who said, "That's what I want my politicians to be like."

Ralph Yarborough   John F. Kennedy should be remembered for what he accomplished as president. I watched him talking to people; I heard his speeches in the campaign. He was different. He was growing in that campaign. A man's got to be someone to do that. You can't just put something over on the people by lying. He was getting into the spirit of the thing—the spirit of the people: Elderly people would come to him with their money and say, "That's my last dollar."

Bernard Boutin   He should be remembered as a charismatic leader—a man who had instincts that corresponded to the needs of the common people, who had a great love for the United States and a great dedication to duty, and who inspired others to perform up to, and even way beyond, their abilities. He gave people hope. The fact of his assassination, through no fault of Lyndon Johnson, took hope away. I remember being at the Indian Embassy not long after the assassination, and as the ambassador was talking to me, tears rolled down his face. It was a scene of loss, not only in a national or international sense but also in a personal sense.

William Sullivan   Kennedy was the symbolism of postwar America; the symbolism of a new, dynamic, and creative generation that was taking over—a generation that looked on the outside world with less concern and sense of insecurity than previous generations. He was also, in political terms, a new breed of politician, who knew how to use television in the same way that Roosevelt knew how to use radio. He was a man who radiated self-confidence and in whom it was contagious to others, so I personally feel had he lived, and had he had two terms, that he would have been one of our great presidents. Now, that is a thoroughly subjective judgment from one of his Irish Mafia, but someone who felt we were doing something important at that time and never since has had the same sense of assurance that we had in those years. They were great years for those of us who had an opportunity to live them.

Charles R. Ross, member, Federal Power Commission   The thing the Kennedy administration should be known for is that they hired a lot of very intelligent, very articulate young government officials who were very anxious to carry out the laws and protect the consumer. This is what the Kennedy administration stood for: that a capitalistic system needs good, strong regulation in certain industries to protect the consumer from some of the very large industrial complexes. We got all kinds of encouragement from the staff at the White House.

Dean Rusk   John F. Kennedy will go down as one of our potentially great presidents, but this would remain potentiality rather than actual performance, particularly on the domestic side. When you compare Kennedy's domestic program to LBJ's Great Society, there's just no comparison of the two. LBJ's Great Society set the domestic agenda for the U.S. for the next generation. But I would think Kennedy would rate in the top ten, based largely upon his performance in the foreign policy field, and particularly the solution to the Cuban missile crisis without a nuclear war. That has to be a massive achievement of President Kennedy.

It was a special moment in the life of the country for various reasons, and we have not had a comparable period since then with the same sense of morale, same sense of good humor, same sense of reconsideration of conventional wisdom and things of that sort. He was an extraordinary man; we all felt it; we knew it. I suppose in one sense his thousand days were a special moment in the life of the country.

Walt Rostow   Kennedy had this sense of historical imagination. The Peace Corps is an example of this, and civil rights. Eisenhower did the civil rights thing reluctantly when he was pressured by Lyndon Johnson;

he didn't expect to get that 1957 legislation. But Kennedy meant it. Kennedy and Johnson wanted to move certain big problems in the world. Kennedy did get us around the corner and begin the arms control business. He did stand for a democratic world. He moved things much more than people realize.

George Romney   I don't think the extent to which their policies have basically influenced the course of the country since President Kennedy's election has been in the right direction. I think we see too great a growth in the federal government; too great a reduction in personal responsibility. Given the assumption that the Great Society and the poverty program were formed in the Kennedy years, basically what they have done is to undertake to use money to solve almost any problem where they thought there was a group who could be influenced politically by using money for their benefit. Ted Kennedy is still doing that. I don't think the Kennedys had the background necessary to understand the dynamics of our society fully. They had been basically political creatures all their lives.

Ralph Dungan   I think that President Kennedy should be remembered as a guy who showed fantastic potential that never really came to full fruition. I think his potential was limitless, despite all the personal stuff that is now coming out. Normally I would say that if you want to find out if a guy is okay, you look at his whole life. In Kennedy's case—having been with him—whatever all those shenanigans were, I could never see that they had any effect at all on the way he made judgments about the things that he was involved in in his public life. This may say something about his psyche and emotional life: Indeed, I have speculated at times that he was really an adolescent in terms of sexual relations; he was emotionally immature. Normally I would say, "That's terrible." But maybe he was two people: I saw the professional level, and he kept those two sides very separate. I don't think you could live that kind of double life today that he apparently did. Not often, but a couple of times he would slip out of the White House and go downtown to see a movie. I don't think that could happen today.

Martin Hillenbrand   I think he should be remembered as a young president who demonstrably grew in office. He obviously had a certain matinee-idol appeal, which few presidents have had. He was young, seemingly vigorous, with a good war record. He had a charming, handsome wife. He seemed to be able to rise to the exigencies of crisis situations as required.

Adam Yarmolinsky   He managed to combine popular appeal with an intelligent weighing of values and possibilities, and good instincts—humane instincts. That's a rare combination. We had it with Roosevelt; we had it with Truman; we didn't have it with Carter. We certainly haven't had it in the last three administrations.

I'm not a yellow-dog Democrat. I suppose I would have to characterize myself as a liberal, if a skeptical liberal, maybe a neoliberal, whatever that means. Woodrow Wilson's first administration was something of that kind, although Wilson must have been an awful stuffed shirt, and Kennedy was never a stuffed shirt. That was one of the wonderful things about him.

Viktor Sukhodrev   I certainly could not but admire President Kennedy—his bearing, his manner of speaking, his naturalness. He was not playing at being America's leader. He was, and it came to him naturally. He spoke naturally. The crown was simply made for him, or he was made for the crown.

George McGovern   To me the most statesmanlike effort in the Kennedy administration began with the American University speech, June 10, 1963. The willingness to take another look at the cold war, to try to see it through the eyes of the country that lost twenty million people. This was followed up with the limited nuclear test ban; this was followed up by the hot line; the Russian wheat deal. I thought we were on the way to a resolution of the cold war in the summer of '63. Unfortunately Vietnam turned things the other way. But for me that was the high point of the Kennedy administration.

Bradford Morse   I think he will be remembered as a guy who stood as a shining beacon for a generation, whether or not that was deserved, or otherwise. That is a fact. If his accomplishments, or the lack of them, are carefully analyzed, it will grow a little dimmer. But they are two entirely separate things. I don't think that there was a great deal accomplished, in all respects. Of course, it would have improved with more time. But quite apart from that is his stature as a person who inspired the trust and confidence of a large number of people.

Najeeb Halaby   He was the last of the American leaders who thought everything that had to be done could be done if he mobilized the people—a man who wasn't afraid to take on difficult issues, appoint independent people. And he had the perspicacity and discrimination to select the major issues, a wonderful ability to mix substance and humor, wisdom and wit, and get people with him, and to challenge the country. Today, on issues where I am prepared to pay more taxes or endure some constraint, nobody has asked me lately to do more because it is important. We talk about a thousand points of light. These lights light themselves—are not lit by the president.

It was a contrast between the sort of slow, old-fashioned Eisenhower or the snaky Nixon. This was fresh, clear, challenging inspiration in words: We can do it, and in doing it we are prepared to make the sacrifices to make it happen.

Marcus Raskin   He reflected, as much as anything, hope and possibility. As a person he was funny—clever in the best sense. He seemed to be a man who represented what the Americans wanted to think they were. It was done, in part, by various kinds of speeches, which were—on the one hand—Roman speeches. On the other hand they also had a touch of the artistic and the aesthetic. There may not have been enough wisdom, but there was no fear of intelligence. So that, in effect, brought in the educated classes in the country, which pretty well controlled the myths of the country. Finally, there is nothing more believable than interrupted promise. When Kennedy died, what died with him was that sense of promise for the society: It didn't have to be that way. Johnson attempted to pick it up. The Great Society was a profound and very, very great thing in many ways. One should read Johnson's speech at the University of Michigan—it was astonishing—as to what he expected a society to be. In a funny way you could say the same thing about Kennedy. There was that sense of understanding the possibility of this country. And all of that stopped—all of that notion of what a society could be.

Dean Rusk   Kennedy had an extraordinary ability to enlist the interest and enthusiasm of young people for public service and politics. I interviewed a good many young people at the beginning of the Kennedy administration asking for jobs in the State Department. The trouble is, most of them wanted to start at the top—young people who had never made a decision, never negotiated anything, never written an aide-mémoire, wanted to start out as assistant secretaries of state. There was no sense among a lot of them that there was an apprenticeship to be served in getting ready for a job of that sort. But nevertheless, the enthusiasm of young people for President Kennedy, as reflected for example in the Peace Corps, was remarkable, and we have not seen anything comparable to that in the years since.

Norman Podhoretz   I have a different perspective than I did then. In terms of achievement, which is the normal criterion by which you would measure a presidency, I think he has to be remembered as a not very good, not very successful president, highly overrated in the imagination of many people. I think that the declaratory policies of that administration were very sound. They represented almost the last expression of what used to be called liberalism in the pre-1965 period—a much healthier political tradition than what came to be called liberalism later on. He was the heir to that tradition. He was an exponent of those values. They were later discarded by the Democrats, and by the liberal community generally, and were lying in the dust until a former Democrat who became a Republican in his early fifties, named Ronald Reagan, picked them up. In 1980 he ran on a platform that was uncannily similar to the platform that Kennedy ran on in 1960. Kennedy said, "Let's get the country moving again," by which he meant an arms buildup, a more aggressive policy toward the Soviet Union, a tax cut to promote economic growth, and a solution to the race problem by fighting external barriers of discrimination. Those were Reagan's appeals. In a funny way you have to say that Reagan was the heir of the Democratic tradition of which Kennedy was the last spokesman.

Wayne Fredericks   I look back upon the first part of the Kennedy-Johnson years as the most exciting of my life. I was working with what I considered the most interesting group of people I have ever worked with. Whether they were the best and brightest, I cannot judge. But it was a very interesting and good cut of people—stimulating and challenging—so for me it was a very special time. There was a great desire for people to come to Washington; it must have had something to do with the president. Also, there was a certain spirit of youth in it: There was a young president grappling with new problems.

George McGovern   Looking back, I think there probably wasn't the intellectual depth and wisdom there that we thought at the time. I think that, for example, a person like Fulbright brought considerably more wisdom and experience and insight to international problems than, let's say, a McGeorge Bundy or a Walt Rostow, even though they were all professors and thought of themselves as intellectuals. I think you needed to match this bright, quick brilliance that they had at the White House and on the National Security staff with people like Mike Mansfield, Fulbright, George Aiken [U.S. senator (R., Vt.)]—some of the others in the Senate. It always puzzled me why first Jack Kennedy, and then Lyndon, tended to ignore some of the countervailing voices in the Senate and to embrace these so-called tough-minded guys that were around the National Security Council and the White House.

There was a kind of ideological quality about them, too, at times— this total commitment to the cold war and the development of counterinsurgency techniques that seemed to me a little bit too close to the military reaction to international problems and not enough attention to historical, social, economic, or political forces that we had to contend with around the world. I think that all through the sixties, the greatest wisdom on international affairs, on the Third World, and on Vietnam was in the United States Senate and not in the best and brightest at the White House.

I would not put him on the level of a Roosevelt or a Woodrow Wilson; he was not one of the half dozen great presidents. But I think he was on the level of a Truman or an Eisenhower, or a Theodore Roosevelt. I think he was one of the near-great presidents. He had the capacity to inspire the country. I think that was his great strength—to give them hope and pride. I can remember traveling abroad during the Kennedy administration and being proud that I was an American and pleased that we had this gallant, young president. I really haven't felt that way since. That capacity to stir the country, to arouse them to greater effort, probably entitles him to a position, in history, of near greatness. But the mistakes on Vietnam, on the Bay of Pigs, the slowness in recognizing the need to fundamentally change the cold war—probably even the inability to move Congress on his domestic programs effectively, as Johnson did—all of those things would cause me to stop short of labeling him a great president. I don't think he was a great president.

Morris Abram   As Reagan changed America's view of itself and established a degree of confidence and exhilaration, I think Kennedy added excitement to American life, and I think it was largely hype. He did gather some extraordinarily able people around him, but I don't know that the ablest academics are the best people to run a country. Harry Truman never went to college, and he did a pretty good job. Kennedy was committed to intellectualism, not that he was an intellectual. He was committed to the arts, because he realized that gave his administration a kind of class. As compared to Eisenhower, he was a public relations manipulator supreme. But his accomplishments? I don't know. They were not as great as his reputation, though I must say, sitting here in Europe, he is very well remembered and affectionately remembered.

Norman Podhoretz   They were neither the best nor the brightest. If you just look at the colossal misjudgments they made on Vietnam alone, aside from the other issues, it's staggering. I was against the war in those days. I wasn't against it ideologically so much: It was the wrong war in the wrong place at the wrong time. As people used to say, it was not winnable; we shouldn't have gone in there altogether. That was my position at the time. Retrospectively I think that judgment was right; it's borne out by the history of the war. On the other hand I have a far better opinion of the war, and purposes for which it was fought, than I did then. But whether you were for the war or against it, whether you thought the war was a noble cause or an evil act of American imperialism, doesn't matter. The analytic judgments that were made by people like Bundy, McNamara, two of the best and the brightest; my old friend Dick Goodwin, Arthur Schlesinger, Galbraith—the misjudgments take your breath away. The misjudgment of Diem, the misjudgment of what was going on in the north, the balance of forces, what was required to win that war, the political problems there and at home—they got virtually everything wrong.

I had good relations with many of those people: If you were a critic from the left, you were paid a certain deference by the Kennedy crowd; a critic from the right they despised. So I was certainly persona grata to the people I knew in the administration; I got treated very nicely by them. I would argue with them sometimes about the antiwar sentiment in this country, and they were very dismissive: They had no sense of what was brewing in the culture, and to the extent that they noticed it, they just dismissed it. Later on, in compensation, some of them went all the way over to the other side. As I once wrote, they thought there was no power in the streets. Later they thought the only power that existed was in the streets.

They were very, very arrogant, very cocksure of themselves. When you stop to think, not a single one of those people knew the Vietnamese language or anything about the history of that country. What made them so sure that they knew not only how to fight a war in that country but how to reshape that society? They knew nothing about it, yet this didn't bother any of them at all. They were just proceeding; they *knew*. That arrogance is in itself a mark of a limited intelligence—a limited imagination. Maybe they were no worse than other courtiers or White House entourages, before and after, but certainly they were nothing to write home about.

John Kenneth Galbraith I would put JFK up with the majors. We should measure presidents in accordance with the sense of the country, and esteem the country felt: the spirit of change that emanated from Washington. And when you think of how short the Kennedy years were and you go over the whole range, foreign policy, the test ban, easing relations with the Soviet Union after the missile crisis, escape from the Cuban preoccupation, the emerging civil rights movement at home—and the sympathy that that got, the sense he conveyed that the government was a positive force—I would put him with the best.

Alexis Johnson As far as Kennedy was concerned, he was growing enormously in the job. I think the making of an icon out of him is a little overdrawn.

Joseph Sisco I have never bought on to the view of his closest political supporters that the Kennedy presidency was going to bring about the millennium and halcyon days; I think that this is largely overdrawn. It is romantic and doesn't take into account the realities of the world. But having said that, I did not view President Kennedy as a romantic possessing a great degree of sentimentality. He was a hard-headed politician in the best sense of the word. He was intelligent, a quick study, shrewd, sensitive to both domestic and external considerations and—to a degree—he could do a certain amount of synthesizing, in a broader strategic way, as well as day-by-day implementation. He did view international problems largely from what had been his dominant experience: namely domestic experience. That is not unusual. There are a good many presidents who come into the White House with relatively little experience of the world out there and how to operate in it.

I view President Kennedy as a very able president; one who would have faced up to problems with the foremost operating principle being: What will work pragmatically? He was a pragmatic problem solver. He wasn't given to broad sweeps of conceptual world orders, even though he had a view of the world and the position of the United States in it. He believed in leadership. He was an internationalist, and certainly enjoyed playing the international stage, as many presidents do.

Phillips Talbot   I'm still very high on him. Clearly there were faults, and faults that some of us didn't know about at the time. Clearly he didn't have the skills in driving his programs home that Lyndon Johnson had. Clearly a number of people around him were romantics. I think this was demonstrated when so many of them left the administration after he died, rather than sticking with a president who had inherited a terribly difficult situation. I think that the revisionism has been based mainly on two things: One is that he was ineffective in opening up opportunities for his programs—of course, he had only one thousand days—but at any rate, he wasn't the implementer to that same degree that Johnson was; and then there is the question of his personal behavior. But that was not a factor in our thinking, in working in his administration.

William Sloane Coffin, Jr.   He wasn't a great legislator. Even Teddy's enemies say that Teddy is the great legislator of the Kennedy boys. I feel very mixed about him. He was there too short a time. If he had dragged us further into the war in Vietnam, it would have been a terrible disaster. But it seems to me for all his privilege, and for all his obsession with power—which is so common among politicians—he had high intelligence.

Gerald Ford   I liked Jack Kennedy. Therefore I think he should be looked on positively. I wouldn't say he was a great president. He was there two and a half years, and I know something about being there for two and a half years, so it's pretty hard to say from a two-and-a-half-year record that Jack Kennedy was a great president. He had a potential. I think history will show that he didn't do as well as many people thought he would do, but I think in the short time he was there, it was premature to judge him as if he had been there for four or eight years.

Norman Podhoretz   I feel much more approving of the Kennedy administration, in retrospect, than I did then, although I would still— even from my present perspective—have criticisms. Just as I would have said from the left that he was too cautious and timid—and even cowardly—I would now say it from the right. Kennedy characteristically tried to do things on the cheap. He was never willing to adopt the means that were necessary to the ends he said he was pursuing. The best example of that, of course, is the Bay of Pigs, where he could either have invaded and provided air cover in order to win—which he didn't—or he could have called off the invasion. Instead, he tried to get away with doing it and not doing it and, therefore, he failed. Something similar happened in Vietnam. The same was truer in his social policies: There was always some large goal being announced, but never the means adequate to the pursuit of that goal.

Lee White   It was a very exciting presidency; it was building and going somewhere. It's just unfortunate it was aborted so early. He had good intentions, good judgment. He wanted to accomplish goals and found ways to do that. He was not as effective as Lyndon Johnson was in terms of legislative achievement, but we were moving; we were getting there. I think he would have been reelected with a good, solid majority. I think we have to remember him as a tragic character. I don't know anything about all the revelations about his sexual activities; I don't know if they're true, or not. As far as the presidency is concerned, it's hard to rank him—we have a penchant for wanting to rank presidents: the very top, good, the mediocre, the poor, and the bad. He wasn't president long enough to put him there. But if I had to I'd put him right up at the good category, and if things had worked out right he'd have been a great president. Part of a president's greatness is dependent on what's going on in the world, over which he has no control. His legacy will be in the foreign affairs field.

Above all it was terrific the way he could move people. He could read any speech—one that Sorensen had written, or somebody else had—and really make it come alive. He had become a first-rate orator by the time he was killed. That's an important responsibility and opportunity for a president—to get people charged up, to move them.

Richard Bissell   He was in office too short a time to have made a big difference. He brought a number of new people into the government— he did have an awfully bright set of people around him: the two Bundys, Walt Rostow, General Taylor, and McNamara, who, I think, is perhaps the most notable. But I don't think that Kennedy can be remembered for what was done in economic policy, although I think that it was an enlightened and successful policy. In international policy, he should be remembered for the Cuban missile crisis, and to some degree, for U.S. policy toward Berlin. I think he is probably going to be remembered— and ought to be remembered—for his personal characteristics, his personality.

George Wallace   John F. Kennedy should be remembered as a man who had guts enough to back Khrushchev down. If he had had a further chance, he would have been a very good president. But just doing that was in itself a big accomplishment. Nixon backed Khrushchev down, too. That debate in the kitchen.* Nixon wasn't afraid of any of them. I damn near voted for Nixon.

JFK wasn't president long enough. If he had become president when Roosevelt did, he would have also brought the people's faith back in the system. The people in the South didn't like Truman at all, and when he passed away he was very unpopular there. There is a more sympathetic attitude toward him now than there was then.

Edmund Brown, Sr.   He should be remembered as a fine human being and one of the best presidents of the United States. And a personable young man. Of all the men that I have ever met in my political life, I have more respect—not that he was the greatest thinker or the best this or that—but in the totality of a human being, I thought Kennedy was the best. And I've met some great people: Stevenson, and all the presidents,

*In late July 1959, Vice President Richard M. Nixon, while on a visit to Moscow, engaged in an impromptu debate with Soviet leader Nikita S. Khrushchev in a model kitchen at an American exhibition in Skolniki Park.

while governor of California, going back to 1950. In forty years I met a lot of people, none better than Jack Kennedy. He was a great president, in my opinion.

Tom Wicker   I think Kennedy really was growing in office and that a second term might really have been something quite different. I advanced in a book that Kennedy might not have carried out the war in Vietnam, not because he was soft on communism—quite the opposite— but because he had gone through the Cuban missile crisis and that was his war, like the Middle East was Bush's war, and so he has proven himself a tough guy, so he did not have to prove that again, which every president needs to do.

Martin Hillenbrand   Because he was assassinated when he was, and because so much of his time had been involved in foreign policy problems—the Berlin problem, the Cuban missile problem, and so on—I don't think domestic affairs ever got the amount of attention which they needed, although obviously he had to get involved in strike situations, for example.

When looking back now at the Kennedy administration, you have the impression it was only a partially completed administration, which is not surprising since it was cut off even a year short of the first term ending. Therefore the judgment of history has to be one of lack of completeness, large areas of responsibility which were only marginally affected by the Kennedy administration because he didn't have the time to focus on all of these problems that were just beginning to emerge: the idea that the U.S. was beginning to lose its economic hegemony in the world, that we were now beginning or threatening to run negative balances on trade and current accounts, that we needed some help from the Germans in order to help pay for part of the bill for our forces there—something that McNamara, for example, pushed very hard—the so-called offset agreement. All of these things, you had the impression, were not thoroughly digested yet as a part of fixed policy, because the president didn't survive, because during the time he was in office he was preoccupied by seeming crises of one sort or another.

So that's generally the way I would assess him, and I leave out of consideration all of the criticisms of personal behavior that have been raised more recently; I think that's not relevant to judging his performance as president.

Orville Freeman   The aura is there. Everywhere around the world people have felt his impact. Every place you go, there is hardly anybody who doesn't remember where they were or what they were doing at the time of the assassination. The impact was so overwhelming that young people come up to me and ask questions about Kennedy. People everywhere want to talk about Kennedy. The aura is one of great respect, and he was the greatest of the great.

William Colby   I think that Kennedy's real effect can be measured by the number of Avenue Kennedys there are around the world; in every obscure place around the world, you will find an Avenue John Kennedy. Everybody in the world looked to Kennedy as the embodiment of a good America. People talk about multinationalism and imperialism, but get a guy like Kennedy and they want to be a part of America.

He should be remembered as a man who inspired the entire world; the entire world was excited by his personality. He saw how to use America's moral and political power to make the place work better. The Alliance for Progress, the Peace Corps—all of those things were inspirational. With his death a lot of that disappeared. We still did much of it, but the spark went out.

Thomas Mann   Kennedy was a genius for public relations; I don't think there has ever been anybody who can touch him in public relations. The legend survives to this day. He was an honest man. I don't know if he was always right. Had he lived, he would have gone down as a great president. When he was killed, the line outside the embassy went on for days. He had a genius for capturing the imagination and the loyalty of people—Americans and others. He was a very unusual man.

Roger Hilsman   Periodically historians get together and rank the presidents, and it is always kind of funny to me. So much depends on what the problems are at the time they are ranking, and the presidents who would have been good for their time go higher than others. In the future rankings I think Lincoln is going to be up there; [Franklin Delano] Roosevelt is going to be way up there; Washington will be up there—not because he really was that good, but because he was the first president. There will be the lousy ones, and Carter will have a place, and so will Harding and Taft. There is going to be a little special niche out there. You know the poem, A. E. Housman's "On an Athlete Dying Young"? Lucky fellow. He died while the wreath was still green—the unfulfilled promise. President Kennedy had a lot of promise, but he never really had a chance to prove himself.

He had a couple of bad failures: the Bay of Pigs; a couple of enormous successes: the Cuban missile crisis, the test ban treaty. I think Laos was a success, but now, essentially, I think the judgment of history will be of the young athlete dying young.

Arthur Schlesinger, Jr.   Here was a man who flashed across the sky for a brief moment. His life was unfulfilled. He was struck down by a tragic fate. It is the stuff of legend. He remains a symbol of hope and possibility and youth. When you think that a third of the country was born after his death, he still stands for some sort of unfulfilled possibility in America.

George Ball   From the historical point of view, he was singularly fortunate: He was shot at the right time—before the legislation crumbled in the Senate and after the missile crisis had given him a great sense of triumph.

Morris Abram   There are myths around assassinated presidents. I think Lincoln was probably one of the greatest presidents, but I think he was ennobled by his myth, and he might have been caught up by the problems of Reconstruction in a second term. Assassination is a powerful, powerful mythmaker.

Angier Biddle Duke   I think the day will come when we will feel very much like we did after the assassination; we'll again realize that we lost a great man and that the history of our country would have been very, very different if he had lived. We lost a great man—a great opportunity—and our country has taken a terrible turn, both domestically and in foreign policy since. I don't think we've recovered from his death.

Julian Bond I did have a sense that this was a new age, but it seemed to me that this was so more in a cultural than actual political sense: Here's this bright, attractive couple, so different from Richard Nixon. I felt that the Kennedys were part of a cultural change that was taking place in the United States. It didn't necessarily represent a political change, and it didn't necessarily mean that conditions for black Americans were going to improve. But it was just so much better than having Richard Nixon. And even though President Kennedy was twenty-six years older than I am, I still remember thinking of him as being young—very young—close to my age. It was a breath of fresh air.

Marcus Raskin There is one period that is very important, which I call the "We shall overcome" period, from June 1963—from the American University speech—to the fall of 1964, where everything seemed possible; where civil rights was a clear moral issue, both for the government and the people; where there was a sense of possibility in terms of international affairs; where you could cut a deal with the Soviets; where the United States was not overtly fighting a war; where the nuclear test ban agreement had occurred. There was a spirit in the country which had as much to do with the civil rights movement and young people in the country as it did with the administration. That period was a great moment in American history. The blacks were the vanguard, and it carried over to what happened in the universities, what happened with women, what happened across the board over the course of the sixties.

Very powerful social forces were unleashed during that period. Often politicians just ride the waves of those forces. In the case of Kennedy, for example, there were a great many people who were frightened by the March on Washington: God knows what this was going to mean. Where would this lead? But he rode that, and he had the intelligence and the judgment and, I think, the innate decency to understand what this really meant. Although he had no real contact with the problem at all, at least there was that understanding that if he chose the wrong side of that issue he would go down in history as a very bad man.

Joseph Rauh, Jr. He believed that government could function to the benefit of all the people, and that's the real reason that I still look back on the Kennedy administration as a real success. It would have been a greater success had he lived through the second term, which I think he would have won by a landslide. But the anomaly is that while he wanted government to do these things, he was held back until he died by the narrowness of his election, by feeling he had to hold back on divisive issues. But he still accomplished a great deal.

Kennedys are winners, and they are winners because they don't overestimate what they can do. I think they are winners in every field; they sure don't like to lose.

I will always remember him as the president who thought the government could remedy the wrongs of our society—most of the wrongs, I guess—and who demonstrated, when it was finally brought home to him, that he had to move on civil rights, that he could move, and that he would be flexible enough to move. At the meeting—I think on June 21, 1963—at the White House, where he invited about twenty civil rights people, he said—and nobody has ever found this—he said, "I have a poll in my pocket that suggests I'll lose the election next year on the civil rights issue." But, he added, "This is a moral issue and we can do nothing else."

John Lewis He should be remembered as the president who embodied the best of America. To me he was this person who gave you the energy and strength to walk in faith—he created this extraordinary faith that we could do anything: "We're going to the moon!" And I didn't know in 1961 if I would go on a Freedom Ride. He got involved in the circumstances of others.

Robert Moses Kennedy represented a new generation to take power. He called forth the sense that this country was going to embark on a new course. That was not spelled out in terms of internal policy, but what it did was to feed into—and be part of—this general revolution of rising expectations that was sweeping the world. So young black people may have stepped into that energy in quite an unexpected way. In saying this there is also a new generation which is going to exercise some power; it's going to take some steps on its own. It's going to answer this question of "What can I do for this country?" in a very unexpected way. I don't think Kennedy anticipated in saying it that it would touch into a deep feeling of people who were looking for new expectations from this country.

I am sure that they did not think that this would take priority over how they were going to have to deal with Russia and affairs of state. That's what happened.

His generation, which was to provide leadership, and which he symbolized, got decapitated with his assassination. That generation did not provide the leadership. The leadership reverted to the older generation—to Johnson, Nixon, Reagan. A whole generation of leadership got decapitated with Kennedy. He really symbolizes a very deep quandary for this country, which is whether or not there was a discontinuity in its history which has affected it in ways in which people are really not quite ready to delve into.

James Meredith   The Kennedy era can be credited with the egalitarian ideal that makes me believe that race is no longer a factor in America. I think we can point to professional sports, to television—we can turn to Oprah Winfrey, Bill Cosby, Eddie Murphy—these are all results of the Kennedy frontier mentality. The worst thing in the Kennedy era was his assassination. The key issue in Western Christian civilization has always been the black issue. The only people who understood the issue were the British, and certain people educated at Harvard University. I think John Kennedy was one of those people. I know Edward Kennedy wasn't; I don't think Bobby was, either.

Fred Shuttlesworth   He was the man that God had to lift American idealism and American standards at that time. Without him, we might have wound up in civil war in this country. And although Johnson came in in an emotional climate, and he passed the civil rights bill, and espoused the Great Society, he couldn't fund the Great Society and the war, at the same time. Kennedy was God's man for that brief moment, though it was in history.

Louis Martin   The Kennedys were good for America. Jack ended that Catholic bias; they were basically straight on the issues. They were subject to all of the problems of wealth. Everybody was after them. You had several hundred people involved in the White House. All of the girls wanted to make one of them. It was a two-sided street there. It might not have sounded that way, but it was.

On the race issue they didn't have the commitment that Johnson had. They were sincere in wanting to move America. They had every-thing; they didn't need anything, so they gave their lives to public ser-vice. JFK was rich. Up there in the ambassador's place, Jesus Christ, they had a floor full of flunkies. I had never seen characters like that. A snap of the finger, and a thousand people would move.

Donald Wilson   I have often thought about how history will treat John F. Kennedy. I don't think there is any question that he will become an insignificant person in the history books, because the term was so short. I do think that the missile crisis will last in the history books because that was clearly the moment where the two superpowers came closest to war. I also think it was the moment where he displayed his greatest talents as a diplomat and as a strong foreign policy president. I really think he will be remembered in the history books for a hundred years for that, and maybe not a lot else. As one who worked with him, it is hard not to remember the impact he had on the American people—and perhaps, even more importantly, on the rest of the world—as a symbol of an America that was idealistic and attempting to improve the lot of Third World countries with programs such as the Peace Corps. John F. Kennedy was regarded as an exceedingly admirable person who stood for progress and change, but those are not qualities that will last in his-tory books.

Harry Felt   Each and every one of our presidents has been remem-bered. Some glowingly and others not so, based on what they did while president. Eisenhower, for example, was our "lovable" president. How will they remember Kennedy? Well, what outstanding thing—or things—did Kennedy accomplish?

Nicholas Katzenbach   He will be remembered as a president who had the capacity, but never the chance, for greatness. You couldn't achieve that in only three years. Once a seminar was held at the White House with an expert from Princeton, on the subject of the presidency. JFK, who was seriously interested in history, participated in the discussion. He asked the professor who the great presidents were, and what made for a great president. He finally said, "You know, I think maybe to be a great president, you have to die in office.

Appendix A

SCHEDULE OF INTERVIEWS

Date	Interviewee	Title/Activity During Kennedy Administration	Venue
5/12/92	Morris B. Abram	General counsel, Peace Corps, 1961; U.S. member, UN Subcomission on Prevention of Discrimination and Persecution of Minorities, 1962–64	Telephone
2/27/91	Alexei Adzhubei	Editor in chief, *Izvestia*, 1959–64; son-in-law of Nikita S. Khrushchev	Moscow
1/13/92	Worth Bagley	Assistant to Gen. Maxwell Taylor for Southeast Asia	Telephone
4/2/92	Bobby Baker	Secretary to the Senate majority, Jan. 1955–Oct. 1963	Washington, D.C.
1/9/92	George Ball	Undersecretary of state for economic affairs, Jan. 1961–Nov. 1961; undersecretary of state, 1961–66	Princeton, N.J.
7/27/91	Yuri V. Barsukov	Washington correspondent, *Izvestia*	Moscow
8/20/91	Lucius D. Battle	Assistant secretary of state for educational and cultural affairs, 1962–64	Washington, D.C.
1/22/92	David Bell	Director, Bureau of the Budget, Jan. 1961–Nov. 1962; administrator, Agency for International Development, Jan. 1963–July 1966	Cambridge, Mass.
6/3/91	Richard M. Bissell	Deputy director of plans, Central Intelligence Agency, 1959–62	Farmington, Conn.
11/21/89	Julian Bond	Member, Student Non-Violent Coordinating Committee	Cambridge, Mass.

Date	Interviewee	Title/Activity During Kennedy Administration	Venue
11/29/91	Bernard Boutin	Deputy administrator, General Services Administration, 1961; administrator, 1962–64	Telephone
1/29/92	Ben Bradlee	Washington bureau chief, *Newsweek*	Washington, D.C.
11/29/91	Willy Brandt	Mayor of Berlin	Bonn, Germany
5/6/91	Edmund G. ("Pat") Brown	Governor of California, 1959–67	Beverly Hills, Calif.
3/10/92	McGeorge Bundy	Special assistant to the president for national security affairs, Jan. 1961–Feb. 1966	New York, N.Y.
4/1/92	George A. Carver, Jr.	Vietnam analyst, national estimates, Central Intelligence Agency	Washington, D.C.
1/31/92	Harlan Cleveland	Assistant secretary of state for international organization affairs, 1961–65	Telephone
5/22/92	Ray Cline	Deputy director for intelligence, Central Intelligence Agency, 1962–64	Washington, D.C.
7/24/91	Rev. William Sloane Coffin, Jr.	Chaplain, Yale University; civil rights activist; consultant, Peace Corps	Stratford, Vt.
4/1/92	William Colby	Station chief, U.S. Embassy, Saigon; director, Far Eastern Division, Central Intelligence Agency	Washington, D.C.
4/n.d./89	John Sherman Cooper	United States Senator (R., Ky.), 1956–73; member, Warren Commission	Washington, D.C.
12/18/91	Archibald Cox	Solicitor general of the United States, Jan. 1961–July 1965	Cambridge, Mass.
12/20/91	Carl T. Curtis	U.S. senator (R., Nebr.), 1955–79	Telephone
4/24/91	Lloyd Cutler	Adviser to the president on Cuban prisoner exchange	Washington, D.C.
1/2/92	Cartha DeLoach	Assistant director, Crime Records Division, Federal Bureau of Investigation, 1959–65	Hilton Head Island, S.C.
3/13/92	Bui Diem	Member, South Vietnamese opposition	Telephone

Date	Interviewee	Title/Activity During Kennedy Administration	Venue
12/23/91	Joseph Dolan	Assistant deputy attorney general, 1961–65	Telephone
10/18/89	Angier Biddle Duke	Chief of protocol for the White House and State Department, 1961–64	New York, N.Y.
9/14/91	Ralph Dungan	Special assistant to the president, Jan. 1961–Mar. 1966	Martha's Vineyard, Mass.
5/22/92	Courtney Evans	Assistant director, Federal Bureau of Investigation; FBI liaison with Attorney General Robert F. Kennedy	Washington, D.C.
1/4/90	James Farmer	National director, Congress of Racial Equality	Fredericksburg, Va.
5/9/91	Harry D. Felt	Admiral, U.S. Navy; Commander in Chief, U.S. armed forces in the Pacific, 1958–64	Honolulu, Hawaii
7/22/91	Gerald R. Ford	Member, House of Representatives (R., Michigan), 1949–73; Member, Warren Commission	New York, N.Y.
1/29/92	Henry Fowler	Undersecretary of the treasury, 1961–64	Washington, D.C.
9/19/91	Wayne Fredericks	Deputy assistant secretary of state for African affairs	New York, N.Y.
4/18/91	Orville L. Freeman	Secretary of agriculture, Jan. 1961–Jan. 1969	New York, N.Y.
12/21/89	J. William Fulbright	U.S. senator (D., Ark.), 1945–75; chairman, Senate Foreign Relations Committee, 1959–75	Washington, D.C.
1/21/92	John Kenneth Galbraith	U.S. ambassador to India, 1961–63	Cambridge, Mass.
7/30/91	Raymond L. Garthoff	Special assistant for Soviet bloc, State Department Bureau of Politico-Military Affairs	Washington, D.C.
6/25/91	Mordechai Gazit	Deputy chief of mission, Israeli Embassy, Washington	Jerusalem
7/16/91	Roswell L. Gilpatric	Deputy secretary of defense, Jan. 1961–Jan. 1964	New York, N.Y.

Date	Interviewee	Title/Activity During Kennedy Administration	Venue
4/21/92	Andrew J. Goodpaster	Brig. Gen., U.S. Army; Staff secretary to President Dwight D. Eisenhower; involved in transition to Kennedy administration	Washington, D.C.
7/15/91	Lincoln Gordon	U.S. ambassador to Brazil, Aug. 1961–Jan. 1966	Washington, D.C.
2/24/92	Denis Greenhill (Lord Greenhill of Harrow)	Deputy chief of mission, British Embassy, Washington, D.C.	London, England
12/6/91	Najeeb E. Halaby	Administrator, Federal Aviation Agency, 1961–65	Arlington, Va.
12/19/91	August Heckscher	Adviser to the president on the arts	New York, N.Y.
11/12/91	Richard M. Helms	Deputy to the director for plans, 1952–62; deputy director for plans, Central Intelligence Agency, 1962–65	Washington, D.C.
3/3/92	Rev. Theodore Hesburgh	Member, United States Civil Rights Commission, 1959–72; president, Notre Dame University, 1952–87	Telephone
3/13/91	Martin J. Hillenbrand	Deputy director, Berlin Task Force, U.S. Department of State 1961–62; director, 1962–63	Athens, Ga.
11/15/89	Roger Hilsman	Director, State Department Bureau of Intelligence and Research, Feb. 1961–May 1963; Assistant secretary of state for Far Eastern affairs, 1963–64	New York, N.Y.
10/16/89	U. Alexis Johnson	Deputy undersecretary of state for political affairs, 1961–64	Washington, D.C.
12/31/91	Philip Kaiser	U.S. ambassador to Senegal, Mauritania	Washington, D.C.
1/5/90	Nicholas deB. Katzenbach	Assistant attorney general, 1961–62; deputy attorney general, 1962–64	New York, N.Y.
1/24/92	Clark Kerr	President, University of California, 1958–67	Telephone
12/20/90	Sergei Khrushchev	Son of Nikita S. Khrushchev	Cambridge, Mass.
1/16/92	Philip Klutznick	U.S. ambassador to UN Economic and Social Council	Chicago, Ill.

Date	Interviewee	Title/Activity During Kennedy Administration	Venue
4/25/91	Robert W. Komer	Senior staff member, National Security Council	Washington, D.C.
5/7/91	Victor H. Krulak	Major general, U.S. Marine Corps; special assistant for counterinsurgency and special activities, Office of the Joint Chiefs of Staff, 1962–64	San Diego, Calif.
4/2/92	John Lewis	Chairman, Student Non-Violent Coordinating Committee, 1963–66	Washington, D.C.
1/17/92	Thomas Mann	Assistant secretary of state for inter-American affairs, 1960–61; U.S. ambassador to Mexico, 1961–63	Austin, Tex.
1/22/92	Robert J. Manning	Assistant secretary of state for public affairs, 1962–64	Boston, Mass.
4/9/92	Burke Marshall	Assistant attorney general in charge of the Civil Rights Division, 1961–64	New Haven, Conn.
9/4/91	Edwin M. Martin	Assistant secretary of state for economic affairs, 1960–62; assistant secretary of state for inter-American affairs, 1962–63	Washington, D.C.
5/3/91	Louis Martin	Deputy director, Democratic National Committee; campaign aide	Diamond Bar, Calif.
8/12/91	Eugene J. McCarthy	U.S. senator (D., Minn.), 1959–71	Washington, D.C.
8/13/91	Edward A. McDermott	Campaign aide; director, Office of Emergency Planning; member, National Security Council	Washington, D.C.
7/29/91	George S. McGovern	Director, Food for Peace Program, 1961–62; U.S. senator (D., S. Dak.), 1963–81	Washington, D.C.
12/7/89	James H. Meredith	Civil rights activist	Washington, D.C.
12/30/91	F. Bradford Morse	U.S. congressman (R., Mass.)	Telephone
4/6/92	Robert Moses	Field secretary, Mississippi Student Non-Violent Coordinating Committee, 1961–65; director, Council of Federated Organizations, 1962–65	Telephone

Date	Interviewee	Title/Activity During Kennedy Administration	Venue
12/20/91	Frank E. Moss	U.S. senator (D., Utah), 1959–77	Telephone
5/31/91	Gaylord A. Nelson	Governor of Wisconsin, 1958–62; U.S. senator (D., Wis.), 1963–81	Washington, D.C.
1/3/92	Maurine Neuberger	U.S. senator (D., Oreg.), 1960–66	Telephone
3/6/92	John Patterson	Governor of Alabama, 1959–63	Montgomery, Ala.
4/1/92	Claiborne Pell	U.S. senator (D., R.I.), 1960–	Washington, D.C.
4/25/91	Esther Peterson	Assistant secretary of labor for labor standards, 1961–69	Washington, D.C.
1/9/92	Norman Podhoretz	Editor, *Commentary*, 1960–	New York, N.Y.
11/16/92	Roman Puchinski	U.S. congressman (D., Ill.)	Chicago, Ill.
4/1/92	Marcus Raskin	Member, special staff, National Security Council; staff member, Bureau of the Budget	Washington, D.C.
12/7/89	Joseph L. Rauh, Jr.	Vice chairman, Americans for Democratic Action, 1957–92	Washington, D.C.
5/4/92	Manuel Ray	Member, Cuban Revolutionary Council	San Juan, Puerto Rico
8/26/91	Abraham A. Ribicoff	Secretary of health, education and welfare, Jan. 1961–July 1962; U.S. senator (D., Conn.), 1963–80	New York, N.Y.
11/27/91	George W. Romney	Chairman of the board and president, American Motors Corporation, 1954–62; governor of Michigan, 1963–69	Telephone
12/20/91	Charles R. Ross	Member, Federal Power Commission, 1961–68	Telephone
1/17/92	Walt W. Rostow	Deputy special assistant to the president for national security affairs, 1961; chairman, State Department Policy Planning Council, 1961–66	Austin, Tex.
3/13/91	Dean O. Rusk	Secretary of state, Jan. 1961–Jan. 1969	Athens, Ga.

Date	Interviewee	Title/Activity During Kennedy Administration	Venue
2/24/92	Pierre E. Salinger	White House press secretary, Jan. 1961–Mar. 1964; campaign aide	London
1/21/92	Paul Samuelson	Adviser on economic affairs	Cambridge, Mass.
4/1/92	Terry Sanford	Governor of North Carolina, 1961–65	Washington, D.C.
12/19/91	Walter Schirra	Astronaut, Mercury Program	Telephone
12/23/91	Norbert A. Schlei	Assistant attorney general, Office of Legal Counsel, 1962–66	Telephone
5/21/92	Arthur M. Schlesinger, Jr.	Special assistant to the president, 1961–64	New York, N.Y
2/4/92	Glenn Seaborg	Chairman, Atomic Energy Commission, 1961–71	Telephone
11/21/89	Robert C. Seamans, Jr.	Deputy director, National Aeronautics and Space Administration	Cambridge, Mass.
4/21/91	John Seigenthaler	Administrative assistant to the attorney general, 1961–62	Washington, D.C.
7/23/92	R. Sargent Shriver	Director, Peace Corps	Telephone
12/4/91	Rev. Fred Shuttlesworth	Secretary, Southern Christian Leadership Conference, 1957–70; president, Alabama Christian Movement for Human Rights, 1956–70	Telephone
3/31/92	Joseph Sisco	Deputy assistant secretary of state for international organization affairs	Washington, D.C.
8/20/91	Donald ("Deke") Slayton	Astronaut, Mercury Program	Seabrook, Md.
8/13/91	George A. Smathers	U.S. senator (D., Fla.), 1951–69	Washington, D.C.
12/5/91	William Y. Smith	Major, U.S. Air Force; special assistant to Gen. Maxwell Taylor (General Taylor served as military representative to the president and as chairman of the Joint Chiefs of Staff, July 1961–Oct. 1962), Oct. 1962–June 1964	Washington, D.C.
1/15/92	Adlai E. Stevenson III	Son of Adlai E. Stevenson	Chicago, Ill.
2/1/91	Viktor M. Sukhodrev	Interpreter for Nikita S. Khrushchev	New York, N.Y.

Date	Interviewee	Title/Activity During Kennedy Administration	Venue
11/26/91	William H. Sullivan	Special assistant to the undersecretary of state for political affairs, 1963–64; UN adviser, Bureau of Far Eastern Affairs	Telephone
11/20/89	Phillips Talbot	Assistant secretary of state for Near Eastern and South Asian affairs	New York, N.Y.
4/2/92	Strom Thurmond	U.S. senator (D., S.C.), 1954–64	Washington, D.C.
12/17/91	James Tobin	Member, Council of Economic Advisers, 1961–62	New Haven, Conn.
5/31/91	William Trueheart	Deputy chief of mission, U.S. Embassy, Saigon	Washington, D.C.
7/15/91	Jack Valenti	Adviser to Lyndon B. Johnson	Washington, D.C.
3/5/92	George Wallace	Governor of Alabama, 1963–67	Montgomery, Ala.
12/21/89	Lee White	Assistant special counsel to the president	Washington, D.C.
12/4,11/91	Tom Wicker	Correspondent, Washington Bureau, *New York Times*	New York, N.Y.
1/9/92	Donald Wilson	Deputy director, United States Information Agency, 1961–65	Princeton, N.J.
3/31/89	James Wine	Campaign aide; U.S. ambassador to Luxembourg, 1961–62; Ivory Coast, 1962–67	New York, N.Y.
1/18/92	Ralph Yarborough	U.S. senator (D., Tex.), 1957–71	Austin, Tex.
5/30/91	Adam Yarmolinsky	Member, transition team; special assistant to the secretary of defense, Jan. 1961–Sept. 1965	Catonsville, Md.
12/30/91	Herbert York	Member, General Advisory Council, U.S. Disarmament and Arms Control Agency	Telephone
5/6/91	Sam W. Yorty	Mayor of Los Angeles, 1961–73	Studio City, Calif.

Appendix B

THE INTERVIEWEES: WHERE ARE THEY TODAY?

Morris B. Abram was U.S. representative to the UN Commission on Human Rights; vice chairman of the U.S. Civil Rights Commission, and chief U.S. delegate to the Paris meeting of the Conference on Security and Cooperation in Europe. He has served as chairman of the National Conference on Soviet Jewry and of the Conference of Presidents of Major American Jewish Organizations. He has also served as president of Brandeis University and, since 1989, has been U.S. ambassador to the UN European office in Geneva.

Alexei Adzhubei has published a book on his father-in-law, Nikita Khrushchev. He is retired from *Izvestia*, writes books and articles, and lives in central Moscow.

Worth H. Bagley was commander of a naval task group in the Vietnam War, director of Navy Program Planning, commander in chief of naval forces in Europe, and vice chief of Naval Operations. He retired from the U.S. Navy in 1975 with the rank of admiral. He has been involved in defense and security issues, has written a syndicated newspaper column in partnership with former Adm. Elmo Zumwalt, and has established and headed a nondefense small business.

Bobby Baker pursues business interests from Washington, D.C.

George Ball served as undersecretary of state until 1966. He has been affiliated with Lehman Brothers as a senior partner and as chairman of Lehman Brothers International, Ltd. His book on Middle East affairs, *The Passionate Attachment*, was published in 1992.

Yuri V. Barsukov lives in retirement in Moscow.

Lucius D. Battle was ambassador to Egypt and assistant secretary of state for Near Eastern and South Asian affairs. He was vice president of the Communications Satellite Corporation; chairman of the Foreign Policy Institute at the Johns Hopkins School for Advanced International Studies; and president of the Middle East Institute. He lives in Washington, D.C.

David E. Bell was a vice president of the Ford Foundation. He served as chairman of the Department of Population Sciences at the Harvard School of Public Health and was Director of the Harvard University Center for Population Studies. Since 1981 he has been Clarence James Gamble Professor of Population Sciences and International Health at the Harvard School of Public Health.

Richard M. Bissell has served as president of the Institute for Defense Analysis and as an executive with United Aircraft Corporation. He is currently a business consultant.

Julian Bond was a member of the Georgia House of Representatives and a Georgia state senator. He has appeared as a commentator on public television and has lectured at colleges and universities throughout the United States. He was a visiting professor at Harvard University's Black Studies Program and at Williams College. He is a Distinguished Professor at the American University, Washington, D.C.

Bernard L. Boutin served as deputy director of the Office of Economic Opportunity and as administrator of the Small Business Administration under President Johnson. He was chairman of the New Hampshire State Board of Education and president of St. Michael's College. He has been a member of several presidential committees, including the President's Advisory Committee on the Arts. He lives in Laconia, N.H.

Benjamin C. Bradlee was managing editor of the *Washington Post* and served as the newspaper's vice president and executive editor from 1986 to 1991. He is currently writing two books.

Willy Brandt was chancellor of the Federal Republic of Germany. He was a former president of the Socialist Internationale, and honorary president of the Social Democratic party. He died on October 8, 1992.

Edmund G. ("Pat") Brown, Sr., was governor of California until 1966. He has been a senior partner at the Los Angeles law firm Ball, Hunt, Hart, Brown and Baerwitz, where he now serves as counsel.

McGeorge Bundy left the White House in 1966. He served as president of the Ford Foundation from 1966 to 1979 and was a professor of history at New York University, where he is now a professor emeritus.

George A. Carver, Jr., served three directors of Central Intelligence; was special assistant for Vietnamese affairs; was deputy to the DCI for national intelligence; and was senior U.S. intelligence officer in the Federal Republic of Germany. He is president of C & S Associates, Inc., of Washington, D.C., and John M. Olin Senior Fellow at the Center for Strategic and International Studies.

Harlan J. Cleveland was U.S. ambassador to NATO. He is a professor emeritus at the Hubert H. Humphrey Institute of Public Affairs at the University of Minnesota. He was president of the University of Hawaii from 1968 to 1974, when he became a professor emeritus.

Ray S. Cline has served as director of the State Department Bureau of Intelligence and Research, as well as director of world power studies at the Georgetown University Center for Strategic and International Studies. An expert on terrorism, he has since 1986 been chairman of the United States Global Strategy Council in Washington, D.C., and serves as a professor of international relations in Georgetown University's School of Foreign Services.

Rev. William Sloane Coffin, Jr., was chaplain of Yale University, senior minister of New York's Riverside Church, and president of SANE. He was a cofounder of Clergy and Laity Concerned for Vietnam and is the author of three books. He continues to be active in the civil rights and peace movements and lectures widely throughout the United States.

William E. Colby was chief of the CIA's Far East Division as well as the organization's director of Central Intelligence from 1973 to 1976. He has been a consultant to corporations and governments, has written two books, and has lectured in the United States and abroad. He is counsel to the Washington law firm of Donovan Leisure, Rogovin, Huge, and Schiller.

John Sherman Cooper served in the U.S. Senate until 1973. He was ambassador to the German Democratic Republic and practiced law in Washington. He died in February 1991.

Archibald Cox headed the Watergate special prosecutor's office. He has been Williston Professor of Law and Carl M. Loeb University Professor at Harvard University, where he is now a professor emeritus.

Carl T. Curtis retired as a Republican senator from Nebraska in 1979. He has written two books and lives in Omaha.

Lloyd N. Cutler was counsel to President Jimmy Carter as well as executive director of the National Commission on the Causes and Prevention of Violence. He has served on several presidential commissions, and is today a partner in the Washington, D.C., law firm Wilmer, Cutler & Pickering.

Cartha DeLoach retired from the Federal Bureau of Investigation. He has been a corporate executive and is a business consultant living in South Carolina.

Bui Diem served in the Government of South Vietnam and was that nation's ambassador to the United States. He is a professor at the Indochinese Institute at George Mason University, Fairfax, Va.

Joseph F. Dolan was administrative assistant to Senator Robert F. Kennedy. He was president of Shakeys, Inc.; executive director of the Colorado Department of Revenue; U.S. attorney for the District of Colorado; and executive director of the Colorado Department of Highways. He retired in 1987 and lives in the Denver area.

Angier Biddle Duke was U.S. ambassador to Spain, Denmark, and Morocco. In 1990 he retired as chancellor of Long Island University, Southampton campus.

Ralph Dungan was commissioner of education of the state of New Jersey. He was U.S. director of the Inter-American Bank and served for ten years with the International Executive Service Corps. He is now retired and lives in Barbados, where he is engaged in farming.

Courtney Evans retired from the Federal Bureau of Investigation and practices law in Washington, D.C.

James Farmer was an assistant secretary of health, education and welfare under President Nixon. He has remained active in CORE and continues to be an influential voice for civil rights. He has lectured at campuses throughout the country and is a Distinguished Professor at Mary Washington College, Fredericksburg, Va.

Harry D. Felt retired in 1964 as an admiral in the U.S. Navy. He lives in Hawaii.

Gerald R. Ford was Republican minority leader of the House of Representatives and became vice president of the United States on December 6, 1973, succeeding to the presidency on the resignation of Richard M. Nixon. He served in that office from August 9, 1974, to January 29, 1977. Since leaving the White House he has served on the boards of several corporations, has lectured at more than 175 colleges and universities, and been active in Republican politics. He has also been associated with the Betty Ford Center, the Gerald R. Ford Foundation, and both the Gerald R. Ford Library in Ann Arbor and the Gerald R. Ford Museum in Grand Rapids, Mich.

Henry H. Fowler was secretary of the treasury from 1965 to 1986. He has served on the boards of a number of educational and public interest organizations, and was a general partner of Goldman Sachs and Company. He is today a limited partner with that firm and lives in northern Virginia.

Wayne Fredericks left the Department of State in 1967. He has since headed the Ford Foundation's Middle East and Africa Program, was director of International Relations for Chase Manhattan Bank, and was executive director of international governmental affairs for the Ford Motor Company. Since 1988 he has been counselor in residence at the Institute for International Education in New York City.

Orville L. Freeman was secretary of agriculture until January 1969. He served as president and then Chairman of the Business International Corporation and since 1985 has been a senior partner in the Washington, D.C., law firm Pophan, Haik, Schnobrich, Kaufman and Doty, Ltd.

J. William Fulbright was a U.S. senator from Arkansas until 1975. A recipient of the Onassis International Prize, he has been, since 1975, counsel to the Washington, D.C., law firm Hogan & Hartson.

John Kenneth Galbraith was Paul M. Warburg Professor of Economics at Harvard University. He was president of the American Academy of Arts and Letters and of Americans for Democratic Action. Since 1963 he has written more than twenty books.

Raymond L. Garthoff was counselor for political-military affairs at the U.S. Mission to NATO, executive officer and adviser to the SALT talks, senior foreign service inspector in the Department of State, and U.S. ambassador to Bulgaria. Since 1980 he has been a senior fellow at the Brookings Institution in Washington, D.C.

Mordechai Gazit has served as director general of Israel's Foreign Ministry and as that nation's ambassador to France. He has been associated with Hebrew and Tel Aviv universities and is a consultant to the American Jewish Committee in Jerusalem.

Roswell L. Gilpatric was chairman of the Board of Fairchild Camera and Instrument Corporation and has served as a director of Eastern Airlines as well as of the Corning Glass Company. Since 1977 he has been affiliated with the New York law firm Cravath, Swaine & Moore.

Andrew J. Goodpaster was assistant to the chairman of the Joint Chiefs of Staff; deputy commander of U.S. forces in Vietnam; and Supreme Allied Commander, Europe. He served as superintendent of the U.S. Military Academy, West Point, from 1977 to 1981, and was president of the Institute for Defense Analysis and chairman of the American Battle Monuments Commission. He has been chairman of the Atlantic Council of the United States since 1985.

Lincoln Gordon was assistant secretary of state for inter-American affairs in the Johnson administration. He has served as president of Johns Hopkins University and is a fellow of the American Academy of Arts and Sciences. Since 1984 he has been a guest scholar at the Brookings Institution, Washington, D.C.

Denis Arthur Greenhill (Lord Greenhill of Harrow) was permanent undersecretary of state and head of the diplomatic service of the United Kingdom. In 1974 he was made baron of the Royal Borough of Kensington and Chelsea. He is a director of S. G. Warburg & Co.

Najeeb E. Halaby was president, chief executive officer, and chairman of Pan American World Airways. He is president of Halaby International Corporation and chairman of Janelle Aviation, with offices in the Washington, D.C., area.

August Heckscher was New York City parks commissioner and is a prolific author. His latest book is a biography of Woodrow Wilson.

Richard M. Helms was deputy director of Central Intelligence and served as CIA director from June 1966 to February 1973. He then became U.S. ambassador to Iran. He is president of Safeer Company—an international business consulting firm based in Washington, D.C.

Rev. Theodore Hesburgh retired as president of the University of Notre Dame in 1987. He served on the U.S. Civil Rights Commission until 1972 and was chairman of the U.S. delegation to the United Nations Conference on Science and Technology for Development. He was awarded the Presidential Medal of Freedom and maintains an office in South Bend, Ind.

Martin J. Hillenbrand was U.S. ambassador to Hungary, assistant secretary of state for European affairs, and ambassador to the Federal Republic of Germany. He has served as director general of the Atlantic Institute for International Affairs and since 1982 has been the Dean Rusk professor of International Relations at the University of Georgia.

Roger Hilsman was professor of government and international politics at Columbia University, where he now is professor emeritus. His book *To Move a Nation* remains an important resource on Kennedy administration foreign policy. His most recent book was *George Bush versus Saddam Hussein: Military Success! Political Failure?* He is a director of America Capital.

U. Alexis Johnson served as deputy ambassador in Saigon and as ambassador to Spain in the Johnson administration. He was appointed by President Nixon to head the U.S. delegation to the Strategic Arms Limitations Talks (SALT) in 1973. He is retired from the Department of State and frequently lectures on foreign policy.

Philip M. Kaiser was minister at the U.S. Embassy, London; ambassador to the People's Republic of Hungary, 1977–80; and ambassador to Austria, 1980–81. He is a senior consultant to SRI International, Washington, D.C.

Nicholas deB. Katzenbach, as attorney general in the Johnson administration, drafted the 1965 Voting Rights Act. He later served as undersecretary of state and was senior vice president and general counsel of International Business Machines Corporation. He now practices law in Morristown, N.J.

Clark Kerr served as president of the University of California until 1967. He was chairman of the Carnegie Commission on Higher Education, chairman of the National Committee for a Political Settlement in Vietnam, and a member of the U.S. delegation to observe elections in El Salvador. He is professor emeritus of economics and industrial relations at the University of California, Berkeley.

Sergei Khrushchev has worked on his father's memoirs. He was associated with scientific institutes in the Soviet Union and in 1990 served as a lecturer at the Kennedy Institute at Harvard. He lives in Moscow.

Philip Klutznick was a member of the President's Advisory Council on Indo-Chinese Refugees. He served as secretary of commerce, 1980–81. He is president emeritus of the World Jewish Congress and maintains an office in Chicago, Ill.

Robert W. Komer was deputy special assistant to the president for national security affairs; special assistant to President Lyndon Johnson; a senior U.S. official in Vietnam; U.S. ambassador to Turkey; and undersecretary of defense for policy in the Carter administration. He is a consultant to the Rand Corporation in Washington, D.C.

Victor H. Krulak was commander of the Fleet Marine Force, Pacific, and retired from the U.S. Marine Corps in 1968 with the rank of lieutenant general after thirty-four years of service. He was vice chairman of the U.S. Strategic Institute and president of the Words Ltd. Corporation, San Diego, Calif.

John Lewis was director of the Voter Education Project and headed Volunteers for ACTION under President Jimmy Carter. He served on the Atlanta City Council and in 1986 was elected to the U.S. House of Representatives—from the Fifth District of Georgia—where he is a chief deputy Democratic whip.

Thomas C. Mann served as assistant secretary of state for inter-American affairs in the Johnson administration, where he also had senior responsibilities involving the Alliance for Progress. He retired from the Department of State in 1966 and lives in Austin, Tex.

Robert J. Manning served as editor in chief of the *Atlantic Monthly* and the Atlantic Monthly Press. He was editor in chief of Boston Publication Company. He is a member of the American Academy of Arts and Sciences. His book *The Swamproot Chronicle: Adventures in the Word Trade* was published in November 1992.

Burke Marshall was general counsel and senior vice president of the International Business Machines Corporation. He is a member of the board of directors of the Robert F. Kennedy Memorial and, since 1970, has been a professor of law at Yale University, New Haven, Conn.

Edwin M. Martin served as ambassador to Argentina in the Johnson administration. He was chairman of the Development Assistance Committee and is associated with the Population Crisis Committee in Washington, D.C.

Louis E. Martin was editor of the *Chicago Defender.* He served as special assistant to President Jimmy Carter and was assistant vice president for communications at Howard University and chairman of the board of Calmar Communications. He lives in California.

Eugene J. McCarthy was a candidate in the 1968 Democratic presidential primaries, and ended his service in the U.S. Senate in 1970. He has served as Adlai Stevenson Professor of Political Science at the New

School for Social Research. He has been a syndicated newspaper columnist since 1977, and has written more than ten books. He maintains an
office in Washington, D.C.

Edward A. McDermott served as director of the Office of Emergency Planning until January 1965. He was a partner in the Washington,
D.C., law firm Hogan & Hartson until his retirement in 1988. He is a
member of the board of Mercedes Benz of North America and lives in
South Florida.

George S. McGovern was the Democratic candidate for president in
1972 and served in the U.S. Senate until 1981. He was a contender for
the Democratic presidential nomination in 1992. He has served as chairman of Americans for Common Sense and has lectured at Northwestern
University. He maintains an office in Washington, D.C.

James H. Meredith graduated from the University of Mississippi
with a BA in political science. In a June 1966 voter registration march
from Memphis to Jackson, Mississippi, he was shot from ambush. He
was a special assistant to Senator Jesse Helms (R., N.C.).

Bradford Morse represented the Fifth District of Massachusetts in
the House of Representatives. He served as UN undersecretary general
for political and General Assembly affairs and Administrator of the UN
development program, as well as president of the Salzburg Seminar. He
lives in South Florida.

Robert Moses spent more than six years in Tanzania working for that
nation's Ministry of Education. He is president of the Algebra Project,
helping inner city public school students learn algebra.

Frank Moss served in the Senate until 1977. He was chairman of the
Committee on Aeronautics and Space in the 93d and 94th Congresses.
He lives in Salt Lake City, Utah.

Gaylord A. Nelson served in the U.S. Senate until 1981. He was
chairman of the Senate Select Committee on Small Business. Since 1981
he has been associated with the Wilderness Society, based in Washington, D.C.

Maurine Neuberger has lectured on consumer affairs and on the status of women. She has taught at Boston University and at Reed College.
She lives in Portland, Oreg.

John M. Patterson practiced law in Montgomery until 1984, when
he joined the Alabama judiciary. He is currently chief judge of the
Alabama Court of Criminal Appeals. His Montgomery office is across

the street from the Dexter Avenue Baptist Church, the site of rallies in support of the Montgomery Bus Boycott.

Claiborne Pell continues to serve as the senior United States senator from Rhode Island. He is chairman of the Foreign Relations Committee and an influential force in national Democratic politics.

Esther Peterson left her post at the Department of Labor in 1969. She served President Jimmy Carter as special assistant for consumer affairs and has been active in national and international consumer organizations. A recipient of the Presidential Medal of Freedom, she lives in Washington, D.C.

Norman Podhoretz was chairman of the New Directions Advisory Committee of the United States Information Agency from 1981 to 1987. He is the author of six books, has written a nationally syndicated newspaper column, and has been editor in chief of *Commentary* magazine since 1960.

Roman Puchinski left the House of Representatives in 1972. He served as an alderman in Chicago from 1973 to 1992.

Marcus G. Raskin has written more than a dozen books and has been a member of the editorial board of *The Nation* since 1979. He was on President Nixon's "enemies list" and was indicted and acquitted, along with Dr. Benjamin Spock, for aiding draft resisters. He is a distinguished fellow at the Institute for Policy Studies, Washington, D.C.

Joseph L. Rauh, Jr., who was retired from the private practice of law and served as vice chairman of Americans for Democratic Action, died in Washington, D.C., on September 3, 1992.

Manuel Ray moved to Puerto Rico in the early 1960s. He is a principal in a San Juan architectural engineering concern.

Abraham A. Ribicoff served as a United States senator from Connecticut until 1981. Since then he has been associated with the New York law firm of Kaye, Scholer, Fierman, Hays and Handler.

George Romney was a candidate for the Republican presidential nomination in 1968. He served as secretary of housing and urban development in the Nixon administration. He lives in the Detroit suburbs.

Charles R. Ross was reappointed by President Johnson as a member of the Federal Power Commission. He was commissioner of the International Joint Commission, United States–Canada, under Presidents Johnson, Nixon, Ford, and Carter. He served as a public member of the Administrative Conference of the United States and is a lawyer and consultant in utility and energy, as well as a breeder of Morgan horses.

Walt W. Rostow was President Johnson's special assistant for national security affairs. He was a member of the faculty of the University of Texas at Austin, where he is the Rex G. Baker, Jr., Professor Emeritus of Political Economy. He has written over thirty books and is a member of the American Academy of Arts and Sciences.

Dean Rusk served as secretary of state until 1969. Since 1970 he has been Sibley Professor of International Law at the University of Georgia at Athens. He maintains an office there, at the Rusk Center, and in 1990 published his autobiography, *As I Saw It*.

Pierre Salinger served as U.S. senator from California from August through December 1964. He was senior adviser to the presidential campaign of Robert F. Kennedy and was cochairman of the National Citizens Committee for George McGovern. He is the author of the bestselling books *With Kennedy* and *Secret Dossier: The Hidden Agenda Behind the Gulf Crisis*. He is currently chief foreign correspondent of ABC News and serves as that network's senior editor in Europe.

Paul A. Samuelson was a consultant to the Council of Economic Advisers and the Federal Reserve Board. He was a columnist for *Newsweek* and is lifetime honorary president of the International Economic Association. His text, *Economics*, a standard work in its field, is in its fourteenth edition. He is Institute Professor Emeritus at the Massachusetts Institute of Technology, Cambridge.

Terry Sanford was president of Duke University from 1969 to 1985. In 1986 he was elected to the United States Senate from North Carolina. He is chairman of the Select Ethics Committee and a member of the Senate Committee on Foreign Relations. He was defeated in his bid for reelection in November 1992.

Walter M. Schirra, Jr., was in charge of operations and training, Astronaut Office, NASA, from 1964 to 1969. He was command pilot of *Gemini 6* and in 1968 commanded *Apollo 7*'s eleven-day flight. Since his retirement as an astronaut in 1969, he has held several senior corporate positions and is a business consultant in Southern California.

Norbert Schlei left his post in the Department of Justice in 1966. He has been a partner in Washington and Los Angeles law firms and, since 1983, has been chairman and chief executive officer of Kahala Capital Corporation, with offices in Santa Monica, Calif.

Arthur M. Schlesinger, Jr.'s books *A Thousand Days*, on the

Kennedy presidency, and *Robert F. Kennedy: His Life and Times*, have become standard works. He has won two National Book Awards and the Pulitzer Prize for Biography. In 1992 his book *The Disunity of America* was a bestseller. He is Albert Schweitzer Professor of Humanities at the City University of New York.

Glenn T. Seaborg, a winner of the Nobel Prize in Chemistry, served under Presidents Lyndon Johnson and Richard Nixon as chairman of the Atomic Energy Commission. He continues to work in isotope research, following up his discoveries in the field. He is currently University Professor of Chemistry, associate director of the Lawrence Berkeley Laboratory, and chairman of the Lawrence Hall of Science at the University of California, Berkeley.

Robert C. Seamans, Jr., served in the Johnson administration and was secretary of the Air Force under President Nixon. He was president of the National Academy of Sciences and is senior lecturer in the Department of Aeronautics and Astronautics at the Massachusetts Institute of Technology, Cambridge.

John L. Seigenthaler was editor, publisher, president, and chairman of the *Nashville Tennessean*. He served as editorial director of *USA Today* and is chairman of the Freedom Forum, First Amendment Center, Nashville, Tenn.

R. Sargent Shriver was director of the Office of Economic Opportunity and then special assistant to President Lyndon Johnson. He served as ambassador to France and in 1972 was the Democratic candidate for vice president of the United States. He has received twenty-four honorary degrees, and since 1990 has been chairman of the board of Special Olympics International.

Fred Shuttlesworth is pastor of the Greater New Light Baptist Church, Cincinnati, Ohio. He is cochairman of the Southern Organizing Committee and a national board member of the Southern Christian Leadership Conference.

Joseph Sisco served as assistant secretary of state for international organization affairs, assistant secretary of state for Near Eastern and South Asian affairs, and undersecretary of state for political affairs. He was president and then provost of the American University and is a partner in Sisco Associates.

Donald K. ("Deke") Slayton served in several administrative posts for the U.S. space program. In 1975 he was Apollo Docking Module Pilot of the Apollo-Soyuz Test Project and spent 217 hours in space. He is director of the Space Service Division of EER System and vice chairman of the Mercury Seven Foundation.

George Smathers served in the U.S. Senate until 1969. He practices law in Washington, D.C., and in Florida.

William Y. Smith was staff assistant to the chairman of the Joint Chiefs of Staff, military assistant to the secretary of the Air Force, and deputy commander in chief, U.S. European Command. He retired as a general from the U.S. Air Force in 1983. Since 1985 he has been president of the Institute for Defense Analysis, Alexandria, Va.

Adlai E. Stevenson III was treasurer of the state of Illinois, 1965–70, and served as a Democratic senator from Illinois, 1970–81. He now practices law in Chicago.

Viktor M. Sukhodrev was employed in the Soviet Foreign Ministry and was his country's leading English-language interpreter, serving professionally at summit meetings between seven U.S. presidents and Soviet leaders. He was special assistant to the secretary general of the United Nations and is now an official in the UN office of General Assembly Affairs.

William H. Sullivan was head of the Interdepartmental Task Force on Vietnam and special assistant to the secretary of state. He served as ambassador to Laos, the Philippines, and Iran and was a member of the U.S. negotiating team at the Paris peace talks on Vietnam. He was president of the American Assembly from 1979 to 1986 and is currently living in retirement in Mexico.

Phillips Talbot was ambassador to Greece in the Johnson administration. He served as president of the Asia Society from 1970 to 1981 and is now the organization's president emeritus. He lives in New York City.

Strom Thurmond continues to serve in the United States Senate from South Carolina. In 1964 he switched from the Democratic to the Republican party. He was president pro tempore of the Senate from 1981 to 1987.

James Tobin received the Nobel Prize in Economics in 1981. He was president of the American Economics Association and is a fellow of the American Academy of Arts and Sciences. He was Sterling Professor of Economics at Yale, where he is now a professor emeritus.

William Trueheart retired from the Department of State in 1974. He died on December 24, 1992.

Jack J. Valenti was a special assistant to President Lyndon Johnson. He has served as a director of Trans World Airlines and Riggs National

Corporation. Since 1966 he has been president and chief executive officer of the Motion Picture Association of America, Inc., with offices in Washington, D.C.

George Wallace was governor of Alabama 1963–66, 1971–79, and 1983–87. He ran in Democratic primaries for president in 1968 and 1972. In 1972 he was partially paralyzed when shot during an assassination attempt while campaigning in Maryland. Since 1987 he has held administrative posts at Troy State University, Montgomery, Ala.

Lee White served in the Johnson administration as associate special assistant to the president and as chairman of the Federal Power Commission. He practices law in Washington, D.C.

Tom Wicker was associate editor of the *New York Times* from 1968 to 1985 and a columnist for that newspaper from 1966 to 1992. His books include a 1991 study of former President Richard Nixon. He is currently working on several books.

Donald M. Wilson was general manager of Time-Life International associate publisher of *Life* magazine; and corporate vice president, public affairs, at Time, Inc. Since 1989 he has been publisher of *BUSINESS for Central New Jersey*, a biweekly newspaper on central New Jersey business and businesspeople.

James Wine was special assistant for refugee affairs to the secretary of state in the Johnson administration. He worked in the presidential campaign of Robert Kennedy and then practiced law in Washington, D.C. He died at his home in Linden, Va., on August 23, 1990.

Ralph Yarborough served in the Senate until 1971. He was a member of Texas commissions on constitutional review and on the state library and archives. He practices law in Austin, Tex.

Adam Yarmolinsky was deputy assistant secretary of defense for international security affairs. He served as a professor of law at Harvard University; as Ralph Waldo Emerson University Professor at the University of Massachusetts; as professor, acting provost, and since 1987 as provost of the University of Maryland, Baltimore County.

Herbert F. York was ambassador to the Comprehensive Test Ban negotiations. He served as chancellor at the University of California, San Diego, where he is a professor of physics.

Sam Yorty served as mayor of Los Angeles until 1971 and is credited with the development of the city's downtown area. He maintains an office in the San Fernando Valley.

Index

Abernathy, Ralph, 275, 299

Abram, Morris B., 34–35, 37, 166, 277, 282–83, 491, 498, 511

Acheson, Dean, 165, 172–73, 175–76, 203, 362–63, 367, 380, 382

Adenauer, Konrad, 169, 201, 240, 365, 370, 454

Adzhubei, Alexei: and the assassination, 453, 459; and Berlin crisis, 367; and Cuban missile crisis, 394; and JFK-RFK relationship, 89; and JFK's role in foreign affairs, 238–39, 240–41; and Kennedy appeal, 60, 61; and Khrushchev-Salinger meeting, 239, 240–41; present activities of, 511; and RFK as attorney general, 89; and Salinger evaluation, 169

Africa, 207–14, 289, 446–47, 468

Alliance for Progress, 172–73, 183–84, 217, 222–23, 497

Alsop, Joseph W., 63, 430

Appointments: and blacks, 286; to cabinet, 110–26; how people learned of their, 128–38; of JFK's staff, 138; sub-cabinet-level, 127–38; of women, 196. *See also specific person*

Arabs: refugee problems of, 223–24, 231–32. *See also* Middle East issues

Aspen Institute, 280

Assassination of JFK: and Bay of Pigs mission, 457; and Camelot question, 468, 472; Castro as responsible for, 457, 459–60, 462, 463, 464; and CIA, 458, 459, 462, 463–64; and civil rights, 292, 293; and conspiracy theory, 456–60, 462; controversy about, 435,
456–60, 462; and FBI, 448, 449–50, 459, 460, 462, 463–64; immediate hours after, 445–48; impact of, 435; JFK's associates learn about, 448–56; and JFK's last conversations, 438–40; and Kennedy legacy, 484, 498, 501; and LBJ's swearing in, 443–45; and Mafia theory, 459; and motorcade, 440–43; and Secret Service, 449–50, 460, 463; Soviet Union as responsible for, 458, 459; and Warren Commission, 442, 460, 461–64; and why JFK went to Dallas, 435–37

Assassination: of Castro, 86, 457, 459–60, 463, 464; of King, 456, 460; of Oswald, 457, 460; of RFK, 456, 460

Atomic energy issues, 242–43. *See also* Seaborg, Glenn

Bagley, Worth H., 410–14, 428–29, 511–12

Baker, Bobby: and Ambassador Kennedy's influence on his children, 76; and the assassination, 435, 462; and Bay of Pigs mission, 333; and Catholic issue, 42, 46; and civil rights, 277–78, 287; and Hoover-Kennedy relationship, 268; and JFK-Jackie relationship, 78; and JFK-LBJ relationship, 188, 192; and JFK-RFK relationship, 81; and JFK's role in foreign affairs, 211; and the Kennedy appeal, 55; and LBJ's reasons for accepting vice presidential nomination, 22; and 1960 election, 10, 13, 17–18, 22, 42, 46; present activities of, 512; and RFK-LBJ relationship, 197; and RFK's appointment as attor-

Baker, Bobby (*cont.*)
  ney general, 112, 115; and selection of a
  running mate, 13, 17–18; and Stevenson
  nomination, 10; and Warren Commission,
  462
Baldwin, James, 290, 291, 292
Ball, George: and Ambassador Kennedy's influence on his children, 74; and Bay of Pigs
  mission, 333–34, 346, 350; and Bowles evaluation, 159; and Camelot question, 472; and
  Cuban missile crisis, 381, 382, 392, 398–99;
  and JFK-RFK relationship, 87; and JFK's
  administrative style, 177, 178, 182, 185, 186;
  and Kennedy appeal, 55; and Kennedy
  legacy, 498; and Maxwell Taylor evaluation,
  161; and 1960 election, 9; present activities
  of, 512; and RFK as attorney general, 87;
  and RFK's personality, 91, 93; and Rusk
  evaluation, 165; and Rusk's appointment,
  116–17; and Stevenson nomination, 9; and
  Stevenson's appointment as U.N. ambassador, 123; and sub-cabinet-level appointments, 134; and Vietnam, 403, 409–10, 413,
  414, 417
Barnett, Ross, 302–7
Barsukov, Yuri: and the assassination, 458; and
  Bay of Pigs mission, 342; and Berlin crisis,
  372; and Cuban missile crisis, 385, 392, 400;
  and JFK's role in foreign affairs, 224, 238,
  239; and Kennedy appeal, 54; and
  Khrushchev-Salinger meeting, 239; present
  activities of, 512; and RFK's personality,
  94–95; and Rusk evaluation, 169; and
  Vienna Summit, 356–57
Bartlett, Charles, 78, 97, 197
Battle, Lucius: and Bay of Pigs mission, 328–29;
  and JFK as a 1990s candidate, 481; and
  JFK's administrative style, 174–75, 182, 183,
  184; and JFK's role in foreign affairs, 208,
  223; and JFK staff appointments, 138; and
  Peace Corps, 256, 257; present activities of,
  512; and sub-cabinet-level appointments,
  134; and Vietnam, 427
Bay of Pigs mission: aftermath of, 347–54; and
  American foreign policy, 403; and the assassination, 457; background of, 323–30; and
  Camelot question, 467, 468, 471; and covert
  activities, 432; and Cuban missile crisis,
  389–90, 394, 396; decision to go with,
  330–33; JFK briefing about, 324–30; and
  JFK's administrative style, 144, 149–50; and
  Kennedy legacy, 490–91, 494, 498; objective
  of, 323; and the operation, 337–47; and
  plausible deniability, 345; prisoners in,
  352–53; reasons for failure of, 323; reasons
  for going with, 333–37; and secrecy, 392;
  and test-ban treaty, 262; and Vienna Summit, 356, 359; and Vietnam, 406, 409, 411
Bell, David: and depressed areas issues, 243;

and Dillon's appointment, 121; and economic issues, 243–44, 246; and JFK's
  administrative style, 144–45, 147–48,
  179–80; and JFK's role in foreign affairs,
  206–7; and Kennedy appeal, 60; present
  activities of, 512; and space program, 250;
  and Vietnam, 408–9
Ben-Gurion, David, 201, 227, 231–32
Berle, Adolph, 330, 347, 349
Berlin crisis: and Acheson memoranda, 362–63,
  367; and Berlin Wall, 363–67, 368; and Clay
  as emissary, 365, 367–69; and Cuban missile
  crisis, 366, 367, 372, 375, 388–89; and JFK-
  RFK relationship, 80; and JFK's administrative style, 153, 175; and JFK's role in foreign
  affairs, 201–2, 203–4, 236; and JFK's visit,
  369–72; and Kennedy legacy, 495; and LBJ's
  visit, 365, 367–69; magnitude of the, 372;
  overview of, 360–62, 366–37; and test–ban
  treaty, 262; and Vienna Summit, 236, 356,
  357, 359, 360, 388; and Vietnam, 411, 430
Birmingham, AL: demonstrations in, 271, 272,
  274, 279, 284–85, 288–89, 298, 300, 309–10,
  316, 316n
Bissell, Richard: and the assassination, 457, 462;
  and Bay of Pigs mission, 325, 327, 329, 330,
  331–32, 335, 336, 338, 342, 343, 344, 345,
  349, 350, 351, 352, 353–54; and Cuban missile crisis, 379, 395; and JFK as a 1990s candidate, 480; and JFK's administrative style,
  145–46; and Kennedy legacy, 495; and LBJ's
  unhappiness as vice president, 199–200; present activities of, 512; and Rusk evaluation,
  167; and Schlesinger evaluation, 169; and
  Vietnam, 404; and Warren Commission, 462
Black America: and appointment of blacks, 286;
  and JFK's role in foreign affairs, 210, 211,
  212–14; and Kennedy legacy, 499, 500–501;
  and 1960 election, 20, 28; and RFK–black
  entertainers/writers meeting, 290–92. *See
  also* Civil rights; *specific person*
Blair, William McCormick, 8–10, 178
Blough, Roger, 146, 258
Boggs, Hale, 25, 461
Bohlen, Charles E., 380, 466
Bond, Julian: and the assassination, 446; and
  civil rights, 36, 281–82, 288, 303, 311, 312,
  314, 321; and JFK-RFK relationship, 79–80;
  and Kennedy legacy, 499; and King phone
  call, 36; and 1960 election, 36; and 1964
  election, 474; present activities of, 512
Boutin, Bernard: and the assassination, 436,
  449–50, 462; and Camelot question, 471;
  and Catholic issue, 42–43; and Hoover-
  Kennedy relationship, 268–69; and JFK-
  RFK relationship, 81; and Kennedy dynasty
  question, 105; and Kennedy legacy, 484; and
  1960 election, 6, 8, 42–43; and 1964 election, 473; present activities of, 512; and

Stevenson nomination, 8; and sub-cabinet-level appointments, 134–35; and Warren Commission, 462

Bowles, Chester: appointed undersecretary of state, 116; and Bay of Pigs mission, 346, 348–49; evaluation of, 158–59; and JFK's administrative style, 149–50, 182, 184, 185; and JFK's role in foreign affairs, 207, 211; and 1960 election, 32; and Rusk's appointment, 116–17, 118–19; and sub-cabinet-level appointments, 127, 132

Bradlee, Benjamin C.: and Ambassador Kennedy's influence on his children, 73; and Bay of Pigs mission, 334–35; and civil rights, 287–88, 320; and Cuban missile crisis, 381–82, 393, 394; and JFK-LBJ relationship, 191; and JFK-RFK relationship, 78; and JFK's administrative style, 142, 173; and Kennedy brothers' relationship, 100; and Kennedy dynasty question, 106; and LBJ's reasons for accepting vice presidential nomination, 21; and McNamara evaluation, 162; and 1960 election, 11–12, 17, 21; present activities of, 512; and RFK's personality, 94; and Schlesinger evaluation, 169; and selection of a running mate, 17; and Stevenson demonstration, 11–12; and Vietnam, 427, 430

Brandt, Willy: and the assassination, 453, 457; and Berlin crisis, 360–61, 362–63, 364–65, 366, 367–69, 370, 371–72; and JFK's role in foreign affairs, 201–2; and Kennedy legacy, 484; present activities of, 513

Braun, Wernher von, 250–51, 250n

Brazil, 216, 217–18, 222, 223, 256

Brown, Edmund G. ("Pat"), Sr., 2, 10, 57, 92, 100, 495–96, 513

Bui Diem, 55, 403–4, 423–24, 451, 514

Bundy, McGeorge: and Ambassador Kennedy's influence on his children, 73; and Bay of Pigs mission, 332–33, 343, 344, 350–51, 352; and Berlin crisis, 366; and Camelot question, 469; and civil rights, 275–76; and Cuban missile crisis, 374, 375, 376–77, 378, 382, 392–93, 394, 395, 399; and economic issues, 246; evaluation of, 159–60; and JFK's administrative style, 143–44, 149, 150, 172, 175, 176, 178, 179, 180, 181, 183, 186, 187; and JFK's political philosophy, 67–68; and JFK's role in foreign affairs, 205, 226–27, 229, 233, 235–36; and JFK staff appointments, 138; and Kennedy legacy, 490, 491, 495; present activities of, 513; and Schlesinger evaluation, 169; and sub-cabinet-level appointments, 128–29; and Vienna Summit, 356; and Vietnam, 409, 410, 425, 491

Bunker, Ellsworth, 132, 206

Burke, Arleigh, 332, 342, 381–82

Cabinet: appointments to, 110–26; and Camelot question, 470; and JFK's administrative style, 146

Camelot question, 465–72

Caro, Robert, 321, 446

Carpenter, Liz, 440

Carter, Jimmy, 127, 137, 173, 174, 487, 498

Carver, George A., Jr., 100–101, 161, 354, 388, 513

Castro, Fidel: assassination attempt on, 86, 457, 459–60, 463, 464. See also Bay of Pigs mission; Cuba; Cuban missile crisis

Catholic issue: and civil rights, 313; and JFK-LBJ relationship, 194; and JFK's administrative style, 145; and Kennedy legacy, 501; and 1960 election, 2, 20, 22, 26, 37–46; and 1964 election, 475; and Vietnam, 419

CIA (Central Intelligence Agency): and American foreign policy, 403; and the assassination, 458, 459, 462, 463–64; and Castro assassination, 457; in Laos, 406; and organized crime, 86; and Peace Corps, 256; and Vietnam, 418, 422, 431; and Warren Commission, 462, 463–64. See also Bay of Pigs mission; Cuban missile crisis

Civil rights: and Autherine Lucy case, 305; and Birmingham demonstrations, 271, 272, 274, 279, 284–85, 288–89, 296, 298, 300, 309–10, 316, 316n; and Camelot question, 471; and communism, 315, 318; and congress, 271, 277, 278, 282, 283, 285, 286, 287, 317, 318, 319, 320–22, 482; and Eisenhower administration, 483, 485–86; and FBI, 294, 296–97, 309, 313–20, 349; and foreign affairs, 289, 297; and Freedom Rides, 271, 272, 275, 279, 280, 293–302, 305, 318, 319, 475; and Hoover-Kennedy relationship, 266; and institutionalized racism, 273–74; and Jews, 273, 274; and JFK-LBJ relationship, 190; and JFK-RFK relationship, 78, 80; and JFK's administrative style, 141, 144, 148; and JFK's assassination, 292, 293; and JFK's political philosophy, 64, 65–66, 68; and JFK's role in foreign affairs, 210, 211, 212–14; and Kennedy dynasty question, 106; and Kennedy legacy, 321–22, 482, 483, 485–86, 492, 499, 500, 501–2; and KKK, 274, 296, 300, 307, 318; legislation for, 65–66, 271, 272, 274, 282, 283, 284–87, 294, 310, 320–22; and March on Washington, 308–13, 499; and Meredith case, 277, 302–7; and Montgomery, AL, 298, 299, 300–302, 306, 309; and 1960 election, 26, 28, 30, 34–37, 278; and 1964 election, 271, 277, 285, 293, 307, 321, 474, 475, 477, 478; and Ole Miss, 277, 302–7; overview of, 271–88, 289, 293; and RFK–black entertainers/writers meeting, 290–92; and RFK-LBJ relationship, 197; and RFK's appointment as

Civil rights (cont.)
    attorney general, 110; and RFK-Wallace-
    Burke meeting, 288–89; and Rusk's appoint-
    ment, 118–19; and sit-ins, 273, 276, 277;
    and sub-cabinet-level appointments, 135;
    and Supreme Court, 279, 286, 295, 297,
    321; and Wallace confrontation, 307–8; in
    Washington, DC, 212–14
Civil Rights Acts, 274, 282, 285, 286, 320–22
Clay, Lucius, 365, 367–69
Cleveland, Harlan: and Bay of Pigs mission,
    336, 339–40; and Cuban missile crisis, 390;
    and JFK-LBJ relationship, 190; and JFK's
    administrative style, 181, 186; and JFK's role
    in foreign affairs, 207; and Kennedy dynasty
    question, 106–7; and 1960 election, 10, 13;
    present activities of, 513; and RFK's person-
    ality, 91; and the Stevenson demonstration,
    13; and the Stevenson nomination, 10; and
    Stevenson's appointment as UN ambas-
    sador, 123, 124
Clifford, Clark, 112, 130, 172, 354
Cline, Ray: and the assassination, 463–64; and
    Bay of Pigs mission, 338–39; and Cuban
    missile crisis, 374–76, 378–79, 389–90,
    395–96; and JFK-LBJ relationship, 189; and
    JFK's administrative style, 149; and JFK's
    political philosophy, 67; and JFK's role in
    foreign affairs, 236; and McNamara evalua-
    tion, 163; present activities of, 513; and
    Vietnam, 425, 430; and Warren Commis-
    sion, 463–64
Coffin, William Sloane, Jr.: and the assassina-
    tion, 456, 460; and Bundy evaluation, 160;
    and Camelot question, 469; and civil rights,
    275–76, 278–79, 290, 311, 319–20; and
    JFK-LBJ relationship, 192; and Kennedy
    legacy, 493; and 1960 election, 39; and 1964
    election, 478; and Peace Corps, 256–57;
    present activities of, 513; and steel price
    increase, 258–59; and test-ban treaty, 262;
    and Vietnam, 403
Colby, William: and Berlin crisis, 366; and Har-
    riman evaluation, 160; and JFK as a 1990s
    candidate, 480; and JFK's political philoso-
    phy, 68; and Kennedy legacy, 497; and 1964
    election, 478; present activities of, 513; and
    Vietnam, 406, 417–18, 425–26, 429
Cold war: and Kennedy's political philosophy,
    66–70
Congo, 181, 209–10
Congress: and civil rights, 271, 277, 278, 282,
    283, 285, 286, 287, 317, 318, 319, 320–22,
    482; and Cuban missile crisis, 385–88, 389;
    and JFK's administrative style, 144–45, 147,
    148; JFK's relationship with, 476, 477, 482,
    490–91, 494; and Kennedy legacy, 490–91;
    LBJ's relationship with, 476, 482, 490–91,
    494; and the test-ban treaty, 263

Connally, John B., 18, 132; and the assassina-
    tion, 435, 436–37, 438, 441, 442, 462
Conspiracy theory, 456–60, 462
Convention. See National Democratic Conven-
    tion (1960)
Cooper, John Sherman, 461, 513–14
Council of Economic Advisers, 151, 180, 247.
    See also Heller, Walter
Counterinsurgency, 84, 87, 93, 153, 406–7, 410,
    428–33, 490
Cox, Archibald: appointment as solicitor gen-
    eral, 129; and the assassination, 447; and
    civil rights, 276; and economic issues, 244;
    and JFK's administrative style, 148, 185; and
    Kennedy legacy, 484; and 1960 election, 32;
    present activities of, 514; and RFK's
    appointment as attorney general, 114–15;
    and RFK's personality, 93
Cuba: and JFK's administrative style, 181; and
    JFK's assassination, 457, 459–60, 462, 463,
    464; and JFK's role in foreign affairs,
    215–16, 218–20. See also Bay of Pigs mis-
    sion; Cuban missile crisis
Cuban missile crisis: and back-channel contacts,
    397–98, 400; and Bay of Pigs mission, 350,
    389–90, 394, 396; and Berlin crisis, 366,
    367, 372, 375, 388–89; and Camelot ques-
    tion, 467, 471; and congress, 385–88, 389;
    end of, 400–401; and EXCOM, 377–84; and
    Gromyko-JFK meeting, 384–85; and JFK-
    RFK relationship, 80, 84–85; and JFK's
    address to nation, 385–88; and JFK's admin-
    istrative style, 146, 173, 178; JFK's response
    to, 393–97; and JFK's role in foreign affairs,
    203, 204; and Kennedy legacy, 485, 492,
    495, 496, 498, 502; and 1962 election, 379,
    385–88, 393; prelude to, 373–77; and rea-
    sons for Khrushchev putting missiles in
    Cuba, 388–91; responsibility for, 362;
    secrecy about, 391–93; and Soviet cables,
    398–400; and a summit meeting, 355; and
    test-ban treaty, 259; and Trollope ploy,
    398–400; and Vienna Summit, 388; and
    Vietnam, 404, 430
Curtis, Carl T., 114, 163, 262, 514
Cushing, Richard Cardinal, 38
Cutler, Lloyd, 30–31, 66, 115, 173–74, 352,
    385, 471–72, 514

Daley, Richard, Sr., 28, 31
Dawson, William, 27, 28–29
Defense, U.S. Department of, 176, 246, 403.
    See also McNamara, Robert S.
De Gaulle, Charles, 62, 203, 233, 297, 466
DeLoach, Cartha: and Ambassador Kennedy's
    influence on his children, 71, 75; and the
    assassination, 448, 457–58, 459; and Bay of
    Pigs mission, 331; and civil rights, 289, 309,
    314–15, 316; and Hoover-Kennedy relation-

ship, 264–65, 267–68; and JFK-LBJ relationship, 193; and JFK-RFK relationship, 86–87, 88; and JFK's administrative style, 157–58; and LBJ's unhappiness as vice president, 200; present activities of, 514; and RFK as attorney general, 86, 88, 113–14

Democratic National Committee, 152

Diefenbaker, John, 203

Dillon, C. Douglas, 121–22, 147, 149, 180, 244, 395, 396

DiSalle, Mike, 2

Doar, John, 281, 282, 300, 314

Dodd, Thomas, 210, 211

Dolan, Joseph: and civil rights, 298, 303–4; and Cuban missile crisis, 387; and JFK-RFK relationship, 98; and JFK's administrative style, 171; and Kennedy dynasty question, 105, 107; and LBJ's reasons for accepting vice presidential nomination, 25; and 1960 election, 14, 16–17, 25; present activities of, 514; and RFK's appointment as attorney general, 115; and selection of a running mate, 14, 16–17; and sub-cabinet-level appointments, 127

Donahue, Richard, 143, 144–45

Douglas, Paul, 113, 286–87

Douglas, William O., 88, 89

Duke, Angier Biddle: and Bay of Pigs mission, 333; and Berlin crisis, 370–71; and civil rights, 213–14; and Cuban missile crisis, 386–87; and Harriman evaluation, 161; and JFK-Jackie relationship, 76–78; and JFK-RFK relationship, 98, 101; and JFK's administrative style, 149–50, 154, 155, 185; and JFK's role in foreign affairs, 202, 203, 204, 205–6, 209, 213–14; and Kennedy appeal, 60–61, 62; and Kennedy legacy, 498; present activities of, 514; and RFK's personality, 90; and Rusk evaluation, 168; and sub-cabinet-level appointments, 135–36; and Vietnam, 419

Dulles, Allen: appointment of, 349; and the assassination, 462, 464; and Bay of Pigs mission, 324, 325, 327, 328, 330, 332, 333, 336, 337, 352, 353–54; and Egyptian issues, 224; and Warren Commission, 462, 464

Dulles, John Foster, 67, 166, 224, 333

Dungan, Ralph: and Ambassador Kennedy's influence on his children, 72; and the assassination, 435–36, 455; and Bay of Pigs mission, 343, 348, 350, 353; and Bowles evaluation, 158–59; and Camelot question, 470–71, 472; and Catholic issue, 38, 39, 40; and civil rights, 274, 278, 293, 309; and Cuban missile crisis, 380, 383–84, 394; and Hoover-Kennedy relationship, 270; and JFK-LBJ relationship, 190–91; and JFK-RFK relationship, 89; and JFK's administrative style, 139, 143–44, 150, 157, 158, 171,

187; and JFK's role in foreign affairs, 204, 208; and the Kennedy appeal, 53, 56; and Kennedy dynasty question, 104–5; and Kennedy legacy, 486; and LBJ's unhappiness as vice president, 200; and Lincoln evaluation, 162; and McNamara evaluation, 162; and McNamara's appointment, 120; and 1960 election, 6, 11, 38, 39, 40, 48–49; and 1964 election, 473; present activities of, 514; and RFK as attorney general, 89; and RFK's personality, 90; and Rusk evaluation, 167; and Schlesinger evaluation, 169; and second-term question, 479; and Stevenson demonstration, 11; and Stevenson's appointment as UN ambassador, 122; and sub-cabinet-level appointments, 127, 130, 133–34; and Vietnam, 431

Economic issues: JFK's knowledge about, 243–47; and Kennedy legacy, 495, 496

Egypt, 224–25

Eisenhower, Dwight D.: administrative style of, 140, 148–49; and atomic energy issues, 242; and Bay of Pigs mission, 323–24, 325, 326, 327, 328, 333, 334, 336, 337, 343–44; and Berlin crisis, 367, 372; and civil rights, 275, 295, 302, 305, 306, 319, 321, 483, 485–86; and Cuban missile crisis, 379; and culture, 469; and economic issues, 243; and foreign affairs, 203, 207, 215, 222, 227, 240; JFK compared with, 100; and JFK's administrative style, 171; and Khrushchev, 261, 356; and Laos, 405; legacy of, 483, 488, 490, 491, 502; and Macmillan, 204; and 1960 election, 32, 40–41, 48; Russian feelings about, 261; sense of history of, 63; and space program, 248, 249–50; staff of, 139; as a status quo administration, 482; style of, 372; and Vietnam, 404, 405

Election—1956, 141

Election—1960: and Ambassador Kennedy's influence on his children, 71, 73, 74; and black America, 20, 28; and the Catholic issue, 2, 20, 22, 26, 37–46; and "Checkers" speech, 29, 29n; and civil rights, 26, 28, 30, 34–37, 278; and Daddy King endorsement, 37; debates during the, 26, 31–34; and depressed areas issues, 243; and economic issues, 247; and Eisenhower telegram, 48; and election day/night, 48–49; and foreign affairs, 216; and health issue, 46–48; and Houston Ministers Meeting, 44–46; JFK announces candidacy for the, 1; and JFK-LBJ relationship, 191; and JFK's administrative style, 158; and JFK's private life, 31; and Kennedy dynasty question, 107; and Kennedy legacy, 484, 500; and King phone call, 34–37; and LBJ's reasons for accepting vice presidential nomination, 21–26; and

Election—1960 (*cont.*)
National Convention, 4–26; overview of the, 26–30; and Peace Corps, 255; prelude to, 1–2; primaries for, 3–4; and RFK's personality, 90, 91, 94–95; and selection of a running mate, 13–21; and Sorensen evaluation, 171; and Stevenson nomination/demonstration, 6–13; wiretaps in, 8

Election—1962, 326–27, 379, 385–88, 393

Election—1964: and the assassination, 435–37; and Catholic issue, 475; and civil rights, 271, 277, 285, 293, 307, 321, 474, 475, 477, 478; debates in the, 477; and foreign affairs, 478; if JFK had lived for the, 473–78; and JFK's administrative style, 147, 148; and JFK's private life, 478; and Kennedy legacy, 494; and RKF, 155; and Vietnam, 409, 478

The Enemy Within (RFK), 75–76

Environmental issues, 248

Evaluations of key personnel, 158–71

Evans, Courtney: and civil rights, 315, 317, 320; and Hoover-Kennedy relationship, 265, 266–67, 269; and JFK-RFK relationship, 85–86, 87, 88; and JFK's administrative style, 157–58; present activities of, 514; and RFK as attorney general, 85–86, 87, 88

EXCOM group, 377–84

Exner, Judith, 267, 320

Faisal (king of Saudi Arabia), 224, 225

Farmer, James: and the assassination, 452; and civil rights, 278, 279–81, 284–85, 293–94, 295, 296–97, 299, 319; and JFK-RFK relationship, 80; and 1964 election, 474; present activities of, 514

Faubus, Orval, 279

FBI (Federal Bureau of Investigation): and the assassination, 448, 449–50, 459, 460, 462, 463–64; and civil rights, 294, 296–97, 309, 313–20, 349; function of the, 317; and organized crime, 86; and Warren Commission, 462, 463–64. *See also* Hoover, J. Edgar

Feldman, Myer ("Mike"), 97, 154, 227, 228, 229–30, 231

Felt, Harry D.: and Kennedy appeal, 58, 59; and Kennedy legacy, 502; and McNamara evaluation, 163; present activities of, 514; and RFK's personality, 93–94; and Rusk evaluation, 166; and Vietnam, 406–7, 418, 419–21, 423, 432

Fomin, Aleksandr, 397–98, 400

Food for Peace, 136–37, 172–73

Ford, Gerald R.: and the assassination, 452, 461–62; and JFK as a 1990s candidate, 481; and JFK's administrative style, 145; and JFK's political philosophy, 65; and Kennedy brothers' relationship, 99–100; and Kennedy legacy, 493–94; and LBJ's reasons for accepting vice presidential

nomination, 25; and the 1960 election, 25, 32; and 1964 election, 475–76; present activities of, 515; and Warren Commission, 461–62

Foreign affairs: and civil rights, 210, 211, 212–14, 289, 297; and JFK-RFK relationship, 78, 79, 80, 83; JFK role in, 201–2, 206–7, 277; and JFK's relationship with foreign leaders, 202–6; and Kennedy appeal, 56; and the Kennedy legacy, 483, 485, 489, 490, 492, 493, 494, 495, 496, 499; and 1960 election, 216; and 1964 election, 476, 478. *See also* State Department, U.S.; *specific person, nation, geographical area, or event*

Fowler, Henry ("Joe"), 66, 189, 515

France, 233. *See also* De Gaulle, Charles

Fredericks, Wayne: and civil rights, 212; and Cuban missile crisis, 387; and JFK's administrative style, 157; and JFK's role in foreign affairs, 208–10, 212; and Kennedy appeal, 53; and Kennedy legacy, 489–90; present activities of, 515; and RFK's personality, 90–91

Freedom Rides, 271, 272, 275, 279, 280, 293–302, 305, 318, 319, 475

Freeman, Orville: appointment as secretary of agriculture of, 121; and the assassination, 447–48, 450; and Camelot question, 471; and JFK's administrative style, 146; and Kennedy legacy, 497; and 1960 election, 16, 20; present activities of, 515; and selection of a running mate, 16, 20; and sub-cabinet-level appointments, 136

Frost, Robert, 63

Fulbright, J. William, 116–17, 118–20, 261, 331, 346, 490, 515

Funeral of JFK, 203, 446, 455

Galbraith, John Kenneth: and Ambassador Kennedy's influence on his children, 74–75; and Bay of Pigs mission, 346; and Berlin crisis, 371; and Bowles evaluation, 159; and Camelot question, 468; and Dillon's appointment, 121; and JFK's administrative style, 180; and JFK's knowledge about economic issues, 244, 245, 246; and JFK's role in foreign affairs, 206, 214; and Kennedy appeal, 58; and Kennedy dynasty question, 105–6, 108; and Kennedy legacy, 491, 492; and LBJ's reasons for accepting vice presidential nomination, 23–24; and 1960 election, 9, 23–24, 32; present activities of, 515; and Rusk evaluation, 164–65; and Rusk's appointment, 116–17; and Sorensen evaluation, 171; and Stevenson nomination, 9; and sub-cabinet-level appointments, 127; and test-ban treaty, 261–62; and Vietnam, 413–14, 427, 431–32, 491

Garthoff, Raymond L., 376, 378, 388–89, 398, 399, 401, 515

Gazit, Mordechai, 55, 224, 225–30, 231–32, 515

Germany, 234, 456. *See also* Berlin crisis

Giancana, Sam, 86

Gilpatric, Roswell: and Ambassador Kennedy's influence on his children, 72–73; appointment of, 130–31; and Cuban missile crisis, 378, 379–80, 382, 384, 393, 395, 396; and JFK-RFK relationship, 83–84; and JFK's administrative style, 146–47; and 1964 election, 476–77; present activities of, 516; and steel price increase, 258; and sub-cabinet-level appointments, 132; and Vietnam, 406, 413, 415, 417

Gilruth, Robert, 250–51, 250n

Glenn, John H., 252–53, 254

Goldberg, Arthur: appointment as secretary of labor of, 121–22; appointment as UN ambassador of, 125; and JFK's administrative style, 143, 155–56; LBJ's relationship with, 125; and 1960 election, 9; and steel price increase, 258

Goldwater, Barry, 55, 473, 474, 475, 477

Gonzalez, Henry, 443

Goodpaster, Andrew J., 323–24, 325, 327–28, 331, 334, 516

Goodwin, Richard N.: and Bay of Pigs mission, 353; and JFK's administrative style, 154, 182, 183–84, 186, 187; and JFK's role in foreign affairs, 220, 222, 223; and Kennedy legacy, 491; and Vietnam, 491

Gordon, Lincoln: and Camelot question, 468; and economic issues, 246; and JFK's administrative style, 183; and JFK's role in foreign affairs, 216–18, 220, 222, 223; and 1964 election, 477; and Peace Corps, 256; present activities of, 516

Graham, Phil, 16, 20

Great Britain. *See* United Kingdom

Greenhill, Denis, 204–5, 234, 260, 516

Gromyko, Andrei, 224, 239, 358, 366–67, 384–85, 387–88

Halaby, Najeeb: and civil rights, 303; and JFK's administrative style, 140; and JFK's political philosophy, 66; and Kennedy legacy, 488; and LBJ's reasons for accepting vice presidential nomination, 23; and 1960 election, 23; present activities of, 516; and RFK-LBJ relationship, 197; and RFK's appointment as attorney general, 112–13

Halberstam, David, 192, 410

Harkins, Paul, 407, 420–21, 427

Harriman, W. Averell: evaluation of, 160–61; and JFK's administrative style, 171, 172, 173; and JFK's role in foreign affairs, 228; and 1956 vice presidential nomination, 198; and RFK's personality, 97; and sub-cabinet-

level appointments, 134; and test-ban treaty, 259–60, 261, 262; and Vietnam, 405, 410, 417, 419, 425

Harrington, Michael, 65

Health of JFK, 46–48, 191

Heckscher, August, 62–63, 77, 130, 145, 393, 516

Heller, Walter, 65, 129–30, 149, 180, 182, 244, 247, 258

Helms, Richard: and Bay of Pigs mission, 337, 343–44, 349, 353–54; and Berlin crisis, 363–64, 366, 372; and Camelot question, 472; and Cuban missile crisis, 375, 380, 395; and Hoover-Kennedy relationship, 270; and JFK-RFK relationship, 83; and JFK's administrative style, 149; and JFK's political philosophy, 67; and Kennedy legacy, 482; present activities of, 516; and Vietnam, 415

Henderson, Loy, 133, 225–26

Hesburgh, Theodore: and Ambassador Kennedy's influence on his children, 71; and assassination, 452–53; and Catholic issue, 39–40, 46; and civil rights, 275, 283, 315; and 1960 election, 39–40, 46; present activities of, 516

Hillenbrand, Martin: and the assassination, 454, 456; and Berlin crisis, 361–62, 363, 364–65, 366–67, 368, 369–70, 371, 372; and Cuban missile crisis, 383, 396; and JFK's administrative style, 175–76; and Kennedy legacy, 486–87, 496–97; present activities of, 516–17; and Vienna Summit, 355, 356, 358–59

Hilsman, Roger: and Bay of Pigs mission, 327, 328, 331, 334; and Camelot question, 465–66; and Cuban missile crisis, 375, 382–83, 394, 395, 396, 397, 398; evaluation of, 160; and Harriman evaluation, 161; and Hoover-Kennedy relationship, 271; and Kennedy appeal, 52; and Kennedy legacy, 497–98; and McNamara evaluation, 163; present activities of, 517; and Rostow evaluation, 164; and Rusk evaluation, 167–68; and test-ban treaty, 260; and Vietnam, 415–16, 417, 418, 424, 425

Hollings, Ernest F. ("Fritz"), 19, 34

Hoover, J. Edgar: and Ambassador Kennedy, 265, 266; and Ambassador Kennedy's influence on his children, 75; appointment of, 349; and the assassination, 448, 457–58, 464; and Bay of Pigs mission, 331; and civil rights, 266, 268, 270, 294, 296, 313–20; and Hoffa investigation, 270; and JFK's administrative style, 157–58; and JFK's political philosophy, 66; JFK's relationship with, 85–87, 88, 264–70, 320; and King, 313, 320; LBJ's relationship with, 269, 448; and LBJ's unhappiness as vice president, 200; and Nixon, 264, 265, 270; and organized crime,

Hoover, J. Edgar (cont.)
  266, 267, 269, 270; and RFK as attorney
  general, 85–87, 88, 113–14; RFK's relationship with, 85–87, 88, 264–70, 314–15, 316,
  320, 448; and Salinger, 269; and Warren
  Commission, 464
Houston Ministers Meeting, 44–46
Hughes, Sarah, 196, 444, 445
Humphrey, Hubert: and assassination, 455; and
  civil rights, 286–87; and JFK's role in foreign affairs, 210; and LBJ, 198; and 1960
  election, 3–4, 5, 11, 13, 14, 20, 30; and
  Peace Corps, 255, 257; and selection of a
  running mate, 13, 14, 20; and Stevenson
  demonstration, 11

Inauguration (1961), 177, 482, 483
India, 193, 205–6, 214–15, 217, 431–32, 483
Irish Mafia, 142–43, 144, 158, 159, 177, 353,
  485
IRS (Internal Revenue Service), 112, 267, 298
Israel, 206, 223–24, 225–30

Jackson, Henry M., 17, 20, 233
Jews, 259, 273, 274. See also Israel
Johns, Lem, 443, 444
Johnson, Claudia T. ("Lady Bird"), 18, 23,
  24–25, 437, 445
Johnson, Lyndon Baines: and Ambassador
  Kennedy's influence on his children, 73; and
  the assassination, 435, 436–37, 438, 439,
  440, 441, 442, 443–46, 447, 450, 454,
  459–60, 461, 462; and the Berlin crisis, 365,
  367–69; and black America, 20; and
  Camelot question, 467, 468; and civil rights,
  274, 277, 283, 285, 286, 288, 290, 293, 310,
  312, 320–22, 478, 482, 485–86, 501–2; and
  congress, 476, 482, 490–91, 494; and Cuban
  missile crisis, 380, 383–84; and election
  day/night (1960), 49; and foreign affairs,
  193, 222, 409; and Goldberg's appointment
  to U.N., 125; and Great Society, 485, 488,
  501; and Hoover-Kennedy relationship, 269;
  Hoover's relationship with, 269, 448; India
  trip of, 193; and JFK's political philosophy,
  64; JFK's relationship with, 22, 25, 144, 145,
  146, 147, 188–200; and JFK's staff, 138, 164,
  447; and Kennedy appeal, 51, 52, 53–54, 55;
  and Kennedy dynasty question, 108; and
  Kennedy legacy, 482, 485–86, 488, 490–91,
  493, 494, 501–2; as a leader, 501; and
  McNamara evaluation, 162; and Maxwell
  Taylor evaluation, 161; and National Security Council, 490; and 1960 election, 4, 5, 8,
  10, 13–21, 29–30, 44, 45–46, 49, 126; and
  1964 election, 473, 474, 475, 478; and 1968
  convention, 198; and policy making, 380;
  and reasons for accepting vice presidential
  nomination, 21–26; and religious issue, 44,
  45–46; and RFK's appointment as attorney

general, 115; RFK's relationship with, 193,
  194, 195–98, 290, 384, 447–48; and Rusk
  evaluation, 167, 168; and selection of a running mate, 5, 13–21, 196–97; and space program, 249, 253; and Stevenson nomination,
  8, 10; style of, 29, 51, 52, 53–54, 147, 149,
  154, 174; and sub-cabinet-level appointments, 131, 132, 137; swearing in of, 196,
  443–45; unhappiness of, 198–200; and Vietnam, 407, 409, 413, 425–26; views of the
  presidency of, 189; and Warren Commission, 461, 462; wiretaps on, 197
Johnson, U. Alexis: and Cuban missile crisis,
  376, 382, 383, 384, 387, 396–97, 400; and
  JFK-RFK relationship, 84, 87; and JFK's
  administrative style, 141; and Kennedy
  legacy, 492; present activities of, 517; and
  RFK as attorney general, 87; and Rusk evaluation, 168; and Vietnam, 419
Joint Chiefs of Staff: and Bay of Pigs mission,
  327–28, 336, 338, 343, 347, 350–51, 353,
  394; and Cuban missile crisis, 380, 394; and
  Vietnam, 402, 405, 408, 410, 418

Kaiser, Philip, 27–28, 67, 143, 517
Katzenbach, Nicholas deBelleville: and the
  assassination, 444, 445; and Camelot question, 470; and civil rights, 274, 276–77, 287,
  290, 294, 302, 304, 307–8, 313, 315; and
  Cuban missile crisis, 373; and Hoover-
  Kennedy relationship, 270; and JFK-RFK
  relationship, 79; and Kennedy dynasty question, 107; and LBJ's swearing in, 444, 445;
  present activities of, 517; and Rusk evaluation, 165; and sub-cabinet-level appointments, 134; and Vietnam, 424–25
Kennedy, Caroline, 60, 61, 78, 194, 255
Kennedy, Edward M.: Africa trip of, 82–83; and
  the assassination, 449; and Camelot question, 465; and civil rights, 501; father's influence on, 72; and Kennedy brothers' relationship, 82–83, 99–101; and Kennedy
  dynasty question, 103, 105, 106, 107, 108–9;
  and Kennedy legacy, 486, 493, 501; and
  1960 election, 12–13; and Stevenson
  demonstration, 12–13
Kennedy, Ethel, 93, 97, 453
Kennedy, Eunice. See Shriver, Eunice Kennedy
Kennedy, Jacqueline Lee Bouvier: admiration
  for, 288; and Ambassador Kennedy's influence on his children, 73; and the assassination, 437, 442, 443–44, 445; and Camelot
  question, 465, 466, 468, 469, 470, 471, 472;
  and civil rights, 280; and foreign affairs, 206,
  211, 214, 220, 221; and JFK funeral, 446,
  455; and JFK's administrative style, 146,
  150, 176; JFK's relationship with, 76–78,
  266, 470; and Kennedy appeal, 60, 61; and
  Kennedy legacy, 487; and LBJ's swearing in,
  443–44, 445; and 1960 election, 2, 29; and

space program, 255; and Templesman relationship, 211

Kennedy, Jean. *See* Smith, Jean Kennedy

Kennedy, John F.: access to, 140, 282; announces presidential candidacy, 1; appeal of, 50–63; and happiness, 63, 467; and if he had lived, 473–81; Jacqueline's relationship with, 76–78, 266, 470; and life as unfair, 63; as a 1990s candidate, 479–81; personality of, 50–63, 102, 221; political philosophy of, 64–69; RFK's relationship with, 78–89, 98–101, 157–58; second-term question about, 478–79; sense of history of, 63, 406; wiretaps on, 266

Kennedy, John F.—administrative style of: and access to JFK, 156–58; and the atmosphere, 154–56; and Berlin crisis, 372; and a day in the White House, 150–54; and evaluations of key personnel, 158–71; and JFK's staff, 182–87; and leaks, 182; and 1960 election, 29; overview of, 139–50; and personnel/ agency tensions, 174–87; and "Thanksgiving Massacre," 182–87; and "Wise Men," 171–74

Kennedy, John F., Jr., 59, 78, 108, 109, 255

Kennedy, Joseph P., Jr., 9, 102–3, 108

Kennedy, Joseph P., Sr.: and Catholic issue, 43; and Hoover, 265, 266; influence on children by, 70–76, 335; influence of, 163, 171; and JFK-Jackie relationship, 78; and JFK-LBJ relationship, 191; and JFK's administrative style, 146, 171, 178; and JFK's knowledge about economic issues, 245, 246; and JFK's political philosophy, 66, 69; and JFK's role in foreign affairs, 202; and Kennedy appeal, 52; and Kennedy dynasty question, 102, 103, 104, 105, 106, 107; and McNamara evaluation, 163; and 1960 election, 5, 13, 43; and RFK-LBJ relationship, 195; and RFK's appointment as attorney general, 111, 112; Rose Kennedy's relationship with, 141; and second-term question, 479; and selection of a running mate, 13; and steel price increase, 258; and Stevenson, 178

Kennedy, Robert F.: assassination of, 456, 460; as attorney general, 85–89, 110–15, 121; and Bay of Pigs mission, 327, 331, 340, 348–50, 352, 353, 354; and Camelot question, 469; and Castro assassination, 457; and Catholic issue, 40, 43; and Cuban missile crisis, 84–85, 373, 375–76, 377, 379, 380–81, 384, 387, 391–92, 394, 395, 398, 399; and decision making, 78–85; and election day/night (1960), 49; and environmental issues, 248; father's influence on, 70, 71, 72, 74, 75–76; and foreign affairs, 87, 90–91, 93, 182, 217–18, 221, 238; Hoover's relationship with, 264–70, 314–15, 316, 320, 448; and JFK-LBJ relationship 193; and JFK's administrative style, 142, 149, 158, 171, 178, 182;

and JFK's assassination, 99, 292, 438, 444, 447–48, 452; and JFK's political philosophy, 66, 67, 68, 69; JFK's relationship with, 78–89, 98–101, 157–58; and Kennedy appeal, 51; and Kennedy dynasty question, 102, 103, 104, 105, 106–7, 108, 109; and the Kennedy legacy, 501–2; and LBJ's reasons for accepting vice presidential nomination, 25; LBJ's relationship with, 115, 193, 194, 195–98, 290, 384, 447–48; and LBJ's unhappiness as vice president, 198; and 1960 election, 4, 6, 7, 11, 12–13, 15, 16, 17, 19, 20, 21, 25, 27–28, 43, 49; and 1964 election, 155, 474, 475, 477; personality of, 27, 90–98, 102; and Rusk evaluation, 164, 165; and Rusk's appointment, 118–19; and second-term question, 478–79; and selection of a running mate, 15, 16, 17, 19, 20, 21; and Sorensen evaluation, 171; and space program, 253, 254; and Stevenson demonstration, 11, 12–13; and Stevenson's appointment as UN ambassador, 126; and sub-cabinet-level appointments, 129, 134, 135, 136; and Vietnam, 84, 431

Kennedy, Robert F.—and civil rights: and Aspen Institute incident, 280; and black entertainers/writers meeting, 290–92; and FBI, 314–15, 316, 317; and Freedom Rides, 294, 296–302; and JFK-RFK relationship, 78, 80, 82; and Kennedy legacy, 501; and King, 315; and legislation, 285; and March on Washington, 309; and 1964 election, 475; and Ole Miss case, 7, 302–4; and RFK's commitment, 272, 274, 275, 276, 277, 281, 282, 283, 286, 287, 288, 308, 321, 501–2; and RFK's influence on JFK, 279; and Wallace confrontation, 307, 308; and Wallace meeting, 288–89

Kennedy, Rose, 75, 103, 107, 141

Kennedy dynasty question, 102–9, 479

Kennedy legacy: and the assassination, 484, 498, 501; and Bay of Pigs mission, 490–91, 494, 498; and Berlin crisis, 495; and black America, 500–501; and Catholic issue, 501; and civil rights, 321–22, 482, 483, 485–86, 492, 499, 500, 501–2; and counterinsurgency, 490; and Cuban missile crisis, 485, 492, 495, 496, 498, 502; and economic issues, 495, 496; and foreign affairs, 483, 485, 489, 490, 492, 493, 494, 495, 496, 499; and JFK's private life, 493, 494, 496–97; and Laos, 498; and LBJ's swearing in, 445; and leadership, 501; and 1960 election, 484, 500; and 1964 election, 494; and Peace Corps, 485, 489, 497, 502; and second-term question, 500; and test-ban treaty, 487, 492, 498, 499; and Vietnam, 487, 490–91, 493, 496

Kerr, Clark, 64–65, 467, 482–83, 517

Kerr, Robert S., 21–22, 24, 81

Khrushchev, Nikita S.: and the assassination, 453–54, 456–57, 458; and Eisenhower, 240, 261, 356; and the JFK-RFK relationship, 89; and JFK's political philosophy, 66, 67; and JFK's role in foreign affairs, 203–4, 236–41; and Kennedy appeal, 54; and Nixon, 495; and RFK as attorney general, 89; Salinger meets with, 239–41. *See also* test-ban treaty; Vienna Summit

Khrushchev, Sergei, 54, 204, 261, 354, 356, 384, 460, 517

Khrushchev Remembers (Nikita Khrushchev), 388

King, Coretta Scott, 34–37, 277

King, Martin Luther, Jr.: assassination of, 456, 460; and demonstrations/Freedom Rides, 272, 279, 284, 298, 299, 300, 301; and FBI, 313, 314–15, 318–19, 320; federal influence of, 279, 283; and Hoover, 268, 270; and JFK's role in foreign affairs, 209; and March on Washington, 310, 311; and 1960 election, 34–37; and RFK, 315; wiretaps on, 268, 315

King, Martin Luther, Sr., 37

Kissinger, Henry, 165, 363, 380

Klutznick, Philip, 40, 43, 122–23, 124, 517

Komer, Robert: and Bundy evaluation, 159–60; and JFK-LBJ relationship, 192–93; and JFK-RFK relationship, 88–89; and JFK's administrative style, 154, 176; and JFK's role in foreign affairs, 206, 227, 228, 229–30, 231, 232, 234–36; and Kennedy appeal, 58–59; and Maxwell Taylor evaluation, 162; present activities of, 517–18; and RFK as attorney general, 88–89; and RFK's personality, 90; and Rusk evaluation, 167

Krulak, Victor: and Bundy-Hilsman evaluation, 160; and JFK-RFK relationship, 98–99; and JFK's administrative style, 171; and Kennedy appeal, 59–60, 61–62; and McNamara evaluation, 162; present activities of, 518; and RFK's personality, 93; and Vietnam, 403, 407–8, 409, 416–17, 424, 430–31, 433–34

Lansdale, Edward, 428, 430–31, 457

Laos: CIA in, 406; and Eisenhower administration, 405; and Harriman evaluation, 161; and JFK-LBJ relationship, 194; and JFK's administrative style, 153; and JFK's role in foreign affairs, 205, 239–40; and Kennedy legacy, 498; and Khrushchev-Salinger meeting, 239–40; and Vienna Summit, 358; and Vietnam, 405, 406, 411, 429

Latin America, 215–24

LeMay, Curtis, 381–82, 383

Lemnitzer, Lyman, 327, 328, 410

Lerner, Alan Jay, 465–66

Lewis, John (SNCC): and the assassination, 451; and civil rights, 273, 294–95, 297, 310, 312, 312n, 314, 321; and JFK's role in foreign

affairs, 211; and Kennedy legacy, 500; and 1960 election, 37; present activities of, 518

Lincoln, Evelyn, 81, 157, 162, 169, 235, 440, 441, 443

Lodge, George Cabot, 105

Lodge, Henry Cabot, Jr.: and 1960 election, 33, 40; and Vietnam, 415–20, 421, 423, 424, 426–28, 434

Loewe, Frederick, 77, 465–66

Lovett, Robert A., 72, 120, 172, 173, 225–26

McCarthy, Eugene J.: and Bay of Pigs mission, 335; and Catholic issue, 38–39, 44–45; and civil rights, 321; and Cuban missile crisis, 393; and JFK-RFK relationship, 85; and JFK's role in foreign affairs, 219; and Kennedy dynasty question, 106; and Kennedy legacy, 483; and LBJ's reasons for accepting vice presidential nomination, 23; and 1960 election, 2, 8, 10, 11, 23, 38–39, 44–45; present activities of, 518–19; and Rusk evaluation, 166; and Stevenson demonstration, 11; and Stevenson nomination, 8, 10; and Stevenson's appointment as UN ambassador, 125; and test-ban treaty, 262–63

McCarthy, Joseph R., 68–69, 69n, 90, 91, 92, 112, 114, 335

McCone, John, 84, 354, 381, 416, 433, 464

McDermott, Edward A.: and the assassination, 438–39, 445–46, 447; and Camelot question, 467–68; and Cuban missile crisis, 384, 391–92, 393; and JFK-Jackie relationship, 77; and JFK as a 1990s candidate, 480; and JFK-RFK relationship, 83; and JFK's administrative style, 139–40; and Kennedy appeal, 56; and 1960 election, 11; present activities of, 519; and RFK's personality, 90; and Stevenson demonstration, 11

McGovern, George: and the assassination, 449; and Bay of Pigs mission, 351; and Catholic issue, 41; and Cuban missile crisis, 389; and health issue, 47; and JFK's administrative style, 172–73; and JFK's political philosophy, 69; and Kennedy legacy, 483, 487, 490–91; and 1960 election, 41, 47; and 1964 election, 477–78; present activities of, 519; and sub-cabinet-level appointments, 136–37; and Vietnam, 406, 422–23

Macmillan, Harold, 201, 204–5, 234–36, 260

McNamara, Robert S.: appointed secretary of defense, 120, 121; and Bay of Pigs mission, 328, 331–32; and Cuban missile crisis, 374, 379, 380, 384, 394, 395; evaluation of, 162–63; and JFK-LBJ relationship, 189; and JFK-RFK relationship, 79, 85; and JFK's administrative style, 141, 144, 146, 147, 173, 180; and JFK's role in foreign affairs, 210, 233, 234; and Kennedy appeal, 58; and

Kennedy legacy, 491, 495, 496; and 1964 election, 476; and Rusk evaluation, 168; and skybolt missile, 233, 234; and space program, 249; and sub-cabinet-level appointments, 130–31; and Vietnam, 405, 406, 407, 408, 410, 413, 415, 416, 417, 418, 422, 424, 432, 434, 491

Mafia, 459. *See also* Irish Mafia

Mann, Floyd, 295–96, 306

Mann, Thomas: and the assassination, 458; and JFK's administrative style, 142, 184; and JFK's role in foreign affairs, 202, 218, 220–21, 222–23; and Kennedy legacy, 497; present activities of, 518; and Rusk evaluation, 165–66

Manning, Robert: and the assassination, 447, 450–51, 459; and Camelot question, 469; and JFK's administrative style, 141, 185; and Kennedy Dynasty question, 103; present activities of, 518; and RFK's personality, 91; and Rusk evaluation, 166; and sub-cabinet-level appointments, 130; and Vietnam, 403

Mansfield, Mike, 145, 436, 449, 490

March on Washington, 308–13, 499

Marshall, Burke: and the assassination, 448; and civil rights, 274, 277, 279, 281, 282, 288–89, 294, 297, 299, 301–2, 303, 304, 306, 307, 308, 317, 318, 320; and Hoover-Kennedy relationship, 266; and JFK-RFK relationship, 80; and Kennedy dynasty question, 104; and Kennedy legacy, 484; and LBJ's unhappiness as vice president, 198, 199; present activities of, 518; and sub-cabinet-level appointments, 135

Marshall, George, 23, 117, 177

Marshall, Thurgood, 280, 286

Martin, Edwin: and Cuban missile crisis, 375, 382; and JFK's administrative style, 156, 183–84; and JFK's role in foreign affairs, 215–16, 218; 221–22; present activities of, 518; and RFK's personality, 92

Martin, Louis: and Ambassador Kennedy's influence on his children, 74; and Catholic issue, 43; and civil rights, 274, 281, 287, 291, 310–11; and JFK-LBJ relationship, 194; and JFK-RFK relationship, 82–83, 98, 99; and JFK's administrative style, 143; and Kennedy appeal, 56, 57–58; and Kennedy legacy, 501–2; and 1960 election, 26–27, 28–29, 43, 48; present activities of, 518; and sub-cabinet-level appointments, 128

Meir, Golda, 226, 227, 229

Meredith, James H., 82, 90, 277, 281, 302–7, 501, 519

Mexico, 220–21

Middle East issues, 223–32, 234–36

Minow, Newton, 8–10, 178

Monroe, Marilyn, 320

Montgomery, AL, 298, 299, 300–302, 306, 309

Morse, Bradford: and Ambassador Kennedy's influence on his children, 71; and civil rights, 285; and JFK's administrative style, 141; and JFK's political philosophy, 66–67; and Kennedy dynasty question, 105; and Kennedy legacy, 487–88; present activities of, 519; and RFK's personality, 91; and second-term question, 478–79

Moses, Robert: and the assassination, 460; and civil rights, 272–73, 281, 289, 290–91, 312–13, 314; and Kennedy legacy, 500–501; present activities of, 519

Moss, Frank, 2, 14, 103, 145, 193, 519

Moyers, Bill, 17–18, 44, 257

Moynihan, Daniel Patrick, 65

Murrow, Edward R., 91–92, 93, 140, 332–33, 380–81

Muskie, Edmund, 2

Myrdal, Gunnar, 351–52

NASA (National Aeronautical and Space Agency), 210. *See also* Space program

Nasser, Gamal Abdel, 224–25

National Democratic Convention (1956), 93

National Democratic Convention (1960): and health issues, 191; and JFK-LBJ relationship, 191; and LBJ's reasons for accepting vice presidential nomination, 21–26; prelude to the, 5–6; and selection of a running mate, 13–21, 196–97; and Stevenson demonstration, 10–13; and Stevenson nomination, 6–10, 126, 178; votes at, 4

National Security Council: and Cuban missile crisis, 377–84, 392, 393; and JFK-LBJ relationship, 190; and Kennedy legacy, 490; and tensions in administration, 178, 179; and Vietnam, 416

Nehru, Jawaharlal, 201, 205–6, 214

Nelson, Gaylord: and the assassination, 449; and Catholic issue, 39; and Cuban missile crisis, 377, 386; and JFK's administrative style, 151; and JFK's knowledge about environmental issues, 248; and 1960 election, 19, 39; present activities of, 519; and selection of a running mate, 19

Neuberger, Maurine, 2, 114, 145, 449, 519

Nixon, Richard M.: and Bay of Pigs mission, 326–27, 334, 346; and black America, 499; and Catholic issue, 40–42; and civil rights, 279; and economic issues, 243; and foreign affairs, 222; Hoover's relationship with, 264, 265, 270; JFK compared intellectually with, 100; and JFK as a 1990s candidate, 480, 481; and JFK's political philosophy, 69; and Kennedy legacy, 488; and Khrushchev, 495; and LBJ's reasons for accepting vice presidential nomination, 23; and LBJ's views of presidency, 189; as a leader, 501; and 1960 election, 7, 23, 29n, 30–31, 40–42; and policy making, 380; Soviet view of, 357; and

Nixon, Richard M. (*cont.*)
  sub-cabinet-level appointments, 137; as vice president, 200, 222
Nixon, Russell, 245
Nobel Prize winners' dinner, 467
Nolting, Frederick E., Jr., 414, 426, 427, 428
Nyerere, Julius, 208, 209

Obote, Milton, 386–87
O'Boyle, Patrick A., 312
O'Brien, Lawrence: and the assassination, 437, 438, 444, 445; and civil rights, 277; and JFK-LBJ relationship, 190, 191; and JFK's administrative style, 143, 144–45, 152, 178; and Kennedy appeal, 60; and LBJ's swearing in, 444, 445; and 1960 election, 14, 19; and selection of a running mate, 14, 19
O'Donnell, Kenneth P.: and the assassination, 435–36, 439, 445; and Bay of Pigs mission, 343; and civil rights, 286, 310; and Hoover-Kennedy relationship, 270; and JFK-RFK relationship, 89, 98; and JFK's administrative style, 139, 142, 143, 144, 157; and Kennedy appeal, 55, 57, 60; and LBJ's swearing in, 445; and Lincoln evaluation, 162; and 1960 election, 14, 15, 17; and RFK as attorney general, 89; and selection of a running mate, 14, 15, 17; and steel price increase, 258
Office of Special Counsel, 154. *See also* Sorensen, Theodore C.
O'Leary, Muggsy, 142–43
Ole Miss, 277, 302–8
Organized crime, 86–87, 266, 267, 269, 270
Oswald, Lee Harvey, 446, 451, 457–58, 459, 460, 461, 462, 464

Palestine, 224, 226, 231–32
Patterson, John: and Bay of Pigs mission, 323, 325–27, 345, 350, 352; and civil rights, 271–72, 279, 283–84, 287, 295–96, 298, 300–302, 305, 308; and JFK-RFK relationship, 80, 86; and Kennedy appeal, 52, 58; and 1960 election, 49; and 1964 election, 475; present activities of, 519–20; and RFK as attorney general, 86; and RFK's personality, 92
Peace Corps, 141, 172–73, 255–57, 485, 489, 497, 502
Peale, Norman Vincent, 43
Pearson, Drew, 43, 135
Pell, Claiborne, 52, 55, 66, 520
Peres, Shimon, 55, 197
Peterson, Esther, 54, 90, 130, 148, 155–56, 483, 520
Plausible deniability, 345
Podhoretz, Norman: and the assassination, 462; and Bay of Pigs mission, 494; and Camelot question, 470; and civil rights, 273–74; and

JFK-LBJ relationship, 194; and JFK's political philosophy, 68–69; and JFK's role in foreign affairs, 225, 228; and Kennedy appeal, 51; and Kennedy dynasty question, 108–9; and Kennedy legacy, 489, 491–92, 494; and LBJ's reasons for accepting vice presidential nomination, 24; and 1960 election, 24, 33; present activities of, 520; and RFK's personality, 97–98; and Schlesinger evaluation, 170; and Stevenson's appointment as UN ambassador, 124–25; and test-ban treaty, 262; and Vietnam, 423, 491–92; and Warren Commission, 462
Powers, David F., 143, 150, 169
Private life of JFK: and Ambassador Kennedy's influence on his children, 75, 78; and Camelot question, 471; and Hoover-Kennedy relationship, 264, 267, 268, 269, 320; and JFK as a 1990s candidate, 479–80, 481; and Kennedy appeal, 56; and Kennedy legacy, 486, 493, 494, 496–97; and 1960 election, 31; and 1964 election, 478
Profiles in Courage (JFK), 69, 75, 351–52
Proxmire, William E., 19
Puchinski, Roman, 31, 47, 52, 386, 520

Raskin, Marcus: and JFK as a 1990s candidate, 480; and JFK's administrative style, 150–51, 179; and JFK's political philosophy, 67–68; and Kennedy legacy, 488, 499; and 1964 election, 477; present activities of, 520; and Vietnam, 402, 422
Rauh, Joseph L., Jr.: and civil rights, 272, 278, 286–87, 290; and health issue, 47–48; and JFK's political philosophy, 64, 65–66; and Kennedy legacy, 499–500; and 1960 election, 3–4, 13, 20–21, 47–48; present activities of, 520; and RFK's personality, 92, 93; and Rusk's appointment, 119–20; and selection of a running mate, 13, 20–21
Ray, Manuel: and Bay of Pigs mission, 324–25, 329–30, 338, 341–42, 347–48, 353; and JFK's role in foreign affairs, 218, 219–20; present activities of, 520
Rayburn, Samuel T.: and JFK-LBJ relationship, 188; and JFK's administrative style, 145; and LBJ's reasons for accepting vice presidential nomination, 22–23, 24, 25; and 1960 election, 14, 18, 19, 20, 21, 22–23, 24, 25, 45, 46; and religious issue, 45, 46; and RFK-LBJ relationship, 196; and selection of a running mate, 14, 18, 19, 20, 21
Reagan, Ronald, 58, 137, 148–49, 468, 489, 491, 501
Rebozo, Bebe, 30–31
Religious issue. *See* Catholic issue
Reston, James B., 20, 46, 238, 392
Ribicoff, Abraham: and Ambassador Kennedy's influence on his children, 76; and health issue, 47; and Kennedy appeal, 51; and

LBJ's unhappiness as vice president, 200; and 1960 election, 1–2, 7, 20, 47; present activities of, 520; and RFK's appointment as attorney general, 110, 111–12, 113; and selection of a running mate, 20; and Stevenson nomination, 7; and Stevenson's appointment as UN ambassador, 125; and sub-cabinet-level appointments, 138

Rockefeller, Nelson, 131, 147, 474, 475–77

Romney, George, 25–26, 64, 65, 243, 245, 486, 520

Roosevelt, Eleanor, 8, 10, 11, 12–13, 122

Ross, Charles R., 485, 520–21

Rostow, Walt W.: and Bay of Pigs mission, 342, 349–50, 351–52; and Bowles evaluation, 159; and civil rights, 283, 288; and Cuban missile crisis, 379; and economic issues, 245; evaluation of, 164; and JFK-LBJ relationship, 194; and JFK's administrative style, 148, 153, 174, 182, 183, 185, 186–87; and JFK's role in foreign affairs, 226–27, 236; and Kennedy appeal, 55, 63; and Kennedy legacy, 485–86, 490, 495; and 1960 election, 5–6; and 1964 election, 473; present activities of, 521; and RFK-LBJ relationship, 198; and Rusk's appointment, 117, 119; and sub-cabinet-level appointments, 128; and Vietnam, 405, 410–14, 429–30

Ruby, Jack, 459, 460, 462–63

Rusk, Dean: appointed secretary of state, 116–10, 121; and the assassination, 449, 450–51, 461, 464; and Bay of Pigs mission, 328, 331, 332, 335, 336, 342, 343, 349; and Berlin crisis, 362, 366–67, 369; and Bowles evaluation, 159; and Camelot question, 466; and Cuban missile crisis, 373, 378, 379, 383, 388, 393, 394, 397, 398, 401; evaluation of, 164–69; and JFK-LBJ relationship, 190; and JFK-RFK relationship, 79, 85; and JFK's administrative style, 141, 149, 150, 156, 174–75, 176–77, 178, 179, 180, 181, 182, 183, 184, 185, 186–87; and JFK's role in foreign affairs, 201, 209, 224, 225–26, 228, 230; and Kennedy dynasty question, 107; and Kennedy legacy, 485, 488–89; and Middle East issues, 225–26, 228, 230; present activities of, 521; and RFK's personality, 91; RFK's views of, 118; and Schlesinger evaluation, 170; and sub-cabinet-level appointments, 130, 132, 135, 136; and Vienna Summit, 355, 357; and Vietnam, 403, 405, 406, 410, 416, 417, 418, 422, 423, 433; and Warren Commission, 461, 464

Russell, Richard, 27, 115, 145, 461, 482

Rustin, Bayard, 310, 311

Salinger, Pierre: and Ambassador Kennedy's influence on his children, 71; and the assassination, 437, 449, 450, 451, 454; and Bay of Pigs mission, 348; and Camelot question,

465; and Catholic issue, 38; and Cuban missile crisis, 379, 381, 386, 392, 397, 400; evaluation of, 169; and Hoover, 269; and Hoover-Kennedy relationship, 269; and JFK-LBJ relationship, 188; and JFK as a 1990s candidate, 479–80; and JFK-RFK relationship, 84–85; and JFK's administrative style, 143, 150, 158, 174; JFK's relationship with, 234; and JFK's role in foreign affairs, 203, 238, 239–41; and Kennedy appeal, 61; and Kennedy dynasty question, 102–3; Khrushchev meets with, 239–41; and LBJ's reasons for accepting vice presidential nomination, 25; and McNamara evaluation, 162; and 1960 election, 12, 16, 17, 25, 30, 38, 48; and 1964 election, 477; present activities of, 521; and RFK-LBJ relationship, 196–97; and RFK's appointment as attorney general, 110–11; and Rusk evaluation, 167; and second-term question, 478; and selection of a running mate, 16, 17; and Stevenson demonstration, 12; and sub-cabinet-level appointments, 131; and Vietnam, 423, 430

Samuelson, Paul: and Ambassador Kennedy's influence on his children, 74; and JFK-LBJ relationship, 188; and JFK's administrative style, 148–49, 182; and JFK's knowledge about economic issues, 244–45, 246, 247; and JFK's political philosophy, 69; and Kennedy appeal, 53; and Kennedy brothers' relationship, 100; and 1960 election, 29; present activities of, 521; and Rostow evaluation, 164; and Sorensen evaluation, 171; and steel price increase, 258

Sanford, Terry: and Bay of Pigs mission, 327; and civil rights, 212, 276; and JFK-LBJ relationship, 193–94; and JFK-RFK relationship, 79; and JFK's role in foreign affairs, 212; and LBJ's reasons for accepting vice presidential nomination, 26; and 1960 election, 13, 19, 26, 27; and 1964 election, 474; present activities of, 521; and selection of running mate, 13, 19

Saudi Arabia, 224, 225

Scali, John, 397–98, 400

Schirra, Walter M., Jr., 250–51, 252, 254, 260, 521

Schlei, Norbert A.: and civil rights, 276, 285, 303, 304–5, 316–17; and Cuban missile crisis, 373–74, 377; and Kennedy appeal, 50; present activities of, 521; and sub-cabinet-level appointments, 134

Schlesinger, Arthur M., Jr.: and Bay of Pigs mission, 330, 337, 347, 353–54; and Camelot question, 465–66; and civil rights, 285–86, 291, 297, 317; and Cuban missile crisis, 390; and Dillon's appointment, 121–22; evaluation of, 169–70; and JFK's administrative style, 172, 182; and JFK staff appointments,

Schlesinger, Arthur M. (cont.)
138; and Kennedy dynasty question, 102, 108–9; and Kennedy legacy, 491, 498; and 1960 election, 8–10, 29–30; present activities of, 521–22; and RFK's personality, 91–92; and Rusk evaluation, 168; and Rusk's appointment, 118–19; and Stevenson nomination, 8–10; and Stevenson's appointment as UN ambassador, 123; and sub-cabinet-level appointments, 127, 130; and Vietnam, 430, 491

Seaborg, Glenn, 128–29, 242–43, 249, 259–60, 263, 522

Seamans, Robert C., Jr., 248–49, 250, 251, 252–53, 254–55, 259, 522

Second-term question, 478–79, 500

Secret Service: and the assassination, 436, 442, 443, 449–50, 460, 463; and JFK's private life, 478; and Warren Commission, 463

Seigenthaler, John: and Ambassador Kennedy's influence on his children, 70–71, 72, 73, 75–76; and Bay of Pigs mission, 333, 348–49; and civil rights, 277, 287, 291–92, 297, 300, 318–19; and Hoover-Kennedy relationship, 265–66; and JFK-RFK relationship, 99; and Kennedy dynasty question, 103–4; and LBJ's reasons for accepting vice presidential nomination, 21–22; and 1960 election, 15–16, 21–22, 28; present activities of, 522; and RFK-LBJ relationship, 195, 196; and RFK's appointment as attorney general, 113; and RFK's personality, 95–96; and selection of a running mate, 15–16; and Stevenson's appointment as UN ambassador, 126

Shepard, Alan, 249, 253, 254

Shriver, Eunice Kennedy, 103, 419

Shriver, R. Sargent, Jr.: and Ambassador Kennedy's influence on his children, 74; appointment of, 111–12, 137; and the assassination, 455; and Catholic issue, 43; and civil rights, 277; and Dillon's appointment, 121; and JFK's administrative style, 177; and Kennedy appeal, 53; and Kennedy dynasty question, 104n; and King phone call, 35–36; and McNamara's appointment, 120; and 1960 election, 28, 35–36, 43; and Peace Corps, 255–57; present activities of, 522; and RFK's appointment as attorney general, 111–12; and RFK's personality, 95–96; and steel price increase, 258–59; and sub-cabinet-level appointments, 127, 128

Shuttlesworth, Fred: and civil rights, 274, 297–98, 299, 309–10; and Kennedy appeal, 50; and Kennedy legacy, 501; and King phone call, 36; and 1960 election, 36; present activities of, 522

Sinatra, Frank, 86

Sisco, Joseph: and Bay of Pigs mission, 340; and Cuban missile crisis, 390–91; and JFK as a

1990s candidate, 481; and JFK's administrative style, 185; and Kennedy legacy, 492–93; present activities of, 522; and Rusk's appointment, 117–19; and Stevenson's appointment as UN ambassador, 124, 125

Skybolt missile crisis, 144, 144n, 233–34

Slayton, Donald "Deke", 251–52, 522–23

Smathers, George: and Bay of Pigs mission, 340; and JFK-LBJ relationship, 192, 193; and JFK-RFK relationship, 85; and Kennedy appeal, 56–57; and Kennedy dynasty question, 102; and LBJ's reasons for accepting vice presidential nomination, 24–25; and 1960 election, 18–19, 24–25; present activities of, 523; and RFK's appointment as attorney general, 111; and selection of a running mate, 18–19

Smith, Jean Kennedy, 73

Smith, Stephen E., 104, 326, 465

Smith, William Y.: and the assassination, 459; and Camelot question, 468; and Cuban missile crisis, 385, 389, 399, 401; and JFK-RFK relationship, 80; and JFK's administrative style, 152–53, 186; and JFK's role in foreign affairs, 203–4, 236–37; and JFK staff appointments, 138; present activities of, 523; and Vietnam, 405, 408, 421–22

Sorensen, Theodore C.: and Ambassador Kennedy's influence on his children, 75; and civil rights, 288; and economic issues, 244, 247; evaluation of, 171; and JFK-LBJ relationship, 190; and JFK's administrative style, 147, 148, 149, 150, 154, 175; and JFK staff appointments, 138; and Kennedy appeal, 56, 57; and Kennedy legacy, 494–95; and 1960 election, 48; and Profiles in Courage, 75; and RFK-LBJ relationship, 198; and Schlesinger evaluation, 169; and sub-cabinet-level appointments, 129

South Africa, 208, 210–11

Soviet Union: and JFK's assassination, 458, 459; and JFK's role in foreign affairs, 236–41; and space program, 248–49, 251, 252, 253. See also Bay of Pigs mission; Berlin crisis; Cuban missile crisis; Khrushchev, Nikita S.; Vietnam

Space program, 25, 194, 248–55, 260

State Department, U.S.: and the assassination, 446; and Bay of Pigs mission, 328, 348; and JFK-LBJ relationship, 193; and Peace Corps, 257; tensions with the, 174–87; and Vietnam, 408. See also Rusk, Dean

Steel companies, 88, 144, 146, 258–59, 471

Stevenson, Adlai E.: appointed UN ambassador, 116, 118, 122–26; and the assassination, 438, 455–56; and Bay of Pigs mission, 338, 339–40, 348, 354, 389–90; and Cuban missile crisis, 389–91; death of, 125; demonstration for, 10–13; JFK assessment of, 5; and JFK's administrative style, 141, 144, 177–78,

180, 181; and JFK's role in foreign affairs, 216–17; and Kennedy, Sr., 178; and Kennedy appeal, 50; and Kennedy legacy, 495–96; and 1956 election, 93; and 1960 election, 3, 5, 6–13, 14, 33–34, 126, 178; and RFK's appointment as attorney general, 114; and RFK's personality, 93; and Rusk evaluation, 165; and secretary of state position, 6, 7, 13, 18, 116–17, 118, 119, 122–23, 125, 178; and sub-cabinet-level appointments, 127; visits Texas, 438

Stevenson, Adlai E. III: and the assassination, 455–56; and Bay of Pigs mission, 348; and Camelot question, 472; and Catholic issue, 40–41; and JFK's administrative style, 141, 177–78; and Kennedy appeal, 50–51; and 1960 election, 7–8, 10–11, 12, 18, 33–34, 40–41; present activities of, 523; and RFK's appointment as attorney general, 114; and Rusk's appointment, 118; and selection of a running mate, 18; and Stevenson demonstration/nomination, 10–11, 12; and Stevenson's appointment as UN ambassador, 122, 123–24

Stone, Oliver, 69, 463

Sukhodrev, Viktor: and the assassination, 453–54, 456–57, 458; and Cuban missile crisis, 384–85, 387–88, 399–400; and JFK's role in foreign affairs, 240–41; and Kennedy appeal, 54; and Kennedy legacy, 487; and Khrushchev-Salinger meeting, 240–41; present activities of, 523; and test-ban treaty, 260–61; and Vienna Summit, 356, 357–58, 359

Sullivan, William H.: and Camelot question, 466; and Harriman evaluation, 160; and JFK-RFK relationship, 83; and JFK's political philosophy, 67; and Kennedy legacy, 484–85; present activities of, 523; and sub-cabinet-level appointments, 133–34, 137; and Vietnam, 402–3, 405, 408, 410, 426–27, 431

Symington, Stuart W., 5, 14, 15, 17, 18, 20, 72

Talbot, Phillips: and JFK's administrative style, 148, 149, 176; and JFK's role in foreign affairs, 214–15, 224–25, 227, 231, 232; and Kennedy legacy, 483, 493; and 1964 election, 476; present activities of, 523; and Rusk evaluation, 164–65; and sub-cabinet-level appointments, 132–33

Taylor, Maxwell D.: and Bay of Pigs mission, 353; and Cuban missile crisis, 353, 401; evaluation of, 161–62; and JFK-RFK relationship, 84; and JFK's administrative style, 152–53, 171, 172–73; and Johnson administration, 161; and Kennedy legacy, 495; and Vietnam, 405, 410–14, 415, 416, 428–29, 430, 431

Templesman, Maurice, 211

Test-ban treaty, 259–63, 362, 471, 487, 492, 498, 499

"Thanksgiving Massacre," 182–87

Thomas, Albert, 436, 437, 438–39

Thompson, Llewellyn E., 239, 379, 380, 398, 399

Thurmond, J. Strom, 120, 163, 277, 346, 523

Tobin, James, 53, 65, 121, 129–30, 243, 247, 258, 523

Trueheart, William, 92, 405–6, 412–13, 414, 419, 421, 426, 427–28, 523

Truman, Harry S.: administrative style of, 147; and foreign affairs, 207; JFK compared with, 100; and Kennedy appeal, 63; legacy of, 475, 487, 490, 491, 495; and 1956 vice presidential nomination, 198; sense of history of, 63

Tshombe, Moise, 209–10

Turkey, 214, 382, 401

Turnure, Pamela, 440

Udall, Stewart, 120, 121, 158

Uganda, 386–87

United Kingdom, 233–36, 260–61. See also Macmillan, Harold

United Nations: and Bay of Pigs mission, 339–40, 348; and civil rights, 289; and Cuban missile crisis, 390–91, 397, 401; and Middle East issues, 225, 225n; and South Africa, 208. See also Stevenson, Adlai E.

United States Information Agency. See Murrow, Edward R.; Wilson, Donald

University of Alabama, 307–8

University of Mississippi. See Meredith, James

Urban Affairs, U.S. Department of, 286

Valenti, Jack: and the assassination, 436, 438–39, 440–41, 443, 444–45, 459–60; and Catholic issue, 42, 45–46; and LBJ's reasons for accepting vice presidential nomination, 22–23; and LBJ's swearing in, 444; and 1960 election, 22–23, 42; present activities of, 523–24; and RFK-LBJ relationship, 197–98; and RFK's personality, 96–97

Venezuela, 216, 221–22

Vienna Summit (1961), 201, 236, 297, 355–59, 360, 388, 411

Vietnam: and August cable, 414–19, 423; and Bay of Pigs mission, 350, 406, 409, 411; and Berlin crisis, 411, 430; and Buddhist demonstrations, 414–19, 422, 423, 425, 426, 433, 434; and Camelot question, 468; and Catholic issue, 419; and CIA, 418, 422, 431; and counterinsurgency, 406–7, 410, 428–33; and coup, 415–26; and Cuban missile crisis, 404, 430; early history of involvement in, 404; and fact-finding missions, 433–34; and JFK-LBJ relationship, 189; and JFK-RFK relationship, 83, 84; and JFK's administrative style, 171, 174; and JFK's role in foreign affairs, 203; and Kennedy legacy, 487,

Vietnam (*cont.*)
490–91, 493, 496; and Laos, 406, 411, 429; leaks about, 412; Lodge appointed ambassador to, 426–28; and McNamara evaluation, 163; and Maxwell Taylor evaluation, 161; and 1964 election, 409, 478; and Nixon administration, 380; overview of, 402–10; reasons for going into, 405; and RFK's personality, 92; and Rusk evaluation, 165, 166; and Rusk's appointment, 119; Special Forces/Green Berets in, 430, 431; statistics about, 407; and Taylor mission, 410–14; U.S. advisers in, 404, 412, 413; and Vienna Summit, 411

Wallace, George: and Bay of Pigs mission, 352–53; and civil rights, 275, 277, 284, 287, 288–89, 302, 307–8, 321; and JFK's political philosophy, 66; and Kennedy appeal, 52; and Kennedy legacy, 495; present activities of, 524
Warren Commission, 442, 460, 461–64
Washington, DC: civil rights in, 212–14; March on, 308–13, 499
Weaver, Robert, 286, 287
Webb, James E., 249, 250–51
Westmoreland, William C., 407, 410, 421, 432–33
White, Byron, 27, 115, 196, 297, 298
White, Lee: and civil rights, 293, 308–9, 320; and JFK-LBJ relationship, 191–92; and JFK-RFK relationship, 80; and JFK's administrative style, 142–43, 150, 151–52, 153–54, 156–57; and JFK's political philosophy, 65; and Kennedy appeal, 54, 57; and Kennedy brothers' relationship, 99; and Kennedy legacy, 494–95; and LBJ's unhappiness as vice president, 198–99; and Peace Corps, 257; present activities of, 524
White, Theodore H., 91–92, 465, 466
Wicker, Tom: and Bay of Pigs mission, 336; and Bundy evaluation, 160; and Camelot question, 469; and Catholic issue, 42, 46; and civil rights, 291, 321–22; and Cuban missile crisis, 400–401; and JFK-LBJ relationship, 188–89, 190, 191; and JFK-RFK relationship, 82, 99; and JFK's political philosophy, 69; and Kennedy dynasty question, 106, 107; and Kennedy legacy, 496; and LBJ's reasons for accepting vice presidential nomination, 24; and McNamara's appointment as secretary of defense, 120; and 1960 election, 24, 30, 33, 42, 46; and 1964 election, 475; present activities of, 524; and Schlesinger evaluation, 170
Wiesner, Jerome B., 128–29, 233, 250
Wilkins, Roy, 274, 310

Williams, G. Mennen ("Soapy"), 19, 22, 53, 207, 208, 211
Wilson, Donald: and Bay of Pigs mission, 332–33; and Camelot question, 469–70; and Cuban missile crisis, 380–81, 396; and JFK-LBJ relationship, 190; and JFK as a 1990s candidate, 481; and JFK's administrative style, 140, 142; and Kennedy appeal, 53–54; and Kennedy dynasty question, 108; and Kennedy legacy, 502; and 1960 election, 26, 29, 31–32, 48, 49; present activities of, 524; and RFK's personality, 90, 91–92, 96
Wine, James, 41–42, 43, 44, 46, 446–47, 454–55, 524
Wirtz, W. Willard, 122, 472
"Wise Men," 171–74. *See also specific person*
Wofford, Harris: and civil rights, 274, 275, 276, 277, 283, 287, 294; and King phone call, 34, 35; and 1960 election, 34, 35; and sub-cabinet-level appointments, 128
Women: appointments of, 128, 196; equal rights for, 141; and JFK's administrative style, 141; and RFK-LBJ relationship, 196; and space program, 252. *See also* Private life of JFK

Yarborough, Ralph: and the assassination, 436–37, 438, 440, 441–42, 443–44, 463; and Camelot question, 468; and JFK-LBJ relationship, 194; and JFK's administrative style, 141; and Kennedy appeal, 51; and Kennedy brothers' relationship, 100; and Kennedy legacy, 484; and LBJ's swearing in, 443–44; and 1960 election, 12–13, 20, 30, 44; and 1964 election, 474; present activities of, 524; and religious issue, 44; and RFK-LBJ relationship, 195–96; and selection of a running mate, 20; and Stevenson demonstration, 12–13; and Warren Commission, 463
Yarmolinsky, Adam: and the assassination, 438; and Camelot question, 466–67; and JFK as a 1990s candidate, 481; and JFK's administrative style, 143, 144, 154–55, 156–57, 176, 185; and JFK's role in foreign affairs, 233; and JFK staff appointments, 138; and Kennedy legacy, 487; and McNamara's appointment, 120; and 1960 election, 6–7; and 1964 election, 474–75; present activities of, 524; and second-term question, 479; and Stevenson nomination, 6–7; and sub-cabinet-level appointments, 127, 128, 131–32, 137, 138
Yemen, 224, 225, 234–35
York, Herbert F., 233–34, 249–50, 524
Yorty, Sam, 114, 145, 460, 462–63, 475, 524
Youngblood, Rufus, 440, 442